RADIO OPERATOR'S LICENSE
Q&A
MANUAL

RADIO OPERATOR'S LICENSE
Q&A
MANUAL

ELEVENTH EDITION

MILTON KAUFMAN

HAYDEN BOOKS

A Division of Prentice Hall Computer Publishing

11711 North College, Carmel, Indiana 46032 USA

ELEVENTH EDITION
FOURTH PRINTING—1992

International Standard Book Number: 0-672-48444-7
Library of Congress Catalog Card Number: 89-63734

Acquisitions Editor: *James Rounds*
Development Editor: *C. Herbert Feltner*
Indexer: *Milton Kaufman*

Printed in the United States of America

Contents

Preface

This revised eleventh edition is in complete accordance with the latest FCC Study Guides, the Supplements to the Study Guides, and the latest FCC Rules and Regulations. It is designed to be used in preparing for the radiotelephone license examinations for:

1. the General Radiotelephone Operator License,
2. the Marine Radio Operator Permit, and
3. the Radar Endorsement.

An extensive section on troubleshooting, specially prepared by the author, provides practice in solving problems similar to those given on the the FCC examination. This edition is completely self-contained, with all of the elements necessary to study for any of the above classes of radio operator's license, permit, or endorsement.

Important Changes in the Eleventh Edition:

In August 1986, the FCC made important changes in the examination for the General Radiotelephone Operator license. To successfully pass the new examination, the applicant must be aware of the changes. This edition has been revised to incorporate all of the latest revisions.

The basic changes to the new FCC examinations are summarized as follows:

1. Most vacuum-tube questions have been eliminated.
2. Test questions more heavily emphasize solid-state circuitry and operation.
3. Numerous questions (much more than previously), are asked on the subjects of Marine and Aviation Radiotelephone Rules and Regulations and operating procedures.

Appendix I has been revised and expanded to include R & R sections from the new FCC Part 80, *Stations in the Maritime Services,* and Part 87, *Aviation Services.* (Parts 81 and 83 have been replaced by the new Part 80.) A new FCC-type sample test covering maritime and aviation topics (essential for the new General or Marine Radiotelephone Operator License), will be found in the new Appendix V.

Applicants should obtain (free) from any FCC office, FO Bulletin #32, titled, *Study Guide and Reference Material for the General Radiotelephone Operator License.*

New Rules and Regulations

Here are some Questions and Answers to help you understand the new Rules and

Regulations issued by the FCC (see Appendix III for more details):

Question 1. With regard to two-way radio services, when do the new FCC Rules become effective?

Answer. These rules become effective 180 days after publication of the Report and Order in the Federal Register. (Effective date is August 1984.)

Question 2. With regard to certain broadcast services, when do the new rules become effective?

Answer. These rules become effective 30 days after publication of the Report and Order in the Federal Register (June 1984). See Appendix III for details of these new rules.

Question 3. What is the basic effect of the new FCC Rules' changes with respect to two-way radio operation?

Answer. *All* operating license requirements for private two-way radio services, except those governed by International Treaty, were discontinued as of August 1984. This means that not even a Restricted Radiotelephone Operator Permit is required to install, maintain, or repair stations in the private two-way radio services.

Question 4. Which services will continue indefinitely to require personnel who perform installation, maintenance, or repair at a station, to have a General Radiotelephone Operator's License?

Answer. The following services:
1. Aviation Services (FCC Part 87).
2. Maritime Services (FCC Part 80).
3. International Fixed Public Radiocommunication Services (FCC Part 23).

Question 5. Which services no longer require any licensed personnel to install, maintain, or repair stations of these services?

Answer. The following services:
1. Private Land Mobile Radio Services (FCC Part 90).
2. Private Operational Fixed Microwave Service (FCC Part 94).
3. General Mobile Radio Services (Subpart A of FCC Part 95).
4. Radio Control Services (Subpart C of FCC Part 95).
5. Citizens Band Services (Subpart D of FCC Part 95).

Question 6. After August 1984, who is responsible for the proper operation of the stations listed in the answer to Question 5?

Answer. The licensee of each station is responsible for the proper operation of his station.

Question 7. Does all the above mean that, after August 1984, the FCC no longer gives examinations and issues licenses for the General Radiotelephone Operator License?

Answer. No! The FCC will continue indefinitely to give examinations and issue licenses for the General Radiotelephone Operator License. However, this license is required only in connection with the services listed in the answer to Question 4.

Question 8. What is the current situation with regard to FCC Radio Operator Licenses?

Answer.
1. The FCC no longer conducts examinations for, or issues the Radiotelephone First Class Operator License, the Radiotelephone Third Class Operator Permit, or the Broadcast Endorsement.
2. The FCC has renamed the Radiotelephone Second Class Operator License.

It is now called the General Radiotelephone Operator License. (The examination has been changed as a result of the renaming.)

3. The FCC has established a new license called the Marine Radio Operator Permit. See Appendix III, Appendix V and Question 14.

Question 9. What are the FCC license examination requirements for each current class of Radio Operator License or Permit?

Answer. The following are the license examination requirements for the various classes:

1. *General Radiotelephone Operator License:* Element III. (The Element III examination also includes questions based on the information given herein in Element I and Element II. Category "O"—General.)

In addition, this examination also includes information given herein in Element II, Category "M"—Maritime. Further, it includes a substantial number of questions on additional Marine and Aviation Rules and Regulations and operating procedures as provided herein in Appendices I (Parts 80 and 87), III, and V (self test).

2. *Marine Radio Operator Permit:* Element I and Element II, Category "M"—Maritime. Also, Marine and Aviation questions and information given herein in Appendices I (Parts 80 and 87), III, and V.

3. *Restricted Radiotelephone Permit:* No written or oral examination.

4. *Ship Radar Endorsement on General Radiotelephone (or First- or Second-Class Radiotelegraph) Operator License:* Element VIII.

Question 10. After August 1984, have the FCC license examinations for Elements I, II, III, and VIII been revised?

Answer. The examinations for Elements I and II remain practically the same. However, the examination for Element III has been drastically changed. (See prior discussion under "Important changes in the Eleventh Edition," and the answer to Question 9.) (The examination for Element VIII has not been changed as of the date of this edition.)

Question 11. What do the various FCC examinations consist of?

Answer. The examination for the General Radiotelephone Operator License is 100 multiple-choice questions including Elements I, II, and III, and FCC FO Bulletin #32. The Marine Radio Operator Permit examination consists of 40 questions taken from Elements I, II(M), and FO Bulletin #32. The Ship Radar Endorsement examination is 50 questions taken from Element VIII. The passing grade for each examination is 75 percent.

Question 12. Do I still need an FCC Operator License to be responsible for the installation, maintenance, repair, and operation of the transmitting equipment of AM, FM, and TV broadcast stations?

Answer. Yes, but any type of FCC Commercial Operator License or permit will suffice, with the exception of the Marine Radio Operator Permit or the Alien Restricted Radiotelephone Operator Permit.

Question 13. In Question 12 you say, "any type"! What about the Restricted Radiotelephone Operator Permit which I can obtain without taking an examination?

Answer. The Restricted Radiotelephone Operator Permit is now all that is required for persons who are responsible for any or all technical or operating duties at AM, FM, and TV broadcast stations. The station licensee, rather than the FCC, is now responsible for judging the competence of operators and technical personnel.

Question 14. What stations are the holder of a Marine Radio Operator Permit authorized to operate?

Answer. The Marine Radio Operator Permit authorizes the holder to operate radiotelephone stations on board certain cargo and passenger vessels sailing the Great Lakes, any tidewater, or the open sea. It also authorizes the holder to operate certain aviation radiotelephone stations and certain maritime coast radiotelephone stations. It does *not* authorize the operation of AM, FM, or TV broadcast stations.

Question 15. What stations are the holder of a Restricted Radiotelephone Operator Permit authorized to operate?

Answer. The Restricted Radiotelephone Operator Permit authorizes the holder to operate most aircraft radiotelephone transmitters, marine radiotelephone transmitters on pleasure vessels, and AM, FM, and TV Broadcast stations.

Question 16. What is the schedule for taking FCC Radio Operator License examinations?

Answer.
1. February 3 through February 7: The final filing date is January 15.
2. May 5 through May 9: The final filing date is April 15.
3. August 4 through August 8: The final filing date is July 15.
4. November 3 through November 7: The final filing date is October 15.
    Examinations are conducted *by appointment* only. Contact your local FCC Office to make an appointment and request an application. The office must *receive* your completed application by the *final* filing date indicated above. Appendix III lists the address of each office.
    Contact the FCC Public Service Division at 202-632-7240 (Washington, DC) for the location of an examination location nearest you.

Question 17. For *present* holders of First-Class, Second-Class, and General Radiotelephone Operator Licenses, what special licenses will the FCC issue?

Answer. The FCC is issuing computer-generated, special lifetime, diploma-type General Radiotelephone Operator License Certificates for the 240,000 present holders of the above classes of licenses. If the present license carries a Ship Radar Endorsement, that endorsement will be carried forward to the new lifetime license. Contact your local FCC field office for more detailed information.

Question 18. Will all *new* General Radiotelephone Operator Licenses be issued for a lifetime?

Answer. Yes. Between June 1984 and August 1984, new General Radiotelephone Operator Licenses were issued for a lifetime term on the diploma-type form. After August 1984, the FCC began issuing new General Class Licenses on a card-type form. The card-type form bears the restrictive endorsement, "This license is valid for operation, maintenance and repair of stations in the Aviation, Maritime and International Public Fixed Radio Services only."

Question 19. What about renewals of current Radiotelephone First- and Second-Class Operator Licenses?

Answer. These licenses will remain valid until they expire. Upon your renewal of such licenses, you will be issued a lifetime General Radiotelephone Operator License.

Question 20. What about renewals for present holders of the General Radiotelephone Operator License that expire before the lifetime diploma-type is issued automatically in 1985 by the FCC?

Answer. These licenses will be renewed with a lifetime diploma-type license that will *not* contain any restrictive endorsement. (See card-type license restrictive endorsement in Answer to Question 18.)

Question 21. Do I need to show proof of service to renew any Radio Operator License?

Answer. No proof of service is required. Merely show your current license.

Question 22. What about renewal of a Radiotelegraph Third-Class Operator Permit?

Answer. This will remain valid until it expires. At renewal, you will be issued the Marine Radio Operator License.

Question 23. Has the renewal grace period been extended?

Answer. Yes. It has been extended from one year to five years. Radiotelephone or Radiotelegraph Licenses that require renewal and expired up to five years ago can be renewed without examination.

Question 24. Does the FCC offer any recommendations regarding the type of personnel who should perform installation, service, or maintenance in the Private Land Mobile Radio Services, the Private Operational Fixed Microwave Service, and the Personal Radio Services? (See Answer to Question 5.)

Answer. Yes. By its rule amendments, the FCC encourages station licensees to have adjustments or tests during or coincident with the installation, servicing, or maintenance of the above stations performed by or under the immediate supervision and responsibility of a person *certified* as *technically qualified* to perform these services. (Note that this is encouraged, but *not* mandatory.)

Question 25. With reference to Question 24, how does an individual become certified?

Answer. The FCC endorses and encourages organizations or committees representative of users in the Land Mobile and Fixed Services (see answer to Question 5), to establish industry certification programs for technicians.

To become certified, an individual must meet the requirements of one of these organizations. At the time of this printing, the organizations that have expressed an interest in establishing such certification programs are listed in Appendix IV. (Contact the FCC on 202-632-7240 for possible additional organizations.)

Interested technicians should contact the listed organizations for information regarding their individual requirements.

How to Use the Eleventh Edition

As described previously, important changes have been made in the FCC examination for the General Radiotelephone Operator License.

There are fewer questions on vacuum tubes and considerably more on solid-state and marine rules, regulations, and operation.

The examination for the Ship Radar Endorsement (Element VIII) remains the same as previously.

In accordance with the FCC examination changes and with the requirements of the various private industry certification organizations, this Eleventh Edition has been updated in the following manner:

1. Elements I and II have been revised and updated in accordance with the latest FCC Rules and Regulations.

2. The FCC-type sample test for Element III has been revised. A number of vacuum-tube and other types of obsolete questions have been eliminated. These have been replaced with solid-state and other currently applicable questions.

3. Appendix I has been expanded and updated in accordance with the latest FCC Rules and Regulations. Appropriate sections from the new FCC Part 80, Stations in the Maritime Services, have been included. Parts 81 and 83 are no longer in use and have been incorporated (modified) into Part 80. Appropriate sections from FCC Part 87, Aviation Services, have also been added to Appendix I.

4. A new FCC-type sample test (with answers), covering Maritime and Aviation topics has been added as Appendix V. This test material is essential for applicants for the General Radiotelephone Operator License, or for the Marine Operator Permit.

Note that the new recent and upgraded material *added* to each section of Element III is numbered differently. This material will further assist applicants for FCC and private industry licenses and certificates.

At the end of each major section in Element III, the new "added" material is numbered beginning with the last number of the section, but modified to indicate that it is "added" material. Thus, the last number of the "Audio Amplifiers" section is Q. 3.119 and the first number of the "added" material is Q. 3.119-A1, followed by Q. 3.119-A2, Q. 3.119-A3, etc.

Each section containing the new "added" questions is preceded by an explanatory note, identifying it.

Explanation of Book Contents

Most of the answers to each Question are presented in two separate sections: (1) a short but complete Answer and (2) a Discussion. This enables the student to make reference only to the Answer at first, and then return to the Discussion for more detailed information at a later date. Discussion sections are included for most of the questions in order to present much needed background material that should add considerably to the student's knowledge of radiotelephony. It is hoped that the Discussion material will save the student time that might otherwise be spent in reading various reference books.

Some very important changes and additions have been made to recent editions. Some of these changes and additions are in accordance with the FCC Study Guides (plus addenda), while others are not found in the FCC material but have been added for the student's benefit.

Typical FCC-type practice examinations have been added following each element. These examinations have been structured carefully to cover all the vital topics of each element. Answers for these tests appear in the back of the book, and a text question number directly relating to the particular test question appears next to each answer in order to assist the student in obtaining additional information, or to help the student to better understand a difficult test question. These exams should be of great assistance to the student in passing the actual FCC tests.

Many of the previously existing answers to questions (such as in Q. 3.09 and Q. 3.36) have been expanded or clarified.

It is anticipated that some of the new material added may appear on some FCC examinations. Two additional questions and answers (not found in FCC documents)—much simpler in nature than the original—have been added to Q. 3.09 because they are more representative of the questions that might appear on FCC examinations.

Because of the increasing use of solid-state equipment, FCC examinations contain more questions on transistors and transistor circuitry. Consequently, many solid-state schematics and discussions have been added, beginning with the tenth edition. In addition, a completely new group of transistor questions (not in FCC documents) has been included Q. 3.192(A) through Q. 3.192(U), immediately following original Question 3.192; these are not the *new* "added" questions.) These also originated in the tenth edition.

The student is referred to the unusually comprehensive index, which includes a complete listing of the additional transistor circuits. The student is also urged to read the introduction to the index, in order to benefit fully from the extensive special entries. The index has also been updated to list all of the new "added" questions.

Each element in this book contains a

number of questions directly related to FCC Rules and Regulations. These have been completely updated in this edition. This is also true for the selected FCC Rules and Regulations and other related topics, which are found in Appendices I through IV. In addition, many of the R & R references appearing directly after certain questions for the various Elements have been updated in accordance with the newly revised FCC Rules and Regulations. (The complete text of these newly revised Rules and Regulations may be purchased from the United States Government Printing Office.)

As in previous editions, many of the technical questions (except for the *new* "added" questions) and their order and grouping are precisely the same as in the latest issue of the FCC Study Guide and Supplements.* The technical part of Element III is divided into the following categories:

1. Alternating and Direct Current.
2. Electron Tubes.
3. Indicating Instruments.
4. Oscillators.
5. Audio Amplifiers.
6. Radio Frequency Amplifiers.
7. Transmitters.
8. Amplitude Modulation.
9. Frequency Modulation.
10. Transistors.
11. Antennas.
12. Transmission Lines.
13. Frequency Measurements.
14. Batteries.
15. Motors and Generators.
16. Microwave Equipment.
17. Troubleshooting.

The author is deeply grateful to Mr. Ed Williamson and Mr. Bernard Grob of RCA Institutes, Rossiter Marvier Schoenkfield and Patrick A. Scifo of the Sperry Gyroscope Company, and Nick Marrone of the New York Telephone Company for invaluable assistance and criticism given during the preparation of the manuscript. In addition, the author wishes to express his appreciation to his wife Hazel, for typing the manuscript.

MILTON KAUFMAN
New Hyde Park, N.Y.

* The *new* "added" questions do not appear in any current FCC document. However, the general topics for these questions do appear in an FCC topical outline (not now officially in force).

ELEMENT I

Basic Law

Note: References which appear after questions in all Elements give the law or regulation involved in answering the questions. Abbreviations used are as follows: Sec. refers to a section of the Communictions Act of 1934; Art. refers to an article of the International Radio Regulations (Atlantic City, 1947); R & R refers to a provision of the Rules and Regulations of the Federal Communications Commission; and GLR refers to regulations annexed to the Agreement Between the United States and Canada for Promotion of Safety on the Great Lakes by Means of Radio.

Question 1.01. Where and how are FCC licenses and permits obtained? (R & R 13.11(a))

Answer. In general, an operator license or permit is obtained by making application to the regional FCC office and by passing such examination elements as are required for the particular class of license desired. In the case of a restricted radiotelephone permit, no written or oral examination is required, but proper application must be made.

Discussion. See the Preface for a list of requirements regarding the various classes of licenses and endorsements.

Q. 1.02. When a licensee qualifies for a higher grade of FCC license or permit, what happens to the lesser grade license? (R & R 13.3(b), 13.26)

A. If the higher grade of license is in the same group, the lesser grade will be cancelled upon the issuance of a new license.

Q. 1.03. Who may apply for an FCC license? (R & R 13.5(a))

A. Commercial operator licenses are issued to: United States citizens, United States nationals, citizens of the Trust Territory of the Pacific Islands presenting valid identity certificates issued by the High Commissioner of the Trust Territory, aliens holding Federal Aviation Administration pilot certificates, and aliens holding Federal Communications Commission station licenses. In addition, any person who is eligible for employment in the United States may apply for an FCC radio operator license.

Q. 1.04. If a license or permit is lost, what action must be taken by the operator? (R & R 13.71, 13.72)

A. An operator whose license or permit has been lost, mutilated, or destroyed shall notify the Commission.

D. An application for a duplicate should be submitted to the office of issue embodying a statement attesting to the facts thereof. If a license has been lost, the applicant must state that reasonable search has been made for it, and further, that in the event it be found either the original or the duplicate will be returned for cancellation. The applicant must also give a statement of the service that has been obtained under the lost license.

Q. 1.05. What is the usual license term for radio operators? (R & R 13.4(a))

A. Five (5) years for the Marine Radio Operator Permit and all Radiotelegraph Operator Permits. The General Radiotelephone Operator License is valid for the operator's lifetime.

Q. 1.06. What government agency inspects radio stations in the U.S.? (Sec. 303(n))

A. The Federal Communications Commission.

D. The licensee of any radio station shall make the station available to inspection by representatives of the Commission at any reasonable hour and under the regulations governing the class of station concerned.

Q. 1.07. When may a license be renewed? (R & R 13.11)

A. Within one year before expiration.

D. However, a grace period exists which extends the renewal time to five years after the expiration of the license. Of course, the licensee may *not* operate with an expired license.

Q. 1.08. Who keeps the station logs? (R & R 73.111)

A. The licensee or permittee of each broadcast station.

D. Each log shall be kept by the person or persons competent to do so, having actual knowledge of the facts required. Such person(s) shall sign the appropriate log when starting duty and again when going off duty.

Q. 1.09. Who corrects errors in the station logs? (R & R 73.111)

A. If corrections or additions are made on the log after it has been signed, explanation must be made on the log or an attachment to it, dated and signed by either the person who kept the log, the station program director or manager, or an officer of the licensee.

Q. 1.10. How may errors in the station logs be corrected? (R & R 73.111)

A. See Question 1.09.

Q. 1.11. Under what conditions may messages be rebroadcast? (Sec. 325(a))

A. No broadcasting station shall rebroadcast the program or any part thereof of another broadcasting station without the express authority of the originating station.

Q. 1.12. What messages and signals may not be transmitted? (R & R 13.66, 13.67, 13.68)

A. The following may not be transmitted:

1. Unnecessary, unidentified, or superfluous radio communications or signals.

2. Obscene, indecent, or profane language or meaning.

3. False or deceptive signals or communications by radio, or any call letter or signal which has not been assigned by proper authority to the radio station being operated.

Q. 1.13. May an operator deliberately interfere with any radio communication or signal? (R & R 13.69)

A. No.

D. No operator shall willfully or maliciously interfere with or cause interference to any radio communication or signal.

Q. 1.14. What type of communication has top priority in the mobile service? (Art. 37)

A. Top priority is given to distress calls, distress messages, and distress traffic.

D. The order of priority for other communications is as follows:

1. Communications preceded by the urgency signal.

2. Communications preceded by the safety signal.

3. Communications relating to radio-direction finding.

4. Communications relating to the navigation and safe movement of aircraft engaged in search and rescue operations.

5. Communications relating to the navigation, movements, and needs of ships and weather observation messages destined for an official, meteorological service.

6. Government radio telegrams: Priorité Nations.

7. Government communications for which priority has been requested.

8. Service communications relating to the working of the radio communications previously exchanged.

9. Government communications other than those shown in 6 and 7 above and all other communications.

Q. 1.15. What are the grounds for suspension of operator licenses? (Sec. 303(m) (1))

A. The FCC has authority to suspend the license of any operator upon proof sufficient to satisfy the Commission that the licensee—

1. Has violated any provision of any act, treaty, or convention binding on the United States, which the Commission is authorized to administer, or any regulation made by the Commission under any such act, treaty, or convention; or

2. Has failed to carry out a lawful order of the master or person lawfully in charge of the ship or aircraft on which he is employed; or

3. Has willfully damaged or permitted radio apparatus or installations to be damaged; or

4. Has transmitted superfluous radio communications or signals or communications containing profane or obscene words, language, or meaning, or has knowingly transmitted false or deceptive signals or communications, or a call signal or letter which has not been assigned by proper authority to the station he is operating; or

5. Has willfully or maliciously interfered with any other radio communications or signals; or

6. Has obtained or attempted to obtain, or has assisted another to obtain or attempt to obtain, an operator's license by fraudulent means.

Q. 1.16. When may an operator divulge the contents of an intercepted message? (Sec. 605)

A. Only in the case of a radio communication broadcast transmitted by amateurs or others for the use of the general public; or in the case of messages relating to ships (or aircraft) in distress.

Q. 1.17. If a licensee is notified that he has violated an FCC rule or provision of the Communications Act of 1934, what must he do? (R & R 1.89)

A. Within 10 days from receipt of notice or such other period as may be specified, the licensee shall send a written answer, in duplicate, direct to the office of the Commission originating the official notice. If an answer cannot be sent nor an acknowledgment made within such 10-day period by reason of illness or other unavoidable circumstances, acknowledgment and answer shall be made at the earliest practicable date with a satisfactory explanation of the delay.

D. The answer to each notice shall be complete in itself and shall not be abbreviated by reference to other communications or answers to other notices. In every instance the answer shall contain a statement of action taken to correct the condition or omission complained of and to preclude its recurrence. In addition: If the notice relates to violations that may be due to the physical or electrical characteristics of transmitting apparatus and any new apparatus is to be installed, the answer shall state the date such apparatus was ordered, the name of the manufacturer, and the promised date of delivery. If the installation of such apparatus requires a construction permit, the file number of the application shall be given, or if a file number has not been assigned by the Commission, such identification shall be given as will permit ready identification of the application. If the notice of violation relates to lack of attention to or improper operation of the transmitter, the name and license number of the operator in charge shall be given.

Q. 1.18. If a licensee receives a notice of suspension of his license, what must he do? (R & R 1.85)

A. He may make written application for a hearing to the Commission (FCC) within 15 days of receipt of notice.

D. Whenever grounds exist for suspension of an operator license, as provided in Section 303(m) of the Communications Act, the Chief of the Safety and Special Radio Services Bureau, with respect to amateur operator licenses, or the Chief of the Field Engineering Bureau, with respect to commercial operator licenses, may issue an order suspending the operator license. No order of suspension of any operator's license shall take effect until 15 days' notice in writing of the cause for the proposed suspension has been given to the operator licensee, who may make written application to the Commission at any time within said 15 days for a hearing upon such order. The notice to the operator licensee shall not be effective until actually received by him, and from that time he shall have 15 days in which to mail the said application. In the event that physical conditions prevent mailing of the application before the expiration of the 15-day period, the application shall then be mailed as soon as possible thereafter, accompanied by a satisfactory explanation of the delay.

Q. 1.19. What are the penalties provided for violating a provision of the Communications Act of 1934 or a Rule of the FCC? (Sec. 501, 502)

A.

1. Any person who willfully and knowingly does or causes or suffers to be done any act, matter, or thing, in the Commu-

nications Act, prohibited or declared to be unlawful, or who willfully and knowingly omits or fails to do any act, matter, or thing in this Act required to be done, or upon conviction thereof, shall be punished by such offense, for which no penalty (other than forfeiture) is provided therein, by a fine of not more than $10,000 or by imprisonment for a term of not more than one year, or both. For each subsequent offense the punishment shall be a fine of not more than $10,000, or imprisonment for a term not to exceed two years, or both.

2. For violation of a Rule of the FCC, a fine of not more than $500 per day for each and every day of the offense is stipulated.

Q. 1.20. What acts, when performed by an operator on board a voluntarily equipped ship, may make him liable to a monetary forfeiture? (Sec. 510)

A. The acts are as specified below. If any radio station:

1. fails to identify itself at the times and in the manner prescribed in the rules and regulations of the Commission;

2. transmits any false call contrary to regulations of the Commission;

3. transmits unauthorized communications on any frequency designated as a distress or calling frequency in the rules and regulations of the Commission;

4. interferes with any distress call or distress communication contrary to the regulations of the Commission.

D. The maximum amount of liability for violating any one of the above numbered clauses is $100.

The forfeiture liability described above shall apply only for a willful or a repeated violation.

Q. 1.21. Define "harmful interference." (Section III, Geneva, 1959, Treaty)

A. "Harmful interference" encompasses the following: any emission, radiation, or induction which endangers the functioning of a radionavigation service or of other safety services, or which seriously degrades, obstructs, or repeatedly interrupts a radio-communication service operating in accordance with these Regulations.

Q. 1.22. What is the frequency for aircraft in distress? (R & R 87.183 (f))

A. The aircraft distress frequency is 121.5 MHz.

D. 121.5 MHz is a universal, simplex, clear-channel frequency, for use by aircraft in distress or in a condition of emergency.

Q. 1.23. In the Private Land Mobile Radio Services (FCC R & R Part 90), what is the required station authorization? (R & R 90.113)

A. No radio transmitter shall be operated in the services governed by Part 90, except under and in accordance with a proper authorization granted by the FCC.

Q. 1.24. In the Private Land Mobile Radio Services (FCC R & R Part 90), what changes in authorized stations require an application for modification of license? (R & R 90.135.)

A. The following changes require an application for modification of a license:
1. Any change in frequency.
2. Any change in the type of emission.
3. Any increase in power beyond that authorized.
4. Any increase in antenna height beyond that authorized.
5. Any increase in the number of transmitters or control, points beyond that authorized.
6. Any change in the authorized location of the base or fixed transmitter, or the area of mobile operation.
7. Any change in ownership, control or corporate structure.
8. Any change in class of station.

Q. 1.25. In the Private Land Mobile Radio Services (FCC R & R Part 90), describe the procedure to obtain special temporary

authority to operate the radio facilities. (R & R 90.145)

A. See Appendix I, R & R 90.145.

Q. 1.26. In the Private Land Mobile Radio Services (FCC R & R Part 90), when must a station first be placed in operation? (R & R 90.155)

A. See Appendix I, R & R 90.155.

Q. 1.27. In the Private Land Mobile Radio Services, (FCC R & R Part 90), what is the procedure for permanent discontinuance of station operation? (R & R 90.157)

A. See Appendix I, R & R 90.157.

Q. 1.28. In the Private Land Mobile Radio Services (FCC R & R Part 90), what are the procedures regarding transmitter measurements? (R & R 90.215)

A. See Appendix I, R & R 90.215.

Q. 1.29. What are the regulations regarding the servicing, tests, and adjustments of a CB transmitter? (R & R 95.111) (CB Rule 41)

A.
1. You may adjust your own antenna to your CB transmitter and you may make "radio checks."
2. Each internal repair and each internal adjustment to your CB transmitter should be made by, or under the direct supervision of, a person holding a privately issued certificate of proficiency.
3. Except as provided in paragraph 4 of this section each internal repair and each internal adjustment of a CB transmitter in which signals are transmitted must be made using a nonradiating ("dummy") antenna.
4. Brief test signals using a radiating antenna may be sent to adjust a transmitter to an antenna or to detect or measure spurious radiation. These test signals may not be longer than one minute during any five-minute period.

Q. 1.30. What equipment may be used at a CB station? (CB Rule 19)

A. You must use an FCC type-accepted CB transmitter at your CB station. You can identify an FCC type-accepted transmitter by the type-acceptance label placed on it by the manufacturer. You may examine a list of type-accepted equipment at any FCC Field Office or at FCC Headquarters.

D. You must not make, or have made, any internal modification to a type-accepted CB transmitter. Any internal modification to a type-accepted CB transmitter cancels the type acceptance.

Q. 1.31. May internal modifications be made to a CB transmitter? (CB Rule 42)

A. You must not make or have anyone else make, any internal modification to your CB transmitter.

D. You must not operate a CB transmitter that has been modified by anyone in any way, including modification to operate on unauthorized frequencies or with illegal power.

Q. 1.32. On a ship or aircraft, what is the requirement for obedience to lawful orders?

A. All licensed radio operators shall obey and carry out the lawful orders of the master or person lawfully in charge of the ship or aircraft on which they are employed.

ADDENDUM TO ELEMENT I

The following information, pertaining to Element I, does not appear as part of the preceding questions and answers for Element I. However, such information is given in an FCC Study Guide, where it is described as material which may appear in FCC Element I examinations. The following additional information is therefore presented here for the benefit of the students, to ensure that they will be aware of all the required information for the examination.

Background

The Federal Communications Commission was created by the Communications Act of 1934 for the purpose of regulating interstate and foreign commerce in communication by wire and radio. One of the general powers given to the Commission is the authority to prescribe the qualifications of station operators, to classify them according to the duties to be performed, and, except for alien aircraft pilots, to issue commercial operator licenses only to United States citizens and nationals. (Sections 1 and 303(l) (1))

Posting Operator Licenses

Operator permits are required to be posted at the operator's place of duty. When an application for a duplicate, replacement, or renewal of a commercial operator license is submitted, the license then held, if available, must accompany the application. In this case the operator may post a signed copy of the application submitted by him in lieu of the license document. (R & R 13.72)

Failing an Examination Element

An applicant who fails a commercial operator examination element will be ineligible to retake that same element for a two-month period. (R & R 13.27)

Suspension of Operator Licenses

Upon receipt by the Commission of application for hearing, the order of suspension shall be held in abeyance until the conclusion of the hearing which shall be conducted under such rules as the Commission may prescribe. Upon the conclusion of the hearing the Commission may affirm, modify, or revoke its order of suspension. (Section 303(m) (2) and R & R 1.85)

False Distress Signals

No person within the jurisdiction of the United States shall knowingly utter or transmit, or cause to be uttered or transmitted, any false or fraudulent signal of distress, or communication relating thereto (Section 325(a))

Distress Traffic

Each station licensee shall give absolute priority to radiocommunications or signals relating to ships or aircraft in distress. The control of distress traffic is the responsibility of the mobile station in distress. Any station which becomes aware that a mobile station is in distress may retransmit the distress message when there is reason to believe that the distress call it has intercepted has not been received by any station in a positon to render aid. (R & R 2.401, 2.402, and 2.403)

Operation During Emergency

The licensee of any station (except amateur, standard broadcast, FM broadcast, noncommercial educational FM broadcast, or television broadcast) may, during a period of emergency in which normal communication facilities are disrupted as a result of hurricane, flood, earthquake, or similar disaster, utilize such station for emergency communication service in communicating in a manner other than that specified in the instrument of authorization. (R & R 2.405)

FCC-TYPE SAMPLE TEST FOR ELEMENT I

I-1. When may an operator deliberately interfere with radio communications? (Q. 1.13)
  (a) Between 12 midnight and 6 A.M.
  (b) At no time.
  (c) When sending government radio telegrams.

  (d) When rebroadcasting the program of another station.
  (e) None of the above.

I-2. The penalty for violating a rule of the FCC is: (Q. 1.19)
  (a) A $10,000 fine.
  (b) Revocation of the operator's license.
  (c) Suspension of the operator's license.
  (d) $500 per day maximum for each day of the offense.
  (e) $50 per day for each day of the offense.

I-3. The penalty for violating a provision of the Communications Act of 1934 (first offense) is: (Q. 1.19)
  (a) An official warning.
  (b) Suspension of the operator's license for 90 days.
  (c) A fine of not more than $10,000, or imprisonment for not more than one year, or both.
  (d) A fine of not more than $1,000, or imprisonment for not more than one year, or both.
  (e) A fine of not more than $10,000, or imprisonment for not more than two years, or both.

I-4. One of the grounds for suspension of an operator's license is: (Q. 1.15)
  (a) Has failed to carry out a lawful order of the master in charge of the ship on which he is employed.
  (b) Has failed to keep correct station logs.
  (c) Has failed to put in the correct number of working hours at his station.
  (d) Has permitted his station to operate off frequency.
  (e) None of the above.

I-5. The following messages or signals may not be transmitted: (Q. 1.12)
  (a) Government communications relating to aircraft schedules.
  (b) Unidentified radio signals.
  (c) Communications relative to station log entries.
  (d) Private messages.
  (e) Communications relative to ship schedules.

I-6. Messages may be rebroadcast under the following condition: (Q. 1.11)

(a) If a proper entry is made in the station log.

(b) If requested by the master of the ship.

(c) Only by an operator having a first-class radiotelephone or radiotelegrah license.

(d) By permission of the originating station.

(e) Between 12 midnight and 6 A.M.

I-7. The usual license term for radio operators is: (Q. 1.05)

(a) One year.

(b) Three years.

(c) Two years.

(d) Four years.

(e) None of the above.

I-8. Where may FCC licenses be obtained? (Q. 1.01)

(a) At the regional FAA office.

(b) At any state licensing agency.

(c) At any Federal licensing agency.

(d) At any regional FCC office.

(e) Only at the Washington, D.C., FCC office.

I-9. The following persons may apply for an FCC license: (Q. 1.03)

(a) Holders of any foreign radio operator's license.

(b) Only holders of a restricted radio license.

(c) Persons who are eligible for employment in the U.S.

(d) Aliens who have applied for citizenship.

(e) Persons who have graduated from an approved radio school.

I-10. The three top priority types of communications, in their correct order, are: (Q. 1.14)

(a) Distress, urgency, and safety.

(b) Urgency, distress, and safety.

(c) Distress, safety, and navigation.

(d) Distress, urgency, and navigation.

(e) Distress, urgency, and government.

I-11. An operator may divulge the contents of an intercepted message only: (Q. 1.16)

(a) When authorized by a first-class license holder.

(b) When authorized by the master of a ship or aircraft.

(c) If it relates to distress or is for the use of the general public.

(d) If it relates to government communications.

(e) If it is an internal company message.

I-12. The agency which is authorized to inspect radio stations in the United States is: (Q. 1.06)

(a) The Federal Aviation Administration.

(b) Any authorized Federal agency.

(c) The local State Communications Administration.

(d) The Federal Communications Commission.

(e) None of the above.

I-13. An operator's license may be renewed: (Q. 1.07)

(a) Every three years.

(b) Only after it has expired.

(c) Only if proof of operation is given.

(d) Automatically.

(e) Within one year before expiration.

I-14. Station logs are kept by: (Q. 1.08)

(a) The owner of the station.

(b) The licensee or permittee of each station.

(c) Only the individual in charge of maintenance of the station equipment.

(d) Any individual having a proper operator's license.

(e) Only by an operator who has never been convicted of violating a provision of a rule of the FCC.

I-15. If a licensee receives a notice of suspension of his license, he must: (Q. 1.18)

(a) Immediately cease to operate any station.

(b) Make written application for a hearing within 15 days.

(c) Make written application for a hearing within 30 days.

(d) Immediately mail his license to the FCC, pending a hearing.

(e) Wait for additional instructions from the FCC.

I-16. If a licensee has been notified that he has violated an FCC rule, he must send a written answer: (Q. 1.17)

(a) To the Washington, D.C., office, within 15 days.

(b) To the originating FCC office, within 10 days.

(c) To the originating FCC office, within 15 days.

(d) To the Washington D.C., FCC office, within 10 days.

(e) To the originating FAA office, within 10 days.

I-17. Errors in the station log may be corrected by: (Q. 1.09)

(a) Erasing the erroneous material and writing over it in a neat manner.

(b) Anyone working in the station.

(c) Anyone possessing a first or second-class operator's license.

(d) Only the person originating the entry.

(e) Only a person designated by the manager of the station or the master of a ship.

I-18. If an operator loses his license, he must: (Q. 1.04)

(a) Notify the FCC within 15 days.

(b) Notify the FAA within 15 days.

(c) Notify the FCC immediately.

(d) Not operate any station.

(e) None of the above.

I-19. Unidentified radio communications may be transmitted under the following condition: (Q. 1.12)

(a) For distress messages.

(b) Under no condition.

(c) For urgency calls.

(d) For government communications.

(e) For weather messages.

I-20. If a licensee has a second-class radiotelegraph license and then qualifies for a first-class radiotelegraph license, the lesser grade of license: (Q. 1.02)

(a) Remains in force.

(b) Is needed to perform maintenance on the station.

(c) Will be cancelled.

(d) Must be immediately mailed back to the FCC.

(e) Is still effective for routine communications.

ELEMENT II

Basic Operating Practice

Note: The questions of Element II have been subdivided into two categories. The candidate for a license may elect to answer questions either in the general category (O) or in maritime category (M).

CATEGORY "O"—GENERAL

Question 2.01. What should an operator do when he leaves a transmitter unattended?

Answer. If an operator leaves a transmitter unattended, the transmitter must be made inaccessible or inoperable with respect to all unauthorized persons.

Q. 2.02. What are the meanings of clear, out, over, roger, words twice, say again, and break?

A.
1. The word "clear" signifies that the transmission is ended and that no response is expected.
2. The word "out" signifies that the conversation is ended and that no response is expected.
3. The word "over" signifies "My transmission is ended and I expect a response from you."
4. The word "roger" signifies "I have received all of your last transmission."

5. The words "words twice" means:
a. As a request: "Communication is difficult. Please send every phrase twice."
b. As information: "Since communication is difficult every phrase in this message will be sent twice."
6. The words "say again" signifies repeat.
7. The word "break" signifies a separation between portions of a message.

Q. 2.03 How should a microphone be treated when used in noisy locations?

A. The microphone should be shielded with the hands in order to reduce outside noises thus making communication more intelligible.

D. In severe cases, special noise-canceling microphones may be used.

Q. 2.04. What may happen to the received signal when an operator has shouted into a microphone?

A. Shouting into the microphone is poor practice, because while it probably will not injure the microphone, it may very well overdrive some speech amplifier or cause overmodulation. Either of these effects may cause severe distortion of the speech and possible interference with adjacent channels.

Q. 2.05. Why should radio transmitters be "off" when signals are not being transmitted?

A. To prevent interference with other stations using the channel.

D. Even if an unmodulated carrier is transmitted, it may cause heterodyning interference with other station carriers, making communication very difficult.

Q. 2.06. Why should an operator use well-known words and phrases?

A. The operator should use simple language, and well-known words and phrases to ensure accurate, efficient communications and to eliminate repetition as much as possible.

Q. 2.07. Why is the station's call sign transmitted?

A. The station's call sign should be transmitted in order to clearly identify the originator of messages being transmitted.

Q. 2.08. Where does an operator find specifications for obstruction marking and lighting (where required) for the antenna towers of a particular radio station?

A. Specifications are found in Part 17 of the Rules and Regulations of the FCC. (R & R 17.23, 17.25, 17.27, and 17.43)

Q. 2.09. What should an operator do if he hears profanity being used at his station?

A. He should take steps to conclude the transmission and enter the details in the station log. The incident should be reported to the FCC.

Q. 2.10. When may an operator use his station without regard to certain provisions of his station license? (R & R 2.405)

A. The licensee of any station, except amateur, may, during a period of emergency in which normal communication facilities are disrupted as a result of hurricane, flood, earthquake or similar disaster, utilize such station for emergency communication service in communicating in a manner other than that specified in the instrument of authorization.

Q. 2.11. Who bears the responsibility if an operator permits an unlicensed person to speak over his station?

A. The licensed operator in charge of the station always bears the responsibility for its operation, regardless of who is speaking over it.

Q. 2.12. What is meant by a "phonetic alphabet" in radiotelephone communications?

A. A phonetic alphabet is one in which each letter is associated with a particular word. For example: A—Alpha, B—Bravo, C—Charlie, etc.

D. A phonetic alphabet is used in radiotelephone communication to ensure that certain letters or words are clearly understandable to the receiving station.

LETTER	WORD	PRONUNCIATION
A	Alfa	*AL* FAH
B	Bravo	*BRAH* VOH
C	Charlie	*CHAR* LEE
D	Delta	*DELL* TAH
E	Echo	*ECK* OH
F	Foxtrot	*FOKS* TROT
G	Golf	*GOLF*
H	Hotel	HOH *TELL*
I	India	*IN* DEE AH
J	Juliett	*JOO* LEE *ETT*
K	Kilo	*KEY* LOH
L	Lima	*LEE* MAH
M	Mike	MIKE
N	November	NO *VEM* BER
O	Oscar	*OSS* CAH
P	Papa	PA *PAH*
Q	Quebec	KEH *BECK*
R	Romeo	*ROW* ME OH
S	Sierra	SEE *AIR* RAH
T	Tango	*TANG* GO
U	Uniform	*YOU* NEE FORM
V	Victor	*VIK* TAH
W	Whiskey	*WISS* KEY
X	X-ray	*ECKS RAY*
Y	Yankee	*YANG* KEY
Z	Zulu	*ZOO* LOO

Q. 2.13. How does the licensed operator of a station normally exhibit his authority to operate the station?

A. The original license of each station operator shall be posted at the place where he is on duty or kept in his possession in the manner specified in the regulations governing the class of station concerned.

Q. 2.14. What precautions should be observed in testing a station on the air?

A. The operator should listen on the transmission frequency to ensure that interference will not be caused to a communication in progress.

FCC-TYPE SAMPLE TEST FOR ELEMENT II (CATEGORY "O"—GENERAL)

II-1(O). A station's call sign is transmitted: (Q. 2.07)

(a) For the purpose of testing the transmitter.
(b) To allow the receiving station to tune his receiver properly.
(c) To identify clearly the originator of the messages.
(d) To identify clearly the receiver of the messages.
(e) To fill in "dead" air time.

II-2(O). When an operator leaves his transmitter unattended, he must: (Q. 2.01)

(a) Place it on automatic operation.
(b) Make it inaccessible or inoperable to all unauthorized persons.
(c) Post a notice on the station door, stating when he intends to return.
(d) Be certain it is operating properly and on the correct frequency.
(e) Make prior notification to the regional FCC office.

II-3(O). An operator should check for possible communications in progress on his assigned frequency prior to: (Q. 2.14)

(a) Increasing the power of his transmitter.
(b) Changing the frequency of his transmitter.
(c) Testing his station on the air.
(d) Transmitting station identification.
(e) None of the above.

II-4(O). Accurate and efficient communications are helped by: (Q. 2.06)

(a) The use of simple phrases and well-known words.
(b) The use of the lowest possible transmitting power.
(c) Using low levels of amplitude modulation.
(d) Maximum repetition of phrases.
(e) Selective overmodulation of the transmitter.

II-5(O). If a transmission is ended and no response is expected, the transmission is ended with the word: (Q. 2.02)

(a) Out.
(b) Over.
(c) Roger.
(d) Break.
(e) None of the above.

II-6(O). A phonetic alphabet (ex.: A—Alpha) is sometimes made use of in radio communications to: (Q. 2.12)

(a) Extend the range of transmission.
(b) Reduce the average modulation percentage.
(c) Ensure that certain words or letters are clearly understandable.
(d) Reduce charges for some types of radiotelegrams.
(e) Transmit weather information by radio.

II-7(O). To prevent interference from other transmitters using a common channel: (Q. 2.05)

(a) A low level of modulation should be used.
(b) Only frequency modulation should be employed.
(c) Phase modulation is preferred.

(d) All transmitters not involved in the particular transmission should be off.

(e) The microphone should be held several inches away from the operator's lips.

II-8(O). The word "clear" signifies that the transmission: (Q. 2.02)

(a) Is ended and that a response is expected.

(b) Is ended and that no response is expected.

(c) Cannot be continued because of transmitter problems.

(d) Has been received and completely understood.

(e) Should be repeated.

II-9(O). The original license of each station operator shall be: (Q. 2.13)

(a) Kept in a safe place, such as a safety deposit box.

(b) Duplicated and the the duplicate posted at the station.

(c) Posted at his station, or kept in his possession.

(d) Given into the safekeeping of the station manager or the master of his ship.

(e) Displayed only when he is testing the station.

II-10(O). If an operator shouts into a microphone, this may: (Q. 2.04)

(a) Cause voice strain.

(b) Damage the microphone.

(c) Cause interference with adjacent channels.

(d) Reduce the effective distance of transmission.

(e) None of the above.

II-11(O). If communication is difficult, the receiver may send the following request: (Q. 2.02)

(a) Speak louder.

(b) Speak closer to the microphone.

(c) Speak farther from the microphone.

(d) Increase your transmitter power.

(e) Words Twice.

II-12(O). If an unlicensed person speaks over a station, this is the responsibility of: (Q. 2.11)

(a) The licensed operator in charge of the station.

(b) The Federal Communications Commission.

(c) The manager of the station.

(d) Any license holder at the station.

(e) The Federal Bureau of Investigation.

II-13(O). If an operator hears profanity being broadcast over his station, he should: (Q. 2.09)

(a) Ignore it, as no censorship is permitted.

(b) Report it to the station manager.

(c) Caution the operator, but take no further steps.

(d) Have the transmission concluded and report it to the Federal Communications Commission.

(e) Immediately shut down the transmitter.

II-14(O). When an operator wishes a repeat of a transmission or a portion thereof, he will say: (Q. 2.02)

(a) Say again.

(b) Please repeat.

(c) I did not understand your last transmission.

(d) Your last transmission was not clear.

(e) Your transmission is breaking up.

II-15(O). A separation between portions of a message is signified by the word: (Q. 2.02)

(a) Separate.

(b) Space.

(c) Break.

(d) Hyphen.

(e) Colon.

II-16(O). A microphone should be shielded with the hands: (Q. 2.03)

(a) To protect it from the wind.

(b) To reduce outside noises.

(c) In cold weather.

(d) To improve the high-frequency response.

(e) To increase its output.

II-17(O). Specifications for obstruction marking and lighting for antenna towers are found: (Q. 2.08)
(a) On a plate fastened to the antenna.
(b) In the regulations of the Federal Aviation Administration.
(c) In the regulations of the State Aviation Authority.
(d) In Part 17 of the Rules and Regulations of the FCC.
(e) In Part 57 of the Rules and Regulations of the FCC.

II-18(O). When communications are disrupted as a result of a disaster, the licensee of a station may: (Q. 2.10)
(a) Shut down his station.
(b) Decrease the power of his station.
(c) Utilize the station for emergency communications.
(d) Operate his station with unlicensed personnel.
(e) None of the above.

II-19(O). When an operator has ended a communication and expects a response, he uses the word: (Q. 2.02)
(a) Respond.
(b) Reply.
(c) Roger.
(d) Over.
(e) Break.

II-20(O). When an operator wishes to indicate that he has received all of the last transmission, he uses the word: (Q. 2.02)
(a) Received.
(b) Roger.
(c) Over.
(d) OK.
(e) Clear.

CATEGORY "M"—MARITIME
(See also Appendices I, III, and IV)

Q. 2.01 What is the importance of the frequency 2182 kHz? (R & R 80.389(a))

A. This frequency may be used in two ways:
1. It is the international distress, ur-gency, and safety frequency for radio-telephony, ships, aircraft and survival-craft stations. This frequency is also used by private public coast stations.
2. It is the international general radio-telephone calling frequency for the maritime mobile service.

Q. 2.02 Describe completely what actions should be taken by a radio operator who hears a distress message; a safety message. (R & R 80.321 through 80.324)

A.
1. How to acknowledge a distress message:
a. Stations of the maritime mobile service which receive a distress message from a mobile station which is, beyond any possible doubt, in their vicinity, shall immediately acknowledge receipt. However, in areas where reliable communications with one or more coast stations are practicable, ship stations may defer this acknowledgment for a short interval so that a coast station may acknowledge receipt.
b. Stations of the maritime mobile service which receive a distress message from a mobile station, which, beyond any possible doubt, is not in their vicinity, shall allow a short interval of time to elapse before acknowledging receipt of the message, in order to permit stations nearer to the mobile station in distress to acknowledge receipt without interference.
2. Form of acknowledgment:
a. The acknowledgment of receipt of a distress message is transmitted, when radiotelegraphy is used, in the following form:
(1) The call sign of the station sending the distress message, sent three times.
(2) The word DE.
(3) The call sign of the station acknowledging receipt, sent three times.
(4) The group RRR.
(5) The distress signal SOS.
b. The acknowledgement of receipt of a distress message is transmitted, when radiotelephony is used, in the following form:

(1) The call sign or other identification of the station sending the distress message, spoken three times.

(2) The words THIS IS.

(3) The call sign or other identification of the station acknowledging receipt, spoken three times.

(4) The word RECEIVED.

(5) The distress signal MAYDAY.

3. Information furnished by acknowledging station:

a. Every mobile station which acknowledges receipt of a distress message shall, on the order of the master or person responsible for the ship, aircraft, or other vehicle carrying such mobile station, transmit as soon as possible the following information in the order shown:

(1) Its name.

(2) Its position, in the form prescribed in R & R 80.316.

(3) The speed at which it is proceeding toward, and the approximate time it will take to reach, the mobile station in distress.

b. Before sending this message, the station shall ensure that it will not interfere with the emissions of other stations better situated to render immediate assistance to the station in distress.

4. Transmission of distress message by a station not itself in distress:

a. A mobile station or a land station which learns that a mobile station is in distress shall transmit a distress message in any of the following cases:

(1) When the station in distress is not itself in a position to transmit the distress message.

(2) When the master or person responsible for the ship, aircraft, or other vehicle not in distress, or the person responsible for the land station, considers that further help is necessary.

(3) When, although not in a position to render assistance, it has heard a distress message which has not been acknowledged. When a mobile station transmits a distress message under these conditions, it shall take all necessary steps to notify the authorities who may be able to render assistance.

b. The transmission of a distress message under the conditions prescribed in paragraph (a) of this section shall be made on any of the international distress frequencies (500-kHz radiotelegraph; 2182-kHz, or 156.8 MHz radiotelephone) or on any other available frequency on which attention may be attracted.

c. The transmission of the distress message shall always be preceded by the call indicated below, which shall itself be preceded whenever possible by the radiotelegraph or radiotelephone alarm signal. This call consists of:

(1) When radiotelegraphy is used:

(i) The signal DDD SOS SOS SOS DDD.

(ii) The word DE.

(iii) The call sign of the transmitting station, sent three times.

(2) When radiotelephone is used:

(i) The signal MAYDAY RELAY, spoken three times.

(ii) The words THIS IS.

(iii) The call sign or other identification of the transmitting station, spoken three times.

d. When the radiotelegraph alarm signal is used, an interval of two minutes shall be allowed, when this is considered necessary, before the transmission of the call mentioned.

5. Safety Message: A safety message is one which provides information concerning the safety of navigation, or important meteorological warnings. A radio operator receiving such a message should immediately forward the message to the ship's master.

Q. 2.03 What information must be contained in distress messages? What procedure should be followed by a radio operator in sending a distress message? What is a good choice of words to be used in sending a distress message? (R & R 80.314 through 80.320)

A.

1. The following information must be contained in distress messages:

The message shall include the distress call followed by the name of the ship, aircraft, or the vehicle in distress, information regarding the position of the latter, the nature of the distress and the nature of the help requested, and any other information which might facilitate this assistance.

2. The following procedure should be followed:

a. Distress signals:

(1) The international radiotelegraph distress signal consists of the group "three dots, three dashes, three dots" (· · · — — — · · ·), symbolized herein by SOS, transmitted as a single signal in which the dashes are slightly prolonged so as to be distinguished clearly from the dots.

(2) The international radiotelephone distress signal consists of the word MAYDAY, pronounced as the French expression "m'aider."

(3) These distress signals indicate that a mobile station is threatened by grave and imminent danger and requests immediate assistance.

b. Radiotelephone distress call and message transmission procedure:

(1) The radiotelephone distress procedure shall consist of:

(i) The radiotelephone alarm signal (whenever possible).

(ii) The distress call.

(iii) The distress message.

(2) The radiotelephone distress transmissions shall be made slowly and distinctly, each word being clearly pronounced to facilitate transcription.

(3) After the transmission by radiotelephony of its distress message, the mobile station may be requested to transmit suitable signals followed by its call sign or name, to permit direction-finding stations to determine its position. This request may be repeated at frequent intervals if necessary.

(4) The distress message, preceded by the distress call, shall be repeated at intervals until an answer is received. This repetition shall be preceded by the radiotelephone alarm signal whenever possible.

(5) When the mobile station in distress receives no answer to a distress message transmitted on the distress frequency, the message may be repeated on any other available frequency on which attention might be attracted.

3. A suitable choice of words would be "Mayday, Mayday, Mayday, this is Trans Ocean Airlines Flight 907, 14 miles due East of Cape Hatteras, three engines out, require immediate assistance to pick up all on board after ditching. Estimate ditching to occur in 30 seconds; number 3 engine on fire, Over."

Q. 2.04 What are the requirements for keeping watch on 2182 kHz? If a radio operator is required to "stand watch" on an international distress frequency, when may he stop listening? What are the requirements for keeping watch on 156.8 MHz? (R & R 80.147, 80.148, 80.304(b), 80.305, 80.308)

A.

1. Each ship station operating on telephony on frequencies in the band 1605–3500 kHz must maintain a watch on the frequency 2182 kHz. This watch must be maintained at least twice each hour for 3 minutes commencing at x h.00 and x h.30 Coordinated Universal Time (UTC) using either a loudspeaker or headphone. Except for distress, urgency, or safety messages, ship stations must not transmit during the silence periods on 2182 kHz.

2. Keep a continuous and efficient watch on the radiotelephone distress frequency 2182 kHz from the principal radio operating position or the room from which the vessel is normally steered while being navigated in the open sea outside a harbor or port. A radiotelephone distress frequency watch receiver having a loudspeaker and a radiotelephone auto alarm facility must be used to keep the continuous watch on 2182 kHz if such watch is kept from the room from which the vessel is normally steered.

After a determination by the master that conditions are such that maintenance of the listening watch would interfere with the safe navigation of the ship, the watch may be maintained by the use of the radiotelephone auto alarm facility alone.

3. Keep a continuous and efficient watch on the VHF distress frequency 156.800 MHz from the room from which the vessel is normally steered while in the open sea outside a harbor or port. The watch must be maintained by a designated member of the crew who may perform other duties, relating to the operation or navigation of the vessel, provided such other duties do not interfere with the effectiveness of the watch. Use of a properly adjusted squelch or brief interruptions due to other nearby VHF transmissions are not considered to adversely affect the continuity or efficiency of the required watch on the VHF distress frequency. This watch need not be maintained by vessels subject to the Bridge-to-Bridge Act and participating in a Vessel Traffic Services (VTS) system as required or recommended by the U.S. Coast Guard, when an efficient listening watch is maintained on both the bridge-to-bridge frequency and a separate assigned VTS frequency. (R & R 80.143)

4. Watch required by the Great Lakes Radio Agreement.

Each ship of the United States which is equipped with a radiotelephone station for compliance with the Great Lakes Radio Agreement must when underway, keep a watch on 156.800 MHz whenever such station is not being used for authorized traffic. The watch must be maintained by at least one officer or crewmember who may perform other duties provided such other duties do not interfere with the watch.

Q. 2.05 Under what circumstances may a coast station contact a land station by radio? (R & R 80.453)

A. For the purposes of facilitating the transmission or reception of safety communication to or from a ship or aircraft station.

Q. 2.06 What do distress, safety, and urgency signals indicate? What are the international urgency, safety, and distress signals? In the case of a mobile radio station in distress what station is responsible for the control of distress message traffic? (R & R 80.314 through 80.329)

A.

1. a. The distress signal (MAYDAY) indicates that the ship, aircraft or any other vehicle which sends the distress signal is threatened by serious and imminent danger and requests immediate assistance.

b. The safety signal (SECURITY) announces that the station is about to transmit a message concerning the safety of navigation or giving important meteorological warnings. Hence, it should precede such a transmission.

c. The urgent signal (PAN) shall indicate that the calling station has a very urgent message to transmit concerning the safety of a ship, an aircraft, or another vehicle, or concerning the safety of some person on board or sighted from on board.

2. The control of distress traffic shall be the responsibility of the mobile station in distress or upon the station which, by application of the provisions of the Commission's rules and regulations has sent the distress call. These stations may delegate the control of the distress traffic to another station.

Q. 2.07. In regions of heavy traffic why should an interval be left between radiotelephone calls? Why should a radio operator listen before transmitting on a shared channel? How long may a radio operator in the mobile service continue attempting to contact a station which does not answer? (R & R 80.116)

A.

1. An interval should be left (and is required by law) to permit other stations to share the radio channel. (See R & R 80.116 for details.)

2. He should listen on the shared channel first to avoid disrupting communication which may already be in progress.

3. Calling a particular station shall not continue for more than 30 seconds in each instance. If the called station is not heard to reply, that station shall not again be called until after an interval of two minutes. When a station called does not reply to a call sent three times at intervals of two minutes, the calling shall cease and shall not be renewed until after an interval of 15 minutes; however, if there is no reason to believe that harmful interference will be caused to other communications in progress, the call sent three times at intervals of two minutes may be repeated after a pause of not less than three minutes. In event of an emergency involving safety, the provisions of this paragraph shall not apply.

D. If applicable, the sub-audible tone squelch should be defeated when monitoring a channel before transmitting. This will ensure that no other station is transmitting on the channel.

Q. 2.07(A). How should the volume control and squelch control (if present) on a receiver be set?

A. With the squelch control set to OFF, adjust the volume control for a more comfortable listening level. Then adjust the squelch control so that very weak signals and/or noises are not heard.

Q. 2.08. Why are test transmissions sent? How often should they be sent? What is the proper way to send a test message? How often should the station's call sign be sent? (R & R 80.101)

A.

1. Test transmissions are sent to ensure that the radio equipment is functioning normally.

2. They should be sent each day unless normal use of the radiotelephone installation demonstrates that the equipment is in proper operating condition.

3. The official call sign of the testing station, followed by the word "test," shall be announced on the radio-channel being used for the test, as a warning that test emissions are about to be made on that frequency.

4. The station's call sign shall be sent at the conclusion of each test message, which should not exceed 10 seconds.

D.

1. Ship stations must use every precaution to insure that, when conducting operational transmitter tests, the emissions of the station will not cause harmful interference. Radiation must be reduced to the lowest practicable value and if feasible shall be entirely suppressed. When radiation is necessary or unavoidable, the testing procedure described below shall be followed:

(a) The licensed radio operator or other person responsible for operation of the transmitting apparatus shall ascertain by careful listening that the test emissions will not be likely to interfere with transmissions in progress; if they are likely to interfere with the working of a coast or aeronautical station in the vicinity of the ship station, the consent of the former station(s) must be obtained before the test emissions occur; (see required procedures in subparagraphs (b) and (c) of this paragraph following);

(b) The applicable identification of the testing station, followed by the word "test" shall be announced on the radio channel being used for the test, as a warning that test emissions are about to be made on that frequency;

(c) If, as a result of the announcement prescribed in subparagraph (b) of this paragraph, any station transmits by voice the word "wait," testing shall be suspended. When, after an appropriate interval of time such announcement is repeated and no response is observed, and careful listening indicates that harmful interference should not be caused, the operator shall, if further testing is necessary, proceed as set forth in subparagraphs (d) and (e) of this paragraph;

(d) Testing of transmitters shall, insofar as practicable, be confined to working frequencies without two way communications. However 2182 kHz and 156.8 MHz may be used to contact other ship or coast stations when signal reports are necessary. Short tests, by vessels which continue to rely upon the use of DSB equipment for distress and safety purposes, are permitted on 2182 kHz to evaluate the compatibility of that equipment with an SSB emission A3J system. U.S. Coast Guard stations may be contacted on 2182 kHz for test purposes only when tests are being conducted during inspections by Commission representatives or when qualified radio technicians are installing equipment or correcting deficiencies in the station radiotelephone equipment. In these cases the test shall be identified as "FCC" or "technical" and logged accordingly.

(e) When further testing is necessary beyond the two "test" announcements specified in subparagraphs (b) and (c) of this paragraph, the operator shall announce the word "testing" followed in the case of a voice transmission test by the count "1, 2, 3, 4, * * * etc." or by test phrases or sentences not in conflict with normal operating signals. The test signals in either case shall have a duration not exceeding 10 seconds. At the conclusion of the test, there shall be voice announcement of the official call sign of the testing stations. This test transmission shall not be repeated until a period of at least one minute has elapsed; on the frequency 2182 kHz or 156.8 MHz a period of at least five minutes shall elapse before the test transmission is repeated.

2. When testing is conducted on any frequency within the bands 2173.5 to 2190.5 kHz, 156.75 to 156.85 MHz, 480 to 510 kHz (survival craft transmitters only) or 8362 to 8366 kHz (survival transmitters only), no test transmissions shall occur which are likely to actuate any automatic alarm receiver within range. Survival craft stations shall not be tested on the frequency 500 kHz during the 500 kHz silence periods.

Q. 2.09. In the mobile service, why should radiotelephone messages be as brief as possible?

A. It is a good policy to be brief to permit other stations to operate without interference and also from the standpoint of efficient station operation.

Q. 2.10. What are the meanings of: Clear, Out, Over, Roger, Words Twice, Repeat, and Break?

A. See Q. 2.02, Category "O"—General.

Q. 2.11. Does the Geneva, 1959 treaty give other countries the authority to inspect U.S. vessels? (Art. 21)

A. Yes.
D. The governments or appropriate administrations of countries which a mobile station visits, may require the production of the license for examination. The operator of the mobile station, or the person responsible for the station, shall facilitate this examination. The license shall be kept in such a way that it can be produced upon request. As far as possible, the license, or a copy certified by the authority which has issued it, should be permanently exhibited in the station.

Q. 2.12. Why are call signs sent? Why should they be sent clearly and distinctly?

A.
1. Call signs are sent to enable monitoring stations to identify the station of origin.
2. They should be sent clearly and distinctly to avoid unnecessary repetition and to assist monitoring stations in identifying calls.

Q. 2.13. How does the licensed operator of a ship station exhibit his authority to operate a station? (R & R 80.175)

A. When a licensed operator is required for the operation of a station, the original license of each such operator while he is employed or designated as radio operator of the station shall be posted in a conspicuous place at the principal location on board ship at which the station is operated: Provided, that in the case of stations of a portable nature, including marine-utility stations, or in the case where the operator holds a restricted radiotelephone operator permit, the operator may in lieu of posting have on his person either his required operator license or a duly issued verification card (FCC form 758-F) attesting to the existence of that license.

Q. 2.14. What may a coast station *not* charge for messages it is requested to handle? (R & R 80.95)

A.

1. No charge shall be made by any station in the maritime mobile service of the United States for the transmission of distress messages and replies thereto in connection with situations involving the safety of life and property at sea.

2. No charge shall be made by any station in the maritime mobile service of the United States for the transmission receipt, or relay of the information concerning dangers to navigation, originating on a ship of the United States or of a foreign country.

Q. 2.15. What is the difference between calling and working frequencies? (R & R 80.5)

A. A calling frequency is one to which all stations generally listen, for example 2182 kHz. A working frequency is an assigned frequency other than a calling frequency on which the main body of the communication would take place after the initial calling.

FCC-TYPE SAMPLE TEST FOR ELEMENT II (CATEGORY "M"— MARITIME)

II-1(M). A coast station may contact a land station by radio: (Q. 2.05)
 (a) To facilitate the transmission or reception of a safety communication.
 (b) To facilitate the transmission or reception of an alarm communication.
 (c) For the transmission of a government communication.

(d) If so directed by the station manager.
 (e) If it is having difficulties with its transmitter.

II-2(M). To permit other stations to operate without interference, radiotelephone messages should be: (Q. 2.09)
 (a) Sent by frequency modulation.
 (b) Sent with reduced amplitude modulation.
 (c) As brief as possible.
 (d) Sent with reduced transmitter output power.
 (e) None of the above.

II-3(M). A calling frequency is one on which: (Q. 2.15)
 (a) The main body of communications take place.
 (b) Calls are always made to land stations.
 (c) Communications are always made to aircraft stations.
 (d) Calls are made from land stations to marine stations.
 (e) All stations generally listen.

II-4(M). The licensed operator of a ship station is required to show his authority to operate the station by: (Q. 2.13)
 (a) An FCC registration attached to his outer clothing.
 (b) Posting his license at the main station location.
 (c) Posting a duplicate of his license at the main station location.
 (d) A letter of approval from the FCC.
 (e) A license from the Federal Maritime Authority.

II-5(M). If a ship or other vehicle is in imminent danger, it should transmit the: (Q. 2.03)
 (a) Distress signal (PAN).
 (b) Urgency signal (MAYDAY).
 (c) Distress signal (IMI).
 (d) Distress signal (MAYDAY).
 (e) Urgency signal (PAN).

II-6(M). The frequency 2182 kHz may be used in the following way: (Q.2.01)

(a) To communicate with commercial broadcast stations.
(b) To communicate with the Federal Communications Commissions.
(c) To send telegrams between ship stations and land stations.
(d) For distress calls.
(e) To report on the passing of other ships.

II-7(M). Maritime stations receiving a distress call from a station in their vicinity shall: (Q. 2.02)
(a) Immediately relay the information to a coast station.
(b) Keep radio silence.
(c) Immediately acknowledge receipt.
(d) Immediately notify the Federal Communications Commission.
(e) Send out a series of SOS signals.

II-8(M). Test transmissions should be sent each day unless: (Q. 2.08)
(a) The operator is prevented from doing so by official duties.
(b) The operator is ordered not to do so by the master of the ship.
(c) The power output exceeds the permissible value.
(d) Normal use shows the equipment to be working properly.
(e) Normal use shows that the equipment is in need of maintenance.

II-9(M). A working frequency is one that is: (Q. 2.15)
(a) Used during normal working hours of the operator.
(b) Used for the main body of the communication.
(c) Generally listened to by all stations.
(d) Used only for test purposes during daylight hours.
(e) Known to be transmitting at the FCC required power.

II-10(M). Call signs should be sent clearly and distinctly in order to: (Q. 2.12)
(a) Alert the auto alarm system.
(b) Make possible accurate radio-direction finding.

(c) Conserve transmission power.
(d) Avoid unnecessary repetition.
(e) Avoid excessive amplitude modulation.

II-11(M). Under the Geneva, 1959 treaty, other countries may: (Q. 2.11)
(a) Check the type of radio equipment being used on board a U.S. vessel.
(b) Require the production of a marine operator's license.
(c) Require that a U.S. vessel's transmitter be shut down.
(d) Require that a U.S. vessel not transmit within the 12-mile limit.
(e) None of the above.

II-12(M). A radio operator in the mobile service may continue attempting to contact a station which does not answer: (Q. 2.07)
(a) For a total of three times, at intervals of two minutes each.
(b) For a total of 30 seconds.
(c) Once every 15 minutes.
(d) On a continuous basis.
(e) At the discretion of the master of the ship.

II-13(M). A mobile station which acknowledges receipt of a distress message shall transmit: (Q. 2.02)
(a) Its name, its position, and the master's name.
(b) Its name, its transmitting frequency, and its position.
(c) Its name, its position, and the approximate time needed to reach the distressed vessel.
(d) Its name, its position, and its tonnage.
(e) Its name, its position, and the call signs of other vessels it is in communication with.

II-14(M). Ship stations navigating the Great Lakes and during their hours of service for telephony are required to keep watch on: (Q. 2.04)
(a) 156.8 MHz.
(b) 158.6 MHz.
(c) 2182 kHz.

(d) 8212 kHz.
(e) 1282 kHz.

II-15(M). The urgent signal PAN indicates: (Q. 2.06)
(a) A communication for Pan American Airways.
(b) The calling station has a message relating to the safety of a ship.
(c) The calling station has a message relating to a storm.
(d) The calling station is in distress.
(e) A low priority ship-to-ship communication.

II-16(M). The safety signal SECURITY takes priority over: (Q. 2.06)
(a) All other communications.
(b) The urgent signal PAN.
(c) The distress signal MAYDAY.
(d) No other communications.
(e) None of the above.

II-17(M). A coast station may not charge for the following type of message: (Q. 2.14)
(a) Any U.S. government communication.
(b) Distress messages.
(c) Ship-to-aircraft messages.
(d) Ship-to-shore messages.
(e) Messages to a foreign government official.

II-18(M). When a distress message is being sent, the following information must be included: (Q. 2.03)
(a) Name of the ship; position; nature of distress; and nature of help requested.
(b) Name of the master; country of registry; and nature of help requested.
(c) Country of registry; frequency of the distress transmission; and frequency of the reply transmission.
(d) Magnetic course of the ship; speed of the ship; ship tonnage; and name of the master.
(e) Position of the ship; name of the master; and frequency of the distress transmission.

II-19(M). When may a radio operator stop listening on an international distress frequency? (Q. 2.04)
(a) Whenever directed to do so by the chief radio operator.
(b) Whenever the station is being used for transmission on that channel.
(c) During periods of transmitter maintenance.
(d) When the ship is within the 12-mile limit.
(e) Whenever the ship is not under way.

II-20(M). Test transmissions are sent: (Q. 2.08)
(a) To facilitate direction finding.
(b) To actuate the auto alarms of neighboring ships.
(c) If the called station does not answer immediately.
(d) To check for radar interference.
(e) None of the above.

Basic Radiotelephone

ALTERNATING AND DIRECT CURRENT

Question 3.01. By what other expression may a "difference of potential" be described?

Answer. Common expressions are: voltage, electromotive force, IR drop, voltage drop.

Discussion. Terms such as "voltage" and "electromotive force" usually apply to a source of electrical energy. For example, the terms "generator voltage or emf," and "battery voltage or emf," are in common use. On the other hand, the terms "IR drop" and "voltage drop" usually apply to a circuit or portion of a circuit, to which the voltage is applied. The distinction is not strict, however.

Q. 3.02. By what other expression may an "electric current flow" be described?

A. Electron flow or electron drift may be used, or the term "amperage" is sometimes used.

D. The term "current flow" is not particularly definite as to the direction of the flow or to the polarity of the charges in motion. So called "conventional current" assumes positive charges to be in motion and

the direction externally of the generator is from + to −. On the other hand, the terms "electron flow" or "electron drift" are quite definite. In this case the moving particles are negative charges and the direction external of the generator is from − to +. "Electron flow" is applied most correctly in such cases as vacuum tubes, while the term "electron drift" would more aptly describe the motion of electrons in a solid conductor.

Q. 3.03. Explain the relationship between the physical structure of the atom and electrical current flow.

A. See discussion of Q. 3.04.

Q. 3.04. With respect to electrons, what is the difference between conductors and non-conductors?

A. A good conductor has a large number of "free" electrons, while an insulator or non-conductor has very few free electrons.

D. In any substance, the outer ring of electrons of an atom of that substance determines its electrical characteristics. If the outer ring is lightly bound to the atom, it is possible that one or more electrons in the outer ring will leave the atom without much urging from an external source. Such an electron is called a "free" or conduction electron. If many of these electrons are present within a substance, their movement under an applied emf constitutes an electric current, and the substance is then a good conductor. On the other hand, if there are very few of these "free" electrons, the current will be extremely small; in such a case, the substance is called an insulator or non-conductor.

Q. 3.05. What is the difference between electrical power and electrical energy? In what units is each expressed?

A. Electrical power is the *rate* of doing work (the rate of expending energy) by electricity. Electrical energy is the *capacity* or *ability* to accomplish work by electricity. ("Work" in this sense includes production of heat, or conversion into any other form of energy.)

D. Electrical power is measured by a unit called the *watt*. One watt is the power expended in heat in a circuit when a current of 1 ampere (6.28×10^{18} electrons per second) flows through a resistance of 1 ohm. One watt is 1 joule per second.

Electrical energy is measured by a unit called the *joule*. Energy in electrical circuits is transferred into the form of heat. A joule is the *amount* of energy expended in moving 1 coulomb (6.28×10^{18} electrons) of electricity through a resistance of 1 ohm. One joule $= 0.7376$ ft pound; 3 600 joules $= 1$ watt-hour.

Q. 3.06. What is the relationship between impedance and admittance? Between resistance and conductance?

A. Admittance (Y) is the reciprocal of impedance (Z). Conductance (G) is the reciprocal of resistance (R).

D. Impedance may be defined as "the total opposition to current flow in alternating current circuits" and is expressed by the symbol "Z." The impedance of a circuit may contain resistance, inductive reactance and capacitive reactance. For a series circuit, impedance may be found from the equation:

$$Z = \sqrt{R^2 + (X_L - X_c)^2}$$

and is expressed in ohms.

Admittance is $\frac{1}{Z}$ or Y. Admittance is used as a convenience in analyzing parallel ac circuits and is expressed in mhos. For a parallel ac circuit the admittance may be found from the equation:

$$Y = \sqrt{G^2 + B^2}$$

where

    Y = Admittance in mhos.
    G = Conductance in mhos.
    B = Susceptance (reciprocal of reactance) in mhos.

Note that the susceptance of an inductance is negative and that of a capacitance is positive. These signs are opposite to the situation when handled as reactances.

Resistance is the factor of proportionality between voltage and current, in a dc circuit, giving Ohm's Law: $V = IR$. In an ac circuit, the "in phase" component of current must be used, and the resistance is the quantity which determines the power lost or dissipated.

Conductance is the ratio of current through a conductor to the voltage which produces it. (In a reactive ac circuit, it is the ratio of "in phase" current to the applied voltage.) Conductance of a circuit or component is numerically equal to $1/R$, where R is its resistance in ohms. The unit of conductance is the "mho," and the usual symbol is G. Conductance is a measure of the ease with which a circuit is able to pass current. Conductance is a property of a given circuit and must be distinguished from conductivity, which is a property of material.

Q. 3.07. A relay with a coil resistance of 500 ohms is designed to operate when a current of 0.2 ampere flows through the coil. What value of resistance must be connected in series with the coil if it is to be energized by a 110-volt dc source?

A. A series resistance of 50 ohms is needed.

D. The normal working voltage of the relay coil equals 0.2 × 500 = 100 volts; 10 volts at 0.2 ampere must be dropped in the series resistor,

$$R = \frac{10}{0.2} = 50 \text{ ohms.}$$

Q. 3.08. Draw a circuit composed of a 12-volt battery with 3 resistors (10, 120, and 300 ohms, respectively) arranged in a "pi" network.

1. What is the total current; the current through each resistor?

2. What is the voltage across each resistor?

3. What power is dissipated in each resistor; the total power dissipated by the circuit?

A. See Fig. 3.08.

1. (a) Total current (I_T) = 1.23 amperes.

(b) Current through R1 (I_{R1}) = 1.2 amperes.

(c) Current through R2 (I_{R2}) = 0.0286 ampere.

(d) Current through R3 (I_{R3}) = 0.0286 ampere.

2. (a) Voltage across R1 (V_{R1}) = 12 volts.

(b) Voltage across R2 (V_{R2}) = 3.43 volts.

(c) Voltage across R3 (V_{R3}) = 8.58 volts.

3. (a) Power dissipated in R1 (P_{R1}) = 14.4 watts.

(b) Power dissipated in R2 (P_{R2}) = 0.0981 watt.

(c) Power dissipated in R3 (P_{R3}) = 0.245 watt.

(d) Total power dissipated (P_T) = 14.743 watts.

D.

Part 1. (a) of the answer.

1. (a) Step 1: Find the total resistance (R_T) across the battery.

$$R_T = \frac{R1 \times (R2 + R3)}{R1 + (R2 + R3)} = \frac{10 \times (120 + 300)}{10 + (120 + 300)}$$

$$= \frac{4200}{430} = 9.76 \text{ ohms}$$

Step 2: Find the total current (I_T).

$$I_T = \frac{V}{R_T} = \frac{12}{9.76} = 1.23 \text{ amperes}$$

Part 1 (b) of the answer.

1. (b) $I_{R1} = \frac{V}{R1} = \frac{12}{10} = 1.2$ amperes

Part 1. (c) of the answer.

1. (c) Step 1: Find the series current through R2 and R3.

$$I_{R2, R3} = \frac{V}{R2 + R3} = \frac{12}{420}$$
$$= 0.0286 \text{ ampere}$$

Step 2: Find the current through R2 (I_{R2}) which is the series current, or 0.0286 ampere.

Part 1. (d) of the answer.

1. (d) The current through R3 (I_{R3}) is also the series current, or 0.0286 ampere.

Part 2. (a) of the answer.

2. (a) The voltage across R1 (V_{R1}) is the battery voltage = 12 volts.

Part 2. (b) of the answer.

2. (b) $V_{R2} = I_{R2} \times R_2 = 0.0286 \times 120$
$= 3.43$ volts

Part 2. (c) of the answer.

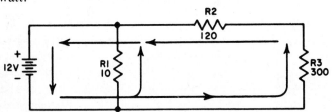

Fig. 3.08. A "pi"-network battery circuit.

2. (c) $V_{R3} = I_{R3} \times R_3$
$= 0.0286 \times 300 = 8.58$ volts

Part 3. (a) of the answer.
3. (a) The power dissipated in R1(P_{R1}) is

$P_{R1} = V \times I_{R1} = 12 \times 1.2$
$= 14.4$ watts

Part 3. (b) of the answer.
3. (b) The power dissipated in R2(P_{R2}) is

$P_{R2} = V_{R2} \times I_{R2} = 3.43 \times 0.0286$
$= 0.0981$ watt, or 98.1 milliwatts

Part 3. (c) of the answer.
3. (c) The power dissipated in R3 (P_{R3}) is

$P_{R3} = V_{R3} \times I_{R3} = 8.58 \times 0.0286$
$= 0.245$ watt

Part 3. (d) of the answer.
3. (d) The total power (P_T) dissipated by the circuit is the sum of the power dissipated in each resistor, or

$P_T = P_{R1} + P_{R2} + P_{R3}$
$= 14.4 + 0.0981 + 0.245$
$= 14.743$ watts

Q. 3.09. To provide additional useful information to the student regarding the solution of typical ac impedance problems, two additional problems have been added to this Question. The original FCC question now appears as **Q. 3.09(A)** and requires the use of j factors for its solution. A series-ac impedance problem (not in FCC Study Guide) is given as **Q. 3.09(B)**, while a series-parallel-ac impedance problem (not in FCC Study Guide) is given as **Q. 3.09(C)**. Neither of the latter two additional problems requires the use of j factors for its solution. In the event that the student is not too well versed in the use of j factors, he should concentrate on the latter two problems only and these will enable him to answer the ac impedance problems given in the FCC examinations.

Q. 3.09(A). Draw a circuit composed of a voltage source of 100 volts—1 000 Hz, a 1-microfarad capacitor in series with the source, followed by a "T" network composed of a 2-millihenry inductor, a 100-ohm resistor and a 4-millihenry inductor. The load resistor is 200 ohms.

1. What is the total current; the current through each circuit element?

2. What is the voltage across each circuit element?

3. What "apparent" power is being consumed by the circuit?

4. What real or actual power is being consumed by the circuit; by the 200-ohm resistor?

A. See Fig. 3.09(a1).

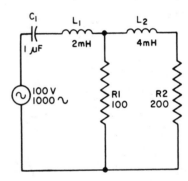

Fig. 3.09(a1). "T" network and load connected to an ac generator.

1. a. The total current (I_T) = 0.63 ampere.
b. The current through C1 and L1 (I_T) = 0.63 ampere.
c. The current through R1 (I1) = 0.43 ampere.
d. The current through L2 and R2 (I2) = 0.21 ampere.

2. a. The voltage across C1 (V_{C1}) = 100.17 volts.
b. The voltage across L1 (V_{L1}) = 7.91 volts.
c. The voltage across R1 (V_{R1}) = 42.65 volts.
d. The voltage across L2 (V_{L2}) = 5.27 volts.

e. The voltage across R2 (V_{R2}) = 42 volts.

3. The apparent power = 63 watts.

4. a. The real power = 27.03 watts.

b. The power consumed by the 200-ohm resistor = 8.8 watts.

D. The solution of this problem requires the use of complex numbers. While there are a fairly large number of steps in its solution, these proceed in logical sequence and are not difficult to follow.

(A). The first answer required is to find the total current (I_T). However, in order to accomplish this, the total equivalent impedance (Z_T) must first be computed. This is the equivalent series impedance of all the circuit elements shown in Figure 3.09(a1). Thus, the series equivalent impedance of C1 and L1 is added vectorially to the series equivalent impedance of R1, R2 and L2 to provide Z_T.

Step 1: Find the equivalent series impedance (Z_p) of R1, R2 and L2.

$$Z_p = \frac{Z1\ Z2}{Z1 + Z2}$$

Expressed as complex numbers; first in rectangular form, we have

$$Z_p = \frac{(100 + j\Theta) \times (200 + jX_{L2})}{(100 + j\Theta) + (200 + jX_{L2})}$$

We must find X_{L2}

$$X_{L2} = 2\pi fL2 = 6.28 \times 1\ 000 \times 4 \times 10^{-3}$$
$$= 25.12\ \text{ohms}$$

$$Z_p = \frac{(100 + j\theta) \times (200 + j25.12)}{(100 + j\theta) + (200 + j25.12)}$$

$$= \frac{20\ 000 + j2,512}{300 + j25.12}$$

In order to reduce this fraction, both numerator and denominator must be expressed in the polar form.

Step 2: Change the numerator to polar form.

$$\tan \theta = \frac{X}{R} = \frac{2\ 512}{20\ 000} = 0.125$$

$$\theta = 7.1°$$

$$Z\ (\text{numerator}) = \frac{X}{\sin \theta} = \frac{2\ 512}{0.1236} = 20\ 323\ \underline{/7.1°}$$

Step 3: Change the denominator to polar form

$$\tan \theta = \frac{X}{R} = \frac{25.12}{300} = 0.084$$

$$\theta = 4.8°$$

$$Z\ (\text{denominator}) = \frac{X}{\sin \theta} = \frac{25.12}{0.0837} = 300.12\ \text{ohms}$$

Therefore, in polar form

$$Z_p = \frac{20\ 323\ \underline{/7.1°}}{300.12\ \underline{/4.8°}} = 67.7\ \underline{/2.3°}$$

(B). It is now necessary to determine the equivalent impedance (Z_S) of C1 and L1.

Step 1: Find the reactance of C1.

$$X_{C1} = \frac{1}{2\pi fC1} = \frac{0.159}{1\ 000 \times 1 \times 10^{-6}} = 159\ \text{ohms}$$

Step 2: Find the reactance of L1.

$$X_{L1} = 2\pi fL1 = 6.28 \times 1000 \times 2 \times 10^{-3}$$
$$= 12.56\ \text{ohms}$$

Step 3: Find the combined impedance (Z_S) of C1 and L1.

$$Z_S = 12.56 - 159$$
$$= -146.44\ \text{ohms (capacitive)}$$

(C). The next step is to combine Z_P and Z_S vectorially to find Z_T, which is the actual load on the generator. With the aid of Z_T, we may determine the generator current (I_T) and then the remainder of the answers to this problem.

Step 1: $Z_T = Z_P + Z_S$

$$Z_T = 67.7\ \underline{/2.3°} + (0 - j146.44)$$

To perform this addition, Z_p must first be converted to rectangular form.

$$Z_P = 67.7\ (\cos 2.3° + j \sin 2.3°)$$
$$Z_p = 67.7\ (0.9990 + j0.0454) = 67.63$$
$$+ j3.07,\ \text{and}$$
$$Z_T = (67.63 + j3.07) + (0 - j146.44)$$
$$= 67.63 - j143.37$$

Step 2: it is now necessary to convert the rectangular form of Z_T (above) to its polar form.

$$\tan \theta = \frac{X}{R} = \frac{143.37}{67.63}$$

$$\tan \theta = 2.1$$

$$\theta = -64.6°$$

$$Z_T = \frac{X}{\sin \theta} = \frac{143.37}{\sin 64.6°} = \frac{143.37}{0.9033} = 158.7 \text{ ohms}$$

Z_T in polar form $= 158.7 \underline{/-64.6°}$

(D). Find the total current (I_T).

$$I_T = \frac{V}{Z_T} = \frac{100}{158.7} = 0.63 \text{ ampere}$$

(E). Find the current through C1 and L1. This is the same as I_T, or 0.63 ampere.

(F). Find the currents 11 and 12 (see Fig. 3.09(a2)).

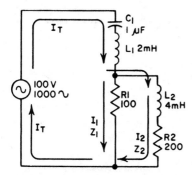

Fig. 3.09(a2). The diagram is redrawn here for clarity in solving the problem.

Step 1: Find the voltage (V_p) across the parallel branch (Z_p) composed of R1 and R2, L2.

$$V_p = I_T \times Z_p = 0.63 \times 67.7 = 42.65 \text{ volts.}$$

Step 2:

$$I1 = \frac{V_p}{Z1} = \frac{42.65}{100} = 0.43 \text{ ampere}$$

Step 3:

$$I2 = \frac{V_p}{Z2}$$

We must find the value of Z2, which is the vector sum of X_{L2} and R2 in series.

$$Z2 = \sqrt{(R2)^2 + (X_{L2})^2} = \sqrt{(200)^2 + (25.12)^2}$$
$$= 201.5 \text{ ohms}$$

$$I2 = \frac{42.65}{201.5} = 0.21 \text{ ampere}$$

This is the current in L2 and R2

(G). We are now ready to find the voltages across each circuit element. (The voltage across R1 is the same as V_P, or 42.65 volts.)

Step 1: Find the voltage across L2

$$V_{L2} = I2 \times X_{L2} = 0.21 \times 25.12$$
$$= 5.27 \text{ volts.}$$

Step 2: Find the voltage across R2

$$V_{R2} = I2 \times R2 = 0.21 \times 200$$
$$= 42 \text{ volts.}$$

Step 3: Find the voltage across C1

$$V_{C1} = I_T \times X_{C1} = 0.63 \times 159$$
$$= 100.17 \text{ volts.}$$

Step 4: Find the voltage across L1.

$$V_{L1} = I_T \times X_{L1} = 0.63 \times 12.56$$
$$= 7.91 \text{ volts}$$

Note: It may appear that the individual voltages add up to more than the generator voltage. However, these are out of phase and must be added vectorially.

(H). Find the apparent power (P_a) consumed by the circuit.

$$P_a = V \times I_T = 100 \times 0.63$$
$$= 63 \text{ volt-amperes}$$

(I). Find the real power consumed by the circuit (P_R)

$$P_R = V \times I_T \times \cos \theta \ (64.6°)$$
$$= 100 \times 0.63 \times 0.4289 = 27.03$$
$$\text{watts}$$

(J). Find the ower consumed by the 200 ohm resistor, R2

$$P_{R2} = I2^2 \times R2 = (0.21)^2 \times 200$$
$$= 0.044 \times 200 = 8.8 \text{ watts}$$

Q. 3.09(B). In a series circuit composed of a series resistance of 40 ohms, an inductive reactance of 80 ohms, and a capacitive reactance of 30 ohms, a current of 0.5 ampere is flowing. What is the applied voltage?

A. The applied voltage equals 32 volts.

D. To solve this problem (see Fig. 3.09(b)), it is first necessary to determine the total series ac impedance (Z_T). Once Z_T is known and since the total current (I_T) is given (0.5 ampere), the applied voltage (V_A) may be easily found from the equation, $V_A = I_T \times Z_T$.

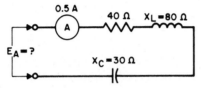

Fig. 3.09(b). An ac series circuit, where the applied voltage (V_A) must be found.

Step 1: Determine the total ac series impedance (Z_T) of R, X_L, and X_C, in Fig. 3.09(b):

$$Z_T = \sqrt{R^2 + (X_L - X_C)^2}$$

$$= \sqrt{40^2 + (80 - 30)^2}$$

$$= \sqrt{40^2 + 50^2} =$$

$$\sqrt{1\,600 + 2\,500} = \sqrt{4\,100} = 64 \text{ ohms}$$

Step 2: Find the applied voltage (V_A):

$$V_A = I \times Z_T = 0.5 \times 64 = 32 \text{ volts}$$

Q. 3.09(C). What is the total impedance of a resistance of 75 ohms in series with the parallel combination of an inductive reactance of 20 ohms and a capacitive reactance of 25 ohms, across a supply voltage of 1 000 volts? What is the line current?

A. See Fig. 3.09(c1)

1. The total (ac) impedance (Z_T) is 125 ohms.

2. The line current (I_L) is 8 amperes.

D. To solve this problem, it is first necessary to separate the series resistor from the parallel circuit. Next, by assuming a

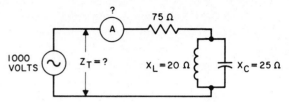

Fig. 3.09(c1). An ac, series-parallel circuit, where the line current (I_L) must be found.

voltage (100 volts) across the parallel circuit (see Fig. 3.09(c2)), its resultant impedance is found. Then, the impedance of the parallel circuit is combined (vectorially) with the resistance to determine the total impedance (Z_T). Finally, the line current (I_L) is determined from the equation,

$$I_l = \frac{V_t}{Z_t}$$

where V_T is the applied voltage in Fig. 3.09(c1), or 1 000 volts.

Note: This problem could have been presented so that only the total impedance (Z_T) was required to be found. In this case, the item of 1 000V given in the question must be ignored. In some FCC questions, added information is sometimes given that is not required for the solution of a problem. It is up to the student to determine if this is the case and to eliminate unnecessary information if required.

Step 1: Assume a voltage of 100V across the parallel branch only and solve for the branch currents (see simplified diagram of Fig. 3.09(c2)):

$$I_1 = \frac{V}{X_L} = \frac{100}{20} = 5A$$

$$I_2 = \frac{V}{X_C} = \frac{100}{25} = 4A$$

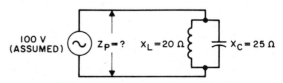

Fig. 3.09(c2). Simplified diagram of Fig. 3.09(c1) to help determine the impedance (Z_P) of the parallel circuit alone.

Step 2: Find the total current (I_T) flowing through the parallel branch: $I_t = I_1 - I_2 = 5 - 4 = 1A$ (inductive).

Step 3: Find the impedance (Z_p) of the parallel branch (only) by the equation:

$$Z_p = \frac{V\ (assumed)}{I_T}$$

$$Z_p = \frac{100}{1} = 100\ ohms\ (inductive)$$

Step 4: Find the total impedance (Z_p) of the entire circuit of Fig. 3.09(c1):

$$Z_T = \sqrt{R^2 + X_L{}^2}$$
$$= \sqrt{75^2 + 100^2}$$
$$= \sqrt{5\ 625 + 10\ 000}$$
$$= \sqrt{15\ 625} = 125\ ohms$$

Step 5: Find the line current (I_L):

$$I_L = \frac{V\ (given)}{Z_T} = \frac{1\ 000}{125} = 8A$$

Note: In some examples it may be required to find the phase angle (θ) of the line current. This is easily done by first finding the cosine of the angle (θ) and then determining the angle from the cosine tables:

$$\cos\theta = \frac{R}{Z_T} = \frac{75}{125} = 0.6$$
$$\theta = 53°$$

(See also Q. 3.235(1).)

Q. 3.10. What is the relationship between wire size and resistance of the wire?

A. The resistance of a wire varies inversely with the cross-sectional area of the wire and directly with its length.

D. The resistance of a conductor varies inversely with the cross-sectional area of the conductor. Thus any increase in the area will decrease the resistance. However, the area varies as the square of the diameter. If the diameter is doubled, the area will be increased by four times. Since the area is four times greater, then the resistance is now four times less, or equal to one-quarter of the original value.

Resistance of a conductor varies in direct proportion to the length of the conductor. For example, doubling the length also doubles the resistance. The resistivity of a material is determined by its atomic structure; some materials have more free electrons than others. The ones with the greater number of free electrons will have less resistance. The resistance of most substances is affected by temperature. Most metals have a positive temperature coefficient: that is, an increase in temperature will cause an increased resistance. Most non-metals, carbon, for example, have lower resistance at higher temperatures; some ceramic substances which are good insulators at ordinary temperatures become fairly good conductors at a red-heat.

Q. 3.11. What is "skin effect"? How does it affect the resistance of conductors at the higher radio frequencies?

A.

1. "Skin effect" is the tendency of alternating currents to exist in the area of a conductor approaching the surface, rather than in the entire cross-sectional area of the conductor.

2. It causes the effective resistance of conductors to increase with the frequency of the applied wave.

D. The term "skin effect" is most generally used in connection with radio frequencies. However, "skin effect" is present at all frequencies, the magnitude of the effect decreasing as the frequency decreases. At extremely high frequencies, the depth of current penetration is very small, most of the current existing practically on the surface of the conductor. It is for this reason that tubular conductors with large surface areas are used at ultra high frequencies. "Skin effect" exists due to the fact that more magnetic lines of force cut the center of the conductor than cut the outer sections. Thus the self inductance of the conductor is greatest at the center and decreases toward the outer edges. There is more counter-emf developed at the center of the conductor and, therefore, the least amount of current exists at this point. As the frequency increases, the cemf at the center approaches the magnitude of the applied voltage and current practically does not exist at the center. Where the conductor is a round wire or tube, the high frequency resistance at high frequencies in ohms per centimeter equals

$$\frac{83.2\sqrt{f} \times 10^{-9}}{d}$$

where

d = the outside diameter in centimeters.
f = the frequency in hertz.

Q. 3.12. Why is impedance matching between electrical devices an important factor? Is it always to be desired? Can it always be attained in practice?

A.
1. Impedance matching is important in certain cases in order to effect maximum transfer of power, minimum VSWR (on transmission lines) and consequently a reasonably flat frequency response of a line (within the practical design limits).
2. Impedance matching is not always desirable, as is the case in some amplifiers.
3. Perfect impedance matching is not always attained in practice since the magnitude and phase angle of the impedances must be matched. However, from a practical standpoint and utilizing a given frequency band of operation, satisfactory impedance matching may be achieved.
D. Impedances should be matched in speech-input equipment in order that maximum transfer of power may take place and to preserve the proper frequency response of the equipment. In short transmission lines, impedance matching is not too important. However, if the line is long and standing waves are present (due to mismatch), the input impedance of the line may change radically and this change will be reflected into the circuit through the matching transformer. This in turn may cause distortion and incorrect frequency response characteristic.

In amplifiers, an impedance match is usually not desirable. For minimum distortion, triode amplifiers require a load impedance several times greater than the plate resistance; while screen-grid amplifiers require a load only a small fraction of the plate resistance. For example, a power amplifier tube, with a plate impedance of 52 000 ohms, requires a load resistance of only 5 000 ohms or less than 1/10 of the plate impedance.

Where distortion is not a factor, a 1-to-1 impedance match is desirable for maximum power transfer between circuits.

Q. 3.13. A loudspeaker with an impedance of 4 ohms is working in a plate circuit which has an impedance of 4 000 ohms. What is the impedance ratio of an output transformer used to match the plate circuit to the speaker? What is the turns ratio?

A.
1. The impedance ratio is 1 000 to 1.
2. The turns ratio is 31.6 to 1.
D. Let the plate circuit impedance equal Z_p (primary impedance). Let the loudspeaker impedance equal Z_s (secondary impedance). The impedance ratio is

$$\frac{Z_p}{Z_s} = \frac{4\ 000}{4} = 1\ 000 \text{ to } 1$$

A basic (approximate) formula relating impedance ratio and turns ratio is:

$$\frac{N_p}{N_s} = \sqrt{\frac{Z_p}{Z_s}}, \text{ or } \left(\frac{N_p}{N_s}\right)^2 = \frac{Z_p}{Z_s}$$

where

N_p = the number of turns in the primary.
N_s = the number of turns in the secondary.
Z_p = the primary impedance.
Z_s = the secondary impedance.

From the above, the turns ratio is found by,

$$\frac{N_p}{N_s} = \sqrt{\frac{Z_p}{Z_s}} = \sqrt{\frac{4\ 000}{4}} = 31.6$$

Q. 3.14. Compare some properties of electrostatic and electromagnetic fields.

A.

1. If two conductors are separated by an insulator and a difference of potential applied between the two conductors, it can be shown that electric energy is stored between the two conductors. This energy is said to exist in an electrostatic field between (mainly) the conductors. If the charging source is removed, the charge (or energy) remains as before and we have a charged capacitor, which stores potential energy in its field. The amount of energy stored is expressed by the equation.

$$W = \tfrac{1}{2}CV^2 \text{ joules}$$

where

C = capacitance in farads.
V = charging potential in volts.
W = energy of the electrostatic field in joules (watt-seconds).

The lines of electrostatic force between two unlike charges (corresponding to magnetic lines of force) are depicted in Fig. 3.14.

The directional arrows on the lines show the direction of force on an electron placed in the field. The electron would be attracted by the positive charge and repelled by the negative charge. Coulomb's law is useful in describing the electrostatic field. This law states that the force between two charges is proportional to the product of the charges and inversely proportional to the square of the distance between them. In Fig. 3.14, if a dielectric material was placed between the unlike charges, some of the electrons in the dielectric would be attracted toward the positive charge and potential energy would now be stored in the dielectric. This process is called "electrostatic induction" and corresponds to the induction caused by an electromagnetic field.

2. If a current of electricity is passed through a wire (or coil), it will be found that an electromagnetic field will build up to a

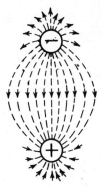

Fig. 3.14 Electrostatic field between unlike charges.

maximum value in the space surrounding the wire. A certain amount of electrical energy will exist in this electromagnetic field and may be expressed by the equation

$$W = \tfrac{1}{2}LI^2$$

where

L = inductance in henrys.
I = current in amperes.
W = energy of the electromagnetic field in joules (watt-seconds).

Unlike the electrostatic field, if the current is cut off, the electromagnetic field shortly ceases to exist, the energy being returned to the wire (or coil). (In actuality, there is always stray capacity across the inductance. Thus, when the excitation is cut off, the energy creates dampened oscillations of this tuned circuit). Since the electromagnetic field requires a current flow to exist, the energy involved is kinetic energy.

If a conductor is moved through the magnetic field (but not parallel to it) magnetic induction will take place and a current will be caused to flow in the conductor. Similarly, if the excitation of the original wire (or coil) is varied, a current will be induced into a stationary wire or coil. In this case, the electromagnetic field is caused to move past the wire and the moving field induces a secondary current. Note an important distinction between electrostatic and electromagnetic fields. An electrostatic field (kinetic energy) may cause induction while stationary. Conversely, an electromagnetic field (or the secondary conductor) must be in motion to produce induction.

D. It is important to note that a radiated wave from a transmitting antenna (or other radiator) is composed of both electrostatic and electromagnetic fields. The total energy content of the wave is constant over one cycle. However, the two fields are 90° apart in phase (as well as in space) and the energy is continuously interchanged between the electrostatic and electromagnetic fields. In the case of a vertical radiator (vertically polarized) the electrostatic lines of force are situated mainly in the vertical plane and the electromagnetic lines of force are mainly in the horizontal plane. For maximum efficiency of a receiving antenna for this wave, the receiving antenna should also be vertical. In this case the maximum induced electrostatic and electromagnetic field energy will occur in the receiving antenna.

Q. 3.15. In what way are electrical properties of common circuit elements affected by electromagnetic fields? Are interstage connecting leads susceptible to these fields?

A.

1. The independent electrical properties of circuit elements are not affected by electromagnetic fields. However, the performance of electrical circuits is sometimes affected by the coupling of electromagnetic fields into common circuit elements, such as coils, capacitors and vacuum tubes. Such coupling may (depending on phase relationships) cause oscillation and/or bandwidth problems. It may also result in such conditions as hum pickup.

2. Interstage connecting leads may pick up electromagnetic fields and cause problems similar to those mentioned above.

D. In the design of electronic circuits, particularly where high-gain stages are involved, one of the most important considerations is the prevention of undesired coupling between stages of the circuitry. As mentioned above, such coupling (or undesired feedback) may be of such phase as to

reinforce the signal appearing at an earlier stage. This can cause instability, regeneration, oscillation and/or a reduction of bandwidth of the circuit. Such undesired coupling can be simple induced currents into common circuit elements, or into inter- or intra-stage wiring. In some situations, the coupling may be through the route of the metal chassis itself. It is not possible in this book to present detailed design information for the avoidance of this condition. However, some of the more common design precautions are:

1. Shielding of glass vacuum tubes in critical circuits.

2. Shielding of selected input or output leads wherever possible and desirable.

3. Shielding of coils and/or of entire stages which may be susceptible to feedback problems.

4. Restriction of the gain of each critical stage to reduce the magnitude of feedback.

5. Shielding the entire bottom of the chassis to eliminate pick up of stray adjacent fields.

6. Use of special circuit grounding procedures, such as all grid-circuit returns to one ground and all plate-circuit returns to another ground, or at least to another portion of the metal chassis.

7. Use of adequate decoupling circuits between stages, including such items as filament-circuit chokes and plate and grid-decoupling RC circuits.

Q. 3.16. Which factors determine the amplitude of the emf induced in a conductor which is cutting magnetic lines of force?

A. There are four basic factors as follows:

1. The flux density, or magnetic strength.

2. The rate or velocity at which the conductor cuts through the magnetic lines of force.

3. The length of the conductor, or if a coil is used, both the number of turns and the length of the coil are important.

4. The angle at which the conductor or coil is cutting through the magnetic lines

of force. Maximum emf is induced if the conductor is moving in a direction perpendicular to the lines of force.

D. The formula to determine the emf induced in a conductor is $V = \dfrac{NBlv}{10^8}$ volts

where

V = the induced voltage.
N = the number of turns.
B = the flux density.
l = the length of conductor.
v = the velocity of cutting.

It is seen that V is *directly proportional* to all above factors.

Q. 3.17. Define the term "reluctance."

A. Reluctance is the opposition to the creation of magnetic lines of force in a magnetic circuit.

D. Reluctance is the same in its relation to magnetic circuits as resistance is to electric circuits. Magnetic flux is analogous to current, and mmf is analogous to emf. Thus the greater the reluctance of a magnetic circuit, the weaker will be the magnetic flux. The total reluctance of a magnetic circuit is the sum of all the reluctances which are in series.

Thus for an iron core with air gap the reluctance is

$$R = \frac{l}{\mu A} + \frac{l_1}{A_1} \text{ units}$$

where

R = the reluctance.
l = the length of iron in centimeters.
μ = permeability of iron.
A = cross-sectional area of iron in centimeters squared.
A_1 = cross-sectional area of the air gap in centimeters squared.
l_1 = length of air gap in centimeters.

Reluctance is the ratio of magneto-motive force to magnetic flux, as

$$R = \frac{\text{gilberts}}{\text{lines per sq cm}}$$

It is the number by which the desired flux is multiplied in order to compute the necessary applied flux.

Q. 3.18. In what way does an inductance affect the voltage-current phase relationship of a circuit? Why is the phase of a circuit important?

A.

1. A series inductance acting alone in an alternating current circuit has the property of causing the circuit current to lag the applied voltage by 90°, and limits the value of current, which is proportional to the voltage and inversely proportional to the frequency and inductance.

2. Phase may be important for various reasons depending upon the application of the circuit. For example, in power circuits, phase angle determines the power factor. In color TV receivers, the correct phase of the demodulation signals is vital to insure proper color reproduction. For other examples, see the discussion.

D. Several other cases where phase is important to the circuitry involved are:
1. Operation of two- or three-phase motors.
2. Operation of servo systems.
3. Correct speaker and circuit phasing in stereophonic audio systems.
4. Synchronization of TV and FM multiplex signals at both transmitter and receiver.
5. Aircraft navigational receivers.

There are numerous other examples where phasing is important. However, there are also many circuits where phasing is not important. For example:

1. Broadcast receivers and transmitters.
2. Ordinary FM receivers.
3. Single-channel amplifiers.
4. Power supplies.
5. Many types of test equipment.

Q. 3.19. Draw two cycles of a sine wave on a graph of amplitude versus time. Assume a frequency of 5 MHz.

1. What would be the wavelength of one cycle in meters; in centimeters?

2. How many degrees does one cycle represent?

3. How much time would it take for the wave to "rotate" 45°; 90°; 280°?

4. If there were a second harmonic of this frequency, how many cycles thereof would be represented on this graph?

5. On the same graph draw two cycles of another sine wave leading the first by 45°.

6. What would be the velocity of this wave or any other electromagnetic wave in free space?

A. See Fig. 3.19.

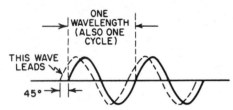

Fig. 3.19. Two cycles of two sine waves, one leading the other by 45 degrees.

1. a. Wavelength in meters = 60 meters.

b. Wavelength in centimeters = 6 000 centimeters.

2. One cycle represents 360°.

3. a. The wave will rotate 45 degrees in 0.025 microsecond.

b. The wave will rotate 90 degrees in 0.05 microsecond.

c. The wave will rotate 280 degrees in 0.155 microsecond.

4. The second harmonic would be represented by 4 cycles.

5. See Fig. 3.19.

6. The velocity would be 300 000 000 meters per second.

D.

1. The wavelength of one cycle in meters is

$$\lambda = \frac{300}{f(\text{MHz})} = \frac{300}{5} = 60 \text{ meters}$$

The wavelength in centimeters is

$$\lambda \text{ (cm)} = \frac{300}{f(\text{MHz})} \times 100$$

$$= \frac{30\,000}{5} = 6\,000 \text{ cm}$$

Note: In common usage, centimeters are used to describe wavelengths at much higher frequencies. For example at 10 000 MHz, the wavelength is 3 cm. This is a matter of convenient notation.

2. One cycle represents 360°, since it may be considered to be derived from a vector rotating inside a 360 degree circle.

3. a. The wave will rotate 45° in $\frac{1}{8}$ $\left(\frac{45}{360}\right)$ of the time required for one complete cycle, which is

$$T \text{ (sec)} = \frac{1}{f \text{ (Hz)}}$$

$$T \text{ (}\mu s\text{)} = \frac{1}{f \text{ (MHz)}}$$

$$= \frac{1}{5} \text{ or } 0.2 \text{ }\mu s \text{ for one}$$

complete cycle

For 45°, $T = \frac{0.2}{8} = 0.025 \text{ }\mu s$

b. The wave will rotate 90° (¼ cycle) in

$$T = \frac{0.2}{4} = 0.05 \text{ }\mu s$$

c. The wave will rotate 280° in

$$T = 0.2 \times \frac{280}{360} = 0.155 \text{ }\mu s$$

4. The second harmonic would be 10 megahertz, each cycle occupying half the time of a 5-megahertz wave. Therefore, 4 cycles of the second harmonic would be shown on the graph.

5. See Fig. 3.19.

6. The velocity of any electromagnetic wave in free space is 300 000 000 meters per second.

Q. 3.20. Explain how to determine the sum of two equal vector quantities having the same reference point but whose directions are 90° apart; 0° apart; 180° apart? How does this pertain to electrical currents or voltages?

A.

1. This may be accomplished by graphical means or by trigonometry (See Discussion.)

2. Electrical currents or voltages are frequently represented by vector quantities in the solution of electrical problems.

D.

1. Two forces (or quantities) acting simultaneously on the same reference point may be summed and replaced by a single quantity. This single quantity will produce the same effect on the reference point, as the two individual quantities. The two initial quantities being added are vectors. That is, they have both magnitude and direction. The resultant of the two vectors will also be a vector and must be expressed in magnitude and direction. Two vectors 90° apart are illustrated in Fig. 3.20.

In order for this example to have the greatest meaning, quantities involving actual electrical elements are used. Thus the figure shows a resistance of 100 ohms and an inductive reactance of 100 ohms at right angles and as they are normally depicted in graphical form. The resultant quantity (Z) will be the impedance of a series circuit of the two elements. The determination of the sum of R and X_L may be done graphically, that is, by drawing Fig. 3.20 to any convenient scale and measuring the magnitude and direction (phase angle) of Z. The more usual method is by means of a common trigonometric theorum which yields the equation

$$Z = \sqrt{R^2 + X_L^2} = \sqrt{100^2 + 100^2}$$
$$= 141.4 \text{ ohms}$$

The direction (phase angle) is

$$\Theta = \tan^{-1} \frac{X_L}{R} = \tan^{-1} 1$$

$$\Theta = 45°$$

2. Two vector quantities which are 0° apart (in phase) are simply added arithmetically. The direction remains unchanged.

3. Two vectors which are 180° apart (180° out of phase) are added algebraically.

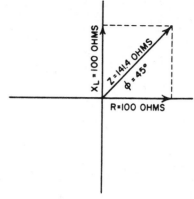

Fig. 3.20. Illustrating the solution of two vectors that are 90° apart.

For example, if vector 1 equals +100 and vector 2 equals −150 the resultant is 100 −150 = −50.

4. A vector may represent any type of quantity having both magnitude and direction. In electrical circuits, there is no physical direction involved. However, there is frequently the problem of phase angle. A typical example of a phase angle has been given in this discussion. (See also Q. 3.09, 3.18 and 3.19, above.) Generally, the problem of most frequent interest is the phase angle between the voltage and current in a circuit. In the solution of electrical problems, vectors are commonly employed and the student should acquire a working knowledge of vectors and complex numbers.

Q. 3.21. Explain how the values of resistance and capacitance in an RC network affect its time constant. How would the output waveform be affected by the frequency of the input in an RC network?

A.

1. The charging time is determined by the value of the capacitor and resistor in the circuit and both of these elements directly affect the time constant. Assuming R and C to be in series with the dc supply voltage; if the resistor is increased in value, the charging current is reduced. This increases the time required to charge the capacitor to any given voltage level. On the other hand,

increasing the value of capacitance (storage tank) with a fixed resistor, requires the current (which is limited by the resistor) to flow for a greater period of time.

2. If the waveform is a sine wave, the shape of the wave is unaffected by the RC network, regardless of its frequency. However, the amplitude of the output waveform may be reduced as the frequency is reduced below certain limits.

D.

1. The "time constant" of an RC circuit is defined as the length of time (in seconds) which is required for a capacitor to attain a voltage across its terminals which is equal to 63.2 percent of the applied voltage. The "time constant" may also be defined as the time required for a capacitor to discharge 63.2 percent of the original charge in the capacitor. (The remaining charge at the end of one "time constant" is therefore 36.8 percent.) In each succeeding time constant, the charge in the capacitor will again change (charge or discharge) by 63.2 percent. For all practical purposes a capacitor may be considered to be fully charged or discharged in 5 "time constants." The "time constant" is T = RC seconds, where R is the resistance in ohms and C is the capacitance in farads. If R is in ohms and C is in microfarads, then T is in microseconds. The voltage across a capacitor under charge, at any instant may be found from the formula,

$$V_C = V_A (1 - \varepsilon^{-t/RC})$$

where V_C is the voltage across the capacitor, V_A is the applied voltage, $\varepsilon = 2.718$, t is the elapsed time, RC equals one time constant.

2. As a rule of thumb, if the waveform period of one cycle is equal to or less than ⅕ of the time constant, the waveform will be passed by the RC network undistorted and without loss of amplitude. As the length of a cycle increases (frequency decreases), the period becomes less than ⅕ of the given time constant. The result in the case of a sine wave was given above. For other waveforms, the waveform will be differentiated

as the frequency decreases. The possibilities and theoretical concepts are too lengthy to be completely enumerated here. However, a familiar case of extreme differentiation occurs when a square wave is fed into an RC network and the output consists of sharply peaked positive and negative "pips." In such a case, the time constant may be only a fraction of the period of one cycle of the square wave.

Q. 3.22. Explain how the values of resistance and inductance in an RL network affect its time constant.

A. The time constant of an RL network is defined as the time (in seconds) required for the current to reach 63.2 percent of its maximum possible value. An increase in the value of inductance will directly increase the time constant. This is true because an inductance tends to resist any change of current and this property is directly proportional to the value of inductance. However, unlike the RC case, an increase of resistance will actually decrease the time constant. The reason an increase of resistance causes a decrease of the RL time constant is that the magnitude of the current at any given time is reduced. A reduced current results in a lesser rate of change of current at any given time. Since the rate of change of current determines the counter emf and therefore the opposition to current flow, a lesser rate permits the current to rise faster; hence a shorter time constant is attained. Of course, the converse is also true and a smaller resistance will result in a longer time constant for an RL circuit.

D. The time constant of an RL circuit may be found by the equation

$$T = \frac{L}{R} \text{ seconds}$$

where

L = inductance in henrys.
R = total series resistance in ohms (including the resistance of the inductance).

When the charging circuit is opened, the time constant of an RL circuit is changed. Assuming current had been at a maximum in the coil when the source was instantaneously disconnected, the energy in the coil is dissipated in the resistance of an oscillating circuit consisting of the coil (with its inherent resistance), the stray capacity of the circuit and the coil itself.

Q. 3.23. Explain the theory of molecular alignment as it affects magnetic properties of materials.

A. The theory of molecular alignment is based on the assumption that magnetic materials contain tiny molecular magnets called "magnetic dipoles." If the dipoles are caused to be in alignment with like poles all pointing the same way, the material is said to be magnetized. In this case magnetic North and South poles appear at opposite ends of the magnetic material.

D. In soft magnetic metals, the molecular alignment must be maintained by an electric current (electromagnet). When the current is removed the alignment becomes largely random and only a small "residual" magnetism remains. Iron is a soft magnetic material. However, there are certain hard magnetic materials, such as Cobalt or Alnico. When these are magnetized, they retain their magnetism indefinitely, if given proper care. It is assumed that in this case the molecular structure of the material is such that it is difficult for the magnetic dipoles to be moved from their aligned position. Such "permanent" magnets can be weakened or demagnetized by being subjected to mechanical shock, excessive heat, or an electromagnetic field which opposes the magnetization of the permanent magnet.

Q. 3.24. What is the relationship between the inductance of a coil and the number of turns of wire in the coil; the permeability of the core material used?

A.
1. The inductance of a coil varies approximately as the square of the number of turns.
2. The inductance of a coil varies directly with the permeability of the core.
D.
1. If the coil consists of only one turn, then its magnetic field will cut this turn, producing a certain counter-emf. However, if the coil consists of 2 turns the flux about *each* turn cuts 2 turns, and the resultant counter-emf is 4 times greater. Therefore, the inductance must also be 4 times greater or vary as the *square* of the number of turns.

Actually, the inductance increases slightly less than proportionally to the number of turns, as in a large many-turn coil, some lines "leak" out and do not cut all the other turns.
2. The permeability of a substance is the ratio of magnetic flux density in that substance to the field strength which produces it. Permeability is a property of a material which is somewhat analogous magnetically to conductivity in an electric circuit. If a magnetic field of strength H exists in a certain space, and the space is then filled with a permeable material, the new field intensity will be $B = \mu H$, where μ is the permeability of the material.

Q. 3.25. What factors influence the direction of magnetic lines of force produced by an electromagnet?

A. There are two main factors involved:
1. The direction of electron flow through the coil.
2. The manner of winding the turns.
D. A simple rule for determining the direction of lines of force of a coil is as follows: With the left hand, grasp the coil so that the fingers curl around the turns in the same direction as electrons are moving through these turns. The thumb of the left hand will then point to the north pole of the magnetic field, or the direction of lines of force *within* the coil. Outside the coil, the lines return to the south pole to form a closed loop.

Q. 3.26. Explain how self and mutual inductance produce transformer action.

A. When current flows through the primary winding of a transformer, the self inductance of the primary causes a counter emf to appear across it because of the expanding magnetic field around the primary. (With a sine wave input into the primary, the primary magnetic field is continuously expanding and contracting at the frequency of the sine wave.) The expanding (or contracting) magnetic field not only affects the primary, but also cuts across the secondary winding of the transformer. This causes a voltage to be induced into the secondary winding by mutual inductance and a current to flow in the secondary winding, if a load is connected across it.

D. The mutual inductance of a transformer may be calculated from the equation

$$M = K\sqrt{L1L2} \text{ henrys.}$$

where

M = mutual inductance in henrys.
K = coefficient of coupling (see Q. 3.27) between the coils.
L1 and L2 = values of self-inductance of the two coils.

In practice, the mutual inductance may be greatly increased by winding the inductances on some form of iron core. This has the effect of increasing the coefficient of coupling greatly, since the magnetic flux generated by the primary will be confined to a large extent by the iron core and will therefore link the secondary winding more completely.

Q. 3.27. What does coefficient of coupling mean?

A. The coefficient of coupling is a number (usually a decimal) which defines the ratio of the amount of magnetic flux linking a secondary coil, as compared to the original magnetic flux generated in the primary coil.

D. Coefficient of coupling is expressed by the equation

$$K = \frac{M}{\sqrt{L1L2}}$$

where

K = coefficient of coupling (a decimal)
M = mutual inductance of the two coils
L1 and L2 = self inductances of the two coils.

The coefficient of coupling may be increased by one or more of several possible expedients:

1. Placing the windings closer together.
2. Winding the primary and secondary wires adjacent to one another (bi-filar winding).
3. Winding the coils on a common iron core.

Where all the flux generated by one coil links the second coil, the value of K = 1. However, typical values of K are 0.05 to 0.3 for air-core coils and K may approach unity for a common wound iron-core coils.

Q. 3.28. How does the capacitance of a capacitor vary with area of plates; spacing between plates; dielectric material between plates?

A.
1. The capacitance varies directly in proportion to the area of the plates.
2. The capacitance varies inversely with the spacing between the plates (thickness of the dielectric).
3. The capacitance varies directly in proportion to the dielectric constant of the dielectric material.

D. To determine the capacitance of a two-plate capacitor, the following formula applies

$$C \text{ (pF)} = \frac{0.225KA}{S}$$

where

C = capacitance in picofarads.
K = dielectric constant of insulating material.
A = area of one plate in square inches.
S = spacing between plates in inches.

For a multi-plate capacitor, the formula is

$$C\,(pF) = \frac{0.225KA\,(N-1)}{S}$$

where N = number of plates.

All dielectric materials are compared to a vacuum, which has a dielectric constant of 1. For practical purposes, the dielectric constant of air is also 1, the actual value being less than 0.06 percent greater. Therefore, if a certain capacitor has a capacity of 0.001 µF with air dielectric, and mica, with a dielectric constant of 7, is placed in the capacitor so as to replace the air completely, its capacity will increase by 7 times and become 0.007 µF. Any increase in the dielectric constant will increase the capacity in direct proportion.

Q. 3.29. Assuming the voltage on a capacitor is at or below the maximum allowable value, does the value of the capacitor have any relationship to the amount of charge it can store? What relationship does this storage of charge have to the total capacitance of two or more capacitors in series; in parallel?

A.
1. The amount of charge which can be stored in a capacitor is directly proportional to its capacitance.
2. The amount of charge which can be stored in two or more capacitors in series is *less* than can be stored in any individual capacitor of the combination, because the *total* capacitance is *reduced*.
3. The amount of charge which can be stored in two more more capacitors in parallel is *greater* than can be stored in any individual capacitor of the combination, because the *total* capacitance is *increased*.

D.
1. The amount of charge stored in a capacitor (or equivalent combination) is expressed by the equation:

$$Q = CV$$

where

Q = charge in coulombs.
C = capacitance in farads.
V = voltage across the capacitor.

The coulomb, not often seen in practice, is a measure of quantity, or charge of electricity. One ampere is a current of 1 coulomb per second. A coulomb is the electric charge of 6.28×10^{18} electrons.

C denotes capacity in farads. This quantity, equal to 1 000 000 microfarads, is defined as that capacity which will have a potential of 1 volt, for 1 coulomb stored in it. The formula above, is actually a working definition of capacity, where V is the applied voltage.

2. Capacitors in series are figured the same as resistors in parallel. Capacitors in parallel are simply additive, as are resistors in series.

In a series circuit, the same current flows for the same time in all parts. Therefore, each capacitor has the same charge, and this value is also the charge in the combination. The voltages are:

$$V_1 = \frac{Q}{C_1} \quad V_2 = \frac{Q}{C_2} \quad V_3 = \frac{C_3}{C_3}\text{, etc.}$$

The voltage on the combination, since it is in series connection, is $V_1 + V_2 + V_3 \ldots$ or

$$V_T = \frac{Q}{C_1} + \frac{Q}{C_2} + \frac{Q}{C_3}\ldots$$
$$= Q\left(\frac{1}{C_1} + \frac{1}{C_2} + \frac{1}{C_3}\ldots\right)$$

but

$$V_T = \frac{Q}{C_T}$$

therefore

$$\frac{1}{C_T} = \frac{1}{C_1} + \frac{1}{C_2} + \frac{1}{C_3}\ldots$$

and

$$C_T = \cfrac{1}{\cfrac{1}{C_1} + \cfrac{1}{C_2} + \cfrac{1}{C_3} \cdots}$$

3. When capacitors are in parallel, each capacitor has the same applied voltage as the combination. The charge in the combination is equal to the sum of the charges on the capacitors. The combination is equivalent to one capacitor which would hold the total of the charges at the applied voltage; such a capacitor would have a capacity equal to $C_T = C_1 + C_2 = C_3 +$ etc.

Q. 3.30. How should electrolytic capacitors be connected in a circuit in relation to polarity? Which type of low leakage capacitor is used most often in transmitters?

A.

1. Electrolytic capacitors must be connected so that the positive terminal is connected to a voltage point which is more positive than the voltage fed to the negative terminal.

2. Where large values are required, oil-filled paper dielectric capacitors are frequently used. For smaller values of capacitance, mica and ceramic dielectric capacitors are frequently used.

D. The properties of the electrolytic capacitor are due to a dielectric film of an oxide which is formed on the positive plate of the capacitor. When connecting electrolytic capacitors the polarity marked on the body of the component must be observed. If this precaution is not observed the capacitor will be ruined. An electrolytic capacitor consists of four basic parts: the anode (positive plate), the cathode (negative plate), the electrolyte, and the dielectric film which is formed electrochemically on the surface of the anode. The dielectric material of an electrolytic capacitor consists of an extremely thin oxide film which is formed upon the surface of the anode. Certain metals, including aluminum, when immersed in special electrolytic solutions, will form a nonconducting film upon the surface when a current is passed through the metal and electrolyte to another metal plate. This film

will be of such a nature as to oppose the flow of current, and will act as an insulator only as long as the same "forming" polarity is maintained. Thus an electrolytic capacitor is formed, utilizing aluminum as the plates and the oxide film as the dielectric. Because the film is very thin, the capacity is very high for a given physical size.

A filter capacitor should be checked for leakage current with its normal operating voltage applied, by means of a milliammeter. While some indication of the condition of a capacitor may be found from a simple ohmmeter check, the proper method involves the application of normal operating potentials. The method of testing a standard 8-microfarad, 450-volt electrolytic capacitor is as follows: The capacitor is connected in series with a 450-volt dc source, a milliammeter (about 10 ma full scale) and a resistance of about 50 000 ohms shunted by a switch. The capacitor is permitted to charge for 5 minutes after which the shunting switch is closed. The milliammeter is then read. A well made electrolytic capacitor will have a very small leakage current when in continuous use. On intermittent operation the normal value of leakage current of an electrolytic capacitor is in the order of 50 to 100 microamperes per microfarad. For example, an 8-microfarad 450-volt electrolytic capacitor in good condition will have a leakage current of about 0.5 milliampere. The maximum leakage current should not exceed about 5 milliamperes.

Q. 3.31. A certain power company charges 7¢ per kilowatt-hour. How much would it cost to operate three 120 volt lamp bulbs, connected in parallel, each having an internal resistance of 100 ohms, for 24 hours?

A. The cost would be 73¢.

D. Step 1: Find the power used by each bulb.

$$P = \frac{V^2}{R} = \frac{14\ 400}{100} = 144 \text{ watts}$$

Step 2: The power used by three bulbs is $144 \times 3 = 432$ watts.

Step 3: Find the watt-hours for the three bulbs. This is $432 \times 24 = 10\ 368$ watt-hours.

Step 4: To find the kilowatt hours, divide the watt-hours by 1 000, or

$$\frac{10\ 368}{1\ 000} = 10.368 \text{ kilowatt hours (kwh)}$$

Step 5: To find the cost, multiply the total kwh by the unit cost per kwh, or 10.368 × 0.07 = 73¢.

Q. 3.32. The output of an amplifier stage having a voltage gain of 30 dB is 25 volts. What is the input voltage level?

A. The input-voltage level = 0.791 volt.
D. Step 1: The input voltage level of an amplifier is equal to the output voltage divided by the gain of the amplifier, or

$$V_{in} = \frac{V_{out}}{Gain}$$

Step 2: Since the voltage gain is given in dB (30 dB), it is necessary to change the dB ratio to a voltage ratio. We have,

$$dB = 20 \log_{10}\left(\frac{V_{out}}{V_{in}}\right)$$

transposing and substituting:

$$\log\left(\frac{V_{out}}{V_{in}}\right) = \frac{30}{20} = 1.5$$

$$\log{-}^1 1.5 = 31.6 \text{ (the voltage gain)}$$

Step 3: Substituting in the original formula.

$$V_{in} = \frac{V_{out}}{Gain} = \frac{25}{31.6} = 0.791 \text{ volt}$$

Q. 3.33. What is the impedance of a parallel circuit which is composed of a pure inductance and a pure capacitance at resonance; of a series circuit at resonance?

A.
1. The impedance of the parallel circuit at resonance is infinite.
2. The impedance of the series circuit at resonance is zero.
D.
1. The assumption is made in the question that zero resistance appears in both legs of the circuit. Under this condition parallel resonance occurs when $X_L = X_C$. These are equal and opposite reactances and the total reactance will then be zero. The impedance measured across the combination will be infinite. Actually this is a theoretical condition since there is always appreciable resistance in the inductance leg of the parallel resonant circuit. In this case the net reactance will be capacitive. In order to have the line current in phase with the applied voltage, X_C must equal

$$X_L + \frac{R}{Q}$$

2. The definition of series resonance specifies that the inductive reactance and the capacitive reactance are equal. Since the inductance tends to cause a 90° lag of current and the capacitance a 90° lead of current, the effect of the two reactances cancel, being equal and opposite, and the net impedance is zero.

Q. 3.34. What is the "Q" of a circuit? How is it affected by the circuit resistance? How does the "Q" of a circuit affect bandwidth?

A.
1. The Q of a circuit is the ratio of the energy stored to the energy dissipated in the circuit over a period of one cycle. In practice, most of the energy is dissipated by coil losses and the coil Q determines the circuit Q.
2. The greater the internal (series) circuit resistance, the lower the Q. The lower the external-shunt circuit resistance, the lower the Q.
3. The bandwidth of a circuit is inversely proportional to its Q.
D.
1. The term "circuit" as used in the question relates most commonly to a parallel resonant circuit and is treated here as such. The "Q" of a parallel resonant circuit is determined mainly by the "Q" of the inductance.
The energy storage is within the field of the pure inductance (no resistance) of the coil while the energy losses are due to a so-called "resistance," made up of several parts. This resistance is designated *effective resistance* and consists of:
a. The dc resistance of the coil.
b. The ac resistance of the coil (skin effect).

c. Dielectric losses in the wire insulation and coil form.

d. Core losses.

e. Radiation from the coil (if an appreciable part of a wavelength long).

From the above, we see that Q may be described by the formula

$$Q = \frac{X_L}{R_{effective}}$$

Sometimes eddy current losses in nearby bodies (such as a coil shield) are included, since the effect on circuit performance is the same as any other loss.

2. The bandwidth of a tuned circuit may be defined as the band of frequencies between the two points on the resonance curve which are three dB down from maximum (or 0.707 of the maximum amplitude of the resonance curve). If we express the two points (frequencies) as f_1 and f_2, then the bandwidth is $(f_2 - f_1)$ and may be expressed by the equation

$$(f_2 - f_1) = \frac{f_r}{Q}$$

where f_1 and f_2 are frequencies at the three dB points and f_r is the resonant frequency of the tuned circuit.

From this equation, it is apparent that the higher the value of Q, the narrower the circuit bandwidth will become (more sharply tuned).

3. In some cases a loading resistor is deliberately placed across a tuned circuit with the intention of increasing its bandwidth response by lowering the Q (increasing dissipated energy). Since this reduces the parallel impedance of the tuned circuit, a pro-

portional reduction in gain takes place. This device is often used in television IF amplifiers to obtain the necessary band pass. A simple formula to determine the value of loading resistance is

$$R = X_r \frac{(2\Delta f)}{f_r}$$

where

2 Δ f = the desired bandwith.

f_r = the resonant frequency.

X_r = the reactance of L at the resonant frequency.

Q. 3.35. Draw a circuit diagram of a low-pass filter composed of a "constant-k" and an "m-derived" section.

A. See Fig. 3.35.

D. Both the "constant-k" and "m-derived" filters are special cases of basic filters (see also Q. 3.36). Basically, such filters are used to achieve the sharper attenuation characteristics. The "m-derived" section is known as the "series-derived" type. There is also a "shunt-derived" type (not shown) where C_2 would be eliminated from the shunt arm and placed across L_1. The "constant-k" section shown is a pi section. Design data for such filters may be found in electrical engineering text books.

Filters are designed to operate into a resistive terminating impedance. When this is true, the impedance looking into the input of the filter has the same impedance value throughout most of the filter pass-band. This constant impedance property (over the pass-band) is more readily achieved by using "m-derived" and "constant-k" filters than with simple filters.

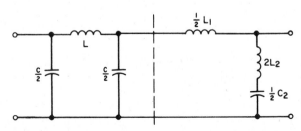

Fig. 3.35. Low-pass filter, composed of a "constant-k" section (left of dotted line) and an "m-derived" section (right of dotted line).

Q. 3.36. In general, why are filters used? Why are the "band-stop," "high-pass," and "low-pass" filters used? Draw schematic diagrams of the most commonly used filters.

A.

1. In general, the purpose of a filter is to select the desired frequency component(s) (from a complex input wave); to reject the undesired frequency component(s) and to apply only the desired component(s) to the circuit(s) where they are required. (This is an idealistic definition, since in practice, some portion of the undesired frequency components will also be present at the output of the filter.)

2. A "band-stop" (also called "band suppression," or "band exclusion") filter is one which discriminates against a band of frequencies within a spectrum and which passes frequencies above and below this band.

3. A "high-pass" filter is one which permits all frequencies above a selected cut-off frequency to be passed without attenuation and rejects frequencies below the cut-off frequency.

4. A "low-pass" filter is one which permits all frequencies below a selected cut-off frequency to be passed without attenuation and rejects frequencies above the cut-off frequency.

5. Schematic diagrams of commonly used filters are given in Fig. 3.36. The most commonly used types are known as, "L," "T," and "Pi" filters. These may be used in single sections or in multiple sections to provide the desired filtering action. In addition to these, there are various other types of filters which provide special filter-response characteristics when needed.

D. Two of the most commonly used filters are known as the "constant-k" and the "m-derived" filters. Various common configurations of these filters as well as three common types of RC filters are shown in Fig. 3.36. In the case of the m-derived filters, note that there are both series and shunt

types and examples are given of each, although space does not permit showing each possible variation. In addition, typical response curves for the four basic variations of constant-k filters are also shown in Fig. 3.36. (See also Q. 3.35 for additional information.)

The constant-k filter (actually a form of artificial transmission line) is designed by the so-called "image-parameter" method (as is the m-derived type). This simply means that the generator (input) looks into its own impedance, while the load (output) also looks into its impedance even though the two impedances may be different. Thus, such

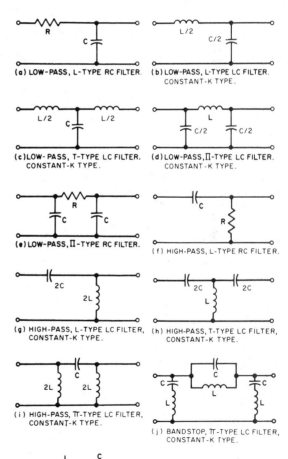

(a) LOW-PASS, L-TYPE RC FILTER.

(b) LOW-PASS, L-TYPE LC FILTER. CONSTANT-K TYPE.

(c) LOW-PASS, T-TYPE LC FILTER. CONSTANT-K TYPE.

(d) LOW-PASS, Π-TYPE LC FILTER. CONSTANT-K TYPE.

(e) LOW-PASS, Π-TYPE RC FILTER.

(f) HIGH-PASS, L-TYPE RC FILTER.

(g) HIGH-PASS, L-TYPE LC FILTER, CONSTANT-K TYPE.

(h) HIGH-PASS, T-TYPE LC FILTER, CONSTANT-K TYPE.

(i) HIGH-PASS, Π-TYPE LC FILTER, CONSTANT-K TYPE.

(j) BANDSTOP, Π-TYPE LC FILTER, CONSTANT-K TYPE.

(k) BANDPASS, Π-TYPE LC FILTER, CONSTANT-K TYPE.

Fig. 3.36. Common types of filters.

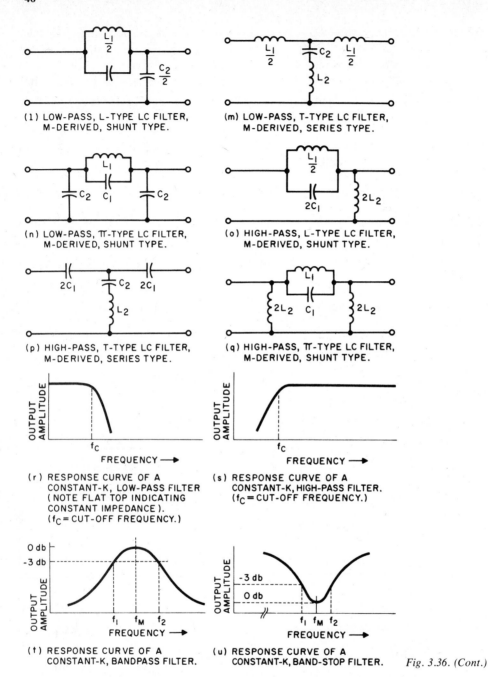

(1) LOW-PASS, L-TYPE LC FILTER, M-DERIVED, SHUNT TYPE.

(m) LOW-PASS, T-TYPE LC FILTER, M-DERIVED, SERIES TYPE.

(n) LOW-PASS, π-TYPE LC FILTER, M-DERIVED, SHUNT TYPE.

(o) HIGH-PASS, L-TYPE LC FILTER, M-DERIVED, SHUNT TYPE.

(p) HIGH-PASS, T-TYPE LC FILTER, M-DERIVED, SERIES TYPE.

(q) HIGH-PASS, π-TYPE LC FILTER, M-DERIVED, SHUNT TYPE.

(r) RESPONSE CURVE OF A CONSTANT-K, LOW-PASS FILTER (NOTE FLAT TOP INDICATING CONSTANT IMPEDANCE). (f_C = CUT-OFF FREQUENCY.)

(s) RESPONSE CURVE OF A CONSTANT-K, HIGH-PASS FILTER. (f_C = CUT-OFF FREQUENCY.)

(t) RESPONSE CURVE OF A CONSTANT-K, BANDPASS FILTER.

(u) RESPONSE CURVE OF A CONSTANT-K, BAND-STOP FILTER.

Fig. 3.36. (Cont.)

filters serve two functions: the elimination of undesired frequencies and the matching of two different impedances. The flat tops on the response curves for the low- and high-pass filters, shown in Fig. 3.36, indicate that the impedance of a properly designed constant-k (or m-derived) filter of these types remains substantially constant throughout the design pass band. The design of the constant-k (and other LC filters) is practical over a range of frequencies from about 1 kHz to 100 MHz. It is important to note that in the case of the filters herein discussed the cut-off characteristics can be made sharper by the use of additional filter sections in cascade. Thus, a three-section filter will have a much sharper cut-off than a single section filter.

M-derived filters (shown in Fig. 3.36)

have an advantage over the constant-k types in that they exhibit a considerable improvement in the sharpness of the filter response. (M-derived and constant-k types may be combined (see Fig. 3.35) to achieve characteristics not achievable with constant-k types alone.) In addition, the frequencies of infinite attenuation are readily selected with the m-derived filters, but not for the constant-k types.

The meaning of the term "constant-k" can be seen readily with the aid of Fig. 3.36(b). If the values of the inductance and capacitance are chosen correctly, any change of reactance of either one (due to change in frequency) will be exactly offset by an equal and opposite change in the other. Therefore, their product will always be a constant, which is here called the "constant-k."

The term "m," from "m-derived," is not as easily explained, but it is a term which is used in the calculation of the value of the reactances used in m-derived filters and is related to the ratio of the filter cut-off frequency to its frequency of infinite attenuation. It is interesting to note that when the value of m becomes one, the filter becomes a constant-k filter.

The uses of filters may be generally listed as follows:

1. Power supply ripple smoothing.
2. Decoupling amplifier stages.
3. Tuned circuits, as in RF or IF stages.
4. Selection of desired products of heterodyning, as in the case of selecting particular sidebands in single sideband transmitters.
5. Harmonic frequency suppression in transmitters.
6. Coupling circuits between amplifier stages.
7. Elimination of undesired frequencies in receivers, as in the case of a 4.5-MHz trap in a TV receiver.
8. Elimination of IF frequencies in a receiver, following detection.
9. Improvement of the high- and low-frequency responses in video amplifiers.

10. Restricting the audio frequency band-pass to be used; such as limiting it to 300 to 3 000 hertz for use in a single-sideband transmitter.
11. Cross-over networks used with loudspeaker arrangements, where lower audio frequencies are fed to a "woofer" and the higher audio frequencies are fed to a "tweeter."
12. Elimination of undesired interference frequencies from motors, generators and other electrical or electronic equipment.
13. A virtually infinite application for other special uses.

Q. 3.37. Name four materials that make good insulators at low frequencies, but not at UHF, or above.

A. The following materials are adequate for low radio frequencies, but not at UHF and above.

1. Rubber.
2. Fiber.
3. Paper.
4. Glass.
5. Bakelite.
6. Cambric.
7. Cotton.

D. Insulators which are more suitable at the higher radio frequencies, include:

1. Ceramics.
2. Mica.
3. Polystyrene.
4. Polyethlyene.
5. Special plastics.

Q. 3.38. In an iron-core transformer, what is the relationship between the transformer turns ratio and primary to secondary current ratio; between turns ratio and primary to secondary voltage ratio? (Assume no losses.)

A.
1. The ratio of primary to secondary currents is approximately in inverse ratio to the turns ratio.
2. The primary to secondary voltage ratio is in proportion to the turns ratio. (In the ideal case, this is true if the secondary is unloaded.)

D. If the losses in the transformer are neglected, it can be assumed that the power which the primary draws from the line is all transformed to the secondary. If the power ratio is the same and the voltage ratio is 1 to 5, then the current ratio must be in inverse proportion to the voltage ratio, or 5 to 1. The voltage ratio is proportional to the turns ratio or

$$\frac{N_p}{N_s} = \frac{V_p}{V_s}$$

The current ratio is inversely proportional to the turns ratio

$$\frac{N_p}{N_s} = \frac{I_s}{I_p}$$

Q. 3.39. What prevents high currents from flowing in the primary of an unloaded power transformer?

A. The relatively high value of inductive reactance of the primary winding.

D. When power is taken from the secondary, the secondary current sets up a magnetic field from this winding. Since the windings have mutual inductance, the secondary field cuts the primary winding and induces a voltage into the primary which causes additional primary current to flow. The additional current is taken from the line to supply the power requirements of the secondary. In effect, the secondary field causes a reduction of primary inductance and the smaller reactance permits additional primary current to be taken from the line.

Q. 3.40. An audio transformer has a resistive load connected across its secondary terminals. What is the relationship between this resistance, the turns ratio and the input impedance at the primary terminals? How is this principle useful in matching impedances?

A.
1. The input impedance is equal to the value of the resistance multiplied by the square of the turns ratio.
2. Any two impedances may be matched (within practical limits) by using the proper turns ratio of a transformer.

D. The impedance ratio which a transformer can match is a function of the transformer turns ratio. A basic formula relating impedance ratio and turns ratio is:

$$\frac{N_p}{N_s} = \sqrt{\frac{Z_p}{Z_s}} \qquad \text{or} \qquad \left(\frac{N_p}{N_s}\right)^2 = \frac{Z_p}{Z_s}$$

where

N_p = the number of turns in the primary.
N_s = the number of turns in the secondary.
Z_p = the primary impedance.
Z_s = the secondary impedance.

This means, for example, that if 5 400 ohms were connected to the secondary of a 1:3 step-up transformer, the apparent impedance, measured at the primary, would be

$$5\ 400 \times \left(\frac{1}{3}\right)^2 \text{ ohms}$$

or 600 ohms.

Q. 3.41. How is power lost in an iron-core transformer? In an air-core transformer?

A.
1. Power is dissipated through the following losses (iron core):
   a. Eddy current losses.
   b. Hysteresis losses.
   c. Copper losses.

2. Power is dissipated through the following losses (air core):
   a. Radiation.
   b. Skin effect.
   c. Absorption through mutual coupling and/or shield losses.
   d. Bandwidth loading resistor, where used in shunt with the coil.

D. Eddy current losses are due to presence of circulating currents throughout the core material. The current in any path is directly proportional to the emf induced in it, and inversely proportional to the resistance of the path. The heat produced is proportional to the square of the induced current. Eddy current losses can be reduced by building the core out of thin laminations individually insulated, and by using material having high specific resistivity. Eddy current losses are proportional to the square of the maximum flux density, the square of the thickness of laminations, and the square of the frequency. This loss is unaffected by dc core saturation.

Magnetic hysteresis is a property of magnetic material by virtue of which the magnetic flux density corresponding to a given magnetizing force (gilberts, ampere-turns) depends on the previous conditions of magnetization of the material. The effect of hysteresis, when the field is alternating, is an energy loss appearing as heat in the material. If a magnetic field is established in air, it will be found that under normal conditions all of the energy stored in the magnetic field will be returned to the circuit upon the collapse of the field. If the field is established in iron or steel, however, only a part of the energy will be returned to the circuit, the remainder appearing as heat in the iron or steel. This heat loss is partly due to the effect of hysteresis. According to the molecular theory of magnetism, the molecules in a magnetic material are haphazardly arranged when the material is unmagnetized. When a magnetizing force is applied, these tiny magnets turn and become aligned with the magnetic field. Their motion is resisted by a force which is called molecular friction. The work done in overcoming this friction is the hysteresis energy loss, which appears as heat. This loss is given by the equation:

$$P = Kf(B_{max})^{1.6} \text{ watts}$$

where

K = a constant of the magnetic material.

f = the frequency in hertz.

B_{max} = the maximum flux density in the material.

The "copper losses" of a transformer are determined by the effective resistance of the primary and secondary windings and the current through each winding. At power frequencies the copper losses may be found by determining the dc resistance of each winding and multiplying this value by the square of the current in the winding.

At radio frequencies, "skin effect" must be taken into account, as the effective resistance may be much greater than the dc resistance alone. At radio frequencies, therefore, the copper loss is found by, $P = I^2 \times R_{eff}$ watts. See also Q. 3.11 for "skin effect."

Q. 3.42. Explain the operation of a "break-contact" relay; a "make-contact" relay.

A.

1. A *break-contact* relay is also known as a "normally-closed" relay. In this type of relay, when the coil is de-energized, one or more sets of contacts are closed and will open only when the relay coil is energized.

2. A *make-contact* relay is also known as a "normally open" relay. In this case, one or more sets of contacts remain open in the de-energized condition and close only when the relay coil is energized.

Q. 3.43. What is the value and tolerance of a resistor which is color-coded (left-to-right): RED, BLACK, ORANGE, GOLD?

A. The value of the resistor is 20 000 ohms. Gold signifies a ±5 percent tolerance.

Q. 3.44. What would be the value, tolerance and voltage rating of an EIA mica capacitor whose first row colors were (from left-to-right): BLUE, RED, GREEN: second row: GREEN, SILVER, RED?

A. In the EIA system, six dots are used to identify the capacitor. The top three dots are read from left-to-right, but the bottom three are read from right-to-left (continuing around the loop). Thus, in the question, the colors should be read in sequence as, (1) BLUE, (2) RED, (3) GREEN, (4) RED, (5) SILVER, (6) GREEN. However, in the EIA system the first dot (1) would be white, identifying the code as that of EIA and not MIL (which would have a black first dot). Therefore, the color sequence should read instead, (1) WHITE, (2) RED, (3) GREEN, (4) RED, (5) SILVER, (6) GREEN.

The value of capacitance (in pF) is taken from dots 2, 3, and 4 and is 2 500 pF.

The tolerance is taken from dot 5 (Silver) and is ± 10 percent.

Dot 6 gives the EIA class (A through G) which specifies temperature coefficient, leakage resistance and other variable factors. The voltage rating is not given by any color dot directly but is generally 500 volts. (Voltage ratings may be found in the manufacturer's data sheets or in supply catalogues, when in doubt.)

EIA are the initials for the Electronic Industries Association, formerly known as the RETMA; which stood for the Radio-Electronics-Television Manufacturers Association.

Q. 3.45. List three precautions which should be taken in soldering electrical connections to assure a permanent junction.

A. Some precautions in soldering are:

1. Clean parts thoroughly, if they are not already tinned. If the parts are not tinned, it is helpful to tin them before soldering.

2. Make a good mechanical connection between the parts.

3. If the solder does not have an inner rosin core, it will be helpful to apply a small quantity of rosin to the joint. (Most electronic-type solders have an inner core of rosin or other non-corrosive flux.)

4. Use a soldering iron or soldering gun of high enough wattage rating so the joint will be adequately heated.

5. Heat the joint so it is hot enough to melt the solder. Don't "paste" molten solder onto a cold joint.

6. Maintain the heat for a sufficient time to permit the solder to flow freely over the entire joint.

7. Use just enough solder to cover the entire joint evenly.

8. Never use acid flux in electrical work, as it is highly corrosive.

9. Be certain the parts of the joint do not move while the solder is cooling.

Note: The following added material numbered Q. 3.45-A1 through Q. 3.45-A33 contains information that may be required to pass the General Radiotelephone Operator's License examination. This added material, as well as the new material added to other sections, has been included to help acquaint students with the current state of the electronics art. It is felt that the added material contains subject matter that may also be required of students who have obtained a General Radiotelephone Operator's License and are seeking employment. Additionally, the added material contains valuable information for private technician certification.

Q. 3.45-A1. Define "volt," "millivolt," "kilovolt," and "microvolt."

A.

1. One volt (V) is the potential difference appearing across a resistance of one ohm, when one ampere of direct current flows through it.

2. One millivolt (mV) equals one-thousandth of a volt.

3. One kilovolt (kV) equals one thousand volts.

4. One microvolt (μV) equals one-millionth of a volt.

Q. 3.45-A2. Define "watt," "milliwatt," "microwatt," "kilowatt," and "megawatt."

A.

1. One watt (W) is the power expended when one ampere of direct current flows through a resistance of one ohm.

2. One milliwatt (mW) equals one-thousandth of a watt.

3. One microwatt (μW) equals one-millionth of a watt.

4. One kilowatt (kW) equals one thousand watts.

5. One megawatt (MW) equals one million watts.

Q. 3.45-A3. Define, "hertz," "kilo-hertz," "megahertz," and "gigahertz."

A.

1. One hertz (Hz) equals one cycle per second.

2. One kilohertz (kHz) equals one thousand (10^3) cycles per second.

3. One megahertz (MHz) equals one million (10^6) cycles per second.

4. One gigahertz (GHz) equals one billion (10^9) cycles per second.

Q. 3.45-A4. Define, "ohm," "kilohm," and "megohm."

A.

1. One ohm (Ω) is the value of resistance through which a potential difference of one volt will produce a current of one ampere.

2. One kilohm (kΩ) equals one thousand (10^3) ohms.

3. One megohm (MΩ) equals one million (10^6) ohms.

Q. 3.45-A5. Define, "farad," "micro-farad," and "picofarad."

A.

1. One farad (F) is the capacitance of a capacitor in which a charge of one coulomb produces a potential difference of one volt across its terminals.

2. One microfarad (μF) equals one-millionth (10^{-6}) of a farad.

3. One picofarad (pF) equals one billionth (10^{-9}) of a farad.

Q. 3.45-A6. Define, "henry," "milli-henry," "microhenry," and "picohenry."

A.

1. One henry (H) is the inductance of a circuit when a current variation of one ampere per second induces one volt across its terminals.

2. One millihenry (MH) equals one-thousandth (10^{-3}) of a henry.

3. One microhenry equals one-millionth (10^{-6}) of a henry.

4. One picohenry (pH) equals one-trillionth (10^{-12}) of a henry.

Q. 3.45-A7. What is the meaning of the term "reactive power"?

A. Reactive (or "wattless" or "quadrature") power is *non-dissipated* power. It is the power that is alternately transferred between the electric field and the reactive component (inductor of capacitor).

The power in a reactance is equal to I^2X. This power is *not* lost in the form of heat as it would be in the case of current passing through a resistance ($P = I^2R$).

D. The unit of reactive power is called the "volt-ampere-reactive," or *var*. For a problem involving reactive power, see 3.45-A26.

Q. 3.45-A8. What is a crystal filter?

A. A crystal filter is a narrow-bandwidth, bandpass filter. They are also called quartz filters. These filters find wide use in single-sideband (SSB) exciters and receiver-IF circuits. The crystal filter is equivalent to an LC tuned circuit.

D. Two simple crystal-filter circuits and their basic response curve are shown in Fig. 3.45-A8. In part (1) of the figure, coil L_1 and resistor R_1 are placed in series with the crystal. This circuit acts as a parallel-resonant tuned circuit with very narrow bandwidth.

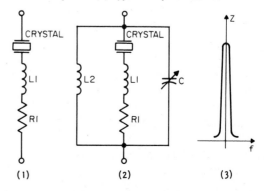

Fig. 3.45-A8. Crystal circuits used for filters: (1) A coil L and its dc resistance R_1 in series with the crystal make it behave as a simple parallel-resonant circuit with a high Q. (2) In this circuit the variable capacitor C tunes the circuit through a narrow range, and coil L_2 lowers the circuit Q for a broader response. (3) Typical response curve.

It will pass most frequencies to either side of the crystal frequency but reject frequencies at and near the crystal frequency.

In Fig. 3.45-A8(2), the Q is lowered and the response broadened by adding coil L_2 in parallel with the circuit. (A resistor could be used instead of the coil.) Capacitor C may be placed across the crystal-filter circuit. This tunes the filter circuit through a narrow frequency range.

Low-cost crystal filters with a passband centered around 9 MHz are commonly used in receiver-IF circuits, transceivers, and much amateur radio equipment. They may replace or supplement conventional tuned circuits.

Circuits employing more than one crystal provide progressively narrower filter bandwidths. As many as 8 (or more) crystals may be used in a crystal filter. Some characteristics of an 8-crystal filter are as follows:

1. 6-dB bandwidth: 2.4 kHz.
2. Passband ripple: less than 2 dB.
3. Insertion loss: less than 3.5 dB.
4. Terminating impedance: 500 ohms.
5. Stop-band attenuation: more than 100 dB.

Q. 3.45-A9. What is a monolithic-crystal filter?

A. A monolithic-crystal filter is fabricated by depositing *several* electrodes on a single quartz wafer. This creates a multi-section crystal filter in a very small package. The filter is equivalent to an LC tuned circuit.

D. A monolithic-crystal filter is compatible with integrated circuits and provides economy in manufacture. Such filters are smaller and cheaper than conventional crystal filters (Q. 3.45-A8). They may be used in many applications in place of conventional crystal filters. They are used in telephone multiplexing, radio receiving, and transmitting equipment.

These filters are available in stop-band frequencies from about 5 to 300 MHz. They are also made for overtone (odd harmonic) operation. Here are some typical characteristics of one type:

1. Frequency: 158 MHz.

2. 3-dB bandwidth: 15 kHz.
3. Insertion loss: less than 2 dB.
4. Passband ripple: less than 1 dB.
5. Terminating impedance: 500 ohms.
6. Stop-band attenuation: greater than 60 dB.

Q. 3.45-A10. What is a ceramic filter?

A. A ceramic filter is a narrow-bandwidth, bandpass filter. It has characteristics similar to those of a crystal (quartz) filter (Q. 3.45-A8). However, the ceramic filter is much smaller in size. The filter is equivalent to an LC tuned circuit.

D. A crystal filter uses quartz for the vibrating (resonant) element. However, the ceramic filter uses the piezoelectric properties of lead zirconate and lead titanate resonators.

A simple three-terminal ceramic filter is shown in Fig. 3.45-A10(1). The input signal is delivered to the *DOT* terminal. The input signal causes the ceramic disk to vibrate at its mechanical resonant frequency. Vibration will only occur if the input signal and the disk resonant frequency are the *same*. As

Fig. 3.45-A10(1). Construction details of a three-terminal ceramic filter.

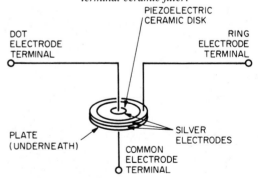

Fig. 3.45-A10(2). An IF stage that uses a ceramic filter in place of an LC tuned circuit.

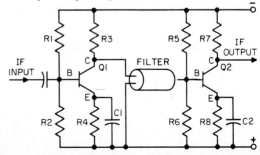

the ceramic disk vibrates, voltages are generated around its edges. These voltages are picked off at the ring-electrode terminal. The common terminal (a silver plate) is normally at ground potential.

An idea of the small physical size of a ceramic filter, a 455 kHz filter has a ceramic disk 0.2 inches in diameter by 0.1 to 0.4 inches thick. Three terminal disks can be stacked to obtain a sharper response. This configuration is called a *ceramic ladder filter*.

Two-terminal ceramic filters are made by placing a silver plate on both sides of the ceramic disk. The signal is fed to one plate and taken from the other. A number of the two-terminal disks can be stacked to provide a sharper response. This configuration is also called a *ceramic ladder filter*.

Figure 3.45-A10(2) shows how a ceramic (or crystal) filter may be used in an IF amplifier by substituting for an LC tuned circuit.

Q. 3.45-A11. Which of the following components has the highest rate of breakdown?
1. **Resistors.**
2. **Capacitors.**
3. **Inductors.**
4. **Piezoelectric crystals.**

A. In descending order of highest breakdown rate first, the answer is:
1. Capacitors.
2. Resistors.
3. Piezoelectric crystals.
4. Inductors.

D. While capacitors may fail of their own accord, resistors generally fail because of excessive current, which may be caused by a shorted capacitor. Piezoelectric crystals may fail naturally, from excessive excitation, or from crystal-holder pressure. Inductors rarely fail naturally, but they can fail from excessive current caused by a circuit defect.

Q. 3.45-A12. What is the total inductance of coils connected in series and having no mutual inductance (no coupling)?

A. The total inductance is equal to the sum of the individual inductances. Thus

$$L_T = L_1 + L_2 + L_3, \text{ etc.}$$

where L_T, L_1, L_2, L_3, etc. are all in the *same* units of inductance. This may be henrys (H), millihenrys (mH), or microhenrys (μH).

D. For example, assume $L_1 = 10$ μH, $L_2 = 20$ μH and $L_3 = 50$ μH. The total inductance (no coupling) is then

$$L_T = 10 + 20 + 50 = 80 \ \mu H$$

Q. 3.45-A13. What is the total inductance of two coils in series that have mutual inductance?

A. The total inductance is dependent upon:
1. The degree of coupling.
2. Whether the coils are connected to be *series aiding* or *series opposing*.

The equation for the total inductance of two coupled coils is

$$L_T = L_1 + L_2 \pm 2L_M$$

where L_M = the mutual inductance.

(See Q. 3.26 and Q. 3.27.) L_M has the *plus* sign, when the two coils are series aiding (increased inductance). L_M has the minus sign when the two coils are series opposing (decreased inductance).

D. Coupling that is series aiding has the common coil current producing the *same* magnetic field direction in both coils.

Coupling that is series opposing has the common coil currents producing *opposite* magnetic field directions in each coil.

The type of coupling is a function of: (1) the method of connecting the coils and (2) the direction of the coil winding. Reversing either (1) or (2) will reverse the direction of the magnetic field.

Q. 3.45-A14. What is the total inductance of two coils connected in parallel and having no mutual inductance (no coupling)?

A. The total inductance is found by the use of the equation

$$\frac{1}{L_T} = \frac{1}{L_1} + \frac{1}{L_2} + \frac{1}{L_3}, \text{ etc.}$$

where L_T, L_1, L_2, L_3, etc. are all in the same units of inductance.

D. For example, L_1 and L_2 are in parallel and each has an inductance of 4 μH. What is the total inductance, L_T?

$$\frac{1}{L_T} = \frac{1}{4} + \frac{1}{4} = \frac{2}{4}$$

$$L_T = \frac{4}{2} = 2\mu H$$

Q. 3.45-A15. What is the total inductance of two coils in parallel that have mutual inductance?

A. The total inductance is dependent upon:
1. The degree of coupling.
2. Whether the coils are connected with their fields *aiding* or *opposing*.

The equation for two parallel coils with fields *aiding* is

$$L_T = \frac{1}{1/(L_1 + M) + 1/(L_2 + M)}$$

The equation for two parallel coils with fields *opposing* is,

$$L_T = \frac{1}{L/(L_1 - M) + 1/(L_2 - M)}$$

D. Given two parallel coils, L_1 and L_2, each having an inductance of 10 μH. The mutual inductance (M), fields aiding between the two coils is, 5 μH. What is the total inductance, L_T?

Substituting in the above equation,

$$L_T = \frac{1}{1/(10 + 5) + 1/(10 + 5)}$$
$$= \frac{1}{1/15 + 1/15}$$
$$= \frac{\frac{1}{2}}{15} = \frac{15}{2} = 7.5 \ \mu H$$

Q. 3.45-A16. What percent tolerance values are available for fixed capacitors?

A. The following are the tolerance classifications for common types of capacitors:
1. Mica: ±0.25 to ±5 percent.
2. Silvered mica: ±10 to ±20 percent.
3. Paper: ±10 to ±20 percent.
4. Plastic film: ±0.5 to ±10 percent (depending on the type of plastic used).

5. Ceramic: low k*, ±5 to ±20 percent, high k, +100 to −20 percent.
6. Aluminum electrolytic: +100 to −20 percent.
7. Tantalum electrolytic: ±5 to ±20 percent.

D. Capacitors may fail in one of three ways: (1) open circuited, (2) leaky, or (3) short circuited. If leaky or shorted, associated components may be damaged. (See also Q. 3.44.)

Q. 3.45-A17. What are some of the important characteristics of the types of capacitors listed in Q. 3.45-A16.

A.
1. *Mica capacitors:* Mica is chemically inert and highly stable. A typical mica capacitor structure is shown in Figure 3.45-A17(1). This is a sandwich structure, which is made up of interleaving layers of tin-lead foil and "ruby" mica.

These capacitors can be used over a wide, ambient temperature range (−55 to +150°C). They have very high insulation resistance and high Q. Their capacitance values range from about 1.0 pF to 0.1 μF. The working voltages range from 500 to 50 000 V. Insulation resistance is greater than 100 000 MΩ.

Fixed types are used in RF circuits up to about 300 MHz. Adjustable types are used as trimmers. The higher-voltage types are used in transmitter circuits.

2. *Silvered mica capacitors*: In this type, a thin layer of silver is fired onto the surface of the mica. The silver is the conducting electrode. Advantages over a mica capacitor include greater mechanical stability and more uniform characteristics.

Characteristics and ratings are similar to mica capacitors discussed in the section on mica capacitors. However, the *maximum* working voltage available is 75 000 V, and the insulation resistance is 1 000 MΩ. Uses are as stated in that same section.

3. *Paper and plastic-film capacitors*: The

* k = relative dielectric constant.

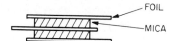

Fig. 3.45-A17(1). The "sandwich" structure mica capacitor.

dielectric material in paper capacitors is *Kraft* paper, which is a very high grade of paper made for this purpose. This type of capacitor is packaged as a "rolled sandwich," as shown in Fig. 3.45-A17(2). The structure is made up of alternate layers of metal foil and paper (or plastic film) dielectric. Their capacitance values range from 500 pF to 50 µF. High-voltage types may be oil filled to increase the breakdown voltage. The working voltages range from 200 to 100 000 V. Insulation resistance is 100 MΩ for paper and 10 000 MΩ for plastic film.

The plastic films used include polyester (Mylar), polystyrene, and polycarbonate. The maximum operating voltages are 100 000 V for paper, 1 000 V for polystyrene, 600 V for polycarbonate, and 600 V for polyester. Operating temperatures are as high as 140°C.

The tolerances are ±10 to ±20 percent for paper; ±0.5 percent for polystyrene; ±1 percent for polycarbonate; and ±10 percent for polyester.

Polyester (Mylar) capacitors are the most widely used plastic film capacitors. They are highly stable and have greater resistance to moisture than Kraft paper.

Paper and plastic foil capacitors are used as coupling, bypass, and filter capacitors. However, because of their "rolled up"

construction, they have a relatively high inherent inductance and stray capacity (to ground). They are also subject to higher-frequency dielectric losses. Consequently, their use is generally in circuits operating below about 2 or 3 MHz. These capacitors frequently are marked with a black band around one end. This marks the connection to the *outer* metal foil. This end of the capacitor should be connected to the *lowest* potential point of the circuit.

4. *Ceramic capacitors*: Ceramic-dielectric materials can have high dielectric-constant (k) values, up to 10 000. Consequently they can provide a given value of capacitance in much less physical space than mica, silvered mica, paper, or plastic film capacitors. The ceramics used are based on the mineral *rutile* (T_1O_2) and on combinations of titanium dioxide and other oxides.

These capacitors are widely used in all types of electronic circuits, up to microwave frequencies (Class I dielectric). They have low self inductance, low shunt capacity (to ground), and low dielectric losses.

Ceramic capacitors come in many forms. Some of these are disk types, tubular types, feedthrough types, and chip types for integrated circuits.

For disk types (see Fig. 3.45-A17(3)), both sides of the ceramic are coated with precious metal paste (platinum, palladium, or silver) and baked at about 1 450°C to form the capacitor. For chip types, the units are stacked with each unit containing several

Fig. 3.45-A17(2). The "rolled sandwich" structure is commonly used for paper and plastic film capacitors.

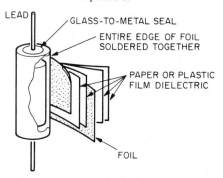

Fig. 3.45-A17(3). Disk-type ceramic capacitor, showing the 5-dot color code system.

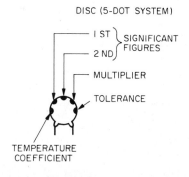

electrodes extending alternately to each cut end. They are then baked as above. Chip capacitors have the highest frequency range.

Tubular ceramic capacitors are formed by firing a precious metal coating on both sides of a ceramic tube.

Voltage ratings for various types, range from 50 to 1 600 V. Disk types have capacitance values ranging from 1 pF to 0.1 μF and voltage ratings from 100 to 1 600 V. The operating temperature range (depending upon ceramic class) may be as great as −55° to +125°C.

Tubular ceramic capacitors have capacitance values ranging from 1 pF to 3.3 μF. Their voltage ratings are from 50 to 200 V. Temperature range is the same as for disk types.

Chip-type, ceramic capacitors have capacitance values ranging from 10 pF to 1 μF. Their voltage ranges are from 25 to 100 V. The temperature range is similar to disk types. The higher capacitance values have the lower voltage ratings. (See Fig. 3.45-A17(4).)

Feed-through ceramic capacitors have capacitance values ranging from 10 to 1 500 pF. The voltage ranges are from 200 to 1 500 V. Temperature ranges are similar to disk types.

An important use for ceramic capacitors is to provide *temperature compensation* of capacity for tuned circuits. The correct choice of a temperature-compensating ceramic capacitor can *neutralize* the normal temperature changes in capacitance of a tuned circuit. This will stabilize the characteristics of the tuned circuit with temperature. The temperature coefficient of a capacitor is defined as the percent change in capacitance over a specified temperature range. It is given in parts per million, per degree Celsius (ppm/°C). It is calculated by measuring the capacitance change between 25° and 85°C and then dividing by 60.

The temperature coefficient may be positive (capacitance increase with increasing temperature) or negative (capacitance decrease with increasing temperature). It can also be zero (no capacitance change with variations of temperature). Negative temperature coefficient capacitors are prefixed by the letter N. For example, N100 indicates a *negative temperature coefficient* of 100 ppm/°C. Conversely, the prefix P indicates a positive temperature coefficient. P100 indicates a *positive temperature coefficient* of 100 ppm/°C. Capacitors having *zero temperature coefficient* are rated as NPO.

Other uses for ceramic capacitors include their use for tuned circuits, coupling, timing, bypassing, and filtering.

5. *Electrolytic capacitors* (see also Q. 3.30): There are two basic types of electrolytic capacitors, *aluminum* and *tantalum*. These capacitors are widely used in circuits where a large value of capacitance in a small volume is required. They may be either *polarized* or non-polarized.

With the polarized type, the lead marked with a plus sign (+) must be connected to a higher dc potential than the other lead. The polarized type can only be used in dc circuits. The non-polarized type can be used in ac or dc circuits. These two types are illustrated in Fig. 3.45-A17(5).

Electrolytic capacitors are constructed as "rolled sandwiches," as shown in Fig. 3.45-A17(6). Note the alternate layers of aluminum (or tantalum) foil and paper (or gauze). The foil is etched to increase its surface area. An extremely thin layer of aluminum (or tantalum) oxide is electrochem-

Fig. 3.45-A17(4). Construction features of a ceramic chip capacitor. (Courtesy West-Cap Division, San Fernando Electric Manufacturing Company)

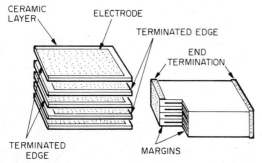

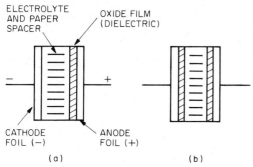
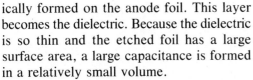

Fig. 3.45-A17(5). An elementary electrolytic capacitor: (a) polarized and (b) non-polarized.

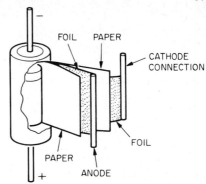

Fig. 3.45-A17(6). The rolled sandwich structure of an electrolytic foil capacitor.

ically formed on the anode foil. This layer becomes the dielectric. Because the dielectric is so thin and the etched foil has a large surface area, a large capacitance is formed in a relatively small volume.

The paper (or gauze) separator is soaked in an electrolyte solution. It acts as a spacer to prevent shorting between the cathode (−) and anode (+) foils.

Aluminum electrolytic capacitors have relatively high dc leakage current (approximately 0.015 to 4.0 mA) and low insulation resistance (less than 1 MΩ). They are low in cost. Their tolerance is from +100 to −20 percent. Capacitance values range from about 1 µF to 1 F, with a working voltage rating from 3 to 500 V. Generally the higher capacitance values have lower working voltage ratings. However, low voltage aluminum electrolytic capacitors are commonly used in transistor circuits. Temperature ranges are commonly from −20° to +85°C, but special types can operate from −55° to +125°C. These capacitors have limited shelf life, and the capacitance deteriorates with time.

These electrolytic capacitors are packaged as single or multiple capacitor units. The multiple units may have three or four different capacitors, with different working voltages in one package. They are frequently used for filtering and bypassing in many types of communications and home entertainment electronic equipment.

Common uses for aluminum electrolytic capacitors are coupling, filtering, and bypassing.

Tantalum electrolytic capacitors are smaller for equivalent ratings than the aluminum electrolytic type, and they are more expensive. They have long shelf life, increased temperature range, and stable operating characteristics. They also have low working voltage ratings and low leakage current. Tantalum electrolytic capacitors have capacitance values ranging from about 0.001 to 2 200 µF. The tolerance is from ±10 to ±30 percent. The working voltages are commonly from 3 to 100 V; special types may go to 450 V. Leakage current is from 1 to 147 µA. Operating temperatures are from −55° to +125°C. Insulation resistance is greater than 1 MΩ.

Common uses for tantalum electrolytic capacitors are coupling, filtering, and bypassing. They are frequently used in transistor circuits in low-voltage ratings. These capacitors come in polarized and non-polarized types.

Q. 3.45-A18. What are the common failure modes of fixed capacitors?

A. Fixed capacitors may become defective in one of three ways: (1) short circuit, (2) open circuit, or (3) leak (partial short).

D.

1. A short-circuited capacitor will read very low or zero resistance between its terminals, as measured on an ohmmeter. This condition can cause other circuit failures be-

cause of possibly excessive current passing through the capacitor.

2. An open-circuited capacitor will read substantially infinite resistance between its terminals. It will not pass a signal, except possibly very high frequencies. If checked with an ohmmeter, the capacitor will not exhibit the "charging" characteristic of a good capacitor.

3. A leaky capacitor will read less than normal resistance across its terminals. This can be caused by a partial short circuit in the dielectric.

Aluminum electrolytic capacitors are particularly prone to developing excessive leakage with time. (See Q. 3.30.) They also have reduced capacitance with shelf life or during use.

Q. 3.45-A19. What is meant by a "variable" capacitor?

A. This term generally refers to a capacitor whose capacitance can be deliberately changed by mechanical means. There are also voltage-variable capacitors (varactors). These are solid-state units whose effective capacitance can be changed by varying their reverse-junction voltage.

D. Mechanically variable capacitors are of two general types; (1) the parallel-plate (single or multisection style) type and (2) trimmer capacitors. For transmitter applications variable vacuum, or gas-filled capacitors of cylindrical construction are used.

1. The parallel-plate variable capacitor uses air as its dielectric. This type is used for tuning receivers and transmitters. The multisection (two, three, or four sections) types are mechanically "ganged." They are used for simultaneous tuning of two to four circuits. These capacitors include fixed metal plates (usually aluminum) connected together to form the *stator*. Meshing with, but insulated from, the stator plates is a set of movable plates, called the *rotor*. The degree of mesh of the two sets of plates is varied by turning a shaft that connects to all the rotor plates. This is the means of varying the capacitance. Full mesh is maximum ca-

pacitance, and minimum mesh is minimum capacitance.

Air-variable capacitors come in a wide variety of capacitance ranges and working voltages. Small units may be variable in capacity from 2 to 10 pF. Larger ones may be variable from 50 to 450 pF. Working voltages may range from 400 V for close-spaced (receiver) types, to thousands of volts for transmitter applications. Piston-type air- or vacuum-dielectric variable capacitors are used for some transmitter applications. Unlike the air-variable capacitors, piston types are made for only occasional adjustment.

2. Trimmer capacitors are physically small units that in general are meant for occasional adjustment. Their capacitance is varied by a screwdriver adjustment, which changes the distance or effective surface area between the trimmer plates. Trimmers are commonly used in circuits where exact capacitance values cannot be readily computed. The trimmer is adjusted in a circuit to provide the needed capacitance.

Trimmer capacitors come in a variety of shapes and sizes. Some trimmer dielectrics are ceramic, glass (and quartz), air, plastic (including Mylar), and mica.

Some trimmer characteristics are:

a. *Air dielectric:* Capacitance range is 1.3–6 to 9.0–143 pF. Working voltage is 250 to 700 V. Temperature range is $-55°$ to $+85°C$.

b. *Ceramic dielectric:* Capacitance range, 1–3 to 7–40 pF. Working voltage is 100 V. Temperature range is $-55°$ to $+125°C$.

c. Plastic dielectric: Capacitance range is 1.0–5.0 to 5.0–150.0 pF. Working voltage is 1 000 V. Temperature range is $-55°$ to $+55°C$.

d. Mica dielectric: Capacitance range is 1.0–15.0 to 1 400–3 055 pF.

e. Glass dielectric: Capacitance range is 0.6–1.8 to 1.0–120.0 pF. Working voltage is 1 500 V. Temperature range is $-55°$ to $+150°C$.

Failure modes for trimmer capacitors are mainly shorts or leakage. Some types experience mechanical failures if adjusted too frequently.

Q. 3.45-A20. What are the general types of fixed resistors?

A. Fixed resistors may be classified as follows:

1. Carbon-composition resistors.
2. Metal-film resistors.
3. Carbon-film resistors.
4. Wire-wound resistors.

D.

1. The carbon-composition resistor is found in discrete circuits. It is made by embedding carbon particles (the resistance material) in a binder, in the form of a slug. The slug is enclosed in an insulated body with a wire lead at each end. The slug and the leads are molded under high pressure and temperature.

Typical carbon-composition resistors are shown in Fig. 3.45-A20(1). These resistors are made in power ratings of one-eighth, one-quarter, 1 and 2 watts.

2. Metal-film resistors are available as thin- or thick-film components. A thin-film resistor, has a resistance element with a thickness in the order of one-millionth of an inch. A thick-film resistor has a resistance element with a thickness greater than one-millionth of an inch. One type of thick-film resistor is illustrated in Fig. 3.45-A20(2). This is a *cermet*-film resistor, made by screening a mixture of precious metals and binder material on a ceramic substrate. These are fired at high temperature. This type has a resistance range of 10 Ω to 1.5 MΩ with a tolerance as low as 1.0 percent. Power ratings from ½ to 3 W are available. Good stability is an important feature.

Thick-film resistor *networks* are in common use. These comprise resistor and conductor networks made of precious metals in a glass-binding system. They are screened onto a ceramic substrate and fired at high temperatures. These networks provide miniaturization at low cost and performance comparable to semi-precision types. They are reliable, rugged, and not subject to catastrophic failure. They are packaged as

Fig. 3.45-A20(1). Typical carbon-composition resistors.

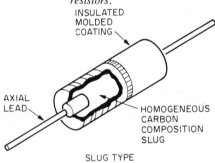

SLUG TYPE

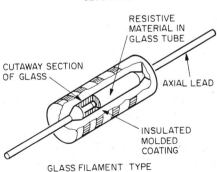

GLASS FILAMENT TYPE

Fig. 3.45-A20(2). A typical metal-film (thick-film) resistor. This is a cermet-*film resistor.*

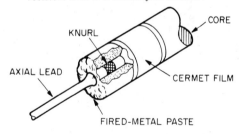

Fig. 3.45-A20(3). A carbon-film resistor. Carbon is deposited on a ceramic (or glass) substrate.

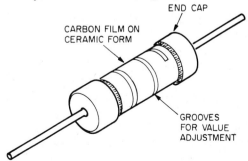

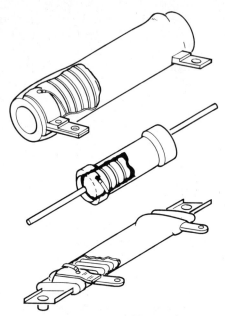

Fig.3.45-A20(4) Basic shapes for coated, wire-wound resistors. Lengths vary from 1¼ to 12 inches.

modular components. Five to 15 resistors in a package are typical.

Some typical applications of thick-film resistor networks include such functions as bias, bleeder, voltage divider, current sensing, and load. They are available as either general-purpose, precision, or power types.

3. Carbon-film resistors are made by depositing a pyrolytic-carbon film on ceramic or glass substrates. The terminals are mostly pressed-on cap and lead assemblies, as shown in Fig. 3.45-A20(3). The film is vulnerable to mechanical damage and atmospheric moisture. Consequently, the film is protected by a varnish coating of the silicone variety.

These resistors provide increased stability, lower noise, and better high-frequency performance than competitively priced, carbon-composition resistors. Resistance values are available from 1 Ω to 125 MΩ for the 1-W size (largest available), from 1 Ω to 400 kΩ in 1/10-W versions, and from 1 Ω to 14 MΩ for intermediate power sizes. Available tolerances are 0.5, 1, and 2 percent.

4. Wire-wound resistors have a broad spectrum of applications and are made in many shapes and sizes. These resistors may

be classified generally as, (a) power-style resistors and (b) precision-style resistors.

a. The power-style, wire-wound resistor is made by winding a single-layer length of special alloy wire in the form of a coil around an insulating core. The unit is then covered with a coating, such as vitreous enamel or silicone. The coating is needed to protect the winding against moisture and breakage. Several types of power resistors are shown in Fig. 3.43-A20(4). Alloys used for the resistance wire include nickel-chromium-aluminum (800 alloy) and nickel-chromium-iron (Nichrome).

Resistance values of power-style resistors range from less than 1 Ω to greater than 1 MΩ. Tolerances range from ±10 to ±20 percent. Power ratings range from 3 to 1 500 W. Power ratings may be increased by enclosing the resistor in a metal case.

Power resistors may be used in power supplies as bleeders and/or voltage dividers. They have a wide use in industrial applications.

b. Precision-style, wire-wound resistors are made as multilayer coils wound on an epoxy coil form or *bobbin*. To improve high-frequency operation and to reduce its inductance, a *bi-filar* winding scheme may be used. In this method one-half of the resistance wire is wound in one direction and the other half in the opposite direction. A bobbin-type, precision-style, wire-wound resistor is shown in Fig. 3.45-A20(5).

Resistance values of these resistors range from a fraction of 1 Ω to 10 MΩ. The tolerance is better than 0.5 percent. The power rating is in the order of 2 W.

Fig. 3.45-A20(5). A precision-style, wire-wound resistor.

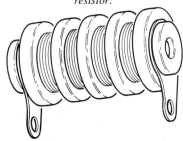

Precision-style, wire-wound resistors are used wherever highly accurate and stable resistance values are needed. They are used in various types of instrumentation. For example, they may be used as meter multipliers and/or shunts.

Q. 3.45-A21. What are the common failure modes for resistors?

A.

1. Carbon-composition resistors may become defective in one of three general ways: (a) increased value from moderately excessive dissipation, (b) open circuited (burned out) from considerably excessive dissipation, (c) water absorption in non-operating storage (baking at 100°C can improve the values), and (d) some types may catch fire. (However, this last possibility has been reduced by the use of non-flammable materials and by some self-fusing resistors.)

2. Metal-film resistors are not affected to any important degree by moisture. They are, however, subject to value changes and burnout by excessive dissipation.

3. Carbon-film resistors can be damaged if moisture accumulates on film surfaces. Changes in resistance value in humid

exposures can range from 1.0 to 1.5 percent and is only partially recoverable. Other failures are as in entry 1 above.

4. Wire-wound resistors may become defective in one of three general ways: (1) melting or burnout of resistance wire from excessive dissipation, (2) melting or cracking of resistor cores or coatings from excessive dissipation, and (3) possible wire corrosion, especially at the terminals.

Q. 3.45-A22. What is the standard color code (EIA) for carbon-composition resistors?

A. The standard color code for carbon-composition (and some axial-type) resistors is illustrated in Table 3.45-A22.

D. The resistance, tolerance, and reliability levels (where applicable) of carbon composition resistors are indicated on the body of the resistor by color bands. Three color bands are used for a 20-percent tolerance resistor and four color bands for 5- and 10-percent tolerance resistors.

As shown in Table 3.45-A22, the first two color bands indicate the first and second digits of the resistance value. The third band indicates the number of zeros (the multiplier) that follow the first two digits. The fourth

Table 3.45-A22. Standard resistor color code.

COLOR	DIGIT	MULTIPLIER	TOLERANCE	RELIABILITY LEVEL [1] (PERCENT PER 1000 HOURS)
BLACK	0	1	–	–
BROWN	1	10	–	M = 1.0%
RED	2	100	–	P = 0.1%
ORANGE	3	1000	–	R = 0.01%
YELLOW	4	10 000	–	S = 0.001%
GREEN	5	100 000	–	–
BLUE	6	1 000 000	–	–
VIOLET	7	10 000 000	–	–
GRAY	8	–	–	–
WHITE	9	–	–	–
GOLD	–	0.1	±5%	–
SILVER	–	–	±10%	–
NO COLOR	–	–	±20%	– [1] WHEN APPLICABLE

band (if present) indicates a 5- or 10-percent tolerance. If there is no fourth band (no color), the tolerance is 20 percent.

For example, colored bands of yellow-violet-orange-silver denote a 47 000 Ω ± 10 percent tolerance resistor. (See also Q. 3.43.)

Where applicable (such as in military use), a fifth color band indicates the reliability level. Reliability is indicated in terms of resistor-failure rate per 1 000 operating hours. For example, a fifth color band of red indicates a 1-percent failure rate, and one of orange indicates a failure rate of 0.01 percent.

Q. 3.45-A23. What are potentiometers?

A. Potentiometers are *variable resistors*. Potentiometers generally serve as *variable-voltage dividers*.

Potentiometers have three terminals, with the center terminal acting as the "output" one.

D. There are three basic types of potentiometers:

1. Single-turn type.
2. Multiple-turn type.
3. Trimmer type.

They all utilize the same basic types of resistance elements.

1. The single-turn carbon-resistance type is illustrated in Fig. 3.45-A23. This has a flat circular resistance element joined to the two outer terminals. A variable wiper arm contacts the resistance element and is electrically connected to the center terminal. The wiper arm rests on the resistance element and selects the desired amount of resistance.

The single-turn potentiometer frequently utilizes a carbon-composition, resistance element. These are the controls that are commonly found on the panels of radios, TV receivers, and some test equipment. Their end-to-end resistance is available in values ranging from about 100 Ω to 5 MΩ. Power dissipation ratings vary from 0.5 W to 5 W. These are the lowest-cost potentiometers. However, they have the poorest temperature coefficient of resistance (TCR) of all types. Tolerance is ±20 percent. Environmentally, they are the poorest.

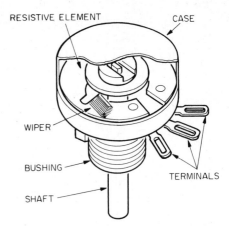

Fig. 3.45-A23. A typical, single-turn carbon-composition potentiometer.

Potentiometers are also available with wire-wound resistance elements. They have excellent TCR characteristics, have power ratings up to 5 W, and are available in resistance ranges from 10 Ω to 100 kΩ. These types have poorer noise performance and resolution than all other types. Tolerance is ±10 percent. Environmentally, these are the best.

Cermet metal-film (thick-film) potentioneters have high resolution (small differences of resistance variation), excellent environmental characteristics and low noise. Their power ratings extend up to 12 W, with resistance ranges from 500 Ω to 2 MΩ. They have moderate values of TCR. Tolerance is ±20 percent.

Potentiometer resistance elements are also available as *conductive plastic*. These feature long rotational life and low noise. Power ratings extend to 2 W with resistance ranges from 1 kΩ to 100 kΩ and moderate values of TCR. Tolerance is ±20 percent.

2. As previously mentioned, the multiple-turn potentiometers can utilize the same types of resistance elements as single-turn potentiometers. They have the same basic characteristics. However, these potentiometers are usually adjusted with a screwdriver and require a number of turns to go through their resistance range. They are meant for infrequent adjustment and feature high resolution and excellent resetability.

3. Trimmer potentiometers are single-turn types employing the same types of resistance elements as single-turn potentiometers. However, these are smaller units, a quarter to a half inch in diameter. They are usually screwdriver-adjusted and are very compact. These units are used in a wide variety of applications where precise resistance values or voltage levels are required. They are also used where circuit functions must be preset or adjusted. Some typical applications include setting transistor bias, adjusting amplifier gain, or adjusting the output of a regulated power supply.

Q. 3.45-A24. What is meant by "preferred values" with respect to resistors and capacitors?

A. This is a series of resistor and capacitor values adopted by the Electronic Industries Association (EIA) and the military services. The purpose is to reduce the number of different values that must be manufactured and/or stocked. If the exact value desired is not on the preferred list, resistors or capacitors may be connected in parallel. However, in most cases a preferred value will be suitable.

D. The *preferred value* number series, as used for resistors and capacitors (and Zener diodes), is shown in Table 3.45-A24. This table has been abbreviated to show the number series for tolerances of 5, 10, and 20 percent. These are the most commonly used. It should be noted, however, that a similar number series exists for tolerances ranging from 0.1 to 2 percent. These series can be found in many electronics handbooks.

Table 3.45-A24. The preferred number series for carbon-composition, fixed resistors.

PREFERRED NUMBER SERIES						
±5% TOLERANCE	10	15	22	33	47	68
	11	16	24	36	51	75
	12	18	27	39	56	82
	13	20	30	43	62	91
±10% TOLERANCE	10	15	22	33	47	68
	12	18	27	39	56	82
±20% TOLERANCE	10	15	22	33	47	68

The number series is applied to resistance in ohms and to capacitance in picofarads. The numbers are applied as shown in the table as is for low values or in decades for higher values: For example, 68 Ω, 680 Ω, or 680 000 Ω (6.8 Ω is also available, but not shown in Table 3.45-A24).

For capacitors, examples are 33 pF, 330 pF, and 3 300 pF. For carbon-composition (general-purpose) resistors, values range from 1 Ω to 100 MΩ.

Mica and silvered-mica dielectric capacitors have values ranging from 1 pF to 0.1 μF. Paper-dielectric capacitor values range from 500 pF to 50 μF. Ceramic-dielectric capacitor values range from 1 pF to 2.2 μF.

Q. 3.45-A25. What percent tolerance values are available for resistors?

A. The following is the tolerance classification for resistors:
1. General-purpose: 5 to 20 percent.
2. Semi-precision: 1 to 5 percent.
3. Precision: 0.5 to 1 percent.
4. Ultra-precision: 0.1 to 0.5 percent (or better).

D. See Q. 3.43, 3.45-A24, and 3.44.

Q. 3.45-A26. Given V = 100 V rms, I = 10 A rms, lagging phase angle of 30°, determine:
1. **Average (real) power (P).**
2. **Reactive power (P_q).**
3. **Apparent power (P_a).**

A. The relationship between the three kinds of power is displayed graphically by a *power triangle,* as shown in Fig. 3.45-A26.

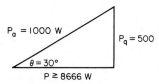

Fig. 3.45-A26. A power triangle for a circuit with net inductive reactance. By the Pythagorean theorem, the relationship of P, P_q, and P_a is $P_a^2 = P^2 + P_q^2$ (see text).

Step 1: Find the average (real) power (P):

$$P = VI_{\cos}\theta = 100 \times 10 \times 0.66 = 866 \text{ W}$$

Step 2: Find the reactive power (P_q).

$$P_q = VI_{\sin}\theta = 100 \times 10 \times 0.5 = 500 \text{ vars}$$

Step 3: Find the apparent power.

$$P_a = VI = 1\,000 \text{ W}$$

Notes:

1. Average (real) power (P) is dissipated only in resistance. ($P = I^2R$)
2. Reactive power (P_q), as mentioned above, is non-dissipative. ($P_q = I^2X$)
3. Apparent power (P_a) is the product of the voltage (V) impressed across the circuit and the current (I) in the circuit. ($P_a = VI$)

Q. 3.45-A27. Draw a vector diagram showing the voltages in a series circuit composed of an inductance, a capacitance, and a resistance.

A. In order for this example to have practical significance, values have been assigned, as follows:

1. L=0.3 H, $X_L = 113.1\ \Omega$.
2. C=50 μF, $X_c = 53.1\ \Omega$.
3. R=40 Ω.
4. V ac = 240 V, 60 Hz.

The vector diagram is shown in Fig. 3.45-A27. The inset of this diagram shows the schematic diagram.

D. The values shown in the vector diagram of Fig. 3.45-A27 are obtained as follows:

Step 1: Find the impedance (Z) of the entire circuit:

$$Z = \sqrt{R^2 + (X_L - X_c)^2}$$

$$= \sqrt{40^2 + (113.1 - 53.1)^2}$$

$$= \sqrt{40^2 + 60^2}$$

$$= 72.1\ \Omega$$

Step 2: Find the current in the series circuit:

$$I = \frac{V}{Z} = \frac{240}{72.1} = 3.33 \text{ A}$$

Fig. 3.45-A27. A vector diagram showing the voltages in a series circuit composed of an inductance, a capacitance, and a resistance. The inset shows the schematic diagram.

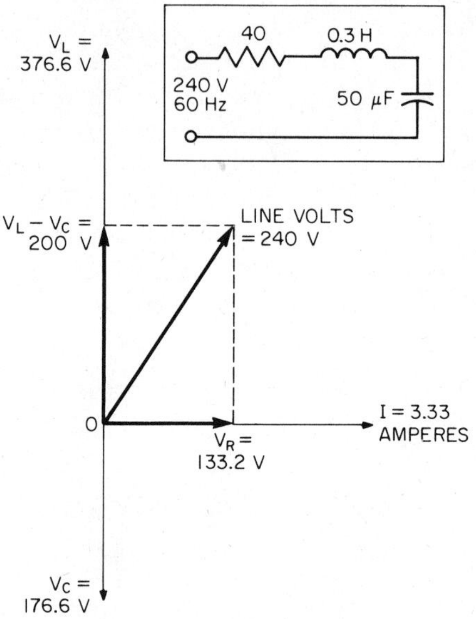

3: Find the voltage across the resistor.

$$V_R = IR = 3.33 \times 40 = 133.2 \text{ V}$$

Step 4: Find the voltage across the inductor.

$$V_L = IX_L = 3.33 \times 113.1 = 376.6 \text{ V}$$

Step 5: Find the voltage across the capacitor.

$$V_c = IX_c = 3.33 \times 53.1 = 176.6 \text{ V}$$

The voltage across the inductor is 180° out of phase with the voltage across the capacitor. Therefore, $V_L - V_c = 376.6 - 176.6 = 200$ V (inductive). The series circuit has a net inductive reactance, and thus the circuit current will lag the line voltage.

The vector sum of V_R (133.2V) and the 200 V across the net inductive reactance ($V_L - V_c$) is equal to the line voltage of 240 V.

$$V_{\text{Line}} = \sqrt{V_R^2 + V_L^2}$$

$$= \sqrt{133.2^2 + (376.6 - 176.6)^2}$$

$$= 240 \text{ V}$$

See also Q. 3.09(B).

Q. 3.45-A28. How do you calculate the impedance of a resistor, an inductor, and a capacitor in series? In parallel?

A.

1. For the series circuit, see Q. 3.45–A27.

2. The following is a method of calculating the impedance of a resistor, an inductor, and a capacitor in parallel. (See Fig. 3.45–A28.)

Step 1: Calculate the current taken by each parallel branch.

 a. Resistance branch:

$$I_R = \frac{V}{R} = \frac{240}{20} = 12 \text{ A}$$

 b. Inductor branch:

$$I_L = \frac{V}{X_L} = \frac{240}{16} = 15 \text{ A}$$

 c. Capacitor branch:

$$I_C = \frac{V}{X_C} = \frac{240}{24} = 10 \text{ A}$$

Step 2: Calculate the line current (I_{Line}):

$$I_{Line} = \sqrt{I_R^2 + (I_L - I_c)^2}$$

$$= \sqrt{12^2 + 5^2}$$

$$= 13 \text{ A}$$

Note: The inductive and capacitive currents are 180° out of phase.

Step 3: Calculate the total impedance (Z):

$$Z = \frac{V_{Line}}{I_{Line}} = \frac{240}{13} = 18.46 \text{ } \Omega$$

Fig. 3.45–A28. Schematic diagram of a circuit used to calculate the total impedance of an R, L, C parallel circuit.

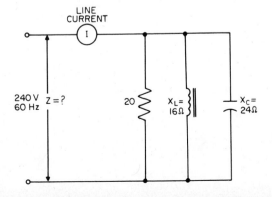

Q. 3.45-A29. What is the formula for calculating the resonant frequency of an inductor and capacitor in parallel?

A. The formula is

$$f = \frac{1}{2\pi\sqrt{LC}}$$

where

 L = inductance in henrys.
 C = capacitance in farads.
 f = resonant frequency in hertz.

D. See also Q. 3.33 and Q. 3.34.

Q. 3.45-A30. Discuss the characteristics and uses of neon lamps.

A. Neon lamps operate on the principle of gas ionization. They give off an orange or red color when operating.

Neon lamps are commonly used to indicate the operating condition of instruments, appliances, and other equipment.

D. The color of a neon lamp is determined by the gas pressure. Also the neon gas may be mixed with a small percentage of argon gas (0.5 percent) to reduce the firing and sustaining voltages. Lamp life is typically 5 000 to 10 000 hours. The usual operating voltages are (1) 65 V ac, 90 V dc for standard brightness types and (2) 95 V ac, 135 V dc and up for high brightness types.

The operating current varies from 0.0005 to 0.003A depending upon the lamp. The firing voltage is generally 20 to 50 percent above the operating voltage.

RC elements can be included in the base to form a relaxation-oscillator type of flashing indicator.

Other uses are as a voltage regulator device for a series-pass transistor regulator and a sawtooth-wave generator.

Q. 3.45-A31. Name some commonly used incandescent pilot lamp bases and pilot lamp ratings.

A. Incandescent pilot lamps are used to indicate an ON or other specified condition of electronic or other equipment. They come in a variety of wattage ratings and bases.

The bases are generally known as bayonet (plug-in), screw-in, and slide-in types.

Some common base types are designated as (1) miniature or miniature flanged, (2) candelabra or bayonet candelabra, (3) bayonet candelabra with prefocusing collar, (4) instrument with lamp integral with screw-in mounting, and (5) slide-in mounting.

Pilot lamps are obtainable with a wide variety of voltage ratings ranging from approximately 1.2 to 120 V. Some popular voltage and current ratings are: (1) 1.2 V at 0.22 A, (2) 2.5 V at 0.15 A, (3) 6 to 8 V at 0.15 or 0.25 A, (4) 12.8 V at 0.2 A, (5) 24 to 28 V at 0.04 A, (6) 120 V at 0.05 A.

Q. 3.45-A32. What are some commonly used (SI) metric units?

A. These are as follows:

Quantity	Unit	Symbol
length	kilometer	km
	meter	m
	centimeter	cm
	millimeter	mm
area	square kilometer	km²
	hectare (10 000 m²)	ha
	square meter	m²
	square centimeter	cm²
volume or capacity	cubic meter	m³
	cubic decimeter	dm³
	liter †	L
	cubic centimeter	cm³
	milliliter †	mL
mass (weight)	metric ton (1000 kg)	t
	kilogram	kg
	gram	g
	milligram	mg
time	day	d
	hour	h
	minute	min
	second	s
temperature	degree Celsius	°C
speed or velocity	meter per second	m/s
	kilometer per hour	km/h
plane angle	degree§	°
force	kilonewton	kN
	newton	N
pressure	kilopascal	kPa
acceleration	meter per second squared	m/s²
rotational frequency	revolution per second**	r/s
	revolution per minute**	r/min
density	kilogram per cubic meter	kg/m³
	gram per liter	g/L

† To be used for fluids (both gases and liquids) and for dry ingredients in recipes. Liter is used for the space within objects such as refrigerators, automobile trunks, etc. Do not use any prefix with liter except milli.

§ For efficiency in calculations the decimal degree is now preferred over the use of degrees, minutes, and seconds, except for cartography; for example, 17.4086° instead of 17°24'31".

**In expressions or operations that involve algebraic manipulation of units (unit analysis), the units of measure are 1/s or 1/min.

Q. 3.45-A33. What are some common (SI) metric prefixes and their meanings.

A. These are as follows:

Multiplication factor		Prefix	Symbol	Pronunciation (USA)*	Term (USA)	Term (Other Countries)
		Common (ST) metric prefixes and meanings				
$1\ 000\ 000\ 000\ 000\ 000\ 000$	$= 10^{18}$	exa	E	ex′a (a as in about)	one quintillion†	one trillion
$1\ 000\ 000\ 000\ 000\ 000$	$= 10^{15}$	peta	P	as in petal	one quadrillion†	one thousand billion
$1\ 000\ 000\ 000\ 000$	$= 10^{12}$	tera	T	as in terrace	one trillion†	one billion
$1\ 000\ 000\ 000$	$= 10^{9}$	giga	G	jig′a (a as in about)	one billion†	one milliard
$1\ 000\ 000$	$= 10^{6}$	mega	M	as in megaphone	one million	
$1\ 000$	$= 10^{3}$	kilo	k	as in kilowatt	one thousand	
100	$= 10^{2}$	hecto	h‡	heck′toe	one hundred	
10	$= 10$	deka	da‡	deck′a (a as in about)	ten	
0.1	$= 10^{-1}$	deci	d‡	as in decimal	one tenth	
0.01	$= 10^{-2}$	centi	c‡	as in sentiment	one hundredth	
0.001	$= 10^{-3}$	milli	m	as in military	one thousandth	
$0.000\ 001$	$= 10^{-6}$	micro	μ	as in microphone	one millionth	
$0.000\ 000\ 001$	$= 10^{-9}$	nano	n	nan′oh (an as in ant)	one billionth†	one milliardth
$0.000\ 000\ 000\ 001$	$= 10^{-12}$	pico	p	peek′oh	one trillionth†	one billionth
$0.000\ 000\ 000\ 000\ 001$	$= 10^{-15}$	femto	f	fem′toe (fem as in feminine)	one quadrillionth†	one thousand billionth
$0.000\ 000\ 000\ 000\ 000\ 001$	$= 10^{-18}$	atto	a	as in anatomy	one quintillionth†	one trillionth

*The first syllable of every prefix is accented to assure that the prefix will retain its identity. Therefore, the preferred pronunciation of kilometer places the accent on the first syllable, not the second.

†The terms should be avoided in technical writing because the names for denominations above one million and below one millionth are different in other countries, as indicated in the last column.

D. The abbreviation "SI" comes from the French name, Le Systeme International d'Unites. This is the name of the modernized metric system established in 1960 by international agreement. Most countries are either converting from non-metric systems to SI or updating their metric standards to conform to SI. (See also Q. 3.45-A32.)

Q. 3.45-A34. In relation to ac circuits, what is the relationship between (1) rms values, (2) maximum and minimum values, (3) peak values, and (4) peak-to-peak values?

A.

1. The rms (or effective value) of a current or voltage is equal to 0.707 of the peak value of the wave. The peak value equals 1.414 times the rms value.

2. Maximum and minimum values are the highest and lowest values of a portion of a waveform, or of a train of waveforms.

3. The peak value is equal to 1.414 times the effective (rms) value. The peak value is also equal to 1.57 times the average value; or, the average value equal 0.636 times the peak value.

4. The peak-to-peak value equals twice the peak value. Also, it equals 2.828 times the rms value.

D.

1. The conventional type of ac ammeter is calibrated to indicate effective (rms) values of current. Effective value is equal to 0.707 of peak value, in the case of sine-wave currents.

The meter itself responds to the average torque. For pure sine-wave currents, the indicated reading is dependent upon the scale calibration, which usually gives the rms value. What a meter does, relatively, on non-sine-wave currents depends on the meter, but in the usual case, the meter indicates the effective value of current.

An ac voltmeter has a scale which is calibrated to read the rms value or 0.707 of peak. The average value equals 0.636 of peak and the ratio of the two equals

$$\frac{0.636}{0.707} = 0.9.$$

The scale reading must therefore be multiplied by 0.9 to obtain the *average* value. It is understood that this is the average value over one-half cycle; the average value of a sine wave over a full cycle is of course zero.

ELECTRON TUBES

Q. 3.46 Discuss the physical characteristics and a common usage of each of the following electron tube types:
1. **Diode.**
2. **Triode.**
3. **Tetrode.**
4. **Pentode.**
5. **Beam power.**
6. **Remote cut-off.**
7. **Duo-triode.**
8. **Cold-cathode.**
9. **Thyratron.**

A.
1. Diode: A two-electrode vacuum tube (Fig. 3.46(a)) containing a cathode and a plate housed in a glass or metal-evacuated envelope. Connections from the elements are brought out to a plug-in base, or to wires in the case of sub-miniature tubes. The cathode may be a directly heated wire or an indirectly heated metal sleeve. In the case of the sleeve, this is given an oxide coating which is an efficient electron emitter. (Directly heated cathodes are also oxide coated to improve their emission characteristics.) Indirectly heated cathode sleeves are brought up to operating temperature by a heated filament wire inside of, but insulated from the emitter sleeve. Diodes are rectifiers and are used as RF detectors, peak detectors and power-supply rectifiers. They are also commonly used as dc restorers (clampers), limiters and clippers.

2. Triode: A triode is a three-element tube. It contains either a filament or cathode structure, a grid, and a plate (Fig. 3.46(b)). If the emitter is of the filament type, it is usually made of thoriated tungsten. This is formed by dissolving a small amount of thorium oxide and carbon in a tungsten filament. The conventional cathode is formed in two sections. The outer section consists of a hollow nickel cylinder which is coated with thorium oxide. Within the cylinder is a tungsten wire suitably insulated from the cylinder. This wire may be heated by either ac or dc and in turn causes the cylinder to become properly heated. The usable emission comes from the outer surface of the cylinder. The grid which surrounds the cathode is usually made of molybdenum wire which is spirally wound upon two vertical supporting wires. The plate is usually made of nickel or iron pressed out of sheet material and crimped or flanged to increase rigidity. It is usually blackened to increase the heat radiation. Some large power tubes have graphite plates which are superior under high temperature conditions. Connections to all

Fig. 3.46(a). Cross section of a diode.

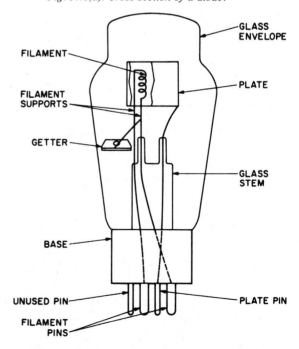

elements are usually made through a base at the bottom of the tube. Triodes are used for a variety of functions. Some of these are: oscillator, RF or AF amplifier, clamper, voltage regulator and cathode follower.

3. Tetrode: A tetrode is similar in physical construction to a triode, but with the addition of a spirally wound screen grid placed between the plate and control grid. Connections to elements are usually made to a base at the bottom, although in some high frequency tubes connections to grid and plate are brought out through the side and top. Tetrodes are seldom if ever used in receiving circuits. They are sometimes used in transmitters as power RF amplifiers or modulators.

4. Pentode: The pentode has five elements. (See Fig. 3.46(c).) These are four elements identical to tetrode arrangements plus another spirally wound wire grid which is located between the screen grid and the plate. This addition is called the suppressor grid. Pentodes have a very wide variety of uses. Some of these are: RF amplifier, video

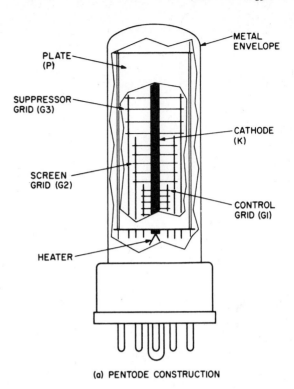

(a) PENTODE CONSTRUCTION

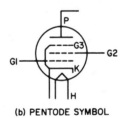

(b) PENTODE SYMBOL

Fig. 3.46(c). Cross section of a pentode.

Fig. 3.46(b) Cross section of a triode.

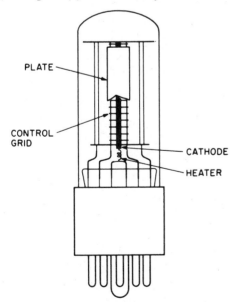

amplifier, cathode follower, audio amplifier (usually pre-amplifier or speech amplifier), IF amplifier, oscillator (generally crystal), mixer and control tube for voltage regulator.

5. Beam Power: A tube usually consisting of a cathode, control grid, screen grid, plate, and two "beam forming" plates on either side of the cathode (Fig. 3.46(d)). These plates are operated at cathode potential. The control grid and screen grid wires are aligned with each other so that the electron stream flows through them in "sheets." This reduces the screen grid current and thus increases the tube efficiency. These "sheets" diverge beyond the screen grid and cross the paths of other sheets thus forming an area of high

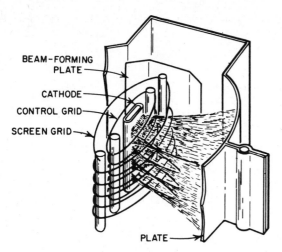

BEAM-FORMING PLATE

CATHODE

CONTROL GRID

SCREEN GRID

PLATE

Fig. 3.46(d). Cross section of a beam power tube.

electron density just short of the plate. This dense negatively charged area serves the same purpose as a suppressor grid, but permits more linear tube operation, with a reduction of third harmonic distortion. The "beam forming" plates confine the electrons to beams and also serve to prevent any stray secondary-emission electrons from approaching the screen grid from the sides of the tube.

6. Remote Cut-Off: Generally refers to pentodes with special control-grid spacing (Fig. 3.46(e)). The grid turns are closer together at both ends, but have a wider spacing in the center. A common application for these tubes is in AGC (or AVC) controlled IF amplifiers. Another use would be in audio volume expander or compresser circuits. In general they are used in circuits where an automatic (or manual) control of circuit gain is desired, by changing the control-grid voltage(s) of the stage(s).

7. Duo-Triode: This merely indicates that two triodes are in one tube envelope. The primary advantages are the savings in space, parts and cost. The uses are the same as given in part 2.

8. Cold Cathode: A typical cold-cathode gassy-diode rectifier tube consists of a large area cathode (which is coated with suitable emitting material such as barium or strontium), a small diameter rod-shaped

pointed anode, and a starter anode. (See Fig. 3.46(f).) These elements are enclosed in an envelope containing a gas such as helium, acetylene, argon, or neon. The gas pressure is critical for correct operation. Common uses for these tubes are as voltage regulators and rectifiers.

9. Thyratron: A mercury vapor or gas-filled tube (Fig. 3.46(g)) having special characteristics which make it adaptable for power or voltage control in electronic devices. The thyratron may be found in either triode or tetrode form. However, the nature of the grid control is considerably different from the normal control as found in conventional amplifier tubes. In a thyatron, the grid is

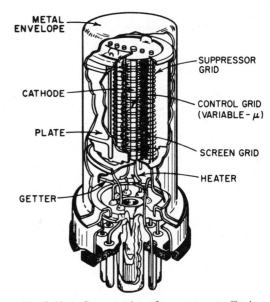

METAL ENVELOPE

SUPPRESSOR GRID

CATHODE

CONTROL GRID (VARIABLE-μ)

PLATE

SCREEN GRID

HEATER

GETTER

Fig. 3.46(e). Cross section of a remote cut-off tube.

capable only of controlling the start of plate current. Once the current has started, the grid can neither stop it, nor alter its magnitude. The current can be stopped only by making the plate potential zero or negative for a short period of time. In the case of a tetrode thyratron the purpose of the screen grid is to reduce the control grid current which flows during periods of non-conduction. In another type of tetrode thyratron, both grids must receive positive triggering voltages simultaneously for the tube to fire.

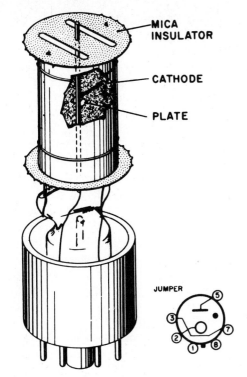

Fig. 3.46(f). Cross section of a cold cathode tube.

MICA INSULATOR

CATHODE

PLATE

JUMPER

This type is sometimes called a "coincidence tube." One use of a small thyratron is as a sawtooth generator in an oscilloscope. In this case, the control grid serves as a synchronizing device. The larger thyratrons are used as inverters, as dc motor control devices, and to fire ignitrons. The "coincidence tube" is used wherever it is desired to initiate an operation when two signals are in the correct phase and amplitude. It is used in radar, beacon-AFC circuits and in industrial electronics circuits.

D.

1 and 2. Diode, Triode: Take first the diode conditions. Assume the plate voltage is zero and that the cathode is properly heated. Electrons will be emitted by the cathode, and attracted back to the cathode in such a way that an electron "cloud" of constant density will form around the immediate vicinity of the cathode. This "cloud" is called the space charge. If a relatively low positive potential is applied to the plate (with respect to the cathode), the plate assumes

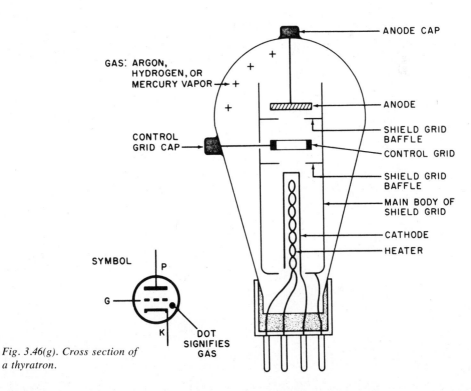

GAS: ARGON, HYDROGEN, OR MERCURY VAPOR

CONTROL GRID CAP

ANODE CAP

ANODE

SHIELD GRID BAFFLE

CONTROL GRID

SHIELD GRID BAFFLE

MAIN BODY OF SHIELD GRID

CATHODE

HEATER

SYMBOL

P

G

K

DOT SIGNIFIES GAS

Fig. 3.46(g). Cross section of a thyratron.

a positive charge, as in any capacitor, and an electrostatic field will exist between the plate and cathode. The forces acting in this field will be in such a direction as to urge electrons to move toward the plate and away from the space charge. With a low value of plate voltage applied, the forces will be relatively weak and a comparatively small number of electrons will move into the plate and produce a small value of plate current in the external circuit. If the plate voltage is increased, the positive charge of the plate will also be increased and this in turn will increase the forces acting in the electrostatic field. More electrons will be removed from the space charge during any given period of time (and replenished from the cathode emission) and thus cause an increased plate current. On the other hand if the original plate voltage were maintained, but the spacing between the plate and cathode were reduced, the plate current would again be increased in inverse proportion to the spacing. (This would be similar to decreasing the spacing between the plates of a capacitor and thereby increasing its charging capabilities by increasing its capacitance.) A simple expression which describes the electrostatic forces acting upon the space charge is

$$F = \frac{V}{300d}$$

where

F = the force acting upon the space charge and is measured in dynes (1 dyne = 1/28,000 ounce).
V = the potential difference between cathode and plate.
d = the plate-to-cathode spacing in centimeters.

The formula shows that the electrostatic forces acting upon the space charge (and producing plate current) vary directly as the applied plate potential, and inversely as the plate-to-cathode spacing. For example, if the plate potential and the plate-to-cathode spacing were simultaneously cut in half, the plate current would remain unchanged. If the plate-to-cathode spacing were reduced to 1/10 of its original distance, the original plate current magnitude could be maintained with only 1/10 of the original plate potential. In other words, for any given applied potential, the degree of control which an electrode possesses with regard to the space charge increases as the electrode is brought closer to the space charge.

The triode has three elements: a cathode; a plate, which is relatively distant from the cathode; and a grid located quite close to the cathode. The grid might be considered to be another plate, but so constructed as to permit the passage of electrons through its wires. The fact that the grid is located so much closer to the cathode than the plate means that, for a given applied potential, the grid will exert a much greater influence upon the space charge and plate current than the plate. Thus a relatively small change of grid voltage is capable of producing a large change in plate current. If an impedance is placed in series with the plate current flow, a relatively large voltage drop will appear across its terminals for each small change of grid potential. Thus, the tube is able to amplify because the control electrode (grid) is placed relatively close to the cathode, in comparison to the plate.

3. Tetrode: The tetrode has an additional screen grid usually operated at about ⅓ of plate supply voltage for voltage amplifiers, and approximately equal to plate supply voltage for power amplifiers. The screen grid has two important functions: first, it greatly reduces the grid to plate capacitance, thus making it unnecessary to neutralize RF amplifiers except at very high frequencies, and second, it makes the plate current substantially independent of plate voltage. This factor makes it possible to obtain much higher values of amplification than with triodes. The plate efficiency is about 10 percent greater than with triodes.

4. Pentode: This is a five-element tube, the added element being a suppressor grid. The suppressor grid is usually at cathode

potential making it extremely negative relative to the plate. The suppressor grid further reduces interelectrode capacitance between control grid and plate, and also makes possible greater power output and higher gain than a tetrode tube. Primarily the suppressor grid acts to return secondary electrons to the plate rather than to permit them to be picked up by the screen grid. Pentodes can be operated at higher RF frequencies without neutralization than tetrodes.

5. Beam Power: The variations of plate current with changes in plate voltage in a beam power tube are similar to those of a normal pentode, the main difference being that in circuits where there is considerable plate current flow, the plate current in a beam power tube will be relatively independent of plate voltage down to a lower value of plate voltage than the plate current in a pentode. Thus, the effective operating range of a beam power tube is somewhat greater than that of an equivalent or similar pentode. By concentrating the electrons in smooth beams or sheets (as contrasted with the uneven structure of a suppressor grid), the suppressor action of the space charge formed in a beam power tube provides superior action to that offered by a suppressor grid of the conventional type.

The beam power tube is commonly used as an audio amplifier in the output and power stages of circuits having low- to moderately high-output ratings. The beam power tube is less frequently used as a radio-frequency power amplifier.

6. Cold Cathode: Electron emission from the cathode is due to two major factors:

a. If the electrostatic field produced by the starter anode is sufficiently great, electrons will be pulled from the cathode coating by force of attraction.

b. Any gas is always in a state of partial ionization. The existing positive ions are accelerated by the cathode to starter-anode voltage so that they strike the cathode with sufficient force to aid in the emission of electrons. The rectifying action of such a tube

makes use of the fact that the current which ionization causes to exist between two electrodes in a low-pressure gas is approximately proportional to the area of the cathode. If one electrode has a very large area (cathode) and the other electrode a very small area (anode), electrons will flow in the direction from cathode to anode. Conduction occurs on that half cycle which makes the anode positive with respect to the cathode.

Q. 3.47 What is the principal advantage of a tetrode tube over a triode tube as a radio-frequency amplifier?

A. The lack of necessity for neutralizing, except possibly at ultra high frequencies.

D. If an RF amplifier is operated with its plate and grid circuits tuned to approximately the same frequency, there is a strong likelihood that the amplifier will act as a tuned-grid tuned-plate oscillator. This is particularly true of triode amplifiers, where the value of grid-to-plate capacitance is relatively large; this would cause large energy feedback from the plate to the grid circuit, and thus permit sustained oscillations to occur. The problem is less serious in tetrodes or pentodes, where the grid-to-plate capacitance is much smaller.

Q. 3.48. Compare tetrode tubes to triode tubes in reference to high plate current and interelectrode capacitance.

A.

1. Tetrode tubes of similar construction to triodes, are capable of higher plate currents, because the plate current is largely dependent upon a constant value of screen-grid voltage. (See Discussion.)

2. Tetrodes have greatly reduced values of control grid-to-plate capacitance compared to triodes. (See Discussion.)

D.

1. Maximum plate current characteristics of tetrodes versus triodes cannot be directly compared, since this is largely a

function of the permissible plate dissipation of a particular tube. However, all other conditions being equal, the effect of the screen grid operation is to make the plate current relatively independent of the plate voltage and to reduce the space charge in the vicinity of the plate. When the actual plate voltage of a triode is reduced because of high current through the plate load, this in turn tends to limit the maximum possible plate current. However, in the tetrode (or pentode), the plate current is more dependent upon screen-grid (than plate) voltage and may therefore be driven to a higher value, since the screen-grid voltage remains at a relatively fixed value, regardless of the plate current.

2. In the tetrode, the screen grid is interposed between the control grid and the plate. The ac ground of the screen grid is returned to ground or to the cathode and has the effect of an electrostatic shield between the plate and control grid. The effective grid-to-plate capacitance now consists of two small capacitances in series, the control grid-to-screen grid capacitance and the screen grid-to-plate capacitance. The resultant capacitance (control grid-to-plate) is smaller than either capacitance and may be in the order of .01 pF. In comparison, a triode of similar dimensions and ratings may have a grid-to-plate capacitance of 2.0 pF. The lower capacitance of the tetrode greatly reduces plate to control grid feedback and consequently the possibility of sustaining oscillations or regeneration in the stage. See also Questions 3.46 and 3.47, above.

Q. 3.49. Are there any advantages or disadvantages of filament-type vacuum tubes when compared with the indirectly heated types?

A.
1. Filament-type tubes—advantages:
a. Quick heating.
b. More efficient in converting heating power into thermal emission.
c. Used to provide high values of current (i.e., in rectifiers, or high power tubes).

2. Filament-type tubes—disadvantages:
a. Prone to hum problems.
b. Lower gain.
c. Prone to filament breakage.
d. Require higher operating temperatures for efficient emission.

3. Indirectly heated tubes—advantages:
a. Elimination of heater hum problems.
b. Operates at relatively low temperatures.
c. Can be made with much higher gains, since grid can be wound closer to the cylindrical cathode.
d. Cathode can be coated with a material which is an efficient electron emitter; such as barium, calcium, and strontium oxides.

4. Indirectly heated tubes—disadvantages:
a. Longer warm-up time.
b. Cathode surface is not as rugged as a directly heated filament.
c. Cannot be used to supply very high values of current.

Q. 3.50. Draw a simple circuit diagram consisting of each of the following and describe its operation. Show a signal source and include coupling and by-pass capacitors, power supply connections and plate load.

1. AF "grounded-cathode" triode amplifier with cathode resistor biasing, as for "Class A" operation.
2. AF "grounded-cathode" pentode amplifier with battery biasing, for "Class A" operation.
3. RF "grounded-grid" triode amplifier with LC tank plate-load for "Class B" operation.
4. AF "cathode-follower" triode amplifier.
5. AF "push-pull" pentode amplifier operated "Class B" with transformer coupling to a speaker.

A.

1. See Figure 3.50(a) for diagram of the triode amplifier. The incoming audio frequency signal is applied to the grid through coupling capacitor, C_c, and the grid resistor, R_g. The actual tube-grid signal is developed across R_g which also provides the necessary dc ground for the grid. The time constant of $R_g \times C_c$, is chosen to pass the lowest desired audio frequency with minimum attenuation. The correct bias for Class A operation is provided by the voltage drop across R_K which occurs because of plate current passing through it. The cathode is thus caused to become positive with respect to the grid (grid is negative with respect to cathode). To prevent degeneration (loss of gain) in the amplifier, R_K is bypassed by a suitable value of capacitor, C_K. The time constant $R_K \times C_K$ is chosen to be at least five times as long as the period of the lowest frequency involved. (The same is true for the time constant of $C_c \times R_g$.) The input signal is amplified and inverted in polarity in the plate circuit and appears across the plate load resistor, R_L. The output signal is coupled from the amplifier via coupling capacitor, C_o. (See also Q. 3.46b, above.)

2. See Figure 3.50(b) for diagram of the pentode amplifier. The basic operation of the pentode is the same as the triode (above). However, fixed battery-grid biasing is used. This scheme for biasing is not commonly used in Class A audio amplifiers, but has the advantage of being independent of plate and screen grid currents. Fixed bias schemes are seen more frequently in transmitters and for Class AB and Class B audio amplifiers. The correct screen-grid voltage is obtained by the correct value of screen-grid dropping resistor (R_{sg}). Capacitor C_{sg} prevents screen grid degeneration and provides an ac ground for the shielding effect of the screen. (See also Q. 3.46 (d), above).

3. In the grounded-grid amplifier, the grid is at signal ground and the signal is fed into the cathode circuit. In the schematic, Fig. 3.50(c), fixed bias is employed to achieve Class B operation.

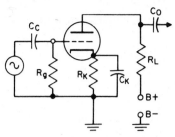

Fig. 3.50(a). Triode-audio amplifier, with cathode bias.

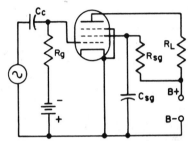

Fig. 3.50(b). Pentode-audio amplifier, with battery bias.

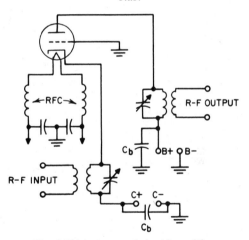

Fig. 3.50(c). A grounded-grid amplifier.

In the grounded-grid amplifier the input voltage is actually in series with the external load impedance connecting the plate and cathode (plate load, power supply, and cathode load) and the tube acts as though it were excited at the grid, but had an amplification factor of $(\mu + 1)$ instead of μ. The input (cathode impedance) of the grounded-grid amplifier is low, being approximately the reciprocal of the g_m of the tube. For a g_m of 6 000 micromhos, the input impedance is 166 ohms. Thus it may be seen that the input may exert a considerable loading effect upon the driving source. The formula for computing the gain of a grounded-grid amplifier is:

$$G = \frac{R_L(\mu + 1)}{R_L + r_p}$$

Note the similarity to the equation for the gain of a grounded-cathode amplifier.

Grounded grid amplifiers are sometimes used at very high frequencies because it is often possible to utilize triode tubes without the necessity for neutralization. In the grounded-grid amplifier the feedback capacitance is not the plate-grid capacitance, but is the much smaller plate-cathode capacitance. This smaller capacitance is less likely to cause oscillations, even at extremely high frequencies when special triodes (Lighthouse type) are used.

4. The triode cathode-follower diagram is given in Fig. 3.50(d). The gain of a cathode-follower is always less than unity.

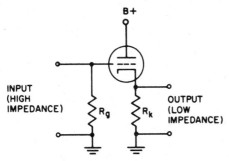

Fig. 3.50(d). Simplified schematic diagram of cathode-follower.

As shown in the figure, the output of a cathode-follower is taken across the cathode resistor (R_K). The output voltage is in phase with the input and is degenerative. Thus, the output voltage is always less than the input voltage. The gain is largely dependent upon the value of R_K and is given by the equation:

$$G = \frac{\mu R_K}{r_p + R_K(\mu + 1)}$$

An important characteristic of a cathode-follower is its very low output impedance which is approximately equal to R_K in parallel with the reciprocal of the tube's transconductance. Typical values for triodes are 200 to 400 ohms and for pentodes may be as low as 50 to 100 ohms. The low-output impedance coupled with the high-input (grid) impedance, makes the cathode-follower useful as an impedance-matching device when driving transmission lines or other low-impedance devices.

5. In a Class B push-pull audio amplifier, both tubes are biased close to cut-off (this is known as extended cut-off). Bias is generally supplied by an external bias supply to provide a stable operating point. The grid-excitation voltages are higher than those used for Class A operation since they must cause grid current to flow in each tube. Because of the bias, each tube will draw plate current for slightly more than 180° and will be cut off for the remainder of the input cycle. Grid current may flow in each tube for as much as 30° of the input cycle. Although each tube conducts for only about one-half cycle, they conduct alternately and produce a full cycle of the input wave when combined in the output transformer. For diagram, see Fig. 3.50(e).

Class B operation for an audio amplifier provides maximum efficiency and power output, but this is coupled with higher audio distortion than Class AB or Class A operation in push-pull. Class B single-ended operation cannot ordinarily be used for audio frequencies because of extreme distortion. (The plate efficiency of a Class B amplifier may be in the order of 50 to 60 percent, compared to about 25 percent efficiency for a Class A amplifier.)

In the usual Class B operation, grid current flows for an appreciable portion of each cycle, thus presenting a low input impedance to the driving source. This requires that the driver be capable of delivering power to the grid circuits without being overloaded, to maintain low distortion at the input circuits. To provide a match from the relatively high output driver impedance

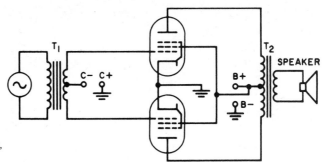

Fig. 3.50(e). Audio-frequency, push-pull pentode, Class B amplifier.

to the lower grid input impedance of the Class B stages, a step-down transformer is generally employed. A well-regulated power supply is needed to supply Class B tubes because the average plate current varies in proportion to the grid signal. Class B operation is not usually designated as B1 (no grid current) or B2 (grid current) since Class B operation almost always requires that grid current be drawn to obtain maximum efficiency.

Tubes which are specifically designed for use as Class B amplifiers operate at either zero or at very low bias potential. This eliminates the need to provide a special, well-regulated bias supply, since the tubes generally operate at zero bias. With such tubes, grid current is drawn during almost the entire positive half of each cycle.

Q. 3.51. What kind of vacuum tube responds to filament reactivation and how is reactivation accomplished?

A. It is usually considered that only thoriated tungsten filaments may be reactivated. This is not necessarily true as many oxide coated cathodes have been reactivated.

The method of reactivating a thoriated tungsten filament is as follows: The filament voltage is raised to about 3½ times normal and kept there for about 1 minute. It is then reduced to about 1½ times normal and held there for about 1 hour. This method is not recommended for tubes with normal filament voltages above 5 volts.

D. The following method of reactivating cathodes of cathode ray tubes proved suc-cessful in at least 50 percent of the cases in which it was tried. A source of about 400 volts dc is connected in series with a mil-liammeter between the intensity grid and the cathode, with the positive terminal going to the intensity grid. The filament voltage is then raised by about 50 percent and the mil-liammeter is constantly observed. After some period of time, sometimes as long as 5 min-utes, the milliammeter reading will be ob-served to be slowly and then rapidly in-creasing. When the reading reaches about 70 milliamperes the supply voltage should be instantly disconnected. The intensity grid may become red momentarily, but this is of little consequence.

Q. 3.52. Draw a rough graph of plate-current versus grid-voltage (I_p vs. V_g) for various plate voltages on a typical triode vacuum tube.

1. a. How would output current vary with input voltage in Class A amplifier operation?

b. Class AB operation?

c. Class B operation?

d. Class C operation?

2. Does the amplitude of the input signal determine the class of operation?

3. What is meant by "current-cutoff" bias voltage?

4. What is meant by plate-current "saturation"?

5. What is the relationship between distortion in the output current waveform and:

a. The class of operation?

b. The portion of the transfer characteristic over which the signal is operating?

c. Amplitude of input signal?

6. a. What occurs in the grid-circuit when the grid is "driven" positive?

b. Would this have any effect on biasing?

7. In what way is the output current related to the output voltage?

A. The plate-current versus grid voltage graph is given in Fig. 3.52(a). A transfer characteristic curve drawn for one particular value of plate-load resistance is given in Fig. 3.52(b). The bias points for class A, B and C operation are shown.

D. Class A is usually near the center of the linear portion of the curve.

Class B can be either at actual cut-off bias or as shown in the figure at "projected cut-off" for linear operation.

Class C can be any value greater than cut-off bias but is frequently about 2 × cut-off.

1. a. Class A operation: A class A amplifier is one in which the grid bias and alternating grid signal are such that plate current flows for the entire 360° of an input sine wave voltage applied to the grid. Operation is confined as nearly as possible to the most linear portion of the tube characteristics.

b. Class AB operation: In class AB operation (refer to Fig. 3.52(b)) the bias is approximately half way between the class A and class B points. In this case, plate current will flow for approximately 270 de-

grees of the input wave. The *average* plate current will not be constant as with class A operation (see (1.a.) above), but will increase with increasing amplitudes of the input grid signal. This type of operation is most commonly used for audio output amplifiers. In this case, two tubes in push-pull must be used to eliminate the high level of distortion which would occur were only one tube used.

c. Class B operation: In class B operation, the bias is set slightly above the actual cut-off value, so that plate current flows for slightly more than 180 degrees of the input wave. Class B operation is frequently used in modulators and RF amplifiers and in high-power audio amplifiers (push-pull) where low distortion is not the prime consideration. The average plate current of a class B amplifier varies normally during operation, where the input signal is not a constant amplitude, sinusoidal voltage. (It practically never is, except possibly during tests.) With no input signal applied to the class B amplifier grids, the plate current will be extremely small. (This is an advantage in portable or high power equipment where conservation of the power supply is essential.) The plate current will vary in direct proportion to the amplitude of the grid signal, and since an audio wave contains many harmonic frequencies, the shape and amplitude of the modulating signal is constantly changing. This in turn causes consequent variations of plate current. If the modulator were op-

Fig. 3.52(a). Graph of plate current versus grid voltage for various values of plate voltage for a typical triode. (Transfer characteristics.)

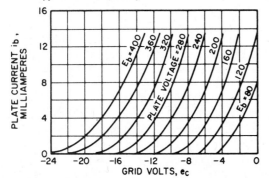

Fig. 3.52(b). Tube characteristic curve, with certain significant bias points.

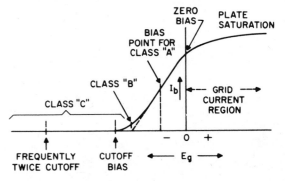

erated class A, the plate current would remain substantially constant, with or without excitation.

d. Class C operation: In class C operation, the bias is set at some value greater than cut-off bias. Thus, the plate current flows for less than 180 degrees of the input wave, and is permitted to flow *only* during the time that the instantaneous value of plate voltage is at or near its *minimum* value. At all other times the tube is non-conducting. This permits a relatively small loss on the plate and high plate efficiency. However, in order that the above conditions be met, a large value of bias must be used, in some cases equal to 4 times cut-off value, but usually about twice cut-off value. Since grid current must flow at some time in each cycle, a relatively large value of grid driving power must be available from a low impedance source. Appreciable RF power is consumed in the grid circuit. Although the plate current wave is a pulse and rich in harmonics, the plate voltage waveshape will be sinusoidal since the plate load will in most cases be a tank circuit with a reasonably high Q. An interesting feature is that the maximum positive value of grid voltage ($v_{c\ max}$), is approximately equal to the minimum value of the plate voltage ($v_{b\ min}$). Class C amplifiers may not be used in audio amplifiers due to the high distortion, but are commonly used for RF amplification in transmitters; they are often applied to special circuits such as clippers and peakers.

2. No. The class of operation is determined basically by the grid-bias value. It is possible to overdrive an amplifier, but this does alter its class of operation.

3. Theoretically, this is the value of bias which will prevent plate current from flowing (no signal input). The amount of bias needed for a given class of operation is inversely proportional to the amplification factor (μ) of the tube. For example, in Class C operation where the bias is equal to twice cut-off, it may be found from the formula,

$$V_c = \frac{2\ V_b}{\mu}$$

4. For any given filament or cathode temperature "plate saturation" occurs when the plate current is equal to the electron emission. Under normal operating conditions for an amplifier tube, the cathode temperature and plate supply voltage are fixed. Saturation effects may occur when a further positive swing of the grid can no longer produce an appreciable increase of plate current.

5. a. In true class A operation, the output waveform is essentially an undistorted reproduction of the input waveform. In classes AB, B and C (see part 1 above), plate current flows for only a portion of the cycle. Distortion in an audio amplifier is greatest for class C and less for classes A and AB respectively. Distortion for class AB and class B audio amplifiers can be greatly reduced by using two tubes in push-pull. Where the plate load is a resonant tank circuit of reasonable Q (10 or more), single-ended class B or C amplifiers produce very little distortion in the output.

b. The transfer characteristics are shown in Fig. 3.52(b). For minimum distortion, operation should not extend into the lower curved portion of the characteristic, for any given plate voltage. Neither should the tube be driven into the region of plate saturation.

c. For an undistorted output signal the input signal amplitude and bias must be such that operation will occur along the linear portion of the transfer characteristic (Fig. 3.52(b)). If the grid signal is increased beyond these limits, the grid swing will extend into the regions of plate current cut-off and saturation. If this occurs, the output waveform will be distorted; the distortion increasing with further increases of the amplitude of the grid signal.

6. a. Grid current flows in the driven tube. This causes the tube (grid-to-cathode) to present a low impedance to the driving circuit and may cause distortion in audio amplifiers.

b. If the input circuit were RC coupled, the input coupling capacitor would charge and this would tend to increase the stage bias. Assuming the stage to be an audio amplifier, the RC time constant of the coupling capacitor and grid resistor would be large enough to maintain the charge between high positive peaks of the signal. The charge is therefore averaged in the coupling capacitor and the capacitor voltage is added to the normal bias voltage. The greater the positive signal peaks, the higher the average capacitor voltage will be, and the greater the increase of bias.

7. The output current is the current in the tubes' output load, while the output voltage appears across this load. The output current is also the tubes' plate current. This current passing through the load impedance creates the output voltage. This may be expressed as

$$V_o = I_o \times Z_o$$

where

  V_o = output voltage.
  I_o = output current.
  Z_o = load impedance.

If the plate load is purely resistive, the plate current will be in phase with the plate voltage across the load. An increase of plate current will result in a proportional increase of output voltage change across the load. If the plate load is a pure inductance, the plate current will lag the output voltage by 90°. A parallel resonant circuit in the plate presents a resistive load at resonance, but acts like an inductive load when tuned above the input frequency, and like a capacitive load when tuned below this frequency.

Q. 3.53. What is meant by "space charge?" By "secondary emission"?

A.

1. "Space charge" is a charge due to the accumulation of negative electrons in the space between certain vacuum tube elements.

2. "Secondary emission" is the emission of electrons from a material, due to the impact of high velocity electrons upon its surface. The original electrons are called primary electrons.

D.

1. In a diode which is not operating under saturation conditions, it will be found that a "cloud" of electrons exists between the cathode and the plate; the cloud is concentrated in a thin layer immediately surrounding the emitting surface. This cloud of electrons is called the "space charge" and exists due to the inability of the plate potential to attract all of the electrons leaving the emitter. The space charge has a negative potential and partially cancels the effectiveness of the plate potential in attracting electrons. Under conditions of equilibrium it is found that the space charge is continuously returning electrons to the emitter as well as receiving them from the emitter so that the total space charge remains constant.

In beam power tubes the space charge effect produces a negative gradient of potential at the plate that eliminates the necessity of utilizing a suppressor grid to reduce secondary emission from the plate. Beam power tubes are constructed so that the wires of the control and screen grids lie in the same plane. This causes the electrons to move in concentrated layers. The screen-plate distance is considerably greater than in conventional screen grid tubes, and so-called "beam forming" plates are employed, at cathode potential, to assist producing the desired "beam" effect.

2. If an electron is in an evacuated space containing a positively charged material, the electron will be attracted with ever-increasing velocity until it strikes the surface of the material. At the point of impact, the moving electron will impart its kinetic energy to other electrons and atoms within the material. If the impact is great enough, one or more electrons within the material will be dislodged with enough energy to be emitted from the surface. The number so emitted will depend upon the velocity of the primary

electron and upon the type and temperature of the material. While secondary emission in an amplifier tube is usually detrimental, such is not always the case. For example, the dynatron oscillator relies upon one effect of secondary emission, called "negative resistance," for its feedback energy. Some structures are built to take advantage of this effect. For instance, in the RCA "image orthicon" television camera tube, there is incorporated an electron multiplier which deliberately produces secondary emission in order to amplify the magnitude of the camera signal.

Q. 3.54. What is meant by the "amplification factor" (mu) of a triode vacuum tube (amplifier)? Under what conditions would the amplifier gain approach the value of mu?

A.

1. The "amplification factor" (mu) of a triode vacuum tube is the ratio of a change of plate voltage which produces a given change of plate current, to the change in grid voltage which will produce the same change of plate current. It represents the theoretical maximum voltage gain of an amplifier.

2. The amplifier gain will approach the value of mu if the ratio of plate load impedance to dynamic-tube plate impedance is high (10 or more).

D.

1. Amplification factor: The actual voltage gain of an amplifier tube can never be equal to the amplification factor because the drop across the plate impedance of the tube must be subtracted from the total available output signal. This amounts to a voltage divider with r_p in series with the plate load resistance. The only output voltage available is that across the plate load resistance. This means that in order for the voltage gain to be equal to the amplification factor, the load resistance must be infinitely large. The formula for amplification factor is

$$\mu = \frac{\Delta v_b}{\Delta v_c} \quad |i_p|$$

2. The voltage amplification factor of a tube equals, $\mu \times V_8$, where V_8 is the input grid signal voltage. Since every tube has an internal impedance some of the output voltage is "lost" in the tube impedance and is not available in the plate load. From a practical standpoint the load resistance should be relatively high with respect to the internal tube impedance (in triodes) if maximum gain is to be achieved. The mid-frequency gain may be calculated from the formula, $G_{mid} = g_m \times R_{eq}$, where g_m is the tube transconductance and R_{eq} is the resultant parallel impedance of the internal tube impedance, the plate load resistance and the grid resistance of the following stage. This applies only to an RC coupled amplifier.

Q. 3.55. What is meant by "plate resistance" of a vacuum tube? Upon what does its value depend?

A.

1. The "plate resistance" of a vacuum tube is the ratio of a small change of plate current to the change of plate voltage producing that current. The grid voltage is a constant.

2. The value of "plate resistance" is an indication of the effectiveness of the plate voltage in causing a change in the plate current. The plate resistance of triodes is much less than that of tetrodes or pentodes because the action of the screen grid makes the plate current relatively independent of plate voltage changes. When a screen grid is present it takes a much larger plate-voltage change to produce a given plate-current change.

D. Plate Resistance: Plate impedance or plate resistance of a vacuum tube is a function of the physical and electrical properties of the tube, and is the ratio between a small change of plate current to the change in plate voltage producing it, with the grid voltage held constant. If normal operating voltages are applied to a tube a certain definite value of plate current will flow. If the plate voltage is divided by the plate current the result is called the dc plate resistance. Thus

$$R_p = \frac{V_b}{I_b}$$

While this value is of some limited use, such as in regulated power supplies, a more general term is needed which more accurately states the operating characteristics of a tube. This more general term is r_p or plate impedance. It represents the impedance offered by the cathode-to-plate path within a tube to a varying voltage. Thus

$$r_p = \frac{\Delta v_b}{\Delta i_b} \ |v_c|$$

where

Δ = a "small change of."
r_p = plate impedance in ohms.
v_b and i_b = instantaneous values of plate voltage and current.
v_c = instantaneous value of grid voltage, which is here held constant, as indicated by the parallel vertical lines enclosing v_c.

The plate impedance may be considered to be the internal resistance of an equivalent ac generator.

Q. 3.56. What is meant by the voltage "gain" of a vacuum tube amplifier? How does it achieve this gain?

A.

1. The voltage "gain" is the ratio of the output voltage to the input voltage, or

$$\text{Gain} = \frac{V_{\text{output}}}{V_{\text{input}}}$$

2. Gain is a measure of the capability of vacuum tubes (except diodes) to produce "voltage amplification" of the input grid signal.

D. 1. Assuming normal plate and grid voltages to be present, the gain of a triode audio amplifier is a function of (1) tube transconductance, (2) plate load impedance, and (3) transformer step-up ratio (if used). While it is true that radical changes in plate supply voltage will change the voltage gain to some extent, this factor is of minor importance in comparison to those mentioned above. For resistance coupled amplifiers the gain is G

$= g_m \times R_{eq,}$ where g_m is the transconductance, and R_{eq} is the internal plate impedance, the plate load impedance and the grid resistance of the following stage taken in parallel. This formula only holds for mid-range frequencies, that is the *flat* portion of the frequency characteristic of the amplifier. For transformer coupled amplifiers, the gain with a triode and well-designed transformer is $G = \mu \times N$, where N is the turns ratio. Pentodes are not generally used with transformers, the usual exception being the output audio power amplifier. However, there is no question here of voltage gain. The only consideration is one of impedance matching for maximum power transfer.

2. See Q. 3.54, Discussion 1. and 2.

Q. 3.57. Draw a rough graph of plate current versus plate supply voltage for three different bias voltages on a typical triode vacuum tube.

1. Explain, in a general way, how the value of the plate load resistance affects the portion of the curve over which the tube is operating. How is this related to distortion?

2. Operation over which portion of the curve produces the least distortion?

A.

1. As shown in Fig. 3.57, the higher the value of plate-load resistance, the lower the position of the load line on the graph. The load line is plotted from the maximum plate current point (V_b/R_L) to the plate voltage point (V_b). When a grid signal is applied the tube operates along the load line. Thus, the value of load resistance determines the operating portion of the curves.

As indicated in Figure 3.57, load lines have been drawn in for 30 000- and 300 000-ohm plate-load resistors. Note that the 30 000-ohm load line passes through the grid-bias lines in an area where these are most linear and most evenly spaced. This of course is not true for the 300 000-ohm load line. Changes in grid voltages (input signal) produce corresponding changes in plate currents (output currents) and consequently in plate

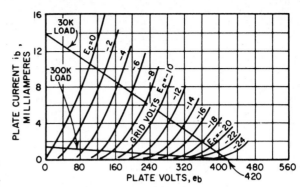

Fig. 3.57. Graph of plate current versus plate supply voltage for a typical triode.

voltages (output voltages). The least amount of output wave distortion (versus input) will occur when the operation occurs between grid bias lines which are the most evenly spaced and most linear. Therefore, in this example (for least distortion), the 30 000 ohm load would be preferred.

    2. See entry 1 above.

Q. 3.58. A triode, "grounded cathode" audio amplifier has a mu (amplification factor) of 30, a plate impedance of 5 000 ohms, load impedance of 10 000 ohms, plate voltage of 300 volts, plate current of 10 mA, and cathode-resistor bias is used.

    1. What is the stage gain of this amplifier?

    2. What is the cut-off-bias voltage, V_{co}?

    3. Assuming the bias voltage is one-half the value of V_{co}, what value cathode resistor would be used to produce the required bias?

    4. What size capacitor should be used to sufficiently by-pass the cathode resistor if the lowest approximate frequency desired is 500 hertz?

    A.

    1. The stage gain = 20.

    2. The cut-off bias = -10 volts.

    3. The cathode resistor = 500 ohms.

    4. The cathode by-pass capacitor = 6.4 microfarads.

    D.

    1. Step 1: Find the stage gain of the amplifier,

$$A = \frac{\mu \times R_L}{R_L + R_p}$$

where

    A = gain of the stage.

    μ = amplification factor (mu).

    R_L = load impedance, in ohms.

    R_p = plate impedance of tube in ohms.

$$A = \frac{30 \times 10\ 000}{10\ 000 \times 5\ 000}$$

$$= \frac{300\ 000}{15\ 000} = 20$$

    2. Step 2: Find the cut-off bias (V_{co})

$$V_{co} = \frac{V_b}{\mu}$$

where

    V_{co} = grid cut-off bias, in volts.

    V_b = plate (supply) voltage, in volts.

    μ = amplification factor (mu).

$$V_{co} = \frac{300}{30} = -10 \text{ volts}$$

    3. Step 3: Find the cathode resistor value for one-half of E_{co}, or -5 volts

$$R_K = \frac{V_K}{I_p}$$

where

    R_K = cathode resistor, in ohms.

    V_K = cathode bias, in volts.

    I_p = plate current in amperes.

$$R_K = \frac{5}{0.01} = 500 \text{ ohms}$$

    4. Step 4: Find the value of cathode by-pass capacitor.

    a. To be effective, the capacitor should have a reactance at least one-tenth or less of the value of the cathode resistor (or in this case, $XC_K = 100$ ohms) at the lowest frequency (or 500 hertz).

b.
$$XC_K = \frac{1}{2\pi fC_K}$$

or

$$C_K = \frac{1}{2\pi fXC_K}$$
$$= \frac{0.159}{500 \times 50} = \frac{0.159}{25\,000}$$
$$= 6.4 \text{ microfarads}$$

Q. 3.59. Why is the efficiency of an amplifier operated Class C higher than one operated Class A or Class B?

A. In Class C amplifiers the plate current is permitted to flow *only* during the time that the instantaneous value of plate voltage is at or near its *minimum* value. At all other times the tube is non-conducting. This permits a relatively small loss on the plate and high efficiency.

D. The outstanding characteristics of a Class C amplifier are:
1. High plate circuit efficiency, up to 85 percent.
2. Large grid driving power.
3. Plate current exists for less than 180° of the grid excitation cycle, usually for approximately 120°.
4. Grid bias on the average is about twice cut-off value.
5. Large power output in comparison to Class A.
6. Great distortion of plate current waveshape.

However, in order that the above conditions be met, a large value of bias, must be used, in some cases equal to four times cut-off value, but usually about twice cut-off value. Since grid current must flow at some time in each cycle, a relatively large value of grid driving power must be available from a low impedance source. Appreciable RF power is consumed in the grid circuit. Although the plate current wave is a pulse

rich in harmonics, the plate voltage waveshape will be sinusoidal, since the plate load will in most cases be a tank circuit with a reasonably high Q. An interesting feature is that the maximum positive value of grid voltage ($v_{c\,max}$) is approximately equal to the minimum value of the plate voltage ($v_{b\min}$).

Q. 3.60. The following are excerpts from a tube manual rating of a beam pentode. Explain the significance of each item:

1.	Control grid-to-plate capacitance	1.1 pF
2.	Input capacitance	2.2 pF
3.	Output capacitance	8.5 pF
4.	Heater voltage	6.3 volts
5.	Maximum dc plate-supply voltage	700 volts
6.	Maximum peak positive pulse voltage	7 000 volts
7.	Maximum negative pulse plate voltage	1 500 volts
8.	Maximum screen grid voltage	175 volts
9.	Maximum peak negative control grid voltage	200 volts
10.	Maximum plate dissipation	20 watts
11.	Maximum screen-grid dissipation	30 watts
12.	Maximum dc cathode current	200 mA
13.	Maximum peak cathode current	700 mA
14.	Maximum control-grid circuit resistance	0.47 megohm

A. Examination of an RCA tube manual shows these ratings to be almost identical for type 6CD6-GA television, horizontal-output tube. However, in two instances, the decimal points appear to have been misplaced. Input capacitance should read 22 pF, instead of 2.2 pF. Also maximum screen dissipation should read 3.0 watts, not 30 watts. The following is the significance of each listed item:
1. Control grid-to-plate capacitance: The measured capacity from the control grid to the plate, with other grids connected to the cathode.
2. Input capacitance: The sum of control grid-to-cathode, control grid-to-screen grid and control grid-to-suppressor grid (or beam plates) capacitances.

3. Output capacitance: The sum of plate-to-cathode, plate-to-screen grid and plate-to-suppressor grid (or beam plates) capacitances.

4. Heater voltage: The nominal cathode heater voltage. It may vary ± 10 percent.

5. Maximum dc plate-supply voltage: The maximum steady-state, power-supply voltage permitted to be applied to the plate to restrict the plate dissipation to a safe value.

6. Maximum positive pulse voltage: In the TV circuit, this occurs during the horizontal flyback time (about 10 μs) when the high voltage builds up. This (7 000 V) is the maximum safe value to prevent internal tube arcing.

7. Maximum negative pulse voltage: In the TV circuit, this occurs during the horizontal trace (about 53 μs) and is limited for the same reason as in item 6 above.

8. Maximum screen-grid voltage (dc): The maximum steady-state, dc supply voltage permitted to be applied to the screen grid. The screen voltage largely determines plate current (and plate dissipation) as well as screen-grid current and dissipation.

9. Maximum peak negative control-grid voltage: The maximum safe value to prevent control grid-to-cathode arcing.

10. Maximum plate dissipation: The maximum safe wattage the plate can dissipate continuously, without causing tube damage (or short life).

11. Maximum screen-grid dissipation: Same as item 10 above, but for screen grid.

12. Maximum dc cathode current: The maximum continuous current which the cathode can supply without serious deterioration of the oxide coating of the cathode. The dc (average) current must be limited to this value.

13. Maximum peak-cathode current: Within the pulse-width limitations of the TV receiver operation, this is the maximum pulse current the cathode can supply without serious deterioration.

14. Maximum control-grid circuit resistance: The maximum value of grid to ground resistance. Higher values may result in an excess positive grid voltage caused by positive ion-grid current, which would cancel out the bias and might damage or destroy the tube.

Q. 3.61 Name at least three abnormal conditions which would tend to shorten the life of a vacuum tube; also name one or more probable causes of each condition.

A.

1. a. Excessive heater voltage.
   b. Excessive plate current.
   c. Inadequate cooling.
   d. Excessive screen-grid current.
   e. Exceeding maximum pulse-current ratings.

2. The causes listed below are keyed to the same letters in 1, above.

   a. Line voltage too high; shorted series-dropping resistor; filament transformer voltage too high.

   b. Bias too low; plate voltage too high; screen grid voltage too high.

   c. Tube shield left off; cooling fan or other cooling scheme not operating.

   d. Bias too low; screen-grid voltage too high.

   e. Pulse-duty cycle too high. In some cases, especially where high voltages are involved, too low a heater voltage may cause cathode damage. In this case, particles of the cathode-oxide coating may be stripped off by the electrostatic field in the tube.

Q. 3.62. Name at less three circuit factors (not including tube types and component values) in a one-stage amplifier circuit, that should be considered at VHF which would not be of particular concern at VLF.

A. The following should be especially considered at VHF:

1. The possibility of circuit oscillation or regeneration due to stray capacitive feedback.

2. The use of low-loss components, such as coil forms, tube sockets, ferrite cores.

3. The use of non-inductive and low-loss by-pass and coupling capacitors, such as ceramic and mica types.

4. Neutralization may be required in some circuits.

5. Use of grounded-grid type of amplifier to reduce feedback problems.

6. Signal lead lengths must be short, to reduce lead inductance.

D. An additional circuit factor of concern at VHF and above is the manner in which the circuit is grounded. Very short and direct ground leads having negligible inductance must be used. In some cases, all grounds are returned to a common point on the chassis. This is done to avoid chassis ground currents which might result in amplifier instability. In multi-stage amplifiers, it may be necessary to run all grid, cathode and filament grounds to one part of the chassis and screen grid and plate ground to another part of the chassis. This helps to prevent feedback currents in the chassis from causing oscillation or instability of the amplifier.

In general, an amplifier for use at these high frequencies should be built in a very compact manner to minimize lead lengths and therby assure minimum lead inductance. In addition, the effect of stray capacitance may be appreciable at the very high frequencies involved and these too must be kept to a minimum. Stray capacitance is developed between wires, parts and ground, as well as between parts and between wires and parts. In a multi-stage amplifier, it is often necessary to shield tubes and RF transformers to prevent regeneration or oscillation, due to coupling between these units.

Q. 3.63. What is a "lighthouse" triode? An "acorn" tube? These tubes were designed for operation in what frequency range?

A.

1. A "lighthouse" triode (or disk-seal tube) is a tube designed especially to operate at UHF and is shown in Fig. 3.63(a). The plate, grid and cathode are assembled in parallel planes instead of coaxially. Extremely close electrode spacing reduces electron transit time. In addition, the electrodes are connected to parallel discs, prac-

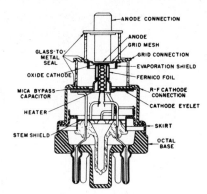

Fig. 3.63(a). Cross-section of a "lighthouse" triode tube.

tically eliminating tube lead inductance. The use of small internal elements results in very low interelectrode capacities. These tubes will amplify up to about 2 500 megahertz.

2. Acorn tubes are seldom used in modern electronic equipment. They will amplify up to about 600 megahertz. Acorn tubes are very small (about half the size of a golf ball) and have no base. Electrode connections are brought out to short wire pins which are sealed in a glass rim around the lower portion of the tube. An "acorn" tube is illustrated in Fig. 3.63(b).

D. "Lighthouse" tubes are also known as "disc-seal" and "planar-disc" tubes. The name "lighthouse" is derived from the appearance of the basic tube although a variety of the tubes have been made and may differ widely in appearance. The very close spacing of electrodes is exemplified by one type of lighthouse tube in which the grid and cathode are separated by only 0.004 inch. Because of the close electrode spacing, very low values of transit time are achieved. If the cathode-plate transit time is greater than one-tenth of a cycle at the operating frequency, the tube efficiency begins to drop. Efficiency decreases as the percentage of transit time to cycle increases. For a tube operating at 2 500 megahertz, the time for one cycle is 4×10^{-4} microsecond and the maximum allowable transit time is 4×10^{-5} microsecond (see Q 3.64 following).

As the transit time becomes greater

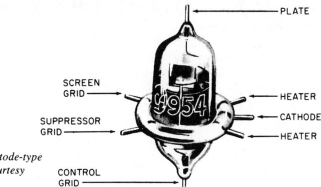

Fig. 3.63(b). A pentode-type
of acorn tube. (Courtesy
RCA)

than one-tenth of a cycle, the plate current lags the plate voltage by greater than 36 degrees. This results in an important decrease of power output and consequent increase of tube-plate dissipation. The condition becomes worse with increasing values of transit time. In the case of oscillators, it is usually found that oscillation ceases as the transit time approaches a quarter of a cycle (90 degrees).

The physical configuration of a lighthouse tube is ideally suited for insertion into resonant coaxial-line tuners. The tuner may consist of coaxial line, cathode-grid, and plate-grid cavities. The assembly of a "lighthouse" tube in its coaxial tuner is shown in Fig. 3.63(c). Note in the figure, that the assembly comprises three concentric cylinders fitted to the end of the tube. Tuning of the cavity is accomplished by a cathode-grid shorting plunger and by a plate tuning rod which slides the plate cylinder over the

plate terminal of the tube. Because of the high operating frequency (about 2 500-3 000 MHz) mechanical problems dictate the use of tuning lines which are multiples of a quarter wavelength. As shown, the cathode line is about ¾ wavelength and the plate line about one full wavelength. (See also Q 3.62 above and Q 3.64 following.)

POWER SUPPLIES

Q. 3.64. Why are special tubes sometimes required at UHF and above?

A. Special tubes or tube types are usually required at UHF or higher frequencies. At frequencies above about 100 megahertz, the interelectrode capacitances of ordinary tubes will attenuate the signals greatly. In addition, the ordinary cathode-to-plate, electron-transit time of one-thousandth of a

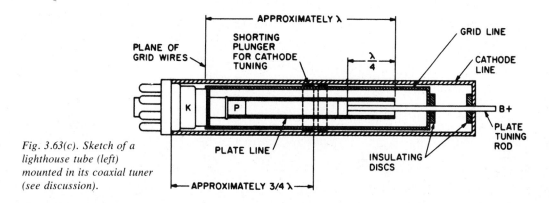

Fig. 3.63(c). Sketch of a
lighthouse tube (left)
mounted in its coaxial tuner
(see discussion).

microsecond becomes excessive. At UHF this time approaches or may equal the time of one cycle of the operating frequency, causing undesirable phase shifts within the tube. In addition, the relatively large lead inductance of ordinary tubes limits their operating frequency.

D. Desirable characteristics of UHF tubes are:

1. Closely spaced electrodes.
2. Small elements.
3. Low-inductance leads.
4. No tube base.

In special VHF and UHF tubes, such as "traveling-wave" tubes, klystrons and magnetrons, the transit time of electrons is utilized to provide proper operation. For a description of these tubes, see Q. 3.246, Q. 3.247 and Q. 3.248 following. See also Q. 3.63 above.

Q. 3.65. Draw a diagram of each of the following power supply circuits. Explain the operation of each, including the relative input and output voltage amplitudes, waveshapes, and current waveforms.

1. Diode, half-wave rectifier with a capacitive-input "pi-section" filter.

2. Diode, full-wave rectifier with choke input (RC) filter.

3. Silicon diode, doubler-circuit rectifier with a resistive load.

4. Non-synchronous-vibrator power supply, with silicon diode, bridge-circuit rectifier and capacitive input "pi-section" filter.

5. Synchronous-vibrator power supply with capacitive input "pi-section" filter.

A.

1. See Fig. 3.65(a1). The following description applies to a half-wave rectifier system as illustrated. The first problem to be considered is that of rectification, or changing alternating current into unidirectional (dc) current. A rectifier is essentially a one-way device, since its reverse (or inverse) current conduction is almost zero. The rectifier conducts only when its anode is positive with respect to cathode, and is a noncon-

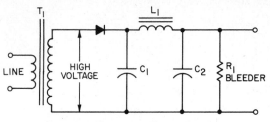

Fig. 3.65(a1). Half-wave rectifier, with "pi-section" filter.

ductor when the anode is negative with respect to cathode. When an alternating voltage is applied to such a rectifier, its output consists of a series of current pulses, which are unidirectional in character. See Fig. 3.65(a2) for waveshapes of operation. Due to the action of the filter, these pulses are considerably less than ½ cycle in width and are separated by spaces more than ½ cycle in width. The output of a rectifier must be filtered to a large degree in order to eliminate the fundamental and harmonic frequency components from the rectifier-filter system output. The usual method for accomplishing this is to insert a suitable *LC* low-pass filter in series with the rectifier output whose cut-off frequency is well below

Fig. 3.65(a2). Current and voltage waveforms for a half-wave rectifier with capacitor-input filter.

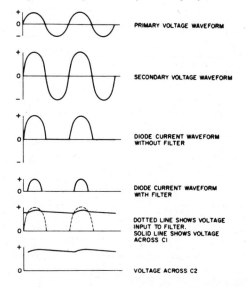

PRIMARY VOLTAGE WAVEFORM

SECONDARY VOLTAGE WAVEFORM

DIODE CURRENT WAVEFORM WITHOUT FILTER

DIODE CURRENT WAVEFORM WITH FILTER

DOTTED LINE SHOWS VOLTAGE INPUT TO FILTER. SOLID LINE SHOWS VOLTAGE ACROSS C1

VOLTAGE ACROSS C2

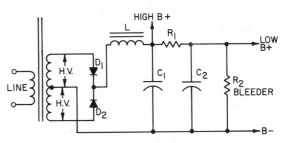

Fig. 3.65(b1). Full-wave rectifier with choke-input RC filter.

the line frequency. The type shown in the figure is a capacitor-input "pi"-type filter. The input capacitor of the filter charges up practically to the peak value of each positive alternation applied to the anode of the rectifier. The rectifier stops delivering current to the filter until the next positive alternation exceeds the potential of the input capacitor. During this interval of time, the power is supplied by the input capacitor, whose voltage drops in a linear manner due to the constant current action of the filter choke. The output capacitor of the filter must be large enough to offer very little reactance at the lowest frequencies to be amplified, so as to reduce the possibilities of feedback through the medium of the common power supply impedance, and also to supply peak demands from the load.

In a half-wave rectifier, the ripple frequency is equal to the line frequency, i.e., a line frequency of 60 hertz will produce a ripple frequency of 60 hertz. A half-wave rectifier is the simplest and least expensive type. However, it is more difficult to filter and ordinarily has poorer regulation than a full-wave type. The dc output voltage of this supply depends upon the extent of current taken from it. If the loading is light, the dc voltage may equal the peak value (not peak-to-peak) of the secondary voltage. As the loading increases, the dc voltage output drops and the ripple voltage increases. If the supply is heavily loaded, the dc voltage may drop to 0.9 or less of the rms value of the secondary voltage.

2. For diagram, see Fig. 3.65(b1). This arrangement may be used where the highest voltage taken from the power supply is at a high current drain and fed to a stage

which is insensitive to a fairly high ripple voltage. Such a stage would be the power output stage of an audio amplifier. Stages of higher gain and low-current requirements require a lower ripple voltage and this may be supplied by an additional RC filter, as shown. A typical stage meeting these requirements is an audio pre-amplifier. (See Q. 4.24.)

The waveforms for the full-wave rectifier are shown in Fig. 3.65(b2). Referring to the schematic (Fig. 3.65(b1)) it may be seen that the high-voltage secondary is center-tapped, the centertap becoming the negative side of the dc output voltage. Note that the *total* secondary voltage must be twice that

Fig. 3.65(b2). Current and voltage waveforms for a full-wave rectifier with choke-input filter.

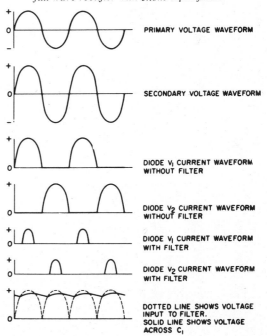

required for a half-wave rectifier, because of the centertap. (See part 4 of this question for comparison to bridge-type rectifier.) However, the diodes conduct alternately for each half of every cycle and the output voltage (ripple frequency) is applied to the filter at twice the line frequency. The ripple frequency for a 60-hertz line will be 120 hertz. The higher ripple frequency permits a less expensive filter to be employed than in the case of a half-wave rectifier having the same ripple voltage requirements. The full-wave rectifier will also have improved regulation over the half-wave type. For comparative characteristics of choke and capacitor input filters, see Q. 3.69.

    3. See Fig. 3.65(c).

    Cascade Doubler, Figure-Group A. During the first negative half cycle, capacitor C_1 charges through diode D1 to approximately the peak value, V, of the transformer secondary voltage (Figure A'). As soon as the negative peak has gone by and the wave starts in the positive direction, capacitor C_1

begins to charge C_2 through D2 (Figure A''). When the wave reaches its positive peak, the voltage across the transformer secondary in series with the voltage across C_1 (totaling $2V$) charges C_2 to approximately double the peak secondary voltage. This doubler is a half-wave device.

    Conventional Doubler, Figure-Group B. For simplicity of explanation it is assumed that the circuit has been in operation for some time and that we are considering a positive-going half cycle (Figure B'). C_2 has been previously charged through D2 and the transformer secondary to approximately the peak value of secondary voltage. As soon as the transformer voltage starts in the positive direction, C_2 begins to discharge through D1 into the load and filter. When the transformer reaches its maximum positive value, it adds its voltage to that of C_2 and charges the filter capacitor (not shown) to approximately double the peak secondary voltage. During this same positive-going half cycle, capacitor C_1 is being recharged to the peak

Fig. 3.65(c). Group A shows a cascade doubler; group B shows a conventional doubler circuit.

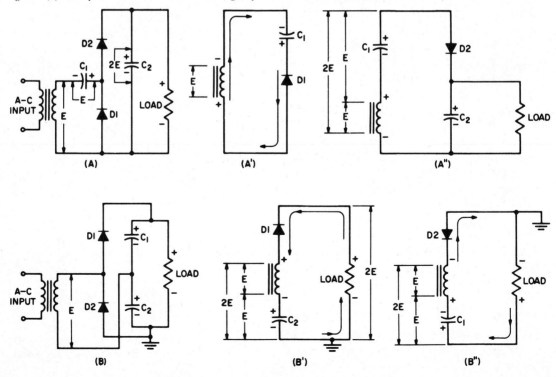

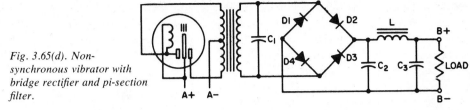

Fig. 3.65(d). Non-synchronous vibrator with bridge rectifier and pi-section filter.

secondary voltage through D1 and the transformer secondary.

As soon as the wave starts in the negative direction (Figure B''), capacitor C_1 begins discharging through D2 into the load (and filter, not shown); when the transformer reaches it maximum negative value, its voltage is added in series to that of C_1 charging the filter capacitor (not shown) to approximately double the peak secondary voltage. During this same negative-going half cycle, C_2 is being recharged to the peak secondary voltage through D2 and the transformer secondary. This completes one cycle of full-wave operation.

4. *Note:* Although there are some vibrator power supplies in present use, it should be realized that this type of supply is rapidly being replaced by transistor power supplies which have no moving parts and are far more reliable. Refer to Fig. 3.65(d). When power is applied to the vibrator coil and transformer primary, the armature is pulled to the left. This shorts out the vibrator coil and the armature springs to the right and touches the right-hand contact, after which the magnetic field of the coil and the spring action cause it to touch the left-hand contact. This action becomes cyclical at about 150 to 250 Hz. Note that the armature action causes current to flow first in the top half of the primary

and then in the bottom half, but in opposite directions. This constitutes an alternating current in the primary which is stepped up in the secondary winding to the desired value. The bridge rectifier shown is a full-wave rectifier and operates as follows:

a. When the top of the secondary is positive and the bottom negative, electron flow is through the secondary from top to bottom, through D4 to B–, through the load and L, through D2 and back to the top of the transformer.

b. When the polarities are reversed, electron flow is through D3, up through the secondary, through D1 to B–, through the load and L and back to D3. For filter operation, see part 1 of this question.

5. See Fig. 3.65(e). The usual synchronous rectifier is the synchronous vibrator, consisting of a "U" frame designed to permit the mounting of a coil with pole piece at the closed end. A vibrating reed and insulated side springs with contacts are mounted at the opposite end. The reed carries contacts mounted on either side in pairs, corresponding to the stationary side spring contacts. The vibrating reed is usually so connected as to keep it at ground potential. The "driver" coil is a high resistance winding which is placed in series with one-half of the centertapped primary of the transformer

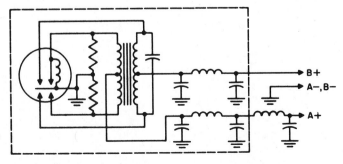

Fig. 3.65(e). Schematic diagram of a synchronous vibrator power supply, using capacitor-input filter.

and the battery. Both primary and secondary windings of the transformer are centertapped. The centertap of the primary is connected to the "hot" side of the dc input line, while the centertap of the secondary is the take-off point for the positive high-voltage rectified dc. The operation is as follows: All contact pairs are open normally and the starting of the reed movement depends upon the magnetic attraction of the "driver" coil. This movement is sufficient to cause the reed to make good electrical connection with a side spring contact which is connected to the same side of the transformer as the driver coil. This shorts the driver coil, destroys the magnetic field and releases the reed which now swings in the opposite direction beyond its original resting position. The reed now contacts the opposite side spring connections, and the driver-coil field pulls it back. In this manner the reed sets up vibrations, usually designed to be 135 hertz. As the reed moves, the secondary side spring contacts alternately reverse the primary and secondary transformer connections so that the output is a uni-directional current (dc). For filter operation, see part 1 of this question.

Q. 3.66. What advantage may a bridge rectifier circut have over a conventional full-wave rectifier?

A. See Q. 3.65(d), above for diagram of bridge rectifier and (b) of that question for diagram of a full-wave rectifier. The advantages are as follows:

1. A bridge circuit produces almost double the output voltage, using the same transformer. (Centertap of secondary is not used.)

2. For the same output voltage, the inverse-peak voltage is only one-half as much across each tube in a bridge rectifier (four tubes), compared to a conventional full-wave rectifier (two tubes).

D. The same advantage is true when solid-state rectifiers are used for both (1) and (2) above. Solid-state rectifiers are preferred for bridge circuits for the elimination

of the three filament transformers which would be required for vacuum tubes and for their greater reliability and lower internal drop.

Q. 3.67. What are "swinging chokes"? Where are they normally used?

A.

1. "Swinging chokes" are power-supply filter chokes, whose inductance varies inversely with the load current in the choke.

2. They are used to improve the voltage regulation of a power supply which is operating under conditions of varying loads.

D. A swinging choke is one whose inductance varies inversely with the amount of dc current flowing through it. The main reason for using a swinging choke is economy, as compared with the use of a conventional or smoothing choke. Where a varying load is present, less filtering is required at heavy loads. As the load decreases, it is necessary to have an increasing value of inductance if the choke is to continue to filter properly, otherwise the output voltage will rise sharply at low current values. A swinging choke may be chosen to fulfill these requirements much more economically than a smoothing choke which would have to be designed to present a constant maximum inductance under all load conditions. This would mean a large, expensive choke. A swinging choke must be the one nearest the rectifier tube, and is generally followed by a smoothing choke in order to satisfy filtering conditions. A system like this is still considerably more economical than if two smoothing chokes had to be used. The inductance is made to vary by having a very small gap, such as the thickness of a piece of fish paper, inserted in the iron core.

Q. 3.68. Show a method of obtaining two voltages from one power supply.

A. See Fig. 3.68(a).

D. The following example illustrates the method of determining the voltage divider resistance.

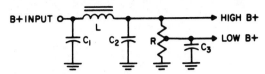

Fig. 3.68(a). A simple divider method for obtaining two voltages from one power supply.

A rectifier-filter power supply is designed to furnish 500 volts at 60 milliamperes to one circuit and 400 volts at 40 milliamperes to another circuit. The bleeder current in the voltage divider is to be 15 milliamperes. What value of resistance should be placed between the 500- and 400-volt taps of the voltage divider?

Refer to Fig. 3.68(b). It will be seen that two currents are present in the 400- to 500-volt section. These are the bleeder current of 15 mA plus the 400-volt load current of 40 mA or a total of 55 milliamperes. The value of resistance is found by Ohm's Law.

$$R = \frac{V}{I} = \frac{100}{0.055} = 1818.2 \ ohms$$

The value of resistance should be 1818.2 ohms.

The power rating is found as follows: $V \times I = 5.5$ watts actual dissipation. Use a 10-watt resistor as a safety factor.

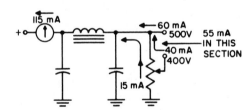

Fig. 3.68(b). A rectifier-filter system which can supply 500 volts at 60 milliamperes and 400 volts at 40 milliamperes to another circuit.

Q. 3.69. What are the characteristics of a capacitor-input filter system as compared to a choke-input system? What is the effect upon a filter choke of a large value of direct current flow?

A.

1. The primary comparative characteristics of a capacitor-input filter are:
   a. Higher dc output voltage. (About 1.4 times rms value of secondary voltage under light loads.)
   b. Poorer voltage regulation.
   c. Higher peak surge currents.
   d. Not suitable for use with mercury vapor tubes.

2. The effect depends upon the original design of the choke. If it was designed to carry a large value of direct current, there would be no adverse effects. However, if the normal rating of the choke was being exceeded, dc core saturation would occur, the value of inductance would be reduced, and the choke might overheat.

D. The characteristics of a choke-input filter as compared with a capacitor-input filter, are:

1. Lower output voltage, about 90 percent of rms secondary voltage.
2. Better voltage regulation.
3. Lower peak current surges.
4. More efficient utilization of tubes and transformers.

When a capacitor-input filter is used, the capacitor charges to 1.414 times the rms value of the secondary voltage of the power transformer. Neglecting any drop in the dc resistance of the choke, this will be the output dc voltage with a light load. If the load increases, however, this voltage may drop to 0.9 of the rms secondary value or less. The choke input filter starts with a dc voltage of 0.9 rms secondary voltage and will vary very much less, thus affording better regulation. See Q. 3.65. If the rectifier has mercury-vapor tubes, a choke-input filter must be used, as otherwise the initial current may be high enough to damage the tube. At the first starting cycle of the rectifying voltage, the input capacitor has no charge. This means that it is practically a short circuit for the initial current until it becomes charged. Thus there is nothing to limit the initial current except the impedance of the tube which is very low and the impedance of the high voltage secondary winding which is also very low. This means that the initial current value will be extremely high and may damage the tube.

Where the input capacitor is removed and a choke-input filter is used, the initial current will be very much lower. This is because, when the initial charging current flows, it must flow through the inductance of the choke oil. The sudden surge of current develops a high reactive drop across the choke coil which opposes the original secondary voltage and thus limits the current in the system to a safe value. Sometimes, in low current systems, a current limiting resistor may be used in series with the rectifier tube. This, however, has an adverse effect on the regulation.

Q. 3.70. What is the purpose of a "bleeder" resistor as used in conjunction with power supplies? Which type of resistor is preferable, carbon-composition, or wire-wound? Why?

A.
1. The primary purpose of a "bleeder" resistor in conventional power supplies is to improve the regulation of the voltage output.

2. Other factors being equal, a wire-wound resistor is preferable, because the wire-wound type is generally more reliable over time. In addition, wire-wound resistors are made in higher wattage ratings, which may be required in some applications.

D.
1. A bleeder resistor is connected directly across the load terminals. It is usually designed to draw at least 10 percent of the total current. In this way the bleeder acts as a minimum load on the power supply when the normal load is removed. Since the output voltage of a rectifier tends to rise when the load is removed, the bleeder draws a constant current and prevents the voltage from rising as much as it would if no bleeder were present. The bleeder also serves the important function of discharging the filter capacitors when the power is turned off.

2. Although a wire-wound bleeder is generally preferred, it is not always feasible to use this type. One drawback is cost, since the wire-wound type is appreciably more expensive. In large production runs, cost could be a factor if a carbon substitute is available. Also, the wire-wound types are generally larger and heavier, which may be important in some devices. Another factor is the required resistance values. Wire-wound types are generally not available in high ohmic values exceeding 1 megohm.

Q. 3.71. Would varying the value of the bleeder resistor in a power supply have any effect on the ripple voltage?

A. Varying the value of the bleeder resistor might affect the ripple voltage output of a power supply.

D. If a bleeder resister of too low a value were employed, then the bleeder current plus the load current might exceed the normal current rating of the power supply. This would decrease the output voltage and increase the ripple voltage. The dc current rating of the filter choke(s) might also be exceeded, reducing the choke inductance and increasing the ripple voltage.

Q. 3.72. What effect does the amount of current required by the load have upon the voltage regulation of the power supply? Why is voltage regulation an important factor?

A.
1. The greater the amount of current required by the load, the poorer the regulation will tend to be. (Of course a supply can be designed to maintain the required regulation for any practical load).

2. Regulation is important to maintain virtually constant output supply voltages under varying loads. This prevents intermodulation of circuits due to power-supply voltage variations as well as possibly insufficient or excessive supply voltages.

D. "Voltage regulation" expresses the ratio between the amount of voltage drop under full load conditions from the no-load value, to the full load voltage. This ratio is multiplied by 100 to express it as a percentage. Poor regulation may be caused by:

1. High resistance filter chokes.
2. Insufficient filter capacity.
3. Saturation of iron core of filter chokes.
4. No bleeder resistor.
5. Varying drop in rectifier tube with changing load (high-vacuum type).

Regulation is usually expressed as a percentage according to the formula:

$$\text{Reg.} = \frac{V_{NL} - V_{FL}}{V_{FL}} \times 100$$

where

V_{NL} = the no-load voltage.
V_{FL} = the full-load voltage.

Q. 3.73. What is meant by the "peak-inverse-voltage" rating of a diode and how can it be computed for a full-wave power supply?

A.
1. "Peak-inverse-voltage" rating of a rectifier tube is the maximum safe peak voltage which can be applied in the reverse direction without causing "arc back" or "flash back."
2. In a capacitor input full-wave rectifier power supply, the peak-inverse-voltage across the non-conducting tube equals the peak-to-peak ac voltage of one-half the secondary winding, or the rms value of the entire secondary winding times 1.414, less the drop in the conducting tube and the dc drop in the half of the transformer which is conducting.

D. In a half-wave rectifier system the peak-inverse-voltage is simply equal to the rms secondary voltage times 1.414.

Q. 3.74 Discuss the relative merits and limitations as used in power supplies of the following types of rectifiers:
1. **Mercury-vapor diode.**
2. **High-vacuum diode.**
3. **Copper oxide.**
4. **Silicon.**
5. **Selenium.**

A.
1. Advantages of mercury-vapor rectifier tubes are:
   a. A low internal voltage drop of 10 to 15 volts, which remains constant under varying load conditions, thus making for good voltage regulation.
   b. Permits the use of oxide coated cathodes, with their lower filament power requirements.
   c. Cooler operation due to the low internal drop.
   d. Greater efficiency and economy in high-voltage, high-current operation.

2. Disadvantages of mercury-vapor rectifier tubes are:
   a. Produces radio frequency interference due to ionization of mercury or gas.
   b. Relatively low peak-inverse-voltage rating.
   c. Filament may be damaged if not pre-heated before plate voltage is applied.

3. Advantages of high-vacuum rectifier tubes are:
   a. Higher peak-inverse-voltage rating for a given size of tube.
   b. Will stand more abuse without breakdown.
   c. Does not generate RF interference (hash).

4. Disadvantages of high-vacuum rectifier tubes are:
   a. Voltage drop across the tube varies with load current changes making for poorer voltage regulation.
   b. Higher filament power requirements.
   c. Tube runs hotter due to larger voltage drop.

5. Copper-oxide rectifiers: The merit of this type is that they can (for a given size) supply a relatively large direct current. Limitations of this type are: (a) there is a large shunt capacitance, and (b) its characteristics vary widely with temperature.

Note: These rectifiers are rapidly being replaced in many uses by germanium and silicon diodes.

6. Silicon rectifiers: The merits of this type are:

a. Compact size.

b. High-current ratings (up to several amperes for larger units).

The major limitation is the relatively low peak-inverse-voltage rating of a junction. By stacking units in series, peak inverse ratings up to several thousand volts can be achieved.

7. Selenium rectifiers: The merits of this type are:

a. Higher junction break-down voltage than copper oxide.

b. Lower forward resistance than copper oxide and, therefore, greater current-carrying capacity.

c. Can be used for high-voltage applications by stacking units in series.

d. Compact in size (for its type).

e. Low voltage drop across rectifier (about 5 volts).

8. Some limitations of selenium rectifiers are:

a. Require appreciable space and special mounting facilities.

b. Must be mounted to obtain adequate cooling.

c. Appreciably larger size than silicon rectifiers, where they are interchangeable for the same function.

d. High-shunt capacity, limiting use to power and audio frequencies.

D.

1. It is important to operate a mercury-vapor tube within specified temperature limits in order to realize maximum tube life and efficiency. Mercury-vapor tubes are built with an excess of liquid mercury to maintain a saturated condition of the vapor. The temperature of this vapor determines the pressure in the tube. If the pressure (or temperature) is too low, ionization is incomplete and the space charge is not sufficiently neutralized. Under those conditions the tube drop becomes excessive. With a high voltage drop, the ion velocities become very great, and bombard the cathode with enough energy to damage it. The minimum temperature at which the condensed mercury may be operated without causing disintegration of the cathode is about 20°C. If the operating temperature is excessive, an increase of vapor pressure will occur which will decrease the peak inverse voltage and may cause "flash-back." The maximum operating temperature is usually in the order of 75°C.

In a mercury-vapor rectifier tube positive ions are produced which tend to neutralize the negative space charge and thus permit higher conduction currents to take place. Electrons which are removed from the positive ions also add to the plate current. When operating two mercury-vapor rectifier tubes in parallel, small resistors must be placed in series with each plate lead.

The operating characteristic curve of a mercury-vapor rectifier tube is so steep that any slight difference in the characteristics of two tubes would cause a very large difference in the currents taken by each tube. The tube with the smaller voltage drop would take almost the entire load current. The difficulty can be overcome by connecting a small resistor in series with each tube before connecting them in parallel.

2. For use in circuits operating under 400 volts dc, the high-vacuum type can be designed to have an internal drop which is little, if any, greater than the internal drop of a mercury-vapor tube. However, this is not true of higher voltage operation in which high-vacuum tubes have a greater voltage drop than the mercury-vapor tube. The peak inverse voltage is the maximum safe negative voltage which can be applied to the plate of a rectifier tube without danger of arcing from plate to cathode. This value is always lower, for a given size, in a mercury-vapor tube due to the ionization of the mercury, which offers a better conduction path than a vacuum. The mercury-vapor tube generates RF interference as a result of ionization, and it must be properly shielded and its output filtered.

3. The most common use of copper oxide rectifiers is their use in rectifying ac voltages of low and medium frequencies so that ac measurements can be made with dc meters.

4. Silicon rectifiers are frequently being used to replace vacuum tube rectifiers. They require no filament supply or tube socket and have a very low voltage drop. It is frequently necessary to protect silicon rectifiers against peak capacitor charging surges by a small series resistor. The use of such a resistor has an adverse effect on voltage regulation and must therefore be kept to the smallest permissible value.

5. Selenium rectifiers have definite advantages over copper oxide types (as stated above) and have replaced the latter in many instances. However, selenium rectifiers are frequently being replaced by solid-state rectifiers, such as the silicon type.

Q. 3.75. Explain the action of a voltage regulator (VR) tube.

A. Refer to Fig. 3.75(a) and (b). A VR tube regulates by virtue of the fact that a constant (relatively) voltage drop appears across the tube as long as the tube current remains within the proper limits (usually 5 to 30 mA). As shown in the figures, the output voltage supply is taken across the tube(s) itself. Variations in either input voltage or output-load current cause varying voltages across the series resistor (R_1), but not across the tube itself. The regulation obtained by this means is poorer than when an amplifier-type of regulator is used, but is adequate for many non-critical, low current circuits.

D. A cold-cathode gassy-diode rectifier tube (see Q. 3.46(f)) consists of a large area cathode (coated with suitable emitting material such as barium and strontium), a small diameter rod-shaped pointed anode and a starter anode. These elements are enclosed in an envelope containing a gas such as helium, acetylene, argon, or neon. The gas pressure is critical for correct operation. Electron emission from the cathode is due to two major factors:

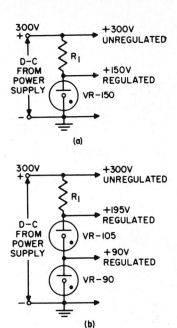

Fig. 3.75. Applications of cold-cathode electron tubes.

1. If the electrostatic field produced by the starter anode is sufficiently great, electrons will be pulled from the cathode coating by force of attraction.

2. Any gas is always in a state of partial ionization. The existing positive ions are accelerated by the cathode to starter-anode voltage so that they strike the cathode with sufficient force to aid in the emission of electrons. The rectifying action of such a tube makes use of the fact that the current which ionization causes to exist between two electrodes in a low-pressure gas is approximately proportional to the area of the cathode. If one electrode has a very large area (cathode) and the other electrode a very small area (anode), electrons will flow in the direction from cathode to anode. Conduction occurs on that half cycle which makes the anode positive with respect to the cathode.

Q. 3.76. If the plate, or plates of a rectifier tube suddenly became red hot, what might be the cause, and how could remedies be effected?

A. If the plate of a rectifier tube became

red hot, it would be due to excessive current demand upon the tube.

D. The filter components should be checked as indicated in Question 3.77. If these are in good order the current demands of all the supplied circuits should be investigated. A screen or plate bypass capacitor might be shorted. The coupling capacitor to a high power tube might be shorted. In the case of an RF power amplifier the plate tank might be mistuned or overloaded.

Q. 3.77. If a high vacuum type, high voltage rectifier tube suddenly became red hot, what might be the cause, and how could remedies be effected?

A. The following should be checked:

1. The filter capacitors should be checked for leakage or short circuit.

2. If these are good the choke or chokes should be checked for possible insulation breakdown.

3. The rectifier tube itself should be checked for gas and shorts.

D. See Q. 3.76.

Q. 3.78. What does a blue haze in the space between the filament and plate of a high-vacuum rectifier tube indicate?

A. A blue haze indicates the presence of gas in the tube.

D. The blue color is due to the ionization of free gas within the tube and is caused by electron bombardment. If the tube is operating under normal conditions, it should be replaced, as its peak-inverse-voltage rating is decreasing and it may soon become unsuitable as a rectifier under the existing conditions.

A blue color is a normal condition of operation in tubes such as mercury-vapor rectifier tubes and voltage regulator tubes.

A glow from within the tube, often a purplish color, indicates a "soft" tube. If the tube was not originally designed to be a "soft" tube, other indications would be: excessive plate current, erratic or non-operation, and a possible red heat observable in the plate. In certain applications the cath-

ode or filament may be destroyed due to positive-ion bombardment. Sometimes fluorescence occurs in the glass itself, also bluish or purplish; this does not indicate a soft tube.

During the manufacturing processes, many precautions are taken to exclude the presence of air from tubes, even those which are designed to contain gas after evacuation. The presence of such air or other undesired gases will interfere with the normal action of the tube due to ionization under the impact of the emitted electrons. Most gases are driven off by heating the tube to a high degree during evacuation. Any gases which remain are absorbed by the "getter," usually consisting of barium, "flashed" inside the tube after evacuation is complete. Deliberate introduction of gas is then made if desired.

Note: The following added material numbered Q. 3.78-A1 through Q. 3.78-A18 contains information that may be required to pass the General Radiotelephone Operator's License examination. This added material, as well as the new material added to other sections, has been included to help acquaint students with the current state of the electronics art. It is felt that the added material contains subject matter that may be required of students who have obtained a General Radiotelephone Operator's License and are seeking employment. Additionally, the added material contains valuable information for private technician certification.

Q. 3.78-A1. What are power supply "smoothing" chokes?

A. Power supply "smoothing" chokes are iron-core chokes used as part of power supply ripple filters. Unlike "swinging" chokes (see Q. 3.67), smoothing chokes are designed to present a practically *constant* inductance over varying power supply loads.

D. The inductance value required of a particular smoothing choke in a power supply is dependent upon:

1. Ripple frequency.

2. Half- or full-wave rectification (which affects ripple frequency).

3. Load current.

4. Permissible output ripple voltage (also a factor of the filter capacitors).

Common values of smoothing choke inductance in 60-Hz power supplies range from approximately 3 to 30 H.

The dc resistance of a choke is an important factor in its design. This is because the load current produces an IR drop across the choke which subtracts from the power supply output voltage. A relatively high dc choke resistance also adversely affects the power supply regulation. (See Q. 3.72.)

Another important design factor is the distributed capacitance across the two terminals of the choke. An excessive value will tend to partially by-pass the choke inductance, reducing its filtering effectiveness.

If the iron core of the choke becomes magnetically saturated, the inductance drops greatly. To reduce this effect, particularly with high load currents, the magnetic path of the iron core is interrupted. This is done by introducing a small gap in the iron core. To maintain the discontinuity, a thin strip of insulating material is inserted into the gap.

Some power supply filters employ two smoothing chokes in series (with filter capacitors), or one swinging choke followed by a smoothing choke. (See also Q. 3.65(2), Q. 3.67 and Q. 3.69.)

Note: A swinging choke for 60-Hz power supplies may have inductance values that *swing* from about 4 H with maximum load current to about 25 H with minimum load current.

Q. 3.78-A2. What are transformer cores made of?

A. Transformer cores are basically made of iron. In some cases nickel or cobalt is added to the iron, as well as other elements.

D. The cores of power, audio, and the larger pulse transformers are made from thin sheet or strip laminations. The laminations are insulated from each other to reduce eddy current losses. The thickness of the laminations depends upon the transformer op-

erating frequency, being thinner for higher frequencies.

Transformer cores may also be made of powdered metal bonded with a resin. Oxides in a ceramic structure, called ferrites, are also used as cores. Powdered iron and ferrite cores are used for higher-frequency applications.

Q. 3.78-A3. How can the size and weight of power transformers be reduced?

A. The following methods can be used:

1. By use of a higher operating frequency such as 400 Hz instead of 60 Hz.

2. By using high temperature materials, which permit higher temperature operation.

3. By operating in a lower-ambient temperature.

4. By making regulation requirements less stringent.

D. See also Q. 3.38, Q. 3.39, and Q. 3.41.

Q. 3.78-A4. What is a "constant-voltage transformer"?

A. A "constant-voltage transformer" is a special transformer that functions to maintain a constant secondary voltage with primary voltage variations of ±15 percent.

D. These are magnetic, voltage-regulating transformers that operate on the principle of ferro resonance. They have no transistors, diodes, or moving parts. They are not manually adjustable.

Constant-voltage transformers have a wide range of ratings. They are rated from less than 1 volt-ampere (VA) at 5 V output, to several thousand volt-amperes at 115 or 230 V. They will hold their output voltages to within 1 percent with an input voltage variation of ±15 percent.

Q. 3.78-A5. With respect to power transformers, what is meant by "percent regulation"? "Efficiency"? "Power factor"?

A.

1. Transformer regulation is the ratio of the difference in secondary voltage be-

tween no load and full load, to the full-load voltage, expressed as a percentage, or

$$\text{Percent regulation} = \frac{100\,(V_{NL} - V_{FL})}{V_{FL}}$$

2. Transformer efficiency (n) is the ratio of the power out of the transformer to the power into the transformer, or

$$n = \frac{\text{Output power}}{\text{Input power}}$$

The input power is equal to the output power plus transformer losses.

3. Transformer power factor is the ratio of the transformer input power to the input volt-amperes, or

$$\text{Power factor} = \frac{\text{Input power}}{\text{Input volt-amperes}}$$

Q. 3.78-A6. If a power supply has an output voltage of 140 V at no load and the regulation at full load is 15 percent, what is the output voltage at full load?

A. The output voltage at full load is 121.73 V.

D. The equation for power supply regulation is

$$\text{Regulation} = \frac{V_{NL} - V_{FL,}}{V_{FL}}$$

where

V_{NL} = the no-load voltage.
V_{FL} = the full-load voltage.

Using the figures given in the problem, we have

$$0.15 = \frac{140 - V_{FL}}{V_{FL}}$$
$$0.15\,V_{FL} = 140 - V_{FL}$$
$$1.15\,V_{FL} = 140$$
$$V_{FL} = \frac{140}{1.15}$$
$$V_{FL} = 121.73 \text{ V}$$

D. See Q. 3.72 and Q. 3.69.

Q. 3.78-A7. Draw a schematic diagram of a transistor "inverter" power supply and explain its uses and operation.

A. For the schematic diagram, see Fig. 3.78-A7(1).

An "inverter" power supply is used to convert a dc input voltage (usually battery voltage) to an ac output voltage. If the ac voltage is rectified and filtered, we then have a dc-to-dc "converter" power supply. (See Q. 3.78-A8.) An inverter is frequently used to change a 6-V or 12-V (battery supply) to 117 V, 60-Hz ac current.

D. Refer to Fig. 3.78-A7. This is a voltage feedback, one-transformer inverter circuit. The circuit is an overdriven, push-pull, transformer-coupled oscillator. The transformer is of the *saturable-core* type. The output ac has a square waveform. The oscillator frequency depends upon the in-

*Fig. 3.78-A7. A basic, voltage feedback, one-transformer inverter circuit: (1) the schematic diagram, (2) the saturable-transformer B-H curve, and (3) the collector-to-collector voltage (V*primary*).*

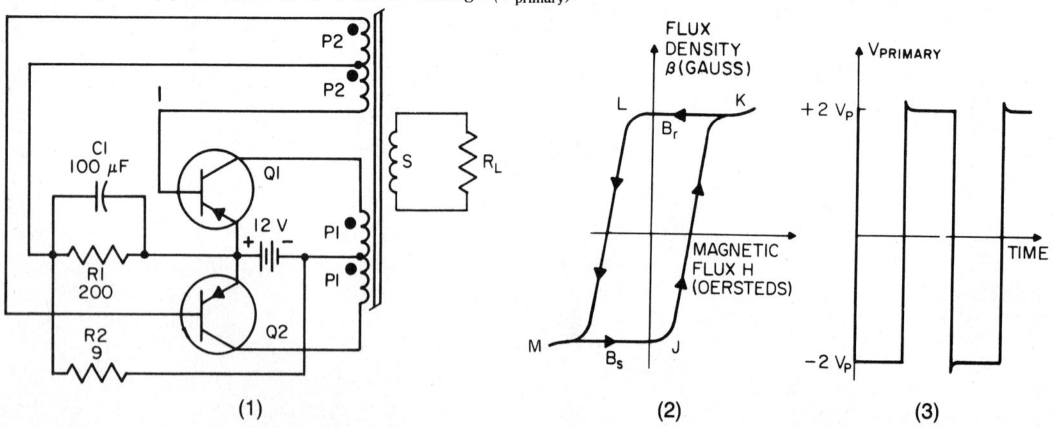

(1)   (2)   (3)

ductance of the transformer windings: the larger the inductance, the lower the frequency.

In order for the oscillator to be self-*starting*, both transistors (Q_1 and Q_2) must be forward-base biased. This base-starting bias is provided by means of the voltage dividers R_1 and R_2. Capacitor C_1 across R_1 offers a low-impedance path for the high-frequency components of the oscillating square wave. The base-starting bias for this circuit is 0.3 V for germanium transistors and 0.5 V for silicon transistors.

When power is applied to the circuit, one transistor will initially conduct more collector current (I_c) than the other. Assume this is Q_1. The expanding magnetic field produced by the I_c of Q_1 is dominant in the upper half of the transformer primary windings (P_1). As a result, a voltage is induced in the feedback windings (P_2). Now the upper P_2 winding voltage forward biases Q_1 more, and the lower P_2 winding voltage forward biases Q_1 less. This is a *regenerative* action that *very rapidly* brings Q_1 to saturation and Q_2 to cut-off. The transformer is now (negatively) saturated at point J (Fig. 3.78-A7(2).)

At this point a constant (square-wave) voltage is applied to the upper half P_1 (see Fig. 3.78-A7(3)) from Q_1. By inductive action, the flux in P_1 must *increase* at a *constant* rate from point J toward point K (positive core saturation). At point K, Q_1 can no longer supply adequate I_c. This is because the current required at point K (core saturation), plus the reflected load current, now exceeds the Q_1 saturation current (I_c).

Now the flux in the transformer begins to *collapse* from point K to point B_r. This induces voltage into N_3 such that Q_1 receives *less forward bias,* reducing its conduction (I_c). At the same time, Q_2 receives *more forward bias*, bringing it into conduction. Because of the regenerative action, Q_1 is quickly cut off and Q_2 saturates while it continues to conduct, applying a constant voltage to the lower half of N_1. The core is driven to negative saturation at point M.

At point M, Q_2 cannot supply the required current (as for Q_1 at point K), and the flux begins to collapse. This turns on Q_1 and turns off Q_2, completing the cycle.

The transformer primary waveform is a square wave, and this same waveshape appears at the secondary.

D. Many inverters have a square-wave output. This is suitable to power such devices as test equipment, shavers, phonos, stereo amplifiers, TV receivers, mobile communications equipment, radios, and small tools. Some types of equipment, such as certain motors, require a sine-wave input. Thus some inverters incorporate an added reactor and capacitors which form a true sine-wave output.

Semiconductor devices used in inverters are generally one of two types: thyristor (usually SCR) or transistor. (Some designs use both types.) Transistor inverters are generally used with dc-input voltages ranging from about 1 to 100 V. SCR inverters work best with an input voltage from 50 to 600 V dc and an input current of 1 to 20 A.

Output power ranges from 1 W to 1 kW. The range of output frequencies is from 60 Hz to 100 kHz. The output ac voltage can be almost any required value. It is determined by the input voltage and the output transformer turns ratio.

Higher-frequency outputs (where permissable) are easier to filter. They also make possible the use of smaller and lighter transformers and filters. For output power in excess of about 100 W, a two-transformer circuit may be preferable.

Q. 3.78-A8. Draw a schematic diagram of a transistor "converter" power supply for mobile radio equipment, and explain its operation.

A. The schematic diagram is shown in Fig. 3.78-A8. A "converter" is a dc-to-dc power supply. Basically it consists of an inverter (see Q. 3.78-A7) followed by one or more rectifiers and filters. The inverter frequency in this case is about 1 000 Hz.

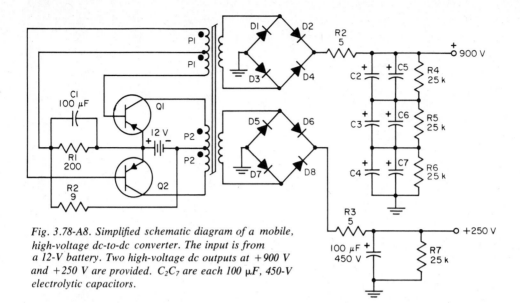

Fig. 3.78-A8. Simplified schematic diagram of a mobile, high-voltage dc-to-dc converter. The input is from a 12-V battery. Two high-voltage dc outputs at +900 V and +250 V are provided. C_2C_7 are each 100 μF, 450-V electrolytic capacitors.

This relatively high frequency permits the use of small transformers and less filtering. The inverter portion of the diagram is the same as the one described in Q. 3.78-A7.

Two secondary windings are provided on the saturable core transformer. The upper winding (S_1) is connected to a bridge rectifier (D_1-D_4). (See Q. 3.65(d) and Q. 3.66.) Filtering is provided by six series-parallel capacitors (C_2-C_7). This arrangement is used to secure adequate filtering and to insure that the capacitors operate well within their voltage rating. Resistors R_4, R_5, and R_6 form a bleeder. They also divide the output dc voltage (+900 V) equally among the filter capacitors. This +900 V dc is used for high-voltage transmitter power.

Q. 3.78-A9. How may a series circuit of silicon diodes be protected against voltage transients? Against unequal peak-reverse voltages?

A.

1. Protection against voltage transients is achieved by connecting a capacitor in shunt with each diode.

2. Protection against unequal peak-reverse voltages is achieved by connecting either a resistor or a capacitor in shunt with each diode.

D. When silicon diodes are connected in series, the most important consideration is for the applied voltage to be divided equally across the individual diodes. If an instantaneous voltage is not equally divided, one of the diodes may be subjected to an excessive reverse voltage and may be destroyed. Uniform voltage division can be achieved by connecting either a capacitor or a resistor across each diode. Resistors are used in steady-state conditions, and capacitors are used where transient voltages are expected. Both resistors and capacitors are used in shunt with each diode, if both ac and dc components are present.

Q. 3.78-A10. How is the minimum safe voltage rating determined for power supply filter capacitors?

A.

1. For a capacitor input filter, the safe voltage rating is as follows:

1.414 × rms secondary transformer voltage × 1.5 to 2 (for safety)

2. For a choke input filter, the safe voltage rating is as follows:

0.9 × rms secondary transformer voltage × 1.5 to 2 (for safety)

D. For a full-wave rectifier, the secondary transformer voltage is measured from either end of the secondary to the center tap. For a half-wave rectifier, the secondary transformer voltage is measured across the entire secondary winding.

For example, assume we have a full-wave rectifier with a *total* rms secondary voltage of 400 V. The safe dc capacitor voltage rating is:

$$\frac{400}{2} \times 1.414 \times 1.5 = 424 \text{ V (working)}$$

The term "working" voltage is commonly applied to the rating of an electrolytic filter capacitor. In this case, a standard value of 450 V could be used.

In the case of a half-wave rectifier, assume the full secondary rms voltage is 200 V. The safe dc capacitor voltage rating is

$$200 \times 0.9 \times 1.5 = 270 \text{ V}$$

A standard value of 250 V could be used in this case. (See also Q. 3.69.)

Q. 3.78-A11. Draw a simple voltage-regulating circuit using a zener diode. Label the input and output voltages and the diode-voltage rating.

A. The schematic diagram is shown in Fig. 3.78-A11. With an unregulated dc voltage input of 30 V, the output is a regulated 20 V dc.

D. The zener regulator will maintain a constant-load voltage for both varying load currents and changes in the unregulated dc input voltage. The zener does this by varying its current and thus the voltage drop across R_1. For the nominal conditions shown in Fig. 3.78-A11 the drop across R_1 is 10 V, thus the output voltage is 30 V − 10 V = 20 V. The total current through R_1 is

$$\frac{10 \text{ V}}{50 \text{ mA}} = 200 \text{ mA.}$$

Now suppose the unregulated dc voltage rises to 35 V. The additional 5 V will be dropped across R_1. The current through

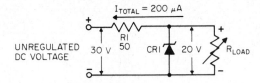

Fig. 3.78-A11. Schematic diagram of a simple voltage-regulating circuit using a zener diode.

R_1 will now be $\dfrac{15 \text{ V}}{50 \text{ ohms}} = 300$ mA. This means that the zener is now conducting an additional 100 mA, and the output voltage remains at 20 V. If the unregulated dc voltage drops, the zener conducts less current, the voltage drop across R_1 decreases, and again, the output voltage remains at 20 V.

Now consider an increase of load current through R_{Load}. This would increase the voltage drop across R_1 and tend to reduce the output voltage. However, the reduced voltage across the zener would make it draw less current, by an amount equal to the load current increase. Thus the total load current, I_{Total}, would remain at 200 mA and the output voltage at 20 V. If the load current should decrease, the drop across R_1 would decrease tending to raise the output voltage. In this case, the zener will conduct more heavily, and the total current would remain constant at 200 mA.

Of course, the ability of the zener voltage regulating circuit to maintain the constant output voltage is subject to the limitations of the circuit.

Q. 3.78-A12. Explain the use of three-terminal integrated circuit voltage (IC) regulators.

A. Three-terminal IC voltage regulators have a wide range of applications. These include (1) local on-card regulation, (2) logic systems, (3) instrumentation, (4) hi-fi, and (5) other solid-state electronic equipment.

D. These IC voltage regulators may be preadjusted for a specific output voltage, or they can be made adjustable with the addition of simple external circuitry. A typical sampling of preadjusted voltages include 5 V,

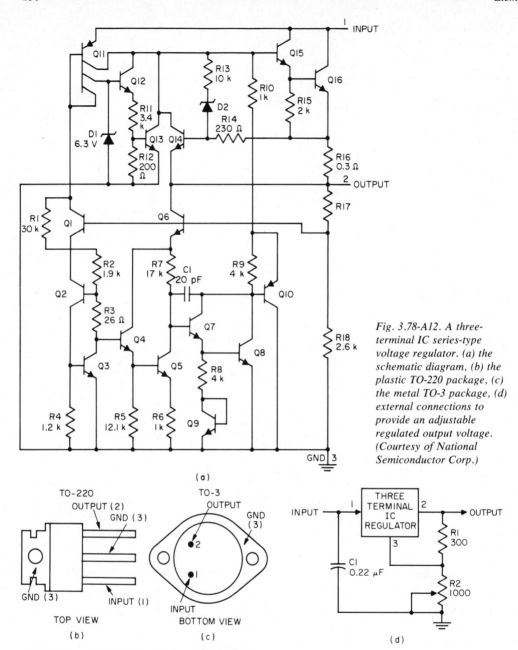

Fig. 3.78-A12. A three-terminal IC series-type voltage regulator. (a) the schematic diagram, (b) the plastic TO-220 package, (c) the metal TO-3 package, (d) external connections to provide an adjustable regulated output voltage. (Courtesy of National Semiconductor Corp.)

(a)

TO-220
OUTPUT (2)
GND (3)
GND (3)
INPUT (1)
TOP VIEW
(b)

TO-3
OUTPUT
GND (3)
2
1
INPUT
BOTTOM VIEW
(c)

INPUT   THREE
              TERMINAL
              IC
              REGULATOR   OUTPUT
C1
0.22 μF   R1
                300
                R2
                1000
(d)

6 V, 8 V, 12 V, 15 V, 18 V, and 24 V. The output current can be in excess of 1 A.

Fig. 3.78-A12 shows the schematic diagram and packages for a typical regulator. It also shows the external connections required to provide for an adjustable voltage output. These units are provided with internal thermal overload protection. Current limiting keeps the peak output current within safe limits.

Q. 3.78-A13. Draw a schematic diagram of a transistor voltage regulator using a pass transistor and a zener diode. Explain its operation.

A. A block diagram of this circuit is shown in Fig. 3.78-A13(a), and the schematic diagram in Fig. 3.78-A13(b).

D. In the Figure, Q_1 is the series-pass transistor, Q_2 is the error amplifier, and zener diode D_z, provides the fixed reference voltage required. The voltage monitor network consists of the effective resistance of R_3 and R_4. The desired output voltage is obtained by adjusting the potentiometer portion of R_3 and R_4. The element that actually controls (and stabilizes) the dc output voltage of the regulator is series-pass transistor, Q_1. Q_1 accomplishes this by changes in the voltage drop from collector to emitter, V_{CE1}. These changes add to or subtract from the output voltage (V_0), as required, to maintain a constant output voltage. Changes of V_{CE1} are caused by initial changes of the base-to-emitter voltage of Q_1, (V_{BE1}). This is discussed further below.

The output voltage will tend to rise because of either an increase of the input dc voltage V_i or a decrease in the load (increase of R_{load}). In this case, V_4 will rise. Since V_4 is the base-to-emitter voltage (V_{BE2}) for Q_2, the collector current of Q_2 will increase through R_1. This causes a drop in the base-to-emitter voltage (V_{BE1}) for Q_1, decreasing the emitter-to-collector current of Q_1. This increases the voltage drop across Q_1 (V_{CE1}), and the output voltage (V_o) is reduced to its nominal value.

The output voltage will tend to fall because of either a decrease of the input voltage V_1 or an increase in the load (decrease of R_{load}). Now V_4 will drop, as will V_{BE2}. The reduced current through Q_2 and R_1 will cause an increase of V_{BE1}. In turn, the current will increase through series-pass transistor Q_1. This decreases the voltage drop across Q_1 (V_{CE1}), and the output voltage (V_o) is increased to its nominal value.

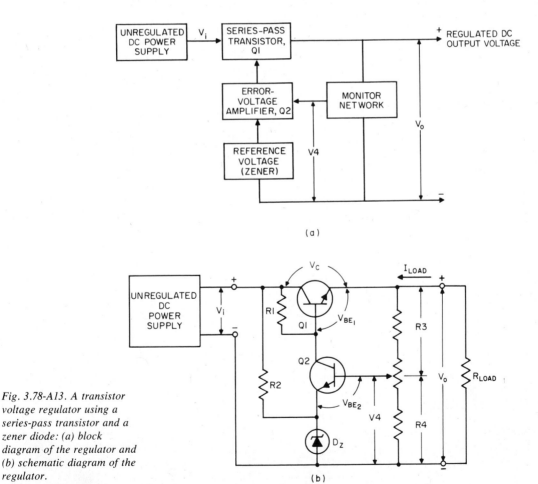

(a)

(b)

Fig. 3.78-A13. A transistor voltage regulator using a series-pass transistor and a zener diode: (a) block diagram of the regulator and (b) schematic diagram of the regulator.

Since the load current passes through Q_1, this transistor may have to dissipate appreciable amounts of power. Therefore, a power transistor is used for Q_1, which is mounted on a heat sink.

Q. 3.78-A14. What would happen if the pass transistor of a transistor voltage regulator short circuited? Draw a schematic diagram of a circuit to protect against damage to the load in the event of a pass transistor short circuit.

A.

1. If the pass transistor short-circuited and no protection circuit were present, the dc output voltage would rise. The output voltage would then assume the value of the unregulated dc power supply (V_i, in Fig. 3.78-A14).

2. The block and schematic diagrams are shown in Fig. 3.78-A14. Note that this circuit is actually a modification of the circuit of Fig. 3.78-A13.

D. The operation of the regulator circuit is the same as described in Q. 3.78-A13. Only the operation of the protection circuit is given here.

Two kinds of protection are provided by this protection circuit. (a) It protects against damage to the load in the event of a pass transistor short circuit. (b) It prevents damage to the pass transistor Q_1, in the event that excessive-load current tends to be drawn. Note that many protection circuits only protect against pass transistor damage.

Refer to the block diagram of Fig. 3.78-A14(1). Note that the protection circuit is in *series* with the negative leg of the power supply. (The same power supply current flows through the negative and positive legs.) Basically, here is how the protection circuit works. In the event of either kind of damages, the tendency is for the output voltage and current to rise. At this time (as explained below), the protection circuit acts to increase the effective series resistance of Q_3. This reduces the power supply output voltage and current to a safe value. Note that Q_3 operates only if either type of damage occurs.

1. Now refer to the schematic diagram of Fig. 3.78-A14(2). During normal operation, protection transistor Q_3 is saturated due to the selected value of R_5. Thus its emitter-to-collector resistance is practically zero. The protection circuit does not now affect the operation of the regulator. If there should be an emitter-to-collector short circuit in the series pass transistor, the output voltage (V_O) and current (I_{load}) will rise. Thus the current through R_6 and the voltage across it will increase. Normally, diode D_1 does not conduct because of its inherent reverse barrier voltage (about 0.7 V). However, increased current through R_6 due to the short-circuited Q_1 increases the voltage across R_6 sufficiently to overcome the barrier voltage. Now D_1 conducts through R_5, reducing the base voltage (and current) of Q_3, and Q_3 comes out of saturation. As a result, the emitter-to-collector resistance of Q_3 is increased and

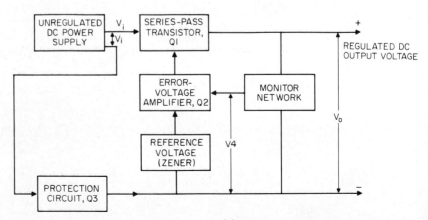

Fig. 3.78-A14. The series-regulator circuit of Fig. 3.78-A13, modified by adding a protection circuit: (1) the block diagram and (2) the schematic diagram. (See text.)

(1)

the power supply current (and voltage) is reduced to a safe value that will protect the load from damage. Resistor R_6 is preadjusted so that if Q_1 short circuits (or if there is an excessive current demand from the load), D_1 will conduct and cause the emitter-to-collector resistance of Q_3 to increase. This, of course, will limit the output current (and voltage) to a safe value.

2. The protection circuit operates to protect Q_1 from excessive load current in the same manner as described above. If the load across the regulator short-circuited, or if the load current simply increased beyond a safe value, the current through R_6 would cause D_1 to conduct and Q_3 to increase its emitter-to-collector resistance. This would, of course, limit the output current to a safe value.

Q. 3.78-A15. What is a circuit breaker?

A. A circuit breaker is a thermally activated or electromagnetic device. It functions to open a circuit automatically when the current through it exceeds its rating. It can be manually reset after the overload has been corrected. This device is not damaged (as a fuse is) by functioning to protect its load. Some types automatically reset after a specified time.

D. To protect some devices, such as TV receivers, transmitters, and power supplies, circuit breakers may be preferable to fuses because of their easy resetability. Thus the need to replace a fuse (and stock it) is eliminated.

Circuit breakers for electronic equipment are available in current ratings from 0.5 to 7 A. The tripping time under overload is a maximum of 10 sec. They can be reset by pressing on an extended rod.

Q. 3.78-A16. What is the function of cartridge-type fuses in electronic circuits?

A. Fuses are inserted in series with circuit leads that pass current from a power source to a load. They function to protect specific parts or circuits against overloads or short circuits.

D. Fuses are *overcurrent* protective devices. They are almost zero resistance devices while carrying currents within their normal ratings. However, should *overcurrent* occur through the fuse, a circuit-opening *fusible* part is heated and *severed,* thus providing protection for the load.

Common "blowing" specifications for the standard cartridge fuses are: (1) 110 percent of rating, 4 hours minimum; (2) 135 percent of rating, 1 hour maximum; (3) 200 percent of rating, 10 seconds maximum.

Q. 3.78-A17. What are the common categories of fuses with regard to "blowing" time?

A. These may be generally listed as:
1. Slow-blow fuses.
2. Medium-lag fuses.

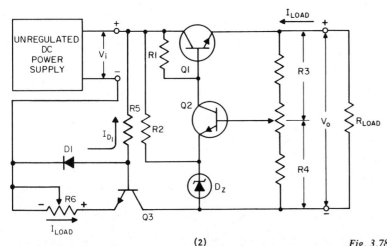

(2)

Fig. 3.78-A14 (cont.)

3. Standard-blow fuses.

4. Fast-action instrument fuses.

D.

1. Slow-blow fuses have a high time lag to withstand high current surges. However, they blow quickly upon short circuits.

2. Medium-lag fuses may be used for TVs, amplifiers, and similar equipment. Some are steatite-enclosed and filled with arc-quenching powder. They are shatter-proofed against quick shorts.

3. Standard-blow fuses are used for TVs, radios, amplifiers, and transmitters. They are unaffected by high operating temperatures.

4. Fast action instrument fuses have the highest blowing speed. This feature makes them ideal for protecting delicate equipment, ammeters, wattmeters, radio and TV B+ circuits, small rectifiers, and power tubes.

Two types of fast-blow fuses are used to protect power tubes. They are "exploding wire" and "exothermic" fuses. Exploding wire fuses require several milliseconds to operate. Exothermic fuses have faster action. Exothermic fuses depend upon the heating of a *chemical* to open the circuit. These may be called simply "chemical fuses."

Cartridge fuses may be enclosed in glass (most common), ceramic, or fiber. Their sizes range from 0.25×1.25-inch down to 0.145×0.300-inch (sub-miniature pigtail fuses, glass-enclosed and hermetically sealed).

"Indicating" fuses have a silverplated pin that pops out when the fuse is blown. This pin can be used to activate an alarm.

Q. 3.78-A18. How are fuses rated?

A. Fuses are rated as follows:

1. Current rating.

2. Voltage rating.

3. Blowing speed (see Q. 3.78-A16 and Q. 3.78-A17).

D.

1. Slow-blow fuses are rated from 1.2 to 30 A, medium-lag fuses from 5 to 25 A, standard-blow fuses from 2 to 30 A, and fast-action fuses from 1/500 to 5 A.

2. The voltage rating is the maximum voltage that should appear across an *open* fuse. This prevents open-fuse arcing, which would defeat the purpose of the fuse. Common voltage ratings are 32, 125, and 250 V. *High-voltage* fuses are available. These protect circuits up to 20 kW on dc and 30 kVA on ac. The current rating ranges from 1/16 to 2 A.

INDICATING INSTRUMENTS

Q. 3.79. Make a sketch showing the construction of the D'Arsonval-type meter and label the various parts. Draw a circuit diagram of a vacuum-tube-voltmeter and a wattmeter.

A.

1. For the sketch of a D'Arsonval meter, see Fig. 3.79(a). The D'Arsonval type of meter consists of three basic parts: (1) a permanent magnet, (2) a movable coil with pointer attached, rotating in jewel bearings, (3) two spiral springs, one at each side of the movable coil. The current to be measured is caused to flow through the movable coil, connection to which is made through the two spiral springs. The magnetic field set up in the movable coil is proportional to the current flowing through it, and causes the coil to turn against the two spiral springs by reacting against the field of the permanent magnet. The amount of coil rotation (and needle), therefore, depends upon the motor force developed to overcome the resistance of the spiral springs. The movable coil rotates about a stationary soft iron core, to increase the magnetic force and thus the sensitivity of the meter. The movable coil is wound of very fine silk covered copper wire upon a light aluminum frame. The frame also performs the function of damping. As the coil moves in the permanent magnetic field, eddy currents are set up in the frame which in turn produce magnetic fields tending to oppose the original field of the permanent magnet, thus tending to stop the rotation. Without such damping, the needle would oscillate many times before finally coming to rest at the proper reading.

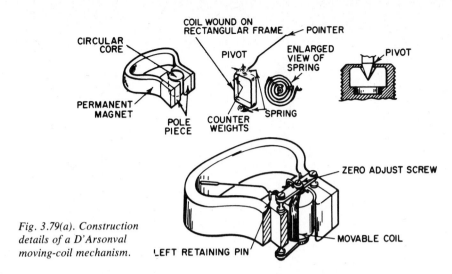

Fig. 3.79(a). Construction details of a D'Arsonval moving-coil mechanism.

2. For the circuit diagram of a vacuum-tube voltmeter, see Fig. 3.79(b). The major advantage of a vacuum-tube voltmeter over a conventional (simple) voltmeter is the VTVM's high input resistance which is commonly 11 megohms on all scales. The vacuum-tube voltmeter thus draws negligible current from the circuit being tested and thereby avoids erroneous readings. Generally speaking, the impedance of the meter should be ten times greater than that of the circuit it is shunting for test. Contrast the 11-megohm impedance on a 1.5-volt scale of a VTVM, with the 30 000-ohm impedance of a 20 000-ohm-per-volt meter, and with the 1 500-ohm impedance of a 1 000-ohm-per-volt meter. This last meter, measuring voltage across a one megohm resistor, would provide a completely erroneous reading by changing the circuit impedance from 1 000 000 ohms to approximately 1 500 ohms.

3. For the circuit diagram of a watt-meter, see Fig. 379(c).

A wattmeter is basically a voltmeter and an ammeter so connected that power factor is automatically compensated for in the indicating device. The usual type of wattmeter consists of two stationary coils made of a few turns of heavy wire which are connected in series with each other and with the line, and a movable coil inside of the two fixed ones, which is connected in series with a high resistance across the line as a voltmeter. The current in the stationary coils produces a field which is proportional to the line current, while the current in the movable coil produces a field which is proportional to the line voltage. The torque tending to deflect the needle of the moving coil is proportional to the product of the instantaneous line voltage and current, or to the instantaneous power. However, the

Fig. 3.79(b). Simplified diagram of a balanced triode dc vacuum-tube-voltmeter.

Fig. 3.79(c). Circuit diagram of a wattmeter.

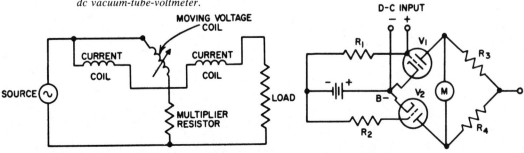

moving element has sufficient damping so that the needle indicates only the *average* power, and thus compensates for power factor. Wattmeters of this type may be used on either ac or dc.

Q. 3.80. Show by a digram how a voltmeter and ammeter should be connected to measure power in a dc circuit.

A. For the diagram, see Fig. 3.80

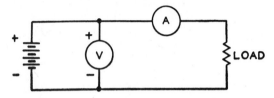

Fig. 3.80. Dc power measurement with voltmeter and ammeter.

D. In a dc circuit, as shown, the power in watts is equal to the product of the voltage in volts and the current in amperes, or

$$P = V \times I$$

Q. 3.81. If a 0-1 dc milliammeter is to be converted into a voltmeter with a full scale calibration of 100 volts, what value of resistance should be connected in series with the milliammeter?

A. The series resistance should equal 100,000 ohms, minus the meter resistance which is usually small enough to neglect in this case.

D. The value of series resistance can be found from the formula,

$$R = \frac{V \text{ (full scale)}}{I \text{ (full scale)}} = \frac{100}{0.001}$$

$$= 100\ 000 \text{ ohms}$$

All standard voltmeters are basically milliammeters or microammeters. The resistance of the meter would probably not be known, but could be measured if equipment were available. However, the full scale current rating is always available on the face of the meter. Neglecting the meter resistance, the value of multiplier resistor could be calculated from

$$R = \frac{V_{fs}}{I_{fs}}$$

where

R = the value of multiplier resistance.
V_{fs} = the full-scale voltage reading desired.
I_{fs} = the full-scale current rating of the meter in question.

Q. 3.82. A 1-milliampere meter having a resistance of 25 ohms was used to measure an unknown current by shunting the meter with a 4 ohm resistor. It then read 0.4 milliampere. What was the unknown current value?

A. The unknown current was 2.9 milliamperes.

D. A basic formula to use in these problems is

$$R_m I_m = R_s I_s$$

where

R_m = resistance of the meter.
I_m = current flowing in the meter.
R_s = resistance of the shunt.
I_s = current in the shunt.

This is because $R_m I_m$ is the voltage across the meter ($V = IR$) and $R_s I_s$ is the voltage across the shunt. The two voltages must be the same because the two are connected. The meter drop is $R_m I_m = 25 \times 0.0004 = 0.01$ volt.

Then $R_s I_s = 0.01$ $I_s = \dfrac{0.01}{4} = 0.0025$ A

Both together take 0.0025 A + 0.0004 A = 2.9 milliamperes, the total current.

Q. 3.83. An RF VTVM is available to locate resonance of a tunable primary tank circuit of an RF transformer. If the VTVM is measuring the voltage across the tuned secondary, how would resonance of the primary be indicated?

A. Resonance will be indicated by the peak reading of the meter.

D. At resonance the primary tank will offer maximum impedance to the wave and therefore the maximum voltage will be developed across it and coupled to the secondary.

Q. 3.84. Define the following terms and describe a practical situation in which they might be used.

1. **RMS voltage.**
2. **Peak current.**
3. **Average current.**
4. **Power.**
5. **Energy.**

A.

1. RMS (or root-mean-square) is also known as the "effective" value of a waveform. In the case of a sine wave, it equals 0.707 of the peak value of the wave. Many meters are calibrated in terms of RMS values because this is the "working" or "heating" value of the current. The effective value of an ac current is that value which would cause the same heating effect as a dc current of the same numerical value.

2. The peak current of any waveform is the greatest instantaneous value of the current. For a sine wave, the peak current equals 1.414 times the RMS value.

Peak currents are important in rectifying devices. The rated peak value should not be exceeded to avoid damage.

3. The average current in an ac circuit is equal to 0.636 of the peak value, or 0.9 of the RMS value.

The rotation of the moving coil in a dc meter is proportional to the average value of current flowing in it. However, the scale is generally calibrated in the effective (RMS) value, which is the working or heating value of the current.

4. Electrical power is the *rate* of doing work (the rate of expending energy) by electricity. Electrical power is measured by a unit called the *watt*. One watt is the power expended in heat in a circuit when a current of 1 ampere (6.28×10^{18} electrons per second) flows through a resistance of 1 ohm. One watt is 1 joule per second.

5. Electrical energy is the *capacity* or *ability* to accomplish work by electricity. ("Work" in this sense includes production of heat, or conversion into any other form of energy.) Electrical energy is measured by a unit called the *joule*. Energy in electrical circuits is transferred into the form of heat. A joule is the *amount* of energy expended in moving 1 coulomb (6.28×10^{18}) of electricity through a resistance of 1 ohm. One joule = 0.7376 ft pound; 3 600 joules = 1 watt-hour.

Q. 3.85. Describe how horizontal and vertical deflection takes place in a cathode ray oscilloscope. Include a discussion of the waveforms involved.

A. The usual test oscilloscope has a cathode ray tube utilizing electrostatic deflection plates. (This discussion is keyed to the illustration in Fig. 3.85.)

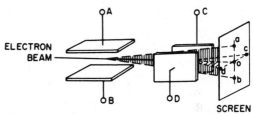

Fig. 3.85. *Deflection plates for electrostatic cathode ray tube.*

There are two sets of deflection plates, the vertical deflecting plates (A-B) and the horizontal deflecting plates (C-D). The effect of these deflection plates is based on the fact that an electron beam can be deflected by an electrostatic field. The negative electron beam will be attracted toward the positive plate and repelled from the negative plate. Since the beam is accelerated toward the screen, its electrons are merely shifted in their path and are not ordinarily picked up by the positive deflection plate. If plate A is more positive than plate B, the beam will be deflected upward and will strike the point "a" on the screen. If the potentials are equal (or zero), the beam will strike point "o." Conversely, if plate B is more positive than plate A, the beam will strike at point "b." In the same manner, the beam may be moved horizontally from point "d" to point "c" on the screen.

In practice, a sawtooth deflection voltage is applied to plates C-D. This causes a relatively slow movement of the beam from "d" to "c" and a much more rapid return of the beam from "c" to "d." The rate of this movement is synchronized with the waveform repetition rate of the input waveform to be viewed. This waveform is applied to the vertical deflecting plates, and may be any wave within the limitations of the oscilloscope. The combination of the horizontal (sweep) movement and the vertical signal input causes the input waveform to be traced out on the screen.

Note: The following added material numbered Q. 3.85-A1 through Q. 3.85-A22 contains information that may be required to pass the General Radiotelephone Operator's License examination. This added material, as well as the new material added to other sections, has been included to help acquaint students with the current state of the electronics art. It is felt that the added material contains subject matter that may also be required of students who have obtained a General Radiotelephone Operator's License and are seeking employment. Additionally, the added material contains valuable information for private technician certification.

Q. 3.85-A1. Explain the meaning of "ohms-per-volt" in reference to a voltmeter.

A. "Ohms-per-volt" is a measure of voltmeter sensitivity. For example, current meters having a full-scale deflection of 1 mA are used as voltmeters. This meter, without a *series-multiplier* resistor, will measure 1 V full scale. Its sensitivity is

$$\text{Ohms-per-volt} = \frac{1 \text{ V}}{\text{Full-scale current}}$$

$$= \frac{1 \text{ V}}{1 \times 10^{-3}}$$

$$= 1\ 000 \text{ ohms per volt } (\Omega/\text{V})$$

To find the resistance of the above meter for any voltage scale, simply multiply the full-scale voltage by the sensitivity. For example, for a 100 V full-scale reading, the sensitivity is $100 \times 1\ 000 = 100\ 000$ ohms-per-volt. Thus, with a 100 000Ω resistor placed in series, the 1 000 ohms-per-volt meter can measure 100 V full scale. This resistor is what we referred to as a series-multiplier resistor (or simply a "multiplier"). The required multiplier for other desired full-scale readings can be calculated in the same manner.

Another meter, which is considerably more accurate in high-impedance circuits, is one that has a full-scale current range of 50 μA (50×10^{-6} μA). This meter will also measure 1 V full scale without a multiplier. Its sensitivity is

$$\text{Ohms-per-volt} = \frac{1 \text{ V}}{\text{Full-scale current}}$$

$$= \frac{1}{50 \times 10^{-6}}$$

$$= 20\ 000 \text{ ohms-per-volt}$$

To measure 100 V with this meter, we need a multiplier with a resistance of $100 \times 20\ 000 = 2\ 000\ 000$ Ω. Note the much higher resistance here, which will cause considerably less loading of the circuit to be measured.

D. In calculating the multiplier for any range, bear in mind that the resistance value as calculated should, strictly speaking, include the resistance of the meter itself. However, from a practical standpoint this is not necessary (except perhaps for very low voltage ranges). This is true because the actual meter resistance will generally be negligible compared to the multiplier resistance.

To maintain the accuracy of the meter, precision multipliers should be used. However, because of the cost, it is generally satisfactory to use 1-percent composition resistors. (See also Q. 3.79 and Q 3.81.)

Q. 3.85-A2. Draw a diagram of a simple ohmmeter and explain its operation.

A. The schematic diagram is shown in Fig. 3.85-A2(1).

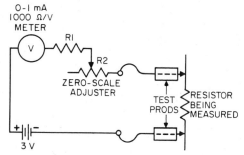

Fig. 3.85-A2(1). Schematic diagram of a simple ohmmeter.

A simple ohmmeter, as shown in the figure, consists of a voltmeter, multiplier resistance R_1, zero-scale adjuster R_2, and a 3-V battery. When the probes are shorted together (zero resistance), the zero-scale adjuster (R_1) is set so that the meter reads *full scale* (3 V). However, on the ohmmeter scale, this point is marked O Ω (see Fig. 3.85-A2(2). Assuming the meter has a sensitivity of 1 000 ohms-per-volt (1.0 mA full scale), the total resistance of R_1+R_2

$$= \frac{3 \text{ V}}{1 \text{ mA}} = 3\,000 \text{ } \Omega.$$ If the two probes are now connected across a 3 000-Ω resistor, the total resistance in the circuit is now 6 000 Ω. The meter current drops to half and the needle to half scale. This is marked as 3 000 Ω in Fig. 3.85-A2(2).

The meter deflection can be computed from

$$D = \frac{R_1 + R_2}{(R_1 + R_2) + R_X} \times 100$$

Fig. 3.85-A2(2). A typical ohmmeter scale. Note that O Ω is at the right (full scale) and infinite ohms at the left (open circuit).

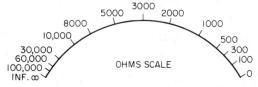

where

D = meter deflection in percent.
$R_1 + R_2$ = total multiplier resistance.
R_X = ohmic value of unknown resistance.

For example, if the probes are held across a 10 000-Ω resistance, then

$$D = \frac{3\,000}{3\,000 + 10\,000} \times 100$$
$$= 23 \text{ percent}$$

D. A simple ohmmeter (as depicted here) will not read resistance values accurately above about 60 000 Ω, since this represents only a 5-percent deflection. Neither will it give accurate readings under about 100 Ω. Somewhat more elaborate circuits will provide accurate readings from 1 Ω to several megohms. A 20 000 ohm-per-volt meter (50 μA) is generally used in the latter case.

R_2 in Fig. 3.85-A2(1) is made adjustable to compensate for differing battery terminal voltages and also for battery aging (voltage drop-off). Before each ohmmeter use, it is necessary to hold the probes together and adjust R_2 for full scale. This assures accurate ohmmeter readings. (See also Q. 3.79, Q. 3.81, Q. 3.85-A1.)

Q. 3.85-A3. What is a multimeter?

A. A multimeter is an instrument having a number of measuring functions. These frequently include: (1) ac and dc voltages, (2) ac and dc currents, (3) dc resistances, and (4) decibel measurements.

D. The two general types of multimeters are *analog* and *digital*. An *analog* multimeter provides measurement indications over a *continuous* range, typically, by means of a meter movement. The needle of the meter movement is caused to move across the face of calibrated scales.

A *digital* multimeter provides measurement indications directly in discrete numbers. This is generally provided by a panel containing a number of LEDs (light-emitting diodes). (See also Q. 3.85-A4 and Q. 3.85-A5.)

Q. 3.85-A4. What are some important characteristics of a solid-state (FET) analog multimeter?

A. A typical solid-state analog (meter-type) multimeter incorporates FETs, an IC, and LEDs. It provides automatic polarity indication, as well as overvoltage and over-current protection. The instrument can be operated from the ac line, a self-contained rechargeable battery, or a "D" size flashlight cell.

D. Typical meter ranges are as follows (in steps):

1. Ac or dc voltages (on same scale): 0.03 V to 300 V. 1 000 V ac and 1 000 V dc ranges available on separate jacks.

2. Input resistance: 10 MΩ on all switchable ac and dc ranges: 31.9 MΩ on the 1 000 V ranges.

3. Ac, dc current ranges: 30 μA to 30 mA. 1 A and 10 A ranges available on separate jacks.

4. DB ranges: −50 dB to +62 dB. (OdB reference is 0.775 V across 600 Ω (1 mW).)

5. Ohms range: 0.2 Ω to 1 000 MΩ.

6. Accuracy of readings = ± 2 to 3 percent, full scale.

The LEDs on the meter panel provide automatic indication of positive or negative dc voltages or currents.

Q. 3.85-A5. What are some disadvantages of analog multimeters? How do digital multimeters overcome these disadvantages?

A. Analog meters are widely used and very practical. However, they do have several disadvantages. Some of these are: (1) difficulty in locating and reading the correct scale, (2) interpolation between printed numbers, (3) limited accuracy and (4) possible parallax errors.

Digital multimeters overcome all these disadvantages. These instruments have large, easily read numbers, and automatic placing of the decimal point. A plus or minus sign appears before the numbers. This indicates the polarity of the measured voltage, au-

tomatically. Accuracies of 0.1 percent to 0.5 percent are common for digital multimeters, ± 2 or 3 percent for analog multimeters.

D. See Q. 3.85-A3 and Q. 3.85-A6.

Q. 3.85-A6. What are some important specifications of a typical basic analog multimeter?

A. The following are some important specifications of a typical basic analog multimeter. (This is *not* an "electronic" multimeter, which employs FETs or vacuum tubes.)

1. Sensitivity: 20 000 Ω/V dc meter deflects to full scale with a current of 50 μA. (For example, On a 10-V scale, input impedance is 20 000 × 10 = 200 000 Ω.)

2. Accuracy: dc = ± 3 percent full scale;, ac = ± 4 percent full scale.

3. Ac or dc voltage (in steps), 2.5 to 1 000 V.

4. Dc current (in steps), 10 to 1 000 mA.

5. Fuse protected ohms range.

6. Ohms range: 0.5 to 10 MΩ (in steps).

(Some units have a decibel scale.)

D. See Q. 3.85-A3, Q. 3.85-A4, and Q.3.85-A5.

Q. 3.85-A7. What are some important specifications and characteristics of a digital multimeter?

A. The following are important specifications of a typical digital multimeter.

1. *Meter Ranges* The limits of the various digital multimeter ranges are as follows (in steps):

a. Dc voltage: 0.2 V to 1 000 V (plus or minus polarity). (Reads from 100 μV to 1 000 V.) Accuracy, 0.5 percent ± 1 digit.

b. Ac voltage (40 Hz to 20 kHz): 0.2 V to 600 V. (Reads from 100 μV to 600 V.) Accuracy, 1.5 percent ± 1 digit.

c. Resistance, low power (max. 350 MV): 2 kΩ to 2 000 kΩ. (Reads from 1 Ω to 2 M/Ω.) Accuracy, 1 percent ± 1 digit.

d. Resistance, standard power (max. 2.5 V): 2 kΩ to 20 M/Ω. (Reads from 1 Ω to 20 M/Ω.) Accuracy, 1 percent ± 1 digit.

e. Dc current: 0.2 mA to 10 A. (Reads from 100 nA to 10 A.) Accuracy 1 percent ± 1 digit.

f. Ac current: 0.2 mA to 10 A. (Reads from 100 nA to 10 A.) Accuracy 1.5 percent ± 1 digit.

2. *Input Impedance:* 15 MΩ, 30 pF.

3. *Frequency Response:* 40 Hz to 3 kHz(± 1 dB).

4. *Display:* 3½ digit, 0.3 in LEDs.

5. *Features:* Automatic polarity, decimal, and overrange indications. Has autoranging.

D. *Autoranging*: Many digital voltmeters have a feature known as "autoranging." This indicates that for all ac and dc voltage and current measurements, as well as resistance measurements, the meter automatically switches to the correct range required to perform the specific measurement. Other units without autoranging provide push buttons to select the desired range.

3½ Digits: Many digital multimeters have a display rating of "3½" digits. With a three-digit meter, the maximum display number is 999. The decimal point is always correctly positioned automatically. Other three-digit displays could be 1.23, 9.99, 67.8, etc.

For relatively little added expense and circuitry, an additional digit can be provided to appear *in front* of the above-mentioned three digits. The added digit can only be programmed to be either unlighted (no reading) or to indicate a 1. If energized, this so-called "½ " digit can practically double the reading for a particular range. Thus a 1-V range could now read 1.999 V; for all practical purposes, a 2 V range. Similarly, a 100 kΩ range could now read 199.9 kΩ (almost 200 kΩ).

Q. 3.85-A8. What is a digital frequency counter?

A. A digital frequency counter is an instrument that measures the frequency of a wave and displays the result digitally on an LED display.

D. A digital frequency counter is a convenient and accurate means of measuring frequencies. Other frequency-measuring procedures that utilize either WWV and a frequency meter, or a calibrated-absorbtion wavemeter, or a heterodyne-frequency meter are much more lengthy and difficult. With the digital frequency counter, no calibration prcedures are required. The correct frequency is instantly displayed on the LED panel.

A digital frequency counter can measure the frequency of virtually any shape of repetitive wave. It measures by counting each cycle of a signal for a precise interval of time (the time base). Further details are given below.

Block Diagram: A simplified block diagram of a digital frequency counter is shown in Fig. 3.85-A8. The input wave (regardless of form) is fed into the *signal conditioner* circuits. The output of these circuits is one (and only one) electrical pulse per input cycle. These output pulses have a constant amplitude and width to properly drive the decade counters.

The output pulses from the signal conditioner are fed to a "signal gate" which is controlled by a *precise* timebase generator. The signal gate opens only for *precise* periods, to pass the signal conditioner output

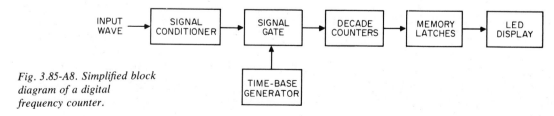

Fig. 3.85-A8. Simplified block diagram of a digital frequency counter.

pulses through to the decade counters. These precise periods are repetitive in nature. Typical periods are 1 s and 0.1 s (selectable on front panel). Thus, if a 1-s gate passes 1 000 000 pulses, the counter reads 1 MHz.

The gated pulse output from the "signal gate" is fed into a set of decade counters, which total the input pulses. For example, a typical digital frequency counter may have an eight-digit LED display. Here, eight decade counters are employed, each one corresponding to a digit position on the LED panel. The decade counters step up the count as the pulses come through. For example, the "ones" counter counts from 0 through 9, automatically resets to 0, and "carries" a 10 to the "tens" counter. The tens counter counts from 10 to 90, automatically resets to 10, and "carries" a 100 to the "hundreds" counter. This process continues until all the pulses within the gate period are counted.

The next step is to feed the eight digits into individual memory latches. The memory latches store each digit's information and activate the eight LEDs with the proper digits representing the measured frequency.

Automatic circuits place the decimal point and light indicators reading "Hz" or "MHz," depending upon the input frequency.

Applications: Some applications of a digital frequency counter are:

1. Measuring digital-counting circuits.

2. Measuring phase-locked loop (PLL) circuits.

3. Setting and checking oscillator frequency and stability for crystal and LC oscillators.

4. Calibration of tone-activated control systems.

5. Calibration of microprocessor systems.

6. Adjustment of cable television (CATV) modulator frequencies.

Typical Specifications:

1. Frequency range (depends on the particular model): Some typical models offer ranges of: (a) 100 Hz to 30 MHz (small hand-held unit), (b) 5 Hz to 80 MHz, (c) 5 Hz to 520 mHz using prescaler (prescaler divides high frequencies to be within normal range of the counter), (d) some counters can measure frequencies above 40 GHz, by using frequency-dividing or "zero-beating" techniques.

2. Sensitivity: 25 mV rms, or 75 mV peak-to-peak with minimum pulse width of 200 ns.

3. Resolution: $\pm$ LSD (least significant digit).

4. Accuracy: $\pm$ LSD $\pm$ (time-base error) $\times$ Frequency.

5. Impedance: 50 Ω or 1 MΩ (switchable).

6. Signal Operating Range: ± 2 V to -2 V.

7. Number of digits displayed: (depends on model) 5, 6, 7, 8, or 9.

Q. 3.85-A9. Briefly discuss some important characteristics of dynamic vacuum tube testers.

A. A typical dynamic vacuum tube tester can perform the following tests:

1. Dynamic-mutual conductance (gm).

2. Gas, grid emission, and grid-to-cathode leakage.

3. Life test (with 10 percent reduced operating voltages).

D. The types of tubes that can be tested with a dynamic vacuum tube tester include:

1. Almost all TV and radio tubes. A meter indication of "GOOD-?-BAD" is actually in terms of the tube's mutual conductance (gm).

2. All new and less popular tube types (by setting the program switches in accordance with the updated charts).

3. High-voltage and gas regulator tubes.

4. Nuvistors, Novars, Magnovals, 10-pin tubes, 12-pin Compactrons.

5. Imported high-fidelity tubes.

6. Industrial and special applications tubes.

Some of these testers feature automatic line voltage compensation for reliable and repeatable test results.

Leakage paths up to 1 MΩ will light a "SHORTS" lamp. The tester's meter may detect leakage currents as low as 0.5 μA.

These testers are commonly furnished with charts indicating tester settings for possibly several thousand tubes.

Note: Many tube tester manufacturers provide a new tube information service to continually update the usefulness of their instruments.

Q. 3.85-A10. Explain how the intensity of the trace of a cathode ray tube is varied.

A. Refer to the simplified drawing of a cathode ray tube (CRT) used in an oscilloscope, in Fig. 3.85-A10. For simplicity, the horizontal and vertical deflection plates are not shown. (For these, see Fig. 3.85.) The intensity of the trace is varied by making the cathode more or less positive with respect to the grid. (This has the same effect as making the grid more or less negative with respect to the cathode.) As the cathode is made more positive, few electrons can be accelerated through the grid opening by the accelerating anode and thus few reach the fluorescent screen. This causes a reduction of display intensity. The opposite effect is also true.

Fig. 3.85-A10. Simplified drawing of a cathode ray tube (CRT). The deflection plates are not shown.

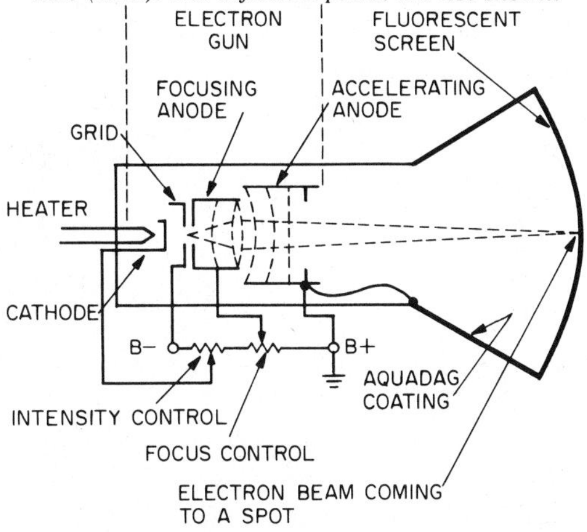

D. In Fig. 3.85-A10, we show the *electron gun,* fluorescent screen, internal aquadag (carbon) coating, and glass envelope. The deflection plates (not shown here, see Fig. 3.85) are positioned just to the right of the accelerating anode.

The electron gun consists of the heater, cathode, grid, focusing anode, and accelerating anode. Its function is to generate, control, focus, and accelerate an electron beam that will arrive at the fluorescent screen as a very fine stream. The finer the stream and the illuminated spot it produces, the more detailed display that is possible.

The heated cathode emits electrons from a small circular area on its surface. The electrons are attracted in the direction of the focusing and accelerating anodes because these are at increasing positive potentials. They pass through a small opening in the grid cylinder. (The action of the grid has been discussed above.) Because of the shape and dimensions of the focus and accelerating anodes and of their respective potentials, an *electrostatic lens* is created. The effect of this lens on the electron stream is similar to that of an optical lens on light rays. By virtue of the electrostatic lens action, the electrons are focused to a fine point when they impinge upon the fluorescent screen. The accelerating anode (at 1 000 to 2 500 V) has the additional function of causing the electron beam to attain high velocity before striking the fluorescent screen. The higher the velocity, the brighter will be the spot on the screen. Note in Fig. 3.85-A10, that the aquadag coating on the inside forward portion of the glass envelope is electrically connected to the accelerating anode potential. This connection assists in the electron acceleration. In addition, secondary electrons released from the screen, due to the electron beam striking it, are picked up by the aquadag coating and returned to the power supply.

Cathode ray tubes are made in a variety of sizes, ranging from about 1 in. to 12 in. or more in diameter, for oscilloscope use.

Q. 3.85-A11. What are some of the general classifications of oscilloscopes?

A. Some general classifications are:

1. Single-trace oscilloscope.

2. Dual-trace oscilloscope.

3. Free-running sweep (recurrent sweep) oscilloscope.

4. Triggered-sweep oscilloscope.

5. CRT-storage oscilloscopes.

6. Digital-storage oscilloscopes.

D.

1. A single-trace oscilloscope is one on which the observed waveform is traced out on a single baseline. Only one waveform at a time can be viewed.

2. A dual-trace oscilloscope is one on which two separate waveforms are traced out on two separate baselines, one beneath the other. The two waveforms can be compared for shape, timing, and relative amplitudes.

3. A free-running sweep (recurrent sweep) oscilloscope is one in which a sweep line is always present, whether or not a signal is being viewed. When a signal is viewed, it is also used to synchronize the sweep rage.

4. A triggered-sweep oscilloscope is one in which no sweep is present without the input of the test signal. As each test signal waveform appears, it triggers the start of a sweep. A delay line delays the appearance of the viewed signal so its leading edge can be seen in its entirety.

5. A CRT-storage oscilloscope will retain a waveform for up to several hours at a time. Two general types are:

a. Bistable-CRT storage. In this type, the phosphor will glow for several hours or until erased by the operator.

b. Storage-mesh type: Here the electron beam (writes) the waveform on a storage mesh. Then an electron gun in the CRT "paints" the waveform on the screen in accordance with the electrical pattern on the storage mesh.

Most bistable storage oscilloscopes have *split screens*. Thus a reference waveform can be stored on one half of the screen.

The other half can be used to see the effect of changes being made in a circuit.

6. Digital-storage oscilloscopes store waveforms in a digital memory. They are easy to use and provide crisp, clear displays. The storage time is essentially unlimited. These oscilloscopes can perform certain functions not possible with other types of storage oscilloscopes. Some of these are:

a. Viewing events prior to the trigger.

b. Capturing events when the oscilloscope is unattended.

c. Dump its waveforms into a computer memory for permanent storage.

d. Signal processing, including rms calculations and averaging several samples of the signal.

e. Catch quick transient events for long storage periods.

Q. 3.85-A12. Draw a simple block diagram of an oscilloscope and explain its operation.

A. For the block diagram, see Fig. 3.85-A12. As shown in the block diagram, a basic oscilloscope consists of four sections: (1) the vertical section, (2) the horizontal section, (3) the trigger system, and (4) the display (or CRT) system.

1. *Vertical Section:* The vertical section provides the display (CRT) system with the "Y" or vertical axis of information for the waveform on the CRT screen. The input to the vertical section is the signal to be viewed. The vertical section amplifies the signal and develops vertical deflection voltages that deflect the CRT electron beam in the vertical direction. The vertical system also provides the signals for the trigger system (discussed below).

In a dual-trace oscilloscope, the vertical system consists of two identical channels. Each channel can cause a waveform to be displayed on its particular sweep.

The vertical system must not only amplify the test signal, it must also produce minimum amplitude and phase distortion of the test signal. In addition, it must have adequate frequency responses in order not to distort the test signal. The frequency response may be from about 1 to 100 mHz depending upon the specific oscilloscope and its required uses.

To control the sensitivity of each vertical channel, a "volts/division" attenuator *switch* is provided. Thus the oscilloscope will be capable of accurately displaying input signal levels ranging from a few millivolts to many volts. The volts/division switch is calibrated in terms of volts per each major division of the graticule. For example, with a setting of 2 mV, each major graticule division will represent 2 mV and the eight vertical divisions can then display 16 mV.

2. *Horizontal Section:* To produce a waveform, an oscilloscope must have the means to cause the CRT to trace in the horizontal as well as in the vertical direction. The function of the horizontal section is to provide deflection voltages to move the CRT beam horizontally.

In many modern triggered-sweep oscilloscopes, the horizontal section contains a sweep generator (or time base) that produces a *linear* sawtooth wave (ramp). This deflection wave moves the CRT beam *linearly* across the CRT with respect to time. This means that the horizontal beam movement can be calibrated directly in *units of time*. This makes it possible to accurately measure the width of waveforms in time. The time intervals that can be measured may vary from nanoseconds and microseconds to several seconds, depending upon the particular oscilloscope.

With a triggered-sweep oscilloscope, a "seconds/division" switch is provided. This switch permits you to select the rate at which the beam sweeps across the CRT screen. By changing the switch settings, you can look at shorter or longer time intervals of the input signal. The markings on this switch refer to the calibration marks on the graticule. For example, if this switch is set to 1 ms, each horizontal major division represents

one millisecond. Also the total horizontal graticule represents 10 ms.

Many oscilloscopes offer a means of "horizontal magnification." As the term implies, this feature gives you a faster sweep speed (example $10\times$). By this means, the input signal is effectively "stretched" to examine details that are close together.

In oscilloscopes with recurrent (non-triggered) sweep, sweep rates are provided for horizontal frequencies ranging from about 1 Hz to 100 kHz. However, in this type of oscilloscope, the horizontal sweep is not calibrated accurately in time.

3. *Trigger Section:* With a triggered-sweep oscilloscope, each horizontal sweep must be started at exactly the same time relative to the signal being viewed. This ensures that a single, clear pattern will appear on the screen. In addition, it makes it possible to measure time intervals on the screen.

With a recurrent-sweep oscilloscope, we must synchronize the sweep rate to that of the test signal. With the sweep rate *locked* to the input signal rate, a single pattern will be seen on the screen.

With both types of oscilloscopes, the trigger section supplies the correct signal to the horizontal section to control the sweep.

The trigger section may receive its input signal in either of two ways: (a) from the vertical section (this trigger comes from the test signal) or (b) from an external signal source. Generally, internal triggering is used. However, in some cases, such as looking at a train of digital pulses, it will be useful to trigger externally from an external clock or with a signal from another part of the circuit.

4. *The Display (CRT Control) System:* The grid of lines appearing at the front of the CRT is called a *graticule*. This is usually etched or silkscreened on the *inside* of the CRT faceplate. By having the graticule inside the faceplate, parallax errors are eliminated. Graticules are usually laid out in an 8×10 pattern. (See block diagram.) Each of the eight vertical and ten horizontal lines block

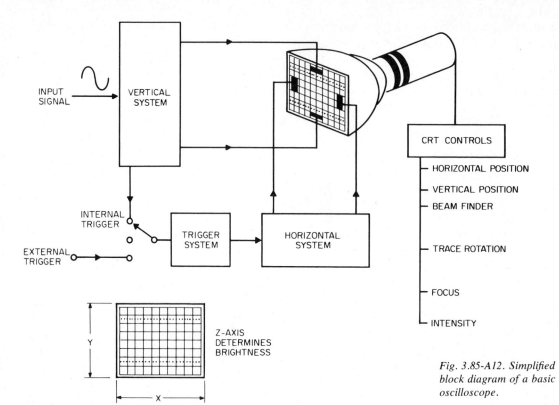

INPUT SIGNAL

VERTICAL SYSTEM

INTERNAL TRIGGER

EXTERNAL TRIGGER

TRIGGER SYSTEM

HORIZONTAL SYSTEM

CRT CONTROLS

— HORIZONTAL POSITION

— VERTICAL POSITION

— BEAM FINDER

— TRACE ROTATION

— FOCUS

— INTENSITY

Y

X

Z-AXIS DETERMINES BRIGHTNESS

Fig. 3.85-A12. Simplified block diagram of a basic oscilloscope.

off major divisions of the screen. Minor divisions are indicated by "tick" marks on the center vertical and horizontal graticule lines. Many oscilloscope graticules include pulse rise time measurement markings.

The common controls for the CRT are for intensity and focus. In addition, there are vertical and horizontal display positioning control. Their function is obvious. Less common are beam finder and trace rotation controls.

The *intensity* control adjusts the brightness of the display. This control is required because the oscilloscope is used under various ambient light conditions and with many different types of signals. In addition, different sweep speeds affect the intensity of the display. The faster the sweep speed, the dimmer the display tends to be.

As the name implies, the *focus* control is used to obtain the sharpest possible display. Focus may also be affected by the setting of the intensity control.

The *beam finder* control permits you to locate the electron beam if it is off screen. Pressing the beam find button brings the beam within some portion of the graticule. Seeing this, the operator knows which direction to turn the CRT horizontal and vertical positioning controls to bring the trace back on the screen.

The *trace rotation* control is used to align the trace with the fixed, horizontal graticule lines. Trace rotation can be affected by the earth's magnetic field. If the scope is moved to different locations, the trace rotation may have to be readjusted.

Q. 3.85-A13. Describe briefly transistor testers and their use.

A. Transistor testers may be found in three basic types: (1) static testers, (2) dynamic testers, and (3) curve-tracer testers. Many types can measure transistors "in circuit" and "out-of-circuit." Since most semiconductors are soldered into the circuit, it is important to be able to test them while in circuit. An out-of-circuit test can be made on parts not in a circuit.

Many transistor testers can test bipolar transistors, FETs, SCRs, Darlingtons, and diodes. Automatic indication of silicon or germanium transistors is provided by some testers.

D.

1. *Static-Transistor Testers:* Static-transistor testers measure the following: (a) transistor short circuits, (b) transistor open circuits. (c) dc leakage current (I_{CBO}) (out-of circuit test only), and (d) dc beta (h_{FE}).

When this type of tester is used, a typical procedure is to: (a) select NPN or PNP type by panel switch, (b) connect all three external leads correctly to the transistor, (c) choose the appropriate transistor power range, and (d) keep the test time short to reduce raised-temperature effects for I_{CBO} and h_{FE} tests. Beta should meet the minimum specified. However, I_{CBO} may be five to ten times the nominal ratings and still be acceptable.

2. *Dynamic-Transistor Testers:* These come in two general types: (a) the oscillator tester and (b) the transistor analyzer.

The *oscillator tester* provides an in-circuit test of a transistor. The transistor completes the circuit of an audio oscillator. An audio tone is heard *only* if the transistor is good. This happens only if the beta is adequate to produce oscillation.

A *transistor analyzer* is more complicated to use, but it gives more total information about the unit being tested. The tester measures transistor parameters with quantitative numbers. A front panel layout of a transistor analyzer is shown in Fig. 3.85-A13(1).

The three major tests performed by the transistor analyzer are: (1) I_{CBO} (reverse-leakage current, collector-to-base), (2) h_{FE} (beta: amplification, base-to-collector), and (3) r_{in} (transistor input resistance).

To measure I_{CBO}, first select for NPN or PNP type. The I_{CBO} meter range switch is then set to the desired full-scale meter range. This can vary from 50 μA to 5 mA for the unit pictured. I_{CBO} is then measured on the meter.

Beta is measured on the ac voltmeter scale. In the ''Beta cal.'' position of the ''Modes'' switch, the meter is calibrated to ''1.'' Then the ''Modes'' switch is turned to ''Beta test,'' and beta is read directly on the meter.

R_{in} is measured by an ac bridge network. The meter is connected now as an ac voltmeter. To measure r_{in}, adjust the ''R_{in}'' dial to obtain a null reading on the meter. The value of r_{in} is then read directly on the calibrated R_{in} dial.

Note: A transistor analyzer can measure r_{in} and h_{FE} in-circuit. It can measure I_{CBO}, r_{in}, and h_{FE} out-of-circuit.

3. *Curve-Tracer Testers:* A curve-tracer transistor tester displays the characteristic curves of the transistor under test. The display is on a cathode ray tube. A front panel layout of a curve-tracer tester is shown in Fig. 3.85-A13(2) along with typical displays for good and bad transistors. Although three connector inputs labeled C (collector), B (base), and E (emitter)—are shown in the figure, other testers will provide standard sockets for various transistor packages.

Fig. 3.85-A13(1). The front panel layout of a transistor analyzer.

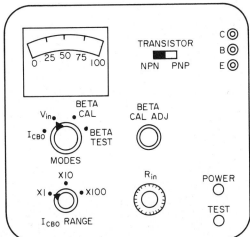

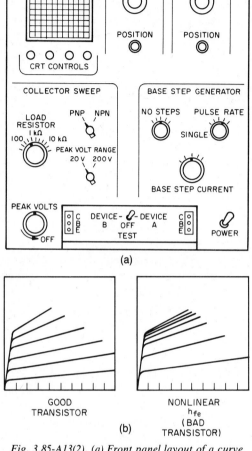

(a)

(b)

GOOD
TRANSISTOR

NONLINEAR
h_{fe}
(BAD
TRANSISTOR)

Fig. 3.85-A13(2). (a) Front panel layout of a curve tracer transistor tester. (b) Typical displays for a good transistor and a bad transistor.

These include TO-3, TO-5, and TO-18 packages.

Controls in the "collector sweep" area on the panel are set first in accordance with the transistor being tested. (Manufacturers instructions must be followed.) Next adjust the "Vertical Current/div.," the "Horizontal Volts/div.," and the two "position" knobs to produce a properly centered display. The next step is to adjust the controls in the "Base Step Generator" section of the panel. These set the number of steps (curves) displayed and the rate of pulsing the transistor (1 to 240 Hz) with these steps.

Q. 3.85-A14. Describe some of the important characteristics and uses of a sine/square-wave audio generator.

A. A sine/square-wave audio generator is an instrument whose output may be selected to be either a sine wave or a square wave. Although frequently called an "audio" generator, its output frequency may range from 20 Hz to 200 kHz or more.

Typical uses for this generator are: (1) measuring gain in audio amplifiers, (2) measuring frequency response in audio amplifiers, (3) as an external modulator for RF signal generators (4) as a signal source for troubleshooting audio amplifiers, and (5) as a signal source for measuring harmonic distortion in audio amplifiers. The square-wave output is particularly useful in measuring the frequency and phase response of audio amplifiers.

D. The characteristics of a typical sine/square-wave audio generator are as follows:

1. Frequency range (sine and square wave): 20 Hz to 200 kHz in four decade ($\times 10$) steps.

2. Frequency Accuracy: ± 3 percent.

3. Sine Wave Output Amplitude: 10 V rms ± 10 percent at 1 kHz.

4. Sine Wave Distortion: 0.5 percent, 50 Hz to 100 kHz; 1 percent 20 Hz to 200 kHZ.

5. Square Wave Output: 10 V peak-to- peak.

6. Square Wave Tilt: 10 percent or less at 20 Hz.

7. Square Wave Rise and Fall Times: 500 ns or less.

8. Stability with ± 10 percent Line Voltage Variation: Less than ± 0.5 percent frequency drift; less than ± 0.5 dB output level variation.

9. Power Requirements: 117 V ac, 50-60 Hz; 30 W.

Q. 3.85-A15. Describe some of the important characteristics and uses of an RF signal generator.

A. An RF signal generator is an instrument whose output is a sine-wave voltage. This output is at a selectable wide frequency range and calibrated amplitude. Both of these characteristics are provided with a high degree of accuracy. These instruments have provision to modulate the RF output generally with 400 or 1 000 Hz.

RF signal generators have many possible uses. Some uses are: (1) alignment of radio and television equipment, (2) calibrating the frequency of other test equipment, (3) signal substitution, (4) measurement by comparison of an unknown frequency, (5) marker generation for sweep waveforms, (6) frequency response of RF, IF, and video amplifiers, and (7) testing sensitivity of radio and television receivers.

D. A typical RF signal generator has all solid-state circuitry. It may have a frequency range of about 100 kHz to 100 MHz on fundamentals and up to 300 MHz on harmonics. Some units can be modulated either internally at 400 Hz or 1 000 Hz, or externally at 50 Hz to 20 kHz. In addition, some RF signal generators have provision for a single frequency, crystal oscillator output. Crystals with frequencies from 1 MHz to 15 MHz can be plugged into the front panel.

The desired frequency is selected in two steps: (1) by a switch that gives you the desired *range* of frequencies and (2) by a variable pointer that indicates the *exact* frequency on a calibrated dial.

The output amplitude is read directly on a meter in conjunction with a calibrated step attenuator and variable amplitude control.

Other RF signal generators are available with output frequencies well up in the microwave region.

Q. 3.85-A16. What is a field strength meter?

A. A field strength meter is an instrument that measures the relative power being radiated from an antenna.

D. A schematic diagram of a simple field strength meter is shown in Fig. 3.85-A16. A pickup antenna is connected to the unit as shown. A half-wave (at the transmitted frequency) antenna will give good readings. Longer antennas will increase the field strength meter sensitivity.

When in use, the protective meter short is removed, the antenna attached, and the instrument placed 100 ft or more from the transmitting antenna. Capacitor C_2 is varied until maximum meter reading is obtained. Adjustments are then made to the antenna system, including matching elements for maximum field strength indication.

Rotating the antenna gives a rough idea of the antenna pattern if the user notes the readings at various antenna positions.

Field strength meters are commonly used in checking the signal level at different points on a cable television system. The field strength meters used for this service are more complicated than the one shown in Fig. 3.85-A16. These latter units tune through a wide range of frequencies and are calibrated directly in microvolts.

Q. 3.85-A17. What is a spectrum analyzer?

A. A spectrum analyzer is a frequency-*swept* receiver. It provides a visual display of amplitude versus frequency of a signal on a cathode ray tube.

A typical display on a spectrum analyzer is shown in Fig. 3.85-A17. This display is of a 50-percent modulated AM wave.

Fig. 3.85-A16. A simple field strength meter. Capacitor C2 tunes the meter to the transmitted frequency.

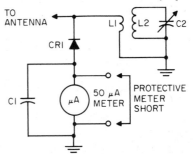

D. A spectrum analyzer should be able to:

1. Make absolute frequency measurements: 1 percent of full scale on a slide rule frequency dial.

2. Make absolute amplitude measurements: The unit indicates what the log/reference level or linear sensitivity is, regardless of control settings.

3. Operate over a large amplitude dynamic range: The dynamic range of a spectrum analyzer is defined as the difference between the input signal level and the average noise level or distortion products, whichever is greater.

4. Have high resolution of frequency and amplitude: Frequency resolution is the ability of the analyzer to separate signals closely spaced in frequency. Amplitude resolution is a function of the vertical scale calibration. Both log and linear calibrations are provided.

5. Have high sensitivity: Sensitivity is a measure of a spectrum analyzer's ability to detect small signals. It may have a sensitivity of − 150 dBm to -125 dBm.

6. Provide variable persistence on CRT screen and digital storage capability: Variable persistence allows the user to vary the length of time that a trace remains on a CRT. Digital storage simplifies measurements and CRT photography.

Fig. 3.85-A17. A typical display on a spectrum analyzer.

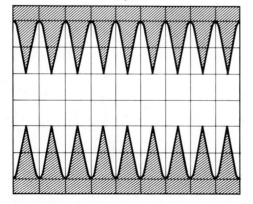

Q. 3.85-A18. What is a directional coupler?

A. A directional coupler is a device inserted into a transmission line or waveguide. It samples a fraction of the power traveling in *one* direction only (either forward *or* reflected power). Directional couplers are used in the measurement of RF power and SWR.

D. A directional coupler can be reversed in position to sample the alternate traveling wave. The coupler rejects the undesired traveling wave to a degree of 30 dB or more.

Directional couplers are rated in decibels of attenuation in passing through it to the measuring device. Thus, a 3 dB coupler transmits one-half of the power; a 20 dB coupler, one-hundreth of the power; and a 30 dB coupler, one-thousandth of the power.

Coaxial lines use loop-type or two-hole directional couplers.

A *two-hole coupler* consists of two parallel coaxial lines in contact. These have holes or slots through their contacting walls, spaced one-quarter wavelength apart. This permits energy to be extracted that is traveling in one direction only.

Waveguide *directional couplers* use an arrangement that is comparable to a two-hole coupler.

Q. 3.85-A19. What is a reflectometer?

A. A reflectometer is an instrument that is used to measure the reflection coefficient or standing-wave ratio (SWR) of a transmission line.

D. See Q. 3.85-A18 and Q. 3.85-A20.

Q. 3.85-A20. Briefly describe an RF wattmeter and its uses.

A. An RF wattmeter is an instrument that may be used to measure RF-output power of a transmitter and standing-wave ratio (SWR) (see Q. 3.215) on its transmission line.

D. With this instrument, coupling circuits sample the traveling waves between the transmitter and antenna (or dummy load). The RF energy is rectified by a diode. The rectified current is then indicated on a meter calibrated in terms of power (watts).

Forward (incident) power to the antenna (or dummy load) is measured by means of a directional coupler (see Q. 3.85-A18). This device, when set to measure *forward* power, discriminates against *reflected* power by greater than 30 dB. Thus, basically, only *forward* power is measured at this time.

Reflected power may be measured only by reversing the directional coupler: In many RF wattmeters this reversal is accomplished electronically. The relationship between forward and reflected power is a measure of SWR. SWR can thus be indicated directly on the instrument meter.

To convert from forward and reflected power to SWR, use the following equation:

$$SWR = 1 + \cfrac{\cfrac{\text{Reflected power}}{\text{Forward power}}}{1 - \cfrac{\text{Reflected power}}{\text{Forward power}}}$$

If forward (F) and reverse (R) standing-wave current (or voltage) is known, use the following equations:

$$ISWR = \frac{I_F + I_R}{I_F - I_R}$$

or

$$VSWR = \frac{V_F + V_R}{V_F - V_R}$$

Note: SWR = ISWR = VSWR. (See also Q. 3.215, and Q. 3.216.)

Many RF wattmeters are the so-called "in-line" type. They are designed to be connected in the series with the coaxial cable between the transmitter and antenna (or dummy load).

Some characteristics of a typical RF wattmeter are:

1. Used with 50-Ω coaxial line.
2. Unit insertion SWR is less than 1.05:1, up to 1 000 MHz.
3. Direct reading in watts (and also in SWR for some instruments).
4. Wattage ratings (in steps) from 2.5 to 500 W.

Some RF wattmeters measure only average power output. However, other units can measure peak-to-peak power for single-sideband transmission. In addition, some wattmeters can capture and hold modulation peaks to indicate the peak power of the transmission.

Q. 3.85-A21. What is a communications-service monitor?

A. A communications service-monitor is a composite test unit. It provides every test function required to service any two-way communications system. This unit can service FM, AM, or single-sideband systems (SSB), in the frequency range from ultrasonic to about 550 MHz.

D. These units have the accuracy and stability of a laboratory standard. However, they are usually battery-operated and portable for field service.

A typical communications service monitor may include the following:

1. A signal generator employing frequency synthesis to provide continuous frequency coverage of the specified range: Typically, a single 10-MHz, temperature-compensated crystal oscillator is used to provide the stable source from which all frequencies are derived. The frequency tolerance is 0.0001 percent $\pm$ 5 Hz at 25°C. Rated accuracy is maintained over a temperature range of 55°C.
2. A frequency meter of great accuracy: It can measure an unknown frequency to a fraction of a hertz.
3. Generator of a modulated FM or AM carrier: The degree of modulation is adjustable.
4. An audio oscillator with selectable audio frequencies.

5. A 1 kHz tone adjustable in amplitude for precision modulation measurements.

6. An FM deviation tester.

7. Measurement of modulation symmetry.

Q. 3.85-A22. What is a CB performance tester? Briefly describe its uses.

A. A CB performance tester is a test instrument that measures basic operating parameters of a CB transmitter.

Typical measurements made by this type of instrument include: (1) transmitter frequency, (2) RF power output, (3) VSWR, and (4) percentage of modulation.

D. The basic purposes of a CB performance tester are:

1. To make quick checks of CB transmitter operation,

2. To make these checks (usually) in the CB installed position,

3. To show whether or not the CB transmitter is matched to the antenna and is delivering the proper power to the antenna.

A CB *Analyzer* is more complex than a CB performance tester. A CB Analyzer contains facilities for making receiver as well as transmitter measurements. It also contains facilities for troubleshooting. In addition, some analyzers have an oscilloscope adapter output for carrier wave and modulation checks, which can be made with a 1 mHz response oscilloscope. Other functions may include: (1) digital readout of crystal frequency, (2) RF power, (3) audio power, (4) SINAD receiver sensitivity test, and (5) RF and IF signal generation.

Some measurement characteristics of a well designed CB performance tester are as follows:

1. Frequency measurement accuracy: 1 part per million (ppm).

2. Frequency stability with time: ±1 ppm per year (temperature-compensated instrument).

3. Modulation percentage: ±1 percent.

4. Standing wave ratios (SWR): ±1 percent.

OSCILLATORS

Q. 3.86. Draw circuit diagrams of each of the following types of oscillators (include any commonly associated components). Explain the principles of operation of each.

1. Armstrong

2. Tuned plate-tuned grid (series fed and shunt fed, crystal and LC controlled)

3. Hartley

4. Colpitts

5. Electron coupled

6. Multivibrator

7. Pierce (crystal controlled)

A. *General:* All oscillators (except relaxation types) require a tuned circuit made up of inductance and capacitance for their operation. It is this tuned circuit which is actually the oscillator. The frequency of an oscillator with reasonably high Q (greater than 10) is found from the approximate formula

$$f = \frac{1}{2\pi\sqrt{LC}}$$

where

f = in hertz.
L = in henrys.
C = in farads.

A conventional type of oscillator operates as follows: when the power switch is turned on, high-frequency current surges pass through the tuned circuit (tank) and shock-excite it into oscillation. If no means were provided to make up energy losses, this oscillation would gradually die out at a rate which would be proportional to the Q of the tank, and the resultant wave train would be called a "damped wave." In order to produce sustained oscillations, it is necessary that the losses which occur in the tuned circuit be replenished from the power supply by means of a vacuum tube. These losses are mainly due to: (1) dc resistance, (2) ac resistance (skin effect), (3) coupling into a load, (4) grid power requirements, (5) radiation.

The function of the vacuum tube is to act as a valve which releases pulses of energy into the tank circuit in the correct phase. This energy is usually applied indirectly to the tank circuit by means of a feedback network. These networks usually consist of inductive or capacitive coupling elements which connect the tube with the tank circuit. Many oscillator tubes operate as Class C amplifiers and are "cut off" for a large percentage of each cycle. When the potential at the grid side of the tank circuit is passing through its most positive values, the Class C bias is overcome and the tube is permitted to conduct for a short period of time, feeding energy into the tank circuit. It should always be borne in mind that the tube itself is *not* the oscillator; the tuned circuit *is*.

Grid leak bias is developed in an oscillator by the charging of the grid capacitor from grid current and its discharging through the grid leak resistor. The average value of the capacitor voltage is the bias. Before the oscillator starts into operation there is no charge in the grid capacitor and the initial bias is, therefore, zero. When the tank circuit starts oscillating the first cycle has a small amplitude which increases at a definite rate depending upon the Q until a maximum value is reached a number of cycles later. Since the initial bias was zero, the effect of the first positive swing of the tank circuit, on the grid, is to cause grid current to charge the grid capacitor to some small value. In a like manner the grid capacitor continues to charge to the increasing positive swings of the tank circuit until the capacitor voltage is equal to some value of the steady-state tank-circuit positive swings, which depends upon the value of grid-leak resistance. The polarity of the charged capacitor is such that it is negative at the grid side, and thus provides the bias potential. The maximum steady state bias depends upon a number of factors such as type of tube, effective Q of tank circuit, amount of feedback, and tube operating voltages. One method of calculating grid bias constants is given below (assuming that the average grid current is known), is given in a tube manual, or can be found experimentally.

1. a. For Class C,
$$V_c = \frac{2V_b}{\mu} \text{ (for twice cut-off)}$$
where
V_c = the dc grid bias.
V_b = the dc plate voltage.
μ = the amplification factor of the tube.

b. For Class B,
$$V_c = \frac{V_b}{\mu} \text{ (at cut-off)}$$

c. For Class A2,
$$V_c = \frac{0.6V_b}{\mu}$$

2.
$$R_g = \frac{V_C}{I_g}$$
where
R_g = the grid resistance in ohms.
I_g = equal to the average dc grid current in amperes.

3.
$$C_c = \frac{5\ 000}{F_r \times R_g}$$
where

C_c = the grid capacitor in microfarads.
F_r = the lowest operating frequency in kilohertz.
R_g = the grid resistor in ohms.

a. Fig. 3.86(a1) shows a shunt-fed Armstrong oscillator and Fig. 3.86(a2) shows a series-fed Armstrong oscillator.

Feedback is accomplished by magnetic coupling between L_2 and L_1 and may be varied by changing the degree of coupling. The frequency is determined mainly by L_1C_1. C_b prevents short circuiting the power supply and provides an easy path for RF plate current to return to the cathode. The radio-frequency choke, *RFC*, prevents RF plate current from entering the power supply; R_g-C_c is the bias network.

The transistor equivalent of the tuned-grid Armstrong oscillator, with shunt-fed plate, is shown in Fig. 3.86(a3). While the circuits are basically similar, there are some important differences.

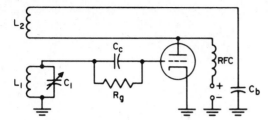

Fig. 3.86(a1). A tuned-grid Armstrong oscillator with shunt-fed plate.

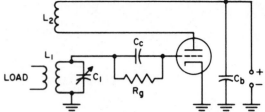

Fig. 3.86(a2). A tuned-grid Armstrong oscillator with series-fed plate.

With a vacuum-tube oscillator, employing only grid-leak bias, the tube is at maximum conduction when the bias is zero. In the case of a transistor oscillator, this would not be true, since the transistor would be biased Class C at zero bias (see Q. 3.192(S)). In order that transistor oscillator will be self-starting, it is essential to provide some forward bias for the base-emitter circuit. Thus, most transistor oscillators are operated either class AB or class A.

In Fig. 3.86(a3), forward bias is provided by the voltage divider consisting of R_F and R_B. The emitter resistor R_E has been included to provide thermal transistor stabilization (see Q. 3.189). The emitter capacitor, C_E, is necessary to prevent degeneration from the voltage which would otherwise appear across R_E.

Note that the function of the RF choke in Fig. 3.86(a1) is performed by the resistor R_C, in Fig. 3.86(a3). The operation of the transistor oscillator is the same as the tube type.

Fig. 3.86(a3). A tuned-base Armstrong oscillator with shunt-fed collector. (This circuit is similar in operation to Fig. 3.86(a1).)

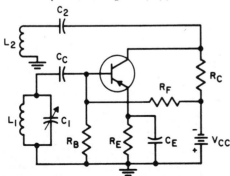

b. (1) For the diagram of a tuned-plate, tuned-grid, series-fed, LC controlled oscillator, see Fig. 3.86(b1).

Feedback is accomplished through the interelectrode capacitance C_{gp}. The output frequency is slightly lower than the resonant frequency of either L_1C_1 or L_2C_2. L_2C_2 is tuned slightly higher than L_1C_1. C_b offers a low impedance path for the RF to return to the cathode, by-passing the power supply. R_g—C_c is the bias network. Tetrodes or pentodes will not be suitable except at very high frequencies because of the low values of C_{gp}.

(2) For the diagram of a tuned-plate, tuned-grid, shunt-fed, LC controlled oscillator, see Fig. 3.86(b2). (See also part b(1) of this question.) C_b prevents short circuiting of the power supply. The value of the inductance of the radio-frequency choke, RFC, should be at least 10 times greater than the inductance of L_2 so as not to change the frequency of L_2C_2.

(3) For circuit diagrams of tuned-grid, tuned-plate, crystal-controlled oscillators, see Figs. 3.86(b3) and 3.86(b4).

Figure 3.86(b3) is a diagram of a tuned-plate, tuned-grid oscillator with the crystal and its holder replacing the original grid tank circuit. Feedback is accomplished through C_{gp}. The bias capacitor here is C_h, the capacity of the crystal holder, and the bias resistor is R_g. The purpose of the RF choke, RFC, is to maintain a high impedance across the crystal and so maintain a high Q. A pentode or tetrode has a higher power sensitivity and a much lower value of C_{gp} than a triode. This means that it is possible to reduce the

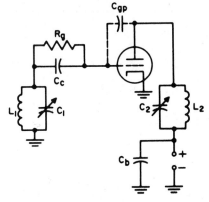

Fig. 3.86(b1). A tuned-plate tuned-grid oscillator
with series-fed plate.

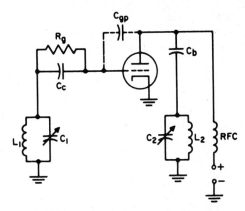

Fig. 3.86(b2). A tuned-plate tuned-grid oscillator
with shunt-fed plate.

amount of crystal voltage and current for a given output power and consequently reduce crystal heating. The grid circuit is also less affected by changes in load than when a triode is used, due to the reduced C_{gp}. However, C_{gp} may be too small to allow sufficient feedback especially at the lower frequencies, and in this case a small capacitor in the order of 2 pF should be connected between grid and plate.

  c. For the circuit diagram of a shunt-fed Hartley oscillator, see Fig. 3.86(c).

  To find whether the oscillator or amplifier is shunt or series fed, merely trace the path of *dc* plate current. If it passes through any part of a tuning inductance, the circuit is series fed. Otherwise it is shunt fed. Feedback is accomplished by magnetic

coupling between L_a and L_b,, and may be increased by lowering the tap, or decreased by raising the tap. The "tank" circuit which mainly determines the resonant frequency, consists of C_1 across the *entire* inductance of $L_a + L_b$. C_b offers a low impedance path for RF plate current to return to the cathode through L_a. The radio-frequency choke, *RFC*, prevents RF plate current from passing through the power supply. R_g-C_c is the bias network.

  For the schematic diagram of a transistor, shunt-fed Hartley oscillator, see Fig. 3.283. Note the great similarity to the tube version shown in Fig. 3.86(c). The operation for the two types is the same. The discussion in part a of Question 3.86, regarding forward bias, the emitter network and resistor

Fig. 3.86(b3). A crystal-controlled vacuum tube
oscillator.

Fig. 3.86(b4). A pentode tube used as a crystal-
controlled oscillator.

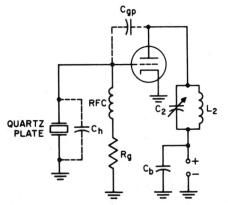

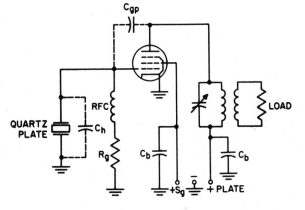

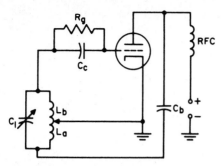

Fig. 3.86(c). A Hartley oscillator with shunt-fed plate.

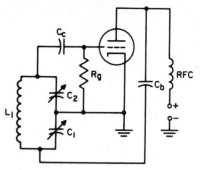

Fig. 3.86(d). A Colpitts oscillator with shunt-fed plate.

R_C, applies equally to this transistor oscillator.

A comparison between the Hartley oscillator shown in Fig. 3.86(c) and the Colpitts oscillator shown in Fig. 3.86(d) follows.

The basic difference between the Colpitts and Hartley oscillators is the method of adjusting the feedback. In both the Colpitts and Hartley oscillators, the tank circuit is effectively connected between the grid and plate of the vacuum tube. In both cases the amount of feedback is adjusted by varying the point at which the cathode is effectively tapped into the tank circuit. In the Hartley oscillator this is done by tapping into the coil proper, while in the Colpitts oscillator the tap is made by means of a capacitive voltage divider. This consists of two series capacitors connected across the tuning inductance, with the cathode connected between the two. By varying the *ratio* between the two capacitors, the feedback voltage may be varied. Once the feedback ratio is determined, the two capacitors may be "ganged" together for tuning. Other differences include: (1) The Colpitts oscillator *must* be shunt fed, while the Hartley oscillator may be shunt or series fed. (2) In the Colpitts oscillator the grid leak resistance must be connected from grid to cathode, while in the Hartley oscillator it may alternatively be connected across the grid capacitor. (3) The Colpitts oscillator seems to be preferred for use in the very low frequencies and the very high frequencies (ultraudion), while the Hartley oscillator is used between these two extremes.

d. For a circuit diagram of a shunt-fed Colpitts oscillator, see Fig. 3.86(d).

Feedback is accomplished by a capacitive voltage divider action between C_1 and C_2. To increase feedback, decrease the value of C_2 in relation to C_1. To decrease feedback, increase C_1 in relation to C_1. R_g must be connected between grid and cathode otherwise the grid will have no dc return to ground. C_e is often eliminated, in which case C_2 will also serve the function of bias capacitor. The frequency is determined mainly by L_1 in parallel with the series combination of C_2 and C_1. In changing frequency, C_2 and C_1 are moved simultaneously. C_b offers a low impedance path for RF plate current through C_1 to the cathode. The RF choke, *RFC,* keeps RF plate current out of the power supply. See also part (c) above.

For the schematic diagram of a transistorized Colpitts crystal oscillator, see Fig. 3.286. While a crystal oscillator is shown, this could be easily changed to an LC oscillator by replacing the crystal by a coil and insuring that capacitors C1 and C2 are correct to tune the coil to the desired frequency range.

The discussion in part a of Q.3.86, regarding forward bias, the emitter network and resistor R_c, also applies to this transistor oscillator.

e. For the circuit diagram of an electron-coupled oscillator, see Fig. 3.86(e).

The oscillator proper is a series-fed Hartley with the screen grid acting as the plate of the oscillator. Coupling into the plate tank circuit occurs by virtue of the electron

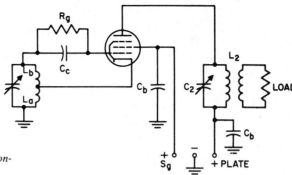

Fig. 3.86(e). An electron-coupled oscillator.

stream variations caused by the swing of the control grid, hence the name "electron-coupled." The main advantage of this circuit arrangement is its excellent frequency stability. Its features are: (1) Buffer action because the oscillator tank is isolated from the load; (2) frequency multiplication may be obtained by tuning L_2C_2 to a harmonic oscillator frequency; (3) frequency is substantially independent of power supply variations; (4) combination of oscillator and amplifier using only one tube.

f. For the circuit diagram of a symmetrical, plate-coupled, free-running multivibrator, see Fig. 3.86(f1). The waveforms used in conjunction with the explanation of its operation are given in Fig. 3.86(f2).

A multivibrator is a form of relaxation oscillator which is rather unstable in the free running condition, but which may be completely stabilized by the application of suitable synchronizing voltages. It requires two tubes for its operation and has a frequency

range extending approximately from 1 cycle per minute to 100 000 (or more) hertz. The operation of this circuit follows.

It is assumed that V_1 initially conducts more heavily than V_2 when power-supply voltages are applied. This causes an increase in the voltage drop across R_{L1} and a *decrease* of the plate voltage of V_1 (e_{p1}). This decrease of e_{p1} voltage is coupled by capacitor C_{c2} to the grid of V_2. The negative-going voltage (e_{g2}) causes a reduction in the plate current of V_2 and an *increase* of its plate voltage, e_{p2}. The increase of e_{p2} is coupled through capacitor C_{c1} as a "positive-going" voltage at the grid of V_1, which further increases the plate current of V_1 and further decreases its plate voltage.

Fig. 3.86(f2). Waveforms of a symmetrical, plate-coupled, free-running multivibrator.

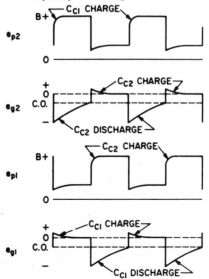

Fig. 3.86(f1). Circuit diagram of a symmetrical, plate-coupled, free-running multivibrator.

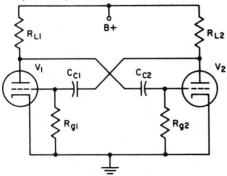

The action just described is regenerative and ends with V_2 being cut off and V_1 conducting at its maximum value (see waveforms). This regenerative (or switching) operation occurs in a fraction of a microsecond. Capacitor C_{c2} now begins to *discharge* to the reduced plate voltage of V_1 through R_{g2}. As C_{c2} discharges in accordance (mainly) with the time constant of $C_{c2}.R_{g2}$, the negative voltage at the grid of V_2 *decreases*. This discharge continues (with V_2 cut off and V_1 conducting heavily until e_{g2} reaches the *cut-off bias* value for V_2. At this point, a new switching action begins. As e_{g2} begins to rise above the cut-off value for V_2, this tube begins to conduct. This initiates another switching action which will be concluded when V_1 is cut off and V_2 conducts heavily.

The conduction of V_2 results in a *decrease* of its plate voltage, e_{p2}. This "negative-going" voltage is coupled to the grid of V_1, reducing its plate current. The reduced V_1 plate current results in an *increase* of its plate voltage and this "positive-going" voltage change is coupled through capacitor C_{c2} to the grid of V_2, further *increasing* its plate current and further *reducing* its plate voltage. Once again the action is regenerative and results in the situation where V_1 is now cut off and V_2 is conducting heavily. The beginning of the next switching action starts when e_{g1} rises just above cut-off and completes one full cycle of operation.

Since this is a "free-running" multivibrator, the above described action continues until the power supply voltages are removed.

As can be seen in Fig. 3.86(f2), the plate waveform is basically a square wave. This arrangement, with and without additional squaring procedures, is frequently used when square wave pulses are desired. The waveforms shown are symmetrical, because both halves of each cycle are equal in time duration. This occurs primarily because the time constant of C_{c1} and R_{g1} is equal to that of C_{c2} and R_{r2}. In many applications (e.g., sawtooth generators and pulse generators),

it is desirable to have the positive portion of the plate waveform either narrower or wider than the negative portion. This is accomplished by choosing unequal time constants for the two grid circuits.

A symmetrical, free-running, collector-coupled transistor multivibrator is shown in Fig. 3.86(f3). Note the great similarity to Fig. 3.86(f1). The operating principles are the same as for the tube counterpart, with one major exception. For oscillations to begin (as with a transistor LC oscillator), it is necessary to forward bias both transistors. This is accomplished by connecting the two base resistors to $-V_{cc}$. (See part 3(a) of Q. 3.86 for a discussion of the requirement for forward bias.)

Some uses for multivibrators are:

(1) As frequency dividers.

(2) As sawtooth generators.

(3) As harmonic generators.

(4) As square wave and pulse generators.

(5) As a standard frequency source when synchronized by an external crystal oscillator.

(6) Many specialized uses in radar and television circuits.

There are two general classifications of multivibrators. These are the *free running* or non-driven type, and the *driven* or monostable type. The former type is capable of generating continuous oscillations, while the latter type requires a driving pulse to start the operation after which it will complete

Fig. 3.86(f3). Circuit diagram of a symmetrical, collector-coupled, free running (astable) transistor multivibrator.

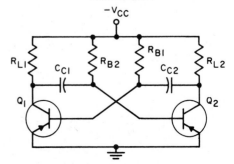

one full cycle and then stop and wait for the next driving pulse.

Multivibrators are also classified as to the manner of feedback. These divisions generally speaking are: (1) plate coupling, where feedback is taken from the plate circuit of each tube and fed into the grid of the opposite tube, and (2) cathode coupling where feedback is provided by means of a common cathode resistor for both tubes and plate coupling for one tube. When used as a frequency divider, the free running frequency of the multivibrator is set so as to be slightly lower than a whole sub-multiple of the synchronizing frequency. A frequency division of 10:1 or so is usually considered to be the maximum obtainable with reliable stability of the multivibrator. For example, an original source of 100 000 hertz could be used to synchronize a multivibrator operating at 10 000 hertz. Due to the very high harmonic content of the non-sinusoidal multivibrator output voltage, harmonics in the order of one hundred or more may be obtained. Thus if the 100 000-hertz synchronizing voltage was supplied by a very stable crystal oscillator, a series of standard harmonic frequencies would be available ranging from 10 000 hertz (fundamental) and increasing in steps of 10 000 hertz to possibly 1 000 000 hertz. No definite simple formula may be given for the frequency of a multivibrator since there are too many variables. However, it can be said that the grid coupling elements (capacitor and resistor) have the greatest effect upon the determination of the frequency. Increasing or decreasing the time-constant of this combination causes proportional increases or decreases of frequency.

g. For the circuit diagram of a crystal-controlled Pierce oscillator and its operation, see Figs. 3.86(g1) and 3.86(g2).

Figure 3.86(g2) is an explanatory diagram for the circuit given in Fig. 3.86(g1). The dotted lines indicate capacity between the tube elements. C_2 blocks the dc plate voltage from the crystal. C_1 decreases the

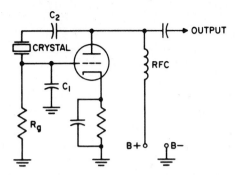

Fig. 3.86(g1). Pierce oscillator.

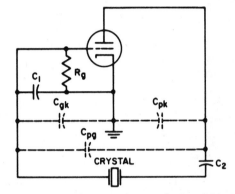

Fig. 3.86(g2). Explanatory diagram for Fig. 3.86(g1).

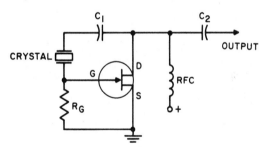

Fig. 3.86(g3). A Pierce oscillator employing FET (Field-Effect Transistor). (See text.)

capacitive reactance between grid and cathode, to keep the feedback down to its proper value. Since the crystal acts as a tank circuit, with the cathode returning to an intermediate point, determined by the relation of C_{pk} to C_1 and C_{gk}, its operation is electrically equivalent to a Colpitts oscillator (part d above).

A transistor version of the Pierce oscillator is shown in Fig. 3.86(g3). This circuit employs a junction, field-effect transistor

(JFET), which has certain characteristics that are very similar to a triode vacuum tube. The gate (G) is similar to a grid; the source (S) is similar to a cathode; and the drain (D) is similar to a plate. The similarities apply both to their functions and to their relative impedance levels. Like a vacuum tube, a FET has a high input impedance and a lower output impedance. (This contrasts with the conventional transistor, which has a low input impedance and a higher output impedance.)

This transistor version of the Pierce oscillator functions in the same manner as the vacuum-tube version, previously described.

Q. 3.87. What are the principal advantages of crystal control over tuned-circuit oscillators?

A. The principal advantages of crystal control are improved frequency stability and compactness of the crystal as compared to a conventional tuned circuit.

D. The quartz crystal, its holder capacitance and associated tube and stray capacitance actually form an equivalent tank circuit of very high Q. Etched crystals with plated electrodes, mounted in a vacuum, have been found to give Qs in the order of 500 000. This is exceptional, however, and ordinary crystal installations have a Q (unloaded) in the order of a thousand or more. Crystal oscillators are generally found in two forms. One is the tuned-plate variety, in which the crystal takes the place of the grid tank circuit (Q. 3.86(b)(3)). The other type is the Pierce oscillator (equivalent to the "ultraudion"), in which the crystal is the sole tuned circuit in the oscillator (Q. 3.86(g)). In any event the very high Q of the crystal makes for excellent oscillator stability, especially when a constant temperature is maintained.

A serious disadvantage of crystal control is the difficulty of changing operating frequencies. This entails the use of a cumbersome crystal changing switch, or the actual plugging in of separate crystals. Small changes in the crystal operating frequency may be made by changing the pressure of the crystal holder or by having a small variable capacitor across the crystal, or by the use of a special diode whose capacity varies with a change of bias voltage.

Q. 3.88. Why should excessive feedback be avoided in a crystal oscillator?

A. The crystal might overheat and break.

D. In the conventional (tuned-plate, tuned-grid) crystal oscillator, discussed in Q. 3.86(b)(3), this means a relatively large value of grid to late capacitance for the particular operating frequency. This in turn might cause excessive feedback into the crystal circuit, overheating and possibly cracking the crystal. The use of a tetrode or pentode greatly reduces this possibility because of the small value of grid to plate capacitance.

Q. 3.89. Why is a separate source of plate power desirable for a crystal oscillator stage in a radio transmitter?

A. To prevent "dynamic instability" of the crystal oscillator.

D. "Frequency shift" or "dynamic instability" refers to the instantaneous changes of oscillator frequency due to corresponding changes of plate and screen grid voltages of the oscillator tubes and is caused by improper regulation of the power supply.

If a common power supply ere used for the oscillator, RF amplifiers, and modulator stages, it would be difficult to prevent "dynamic instability," especially if the modulator was not operating strictly class A. Any changes in loading due to any cause, or any changes in modulator power requirements will create a change in power supply output voltage. This in turn may cause the oscillator frequency to shift, creating undesired frequency modulation. In general, an increase of oscillator plate voltage (with screen voltage constant) will cause the oscillator frequency to increase because of a decrease of tube input capacity. A proportional increase of screen voltage would have the opposite effect on the frequency, and this factor is taken advantage of in the electron-coupled oscillator to maintain frequency stability and reduce "dynamic instability." Dynamic instability can also be reduced by: (1) using an oscillator tank circuit with a high C/L ratio, (2) by light loading of the oscillator circuit, (3) by using a high value of grid leak, (4) by using separate power supplies for oscillator, modulator, and RF amplifiers, or at least for the oscillator.

Q. 3.90. What may result if a high degree of coupling exists between the plate and grid circuits of a crystal controlled oscillator?

A. See Q. 3.88.

Q. 3.91. Explain some methods of determining if oscillation is occuring in an oscillator circuit.

A. The following methods may be used:
1. Tuning a radio receiver to the oscillator frequency.
2. Tuning a heterodyne frequency meter to the oscillator frequency. A sensitive wavemeter (loosely coupled) may also be used.
3. Certain grid-dip meters have phone jacks and provisions for detecting a zero-beat condition. When the grid-dip meter is tuned to the oscillator frequency (if operating), a "zero-beat" condition will be observed.
4. A neon bulb or low current flashlight bulb connected to a loop of wire and loosely coupled to the oscillator circuit will light if the oscillator is functioning.
5. Check the grid bias with a high-impedance voltmeter. It will be considerably higher when the circuit is oscillating than when it is not. If the voltmeter is not high-impedance, the oscillations may be stopped when the meter is applied.
6. A grid milliammeter will read grid current. This should be bypassed for RF.
7. The dc plate current of the oscillator

is lower when the circuit is oscillating. This may be checked with a by-passed milliammeter.

Q. 3.92. What is meant by parasitic oscillations; how may they be detected and prevented?

A.
1. Parasitic oscillations are defined as "either high or low frequency oscillations occurring in circuits other than the original tank circuits, and at frequencies other than the desired output frequencies."
2. They may be detected by tuning for them with a receiver (loosely coupled), wavemeter, or heterodyne frequency meter. Excessive or erratic grid or plate current readings, or overheating of components, sometimes indicates the presence of parasitic oscillations.
3. Parasitic oscillations may be either high or low in frequency. High frequency parasitics are present in tuned circuits usually composed of tube and stray capacitance and lead inductance. Many times, this behaves as a tuned-grid tuned-plate oscillator. High frequency parasitic oscillations may be minimized by inserting small non-inductive resistors in series with plate and grid leads, and by making the plate leads considerably longer than the grid leads. Other methods are placing a wave trap in series with the grid, and placing small RF chokes in series with the plate and grid leads. Low frequency parasitics are usually caused by having RF chokes in both plate and grid circuits. These can be minimized by eliminating one of the two chokes, or by making the plate choke larger than the grid choke. Series plate and grid resistors may also help to eliminate low frequency parasitic oscillations.
D. For methods of testing for the presence of parasitic oscillations, see Q. 3.126.

Q. 3.93. What determines the fundamental frequency of a quartz crystal?

A. The fundamental frequency of a quartz crystal is dependent upon the following factors:

1. The crystal's physical dimensions.
2. Capacitance of the crystal holder.
3. The orientation of the slab cut from the natural crystal.
4. The crystal substance.

D. Certain crystalline substances such as quartz, rochelle salts, and tourmaline have a property known as piezo-electricity. If a pressure is applied to such a substance along one of its axes, a potential difference is developed across another axis. Conversely, a potential difference applied across one axis produces a mechanical displacement along another axis. This phenomenon is known as the "piezo-electric effect." Of all the various substances, quartz is the most generally satisfactory for use in oscillators.

There are very many different types of crystal cuts in use each having its own stability characteristics. Most of these change their operating frequency in varying degrees, with changes of operating temperature. Where extreme frequency stability is desired, the crystal may be kept in a constant-temperature oven.

Q. 3.94. What is meant by the temperature coefficient of a crystal?

A. The "temperature coefficient" of a crystal defines the manner in which the frequency of the crystal varies with temperature change. The crystal is rated in terms of hertz per megahertz per temperature change in centigrade degrees (see discussion).

D. A crystal may have a negative, a positive or a zero-temperature coefficient. If the crystal has a negative temperature coefficient, its operating frequency is inversely proportional to its temperature. With a positive temperature coefficient, the crystal frequency is directly proportional to the temperature. A crystal with zero temperature coefficient remains at a relatively constant frequency within stated temperature limits. A typical example involving a negative-temperature coefficient crystal follows.

A standard crystal marking may be as follows: $-50/10^6/C°/$. This means that the crystal frequency will change at the rate of 50 hertz per megahertz, per degree change of temperature in centigrade. The negative sign indicates that the crystal has a negative temperature coefficient. For example, a 7-megahertz crystal has the following marking: $-40/10^6/C°$; find the operating frequency if the temperature increases 5° C. This is done simply as follows: $40 \times 7 \times 5 = 1\ 400$ hertz. The new frequency is 7 000 000 minus 1 400 or 6 998 600 hertz.

Q. 3.95. What are the characteristics and possible uses of an "overtone" crystal? A "third mode" crystal?

A.
1. An "overtone" crystal is one specially ground to oscillate at an odd harmonic of its fundamental frequency. Crystals are available to oscillate at frequencies up to 100 MHz. Most standard crystals will oscillate on their third and fifth overtones using suitable circuitry. Overtone crystals are commonly used for oscillators in VHF transmitters (often in conjunction with frequency-multiplier stages).
2. A "third mode" crystal is one which is operated on the third harmonic of its fundamental frequency.

D. As the fundamental operating frequency of a crystal increases, its thickness decreases. Consequently, at fundamental frequencies above about 25 to 30 megahertz, the crystal tends to become quite fragile and may be unstable. "Overtone" operation is produced when crystals are operated at much higher frequencies. While standard crystals may produce "overtone" operation, the best results are obtained with specially ground "overtone" crystals operated in circuitry designed for such operation. In "overtone" operation, a relatively low-frequency (e.g. 20-megahertz) crystal, is operated on its overtone frequency and may produce (for example) its fifth overtone frequency of 100 megahertz. This procedure permits the use of a relatively thick (and stable) crystal at frequencies not practical for crystals operating at their fundamental frequency.

Q. 3.96. Explain some of the factors involved in the stability of an oscillator (both crystal and LC-controlled).

A. Some of the important factors are:
1. C to L ratio of tank circuit.
2. A stable and separate power supply. See Q. 3.89 above.
3. Components with very low temperature coefficients.
4. Low loss components, including tank circuit elements, by-pass capacitors and tube sockets.
5. Constant temperature operation, such as enclosing critical circuits in a temperature-controlled oven.
6. Use of high-Q, frequency determining elements, including the important factor of stable-crystal control.
7. Isolation of the oscillator from its load.
8. The use of temperature compensating components.

D. A major cause of oscillator "drift" is due to changes in the total tuning capacitance of the oscillator. These include such factors as tube capacitance, wiring capacitance, and reflected reactance. If the original tuning capacitor is made relatively large, then any such capacity changes will cause a smaller percentage change of the total capacitance than if the original tuning capacitance were much smaller. Thus the percentage of oscillator frequency change is less when the oscillator tank has a high C to L ratio. See also Q. 3.87, Q. 3.89, Q. 3.94, and Q. 3.98.

Q. 3.97. Is it necessary or desirable that the surfaces of a quartz crystal be clean? If so, what cleaning agents may be used which will not adversely affect the operation of the crystal?

A. The crystal surfaces must be free of dirt or grease in order to operate properly. The faces of the crystal should not be touched with the fingers, and may be cleaned with soap and water or carbon tetrachloride.

D. Any greasy film upon the surfaces of a crystal will prevent good contact being made with the holder, and will interfere with the correct operation of the crystal.

Q. 3.98. What is the purpose of a buffer amplifier stage in a transmitter?

A. A buffer amplifier is used to improve the frequency stability of the oscillator stage.

D. A buffer amplifier is located immediately following the oscillator. It has low gain and low Q circuits and draws no grid current. Thus it presents a very high impedance load upon the oscillator and does not affect the oscillator Q to any great extent. Any changes in tuning of the succeeding amplifier or antenna stages have little or no effect upon the output frequency of the oscillator. If a buffer amplifier were not present, such tuning changes, or even motion of the antenna, might change the oscillator frequency.

Note: The following added material numbered Q. 3.98-A1 through Q.3.98-A10 contains information that may be required to pass the General Radiotelephone Operator's License examination. This added material, as well as the new material added to other sections, has been included to help acquaint students with the current state of the electronics art. It is felt that the added material contains subject matter that may also be required of students who have obtained a General Radiotelephone Operator's License and are seeking employment. Additionally, the added material contains valuable information for private technician certification.

Q. 3.98-A1. Draw a schematic diagram of an overtone JFET crystal oscillator. Briefly explain its operation.

A. The schematic diagram is shown in Fig. 3.98-A1. Note the similarity to the circuit of Fig. 3.86(b3).

No forward bias is required for a JFET to start oscillations (similar to a vacuum

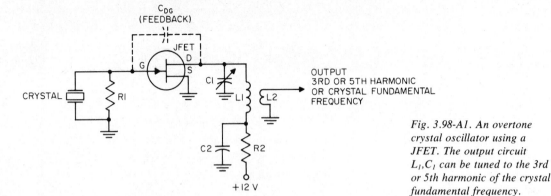

Fig. 3.98-A1. An overtone crystal oscillator using a JFET. The output circuit L_1, C_1 can be tuned to the 3rd or 5th harmonic of the crystal fundamental frequency.

tube). To produce oscillation, the drain-tuned circuit L_1C_1 is tuned slightly above the desired harmonic frequency. This is usually the 3rd or 5th harmonic. R_1 is the gate self-bias resistor. C_2 and R_2 form a decoupling network. Feedback takes place through the drain-to-gate capacitance. (C_{DG}).

D. See Q. 3.95.

Q. 3.98-A2. Draw a schematic diagram of a crystal harmonic oscillator. Briefly explain its operation.

A. The schematic diagram is shown in Fig. 3.98-A2.

Unlike the overtone crystal oscillator, the crystal harmonic oscillator has the crystal operating at its fundamental frequency. The collector-tuned circuit is tuned to the desired harmonic (2nd, 3rd, or 4th). This is another scheme to employ a relatively low-frequency crystal to produce stable oscillations at appreciably higher frequencies. (See also Q. 3.86(e).) To reduce the appearance of undesired harmonics in the output, a double-tuned collector circuit (shown) may

be used. Alternatively a single-tuned circuit followed by a harmonic filter may be used. Vacuum tube, crystal harmonic oscillators may be fashioned using common oscillator circuits such as the Colpitts or Pierce types. In this case, electron-coupled circuits are used, as described for Fig. 3.86(e), which can also be used for harmonic frequency generation.

Q. 3.98-A3. Draw a schematic diagram of a transistor Clapp oscillator. Briefly explain its operation.

A. For the circuit diagram of a transistor Clapp oscillator, see Fig. 3.98-A3.

The Clapp oscillator is a high-stability version of the Colpitts oscillator. Feedback is still determined by the ratio of C_1 to C_2. However, note the small capacitor C_3. The total tuning capacitance across the tank coil L_1 is the *series* value of C_1, C_2, and C_3 and thus is mainly the value of C_3 (slightly less.) Thus, the resonant frequency of the tank circuit is in control of C_3. Consequently, the values of C_1 and C_2 can change up to 20 percent with very little effect on the tuning

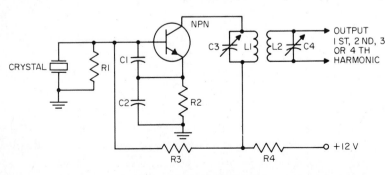

Fig. 3.98-A2. A crystal-harmonic oscillator. The output tuned circuits are tuned to a harmonic of the crystal fundamental frequency.

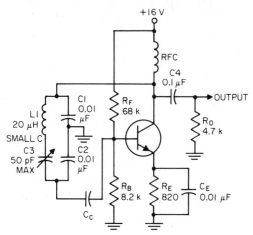

Fig. 3.98-A3. A Clapp (modified Colpitts) high-stability oscillator. The effective tuning capacity is mostly from C_3. (See text.) At maximum C_3 capacity, the oscillating frequency is about 5 mHz.

capacitance and resonant frequency. This fact enables the Clapp oscillator to have improved stability over the basic Colpitts oscillator. In addition, the Clapp oscillator has only a *single* tuning capacitor, rather than a double one as in the basic Colpitts oscillator. In order to gain the best stability of the Clapp oscillator, the smallest value of C_2 must be *at least* 20 times the maximum value of C_3.

Q. 3.98-A4. Draw a schematic diagram of a transistor "tuned-plate, tuned-grid" type oscillator. Briefly explain its operation.

A. A transistor version of a "tuned-plate, tuned-grid" oscillator is shown in Fig.

3.98-A4. This would be properly called a tuned-collector, tuned-base oscillator. For a crystal oscillator version, the base-tuned circuit can be replaced by a crystal and its holder. Because of the low collector-to-base capacitance, an added (small) feedback capacitor C_{cb} may be needed. To make the oscillator self starting, a low forward-base bias is provided by the voltage divider, R_B and R_F. Capacitor C_3 places the bottom of the collector-tuned circuit, C_2L_2, at RF ground potential.

D. See also Q. 3.86(b1), (b2).

Q. 3.98-A5. Draw a schematic diagram of a transistor, shunt-fed Hartley oscillator. Briefly explain its operation.

A. For the schematic diagram of a transistor, shunt-fed Hartley oscillator, see Fig. 3.98-A5. Note the great similarity to the tube version shown in Fig. 3.86(c). The operation for the two types is the same.

D. The voltage divider R_B, R_F is needed to supply self starting base bias. R_E improves transistor temperature stability. Capacitor C_E bypasses R_E to prevent degeneration. Resistor R_C acts to isolate the bottom end of the tuned circuit from the power supply (like an RF choke), while feeding supply voltage to the collector.

Q. 3.98-A6. How may the oscillating frequency of a crystal be varied?

A. The oscillating frequency of a crystal

Fig. 3.98-A4. A transistor- type, "tuned-plate tuned- grid" oscillator. A crystal and its holder can replace the base-tuned circuit L_1C_1.

Fig. 3.98-A5. Schematic of a transistor, shunt-fed Harley oscillator.

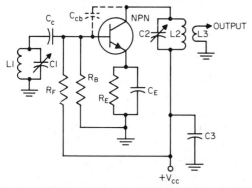

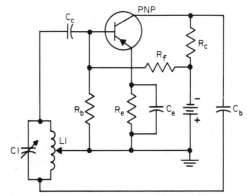

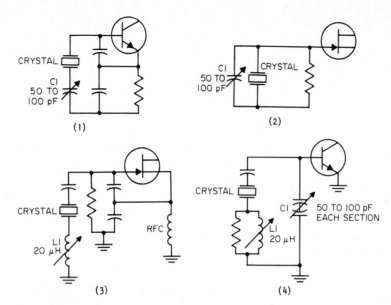

Fig. 3.98-A6. Partial schematics showing methods of varying the frequency of a crystal-oscillator: (1) variable capacitor (C_1) in series with the crystal; (2) variable capacitor (C_1) in parallel with the crystal; (3) variable inductance (L_1) in series with the crystal; (4) variable inductance (L_1) and split-variable capacitance (C_1) used in conjunction. Values are typical but can change according to crystal type and operating frequency.

may be varied by adding a variable capacitance in series or parallel with the crystal. In addition to the added capacitance, a series-variable inductor will increase the possible crystal frequency change. A variable-frequency crystal oscillator is often identified by the abbreviation VXO.

The general methods of varying the frequency of a crystal oscillator are shown in Fig. 3.98-A6. Stray circuit capacitances should be kept to a minimum to obtain the maximum frequency change.

D. In Fig. 3.98-A6. (1), the adjusting capacitor C_1 is in series with the crystal. AT-cut crystals are popular for VXO service. With circuit (1), a frequency change of about 750 Hz (maximum) for each 1 MHz of crystal frequency can be achieved.

About the same performance is obtained with the parallel adjusting capacitor (C_1) in Fig. 3.98-A6(2). Again, it is very important to keep stray circuit capacitances to a minimum.

Figure 3.98-A6(3) shows a method employing a variable inductance (L_1) in series with the crystal. The range varies only from the original crystal frequency to a lower frequency. This circuit will also provide about a 750 Hz change for each 1 MHz of crystal frequency.

In Fig. 3.98-A6(4), both a series-variable inductance (L_1) and a parallel capacitor (C_1) are used. With this arrangement, about triple the frequency change mentioned above can be achieved. L_1 is initially adjusted to provide the maximum frequency change obtainable with C_1.

Q. 3.98-A7. What is the flywheel effect. How does it relate to the operation of RF oscillators and RF amplifiers?

A.

1. The "flywheel effect" refers to the action of a resonant, parallel LC circuit. If this type of circuit is shock-excited by a single electrical pulse, it will produce a series of damped oscillations. The initial energy of the pulse will cause a periodic transfer of energy between the inductance and capacitance, in sine-wave fashion. If there were zero resistance in and no radiation from the LC circuit, the oscillations would continue forever at a constant amplitude. However, both of these *losses* cause the oscillations to constantly lose amplitude and then die out. The tendency of a resonant circuit to continue to oscillate after the initial pulse has ceased, is referred to as the *flywheel effect*. This is somewhat analogous to the action of a mechanical flywheel, which tends

to keep turning after an initial push. With the mechanical flywheel, the lower the total friction forces, the longer it will keep turning. For the LC circuit, the higher the circuit Q (minimum resistance and radiation) the longer it will continue to oscillate. (For a discussion of circuit Q, see Q. 3.34.)

2. With respect to oscillator operation, the flywheel effect is of great importance. An analogy can be made to the balance wheel of a watch. The balance wheel oscillates smoothly back and forth, although it receives energy for only a short period once each cycle. The flywheel effect carries the balance wheel through most of its cycle. In the case of most RF oscillators, the LC circuit (or crystal) also receives a short pulse of energy once each cycle. This pulse overcomes the circuit losses and makes possible constant amplitude oscillation of sinusoidal waves. Because of the flywheel effect in producing sine waves, the production of harmonic frequencies in the output of an oscillator is held to a minimum (the purer the sine wave, the fewer the harmonics).

3. Much RF amplifier operation is under Class B or Class C conditions. Here, the amplifier receives driving energy for only a portion of each cycle. (See Q. 3.86.) However, the flywheel effect of the tuned circuit causes it to continue to oscillate in sinusoidal fashion between the input driving impulses. This is important because it is desired here to amplify sinusoidal signals (not pulses), and operation at Class B and C permits much greater efficiencies than Class A amplification. In addition, by maintaining good sine waveforms, the generation of undesired harmonics is kept to a minimum.

D. See Q. 3.34, Q. 3.52, and Q. 3.86.

Q. 3.98-A8. What is meant by "locking" two oscillators together?

A. Basically, locking refers to synchronizing the frequency of one oscillator with that of another and more stable oscillator. For example, a variable frequency oscillator (VFO) can be locked in frequency by a circuit that refers the VFO to a stable crystal oscillator in a phase-locked loop circuit.

D. The locking process may be accomplished by the use of a phase-locked loop (PLL) system. In another system, two oscillators operating on approximately the same frequency can be caused to operate on exactly the same frequency. This is accomplished by synchronizing the frequency of one oscillator with the output of the other oscillator. This would also be considered as "locking" the two oscillators together.

Q. 3.98-A9. Draw a simple schematic diagram of a crystal RF oscillator, in which each of several frequencies may be selected by diode switching of different crystals.

A. The schematic diagram is shown in Fig. 3.98-A9. In the figure, high-speed silicon-switching diodes (D_1, D_2, D_3) are connected from one side of the crystal to ground. Unless a diode is conducting heavily, the crystal to which it is connected will not be activated. Thus, by means of switch S_1, any one of the three crystals shown, can be selected. On the selected switch position, +12 V is fed to the connected silicon diode through a series resistor (R_1, R_2, or R_3). The value of resistance is selected so its respective diode will conduct heavily, offering essentially zero resistance to ground. In Fig. 3.98-A9, only crystal 1 will operate.

D. Although crystals can be switched mechanically, this entails important disadvantages. First, the mechanical switch must be in the RF path. This severely restricts the possible physical layout of the equipment. The wiring leads from the crystal to the switch can introduce undesirable inductive and capacitive reactances, which may affect crystal frequency. Further, vibrations of such leads may cause oscillator instability.

The scheme shown in Fig. 3.98-A9 eliminates the above disadvantages. In addition, remote operation is facilitated, since only dc is switched.

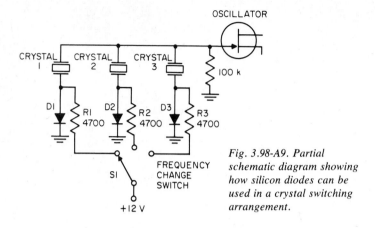

Fig. 3.98-A9. Partial schematic diagram showing how silicon diodes can be used in a crystal switching arrangement.

Q. 3.98-A10. What is the frequency range of commercially available crystals?

A. Commercially available crystals may be found in the range of 1 kHz to 200 MHz. High-precision crystals are readily available in *standard* frequencies of 1.0, 2.5, and 5 MHz. These standard frequency crystals may be used to calibrate electronic devices.

D. Some typical crystal frequency tolerances for a temperature range of 0°C to +50°C are:
1. 1 to 50 kHz: ±0.01 percent.
2. 200 to 500 kHz: ±0.003 percent.
3. 500 to 1 400 kHz: ±0.0025 percent.
4. 1.4 to 20 MHz: ±0.002 percent.
5. 10 to 200 MHz: ±0.002 percent.

The following are designated as standard frequency spectrum allocations by the FCC: 20 kHz, 60 kHz, 2.5 MHz, 5 MHz, 10 MHz, 15 MHz, 20 MHz, 25 MHz.

A radio station of the National Bureau of Standards WWV at Fort Collins, Colorado broadcasts *highly accurate,* standard radio frequencies continuously, night and day. The carrier frequencies broadcast are: 2.5, 5, 10, 15, 20, and 25 MHz. These can be picked up on a short wave receiver and used for calibration purposes. Standard audio frequencies of 440, 500, and 600 Hz are used to modulate each carrier at alternating periods.

Two other transmitters of the National Bureau of Standards at Fort Collins, Colorado broadcast highly accurate, low-frequency carrier signals. WWVL transmits intermittent experimental programs on 20 kHz. WWVB transmits continuously on 60 kHz.

The above frequencies are held to a tolerance of one-tenth of one cycle of the carrier frequency.

AUDIO AMPLIFIERS

Q. 3.99. Draw simple schematic diagrams illustrating the following types of coupling between audio amplifier stages and between a stage and a load.
1. Triode vacuum tube inductively coupled to a loudspeaker.
2. Resistance coupling between two pentode vacuum tubes.
3. Impedance coupling between two tetrode vacuum tubes.
4. A method of coupling a high impedance loudspeaker to an audio-frequency amplifier tube without flow of plate current through the speaker windings, and without the use of a transformer.

A.
1. For inductive coupling, see Fig. 3.99(a).
2. For resistance (RC) coupling, see Fig. 3.99(b).
3. For impedance coupling (rarely used), see Fig. 3.99(c).
4. For high-impedance speaker coupling (rarely used), see Fig. 3.99(d).

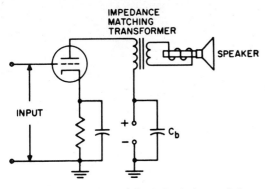

Fig. 3.99(a). An AF amplifier inductively coupled to
a loudspeaker.

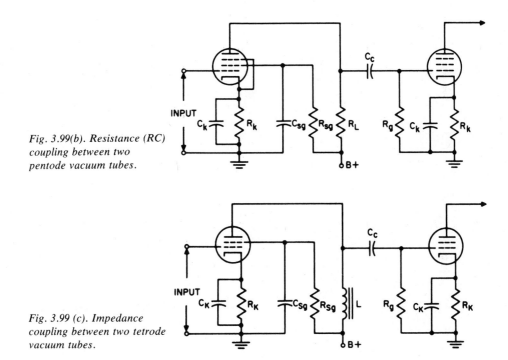

Fig. 3.99(b). Resistance (RC)
coupling between two
pentode vacuum tubes.

Fig. 3.99 (c). Impedance
coupling between two tetrode
vacuum tubes.

Fig. 3.99(d). Method of coupling a high-impedance
loudspeaker to an AF amplifier.

Q. 3.100. What would probably be the effect on the output amplitude and waveform if the cathode-resistor by-pass capacitor in an audio stage were removed?

A. The output amplitude would be reduced and the output waveform might be improved.

D. If the cathode by-pass capacitor is removed, a condition of negative current feedback exists in the amplifier. This is a degenerative voltage, developed across the cathode resistor by the plate current in it.

The results of degenerative feedback in audio amplifiers are:

1. Greater stability of amplifier characteristics.

2. Reduction of harmonic distortion.

3. Reduction of phase distortion.

4. Improvement of frequency response linearity.

5. Reduction of amplifier gain.

6. Reduction of noise output.

7. Reduction of effective r_p with negative voltage feedback.

8. Increase of effective r_p with negative current feedback.

The gain ratio of an amplifier with negative feedback may be determined from the formula

$$a' = \frac{a}{1 + Ba}$$

where

> a' = the gain with feedback. B = the fraction of the total output voltage fed back in opposition to the input signal voltage V_g. a is the gain without feedback. The low-frequency response will be affected according to the formula

$$F_1' = \frac{F_1}{1 + Ba}$$

where

> F_1' = the new low-frequency response with feedback.

The high-frequency response will be affected according to the formula,

$$F_2' = F_2 (I + Ba).$$

If no bypass capacitor were across the cathode resistor, the amplifier would in general have improved performance but at a sacrifice in gain. Placing a capacitor of suitable value across the cathode resistor prevents degenerative effects due to instantaneous bias changes on the cathode, which are in phase with the applied signal. This is due to the fact that the capacitor charges very little on increasing plate currents and discharges very little on decreasing plate currents. This condition requires that the time constant in the cathode circuit be long with respect to the time of the lowest audio frequency desired to be passed through the amplifier without degeneration. A simple formula to calculate the value of cathode capacitor is:

$$C_K = \frac{10\ 000\ 000}{2\pi f_1 R_K}$$

where

> C_K = cathode capacitor in microfarads.
> f_1 = the lowest frequency in hertz desired to be passed.
> R_K = the cathode bias resistance in ohms.

Q. 3.101. Why do vacuum tubes produce random noise?

A. Vacuum tube random noise (or shot-effect noise) is caused by random irregularities in the flow of electrons within the tube.

D. Shot-effect is caused by the fact that electrons are discreet particles which are emitted from the cathode in a random manner, rather than as a smooth continuous "fluid-like" flow. The current resulting from such an emission causes variations in the output circuit, commonly called "noise." The "noise" energy is distributed evenly across the entire frequency spectrum.

Q. 3.102. Why are de-coupling resistors and capacitors used in stages having a common power supply?

A. The purpose of decoupling networks is to prevent oscillations from occurring in a multistage audio amplifier.

D. It is common practice to supply plate and screen grid supply voltages for a multistage audio amplifier from a single power source. The output impedance of a power supply (unregulated) consists mainly of the reactance of the output filter capacitor. This reactance is a common impedance coupling element between all stages. If the amplifier contains high gain stages, there is a possibility of sufficient feedback voltages being developed across the reactance of the output capacitor to sustain oscillations. Since the reactance of a capacitor increases as the frequency decreases, such oscillations, if they occur, will most likely be of a very low frequency.

Q. 3.103. How would saturation of an output transformer create distortion?

A. When saturation of an output transformer has been reached, the inductance value is greatly reduced. This causes two immediate effects:

1. A reduction of load impedance on the output tube which reduces output amplitudes, especially at the low frequencies and thus creates amplitude distortion.

2. The inability of a saturated transformer to pass the waveform through to the speaker, without severe change. This happens because the flux in the transformer is already at its (practical) maximum value and cannot increase to follow the waveform pattern. This causes severe audio distortion.

D. When a transformer core is saturated, the iron contains the maximum number of flux lines it is capable of handling. A further increase in current through the primary does not produce additional flux lines and the effect is a flattening of the signal in the secondary. The transformer may respond in the normal manner to low current signals, but saturate on high current peaks.

Q. 3.104. Why is noise often produced when an audio signal is distorted?

A. Whether or not "noise" is actually present when an audio signal is distorted depends largely upon the actual cause of the distortion. Simple amplitude or frequency distortion will not necessarily produce any noise. Some cases where noise may accompany audio distortion may result from:

1. Defective coupling capacitor.
2. Microphonic tube.
3. Microphonic connections or components.
4. Defective volume control.

D. An apparent increase of the "noise" level of an audio signal may be a consequence of distortion. If appreciable non-linear audio amplification is present, amplitude distortion and possibly intermodulation distortion may result. Amplitude distortion causes the production of harmonics of the original wave. Intermodulation distortion is a result of the production of entirely new frequencies which were not present in the original audio wave. These may be produced by a heterodyning process (non-linear amplification) between original audio frequencies or between original audio frequencies and their harmonics produced by non-linear amplification. In either case, the resultants are the sum and difference frequencies (and harmonics of these) of the various combinations which tend to obscure the original audio tones and thus may be considered a form of audio "noise."

Q. 3.105. What are the factors which determine the correct bias voltage for the grid of a vacuum tube?

A. The following factors apply:
1. The class of operation (A, B, or C).
2. The plate supply voltage.
3. Permissible distortion.
4. Grid signal magnitude.
5. Permissible plate dissipation (in power tubes).
6. Desired amplification factor (in variable μ tubes).
7. The no-signal plate current desired.

8. The desirability or not of drawing grid current.

D. The amount of bias needed for a given class of operation is inversely proportional to the amplification factor (μ) of the tube. For example, in Class C operation where the bias is equal to twice cut-off, it may be found from the formula

$$V_c = \frac{2\,V_b}{\mu}$$

See also Q. 3.52, Q. 3.58 and Q. 3.106 through Q. 3.109.

Q. 3.106. Draw schematic diagrams illustrating the following types of grid biasing and explain their operation.
   1. Battery.
   2. Power supply.
   3. Voltage divider.
   4. Cathode resistor.

A.
   1. For battery bias, see Q. 3.50(b), above.
   2. For power supply bias, see Fig. 3.106(b) and Q. 3.50(c) and (e), above, for diagrams. In this scheme the desired value of bias is provided by means of a separate power supply. The current provided by such a supply is negligible, so that small solid-state rectifiers and simple RC filters may be employed in a half-wave rectifier.

   3. For a diagram of a voltage-divider bias scheme, see Fig. 3.106(c). In this bias scheme, the center-tap of the high-voltage secondary is returned to ground only through the low end of the bleeder resistor. This provides a negative dc voltage with respect to ground, whose amplitude is proportional to the percentage of the bleeder resistance tapped to ground.
   4. For cathode bias, see Q. 3.50(1), above.

   D. See Q. 3.105.

Q. 3.107. Is grid-leak biasing practical in audio amplifier stages?

A. Grid-leak biasing is not practical in audio amplifier stages.

D. The value of grid-leak bias is proportional to the amplitude of the input-grid signal. This type of bias varies whenever the signal changes and thus the operating point of the tube also changes. This condition may cause severe distortion of the audio signal. In addition, the grid current required to produce grid-leak bias causes loading on the driver stage reducing its gain and causing additional waveform distortion. See also Q. 3.52(6), Q. 3.105, Q. 3.121, and Q. 3.122.

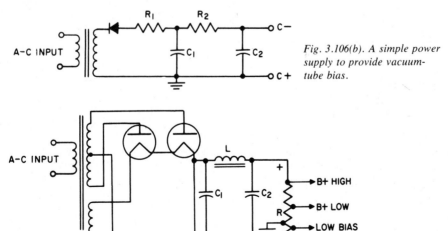

Fig. 3.106(b). A simple power supply to provide vacuum-tube bias.

Fig. 3.106(c). Schematic showing how to obtain voltage-divider bias.

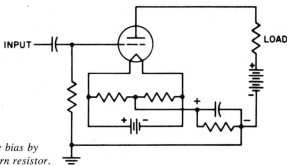

INPUT

LOAD

*Fig. 3.108. Tube bias by
series plate-return resistor.*

Q. 3.108. Draw a diagram showing a method of obtaining grid bias for a filament type vacuum tube by use of resistance in the plate circuit of the tube.

A. For the circuit diagram, see Fig. 3.108.

D. This is actually a type of "cathode" bias scheme. Plate current flows from the plate, through the load resistor, through the battery, then through the series RC network to the filament center tap. The drop across the RC network is such that a positive dc voltage appears at the filament, providing the bias.

Q. 3.109. Explain how you would determine the approximate value of cathode bias resistance necessary to provide correct grid bias for any particular amplifier.

A. The bias is equal to the *IR* drop across the cathode resistance and is found by dividing the desired dc bias voltage by the total dc, no-signal cathode current.

D. For a triode the bias resistance will equal the dc bias voltage divided by the no signal dc plate current or

$$R_K = \frac{V_c}{I_{bl}}$$

where

V_c = dc bias voltage as desired.
I_{bl} = the no signal value of dc plate current.

For tetrode or pentode the screen current must be added to the plate current, giving:

$$R_K = \frac{V_c}{I_{bl} + I_{sg}}$$

Q. 3.110. Draw circuit diagrams and explain the operation (including input-output phase relationships, approximate practical voltage gain, approximate stage efficiency, uses, advantages, and limitations) of each of the following types of audio circuits.

1. Class A amplifier with cathode-resistor biasing.

2. Cathode-follower amplifier.

3. At least two types of phase inverters for feeding push-pull amplifiers.

4. Cascaded Class A stages with a form of current feedback.

5. Two Class A amplifiers operated in parallel.

6. Class A push-pull amplifier.

A.

1. Class A amplifier, with cathode-resistor biasing:

a. For diagram, see Figure 3.50(a).

b. For operation, see Q. 3.50. The output wave is 180 degrees out of phase with the input wave.

c. The actual voltage gain which may be achieved depends upon the tube in use and the circuitry. An example of finding the voltage gain of a stage is given in Q. 3.58.

d. The approximate stage efficiency is 25 percent.

e. This type of amplifier may be used as an audio pre-amplifier, audio-intermediate amplifier, or final audio amplifier. It may also be used as a receiver RF amplifier or

IF amplifier. It also has many uses in various stages of different types of test equipment.

f. Advantages of this circuit are:

(1) Requires practically no grid driving power.

(2) Provides minimum distortion of the output waveform.

(3) Average plate current remains constant with or without an input signal.

(4) Has a high power-amplification ratio.

Limitations of this circuit are:

(1) Low plate circuit efficiency, usually about 25 percent.

(2) Plate current flows for 360 degrees of each cycle (reducing efficiency).

(3) Low power output compared to Class B or Class C.

2. a. For the diagram, see Fig. 3.50(d).

b. For operation and discussion of cathode-follower, see Q. 3.50, Answer (d).

c. The voltage gain is always less than one and depends upon the tube and circuitry in use. For the method of calculating gain, see Q. 3.50, Answer (4).

d. Plate circuit efficiency is not a factor in a cathode follower since the output is taken across the cathode circuit. However, for a Class A-biased stage, the efficiency is comparable to a Class A-biased conventional amplifier, or about 25 percent.

e. A cathode follower is most often used to drive a low-impedance device from a high-impedance input. It is frequently used to feed a low-impedance transmission line from a high-impedance source and is commonly used for this purpose in connection with pulse circuits. Because of its low-impedance output, its output is affected relatively little by the effects of shunt capacities of the load. It is sometimes used to feed a loudspeaker voice coil directly and thus eliminate the need for an output transformer. However, relatively high impedance voice coils are required (25-50 ohms) in this case.

f. The advantage of the cathode follower lies in the fact that it is a simple but highly effective impedance reducer. It also

has a very wide frequency response and passes narrow pulses without appreciable distortion. Its only serious limitation is the fact that its voltage gain is always less than one.

3. Two types of phase inverters: These are covered one at a time, the first one discussed is the single tube (paraphase) amplifier.

a. For diagram, see Figure 3.110(c1.)

b. As shown in the figure, one output is taken from the plate (inverted) and one from the cathode (not inverted). In practice, R_K is made equal to R_L and equal outputs are thus obtained since the same current flows through both resistors.

c. The voltage gain of each output is always less than one because of the negative feedback across R_K.

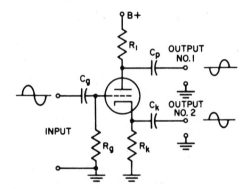

Fig. 3.110(c1). A simple method of supplying signals to double-ended audio amplifier without transformer.

d. Plate circuit efficiency is about 25 percent.

e. The paraphase amplifier is used to drive a push-pull amplifier from a single-ended input.

f. The advantage of this circuit is that it requires only a single tube, and has excellent frequency response. Its limitation is that it has no voltage gain.

Note: The second type of phase inverter to be discussed below is called a cathode-coupled paraphase inverter.

a. For diagram, see Fig. 3.110(c2).

b. Observe in the figure that the com-

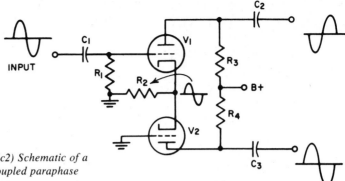

Fig. 3.110(c2) Schematic of a cathode-coupled paraphase inverter.

mon cathode resistor R_2 is unbypassed and that the grid of V_2 is grounded. R_2 is chosen so that the signal across it is equal to one-half of the V_1 grid-input signal. The effective signals applied to both tubes are equal since the R_2 signal is degenerative for V_1, but not for V_2. The output of V_1 is inverted with respect to the input signal. However, the output of V_2 is not because its input signal is applied to its cathode, and not to the grid.

c. The voltage gain of each stage is equal to one-half of its normal gain because of the cathode signal action. For gain-calculation references, see part 1. c. of this question.

d. The approximate plate efficiency of each tube is 25 percent.

e. The use of this amplifier is the same as for the paraphase amplifier discussed above.

f. This circuit has the advantage of providing voltage gain at each plate and good frequency response. However, the frequency response is poorer than in the prior phase inverter and it has only one-half the gain provided by conventional amplifier circuits.

4. Cascaded Class-A stages with current feedback.

a. For diagram of cascaded Class-A stages, see Fig. 3.110(d).

b. In practice, voltage feedback over two stages is generally preferred, or a combination of voltage and current feedback may be found quite often. The circuit of Fig. 3.110(d) employs current feedback in both stages by virtue of the unbypassed cathode resistors. The polarity of signal at each cathode is the same as the appearing at its corresponding grid. Therefore degeneration (negative feedback) occurs in each stage. This is current feedback because the voltage at each cathode depends upon the plate current of each tube flowing through the individual cathode resistors (R_2 and R_5).

c. The voltage gain of each stage is modified (reduced) by the negative feedback and may be found from the equation

$$A' = \frac{\mu R_L}{(\mu + 1) R_K + r_p + R_L}$$

where

A' = Gain with feedback.

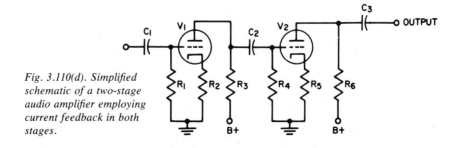

Fig. 3.110(d). Simplified schematic of a two-stage audio amplifier employing current feedback in both stages.

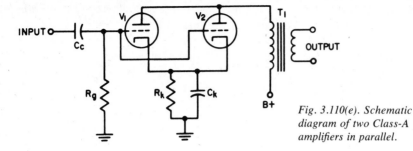

Fig. 3.110(e). Schematic
diagram of two Class-A
amplifiers in parallel.

μ = Amplification factor.
R_I = Plate-load resistance.
R_K = Cathode resistance.
r_p = Plate resistance (internal).

d. The approximate plate efficiency of each stage is 25 percent.

e. This type of amplifier may be used as intermediate audio-amplifier stages in various types of audio systems, or as inter-mediate amplifier stages in an oscilloscope, or other test equipment.

f. Advantages of this type of amplifier include; reduced distortion, improved frequency response, improved stability from regeneration or oscillation, reduction of hum and noise. The only serious limitation is the reduced gain.

5. Two Class-A amplifiers operated in parallel.

a. For diagram, see Figure 3.110(e).

b. Operation is basically the same as for a single tube as discussed in part (a) of this question. However, in this case, the proper cathode bias depends upon the plate current of both tubes. Two tubes in parallel provide double the power output of one tube. Distortion remains the same as for one tube and the grid input voltage remains the same. The effective internal-plate resistance is half

that of one tube and thus the required plate load impedance is cut in half.

c. The voltage gain is unchanged by the use of two tubes in parallel. However, this factor is seldom important since power output is the reason for paralleling the two tubes.

d. The approximate plate efficiency of each tube is 25 percent.

e. This type of amplifier, while not popular, may be used as an audio power-output amplifier. In general the push-pull type is preferred.

f. The principal advantage of this con-figuration is the elimination of the phase splitter required for push-pull operation. Limitations include: double the dc plate cur-rent requiring a special and expensive output transformer, no reduction in distortion as with push-pull operation and the larger cath-ode by-pass capacitor required because of the half value of the cathode-bias resistor.

6. Class A push-pull amplifier.

a. For diagram, see Fig. 3.110(f).

b. The proper inputs could be supplied from a phase inverter (see part 3. of this question), but is here provided by a center-tapped input transformer. The two grids are fed with signals which are 180 degrees out

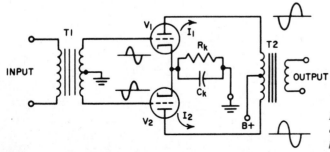

Fig. 3.110(f). Schematic
diagram of a Class-A push-
pull amplifier.

of phase. As a result, the plate signal currents (I_1 and I_2) are also 180 degrees out of phase. However, these currents flow in opposite directions through the primary winding and so are additive in the secondary winding.

c. Voltage gain is not a consideration here, but the power output is twice that for an amplifier using one of the same output tubes.

d. The approximate plate efficiency of each tube is 25 percent.

e. The most common use of this amplifier is as the audio power-output stage feeding a loudspeaker.

f. Advantages of this circuit are:

(1) Cancellation of even harmonic distortion in the output.

(2) Reduction of hum.

(3) Reduction of regenerative feedback.

(4) Elimination of dc core saturation, in output transformer.

(5) Elimination of cathode by-pass capacitor.

Elaborating:

1. Even order harmonic currents flow out of phase in the output transformer and thus cancel. This does not apply to distortion created either before or after the push-pull stage.

2. Hum currents are out of phase in the output transformer and return circuits and, therefore, cancel.

3. There is no ac signal current flowing through the plate supply and return circuits, and thus the tendency for regeneration in a multistage amplifier is reduced.

4. The dc plate currents in the output transformer flow in opposite directions creating opposing magnetic fields which cancel. This enables the size of the iron core to be made much smaller for a given power rating.

5. The fundamental ac signal components flow in opposite directions through the cathode resistor and cancel. Thus no by-passing is theoretically needed. However, a bypass capacitor is often included to compensate for unbalance in the tubes and for heater to cathode leakage.

Limitations of this circuit are:

1. The need to supply out-of-phase grid signals, and matched tubes and transformer windings for best results.

2. Bias controls may be required to assure perfect balancing.

Q. 3.111. Why does a Class B audio frequency amplifier stage require considerably greater driving power than a Class A amplifier?

A. A Class B audio amplifier stage usually operates with a value of grid input signal sufficient to drive the grid positive with respect to the cathode, on the positive peaks of the signal. Thus grid current exists for these positive peaks and appreciable power is dissipated in the grid circuit. The usual Class A amplifier does not operate in the grid current region, and, therefore, requires an insignificant amount of grid driving power.

D. As with most power tubes, it is required that the input grid impedance be kept low, especially where grid current exists. A transformer is generally used to couple into the grid circuit of the push-pull Class B tubes. The turns ratio of this transformer must be correct so that the proper load impedance will be reflected back into the primary of the driver tube (or tubes). A well-regulated power supply is needed to supply the Class B tubes because the average plate current varies in proportion to the grid signal.

Q. 3.112. Show by use of circuit diagrams two ways of using single-ended stages to drive a push-pull output stage.

A.

1. A paraphase amplifier, shown in Fig. 3.110(c1), is one method. The operation of this circuit is discussed in Q. 3.110(3).

2. A second type of phase inverter is shown in Figure 3.112. The voltage divider has a ratio equal to the voltage gain of V_1.

Because of this relationship, the signal output of V_1 is divided by its gain factor. The inverted output-signal amplitude from the voltage-divider is equal to the input-signal amplitude of V_1. The voltage-divider output is applied to the grid of V_2 and since V_1 and

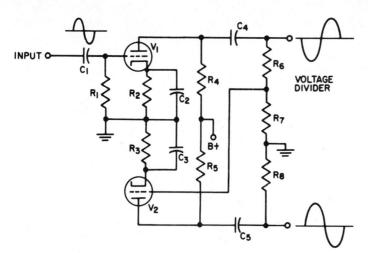

Fig. 3.112. Single-ended
stages arranged to drive a
push-pull output stage.

V_2 have equal gains, the output signals from V_1 and V_2 have equal amplitudes, but opposite phases.

Q. 3.113. Draw circuit diagrams and explain the operation of two commonly used tone control circuits and explain their operation.

A. See Figs. 3.113(a) and 3.113(b).

1. In the circuit of Fig. 3.113(a) the tone-control elements are C_T and R_T. This is a very simple, but popular, circuit and provides high-frequency attenuation only. When the slider of R_T is at the top, C_T is fully effective in bypassing the higher audio frequencies. When R_T is at the bottom end (maximum series resistance), the effect of C_T is nullified and all high audio frequencies are passed to the grid of the tube.

2. The circuit of Fig. 3.113(b) is more complex and provides both bass and treble attenuation. When C_1 goes to the grid side of R_2, low frequencies are attenuated by the effect of the series reactance of C_1, but this effect is limited by the bypass effect of R_1. When C_1 is at the ground end of R_2 high frequencies are attenuated by the bypass effect to ground of C_1.

Q. 3.114. Name some causes of hum and self-oscillation in audio amplifiers and the methods of reducing it.

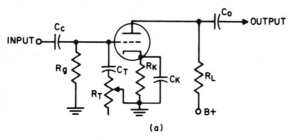

(a)

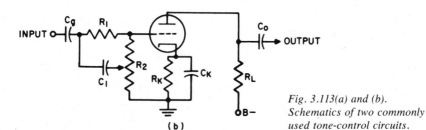

(b)

Fig. 3.113(a) and (b).
Schematics of two commonly
used tone-control circuits.

A.

1. Hum may be caused by:

a. Heater-to-cathode tube leakage. The tube must be replaced to cure this.

b. Filament-wire radiation. When the two wires are twisted together in close proximity, the hum radiation is largely cancelled. The reason for this is that the two wires are carrying currents in opposite directions and thus the magnetic fields will oppose and cancel out to a large degree.

c. Open-grid circuit. The high-impedance grid is susceptible to hum-radiation pickup. The cure is obvious.

d. Faulty filter capacitor (or resistor or choke) in the power supply filter feeding the amplifier. Again, the cure is obvious.

e. Hum pickup from a power transformer due to its inadequate shielding or its close proximity to a high gain stage. This may be corrected by replacing the transformer or by proper shielding of the tube(s) involved and their input (grid) leads. Proper dress of the input leads may also be effective in reducing hum pickup.

f. Hum may be reduced by the use of a push-pull amplifier. See Q. 3.110(6.) for a discussion of this procedure.

g. High-gain amplifiers, e.g., the preamplifier for a stereophonic audio amplifier, are more susceptible to hum pickup problems than are low-gain amplifiers. In such cases, it is common to feed the filaments of such stages with well-filtered dc voltage. This reduces the heater-to-cathode hum pickup problem as well as reducing hum radiation from the filament wires.

2. Self-oscillation may be caused by the following:

a. Open grid resistor (when amplifier draws grid current).

b. Coupling circuit time constant too long (when amplifier draws grid current).

c. Output power supply filter capacitor too small, or defective.

d. Decoupling filter(s) defective.

e. Output of one high-gain stage feeding back to the grid circuit of a prior high-gain stage. This can be prevented by isolating the input grid from output-plate circuits, and by shielding the tubes (and whole stages where necessary). Proper layout of the amplifier stages will provide physical separation of stages which might create oscillation problems.

D. Self-oscillation is an oscillation which is generally of the relaxation type when coupling elements are involved. If the output impedance of the power supply is relatively large and decoupling filters are not used, it represents a common impedance coupling element between the various amplifier stages and thus affords a means for feedback to sustain oscillations. See Question 3.102.

Q. 3.115. What factors should be taken into consideration when ordering a Class-A audio-output transformer; a Class-B audio-output transformer feeding a speaker of known ohmic value?

A.

1. Some important considerations when ordering a Class-A audio-output transformer are:

a. Operating power level in watts, including peak-power level expected.

b. Turns ratio to match speaker voice coil to the output tube(s).

c. Single ended or push-pull power output stage.

d. Frequency response under normal power-output conditions.

e. Harmonic distortion at the lowest frequency involved and at the maximum-output power.

f. Direct current in primary winding(s).

g. Adequate magnetic and electrostatic shielding.

h. Source impedance and load impedance.

2. Important considerations for a Class B output transformer are the same as for Class A (above) with one added consideration. Since the plate currents flow intermittently (180 degrees) in each tube, it is

essential that the leakage inductance between both halves of the primary windings be very small. If this is not true, transients will be produced in the primaries, that may produce severe distortion.

Q. 3.116. Draw a diagram of a single-button carbon microphone circuit, including the microphone transformer and source of power. Draw its cross-section.

A. For the diagrams see Figs. 3.116 (a) and (b).

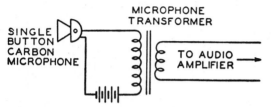

Fig. 3.116(a): Single-button microphone connection.

D. The "carbon-button" microphone depends for its operation upon the characteristics of a pile of carbon granules when subjected to varying pressures. The carbon button proper consists of a small cup completely filled with very fine carbon granules. A tightly stretched duralumin diaphragm is attached to the carbon button (or buttons) in such a way that sound vibrations cause varying pressures upon the button. The resistance of the carbon button varies in proportion to the pressures upon it. A battery

supply is connected in series with the button and a resistance (or transformer primary), so that variations in resistance will cause corresponding variations in the output current from the button. These varying currents will be proportional to the character of the sound waves producing them. The frequency response of a broadcast type is inferior to most other types of microphones, and is in the order of 70 to 6000 hertz. The carbon microphone is no longer in general use because, although it has very high sensitivity, it has a number of serious disadvantages. These are: (1) it is sensitive to vibration, (2) it cannot be handled while in use, (3) it generates a hissing sound in its output, (4) the carbon granules in the buttons are subject to "packing," (5) it requires a battery power supply for operation. Carbon microphones are used wherever high output voltages with restricted frequency response characteristics are desired. A typical example is the use of carbon microphones in aircraft radio transmitters and in other mobile equipment.

Q. 3.117. If low-impedance head telephones of the order of 75 ohms are to be connected to the output of a vacuum tube amplifier, how may this be done to permit most satisfactory operation?

A. Low-impedance head telephones may be satisfactorily coupled to an amplifier

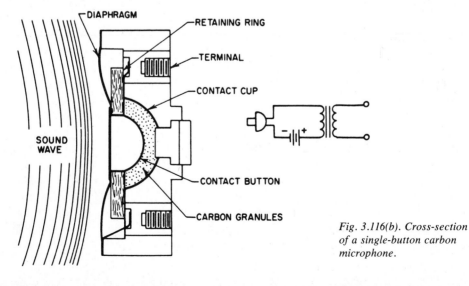

Fig. 3.116(b). Cross-section of a single-button carbon microphone.

tube by the use of an impedance matching transformer.

D. In order to achieve maximum output with tolerable distortion it is necessary that a certain value of plate load impedance be presented to the amplifier tube. An impedance of 75 ohms will not be satisfactory as a plate load with any of the common types of tubes. Therefore, it is necessary for the tube to work into its proper load impedance and for the phones to work into their proper impedance which is 75 ohms. This is accomplished by making use of the impedance reflecting properties of a transformer. If the load across the secondary of the transformer is 75 ohms, then the primary impedance is found by $Z_p = Z_s \times N^2$. Thus if the turns ratio, which is equal to the voltage ratio, is 10 to 1, the primary impedance will be 75×10^2 or 7500 ohms. If it is desired to find the turns ratio the following formula is applied:

$$N = \sqrt{\frac{Z_s}{Z_p}}$$

where

N = the turns ratio.
Z_p = the correct plate load impedance.
Z_s = the impedance of the driven device (headphones).

Another way of using the 75-ohm phones without a transformer is to connect them as a cathode bias resistor in the output stage. In this case, the B+ goes directly to the plate, and there is no cathode bypass capacitor. This is the cathode-follower connection, useful for feeding low impedance loads and to reduce distortion.

Q. 3.118. Describe the construction and explain the operation of a "crystal" type microphone.

A.
1. For sketch of a crystal microphone, see Fig. 3.118.
A "crystal" microphone depends for its operation upon the piezo-electric effect

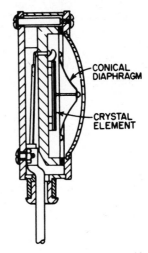

Fig. 3.118. Crystal microphone assembly.

of a suitable crystalline material. Rochelle salts are most commonly used for this purpose in the crystal microphone. The crystal proper is made up of a number of crystal cells arranged so as to increase the sensitivity of the unit. One such unit consists of *two* crystal elements so arranged as to operate in phase when sound vibrations are present, but to generate out of phase potentials when subjected to shock or mechanical vibration. The entire crystal unit is impregnated in wax and enclosed in an airtight chamber. This enclosure, however, does not prevent the crystal from vibrating and thus generating emf's proportional to the sound wave components. The sound vibrations are transmitted to the crystal unit by means of a conical duralumin diaphragm by means of a resilient, intermediate member. The microphone has a flat frequency response over the entire audio range. It is lightweight, reasonably rugged, easily maintained, and requires no power supply. It has a high-impedance output, is non-directional, and has no inherent background noise level. The microphone should be protected against excessive humidity, as Rochelle salts are soluble in water. The wax impregnation of the crystal element is, however, highly efficient in protecting the crystal against moisture.

2. For sketch of a single-button carbon microphone, see Fig. 3.116. For its operation, see Q 3.116.

D. For a discussion of several types of microphones, and their construction, see Q. 3.119-A1.

Q. 3.119. What precaution should be observed when using and storing crystal microphones?

A. The microphone should be protected against excessive heat, shock and humidity.

D. See Q. 3.118.

Q. 3.119-A1. Sketch the physical construction of the following types of microphones and list their advantages and/or disadvantages:
1. Dynamic.
2. Ceramic.
3. Ribbon.
Which types are normally used in the broadcast studio? Why?

A.

1. For a sketch of a dynamic microphone, see Fig. 3.119-A1(a). A "dynamic" or "moving coil" type of microphone is somewhat similar in construction to a small permanent magnet dynamic speaker.

The diaphragm is of the unstretched, non-rigid type and has a number of circular corrugations. These corrugations give the diaphragm a great amount of flexibility and excellent low frequency response. Attached to the diaphragm is a circular coil constructed of a large number of thin aluminum turns held together and insulated by a varnish.

Fig.3.119-A1(a). Cross-section of a dynamic microphone.

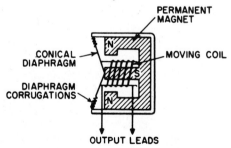

The coil, which moves with the diaphragm, passes between the poles of a strong permanent magnet, with very small clearance. When the diaphragm is actuated by sound waves, the coil moves in the magnetic field of the permanent magnet, and has induced into it a voltage corresponding to the sound variations.

The microphone has a low impedance output (25 to 50 ohms) and may be connected through long shielded cables to a distant amplifier. It is rugged, dependable, requires no power supply, and very little maintenance. The frequency response of those commonly available is approximately from 50 to 15 000 hertz.

Advantages of a dynamic microphone are:
a. Rugged construction.
b. High output level (-55dB).
c. Light weight.
d. Wide frequency response (50–15 000 hertz).
e. Low-hum pickup (-128 dBm).
f. Low impedance (switchable for 30, 150 or 250 ohms in certain broadcast studio types).
g. Relatively insensitive to temperature and humidity.
h. Large dynamic operating range.
i. Does not require power supply.

2. The ceramic microphone is constructed in a similar manner to a crystal microphone and is shown in Figure 3.119-A1(b). The basic difference is that the piezo-electric effect of certain ceramic materials replaces that of Rochelle-salt crystals. Ceramic is much less affected by temperature and humidity than Rochelle salt. However, the ceramic element like the crystal, is frequently enclosed in a moisture-proof case. The basic principle of operation is the same as for the crystal type (see Q. 3.118). The output of ceramic microphones and their frequency response (for similar services) are very similar to the crystal type and they both feature high-impedance outputs. The output level

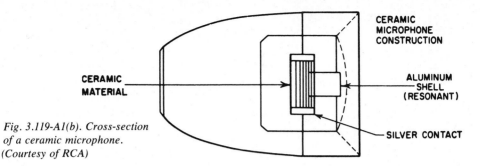

Fig. 3.119-A1(b). Cross-section
of a ceramic microphone.
(Courtesy of RCA)

for a good-quality microphone may be
− 55dB and the frequency response from 50
to 12 000 hertz.

Advantages of a ceramic microphone
are:

a. Relatively inexpensive.

b. High output level (− 55dB).

c. Good frequency response.

d. Does not require power supply.

Disadvantages of a ceramic microphone
are:

a. Tends to be susceptible to temperature and humidity (although less so than
crystal type).

b. May be susceptible to shock.

c. Response may not be as smooth as
the dynamic or ribbon type.

d. Frequency response may not be as
extensive as dynamic or ribbon type.

e. High output impedance, makes it
more susceptible to hum pickup and background noise.

3. For sketch of a ribbon microphone,

see Fig. 3.119-A1(c). The ribbon (or velocity,
or pressure gradient) microphone employs
a very light ribbon of corrugated aluminum
suspended to vibrate freely in a magnetic
field. The ribbon is actually the diaphragm
of the microphone and exposed to the air
on its two opposite faces. The ribbon vibrates
in response to the velocity component of
the sound wave and cuts magnet lines of
force causing proportional voltages to be
induced into the ribbon. These voltages (at
extremely low impedance) are fed to a transformer. The transformer raises the microphone impedance to be compatible with
standard lines and facilities of the broadcast
studio and also raises the microphone output
voltage level to a practical value similar to
a dynammic microphone.

Advantages of a ribbon microphone
are:

a. Wide frequency response (50–15 000
hertz).

b. High output level (− 55 dBm).

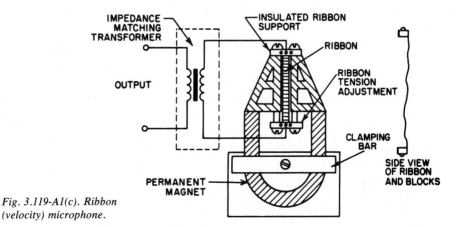

Fig. 3.119-A1(c). Ribbon
(velocity) microphone.

c. Low output impedance (30-150 ohms, switchable).

d. Rugged construction.

e. Light weight.

f. Insensitive to heat and humidity.

g. Large dynamic operating range.

h. Does not require power supply.

i. Low background noise.

Disadvantages of a ribbon microphone are:

a. Ribbon is delicate and should not be subjected to sudden puffs of wind or blasting sounds.

b. Ribbon should not be overstretched or it will lose its elasticity with a consequent reduction of overall performance.

4. The microphones normally used in the broadcast studio are the dynamic and the ribbon types. The reasons for using these are:

a. Light weight.

b. Rugged construction.

c. Low-hum pickup.

d. Indefinite life.

e. Wide and smooth frequency response characteristics.

f. Relatively impervious to shock and vibration, temperature and humidity.

g. Some types are built to have directional characteristics.

h. Low background noise.

i. Low-impedance output.

j. High-level output.

Q. 3.119-A2. What is meant by the "phasing" of microphones? When is it necessary?

A.

1. "Phasing" of microphones indicates that each microphone will have the same output polarity for a given sound-pressure wave acting on the microphones.

2. Phasing is necessary when two or more microphones are connected to a mixer. If this is not done the microphone outputs may oppose each other, causing a reduction of output. In addition, varying amounts of distortion may also be introduced.

D. Phasing may be particularly important when two similar microphones are placed in a symmetrical relationship to a performer. Also, for optimum operation of some amplitude-modulated transmitters, correct phasing may be important. This is true because of the unsymmetrical aspects of speech waveforms.

Q. 3.119-A3. What is the difference between multidirectional, bidirectional, and omnidirectional microphones?

A.

1. A unidirectional microphone has its major lobe of pickup extending in only one direction.

2. A bidirectional microphone has two major lobes of pickup which are separated by 180 degrees.

3. An omnidirectional microphone picks up sounds with equal facility from all directions.

D.

1. A unidirectional microphone is used when it is desired to discriminate against sounds coming from all but one direction. An example is the use of such a microphone for a singer before a large audience.

2. A bidirectional microphone may be used to pick up the voices of two people sitting across from one another, while discriminating against pickup from other directions.

3. An omnidirectional microphone may be positioned in the center of activity when it is desired to pick up sound equally from all directions. For example, the microphone may be placed in the center of a round-table discussion.

Q. 3.119-A4. What is the nominal frequency range for which audio transformers may be used?

A. The nominal frequency range is 20 to 20 000 Hz.

D. An important consideration in the design, size, and cost of an audio transformer is its required frequency response. For analysis, the frequency span can be separated into three ranges: (1) high frequencies, (2) middle (or ''mid'') frequencies, and (3) low frequencies.

In the high-frequency range the most important items are the distributed capacitance and the leakage inductance. In the mid-frequency range (1 000 Hz), the effect of the transformer on frequency response can be neglected. In the low-frequency range, the important consideration is the transformer open-circuit inductance.

Miniaturized audio transformers have inherently low distributed capacitance and leakage inductance. As a result, they generally have excellent high-frequency response. However, with these units the core air gap must be reduced to maintain good low-frequency response (adequate open-circuit inductance). As an example, this parameter may be 32 H with no air gap, down to 12 H with a 0.002-in. gap. *Interlacing* the laminations can bring the open circuit inductance up to 120 H. This procedure staggers the lamination butt joints. However, as the air gap is reduced, the dc current in the transformer winding must be reduced to prevent core saturation.

Q. 3.119-A5. What are audio chokes?

A. *Audio chokes* are used for *impedance* coupling in certain audio amplifiers. These chokes are iron-core units that are generally connected in the output circuit of an amplifier instead of a load resistor.

D. The use of a resistor for an amplifier output load generally provides excellent frequency response for an amplifier. In addition, a resistor is small and inexpensive. However, the dc drop across the load resistor limits the amplifier output. With an audio choke for the output load, there is very little dc drop in the choke resistance. Consequently, greater output can be obtained. However, an audio choke with adequate audio frequency response can be somewhat expensive and bulky. Thus, the resistance type of amplifier output load is generally preferred.

Q. 3.119-A6. Draw a schematic diagram of a basic N-channel FET audio amplifier. Briefly explain its operation.

A. The schematic diagram is given in Fig. 3.119-A6.

The N-channel FET employs self-bias. The bias is provided by the voltage drop $V_S = I_D R_S$ across the drain resistor R_S. This voltage drop makes the source positive with respect to the gate. This is the correct polarity to properly bias the FET.

Resistor R_G places the gate at dc ground potential. It also provides a high-resistance load to the input signal source, permitting the entire input signal to appear at the gate.

On positive half-cycles of V_{in}, the drain current (I_D) increases and the instantaneous value of V_O goes in the negative direction (phase reversal). On negative half-cycles of V_{in}, the drain current (I_D) decreases and the instantaneous value of V_O goes in the positive direction. An amplified version of V_{in} thus appears as V_O. Amplification takes place because a small change of input voltage (V_{in}) produces a larger change of output voltage (V_O). (The input voltage change is effective in causing a substantial drain current change through resistor R_D.)

D. The voltage amplification of this amplifier may be described by the following equation:

$$A_V = \frac{V_o}{V_{in}} = \frac{V_{DS}}{V_{GS}}$$

Fig. 3.119-A6. Schematic diagram of an N-channel FET audio amplifier.

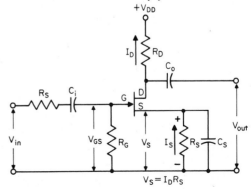

In a typical FET amplifier, a change in V_{GS} of 0.4 V may cause a change of 0.4 mA in I_D. This can cause a change of 8 V in V_{DS}. In this case, the amplification equals

$$A_V = \frac{8 \text{ V}}{0.4 \text{ V}} = 20$$

Q. 3.119-A7. Draw a schematic diagram of a basic MOSFET (metal oxide semiconductor field effect transistor) audio amplifier. Briefly explain its operation.

A. The schematic diagram is shown in Fig. 3.119-A7.

Note that the drain voltage V_{DS} and the gate voltage V_{GS} have the same polarity. Thus, only one power supply voltage is required. The gate bias voltage V_{GS} is obtained from the supply voltage through resistors R_D and R_G.

D. Resistor R_G usually has a very large value, in the order of 10 MΩ or greater. This avoids the possibility of undesirable feedback from drain to gate. The MOSFET operates in the constant current, or saturation, region of its drain characteristics. This condition occurs when the gate voltage exceeds several volts.

The signal voltage V_{in} is coupled to the gate through capacitor C_i. If the signal voltage excursion does not exceed the region of the constant current curves of the MOSFET characteristic, the output voltage V_{out} will be an accurate but amplified version of the input voltage V_{in}.

Q. 3.119-A8. Draw a simplified basic schematic diagram of a complementary-symmetry audio amplifier. Briefly explain its operation.

A. The schematic diagram is shown in Fig. 3.119-A8.

As shown in the figure, a PNP and an NPN transistor are used for this circuit. The complementary-symmetry circuit combines the advantages of conventional push-pull amplifiers, plus direct coupling. No input or output transformer is required. The voice coil of a loudspeaker may be connected in place of resistor R_L shown in Fig. 3.119-A8, without producing excessive distortion.

D. The two transistors are operated in Class B. (For simplicity, two power sources are shown in the figure. A practical circuit would use only one power source and would include the biasing and stabilization circuits, as well as a driver stage.)

On the positive half-cycle of the input signal (V_{in}), NPN transistor Q_2 is forward-biased and conducts through R_L as shown by the arrows. At this time, PNP transistor R_1 is cut off. On the negative half-cycle of the input signal, Q_1 conducts and Q_2 is cut off. Q_1 conduction is now in the opposite direction through R_L. Thus, we see that Q_2 amplifies the positive half-cycle and Q_1 the negative half-cycle of the input signal. Each transistor acts as an emitter follower (low impedance) and delivers power to the load (R_L) on alternate half-cycles.

Fig. 3.119-A7. Schematic diagram of a P-channel enhancement MOSFET audio amplifier.

Fig. 3.119-A8. The simplified basic circuit for a complementary-symmetry audio output stage. R_L can be replaced by the voice coil of a loudspeaker. The arrows indicate electron current.

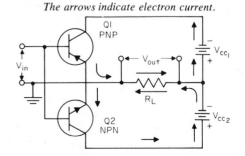

Q. 3.119-A9. Draw a schematic diagram of a direct-coupled audio amplifier using two NPN transistors. Briefly explain the operation.

A. The schematic diagram is shown in Fig. 3.119-A9.

The base voltage of transistor Q_1 is determined by the voltage divider consisting of R_1 and R_2; it is 1.9 V. There is a drop of 0.7 V across the base-emitter junction, making the emitter voltage 1.2 V. The collector voltage (due to the drop across R_3) is here, 3.4 V. This is also the base voltage of transistor Q_2. Since there is, again, a 0.7-V drop across the base-emitter junction, the Q_2 emitter voltage is 2.7 V. Because of the drop across resistor R_G, the collector voltage of transistor Q_2 is 9.0 V. A typical overall voltage gain would be in the order of 70.

D. The basic advantage of a direct-coupled amplifier is its excellent response for very low frequencies or, in some cases, to dc. RC-coupled or transformer-coupled amplifiers have a drop-off at low frequencies because of the reactances of the coupling elements. However, direct-coupled amplifiers require well regulated power supplies. Also, temperature variation of the bias current in one stage may be amplified by another stage, resulting in temperature instability of the amplifier. This latter problem may be reduced by using complementary transistors (NPN and PNP) for the amplifier.

RF AND IF AMPLIFIERS, MIXERS, AGC, AND OPERATIONAL AMPLIFIERS

Q. 3.120. What is an RFC? Why are they used?

A. In general, an RF choke acts as a low-pass filter which permits the passage of dc and low frequency components but prevents the passage of radio frequencies.

D. Chokes are often used to prevent radio frequencies from entering the power supply. They are also used as coupling elements, to help maintain the Q of tank circuits, as in a crystal oscillator, and sometimes as tuning elements, as in a Pierce oscillator.

Q. 3.121. What are the advantages of using a resistor in series with the cathode of a Class C radio-frequency amplifier tube to provide bias?

A. If the exciting signal to a Class C radio-frequency amplifier, using grid-leak bias only, is interrupted for any reason the bias will be reduced to zero and excessive dc plate current will flow; usually with disastrous results. If at least a portion of the total bias is obtained from a resistor in series with the cathode, the bias will not be reduced to zero because the dc plate current, flowing through the cathode resistor, will still provide some bias.

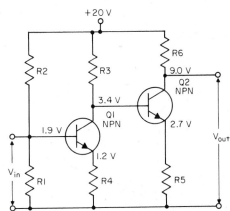

Fig. 3.119-A9. Schematic diagram of a direct-coupled audio amplifier using two NPN transistors.

D. This remaining bias can be made just sufficient to allow no more than the maximum allowable plate dissipation to occur under the dc conditions of no excitation. For example, consider a type 833-A triode being used as a Class C RF amplifier with a plate voltage of 2 500 volts. The maximum allowable plate dissipation for this tube is 300 watts. Under no-excitation conditions, all of the plate power input is converted to plate dissipation which, in this case, will reach the maximum allowable when the dc plate current is 120 milliamperes. Reference to the characteristic curves for the tube will indicate the approximately -40 volts grid bias will produce a dc plate current of 120 mA. Using Ohm's Law, the value of resistance to be used is found to be 40/0.120 or 333 ohms.

If the total grid bias recommended is -300 volts, the remaining 260 volts can be obtained in the usual manner by means of a grid leak.

Q. 3.122. What is the difference between RF voltage amplifiers and RF power amplifiers in regards to applied bias? What type of tube is generally employed in RF voltage amplifiers?

A.

1. Usually an RF voltage amplifier is operated as a Class A amplifier, whereas an RF power amplifier is operated as either a Class B or Class C amplifier. Therefore, an RF voltage amplifier would normally use a bias that is approximately midway between zero and the cut-off bias for the value of plate voltage employed. For a Class B power amplifier the bias would be approximately equal to the cut-off bias and for a Class C power amplifier the bias would be in the order of twice cut-off bias.

2. As power amplification is not required of RF voltage amplifiers, receiving type tubes are normally used for this function. Commonly, these are pentodes, although triodes are sometimes used under special circumstances.

Q. 3.123. Draw schematic diagrams of the following circuits and give some possible reasons for their use.
1. Link coupling between a final RF stage and an antenna. (Include a low pass filter.)
2. Capacitive coupling between an oscillator stage and a buffer amplifier.
3. A method of coupling a final stage to a quarter-wave Marconi antenna other than link or transmission line.

A.

1. Link coupling between a final RF stage and an antenna is most useful when the antenna is located remotely from the transmitter building as is the case in most broadcast stations. This permits placing both the building and the antenna in the most advantageous physical locations. Figure 3.123(a), illustrates the pertinent details of the system.

2. Capacitive coupling between an oscillator and its buffer amplifier is a very simple and easily adjustable method. For greater coupling, the tap on the tank coil of the oscillator may be moved closer to the plate end of the coil. Figure 3.123(b), illustrates the basic scheme for this type of coupling.

3. For shipboard installations where the intermediate frequency ranges are used, the antenna's physical size is such that the connections to it from the transmitter necessarily are part of the complete antenna system. In such circumstances, the antenna

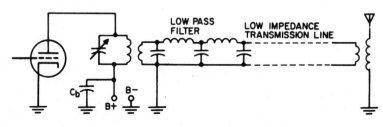

Fig. 3.123(a). Link coupling between a final RF stage and an antenna.

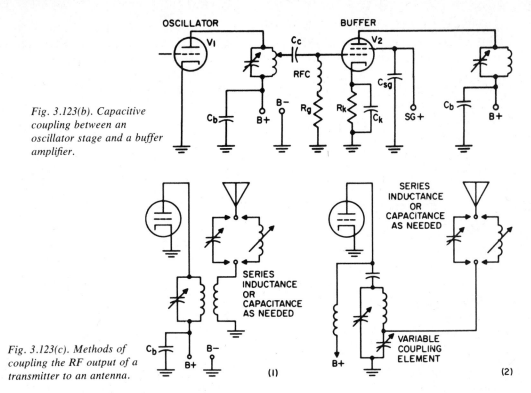

Fig. 3.123(b). Capacitive coupling between an oscillator stage and a buffer amplifier.

Fig. 3.123(c). Methods of coupling the RF output of a transmitter to an antenna.

downlead, which is a portion of the antenna itself, is connected directly to the transmitter output terminals. The diagrams given in Fig. 3.123(c) (1 and 2) illustrate two methods for accomplishing this. It should be noted that all parts shown in the diagrams are included inside the transmitter enclosure and just the antenna and ground connections are made to the transmitter.

Q. 3.124. Draw a schematic diagram of a grounded-grid RF amplifier and explain its operation.

A. For the diagram, see Fig. 3.124. As shown in the figure, the grid is grounded and the input signal is applied to the cathode circuit.

In some circuits, bias is applied to the grid circuit either by a fixed-bias supply, or by means of a grid-leak resistor and grid capacitor connected in parallel from grid to ground. In the latter arrangement, the grid is "grounded" for signal by means of a capacitor, but is not grounded for dc. The fil-

ament chokes prevent bypassing through the filament transformer capacity to ground of the input signal through the cathode-to-filament capacity. The output signal is taken from the plate circuit in the same manner as in a grounded-cathode amplifier. However, since the input voltage is in series with the external load impedance, this signal contains

Fig. 3.124. A grounded grid RF amplifier.

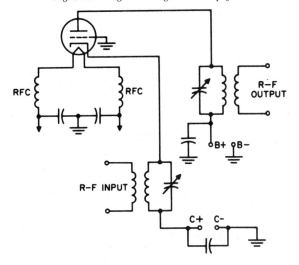

an additional component consisting of the input energy (see discussion below).

D. For an extensive discussion of grounded grid amplifiers see Q. 3.50(c).

Grounded grid amplifiers are sometimes used at very high frequencies because it is often possible to utilize triode tubes without the necessity for neutralization. In the grounded-grid amplifier the feedback capacitance is not the plate-grid capacitance, but is the much smaller plate-cathode capacitance. This smaller capacitance is less likely to cause oscillations, even at extremely high frequencies when special triodes (lighthouse type) are used. See also Q. 3.63 and Q. 3.64.

Q. 3.125. Explain the principle involved in neutralizing an RF stage.

A. The purpose of neutralization in a radio-frequency amplifier is to prevent the amplifier from generating self-sustained oscillations. Without neutralization but with the tuned transformers customarily used, the circuit usually will act as a tuned-plate tuned-grid oscillator. Three common methods of neutralization are known as: (1) Hazeltine or plate neutralization, (2) Rice or grid neutralization, (3) Cross neutralization or push-pull neutralization.

D. Conventional triode RF amplifiers with both plate and grid circuits tuned to the same frequency invariably require neutralization. The reason for this is obvious when the RF amplifier of Figure 3.125(a) is compared with the diagram of a tuned-grid tuned-plate oscillator as shown in Figure 3.86(b1). Except for the neutralization connections, the two circuits are identical. Feedback through C_{gp} will cause the circuit to oscillate. If the amplifier is permitted to oscillate, there will be several undesirable effects: (1) Excessive plate current, (2) Overheating with possible burnout of tube, (3) Possible damage to circuit parts, such as meters, RF chokes, etc., (4) Generation of spurious frequencies, (5) Distortion of a modulated wave (if this stage is modulated)

during peaks of modulation. Since the tendency to oscillate is caused by an RF voltage applied through C_{gp} to the grid, in phase with the original grid voltage, then a bucking voltage must be provided which is equal in amplitude and opposite in phase to the feedback through C_{gp}. The means of providing for such a bucking voltage is to tap the lower end of the plate tank circuit and feed this new voltage into the grid circuit.

1. A schematic diagram and the equivalent bridge circuit of a plate-neutralized amplifier are shown in Figs. 3.125(a) and (b).

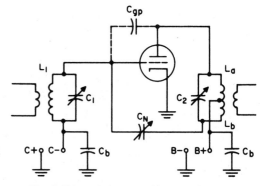

Fig. 3.125(a). Schematic diagram of a plate-neutralized amplifier.

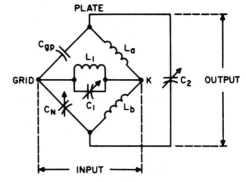

Fig. 3.125(b). Equivalent bridge circuit of a plate-neutralized amplifier.

The currents flowing into the input circuit through C_{gp} tend to cause oscillation. This effect is cancelled by opposing currents fed back to the input circuit through C_n. If the bridge is properly balanced (by adjusting C_n), no oscillations can appear in the output circuit. The relationship for balance is:

$$\frac{L_a}{L_b} = \frac{C_n}{C_{gp}}$$

2. The schematic diagram and the equivalent bridge circuit of a grid-neutralized RF amplifier are illustrated in Figures 3.125(c) and (d). This circuit operates in a manner similar to the plate neutralized system. For a balance

$$\frac{L_a}{L_b} = \frac{C_n}{C_{gp}} \text{ , as before.}$$

3. Push-pull neutralization does not require the addition of any special circuits other than the neutralizing capacitor. A schematic diagram is shown in Figure 3.125(e). It can be considered to be a form of plate neutralization. Advantage is taken

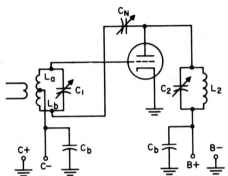

Fig. 3.125(c). Schematic diagram of a grid-neutralized amplifier.

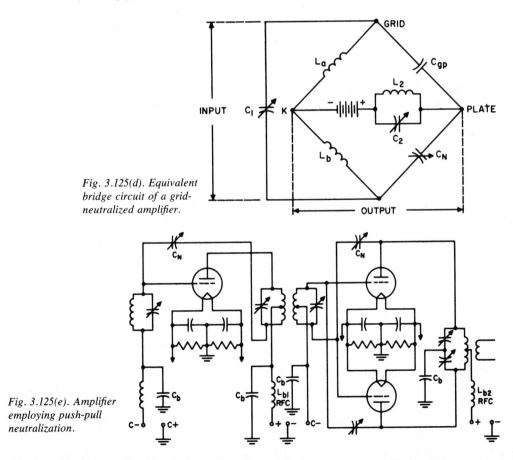

Fig. 3.125(d). Equivalent bridge circuit of a grid-neutralized amplifier.

Fig. 3.125(e). Amplifier employing push-pull neutralization.

of the fact that the voltages on the two sides of a push-pull amplifier are of opposite polarity, and thus automatically provide the correct phase relations for neutralizing.

Q. 3.126. State some indications of, and methods of testing for, the presence of parasitic oscillations in a transmitter.

A.

1. Parasitic oscillations may be indicated by one or more of the following:

a. Generation of spurious frequencies (carrier).

b. Generation of spurious sideband frequencies during modulation.

c. Distortion of the modulated wave.

d. Overheating of the amplifier tube.

e. Reduced efficiency of the amplifier tube at the desired frequency or frequencies.

f. Change of bias (grid leak).

g. High or erratic plate or grid-current readings.

h. Unstable operation of an amplifier stage (or stages).

i. Abnormal tuning characteristic of a stage (or stages).

2. Some methods of testing for the existence of such parasitics are as follows:

a. Using a radio receiver or sensitive wavemeter to explore the frequency spectra on either side of the desired operating frequency during both modulated and unmodulated conditions. Parasitic oscillations will show up as extra frequencies produced in addition to the desired operating frequency.

b. Observing the modulation envelope, preferably using a trapezoidal pattern, with an oscilloscope with and without constant tone modulation. The presence of parasitics will cause unexplained nonlinearities, the degree of which will vary with differing percentages of modulation.

c. Measuring the efficiency of the amplifier tube at the operating frequency. If the tube is operating with rated dissipation and power input, but the output at the operating efficiency is too low, the "missing" power output represents power output at a parasitic frequency.

d. Checking for the overheating of one or more amplifier components. The radio frequency chokes and bypass capacitors are especially suspect.

D. See Q. 3.92.

Q. 3.127. Draw a circuit diagram of a push-pull (triode) final power amplifier with transmission line feed to a shunt-fed quarter-wave antenna and indicate a method of plate neutralization.

A. For the diagram, see Fig. 3.127.

D. For a discussion of transmission line feed, see Q. 3.214; for shunt feed, see Q. 3.209(b); and for push-pull neutralization, see Q. 3.125.

Fig. 3.127. Neutralized push-pull final amplifier; transmission-line fed to a shunt-fed quarter-wave antenna.

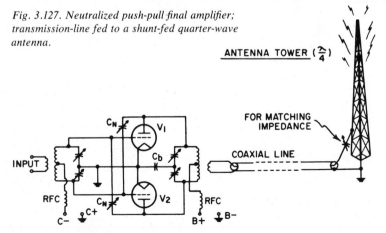

Q. 3.128. Explain, step-by-step, at least one procedure for neutralizing an RF amplifier stage.

A. Two procedures for neutralizing an RF amplifier stage are as follows:

1. a. Remove the plate (and screen) voltage from the stage being tested, but keep filaments lit and grid excitation present. The plate voltage should be removed in order to make the amplifier inoperative. If the amplifier were in the process of being neutralized and the plate voltage were not removed, it would be extremely difficult to determine when neutralization had taken place, since with grid excitation present there would always be RF in the plate tank circuit. The danger of self-oscillations damaging the tube before neutralization is completed is another important factor.

b. If not already present, insert a dc milliammeter of suitable range into the grid circuit of the amplifier under test.

c. Vary the tuning of the plate tank circuit while observing the grid current meter.

d. If sharp variations of grid current are observed while so tuning, the stage is not properly neutralized.

e. Adjust neutralizing capacitor until variations in grid current cease during plate tank tuning.

2. a. This method requires the use of a suitable RF indicator which may be a neon bulb, a small flashlight bulb with a loop of wire attached, a sensitive wavemeter, a sensitive thermocouple meter with a loop of wire attached, or any other suitable indicator.

b. Remove the plate (and screen) voltages from the stage being tested, but keep filaments lit and grid excitation present. (See 1.(a) above.)

c. With any of the indicators mentioned above (a), test for the presence of oscillations in the plate tank while tuning the tank capacitor through its range.

d. While performing the above (c), the grid circuit should be tuned for the maximum grid current, and the preceding plate circuit tuned for maximum drive, indicated by maximum grid current.

e. If oscillations are present in the plate tank circuit, adjust the neutralizing capacitor until they vanish or are at a minimum.

f. After a minimum indication has been reached, the driver and grid tanks should be retuned for maximum grid current and the neutralizing procedure repeated.

D. After the neutralizing procedure has been completed couple the load to the output of the amplifier (if not already coupled) and apply reduced plate and screen grid voltages to the neutralized stage. Tune the plate tank to resonance (as shown by a minimum plate current indication). Then apply normal voltages and readjust the plate tank for resonance. (See also Q. 3.125.)

Q. 3.129. Draw a circuit diagram of a push-push frequency multiplier and explain its principle of operation.

A. For the diagram, see Fig. 3.129. As shown in the diagram, the plates are connected in parallel. Also, the plate tank circuit is tuned to twice the frequency (second harmonic) of the grid-tank circuit. The plate circuit thus completes two cycles to every cycle of the grid circuit. However, because of the "push-push" connection the plate tank receives a pulse of current for each of its two cycles. When the grid of V_1 is positive it provides a pulse of current to the plate tank. One-half cycle of the input wave later, the grid of V_2 is positive and it provides a pulse of current to the plate tank for the second cycle occurring at this time.

Fig. 3.129. A push-push frequency multiplier.

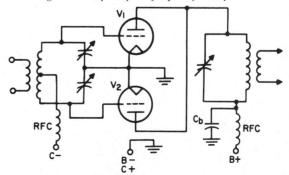

D. In the case of a single-tube frequency doubler (see Q. 3.131 and Q. 3.132), the plate efficiency is about 50 percent and the power output is about 70 percent, compared to a conventional Class C amplifier. The reason for this is that plate current energy is supplied to the plate-tank circuit only every other cycle. For a tripler, energy is supplied only on every third cycle and the power output capability is further reduced. Thus, reduction of power output and plate efficiency becomes increasingly severe as higher orders of frequency multiplication are attempted. As a result, frequency multipliers in transmitters are generally limited to doublers and triplers. Another factor to be considered in relation to the degree of multiplication is the stability of the output wave. For a single tube tripler the tank circuit is "running free" for two out of three cycles and is not under control of the stable driving (usually crystal) oscillator. A tank circuit with a high Q is required to maintain a stable frequency during the "free-running" time. However, if too great a frequency multiplication is attempted, frequency instability may result due to phase or frequency changes of the "free-running" cycles. To improve the efficiency of frequency multipliers, "push-push" circuits are used as frequency doublers (even-order harmonics). and "push-pull" circuits are used as frequency triplers (odd-order harmonics).

Q. 3.130. Push-pull frequency multipliers normally produce what order of harmonics; even or odd?

A. Since the push-pull amplifier has been especially designed to reduce or elim-inate all even-order harmonics, it follows that such an amplifier when used as a frequency multiplier will operate successfully only on odd-order harmonics.

D. See Q. 3.129, Q. 3.131 and Q. 3.132.

Q. 3.131. Draw a schematic diagram and explain the operation of a harmonic generator stage.

A. For the diagram see Fig. 3.131.

A pure sine wave contains only one frequency, the fundamental. However, any distortion of the sine wave indicates the presence of other frequencies, which are multiples of the fundamental and are called harmonics. Thus any amplifier which distorts the input wave is actually a harmonic generator. The desired harmonic may be selected with a suitable resonant circuit. In a frequency doubler the grid tank is tuned to the fundamental while the plate tank is tuned to the second harmonic. In triodes the grid bias for most efficient doubling is 10 times cut-off value, with a plate efficiency of 50 percent, a relative power output (compared to ordinary Class C amplifier) of 70 percent, and a plate current pulse length of 90°.

For a triode tripler, the grid bias is 20 times cut-off, plate efficiency of 50 percent, relative power output of 36 percent, and a plate current pulse length of 75°.

Due to the high bias, very large values of grid excitation voltages must be used.

D. From a practical consideration, a doubler is most often used in connection with crystal oscillators. The high frequency limitations of quartz crystals are due to the fact that the crystal plate becomes thinner as its resonant frequency is increased. Thus

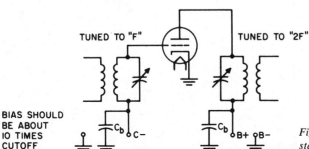

TUNED TO "F"   TUNED TO "2F"

BIAS SHOULD
BE ABOUT
IO TIMES
CUTOFF C_b C− C_b B+ B−

Fig. 3.131. An RF doubler stage.

it becomes extremely fragile and easily subject to overheating and cracking. To overcome this important limitation, the crystal frequency is kept relatively low, usually under 20 megahertz, and the crystal oscillator may be followed by one or a series of doublers to increase the output frequency.

In addition to the triode harmonic generators, beam-power pentodes are also commonly used. Because of its high transconductance, a beam-power tube may deliver a high harmonic content output with a relatively low driving signal. It should be noted that in general, frequency multipliers do not require neutralization (see Q. 3.128). This is so because the plate and grid circuits are tuned to widely differing frequencies and the feedback from plate-to-grid circuits is not of the phase necessary to sustain oscillations.

Q. 3.132. What class of amplifier is appropriate to use in a radio frequency doubler stage?

A. A Class C amplifier.
D. See Q. 3.131. See also Q. 3.129 and Q. 3.130.

Q. 3.133. Describe some factors in connection with the following items, which should be considered at VHF and above but would not be of particular concern at MF or below.
1. Wire diameter and length.
2. Wiring configuration (placement and bending).
3. Coaxial cables and transmission lines.
4. Capacitor types.

A.
1. To minimize the self-inductance of wires carrying VHF currents it is necessary to use conductors that are as short as possible and with as large a diameter as feasible. The diameter, however, should not be increased to the extent of appreciably increasing the capacitance of such conductors to ground or other conductors.
2. Wiring configuration should be such that each conductor is separated by as great a distance from other conductors and ground

as possible to minimize any distributed capacitances.

Any bends in the conductors should be minimum in number and of a maximum in radius as possible within the physical confines of the space available. This is to minimize the self-inductance of such conductors.

3. The insulation of coaxial cables and transmission lines should be of a material having the lowest possible dielectric losses. Certain materials exhibit negligible losses at MF but have substantial losses at VHF. Insofar as is possible, such cables and lines should be air insulated. Where physical support is required, the number of such supports should be as few as possible. If standing waves are normally present on such cables and lines, it is important that insulating supports only be located at points of minimum voltage.

4. Variable capacitors used in VHF service should be air insulated, using a minimum of solid dielectric for supporting the capacitor plates. Such dielectric that is used should have as small a dielectric loss as possible. Fixed capacitors should have low loss dielectrics, such as mica or ceramic.

D. At low RF frequencies only the capacitance of a capacitor is considered and any inductive effects are usually discounted. However, at VHF and above, the inductance of a capacitor may represent an appreciable reactance and will modify the performance of the capacitor. At such frequencies the capacitor may represent a resonant circuit. In fact, in certain by-pass applications at VHF a capacitor may be chosen that is series-resonant at the operating frequency thus offering minimum impedance to ground. Of course, at frequencies differing substantially from resonance, the capacitor may act as a fairly high value of either inductive or capacitive reactance. Thus, so-called "bypass" capacitors under some conditions may not "bypass" at all and may function as a high impedance instead. In the usual case, capacitors used at VHF and above are constructed to have an exceeding low value of self inductance, so that at the operating frequency, the inductive element can be neglected and the very-low value of capacitive reactance is the dominating factor. Typical of these are the "button" ceramic and "feed-through" coaxial- ceramic types, which are widely used in VHF transmitters and receivers. These are made in very small physical sizes with extremely low inductances and act as efficient coupling, bypass or RF filter capacitors.

Note: The following added material numbered Q. 3.133-A1 through Q. 3.133-A30 contains information that may be required to pass the General Radiotelephone Operator's License examination. This added material, as well as the new material added to other sections, has been included to help acquaint students with the current state of the electronics art. It is felt that the added material contains subject matter that may also be required of students who have obtained a General Radiotelephone Operator's License and are seeking employment. Additionally, the added material contains valuable information for private technician certification.

Q. 3.133-A1. What is an RF choke (RFC)? Why are they used?

A. An RF choke (RFC) is a coil that is used to present an inductive reactance in series with a circuit.

D. RF chokes may be placed in series with some portions of an RF circuit to act as a signal "load," as a coupling element, to help maintain the Q of tank circuits (as in a crystal oscillator), and sometimes as tuning elements (as in a Pierce oscillator). They are also used to prevent RF from appearing in a portion of a circuit or the power supply or in some cases to prevent parasitic oscillations. For an RF choke to function effectively, its self resonant frequency must be well above the circuit-operating frequency. It should present an inductive reactance to the circuit. Therefore, the distributed capacity of the RF choke should be kept to a minimum.

With RF chokes having an appreciable number of windings, the "pie" winding technique is used to reduce the distributed capacity. A typical value for a pie-wound RF choke is 2.5 MHz. These chokes are used at frquencies in the order of 1 to 3 kHz.

RF chokes for the VHF range may consist merely of several turns of wire, air-wound. Inductance values in the order of 5 to 35 μH are typical for VHF.

Ferrite-bead RF chokes may be used for VHF and UHF applications. (See Q. 3.133-A4.)

Q. 3.133.-A2. What is a toroid inductor?

A. A toroid inductor (or transformer) is an inductor that is wound in the shape of a doughnut. It is generally wound on magnetic core materials, such as iron alloys, ferrites or powdered iron. See Fig. 3.133-A2.

D. A toroidal inductor wound on a magnetic core material has several important advantages:

1. The maximum magnetic strength is within the core material with little flux externally.

2. It is less sensitive to induction from external magnetic fields.

3. Shielding requirements are reduced.

4. It can obtain the maximum inductance per unit volume.

Toroid inductors (or transformers) are useful over a very wide range of frequencies from about 250 Hz to 1 000 MHz.

Some applications are:
1. As RF chokes.
2. In dc to dc converters.
3. In audio or RF circuits.
4. As broadband transformers.

Fig. 3.133-A2. One example of a toroid inductor.

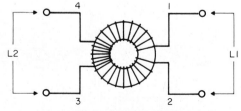

LI—TO OCCUPY ENTIRE CORE
L2—WOUND OVER LI WINDING

5. As transmission line transformers.

Toroid inductors (or transformers) are available in a very wide variety of sizes. These range from microminiature sizes to ones several inches in diameter.

Note: Toroidal deflection yokes are commonly used on the picture tubes of television receivers. They are far more efficient (require less power) than the older "saddle" yokes.

Q. 3.133-A3. What is an RF transformer?

A. An RF (or IF) transformer generally consists of coupled primary and secondary coils, either air wound or having ferrite cores. Either or both coils may be tuned to the desired RF-resonant frequency.

D. When ferrite cores are employed, they are frequently adjustable to vary the resonant frequency of the coils. One or both coils may be individually adjustable. Schematic drawings for an RF transformer with two adjustable ferrite cores are given in Fig. 3.133-A3(1) and (2). This particular arrangement is used for IF (10.7 MHz) transformers in FM broadcast receivers.

RF transformers are generally variable capacitor (or varactor) tuned when they must tune over a band of frequencies, rather than to a fixed frequency such as an IF.

Adjustable ferrite cores are not used for AM broadcast band, receiver IF transformers (455 kHz) because of the large physical size required. These IF transformers are usually air-wound and tuned by small trimmer capacitors mounted on the transformer. See Fig. 3.133-A3(3).

Q. 3.133-A4. What are ferrite beads?

A. *Ferrite beads* as the name implies, are very small bead-like devices made of ferrite and with holes through their centers. In practice, they are slipped over a conductor to present an impedance to RF currents. (Their function is similar to that of RF chokes.) They are useful in the approximate frequency range of 10 to 1 000 MHz. Very small toroids wound on ferrite cores may be used in place of simple beads.

D. The greatest use for ferrite beads (or ferrite toroids) is in low-impedance circuits where it is desired to suppress the flow of conducted RF to avoid circuit malfunctions. The beads represent a limped impedance at radio frequencies, while presenting a very low reactance to audio frequencies and zero impedance to dc Some practical uses are:

1. As VHF and UHF parasitic oscillation suppressors at input and output amplifier points.

2. To suppress radio frequency interference (RFI) and television interference (TVI) in high-fidelity amplifiers and television receivers.

3. To prevent unwanted coupling of RF energy from one section of a circuit to another.

4. As low-Q, transistor-base impedances in VHF and UHF amplifiers.

Typical applications include:

1. on the collector leads of transistors,

2. between stages on a power supply line,

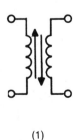
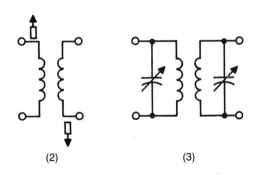

Fig. 3.133-A3. Schematic symbols for an RF transformer. Transformers (1) and (2) have two adjustable ferrite cores. The position of the arrows indicates the location of the adjustment (top or bottom). In transformer (3), the RF transformer is tuned by means of small trimmer capacitors.

(1)   (2)   (3)

3. on vacuum-tube filament leads, and

4. any leads entering a shielded enclosure that should not pass radio frequencies.

In cases where a single bead will not supply enough impedance, multiple beads may be used in a *string*.

Q. 3.133.-A5. In a capacitor-coupled RF amplifier, what symptoms would result if the coupling capacitor shorted? If it opened?

A. Refer to Fig. 3.133-A5, which shows the schematic diagram of an NPN RF amplifier, with coupling capacitor, C_C.

1. If the coupling capacitor shorted, the full +12 V of the power supply would be applied to the base of Q_2 instead of the small value of normal, forward-base bias. The +12 V at the base will throw Q_2 into saturation. There would be little or no RF output and possible damage to Q_2.

2. If C_C opened, this would prevent the RF driver signal from reaching the base

of Q_2. There would be no RF output from Q_2. No damage would result to Q_2, since normal base bias would still be supplied by the divider action of R_1, R_2.

D. See Q. 3.183, Q. 3.187(a), Q. 3.192(N). See also Q. 3.284, Q. 3.286, Q. 3.294, Q. 3.296.

Q. 3.133-A6. Draw a schematic diagram of a common-base RF amplifier and explain its operation.

A. The schematic diagram is shown in Fig. 3.133-A6. In the common-base mode (analogous to grounded grid, Q. 3.124), the base is grounded for RF by C_3. The input signal is fed to the emitter and the output signal is taken from the collector. Forward-base bias is provided by the divider action of resistors R_3 and R_4. Capacitors C_1 and C_5 tune coils L_2 and L_3, respectively, to the operating frequency.

D. In the common-base mode, the current gain is less than 1. There is no need to

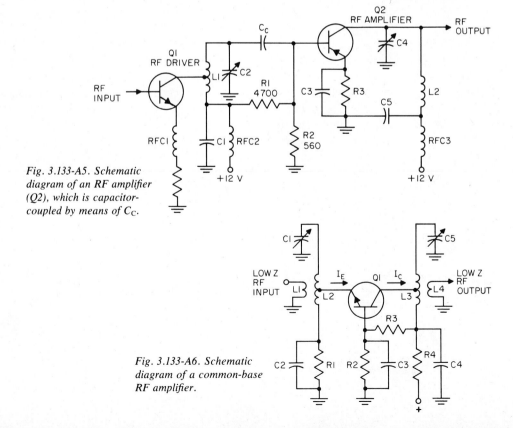

Fig. 3.133-A5. Schematic diagram of an RF amplifier (Q2), which is capacitor-coupled by means of C_C.

Fig. 3.133-A6. Schematic diagram of a common-base RF amplifier.

neutralize an RF amplifier of this configuration because the input and output currents are in phase. The input signal current (I_E) to the emitter must be supplied by the driver. This current is slightly greater than the signal current in the collector circuit (I_C). Thus, the current gain is less than 1. The voltage gain can be as large, or even larger than in a common-emitter circuit (see Q. 3.192(K) for comparison). The input resistance of a common-base amplifier is very low, in the order of 30 to 150 Ω. Note in Fig. 3.133-A6 that the coil L_2 is tapped far down to match this low-input impedance. However, the output (collector) impedance is very high, in the order of 300 000 Ω to 1 MΩ. (Output load impedance is from about 3 000 to 100 000 Ω. Thus, the output transformer L_3, L_4 is a stepdown type, to match the high output load impedance to the following stage (or device). (See also Q. 3.192(J) and Q. 3.192(K).)

Q. 3.133-A7. Draw a schematic diagram of a common-emitter RF amplifier and explain its operation.

A. The schematic diagram is shown in Fig. 3.133-A7. In the common-emitter mode (analogous to grounded cathode, Q. 3.123(2)), the emitter is grounded for RF

by C_3. The input signal is fed to the base and the output signal is taken from the collector. Forward-base bias is provided by the divider, R_1, R_2. C_2 and C_4 tune coils L_2 and L_3, respectively, to the operating frequency.

D. In the common-emitter mode, the current gain can be from 22 to 55 or greater, and the voltage gain can be from 250 to 1 000. The input resistance is appreciably higher than for the commonbase mode, or about 500 to 1 500 Ω. (See Q. 3.192(K) for comparisons.) The output (collector) resistance is about 30 000 to 50 000 Ω. Impedance matching into and out of the amplifier is provided by transformers L_1, L_2 and L_3, L_4 respectively. (See also Q. 3.192(J) and 3.192(K).)

Q. 3.133-A8. Draw a schematic diagram of a neutralized, PNP common-emitter RF amplifier and explain its operation.

A. The schematic diagram is shown in Fig. 3.133-A8. Internal feedback through the collector-to-base capacitance may cause oscillations at high operating frequencies. The circuit may oscillate as a tuned-collector, tuned-base oscillator (similar to the tuned-plate, tuned-grid oscillator shown in Q. 3.86).

To prevent such oscillations, an additional feedback signal is fed back to the

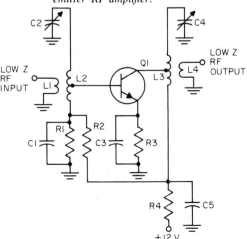

Fig. 3.133-A7. Schematic diagram of a common-emitter RF amplifier.

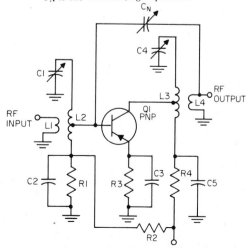

Fig. 3.133-A8. Schematic diagram of a neutralized, PNP common-emitter RF amplifier. C_N is the neutralizing capacitor.

base. This must be of equal amplitude and opposite in phase to the internal feedback signal. This additional signal in Fig. 3.133.-A8 is taken from L_4. The signal phase at L_4 is opposite to that at the collector of Q_1. This feedback signal goes through C_N to the base of Q_1 and cancels the internal feedback signal. The circuit is then said to be *neutralized*. C_N is made variable to obtain the correct amplitude of the feedback signal.

D. See Q. 3.125, Q. 3.127, and Q. 3.128.

Q. 3.133-A9. Draw a schematic diagram of a transistor, RF driver stage, suitable for driving a transistor RF power amplifier. Explain its operation.

A. For the schematic diagram, see Fig. 3.133-A9.

The circuit of Fig. 3.133-A9 is a Class C driver amplifier. Note the absence of forward bias. (Without forward bias, many types of transistors operate Class C.) Input transformer T_1 is a step-down type to match the low base input impedance. The ferrite bead Z_1, is used to suppress parasitic oscillations. Resistor R_1 (perhaps 2–3 Ω) helps prevent transistor thermal runaway. It also provides degenerative feedback as a form of neutralization. The RFC and C_1 and a decoupling network. C_2 resonates the primary of the output transformer T_2 to the desired operating frequency. The step-down secondary of transformer T_2 goes to the base of the RF power amplifier.

D. Transistor drivers and transistor power output amplifiers are commonly found in transmitters with output powers of about 200 W or less. Above this approximate power, vacuum tubes are frequently used for both the driver and power amplifier stages. Higher-power tube amplifiers have the following advantages compared to transistor amplifiers (at the same power level):

1. They are less subject to damage from excessive drive.

2. They are less subject to damage from mismatched loads (high VSWRs).

3. They develop fewer harmonics.

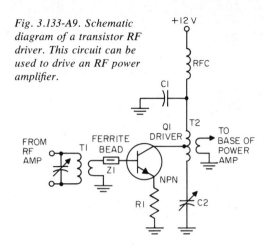

Fig. 3.133-A9. Schematic diagram of a transistor RF driver. This circuit can be used to drive an RF power amplifier.

4. They are less prone to self oscillation.

5. They require less complex power supplies.

6. They are simpler to cool (cooling fans versus heat sinks).

An exception to the use of transistors in higher-powered RF amplifiers is the use of Class D RF transistor power amplifiers. (See Discussion for Q. 3.133.-A10.)

Q. 3.133-A-10 Draw a schematic diagram of a transistor RF power amplifier. Explain its operation.

A. See Fig. 3.133-A10. Transformer T_1 is a step-down type. It matches the output impedance of a transistor driver to the base-input impedance of the power amplifier (Q_2). The stage is operated Class C. Note the absence of forward bias for Q_2. RFC_1 is the collector load for Q_2. RFC_2, C_3, and C_4 decouple the collector circuit from the $+12$ V power supply. L_1, L_2, and C_1 form a T-filter network. This transforms the Q_2-collector impedance (about 5 to 15 Ω) to a 50-Ω output.

D. (See also Q. 3.133-A9.) Because of the advantages of high-power tubes, transistors in Class C operation are not generally used for power outputs above about 200 W. However, an exception is the use of power transistors operated Class D.

In Class D operation, the audio wave is transformed into a pulse-modulated signal

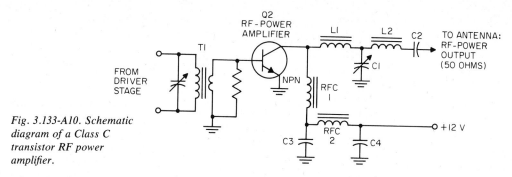

Fig. 3.133-A10. Schematic diagram of a Class C transistor RF power amplifier.

by a pulse width modulator. The output of the modulator is a pulse train having frequency and pulse width variations that are proportional to the amplitude and frequency of the modulating audio signal.

The advantage of using pulse modulation is that the pulse modulation signal produces on-off "switching" of the power amplifier transistors. This permits high-efficiency transistor operation (better than 80 percent). The original shape of the audio-modulating wave is restored by the tuned circuits and a harmonic filter, which follows the power amplifiers.

A system employing pulse modulation is considerably more complex circuitwise than one using Class C vacuum tube amplifiers. For example, in an RCA AM broadcast band 5 000 W transmitter, the pulse modulator incorporates 24 transistors. Also the power amplifier consists of six Class D bridge amplifier modules. Each bridge circuit consists of four solid-state legs with seven transistors in each leg. The total number of transistors in the power amplifier is $28 \times 6 = 168$ transistors.

In spite of the circuit complexity, this transmitter (100 percent solid-state) occupies only half the space of an equivalent tube type. It is lightweight, installs easily, and has a lower ac power consumption than a tube type.

Q. 3.133-A11. Draw a schematic diagram of a common-emitter frequency doubler and explain its operation.

A. The schematic diagram is shown in

Fig. 3.133-A11. A frequency multiplier must be operated Class C to produce the required harmonics and efficiency of operation. In Fig. 3.133-A11, note that the emitter and base are both dc grounded. No forward bias is present providing Class C operation. The collector circuit L_1C_2 is here tuned to the 2nd harmonic $(2 \times f)$, but it could also have been tuned for an output of $3 \times f$ or $4 \times f$.

D. The circuit shown in Fig. 3.133-A11 is not the most desirable for use as a frequency doubler, although it is one of the simplest. A better doubler is the push-push doubler explained in Q. 3.129. A better tripler is the push-pull tripler discussed in Q. 3.130. (Transistors including FETs can be easily substituted for the vacuum tubes of push-push and push-pull multipliers).

The circuit of Fig. 3.133-A11 has lower efficiency than the two latter mentioned circuits. Its efficiency as a doubler is 50 percent, as a tripler 33 percent, and as a quadrupler 25 percent. In addition, the circuit of Fig. 3.133-A11 contains, in its output, harmonics other than the desired one to which L_1C_2 is

Fig. 3.133-A11. Schematic diagram of a common-emitter frequency doubler.

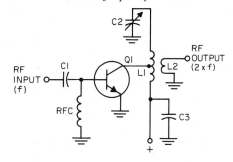

tuned. Thus, it may be necessary to follow the circuit with an effective bandpass filter.

Some transistor frequency multipliers may use forward bias to reduce the excitation (drive) requirements. However, even in this case, Class C operation must be present by applying sufficient drive to the input. (See also Q. 3.129, Q. 3.130, Q. 3.131, and Q. 3.132.)

Q. 3.133-A12. Draw a schematic diagram of a varactor diode, radio frequency tripler. Describe its operation.

A. The schematic diagram of a varactor diode, RF tripler is shown in Fig. 3.133-A12.

The fundamental frequency (f) is fed into the tripler via impedance-matching capacitor C_2. L_1C_1 are tuned to the fundamental. The fundamental frequency current (i_f) flows through the varactor. The varactor has a nonlinear capacitive-reactance characteristic and low series resistance. It thus produces distortion of the fundamental, creating harmonics with high efficiency. L_2C_3 is series resonant to the second harmonic (2f), thus effectively eliminating it from the

output. The output circuit C_4L_3 is tuned to the third harmonic (3f).

D. See also Q. 3.192(U)-A7 for a basic discussion of varactors.

Q. 3.133-A13. Draw a schematic diagram of a transistor IF amplifier. Include the AGC connection. Briefly describe the operation.

A. The schematic diagram is shown in Figure 3.133-A13.

The output of the mixer (first detector) is fed to a tap on the primary of IF transformer T_1. This tap provides the correct match to the output impedance of the mixer. The step-down secondary of T_1 provides a low-impedance input for the base-emitter input of transistor Q_1.

The collector of transistor Q_1 is connected to a tap on the primary of IF output transformer T_2. This is necessary to provide proper collector circuit impedance matching. It also helps to make the stage performance relatively independent of variations between transistors of the same type. The output of

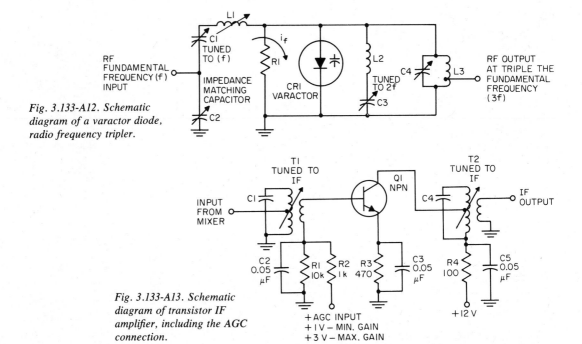

Fig. 3.133-A12. Schematic diagram of a varactor diode, radio frequency tripler.

Fig. 3.133-A13. Schematic diagram of transistor IF amplifier, including the AGC connection.

the transistor IF amplifier is taken from the low-impedance secondary winding of T_2. This low impedance is necessary to drive the following stage properly. The following stage may be another IF amplifier or a detector.

D. The AGC (or AVC) voltage is fed via voltage divider R_2, R_1, to the base of transistor Q_1. Since this is an NPN transistor, the AGC voltage applied to the base must have positive polarity. Thus, $+1$ V AGC results in minimum transistor gain and $+3$ V results in maximum transistor gain.

Common IFs are 455 kHz, 1600 kHz, and 10.7 MHz for single-conversion receivers. For double-conversion receivers, a first IF of 9 MHz and a second IF of 3.3 MHz (sometimes 460 kHz) is used.

If Q_1 was a PNP transistor with AGC voltage applied to the base, the AGC voltage would have negative polarity. (See also Q. 3.155, Q. 3.156, Q. 3.157, and Q. 3.177.)

Q. 3.133-A14. Draw a schematic diagram of an integrated circuit (IC) IF amplifier. Briefly describe its operation.

A. The schematic diagram is shown in Fig. 3.133-A14.

The IC pictured is a Motorola type MC1590G chip. The IF input signal is fed into terminal 1 of the *chip*. A chip such as this may contain several transistors, diodes, and resistors. An external bypass capacitor,

Fig. 3.133-A14. Schematic diagram of an integrated circuit (IC) IF amplifier. (Courtesy of Motorola)

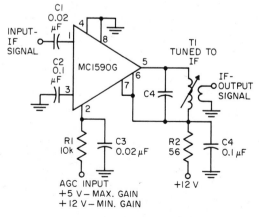

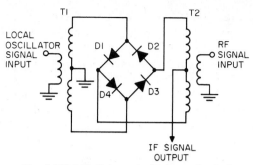

Fig. 3.133-A15. Schematic diagram of a diode doubly balanced mixer.

C_2, is connected to terminal 3 of the chip. AGC voltage is fed to terminal 2 via the decoupling network, R_1C_3. This voltage is fed to the base circuit of a transistor in the chip. A $+5$ V AGC results in maximum gain, while $+12$ V AGC results in minimum gain.

The IF output of the chip is fed to the primary of IF transformer T_1. R_2 and C_4 decouple the primary from the $+12$ V power supply. The IF output signal is taken at low impedance from the secondary of T_1. This output can be fed either to a detector or to an additional IF stage.

D. Some chips used for this type of service may also contain limiters, a detector, an AGC loop, and audio pre-amplifiers.

Q. 3.133-A15. Draw a simple schematic diagram of a doubly balanced mixer. Briefly describe its operation.

A. The schematic diagram is shown in Fig. 3.133-A15.

The basic circuit consists of a diode-bridge circuit (D_1D_4) and two RF transformers with center-tapped secondaries. The local oscillator signal is fed into the primary of RF transformer T_1. The secondary windings of T_1 are connected across one part of the diode bridge circuit.

The RF signal is fed into the primary of RF transformer T_2. The secondary windings of T_2 are connected across the other part of the bridge circuit.

The output of the mixer, the IF signal,

is taken from the center tap of T_2 secondary and ground.

D. The doubly balanced mixer is used up to and beyond 1GHz using hot carrier diodes. It exhibits excellent local oscillator-to-RF-to-IF signal isolation. For example, typical circuits exhibit 30-dB RF-to-IF isolation below 50 MHz. From 50 to 500 MHz, 20-dB iosolation is obtained.

Isolation of local oscillator energy at the RF port prevents excessive local oscillator radiation from a receiver. RF-to-IF port isolation keeps interference in the RF circuits at IF frequency, from penetrating the doubly balanced mixer. Local oscillator-to-IF port isolation prevents local oscillator energy from overloading the first IF amplifier.

Q. 3.133-A16. Draw a simple schematic diagram of a singly balanced mixer. Briefly describe its operation.

A. The schematic diagram is shown in Fig. 3.133-A16.

Transformer T_1 is a tri-filar, toroidal type, having wideband characteristics. The RF input signal is fed to the primary of T_1. The local oscillator input signal is fed to the connection point of the two secondary windings. The IF output is taken from the junction of diodes D_1 and D_2. These diodes can be matched silicon-switching types or hot carrier diodes. Capacitors C_1 and C_2 are adjusted for circuit balance, providing the

Fig. 3.133-A16. Schematic diagram of a singly balanced mixer.

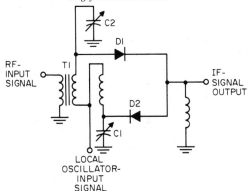

maximum IF output and minimum local oscillator output.

D. The circuit of Fig. 3.133-A16 can be operated up to and beyond 1 GHz, using hot carrier diodes. One advantage of a *balanced* mixer over a single-ended type is the isolation of signals injected into one port from appearing at another port.* In the case of a singly balanced mixer, only the local oscillator input signal is isolated from the other two signals. In a doubly balanced mixer, all three signals are isolated from one another. (See Q. 3.133-A15 for doubly balanced mixer.)

The port-to-port isolation of a balanced mixer prevents signals other than the IF signals from reaching subsequent stages. If the undesired signals were present in the mixer output, they might be heterodyned in subsequent circuits, causing undesirable beat signals.

Isolation of the relatively high local oscillator signal from the RF amplifier prevents signal compression in that stage. In addition, amplitude-modulated noise (if present) on the local oscillator signal is suppressed at the balanced mixer output. This prevents possible detection of such noise at a later stage.

In general, diode mixers are noisier and require a higher-amplitude, local oscillator signal injection than active mixers. Active mixers are those employing transistors. (See Q. 3.133-A18.)

Q. 3.133-A17. Draw a simple schematic diagram of a single-ended diode mixer. Briefly describe its operation.

A. For the schematic diagram, see Fig. 3.133-A17.

In this circuit, a single semiconductor diode acts as the mixer. The RF input signal and the local oscillator input signal are both applied to the diode mixer D_1. Because of the non-linear characteristic of D_1, the two frequencies are heterodyned. The *useful*

---

* A *port* is an input or output terminal of a circuit.

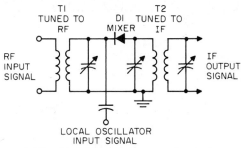

Fig. 3.133-A17. Schematic diagram of a single-
ended diode mixer circuit.

output of D_1 is the difference (or sum) of
the two input frequencies which is the IF.

D. While frequencies other than the
IF are present at the output of D_1, the desired
IF is selected by the tuned circuits of trans-
former T_2.

The semiconductor material of crystal
diodes may be silicon, germanium, or gallium
arsenide.

As shown in Fig. 3.133-A17, the single-
ended diode mixer circuit is quite simple.
However, for the HF and VHF portions of
the frequency spectrum, this type of mixer
is inefficient compared to other types. However, above the VHF band, single-diode
mixers are frequently used in superheterodyne receivers to produce the IF.

Point-contact and Schottky diodes are
commonly used as mixers. Schottky diodes
have better noise figures and are used as
mixers from the UHF band up to and higher
than the EHF band. However, point-contact
diodes have been frequently used as mixers
in microwave receivers.

**Q. 3.133-A18. Draw a schematic dia-
gram of a single-ended active (transistor)
mixer. Briefly describe its operation.**

A. The schematic diagram is shown in
Fig. 3.133-A18.

The RF signal input to the gate of the
JFET is fed from the tuned secondary of RF
transformer T_1. The local oscillator signal
is injected at the JFET source, across resistor
R_2. Mixing occurs in the JFET drain circuit
and the IF is selected by the tuned primary
winding of RF transformer T_2.

D. Bi-polar transistors are seldom used,
and field effect transistors are the preferred
type for mixers. Bipolar mixers have a limited
dynamic range. Thus a strong, undesired
signal at the mixer input will generate many
spurious frequencies, which may interfere
with the desired signal. FET mixers have a
wide dynamic range and low-noise figure.
However, the isolation between the RF signal
and the local oscillator signal is not good in
JFET mixers because the two input signals
are simply combined.

An important advantage of an active
(transistor) mixer lies in its *conversion gain*.
A diode mixer has a *conversion loss*. The
conversion gain (efficiency) of a mixer is the
ratio of its IF output voltage to its RF signal
input voltage. As an example, a doubly balanced diode mixer may have a conversion
loss of 8 dB, while an FET mixer may have
a conversion gain of 15 dB. The advantage
of a conversion gain is that less gain (fewer
stages) is required of the IF section.

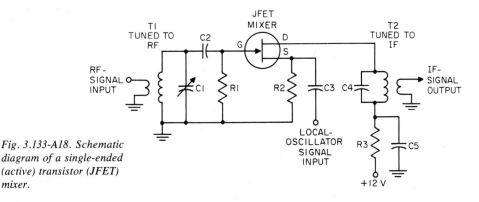

Fig. 3.133-A18. Schematic
diagram of a single-ended
(active) transistor (JFET)
mixer.

Q. 3.133-A19. Briefly compare AGC (AVC) voltages used in vacuum tube and transistor receivers.

A. With vacuum tube AGC (AVC) circuits (see Q. 3.157), the AGC voltage is always negative, as fed to the control grid of RF and IF stages. However, when transistors are the controlled stages, the AGC voltage may be positive or negative.

D. In transistor receivers, either PNP or NPN transistors may be used. For NPN transistors, the AGC voltage will be positive. For PNP transistors, the AGC voltage must be negative. In some receivers, both positive and negative AGC voltages are employed.

With transistor stages, the AGC voltage may be applied either to the base or emitter or a transistor. However, it is preferable to apply the voltage to the base because in that way there will be a greater change of transistor gain for a given change of AGC bias.

In addition, as described in Q. 3.113-A20, a system of *forward* or *reverse* AGC may be used.

Q. 3.133-A20. Describe forward and reverse AGC bias as used with transistor RF and/or IF amplifiers.

A. In a transistor RF or IF amplifier, the AGC voltage may be used to reduce the gain by *reducing the forward bias;* or it may be used to reduce the gain by *increasing the forward bias*. This is illustrated in Fig. 3.133-A20.

D. When the AGC voltage is used to reduce the gain by *reducing* the forward bias, it is called *reverse AGC bias*. When the AGC voltage is used to reduce the gain by *increasing* the forward bias, it is called *forward AGC bias*. The curve in Fig. 3.133-A20 shows that it is possible to decrease the gain of a transistor amplifier by either increasing or decreasing the amount of the emitter-base forward bias. The maximum gain of the amplifier is obtained by setting the bias at point a. Forward bias will be a negative voltage in the case of PNP transistors, and it will be a positive voltage in the case of NPN

transistors. As shown on the graph, decreasing the amount of forward bias will reduce the gain of the amplifier, and the drop-off is quite rapid. On the other hand, the gain will also decrease if the forward bias is increased, in which case the drop-off is more gradual. From this curve, it is obvious that the amplifier can be operated in such a way that either increasing or decreasing the forward bias will be used to decrease the gain. In most cases the amplifier is not actually biased at the peak gain point, but it is biased on the slope in order to assure stability of operation.

Reverse AGC is frequently preferred. This is because it produces a smaller change of the base-collector junction capacitance. In turn, the input and output impedances of the controlled transistor vary less than if forward AGC bias were employed.

Q. 3.133-A21. Draw a simple block diagram of a method of obtaining AGC voltage for a solid-state receiver. Include an S (signal strength) meter. Briefly describe the operation.

A. The block diagram is shown in Fig. 3.133-A21.

IF signal voltage at a low level is fed to the AGC Amplifier. This reduces possible loading on the last IF amplifier output. The IF signal level is raised by perhaps $+30$ dB by the AGC amplifier. It is then changed to dc by the AGC rectifier, D_2.

The dc voltage is raised to a suitable level by one or more dc amplifiers. Any re-

Fig. 3.133-A20. This curve shows how the AGC voltage can reduce transistor gain by either increasing or decreasing the forward bias.

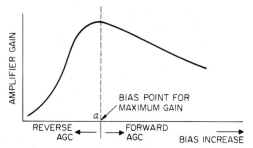

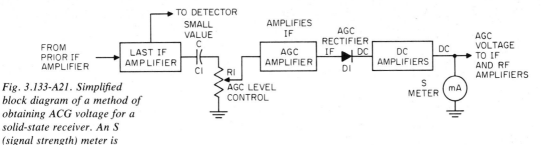

Fig. 3.133-A21. Simplified block diagram of a method of obtaining ACG voltage for a solid-state receiver. An S (signal strength) meter is included.

maining IF variations are filtered out by the dc amplifiers(s).

The output of the dc amplifier(s) is a dc voltage that is proportional to the received signal strength and is the AGC voltage. The AGC is then fed to the IF and RF amplifiers.

The S (signal strength) meter is simply a dc milliammeter, which measures the relative amplitude of the AGC voltage. In this manner it provides an indication of the incoming signal strength.

D. An AGC-level control, R_1, is placed at the input of the AGC amplifier. This control is adjusted to establish the desired received signal level that activates the AGC system. This is frequently set to activate the AGC system at a received signal level of about 1 μV.

Q. 3.133-A22. Draw a schematic diagram of a dual-gate MOSFET IF amplifier. Show how AGC is applied. Briefly describe the operation.

A. The schematic diagram is shown in Figure 3.133-A22.

The output of the mixer (first detector) is fed to the primary of IF transformer T_1. The secondary of T_1 is effectively tapped by capacitors C_1 and C_2. This provides the correct impedance for G_1 (gate 1) of the MOSFET. T_1 is tuned to the IF. This is a high-impedance input.

G_2 (gate 2) receives the AGC voltage and regulates the gain of the MOSFET. +0.5 V at G_2 results in minimum gain, while +4 V provides maximum gain.

The drain of the MOSFET is connected to a tap on the primary of IF output transformer T_2. This tap provides proper drain-circuit impedance matching.

The output of the MOSFET IF amplifier is taken from the low-impedance secondary winding of T_2. This low impedance is necessary to drive the next stage, which may be another IF amplifier or a detector.

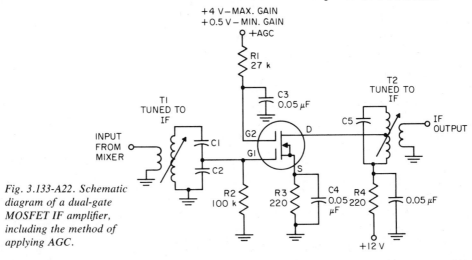

Fig. 3.133-A22. Schematic diagram of a dual-gate MOSFET IF amplifier, including the method of applying AGC.

D. With a dual-gate MOSFET, there is a signal input gate, which is gate 1 (G_1), and a control gate, gate 2(G_2). The dynamic range of the MOSFET is controlled by varying the bias on gate 2. Thus AGC is applied to gate 2. See also Q. 3.133-A21.

Q. 3.133-A23. What is an operational amplifier (op amp)? How are op amps used?

A.

1. An operational amplifier (op amp) is a dc amplifier having very high gain and good stability. External feedback from the output to the input, determines its functional characteristics. The term "operational" is derived from the fact that the first op amps were used to perform mathematical operations in analog computers.

2. The phenomenal development of monolithic (single substrate) IC technology has made the op amp the most versatile component in the electronics industry. The op amp finds its use in countless applications. It is used mostly in analog circuits, but it also has a few digital applications. The op amp is capable of amplifying, controlling, or generating any sinusoidal or non-sinusoidal waveform over a range of frequencies from dc to many megahertz. All classical mathematical functions are possible, including addition, subtraction, multiplication, division, integration, and differentiation. The op amp is used in many applications in control systems, regulating systems, signal processing, instrumentation, and analog computers. A few common uses are:

a. Linear amplifiers, with gains from less than one to several million.

b. Non-linear amplifier (precision rectifier).

c. Comparators.

d. Filters.

e. Log and antilog circuits.

f. All types of multivibrators.

g. Oscillators.

h. Waveform generators.

i. Voltage regulators.

j. Summers.

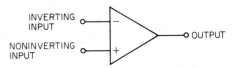

Fig. 3.133-A23. The standard symbol for an operational amplifier (op amp).

D. Internally, an op amp consists of a number of series-connected transistor amplifiers. Externally, the op amp is represented by a standard symbol, shown in Fig. 3.133-A23. The symbol shows two input terminals and one output terminal. The output terminal is controlled by the two input terminals. One input terminal ($-$) is the *inverting* input. A positive voltage applied to this terminal will cause the output to go negative. Likewise, a negative voltage on the ($-$) input will cause the output to go positive.

The other input terminal ($+$) is the *noninverting* input. Whatever polarity is applied to this input, the *same* polarity will appear at the output.

A theoretically perfect (ideal) op amp would have the following characteristics (many physical op amps approach these):

1. Infinite voltage gain.

2. Infinite input impedance.

3. Zero output impedance.

4. Infinite bandwidth.

5. Output signal is zero when input voltage is zero. None of the above ideal characteristics are achieved by any operational amplifier, nor can they ever be achieved. However, in some op amps, these characteristics are closely approached.

Q. 3.133-A24. Draw a block diagram of the internal circuits of one type of commonly used op amp. Explain its operation.

A.

1. For the block diagram, see Fig. 3.133-A24(a). A simplified schematic diagram of this op amp is shown in Fig. 3.133-A24(b).

2. While there are many circuits used inside of op amps, the one shown in Fig. 3.133-A24 is one that is widely used. The first stage of the op amp is the input differ-

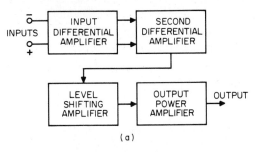

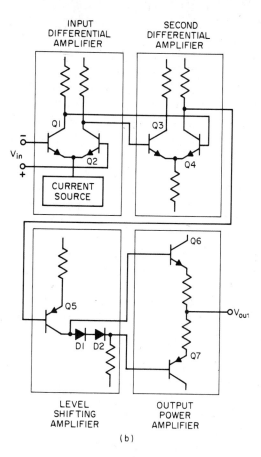

Fig. 3.133-A24(a). Block diagram of a common
method for constructing an op amp. (b) The four
main stages of the op amp in part (a): the input
differential amplifier, the second differential
amplifier, the level-shifting amplifier, and the output
power amplifier.

ential amplifier. This establishes the circuitry
for the inverting and non-inverting inputs.
Q_1 and Q_2 are the transistors involved. (Remember that all the circuitry in Fig. 3.133-
A24 is part of an IC.) This first stage establishes most of the important op amp characteristics. Included are: (a) gain stability,
(b) bias drift, (c) input impedance, (d) bandwidth, and (e) noise figure.

The second differential amplifier
(Q_3,Q_4) is similar to the input stage. It is
much less critical with regard to the characteristics mentioned above for the input
stage. The second stage has only one output,
which is fed to the level-shifting amplifier.

Ideally, the quiescent output voltage
of an op amp should be zero if the input
voltage is zero. The output of the two differential amplifiers *cannot* provide this zero
output voltage. This requirement is accomplished by the level-shifting amplifier
(Q_5,D_1,D_2). This stage provides additional
gain and acts as an impedance transformer.
It transforms the high impedance of the second differential amplifier to a low impedance
capable of driving the output power amplifier.

The output power amplifier is an
emitter-follower of the complementary type.
That is, Q_6 handles the positive output signal
and Q_7 handles the negative output signal.
The emitter-follower provides high-current
gain, wide bandwidth, high-input impedance,
and low-output impedance.

D. See also Q. 3.133-A23 and 3.133-
A25.

**Q. 3.133-A25. Draw a schematic dia-
gram of an inverting amplifier with a gain of
200, using an operational amplifier and two
resistors.**

A. For the schematic diagram, see Fig.
3.133-A25.

D. The voltage gain of an inverting op
amp is given by

$$A_f = - \frac{R_F}{R_1}$$

where

A_f = gain with feedback.
R_F = feedback resistor.
R_1 = series resistor in signal path.

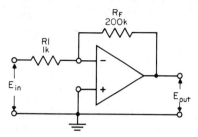

Fig. 3.133-A25. An inverting op amp with a gain of 200.

Thus, the voltage gain of the inverting op amp of Fig. 3.133-A25 is

$$A_f = -\ \frac{R_F}{R_1} = -\ \frac{200\ K}{1\ K} = -200$$

An important point here is that the voltage gain is a function *only* of the resistors R_F and R_1. If these are precision resistors, the gain will remain constant, regardless of any variations in amplifier characteristics, power supply voltage, or other variables. (See also Q. 3.133-A23 and Q. 3.133-A24).

Q. 3.133-A26. Draw a schematic diagram of a low-pass active filter using an integrated circuit operational amplifier. Briefly describe its operation.

A. The schematic diagram is shown in Fig. 3.133-A26. (This type is known as a *second-order* active filter.)

The low-pass active filter shown in the figure has a high-frequency cut-off of 10 kHz. That is, the filter response will be down 3 dB at 10 kHz. Beyond 10 kHz, the filter output drops off rapidly. Note that the filter consists of an IC operational amplifier, two resistors, and two capacitors. No inductors are used.

D. An active filter contains one or more *active* components; generally operational amplifiers are used. As compared to passive filters, active filters have the following advantages:

1. Small capacitors can be used even at low frequencies.

2. Inductors are not used.

3. They may have an amplified output.

4. They have a very low output impedance. Thus, the load does not affect the filter characteristics.

5. Performance is as good as or better than passive filters.

Q. 3.133-A27. Draw a schematic diagram of a high-pass active filter using an integrated circuit operational amplifier. Briefly describe its operation.

A. The schematic diagram is shown in Fig. 3.133-A27. (This type is known as a *second-order* active filter.)

In constructing this high-pass active filter, capacitors have been substituted for resistors and resistors for the capacitors in the prior low-pass active filter. This filter has a cut-off frequency (-3 dB) of 100 Hz. That is, the filter will pass frequencies above 100 Hz without attenuation. Frequencies below 100 Hz will be severely attenuated.

D. The high-frequency response of an active filter is limited by the high-frequency response of the operational amplifier.

Q. 3.133-A28. Draw a schematic diagram of a bandpass active filter, using an integrated circuit operational amplifier. Briefly describe its operation.

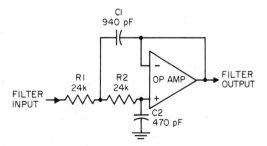

Fig. 3.133-A26. Schematic diagram of a low-pass active filter, using an integrated circuit operational amplifier. The values given are for 10 kHz cut-off (-3 dB level).

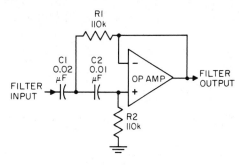

Fig. 3.133-A27. Schematic diagram of a high-pass active filter, using an integrated circuit operational amplifier. The values given are for 100 Hz cut-off (−3 dB level).

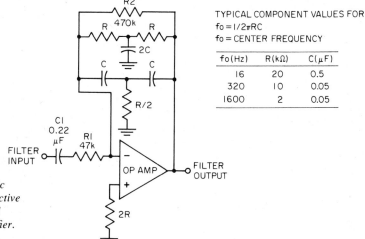

TYPICAL COMPONENT VALUES FOR
$f_o = 1/2\pi RC$
f_o = CENTER FREQUENCY

fo(Hz)	R(kΩ)	C(μF)
16	20	0.5
320	10	0.05
1600	2	0.05

Fig. 3.133-A28. Schematic diagram of a bandpass-active filter, using an integrated circuit operational amplifier. Note the two T networks.

A. The schematic diagram is shown in Fig. 3.133-A28.

A bandpass filter *passes* frequencies close to both sides of the center frequencies. It *rejects* frequencies farther away from the center frequency.

Two T networks provide the required bandpass characteristic. These are shown in the schematic diagram just above the op amp. The currents in the upper and lower Ts are equal and opposite in phase. Thus, at the *center frequency* the feedback loop passes no current and *no attenuation* occurs.

The center frequency $f_0 = \dfrac{1}{(2\pi\,RC)}$ Hz.

For frequencies on either side of the center frequency, feedback current increases. This causes attenuation to *progressively increase*, producing the desired bandpass response.

D. See also Q. 3.133-A26, and Q. 3.133-A27.

Q. 3.133-A29. Draw a schematic diagram of a band reject (notch) filter using an integrated circuit operational amplifier. Briefly describe its operation.

A. The schematic diagram is shown in Figure 3.133-A29.

A band reject (notch) filter *rejects* frequencies close to both sides of the center frequency. It *passes* frequencies farther away from the center frequency.

Two T networks provide the desired response. However, unlike the bandpass filter (Q. 3.133-A28), the T networks are placed in the input section. The rejection response can be very sharp. The center frequency

$f_o = \dfrac{1}{(2\pi\,RC)}$ Hz.

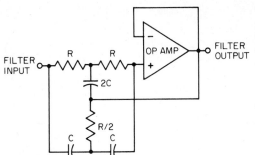

TYPICAL COMPONENT VALUES FOR
$f_o = 1/2\pi RC$
f_o = CENTER FREQUENCY

f_o(Hz)	R(kΩ)	C(μF)
16	20	0.5
320	10	0.05
1600	2	0.05

Fig. 3.133-A29. Schematic diagram of a band reject (notch) filter, using an integrated circuit operational amplifier. The two T networks are at the input.

Q. 3.133-A30. In connection with active filters, briefly describe how op amps using relatively low values of capacitors can act as (1) large capacitors or (2) large inductors.

A.

1. An op amp *capacitance multiplier* circuit is shown in Fig. 3.133-A30(a) and the equivalent input impedance circuit, in Figure 3.133-A30(b). The equivalent input impedance Z_{in} is a resistor R_1 in series with a capacitor C_1. At low frequencies, where R_1 is much smaller than $X_C{}^1$, the circuit acts like

a capacitor with a value $C_1 \times \dfrac{R_2}{R_3}$

$= 1\,000\ \mu$F.

2. An op amp simulated inductor is shown in Fig. 3.133-A30(c) Here, the op amp inverts the phase of the input current by 180°. Thus, the input impedance now appears to be *inductive* instead of capacitive. The equivalent input impedance Z_{in} for the simulated inductance is shown in Fig. 3.133-A30(d). This inductance $L_1 = R_1 \times R_3 \times C_1 = 100 \times 1 \times 10^6 \times 0.1 \times 10^{-6} = 10$ H.

D. By the use of *active capacitors* and active *inductors,* as described above, it is possible to avoid the use (particularly at low frequencies) of relatively expensive and bulky capacitors and inductors. By the use of the proper combinations of active reactances, active filters of any desired characteristics can be constructed.

TRANSMITTERS AND MOBILE RADIO

Q. 3.134. Discuss the following items with respect to their harmonic attenuating properties as possibly used in a transmitter or receiver.
   1. Link coupling.
   2. Tuned circuits.
   3. Degree of coupling.
   4. Bias voltage.
   5. Decoupling circuits.
   6. Shielding.

A.
   1. Link coupling has, to a small degree, some attenuating properties for harmonics

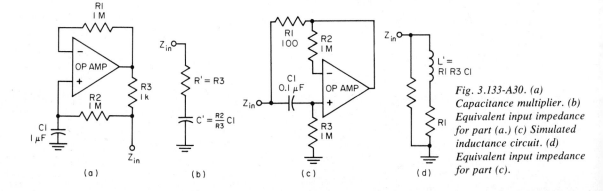

Fig. 3.133-A30. (a) Capacitance multiplier. (b) Equivalent input impedance for part (a.) (c) Simulated inductance circuit. (d) Equivalent input impedance for part (c).

(a)   (b)   (c)   (d)

due to the relatively high capacitance of the low impedance transmission line connecting the two coupling coils. The capacitance will offer decreasing reactance as the frequencies increase and thus tend to bypass harmonics to a greater extent than the fundamental frequency.

A low impedance coaxial-transmission line with a grounded outer conductor is often used, and harmonics tend to be bypassed to ground to a considerably greater extent than the fundamental frequency. Another reason link coupling discriminates against harmonics is the reduction of capacitive coupling between the coils. Harmonics are coupled more readily through capacitive coupling (because of reduced reactance) than the fundamental frequency. The use of physically small link coils reduces capacitive coupling between the resonant circuits and the link coils to a greater extent than if two resonant circuits were inductively (or capacitively) coupled.

2. Tuned circuits, resonant to the fundamental frequency, discriminate against harmonic frequencies to a remarkable degree. This discrimination, and hence harmonic attenuation, is a function of the Q of the tuned circuits and it is therefore desirable to have as high a Q as practical, if harmonic reduction is a prime consideration.

3. In coupled-tuned circuits it is best to use loose coupling to achieve harmonic attenuation. The effect of such loose coupling is to "sharpen" the frequency response curve of the coupled circuits and increase the operating Qs of each of the tuned circuits. Not only is the Q increased but, as discussed in (a) above, the capacitive coupling between the two tuned circuits is reduced, decreasing harmonic transfer between the tuned circuits.

4. Bias voltage in Class A, Class B, and Class B linear RF amplifiers is extremely important from the standpoint of the reduction of harmonic generation. If the bias is incorrect in these amplifiers, a distorted output is obtained and harmonics of the input signal therefore appear. It should be noted, however, that already existing harmonics in the input signal will appear in the output undiminished and therefore the correct bias will not aid in the attenuation of such harmonics. Any harmonic attenuation in these amplifiers will be due to the action of the tuned circuits only.

5. Since decoupling circuits are employed to reduce or eliminate positive feedback in multi-stage amplifiers, distortion in such amplifiers is reduced and, therefore, the generation of harmonics is reduced. However, if harmonics are present in the input signal, harmonics will appear in the output to the same degree despite the use of decoupling circuits. If the amplifiers are tuned, any harmonic attenuation will be due to the tuned circuits only.

6. Shielding, when properly used, can be very effective in harmonic attenuation; especially when used as electrostatic or Faraday shields between coupled tuned circuits. Used in this manner, the shields drastically reduce the capacitive coupling between such circuits and thus reduce the transfer of harmonic energy from one circuit to the other.

D.

1. For the diagram of one type of link coupling see Fig. 3.123(a). See also Fig. 3.168(b) for another type of link coupling.

"Link coupling" is a low impedance transmission line method of coupling together two circuits which may be separated by a relatively large distance. It may be considered to be a step-down transformer and a step-up tranformer interconnected. A link system consists of a very few turns of wire which is coupled to the low impedance point of a tank circuit then connected to a length of low impedance transmission line and terminated by another few turns which is again coupled to the low impedance point of the antenna matching circuit. The amplifier low impedance point is that point to which the RF bypass capacitor is connected. In push-pull operation, the low impedance position is at the center of the tank. Advantages of this system are extreme flexibility of mechanical construction and a reduction of tube capacitance effects on the L/C ratio of the tank circuits.

2. A parallel resonant circuit of fairly high Q will present a high impedance at the resonant frequency and a very much lower impedance at harmonic frequencies. At harmonic frequencies the impedance will be a relatively low capacitive reactance. Thus, the gain of a stage employing a tuned-circuit load will be much lower at harmonic than at the fundamental frequencies. Of course, care must be taken to assure that harmonics are not transferred by means of capacitive coupling between stages (see also (c) and (f) above).

3. See Q. 3.131 for the effect of bias on harmonic generation.

4. For discussion of decoupling circuits, see Q. 3.102 and Q. 3.114.

5. For discussion of Faraday screen, see Q. 3.137(1).

Q. 3.135. Define "transmitter intermodulation," a possible cause (or causes), its effects and steps that could be taken to reduce it.

A. Transmitter intermodulation is the generation, by a transmitter, of a frequency, or frequencies, which is the combination of the fundamental or any of its harmonics with another fundamental or harmonics from a second transmitter that is fairly close by. One common cause of this is the picking up, by the antenna, some of the radiated energy from the second transmitter which is then fed backward into the transmitter over the transmission line. A portion of this energy can then be transferred to the grid of the power amplifier. Since at least the grid of this amplifier is a non-linear circuit, a modulation of one frequency, or its harmonics, by the second frequency, or its harmonics, takes place with resulting sideband frequencies. These sideband frequencies are known as intermodulation products and may be equal to $f_1 \pm f_2$, $f_1 \pm 2f_2$, $2f_1 \pm f_2$, etc.

One obvious manner of reducing such intermodulation would be to locate the transmitters and their associated antennas at greater distances from one another. Economic and other reasons however, often eliminate this remedy. By placing a wavetrap, tuned to the second transmitter's frequency or offending harmonic, in the transmission line close to the transmitter, the picked up energy can be markedly reduced, with a corresponding reduction in the intermodulation. RF power amplifiers using inductive neutralization are prone to these intermodulation effects because the neutralization is only effective for the operating frequency and energy transfer from output to input at frequencies appreciably different from the operating frequency takes place quite easily. Plate or grid neutralization, on the other hand, is effective over quite a large frequency spectrum and such energy transfer is more effectively blocked.

D. For a discussion of the principles of intermodulation involving audio frequencies, see Q. 3.104, D. Generally, the same principles apply to intermodulation involving radio frequencies, as described above. Due to the nature of intermodulation, problems involving this phenomenon may occur within a transmitter, as well as between two transmitters. These may be produced in virtually any stage of a transmitter: audio, video, or radio frequency, if the stage operates in a non-linear fashion. This includes modulator stages, Class C RF amplifiers and even conventional audio and video amplifiers if operated in a non-linear manner. If radiated, intermodulation frequencies may result in interference to other channels or may produce distortion in the originating signal. In the case of audio or video amplifiers, which are generally Class A types, care must be taken to see that the operation of these stages remainss in the linear regions of their characteristic. This dicates, primarily, that the original design be adequate; that the components function properly; that correct bias is maintained; and that there is no overdriving of stages. Many of the RF intermodulation components generated within a transmitter are automatically eliminated by the resonant effect of the RF tank circuits and by the antenna matching network which is normally used between the final RF amplifiers and the antenna and transmission line. Shielding of some transmitter circuits and the use of Faraday screens (see Q. 3.134(6)) are also effective means of reducing RF intermodulation radiation. In addition, circuits used to reduce simple harmonic radiation (see Q. 3.137), may also be effective in reducing RF intermodulation radiation. Obviously, intermodulation components lying within the normal audio, video, or RF pass band cannot be filtered out, but must be eliminated at the source.

Q. 3.136. State a probable cause of and method of reducing transmitter spurious emissions (other than harmonics).

A. There are three general types of spurious emissions, other than harmonics or intermodulation frequencies.

1. Parasitic oscillations: See Q. 3.92 and Q. 3.126 for a complete discussion.

2. Harmonic generator frequencies: Many types of transmitters employ harmonic generators. In some cases the input or output frequencies of intermediate harmonic generator stages exist at sufficiently high altitude to feed through to the antenna. However, most of these frequencies are removed from the transmitted frequency. In many cases, therefore, such frequencies are discriminated against by the RF tank circuit and by the shielding and filtering normally employed against the transmission of harmonics and intermodulation frequencies (see Q. 3.135) In special cases, it may be necessary to employ resonant filters to reduce interference from an unusually strong harmonic generator, from intermediate frequency signals, or from the primary frequency generated by the stable-master oscillator. See Q. 3.128 through Q. 3.132 for a discussion of possible offending stages. See also Q. 3.168(1).

3. Another possible type of spurious emission is due to oscillation of an improperly neutralized RF amplifier. In this case, the stage acts as a tuned-grid, tuned-plate oscillator, with feedback occurring through the plate to grid capacitance of the tube. A similar type of oscillation may occur in a transistor RF amplifier employing tuned input and output circuits, which are resonant to the same frequency. In this case, the feedback is through the collector-to-base capacity and the base-material resistance. For a discussion of neutralization, see Q. 3.125 and Q. 3.128.

Q. 3.137. List several frequently used methods of attenuating harmonics in transmitters and explain how each works.

A.

1. A Faraday screen may be used between the final-tank inductance and the output-coupling coil of the transmitter as shown in Fig. 3.137(a). The Faraday screen is a grounded electrostatic screen which greatly reduces the capacitive coupling between the two coils and thus reduces the transfer of harmonic frequencies. (See discussion below.)

2. The use of tuned wave traps in the transmission line to the antenna. The diagram shown in Fig. 3.137(a) shows how such traps may be connected to the transmission line. The parallel resonant traps shown connected in series with the line present a very high impedance to the harmonic frequency to which they are tuned and therefore reduce the amount of harmonic energy transferred to the antenna. The series resonant traps shown connected from the line to ground exhibit a very low impedance to the harmonic frequency and tend to short circuit the harmonic energy to ground, thus reducing the amount of such energy from reaching the antenna.

3. Low pass RF filters are sometimes used in the transmission line instead of the tuned filters discussed above. The low pass filters are designed to have a cut-off frequency somewhat in excess of the operating frequency. These filters not only reduce the harmonic radiation but have the added advantage of attenuating any other spurious

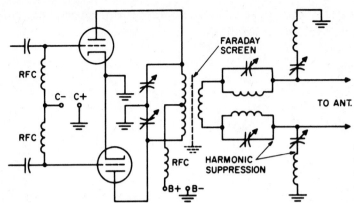

Fig. 3.137(a). RF output of a transmitter may be coupled to a transmission line in this manner, utilizing the Faraday screen to reduce the transfer of harmonic frequencies.

emissions above the filter's cut-off frequency. For diagrams of low-pass filters, see Q. 3.35 and Q. 3.36.

4. The use of a "pi" network for impedance matching between the plate of the output tube and the transmission line has some value in attenuating harmonic output and is shown in Fig. 3.137(b). The output or load adjusting capacitor of the network will have much lower reactance for harmonic frequencies and thus tends to bypass such energy to ground.

D. See Q. 3.134.

1. The purpose of a "Faraday" screen (or shield) is to minimize the transfer of harmonic frequencies between two inductively coupled circuits due to the capacity between the two coils. The two coils in question are usually the plate tank circuit coil of the final RF amplifier and the coupling coil to the antenna system.

In addition to inductive coupling between the two coils, there also exists a degree of capacitive coupling due to the stray capacity existing between the two coils. The amount of capacity coupling increases as the two coils are brought closer together. This capacity coupling offers a relatively low impedance path for the transfer of harmonics, since the capacitive reactance decreases as the frequency is increased. One effective means of reducing harmonic transfer into the antenna circuit is to reduce the capacity between the two coupled coils. The method of accomplishing this is similar to the principle of a screen grid in a tetrode vacuum

tube. A screen or shield which is grounded is placed between the two coils. Such a device is called a "Faraday" screen. It is made up of a flat plate constructed of separate parallel conductors insulated from each other at one end, but joined together physically and electrically at the other end. The conductors are insulated at one end so that no closed circuits will appear in the screen which would also cause magnetic shielding. The insertion of this grounded screen between the two coils greatly reduces the capacitance between the coils and so minimizes harmonic coupling due to the capacitance effect.

2. For discussions of commonly used filters, see Q. 3.35 and Q. 3.36.

Note: The following added material numbered Q. 3.137-A1 through Q. 3.137-A29 contains information that may be required to pass the General Radiotelephone

Fig. 3.137(b). Coupling to an antenna by means of a "pi" network.

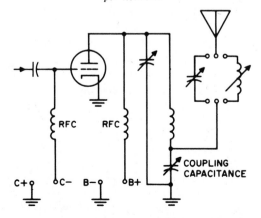

Operator's License examination. This added material, as well as the new material added to other sections, has been included to help acquaint students with the current state of the electronics art. It is felt that the added material contains subject matter that may also be required of students who have obtained a General Radiotelephone Operator's License and are seeking employment. Additionally, the added material contains valuable information for private technician certification.

Q. 3.137-A1. Draw a block diagram of an AM transmitter, complete from the microphone input to the antenna output. State the purpose of each stage, and explain briefly the overall operation of the transmitter.

A. For the block diagram of an AM transmitter, see Fig. 3.137-A1.

1. The crystal oscillator produces a stable carrier frequency at low power. Depending upon the inherent crystal stability, it may or may not require oven temperature control.

2. The buffer amplifier isolates the crystal oscillator to improve its stability. (See Q. 3.98.)

3. The intermediate-power amplifier raises the output RF power of the buffer to a level sufficient to drive the modulated RF amplifier.

4. The Class C modulated RF amplifier supplies the energy required to drive the antenna system at the rated RF power. This stage may be operated as a parallel or as a push-pull amplifier.

5. The modulator driver supplies the necessary audio power to drive the Class B modulator.

6. The Class B modulator varies the plate voltage of the Class C RF amplifier in accordance with the frequency and amplitude of the audio signal. This, in turn, varies the amplitude of the RF output wave to the antenna, producing an amplitude-modulated wave. (See Q. 3.142.)

Q. 3.137-A2. What are the advantages and disadvantages of Class B modulators?

A. Class B modulators generally have greater efficiency but more distortion than Class A modulators.

D. Advantages of Class B modulators are:

1. Greater power output for a given type of tube or transistor.

2. Greater plate or collector efficiency.

3. Lower average power consumption.

4. Smaller tubes or transistors can be used for a given output power.

Disadvantages of Class B modulators are:

1. Power supply must have excellent regulation.

2. Grid bias supply must be low impedance and have good regulation.

3. Input circuit requires considerable driving power.

4. Must use two tubes or transistors in push-pull circuit.

5. More distortion than Class A.

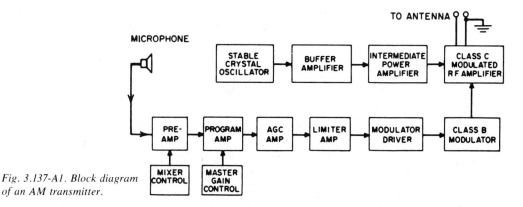

Fig. 3.137-A1. Block diagram of an AM transmitter.

Q. 3.137-A3. Define percentage of modulation for AM and FM.

A.

1. For AM definition of percentage of modulation, see Q. 3.142.

2. For FM, the percentage of modulation is the ratio of the actual frequency swing to the frequency swing, defined as 100 percent modulation, expressed in percentage. For example, for standard FM broadcast stations, a frequency swing of ±75 kHz is defined as 100 percent modulation.

D.

1. For AM, see Q. 3.142, and Q. 3.148.

2. For FM, see Q. 3.163, and Q. 3.158.

Q. 3.137-A4. What undesirable effects result from overmodulation of a transmitter?

A. Some results of overmodulation are:

1. Distortion is produced in the modulation component of the radiated wave, causing distortion of the received signal.

2. Generation of spurious harmonic frequencies.

3. Adjacent channel interference due to extended sidebands.

D. See Q. 3.141.

Q. 3.137-A5. Draw a diagram of a balanced modulator. Explain its operation.

A. For a simplified, basic circuit diagram, see Fig. 3.137-A5.

The function of a balanced modulator is to suppress the carrier wave, while providing an output consisting only of the AM sidebands. Since all of the modulation information is contained in either one of the sidebands, no information is lost by this scheme. (For a discussion of single-sideband, suppressed carrier (SSSC) emission, see Q. 3.152. For SSSC transmission and reception, see Q. 3.153 and Q. 3.154.)

Refer to Fig. 3.137-A5. This is a basic circuit diagram of a balanced modulator. Two modulator devices are connected back-to-back. The audio (or other) modulation signal is injected in *push-pull* fashion (opposite phases). However, the carrier wave is injected in *parallel* fashion (same phases). As indicated in the figure, the output consists only of the two AM sidebands. No carrier is present in the output under ideal circuit operating conditions.

In some types of transmissions both sidebands may be present, with either a completely or a partially suppressed carrier. Alternatively, a single AM sideband with a completely or a partially suppressed carrier may be generated (Q. 3.152). When a partially suppressed carrier is transmitted, it is for the purpose of synchronizing carrier reinsertion oscillators in receivers. An example is the color TV sub-carrier.

There is a great variety of circuits used for balanced modulators. Each has its own particular advantages and disadvantages. Such circuits may employ vacuum tube diodes or triodes, solid-state diodes, or transistors as the non-linear elements. In addition a special vacuum tube, known as a *beam deflection tube,* offers superior carrier suppression (60 dB) when used in a balanced modulator circuit. Other types of circuits offer between 30 and 50 dB of carrier suppression.

Integrated circuits are also used in bal-

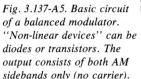

Fig. 3.137-A5. Basic circuit of a balanced modulator. "Non-linear devices" can be diodes or transistors. The output consists of both AM sidebands only (no carrier).

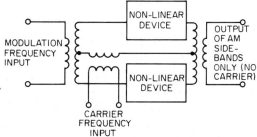

anced modulator circuits. Diode arrays formed on a single silicon chip are closely matched in their characteristics. Thus, they are ideal for use in a balanced modulator requiring good balance for carrier suppression.

When it is desired to suppress one of the AM sidebands, a balanced modulator is followed by filter. This may be of the LC, crystal, ceramic, or mechanical type. (Mechanical filters are designed for use only in the range of about 200 to 600 kHz.)

Q. 3.137-A6. What techniques can be used to measure the percentage of amplitude modulation (AM) of a VHF aircraft transmitter?

A. An oscilloscope is commonly used to measure the percentage of AM of a VHF aircraft transmitter (and of various other types of AM transmitters). Two of the most common methods are,

1. To show the modulation envelope.
2. To produce a trapezoidal pattern that indicates the percentage of modulation. Both of these methods can also indicate certain types of distortion of the modulated wave. Both methods are illustrated in Fig. 3.137-A6.

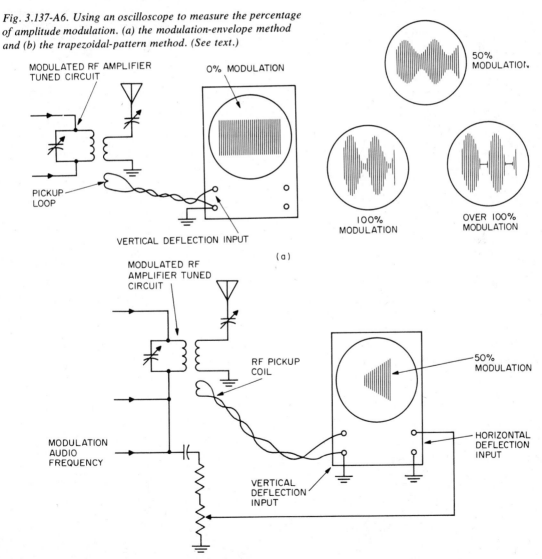

Fig. 3.137-A6. *Using an oscilloscope to measure the percentage of amplitude modulation. (a) the modulation-envelope method and (b) the trapezoidal-pattern method. (See text.)*

D. In part (a) of Fig. 3.137-A6, a small pickup coil is loosely coupled to the modulated RF amplifier circuit or to the antenna circuit. The output of this coil is connected to the vertical deflection input terminals of the oscilloscope. (A wide-band oscilloscope is not required.) Internal horizontal deflection is used. The horizontal frequency should be about one-half of the modulating frequency to show two envelopes, as in Fig. 3.137-A6(a).

If the modulation frequency is 400 Hz, set the horizontal frequency to 200 Hz. Typical patterns for 50-, 100-, and over 100-percent modulation are shown in Fig. 3.137-A6(a). Distortion is indicated if the waveshape deviates from a sinusoidal wave. Overmodulation is indicated when there is an interruption at the baseline.

In the second method, shown in Fig. 3.137-A6(b), the output of the pickup coil is connected as shown in Fig. 3.137-A6(b). However, in this case, internal horizontal deflection is not used. Now, the audio modulation frequency is connected to the horizontal deflection input terminals (external sweep connections). The resultant pattern is trapezoidal in shape, when modulation is present. Trapezoidal displays can be used by calculating the modulation percentage. (See also Q. 3.142.)

Q. 3.137-A7. What is the ratio of unmodulated carrier power to instantaneous peak power, at 100 percent amplitude modulation?

A. The instantaneous peak power under modulation conditions rises to four times the unmodulated peak carrier power.

D. When a carrier is modulated to 100 percent the current (and voltage) vary between twice the original unmodulated value and zero. Since power varies as the square of the current or voltage, the peak power will be increased to four times the original carrier power. (See Q. 3.142 and Q. 3.148.

Q. 3.137-A8. A certain transmitter has an output of 100 W. The efficiency of the final, modulated amplifier stage is 50 percent.

Assuming that the modulator has an efficiency of 66 percent, what plate input to the modulator is necessary for 100-percent modulation of this transmitter? Assume that the modulator output is sinusoidal.

A. The plate input power to the modulator must be 151.5 W.

D. The reasoning behind this answer is as follows: The unmodulated carrier output is 100 W and the efficiency (E) of the final stage is 50 percent. The dc input power (P_{in}) to the final stage is

$$P_{in} = \frac{P_{out}}{E} = \frac{100}{0.5} = 200 \text{ W}$$

For 100 percent modulation the ac power supplied by the modulator must be equal to 50 percent of the dc power to the RF amplifier or 200 × 50 percent = 100 W. The modulator efficiency is 66 percent so the input power to the modulator

$$P_{in} = \frac{P_{out}}{E} = \frac{100}{0.66} = 151.5 \text{ W}.$$

Q. 3.137-A9. If the transmission line current of an FM transmitter is 8.5 A without modulation, what is the transmission line current when the percentage of modulation is 90 percent?

A. The transmission line current is still 8.5 A.

D. Since the power output remains substantially constant with or without modulation, there should be no change of transmission line current.

Q. 3.137-A10. The direct-current input power to the final amplifier stage is exactly 1500 V and 700 mA. The antenna resistance is 8.2 Ω and the antenna current is 9 A. What is the plate efficiency of the final amplifier?

A. The plate efficiency of the final amplifier is 63.25 percent.

D. Plate efficiency equals the output power divided by the input power multiplied by 100.

Step 1: Find the input power

$$P_{in} = V_b \times I_b = 1\,500 \times 0.7 = 1\,050 \text{ W}$$

Step 2: Find the output power

$P_{out} = I_{out}^2 \times Z_{out} = (9)^2 \times 8.2 = 664.2 \text{ W}$

Step 3: Find the plate efficiency

$$PE = \frac{P_{out}}{P_{in}} \times 100 \text{ percent}$$

$$= \frac{664.2}{1\,050} \times 100 = 63.25 \text{ percent}$$

Q. 3.137-A11. If the antenna current of a station is 9.7 A for 5 kW, what is the current necessary for a power of 1 kW?

A. The new antenna current is 4.33 A.

D. Power is proportional to the square of the current.

$$\frac{W_1}{W_2} = \frac{I_1^2}{I_2^2}$$

$$\frac{1}{5} = \frac{(I_1^2)}{(9.7)_2}$$

$$I_1 = \frac{9.7}{\sqrt{5}} = 4.33 \text{ A}$$

(See also Q. 3.195.)

Q. 3.137-A12. An FM transmitter has 370 W plate power input to the last radio-frequency stage and an antenna field gain of 1.3. The efficiency of the last radio frequency stage is 65 percent, and the efficiency of the antenna transmission line is 75 percent. What is the effective radiated power?

A. 304.8338 W.

D. The dc plate power input to the last RF stage is given at 370 W. The efficiency of this stage is given as 65 percent. This means that only 65 percent of 370 W or 240.5 W is available to the transmission line as RF power. The remaining 35 percent or 129.5 W is dissipated in the form of heat on the plate of the last RF stage. If, of the 240.5 W of RF power fed to the transmission line, only 75 percent reaches the antenna (or 180.375 W), the remaining 25 percent or 60.125 W is dissipated on the line. The antenna has a field gain over a simple dipole of 1.3, so that the effective radiated power is then 180.375 times 1.3^2 or 304.8338 W.

Note: Antenna field gain is a measure of voltage. This value must be squared in order to find the power gain.

Q. 3.137-A13. What is effective radiated power? Given transmitter power output, antenna resistance, antenna transmission line loss, transmitter efficiency and antenna power gain, show how ERP is calculated.

A.

1. Effective radiated power is the power actually delivered to the antenna, multiplied by the power gain of the antenna in the direction of interest.

The power delivered to the antenna is the transmitter-output power less the power lost by the transmission line connecting the transmitter to the antenna. The power gain of the antenna and the transmission line losses are usually expressed in decibels (dB). The power gain of the antenna system includes the transmission line; the transmission-line losses in dB are subtracted from the antenna-power gain in dB.

The simplest method of calculating the ERP is to convert the dB power gain of the antenna system into a power ratio and multiply the transmitter power output by this ratio to find the ERP.

2. For example, assume a transmitter with a power output of 10.1 kW feeds an antenna with a power gain of 24.6 dB via a transmission line with a loss of 1.6 dB.

The power gain of the antenna system is 24.6 − 1.6 or 23.0 dB. Using the relationship

$$dB = 10 \log \frac{P_1}{P_2}$$

we can find that the transmitter's power output will be multiplied by 200 times. The ERP is 10.1 × 200 or 2 020 kW.

D. See Q. 3.195.

Q. 3.137-A14. What is meant by frequency translation?

A. *Frequency translation* is the process of changing the frequency of a particular wave to some other desired frequency. In the process the information in the original wave remains intact.

D. Frequency translation is performed for various reasons. For example, an audio or video wave must be *translated* into a modulated RF carrier to be transmitted. Other examples of frequency translation are:

1. Modulation signal into AM RF carrier wave.

2. AM RF carrier wave into modulation signal.

3. Dc translated into ac and vice-versa.

4. One type of satellite (Intelsat) receives frequencies in the band of 5925 to 6425 MHz for ground-to-satellite signals. These are translated to a band of 3700 to 4200 MHz for satellite-to-ground signals.

5. In cable television (CATV) Cablevision systems, all UHF channels are translated to UHF for cable transmission. Further, at each user's location all channels are translated to either channel 3 or 4 (whichever is unused) by a CATV converter.

6. A TV *translator station* consists basically of a TV receiver and a low-power TV transmitter. Programs are received on VHF at a good location and are re-broadcast on an unused UHF channel (70 to 83). The re-broadcast is needed to supply usable signals to areas in valleys, or those that are too far from the originating station to receive good signals.

7. Remote communications or TV pickups may be initially broadcast on VHF or UHF and then translated to frequencies (SHF) utilized by satellites. (See part 4.)

Q. 3.137-A15. What is meant by selective calling?

A. *Selective calling* is a scheme in which code signals are transmitted so that only a *specific* receiving station (or stations) will receive the transmission.

D. One type of selective calling is the continuous tone-coded squelch system (CTCSS) described in Q. 3.181-A7. This scheme may operate a number or receivers simultaneously.

Another type of selective calling can be received by only one specific receiving station. The base station can transmit a different tone-coded signal to each receiving station. Only the receiving station equipped to be actuated by the particular coded tone being transmitted will receive the transmission.

The tone-coded signal may be a continuous tone, a burst, a pulsed tone, or a combination of tones.

With the single burst or pulsed-tone system, the tone is sent only at the beginning of each transmission. A decoder at the receiver opens the squelch circuit, which then stays open by a carrier-operated circuit. Here the tone is in the range of 1 500 to 3 000 Hz.

Some mobile communications systems use a dual-tone method to open a receiver squelch circuit. Typical frequencies used for this system are 600 and 1500 Hz.

Q. 3.137-A16. What are isolators? How are they used? What are circulators? How are they used?

A.

1. An *isolator* is an attenuator in which the RF transmission loss through it in one direction is much greater than in the opposite direction. Energy from the opposite direction is absorbed by the isolator. The basic element of an isolator is the ferrite (a compound of oxides of iron, zinc, and other metals), which operates in conjunction with a permanent magnet. The ferrite molecules have a resonance condition that will either pass the RF energy with little loss or absorb it, depending on the direction of wave travel.

In many applications, *reflected* waves on a transmission line cannot be tolerated because of the high values of VSWR that might occur. The use of an isolator prevents the formulation of high VSWRs by absorbing most of the reflected waves. In addition, an isolator presents a matched load at the output of the transmitter, no matter what the VSWR may be. An isolator helps to reduce trans-

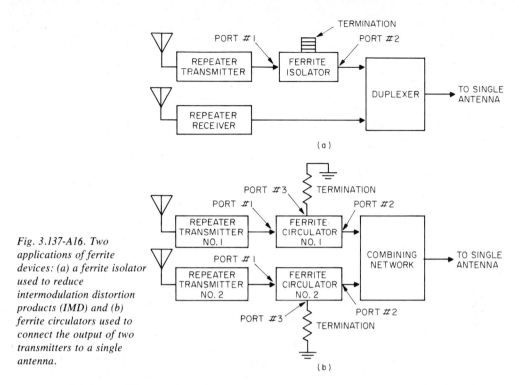

Fig. 3.137-A16. Two applications of ferrite devices: (a) a ferrite isolator used to reduce intermodulation distortion products (IMD) and (b) ferrite circulators used to connect the output of two transmitters to a single antenna.

mitter-generated *intermodulation distortion products* (IMD), which are generated in the last stage of the transmitter (see discussion).

An example of the use of an isolator to reduce IMD is shown in Fig. 3.137-A16(a). The isolator is a two-"port" device. (A *port* is an entrance or an exit for a network.) Here, it is placed between the repeater transmitter and a duplexer. IMD generation is dependent upon externally generated signals being fed from the antenna, back to the transmitter. The isolater, being a "one-way" device, effectively prevents this from happening. As shown in Fig. 3.137-A16(a), the isolator has a built-in termination that absorbs the reflected energy. Rejection of the undesired energy picked up by the antenna is in the order of 25 dB. The insertion (forward) loss is about 0.5 dB.

1. A *circulator* is also a ferrite device, operating with a fixed magnet. It is a three-"port" device. Circulators can be used as *duplexers*. When so used, circulators provide more than 20 db of isolation between the transmitter and receiver, with an insertion

loss of about 0.25 dB. Both isolators and circulators have been designed to handle an average power of as much as many kilowatts. They also can be used to feed the output of two or more transmitters to a single antenna. A block diagram illustrating the latter use is shown in Fig. 3.137-A16(b). By terminating port 3 in a resistance, the circulator functions as an isolator. The termination resistance absorbs the reflected wave energy.

D. Transmitter-generated IMDs are generated within the last power amplifier (PA) stage of the transmitter. This occurs as follows: A strong signal from another transmitter is picked up by the antenna of the repeater transmitter under consideration. This signal travels down the transmission line and into the last PA stage of the latter transmitter. Since this stage is operated in a non-linear fashion (Class C or some form of Class B) for efficiency, the stage acts as a mixer. The interfering frequency then mixes with that of the repeater transmitter or with its second or third harmonic. The last PA stage then acts a high-level mixer and produces strong IMD products. These are then radiated from the antenna of the repeater transmitter. When the second harmonic of the repeater-transmitter frequency mixes with the incoming signal frequency, one of the IMD product frequencies may be fairly close to the repeater-transmitter frequency.

When this is radiated (in appreciable strength), it may be received by another repeater receiver situated in the same general area. This will, of course, interfere with the normal reception of that repeater receiver. The IMD-product frequency in this case may, in the second repeater receiver, cause IMD problems by mixing with its desired signal, in the RF amplifier and mixer circuits. Receiver IMD can give rise to the reception of unwanted signals and to the generation of spurious receiver responses. (For additional discussion of IMD, see Q. 3.135.

Note: IMD product frequencies are also generated that are far removed from the repeater transmitter frequency. However, these seldom cause interference problems. The reason for this is that such frequencies are highly attenuated by the PA-tuned circuit, the duplexer (if used), and the antenna. The resonance characteristics of these components will greatly attenuate IMD product frequencies of this range.

Q. 3.137-A17. How is the operation of a two-way radio system affected by changes in antenna height? Antenna gain? Terrain? Urban environment? Frequency band?

A.

1. Generally speaking the higher the base and/or mobile antenna, the greater the communicating range. The antenna(s) height versus transmission distance is more critical in the VHF and UHF bands than in the HF band.

2. An antenna having a specific gain, when used at a base and/or mobile station will increase the communicating range, when compared to an antenna(s) without a gain factor.

3. Terrain features, such as hills or mountains, which are between and higher than the base and/or mobile station (or stations) will reduce the communicating range.

4. Urban (city) environment consisting of numerous tall buildings can appreciably reduce two-way communication range. This is particularly true on the VHF and UHF bands. The situation will be improved where a base-station antenna can be appreciably elevated.

5. The frequency band used has a definite effect on two-way radio communications. On the VHF and UHF bands, the communicating range is considered to be restricted to approximately "line-of-sight" distances. (In practice it may be somewhat greater.) The HF band will permit appreciably greater communicating distances. In AM systems, the interference problems from atmospheric static is much less on the VHF and UHF bands than on the HF band.

D.

1. The line-of-sight distance, corrected for the actual curvature path of radio waves traveling close to the earth, is given by

$$D = 1.415(\sqrt{h_t} + \sqrt{h_r})$$

where

    D = the line-of-sight distance in miles.
    h_t = the height of the transmitting antenna in feet.
    h_r = the height of the receiving antenna in feet.

Based on the above equation, if the base station antenna is 100 ft high and a mobile-unit antenna is 6 ft high, the communicating range (based upon flat terrain) is about 15 miles. This range may be increased when a mobile unit is operating in an elevated position. The range may be substantially decreased if there exists between units, intervening hills or heavy foliage.

2. Increased range due to antenna gain depends upon the particular gain figure of the base station antenna and mobile unit. For example, the base station antenna has

a power gain of 6 dB (4 times). The effective radiated power (ERP) is then increased by a factor of four. In a practical case, this may increase the VHF range to a mobile unit from 25 to 35 miles. A similar improvement in range from a mobile unit to a base station will be noted, if the mobile unit antenna has a gain of 6 dB. In addition, communicating range between mobile units will be increased if gain antennas are used.

3. Terrain features in the path of propagation will introduce transmission losses and thus reduce communicating range. This loss is called *shadow* loss and increases with frequency. As an example, consider a hill about 500 ft high between a base station and a mobile station. If the top of the hill is about 5 miles from the base station, the shadow loss will result in a reduction of communicating range of the base station to the mobile unit of about 12 miles.

4. Urban environment will produce a reduction of range in proportion to the number, type, and height of the intervening buildings. Buildings with metal frames will cause greater losses than wooden structures. Likewise buildings that are close together will cause greater losses. Gain antennas at base and mobile stations, higher-power transmitters, and elevated antennas at base stations will provide improved range. For covering large areas, many mobile systems operating in the 25 to 50 MHz band use transmitters with a power output of 30 to 100 W. In the 150 to 173 MHz (VHF) band, power outputs of 10 to 30 W are used to cover a medium-sized city with mobile units. In the 450 to 512 MHz (UHF) band, transmitter powers of 5 W or greater will cover a medium-sized city, when using mobile units.

5. The transmitting frequency is an important factor in the communicating range. For example, if the communicating range in the 25 to 50 MHz band is typically 25 to 50 miles; in the 150 to 173 MHz band, it will be 15 to 25 miles; and in the 450 to 512 MHz

band, it will be 10 to 15 miles. These figures are for base-to-mobile stations.

Q. 3.137-A18. Draw a simplified block diagram of a mobile radiotelephone system. Briefly describe its operation.

A. The block diagram is shown in Fig. 3.137-A18.

In this system, both the base station and the mobile station operate duplex. The base station transmits on frequency 1 and receives on frequency 2. The mobile station receives on frequency 1 and transmits on frequency 2.

The base station is tied into the land telephone system for land distribution to a desired called number from the mobile station. The mobile radiotelephone subscriber may use the mobile station in any area where the service is given.

D. This system features automatic call handling in both directions. It also provides access to several different channels by each mobile station.

At each mobile station the receiver *hunts* for an unused channel. It locks onto the unused channel and this condition is identified by a steady 2 000-Hz tone. The mobile station wishing to transmit *seizes* the unused channel by activating its transmitter. Coded tones then automatically transmit its identifying code. This code is recorded for billing purposes. The mobile subscriber then receives a telephone dial tone. He can now

Fig. 137-A18. A simplified block diagram of a mobile radio telephone system. Both stations operate duplex.

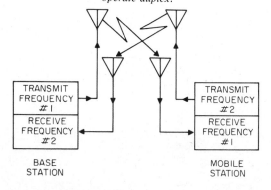

use his touch tone (or dial) to place the call to the desired party.

When the mobile radiotelephone operator wishes to alert a mobile station, he transmits a coded signal over the base transmitter. This may consist of 600- and 1 500-Hz frequency shift tones. When the code combination assigned to a particular mobile unit is received, a decoder activates circuits that operate a buzzer and a light, indicating a waiting call. The decoders are usually solid-state logic devices.

Q. 3.137-A19. Briefly discuss the use of RF control stations associated with land mobile stations.

A. Remote control of a mobile station can be accomplished by radio frequency transmission. Control stations may operate on frequencies available for use by operational fixed stations.

D. At the option of the licensee, control stations may operate at the frequency of the associated mobile station(s).

Note: The following paragraph shall apply only for control stations operating in the 450 to 470 MHz band and located within 75 miles of the center of urbanized areas with a population of 200 000 or more.

If the control station is used to control one or more mobile relay stations located within 45° of azimuth, the control station shall employ a directional antenna with a front-to-back ratio of at least 15 dB. For other situations a directional or omnidirectional antenna may be used.

Q. 3.137-A20. In the Private Land Mobile Radio Services (Part 90, FCC R & R), what are trunked systems?

A. *Trunked* systems are ones in which the base station may communicate with a large number of vehicular and/or portable mobile units. Conversely, a large number of vehicular and/or portable mobile units may communicate with a base station.

D. The minimum number of frequency pairs that may be assigned to a trunked system is five and the maximum number is twenty.

An abbreviated table showing the number of vehicular and/or portable mobile units (loading) versus 5-, 10-, and 20-channel systems for the 806 to 821 MHz and 851 to 866 MHz bands is shown in Table 3.137-A20.

Q. 3.137-A21. Draw a simple schematic diagram showing how a mobile base station can remotely control the transmitter receiver equipment using telephone lines. Briefly describe the operation.

A. The schematic diagram is shown in Fig. 3.137-A21.

In this method, only one pair of telephone lines is used. The audio signal (either direction) is applied to either transformer primary. The control voltages are applied to the wires through split-transformer secondary windings. Note that in this scheme no ground connections are required because they are in a different single-wire pair design.

D. Remote control of the transmitter-receiver location is required when the operating office is at a considerable distance from it. By remote control over wires, a distance of several miles for remote control is possible. Remote control can also be accomplished without a wire line. In this case

Table 3.137-A20. Loading Requirements for Trunked Systems.

	Number of Radio Units		
	5-Channel Systems	10-Channel Systems	20-Channel Systems
Police and fire group	300	750	1 500
Business radio group	500	1000	2000
Motor carrier group (urban and interurban passenger motor carriers only)	800	1600	2500

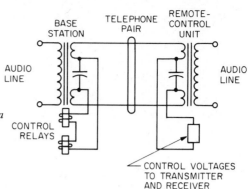

Fig. 3.137-A21. Simplified schematic diagram showing a method of remote control of the transmitter-receiver equipment from a mobile base station, using a pair of telephone lines.

control is accomplished by radio wave transmission.

Q. 3.137-A22. In accordance with FCC Part 90 (Private Land Mobile Radio Services), what are the timing periods permitted for tone or impulse signaling? For this type of signaling, what is the maximum time the transmitter is permitted to be on before being automatically deactivated by a timing mechanism?

A.

1. For Public Safety Radio Services, the duration of any one non-voice signal may not exceed 2 s. It shall not be transmitted more than three times. Any one voice alarm shall not exceed a duration of 6 s and shall not be transmitted more than three times.

2. For tone or impulse signaling service, the transmitter is required to be automatically deactivated, if the carrier remains on for a period greater than three minutes.

When automatically retransmitting messages originated by or destined for hand-carried transceivers, each mobile station shall activate the mobile transmitter with a continuous-coded tone. The absence of the tone will automatically deactivate the mobile transmitter. This tone is not required if the mobile unit being contacted is equipped with an automatic timer that shuts off the transmitter after any uninterrupted transmission period in excess of three minutes.

D. Base, mobile relay, or mobile stations may transmit tone or impulse signals to receivers at fixed locations.

Q. 3.137-A23. What is receiver desensitization? How can receiver limiter current be used to determine if desensitization is occurring. Describe a repeater system.

A.

1. *Desensitization* is the reduction of repeater receiver sensitivity, caused by the reception of a strong signal within or near the RF amplifier bandwidth. This strong signal can cause overload in the RF amplifier and/or mixer stages and thus reduce receiver sensitivity. In a repeater station (see discussion), this condition is most commonly caused by the broadband ("white") noise or RF output from the nearby repeater transmitter—provided the receiver and transmitter antennas are close together. Severe power line noise or strong radiation from an adjacent channel transmitter can also cause desensitization.

2. Checking the performance of the receiver (FM) limiter current provides a ready indication of possible desensitization. Switch the repeater transmitter off and then on. An increase of limiter current when the

Fig. 3.137-A23. Simplified block diagram of a repeater system.

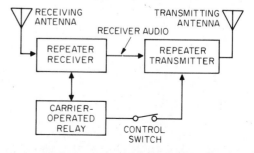

transmitter is on shows that desensitization is occurring.

3. A relay (repeater) system is one that retransmits signals it receives. Its purpose is to improve the range and coverage of communications. This improvement is possible because, unlike mobile units, the repeater can be permanently located at an elevated site. Thus the repeater provides coverage considerably greater than that of mobile stations alone. Repeaters are advantageously used with VHF and UHF mobile stations. The range of mobile stations are limited by virtue of their low antenna heights and also by operation in hilly terrain.

D. A block diagram of a simple repeater is shown in Fig. 3.137-A23. The audio output of the repeater receiver is connected to the audio (modulation) input of the repeater transmitter. Provision is made to control the audio amplitude, in order to achieve the desired percentage of modulation. A carrier operated relay (COR) is connected to the squelch circuit of the receiver. When the input signal exceeds a minimum required value, the squelch circuit is made inactive (receiver operates) and the COR is closed. Contacts on the COR then activate the transmitter.

The control switch is provided when it is desired to manually prevent the transmitter from operating.

Q. 3.137-A24. Discuss the merits of using cavity resonator filters, as opposed to conventional LC filters, for filtering in the transmitter and receiver antenna feedlines of a repeater.

A. At VHF and especially UHF frequencies, the conventional coil and capacitor (LC) filter circuit becomes difficult to construct. This is basically because of the small physical size of the required components. In addition and more important, it is very difficult to construct such filters with the high Q required for this service. Very high Qs with consequent sharp responses are required here.

To obtain the required Q (and tuning stability), cavity resonator filters (or high-Q *stripline* filters-are used. (A basic discussion of resonant cavities used at microwaves is given in Q. 3.251. The principles are the same for VHF and UHF cavities, although for the latter two bands, the physical dimensions will be proportionately larger.) A cavity resonator, tuned to the operating frequency and inserted in the receiver and transmitter feedlines, acts as a highly efficient high-Q filter. A simplified sketch of a typical feedline cavity filter is shown in Fig. 3.137-A24(a). Note that the resonant cavity frequency may be adjusted by moving a metal plunger to increase or decrease the effective cavity dimensions (the smaller the cavity, the higher its reasonant frequency). A resonant cavity not only has a very high Q, but also a low-insertion loss (loss caused by the filter).

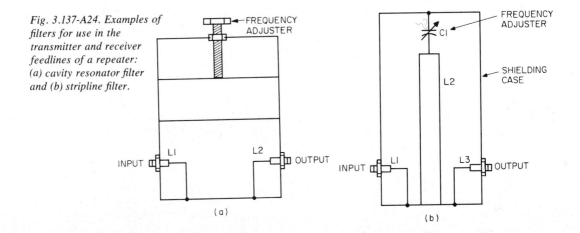

Fig. 3.137-A24. Examples of filters for use in the transmitter and receiver feedlines of a repeater: (a) cavity resonator filter and (b) stripline filter.

D. One method of reducing or eliminating the problem of receiver desensitization (Q. 3.137-A23) is to improve the effective selectivity of both the transmitter and receiver. Basically, this means to restrict the bandwidth of transmission and reception frequencies. Broadband ("white") noise transmission from the transmitter will be greatly reduced by a high-Q cavity filter placed in the *transmitter* feedline. In addition, the reception of "white" noise and undesired carrier emissions may be greatly reduced by the insertion of a cavity filter in the *receiver* feedline. The use of filters in both places will greatly reduce the problem of receiver desensitization.

The use of a *duplexer* containing high-Q cavities is also effective in reducing receiver desensitization. With a duplexer, a single antenna is used for both transmitting and receiving. The high-Q cavities in the duplexer prevent appreciable white noise and transmitter signal energy from reaching the input of the receiver. A duplexer can provide up to 120 dB of isolation between the transmitter and receiver.

A *stripline filter* is a tuned section of a stripline. A stripline consists of a center (printed) copper conductor sandwiched between two outer conducting planes. The outer (ground) planes are formed from copper-clad polyethelyne sheets. Striplines are used as transmission lines and tuned circuits. Stripline filters feature high Q and low-insertion loss. A simple sketch of a stripline filter, which can be used as a repeater feedline filter, is shown in Fig. 3.137-A24(b). The resonant frequency of the filter can be adjusted by varying capacitor C_1.

Q. 3.137-A25. How may repeater transmitter and receiver antenna separation be used to reduce desensitization of the receiver? Why is vertical antenna separation more effective than an equal distance of horizontal separation, in reducing desensitization?

A.

1. The farther the transmitting antenna is from the receiving antenna, the lower will be the signal strength appearing at the receiving antenna. This will, if carried out properly, reduce the problem of receiver desensitization.

2. Vertical antenna separation is more effective than an equal distance of horizontal separation. The reason for this lies in the shape of the radiation pattern of vertical antenna. (See Q. 3.198.) Maximum strength of radiation takes place in angles fairly close to the ground and in a non-directional fashion. Thus, a receiving antenna separated horizontally lies in the path of the strongest radiated waves.

On the other hand, the radiation of a vertical antenna is *minimum* in the vertical direction. Consequently, if the receiving antenna is mounted vertically with respect to the transmitting antenna, it will receive (for the same separation distance) appreciably less radiation.

D. The effectiveness of horizontal versus vertical separation can be seen from the following. In the upper portion of the VHF band (200 MHz), a horizontal spacing of 200 ft will provide a transmitted signal attenuation of about 65 dB at the receiving antenna. However, using vertical separation, a separation of only about 25 ft is required.

Q. 3.137-A26. Draw a circuit diagram of a complete radiotelephone transmitter composed of the following stages:
1. **Microphone input connection**
2. **Preamplifier**
3. **Speech amplifier**
4. **Class B modulator**
5. **Crystal oscillator**
6. **Buffer amplifier**
7. **Class C modulated amplifier**
8. **Antenna output connection**

Insert meters in the circuit where necessary and explain, step-by-step, how the transmitter is tuned.

A. For the diagram, see Fig. 3.137-A26.

The transmitter may be tuned by the method outlined in the following steps:

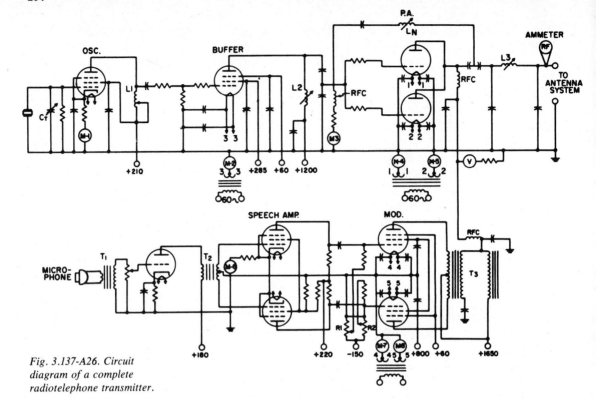

Fig. 3.137-A26. Circuit diagram of a complete radiotelephone transmitter.

1. Turn on all filaments and heaters in the transmitter.

2. Activate the bias supply for the modulator.

3. Apply plate voltage to the oscillator and adjust the oscillator plate inductor (L1) tap to a position giving minimum indication on M-1. Move the tap one position *closer* to the plate end of inductor.

4. After checking for a grid current indication in the buffer by M-2, apply plate, screen and suppressor voltages to the buffer and immediately adjust buffer tank inductor for a minimum reading on M-2, and maximum reading on power amplifier grid meter, M-3.

5. Measure frequency of transmitter. If not correct, make necessary adjustments by means of the trimmer capacitor across crystal (C_T).

6. Adjust the power amplifier tank inductor (L3) for a maximum indication of RF current as shown by ammeter in the output. It is assumed that the transmitter is connected to its antenna system.

7. Adjust neutralizing inductor, L_N, for minimum RF current.

8. Adjust the buffer tank inductor (L2) for maximum RF current.

9. Repeat steps 6, 7, and 8 until the RF current shown by the ammeter is zero or at a minimum.

10. Adjust the bias potentiometers (R1, R2) on the modulator for maximum bias to the modulator tubes.

11. Apply plate voltage to the power amplifier and immediately adjust its tank inductor (L3) for minimum plate current as shown on ammeters M-4 and M-5. RF current at this point should be at a maximum and of normal expected value.

12. With input level control set to minimum, apply plate voltage to the preamplifier and speech amplifier and screen and suppressor voltages to the modulator.

13. Adjust the bias potentiometers in the modulator so that the modulator tubes draw normal and equal plate currents as indicated by ammeters M-7 and M-8.

14. Check the cathode current of the

speech amplifier to see that it is within expected values.

15. Apply a 1 000-hertz tone to the input of the preamplifier in place of the microphone and increase the input level slowly while observing the modulation envelope with an oscilloscope. Observe all ammeters in the power amplifier and modulator to see that they stay within expected values while modulation is increased to 100 percent.

16. Note modulation envelope and see if troughs of modulation reach the zero axis at 100 percent modulation. If not, slightly readjust neutralizing inductor (L_N) until troughs reach zero. At each change of L_N, readjust buffer and power amplifier tank inductors for resonance.

17. Check to see if both modulator tubes are drawing equal cathode currents. If not, readjust bias potentiometers until they do.

18. The transmitter may now be considered tuned.

Q. 3.137-A27. Draw a cross-section diagram of a Vidicon television camera tube.

A. Fig. 3.137-A27 shows a cross section of the Vidicon-television camera tube.

D. The standard vidicon is a relatively simple and compact camera tube. Vidicons may vary in diameter from 0.5 in (1.27 cm) to 1.5 in (3.8 cm), and in length from 3.5 in (8.9 cm) to 8 in (20.3 cm). Vidicons are widely used for closed-circuit television (CCTV) and for TV studio and film cameras. Some vidicons can produce useable pictures operating in near-total darkness, or in near-direct sunlight.

Q. 3.137-A28. Describe the monochrome scanning technique used in United States television transmissions. Why is interlacing used?

A.

1. A frame is a complete picture containing all necessary picture elements. There are a total of 525 horizontal sweep cycles or *lines* in one frame and, therefore, a total of $525 \times 30 = 15,750$ lines per second. Of the 525 lines per frame there are 262.5 lines in each field of which about 242.5 lines contain picture information and about 20 lines do not. These 20 lines are blanked out during the vertical retrace interval. At the transmitter and receiver, the scanning process may be broken down into four distinct periods. These may be referred to as (a) the odd line field trace period, (b) the odd line field retrace period, (c) the even line field trace period, (4) the even line field retrace period during which no picture information is transmitted, about retrace period. The permissible time allowed for each operation is approximately as follows: (a) For the even line field trace period during which picture

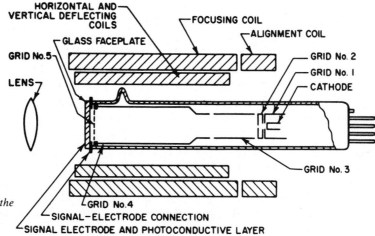

Fig. 3.137-A27. Sketch of the Vidicon television camera tube.

information is being transmitted, about 15,417 microseconds or 242.5 horizontal sweep cycles, (b) for the even line field 1250 microseconds or 20 horizontal sweep cycles. This period is also known as the vertical blanking interval. The even line field trace and retrace periods have the same time allowances and the same number of horizontal sweep cycles as the odd line field trace and retrace periods. Each trace and retrace period constitutes a complete field. There are 60 of these fields (odd and even) per second. An odd line field plus an even line field equals one *frame* of which there are 30 per second.

2. Interlaced scanning is used in order to eliminate flicker from the television picture.

D.

1. The scanning process takes place as follows: A narrow beam of electrons is produced and directed upon an image plate in a camera tube or a fluorescent screen in a kinescope (receiving) cathode ray tube. Due to the presence of various synchronizing pulses, the beam at the camera tube and the beam at the kinescope tube are locked in step with each other and may be considered to be covering the same basic areas of the picture in question, simultaneously. The electron beam is acted upon by electromagnetic coils or electrostatic plates in such a manner that it is caused to move relatively slowly from left to right (trace), during which time picture information is present, and then moves quickly from right to left (retrace) in which time no picture information is present, as the beam is blanked out. During the left to right movement (in 53.34 microseconds) the beam also is moving slightly downwards so that when the retrace takes place (in 10.16 microseconds) the beam returns at the left hand side of the screen slightly below its original starting position. The distance below is equal to the width of two lines, since every other line is skipped in interlaced scanning. In a similar manner the beam moves across horizontally and downward until the entire picture area has been covered in about 242.5 lines. At this point (beginning of vertical

blanking interval) the screen is blanked out and the beam returns horizontally and upwards in about 3 to 5 lines until it reaches the top of the picture. This completes one field. The downward scanning process is now resumed but the beam is now so positioned that it falls into the empty line spaces previously left in the preceding field. About 242.5 lines are again completed in the downward direction until the beam reaches the bottom of the picture. At this time the picture is again blanked out and the beam moves horizontally and upwards in about 3 to 5 lines until it reaches the top. This completes another field and one *frame*. This sequence of events is repeated at the frame repetition rate of 30 hertz.

2. One of the very important factors in transmitting a television signal is the number of complete pictures sent each second. In motion picture practice it is common to show 24 frames or pictures per second to give the illusion of smooth and continuous motion. However, due to the action of a shutter, each frame is shown twice; being blanked out for a short period of time and then shown again. Thus to the eye it appears that there are 48 pictures per second while in reality there are only 24. This optical illusion is necessary in order to eliminate flicker from the picture. Flicker refers to a change of light intensity and not to motion. Reference is made to electric light bulbs operated from a 25-hertz power source. A very noticeable and objectionable flicker may be readily observed by watching the bulbs. On the other hand, bulbs operating from a 60-hertz source apparently have no flicker at all. To eliminate flicker, the repetition rate should be in excess of 40 pictures per second. A system similar to motion picture practice is used in television and this is called interlaced scanning. The frame or picture repetition rate in television has been standardized at 30 per second. This rate is not sufficient to eliminate flicker. Each frame, therefore, has been split into two parts called fields. Thus there are 60 fields per second. Instead of scanning all of the lines which make up

a picture, in sequence, every other line is scanned first. This makes up one field. Then, the alternate lines are scanned completing the second field and one frame. In this way, the illusion of 60 pictures per second is gained and the appearance of flicker is eliminated.

Q. 3.137-A29. Make a sketch showing equalizing, blanking, and synchronizing pulses of a standard U.S. television transmission.

A. For the sketch, see Fig. 3.137-A29.

D. 1. As shown in the figure, six equalizing pulses are present on each side of the serrated vertical synchronizing pulses. These equalizing pulses serve two important functions: One is to maintain correct interlacing of the odd and even fields of each frame. This will enable the scanning lines of one field to fit perfectly between the scanning lines of the following (or preceding) field. Basically, the equalizing pulses permit the vertical synchronizing pulse to begin at the correct time at the end of either odd or even fields. The second function is to maintain a continuous string of horizontal synchronizing pulses to the horizontal scanning circuit. In Fig. 3.137-A29, "H" equals the time from one horizontal line to the next horizontal line, or 63.5 microseconds. "V" equals the time from the start of one field until the start of the next field, or 262.5 "H" periods, or 16 667 microseconds.

2. In general, the purpose of synchronizing pulses is to maintain the correct scanning pattern and to synchronize or lock-in the action of the receiving tube (Kinescope)

scanning beam with that of the camera tube scanning beam.

There are two types of synchronizing pulses, the amplitude of each type being confined to the region between 75 percent and 100 percent of maximum carrier amplitude. The upper tip of the synchronizing pulses is at an amplitude corresponding to 100 percent and the base of the pulses is at an amplitude corresponding to 75 percent. The horizontal pulses are rectangular in shape and extend above the top of the horizontal blanking pulses (see the figure). They have a width equal to about 5.08 microseconds. There is one horizontal synchronizing pulse for each horizontal line, or 525 per frame and 15 750 per second. The horizontal synchronizing pulse normally occurs at the time when the electron beam has progressed to the extreme right hand edge of the picture. The pulse acts upon a horizontal multivibrator or blocking oscillator type of sweep generator in such a way as to initiate the start of the horizontal retrace.

The vertical synchronizing pulse is somewhat more complicated being formed from 6 vertical serrated pulses which are electronically added in an integrating circuit to form a single pulse. There is one complete vertical synchronizing pulse for every field, or 2 per frame and 60 per second. The vertical pulse acts upon a multivibrator or blocking oscillator type of sweep generator in such a way as to initiate the starting of the electron beam to return to the top of the picture from the extreme lower part.

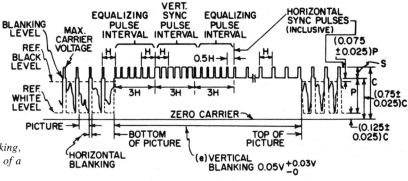

Fig. 3.137-A29. Sketch showing equalizing, blanking, and synchronizing pulses of a standard U.S. television transmission.

3. Blanking pulses are rectangular pulses of short duration used to extinguish the electron beam during the retrace, and are of negative polarity when applied to the intensity grid of the electron gun at both the transmitting and receiving cathode ray equipment. At the end of each horizontal line just before the retrace is initiated, the horizontal blanking pulse extinguishes the electron beam so that it returns to the left side of the picture unnoticed. The horizontal blanking pulse width is 10.16 microseconds, and there are 525 per frame or one for each horizontal synchronizing pulse. When the scanning beam reaches the extreme bottom of the picture and just prior to the vertical retracing, the vertical blanking interval pulse causes the electron beam to be extinguished so that the lines moving upward will not be seen. The duration of the vertical blanking interval pulse is about 1 250 microseconds and there are 60 per second.

4. See also Q. 3.137-A28.

Q. 3.137-A30. Make a sketch which shows the difference between blanking and synchronizing pulses used for color and those used for monochrome.

A. The monochrome synchronizing and blanking pulses are shown in Fig. 3.137-A29. The blanking and synchronizing pulses used for color are shown in Fig. 3.137-A30.

D. The synchronizing and blanking pulses used for color transmission are identical with those used for monochrome television with the exception of the addition of the "color burst" synchronizing signal. This consists of a short "burst" of the chrominance sub-carrier frequency of 3.579545 megahertz. This sub-carrier is superimposed on the "back porch" of the horizontal blanking pulses. This "color burst" signal is separated at the receiver and is used, in conjunction with an AFC system to synchronize the receiver's chrominance-sub-carrier oscillator to the same frequency and phase as the equivalent oscillator at the transmitter. In this manner the reproduction of colors at the receiver is synchronized with those produced at the transmitter.

Q. 3.137-A31. Sketch the amplitude characteristics of an idealized picture transmission of a television station in the United States.

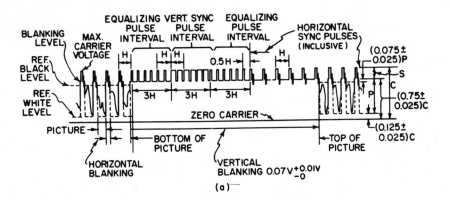

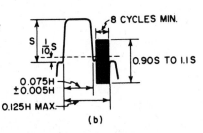

Fig. 3.137-A30.(a) Sketch showing equalizing, blanking and synchronizing pulses used for color-television transmission; (b) details of the "color burst" signal on the "back porch" of the horizontal-blanking pulse.

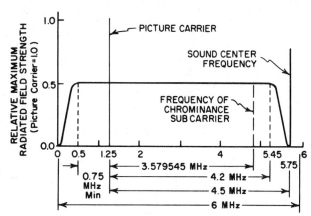

Fig. 3.137-A31. Idealized picture transmission amplitude characteristic.

A. For the sketch, see Fig. 3.137-A31.

D. Referring to the accompanying figure, it is seen that a standard television channel is 6 megahertz wide. Unlike conventional double-sideband amplitude modulation as used for AM-broadcast stations, television picture transmission is accomplished by "vestigial" (partial) sideband transmission. Note that while the upper sideband drops to zero, 4.5 megahertz above the picture carrier, the lower sideband extends to only 1.25 megahertz. This system permits a greater number of TV channels in the allotted frequency spectrum. Since all of the picture information is contained in a single sideband, no loss of information takes place.

Both sidebands are normally produced by the modulation process and the undesired portion of the lower sideband is eliminated at the transmitter by a vestigial side-band filter. It is not feasible to eliminate the entire lower sideband because of undesirable phase shifts which would occur to signals adjacent to the cut-off frequency. At the receiver, the IF response at the picture carrier is at the 50-percent amplitude point to compensate for the unequal sidebands. In a color transmission, the chrominance subcarrier and its sidebands are caused to modulate the picture carrier. The chrominance subcarrier has a frequency of 3.579545 megahertz and is so indicated in the figure. The aural portion of the program is transmitted by FM on a separate carrier which is located 4.5 megahertz above the picture carrier.

Q. 3.137-A32. for what purpose are reflectometers or directional couplers used in TV transmission systems?

A. Reflectometers are used to:

1. Measure standing-wave ratio on the transmission line.

2. Measure the relative power output of the transmitter.

3. Protect the transmission line against high-voltage surge damage, such as a lightning strike on the antenna.

D. The reflectometer is used in both the aural and visual transmitter output circuits, generally at the input to the transmission line. The reflectometer may consist of special peak-reading vacuum-tube voltmeter circuits. Two signal pick-up coils are used to feed energy to the vacuum-tube voltmeter. One is oriented to intercept the incident wave going to the antenna and the other to intercept the reflected wave from the antenna. (The incident and reflected currents are 180° out of phase.) The two waves are compared to provide a standing-wave ratio. To measure the power going to the antenna, the incident-wave circuit is used alone. In addition, the reflected-wave circuit may be used to actuate a protective device. This device protects the transmission line against damage due to high-surge currents and is actuated whenever the return current exceeds a specified value.

Q. 3.137-A33. Explain the operation of a turnstile TV antenna.

A. A simplified sketch of a turnstile antenna is shown in Fig. 3.137-A33(a). The antenna as used in practice actually consists of two antennas at right angles to each other, thus giving the appearance of a turnstile. A single section of a turnstile antenna provides a radiation pattern which is very similar to two vertically stacked horizontal dipoles. That is; it provides a bi-directional pattern (figure 8 pattern) with reduced radiation in the vertical plane. The single section is sometimes called a "batwing" antenna and is shown in simplified form in Fig. 3.137-A33(b). In order to provide an omnidirectional pattern for uniform-area coverage, two antennas are mounted at right angles and are fed 90° out of phase with each other. For greater gain and lower angles of radiation, several turnstile antennas may be stacked vertically on a pole. A six layer antenna provides a gain over a single layer type of

about seven times. The turnstile antenna radiates a horizontally polarized wave for both picture and sound transmissions. (Receiving antennas are of course horizontally polarized.)

D. A complete discussion of the operation of this antenna is not feasible in this book. However, a simplified explanation follows. The "bat-wing" antenna is derived from a "slot" antenna and its operation is briefly as follows: (See Fig. 3.137-A33(c)). The figure shows a solid conducting sheet, one-half wavelength high with a slot in its middle section. The antenna is fed at the center points as indicated (with a coaxial line). When this antenna is excited, voltage and current patterns are set up as shown. Because the currents flow horizontally, radiation takes place from both the front and rear of the sheet. At about one-quarter wavelength from the slot, the current decreases to a negligible amount. The impedance characteristics and vertical and hori-

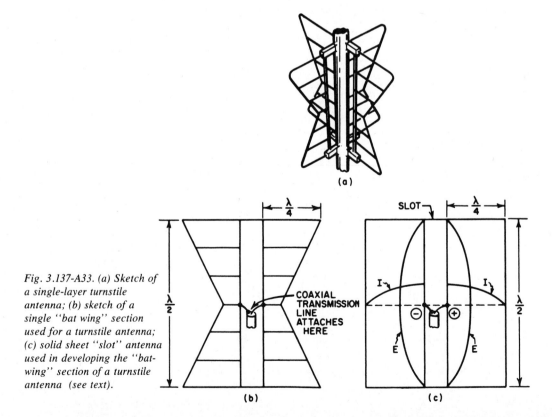

Fig. 3.137-A33. (a) Sketch of a single-layer turnstile antenna; (b) sketch of a single "bat wing" section used for a turnstile antenna; (c) solid sheet "slot" antenna used in developing the "bat-wing" section of a turnstile antenna (see text).

zontal-radiation patterns are similar to those of a conventional dipole. By reducing the width of the antenna at the center (see Fig. 3.137-A33(a), the vertical radiation is decreased. To reduce wind resistance, a framework construction may be used to replace the sheet without changing the antenna characteristics, providing the spaces are a small portion of a wavelength. The antenna is fed with a coaxial line. The inner conductor is connected to one center point of the slot and the outer conductor to the opposite center point. The impedance of the antenna is about 72 ohms at the center-feed points.

Q. 3.137-A34. Draw a block diagram of a monochrome TV transmitter. Briefly explain its operation.

A. For block diagram of a TV broadcast transmitter, See Fig. 3.137-A34.

D.

1. The block diagram shown is of a low-level modulated monochrome visual TV transmitter. Although not shown here, visual transmitters also may employ medium-level or high-level modulation.

2. The first block in the figure is a crystal oscillator operating at one-twelfth of the desired picture carrier frequency. For example, the picture carrier for channel 2 is 55.25 megahertz. In this case the crystal oscillator would operate at one-twelfth of this frequency, or 4.6 (approximately) megahertz. This is done to insure good crystal oscillator stability. Following the crystal oscillator is a series of frequency multipliers consisting of one tripler and two doublers providing a total frequency multiplication of 12 times. Thus, the output of the multipliers is at actual picture carrier frequency and is then applied to the modulated amplifier stage. The modulated amplifier also receives an input consisting of the composite video signal including sync and blanking pulses. The video signal is provided at about 25 volts peak-to-peak level by a five-stage video amplifier. This amplifier receives its input from the studio cameras, relay equipment, or from a line amplifier. Dc restorers are provided to reinsert the dc component of the signal before application to the modulated amplifier.

3. In addition, a video monitor is used to afford continuous monitoring of the composite video signal. Such factors as proper sync level, and white and black levels may be observed on the monitor. Synchronizing and blanking pulses as well as equalizing pulses are generated and keyed in at the appropriate times by the Keyer unit. The sync stretcher controls the amplitude of the sync pulses to compensate for compression or variations in amplitude.

4. The modulated amplifier output is a low-level RF monochrome TV signal. This is brought up to the desired transmitting strength by three stages of intermediate RF power amplification and then by the final RF power amplifier.

5. Note that the final RF power amplifier output is fed through a vestigial sideband filter and a diplexer before being applied to the transmitting antenna. The use of the vestigial (partial) filter assures that the undesired portion of the *lower picture sidebands*

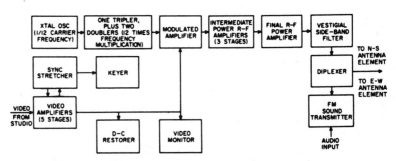

Fig. 3.137-A34. Block diagram of a typical monochrome TV transmitter using low-level modulation.

will be attenuated in accordance with the FCC requirements. This attenuation must be at least 20 dB at a point 1.25 megahertz below the visual carrier to prevent interference with the next lower TV channel.

6. The diplexer is a device used for the purpose of supplying both the visual and aural modulated carriers to the same transmitting antenna without crosstalk. Electrically, the diplexer is a circuit with the aural and visual transmitters connected across opposite arms of the bridge.

Q. Q. 3.137-A35. Draw a block diagram of a color TV transmitter. Briefly explain its operation.

A. For block diagram of a color TV transmitter, see Fig. 3.137-A35.

1. The "Color Camera" contains three separate camera tubes. Filters are employed with each tube so that one tube responds to green, one to blue and one to red. As indicated in the block, amplitude-varying signals corresponding to the green, blue and red picture components are sent separately to the "Matrix Circuits."

2. The "Matrix Circuits" are lumped into one block but actually contain amplifier circuits and resistive networks. The purpose of the "Matrix Circuits" is to produce certain combinations of the green, blue and red camera inputs and to produce three entirely different signals, known as the "Y," "I" and "Q" signals. These signals are produced by addition, subtraction and inversion of the three camera signals.

The "Y" (or brightness) signal has a bandwidth of 0 to 4.2 MHz. It is produced in the matrix by combining the outputs of the three camera tubes in the proportions : 59 percent green, 11 percent blue and 30 percent red. This is the signal viewed on a conventional black and white set. On a color set it supplies fine detail information (above 1.5 MHz bandwidth) which is sent only in black and white.

3. The "Y" signal is sent to the "Y Amplifier and Delay Circuit." Here the 'Y'

signal is amplified and delayed about 1 microsecond. The delay is necessary to match the delay normally imposed by the "Q" filter and by the "I" filter plus its delay circuit.

4. The "Y" inverter is necessary for the operation of the "Matrix Circuits."

5. The "Y" signal is further amplified by a second "Y" amplifier and is then passed to the "Output Mixing Amplifier."

6. The two other outputs of the "Matrix Circuit" are the "I" and "Q" signals (chrominance signals). Each of these signals represents a certain range of colors, which in combination can produce green, blue, red, or any other desired mixture color on the receiver-color tube. The "Q" signal alone is capable of producing colors ranging from yellow-green to purple. The "I" signal alone can produce colors ranging from cyan (bluish-green) to orange. The two signals acting together can produce a very wide range of colors to produce a full-color picture.

7. The "I" signal is fed to the "I Amplifier and Delay Circuit." This delay is necessary to match the delay of the "Q" signal. There is no delay circuit required in the "Q" channel. This is because the inherent delay of the "Q" filter introduces the greatest signal delay (about 1 microsecond) and is the reference time to which the "I" and "Y" signals must be matched.

8. The "I" signal is then passed through the "I" filter. This filter restricts the "I" signal bandwidth to 0 to 1.5 megahertz. This bandwidth restriction is required to fit the color information within the conventional TV transmission channel and also to reduce the possibility of creating an interference pattern on the color tube due to the mixing of the "I" and "Q" signals.

9. The "Q" signal coming from the matrix is fed into the "Q" amplifier and the "Q" filter. The "Q" filter restricts the "Q" signal bandwidth to a range of 0 to 0.5 megahertz. This bandwidth is adequate for reproducing sufficient detail for the colors represented by the "Q" signal. (Fine detail in a color picture is supplied by the black and white, or "Y" signal.)

10. The "I" and "Q" signal outputs from their respective filters are applied to the "I" and "Q" balanced modulators. Each balanced modulator also receives an input voltage from the 3.58 MHz sub-carrier. The sub-carrier input to the "Q" (quadrature) balanced modulator is shifted in phase by 90 degrees relative to the sub-carrier fed to the "I" (in-phase) balanced modulator.

11. In the "I"-balanced modulator, orange-to-cyan range color signals (0 to 1.5 MHz) are heterodyned with the sub-carrier. The sub-carrier is suppressed by the balanced modulator and its output is a set of sidebands ranging from 2.08 to 5.08 megahertz (3.58 MHz ± 1.5 MHz). Frequencies above 4.2 megahertz are later suppressed by the transmitter. The sub-carrier is suppressed to prevent the formation of a fine dot structure on black and white TV receivers. At the color receiver, the sub-carrier is reinserted in synchronous detectors which have as their output, the "I" and "Q" signals, reproduced.

12. In the "Q"-balanced modulator, the yellow-green to purple range color signals (0 to 0.5 MHz) are heterodyned with the 90-degree phase-shifted sub-carrier. Again, the sub-carrier is suppressed and the output is a set of sidebands ranging from 3.08 to 4.08 megahertz (3.58 ± 0.5 MHz). Because of the 90-degree sub-carrier phase shift, the sidebands for the "Q" and "I" signals are 90 degrees out of phase with one another and can be transmitted together without interference. They can then be individually recovered by the receiver synchronous detectors, by using two reinserted sub-carriers, 90-degrees out of phase with one another.

13. The outputs of "I" and "Q" balanced modulators are fed through the "I" and "Q" amplifiers and combined with the "Y" signal in the "Output Mixing Amplifier."

14. To reproduce color accurately at the receiver, the receiver sub-carrier oscillator must be locked in frequency and phase with the transmitter sub-carrier oscillator. This is done by the use of a *color burst sync signal*. This signal consists of a burst of 8 to 11 hertz of 3.58 MHz sub-carrier oscillator

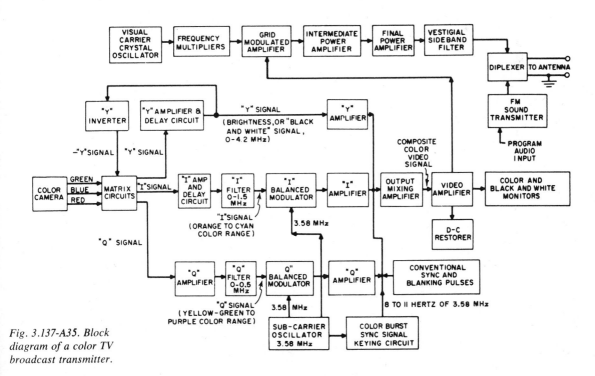

Fig. 3.137-A35. Block diagram of a color TV broadcast transmitter.

signal, which is keyed to be added to the *back porch* of the horizontal blanking pulses. (See Q. 3.137-A30 above.) The keying is accomplished by the block labeled, "Color Burst Sync Signal Keying Circuit." This signal is fed to the "Output Mixing Amplifier."

15. The conventional monochrome TV, horizontal and vertical sync and blanking pulses (see Q. 3.137-A29 above) are generated in the block so marked and are also fed to the "Output Mixing Amplifier."

16. The output of the "Output Mixing Amplifier" is a composite color-video signal consisting of the following signal voltages:

   a. Color burst sync signal.
   b. "Q" signal.
   c. "I" signal.
   d. "Y" signal.
   e. Conventional sync and blanking pulses.

17. The composite-color signal is fed through video amplifiers to the grid-modulated amplifier, dc restorer and to color and black and white monitors.

18. For discussion of the remainder of the blocks in Figure 3.137-A34 see Q. 3.137-A34.

AMPLITUDE MODULATION

Q. 3.138. What is the meaning of the term "carrier frequency"?

A. The *carrier frequency* is the frequency of the carrier wave. The *carrier wave* is the output of a transmitter when the modulating wave is equal to zero.

D. The above definitions hold true in the case of conventially modulated AM or FM transmitters. However, in the case of single-sideband suppressed carrier emission (see Q. 3.152), the carrier is not transmitted. There is a carrier frequency in this case, but it is suppressed prior to transmission.

Q. 3.139. If a carrier is amplitude modulated, what causes the sideband frequencies?

A. The process of modulation can be thought of as a process of heterodyning two or more frequencies and results in beat frequencies. The products of modulation are the two original frequencies plus the sum and difference frequencies. The sum and difference frequencies are known as the sideband frequencies. One of the two original frequencies (the radio frequency) appears unchanged and is termed the carrier frequency. The lower original or modulating frequency is also unchanged, but usually does not appear in the output of the modulated amplifier because the amplifier's load presents practically zero impedance to this low frequency.

D. In a more analytical sense, the modulated wave is a distorted sine wave because its amplitude is varying. Mathematically it can be shown that this distorted sine wave is comprised of three component frequencies; the carrier plus the two sidebands. The amplitude of the modulated wave at any instant is the vector sum of the amplitudes of the three components at the same instant.

Q. 3.140. What determines the bandwidth of emission for an AM transmission?

A. The bandwidth of emission for an AM transmission is always equal to twice the highest modulating frequency being used.

D. Assuming a carrier frequency of 500 kilohertz and a modulating frequency of 800 hertz, the bandwidth of emission is determined as given in the following example.

The total bandwidth is the difference between the upper and lower sideband frequencies. The upper sideband frequency equals $500\,000 + 800 = 500\,800$ hertz. The lower sideband frequency equals $500\,000 - 800 = 499\,200$ hertz. The total bandwidth, therefore, equals 1600 hertz, or the difference between the two sideband frequencies.

Q. 3.141. Why does exceeding 100 percent modulation in an AM transmission cause excessive bandwidth of mission?

A. When 100 percent modulation is exceeded in an AM transmission, the negative peaks of the modulation envelope are clipped. The result of this is to introduce even-order harmonics of the modulating frequencies into the wave. Since these represent higher modulating frequencies, the bandwidth of the emission is correspondingly increased and may become excessive.

D. When an RF amplifier is modulated in excess of 100 percent, there are definite periods of time when the amplifier does not produce any output at all. This factor radically changes the original wavelength of the modulating signal. New frequencies are thus generated which were not present in the original modulating signal. Among these new frequencies are many harmonics, the number and intensity of which vary in proportion to the degree of overmodulation. These in effect create additional sideband frequencies which may extend far beyond the allotted bandwidth, and cause interference to adjacent channels. In addition to creating interference, the change in waveshape of the modulation component also causes distortion of the received signal, the magnitude of which increases with the degree of overmodulation.

Q. 3.142. What is the relationship between percent modulation and the shape of the waveform "envelope" relative to carrier amplitude?

A. The amplitude of the peaks of modulation, expressed as a percentage of the carrier amplitude, is the percentage of modulation. Fig. 3.142 illustrates the relationship between the audio modulating signal, the unmodulated carrier wave and the modulated carrier wave for a 50-percent modulated wave.

D. Assume the carrier amplitude to be 100 volts unmodulated, the value of V_{max} to be 150 volts, and the value of V_{min} to be 50 volts. The percentage modulation is found according to the formula:

$$Mod. = \frac{V_{max} - V_{min}}{2\,E_{av}} \times 100$$

$$= \frac{150 - 50}{200} \times 100 = 50 \text{ percent}$$

For 100 percent modulation V_{max} would be 200 and V_{min} would be zero.

Q. 3.143. Draw a simplified circuit diagram of the final stages (modulator, modulated push-pull linear amplifier) of a type of low-level plate modulated transmitter, utilizing a pentode tube in the modulated stage. Explain the principles of operation. Repeat using a tetrode to provide high-level modulation.

A. Figure 3.143(a) illustrates one possible configuration for a low-level Class C plate-modulated amplifier followed by a push-pull Class B RF linear amplifier. It is believed the question is slightly in error, as a push-pull linear amplifier is not ordinarily modulated.

In a properly adjusted Class C amplifier, the output voltage or amplitude is directly proportional to the applied plate voltage. Examining the diagram, it can be seen that the AF output voltage of the modulator is in series with the applied dc plate voltage to the modulated amplifier. This results in an applied voltage that varies in accordance with the modulating frequency and therefore results in an output from the modulated amplifier whose amplitude also varies in accordance with the modulating frequency.

Fig. 3.142. A 50-percent modulated wave.

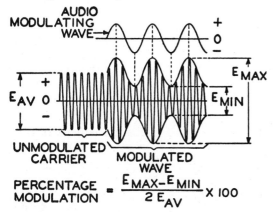

PERCENTAGE MODULATION $= \dfrac{E_{MAX} - E_{MIN}}{2\,E_{AV}} \times 100$

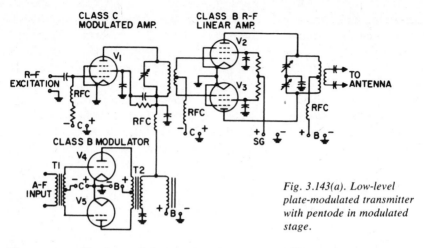

Fig. 3.143(a). Low-level plate-modulated transmitter with pentode in modulated stage.

Thus an amplitude modulated wave is created.

When a pentode is used as a modulated Class C amplifier, it is necessary to vary the applied screen grid voltage in the same manner as the applied plate voltage. One way of doing this is shown in the figure. An inspection of the figure will reveal that the screen voltage is obtained, through a series-dropping resistor, from the applied voltage and therefore both voltages will vary simultaneously.

In the circuit shown, a Class B RF linear amplifier amplifies the already modulated wave. It is necessary to use this particular type of amplifier to prevent distortion of the modulated wave. Such an amplifier has the ability to produce an output voltage that almost exactly duplicates the exciting voltage within certain limits. A Class C amplifier used in this position, of course, would produce intolerable distortion.

Figure 3.143(b) illustrates one possible configuration for a high-level plate-modulated amplifier using a tetrode. High-level modulation is defined as plate modulation of the final power amplifier, hence, in this case, the output of the modulated amplifier is fed directly to the antenna instead of to a following amplifier.

The illustrated circuit operates exactly as described for the foregoing pentode modulated amplifier. An examination of both circuits will reveal that they are similar in all respects except for the suppressor grid connection.

D. Any stages which are required to amplify a modulated wave must be operated as linear amplifiers in order that the modulation components shall not be distorted.

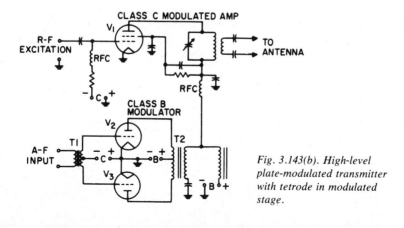

Fig. 3.143(b). High-level plate-modulated transmitter with tetrode in modulated stage.

Class C operation cannot be used because of the extreme distortion which would result. It would be possible to employ Class A except for its very low efficiency. Thus Class B operation is the logical choice both from the standpoint of low distortion and of efficiency. It is usually preferred to operate at least the final Class B amplifier in push-pull. See also Q. 3.139 through Q. 3.142.

Q. 3.144. How does a linear power amplifier differ from other types?

A. It is assumed that the question was meant to be "How does an RF linear power amplifier differ from other types of RF power amplifiers?"

Under the above assumption, the most generally used RF power amplifier is the Class C amplifier with its high distortion produced by using a bias voltage greatly in excess of the cut-off value. As opposed to this, the RF linear power amplifier is a Class B amplifier that uses a bias approximately equal to the projected cut-off bias. Biased in this manner, such an amplifier has an output voltage that is almost exactly directly in proportion to the exciting voltage—hence the name, linear.

D. Occasionally, Class A RF power amplifiers are used. These amplifiers are also linear, but are not able to generate the amount of output power that the Class B amplifiers can, nor do they operate as efficiently. (See also Q. 3.143.)

Q. 3.145. Draw a simple schematic diagram showing a method of coupling a modulator tube to a radio frequency power amplifier tube to produce grid modulation of the amplified RF energy. Compare some advantages or disadvantages of this system of modulation with those of plate modulation.

A. For the diagram, see Fig. 3.145.

Some *advantages* of grid modulation vs. plate modulation are as follows:

1. The amount of audio power required of the modulator for 100 percent modulation is extremely small.

2. Very much smaller modulation transformer may be used.

Some *disadvantages* of grid vs. plate modulation are as follows:

1. The grid modulated amplifier must use tubes having an output rating approximately equal to four times the carrier output power, whereas the plate modulated amplifier must use tubes having an output rating equal to approximately one and a half times the carrier output power. The output power ratings mentioned are those for straight Class C unmodulated or oscillator service.

2. Distortionless modulation, greater than about 85 percent, is very difficult to achieve, whereas with the plate modulated

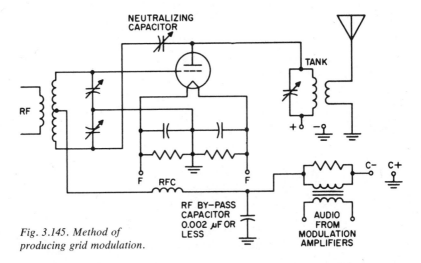

Fig. 3.145. Method of producing grid modulation.

amplifier, 100 percent modulation without distortion is easily accomplished.

D. The efficiency of a grid-modulated amplifier is maximum at complete modulation and minimum at zero modulation.

The plate efficiency of a grid-bias modulated Class C RF amplifier under unmodulated conditions is about ½ of the amplifier efficiency realized during the 100 percent modulation peaks. This averages between 30 and 40 percent in typical cases. When the wave is 100 percent modulated, the plate efficiency averages about 45 to 60 percent. The carrier power obtained from a grid-bias modulated stage is about ¼ of the power obtainable from the same tube operated as an ordinary Class C amplifier.

If maximum output from a grid-modulated amplifier is to be achieved, it is necessary that the grid be driven positive (and draw current) on the modulation crests (peaks). However, it must be realized that grid current may cause distortion due to an impedance drop in the driver. It is essential, therefore, that the impedance presented by the driver be a low value to insure output voltage regulation. Where minimum distortion is desired, the grid is not permitted to draw current. This operating condition results in a reduction of both output and operating efficiency, but this is the price which must be paid for the improved quality.

The dc grid bias is normally adjusted to a value varying from 1½ to 3 times the plate current cut-off value. The actual value of bias used is not extremely critical and is a function of the available modulating voltage, and the desired operating efficiency. The efficiency of a grid-bias modulated Class C amplifier is only about half that of a properly designed unmodulated Class C amplifier and therefore the output is correspondingly less.

Q. 3.146. What is meant by "frequency shift" or "dynamic instability?" with reference to a modulated RF emission?

A. *Frequency shift* or *dynamic instability* refers to the instantaneous changes of oscillator frequency due to corresponding changes of plate and screen grid voltages of the oscillator tubes, and is caused by improper regulation of the power supply.

D. If a common power supply were used for the oscillator, RF amplifiers and modulator stages, it would be difficult to prevent "dynamic instability," especially if the modulator were not operating strictly Class A. Any changes in the loading due to any cause, or any changes in modulator power requirements will create a change in power supply output voltage. This, in turn, may cause the oscillator frequency to shift, creating undesired frequency modulation. In general, an increase in oscillator plate voltage (with screen voltage constant) will cause the oscillator frequency to increase because of a decrease of tube input capacity. A proportional increase of screen voltage would have the opposite effect on the frequency, and this factor is taken advantage of in the electron-coupled oscillator to maintain frequency stability and reduce dynamic instability. Dynamic instability can also be reduced by: (1) using an oscillator tank circuit with a high C/L ratio, (2) by light loading of the oscillator circuit, (3) by using a high value of grid leak, and (4) by using separate power supplies for oscillator, modulator and RF amplifiers, or at least for the oscillator.

Q. 3.147. What would cause a dip in the antenna current when AM is applied? What are the causes of carrier shift?

A.

1. This is called "downward modulation."

With *plate* modulation, "downward modulation" may be caused by any of the following:

a. Insufficient bias at the modulated RF amplifier.

b. Insufficient excitation into the modulated RF amplifier.

c. Excessive overloading of the Class C modulated RF amplifier.

d. Incorrect load impedance for the Class C modulated RF amplifier.

e. Faulty or insufficient value of output capacity in the power supply filter for the modulated RF amplifier.

f. Poor regulation of a common power supply.

g. Defective tube.

With *grid-bias* modulation, a downward "kick" may be caused by any of the following:

a. Excessive RF excitation to the grid of the modulated RF amplifier.

b. Insufficient operating bias on the grid of the modulated RF amplifier.

c. Distortion in the modulator or speech amplifier.

d. Excessive resistance in the grid bias power supply.

e. Faulty or insufficient output capacity in the plate power supply filter to the modulated RF amplifier.

f. Insufficient loading of the plate circuit of the modulated RF amplifier.

g. Too high plate-circuit efficiency of the modulated RF amplifier under unmodulated conditions.

h. Defective tube.

2. "Carrier shift" occurs when the relative amplitudes of the positive and negative modulation peaks are unsymmetrical. The shift is one of amplitude and not of carrier frequency.

D.

1. An upward rise of antenna current when a transmitter is amplitude modulated is a normal condition. However, an upward "kick" of current may occur which is not a normal condition. With plate modulation an upward "kick" may be caused by any of the following:

a. Parasitic oscillations in the modulated RF amplifier.

b. Overmodulation.

c. Incomplete neutralization of the modulated RF amplifier.

With grid modulation an upward "kick" may be caused by any of the following:

a. Overmodulation.

b. Audio system distortion.

c. Incomplete neutralization of the modulated RF amplifier.

d. Excessive grid bias in the modulated RF amplifier.

2. The following are causes of positive carrier shift:

a. High or low frequency parasitic oscillations.

b. Excessive audio drive.

c. Incorrect tuning of final amplifier.

d. Insufficient RF excitation.

e. Incorrect neutralization.

The following may cause negative carrier shift:

a. Distorted modulating wave due to

(1) Improper bias of modulation amplifier.

(2) Overdriving of modulation amplifier.

(3) Poor regulation of modulator power supply.

(4) Defective tube or modulation transformer.

b. Overmodulation.

c. Incorrect load impedance presented to modulator tube by RF amplifier.

d. Improper tuning of tank circuits.

e. Poor regulation of RF amplifier power supply.

f. Insufficient RF excitation.

The term "negative carrier shift" does not denote a change of carrier frequency, although additional harmonic frequencies are produced. Carrier shift occurs when an unsymmetrical distortion of the modulation envelope is present. In "negative carrier shift," the negative portions of the modulation component become greater than the positive portions, resulting in a decrease of the average output power as evidenced by a decreased reading on the dc plate milliammeter of the final RF amplifier. In "positive carrier shift" the positive portions of the modulation component become greater in amplitude than the negative portions, resulting in an increase of the average output power as evidenced by an increased reading on the dc plate milliammeter of the final RF amplifier.

The dc plate current of a modulated

Class C amplifier should remain constant when AM is applied. If no distortion (practically) occurs in the process of modulation, the amount of increase in Class C plate current should be exactly the same as the amount of decrease and therefore the average change is zero. This applies as long as there is no overmodulation present or carrier shift.

Q. 3.148. What is the relationship between the average power output of the modulator and the plate circuit input of the modulated amplifier under 100 percent sinusoidal plate modulation? How does this differ when normal voice modulation is employed?

A.

1. With 100 percent sinusoidal plate modulation, the average audio output power of the modulator is equal to 50 percent of the dc plate circuit input power of the modulated amplifier.

2. With normal voice modulation, the average modulation percentage is only in the order of 30 percent or less. This is due to the ratio of peak to average power in the human voice. Under these conditions, the average power output of the modulator is only about 4.5 percent of the amplifier's dc plate input power. To reproduce the peaks of speech faithfully, however, the modulator must still have the same peak power capability as when called upon to produce 100 percent sinusoidal modulation.

D. Under 100 percent sinusoidal plate modulation conditions, the ac power output of the modulator must equal ½ of the dc power input to the modulated RF amplifier. The modulator output supplies the power for the sidebands, while the dc supply furnishes the power for the carrier wave.

Q. 3.149. What is the relationship between the amount of power in the sidebands and the intelligibility of the signal at the receiver?

A. Since all the intelligence in an amplitude-modulated emission is contained in the sidebands and none in the carrier, the intelligibility of the signal at the receiver is directly proportional to the amount of power in the sidebands.

D. The following are advantages of high percentage modulation:

1. A higher signal-to-noise ratio at the receiver.

2. Greater area coverage for a given carrier power.

3. Greater useful transmitted power for a given carrier power.

4. Higher plate efficiency of the modulated RF amplifier.

5. Less interference at the receiver from other stations operating on the same channel.

It should be realized that the only *useful* power contained in a modulated carrier wave is in the sidebands. At 100 percent modulation the sideband power represents only 33⅓ percent of the total radiated power. The remainder of the power, or 66⅔ percent, is in the carrier wave and is of no value in transmitting intelligence. If the percentage of modulation is reduced to 50 percent, the amount of power in the sidebands is reduced only about 11 percent of the *total* radiated power. (This corresponds to an increase of 12.5 percent over the original carrier power.) It may be seen from the above examples that it is important to keep the average percentage of modulation as high as may be practical for any particular transmitter.

Q. 3.150. What might cause FM in an AM radiotelephone transmitter?

A. See Q. 3.146.

Q. 3.151. Draw a block diagram of an AM transmitter.

A. For the diagram, see Fig. 3.151.

D.

1. The crystal oscillator produces a stable-carrier frequency at low power. Depending upon the inherent crystal stability, it may or may not require oven-temperature control.

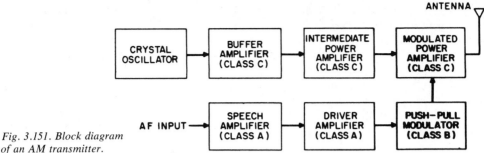

Fig. 3.151. Block diagram of an AM transmitter.

2. The buffer amplifier isolates the crystal oscillator to improve its stability. (See Q. 3.98.)

3. The intermediate-power amplifier raises the output of RF power of the buffer to a level sufficient to drive the modulated RF amplifier.

4. The Class C modulated RF amplifier supplies the energy which is required to drive the antenna system at the rated RF power. This stage may be operated as a parallel or a push-pull amplifier.

5. The speech improves the signal-to-noise ratio before mixing.

6. The modulator driver supplies the necessary audio power to drive the Class B modulator.

7. The Class B modulator varies the plate voltage of the Class C RF amplifier in accordance with the frequency and amplitude of the audio signal. This, in turn, varies the amplitude of the RF output wave to the antenna, producing an amplitude modulated wave.

Q. 3.152. Explain the principles involved in a single-sideband suppressed-carrier (SSSC) emission. How does its bandwidth of emission and required power compare with that of full carrier and sidebands?

A. Either a mathematical or electrical analysis of an amplitude modulated wave will demonstrate that the carrier of the wave is completely unaffected by the presence or absence of modulation. Further analysis will demonstrate that *each* sideband will contain *all* the intelligence that is being transmitted. The foregoing facts lead to the conclusion, that, to successfully **convey intelligence,** it is only necessary **to transmit but one** sideband; the carrier **and the remaining sideband** being suppressed or **not transmitted.**

Since with the single-sideband suppressed-carrier (SSSC) mode of transmission, only one sideband is transmitted, the bandwidth of emission is reduced to only one-half of the bandwidth required for normal amplitude-modulated transmission. The bandwidth required is equal to the highest modulating frequency used.

The signal-to-noise power ratio at the output of a radio receiver depends on several factors, among which are the following:

1. The amount of power contained in the sidebands of the received wave.

2. The width of the receiver's passband or its selectivity.

3. The amount of noise power received by the antenna.

If the above factors are constant, then, for the same peak-power capabilities of the transmitter, an improvement in signal-to-noise power ratio of eight times can be obtained by the use of SSSC. For the same signal-to-noise performance at the receiver, the transmitter must be capable of handling only one-eighth the peak power that would be required of an amplitude-modulated transmitter.

On an average-power, instead of a peak-power basis, the SSSC transmitter must deliver only one-sixth the amount of average power required of an amplitude-modulated transmitter for the same signal-to-noise performance at the receiver.

D. See Q. 3.153 and Q. 3.154.

Q. 3.153. Draw a block diagram of an SSSC transmitter (filter type) with a 20-kHZ oscillator and emission frequencies in the range of 6 MHz. Explain the function of each stage.

A.

1. For the diagram, see Fig. 3.153.

2. The stage functions follow:

a. The *First Balanced Modulator,* because of special circuit balancing, produces a modulated wave containing upper and lower sidebands but no carrier. The carrier, if it were present, would have a frequency in this case of 20 kHz and is supplied by the 20-kHz *Crystal Oscillator.* The output of the first balanced modulator consists of the lower sideband frequencies, from 17.3 kHz to 19.7 kHz, and the upper sideband frequencies, from 20.3 kHz to 23.0 kHz.

b. The *First Bandpass Filter* is so designed as to pass only frequencies of 20.3 to 23.0 kHz. Frequencies outside this pass band are greatly attenuated. Therefore, the first bandpass filter allows only the upper sideband frequencies to pass through and be fed to the *Second Balanced Modulator.* By this action, a single-sideband suppressed-carrier signal has been generated, but it requires further treatment as it is not of the desired frequency range as yet.

c. The second balanced modulator differs from the first balanced modulator only in having an input carrier frequency of 480 kHz instead of 20 kHz. The output of the second balanced modulator consists of lower sideband frequencies of from 457.0 to 459.7 kHz and upper sideband frequencies of from 500.3 to 503.0 kHz.

d. The second bandpass filter, because of its pass band of 500.0 kHz to 503.0 kHz, allows only the upper sidebands of the second balanced modulator to be presented to the input of the *Mixer.*

e. The mixer stage is similar to mixer stages used in superheterodyne receivers and its output consists of the original input frequencies of from 500.3 to 503.0 kHz, the *Crystal Oscillator* frequency of 5500 kHz, the difference frequencies from 4997.0 kHz to 4999.7 kHz and the sum frequencies from 6000.3 kHz to 6003.0 kHz.

f. The *Tank Circuit,* which actually is part of the mixer, is adjusted to be resonant at 6000 kHz. Consequently, the output of the tank circuit is only the upper sideband frequencies of from 6000.3 kHz to 6003.0 kHz. All of the other responses of the mixer are discriminated against or attenuated by the tank circuit.

3. In actual practice, the carrier is not always suppressed completely. For use in receiving a single-sideband signal it is very useful to have a very much attenuated carrier present in the wave as a reference frequency. The carrier may be reduced as much as 20 dB below the sideband power level. Propagation conditions may often dictate a carrier power level that is higher than the usual 20 dB. The carrier is reinserted into the single-

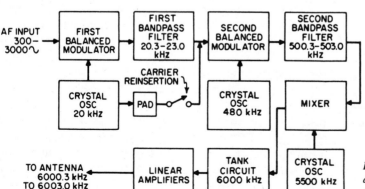

Fig. 3.153. Block diagram of a filter-type SSSC transmitter.

sideband signal at the output of the first bandpass filter as shown in the diagram. The amount of carrier reinserted is controlled by the adjustable attenuating pad.

D. It is normal practice to operate the above-described stages at very low power levels and to use receiving type vacuum tubes in this part of the transmitter. Today, semiconductors are beginning to replace vacuum tubes. The section of the transmitter just described is called various names, among which are "Exciter," "SSB Generator," etc., and has a final power output in the order of tenths of a watt.

The output of an exciter is insufficient to excite the antenna and further amplification is required. Since the signal is already modulated, the normal Class C amplifier cannot be used for this purpose. Therefore, Class B RF linear amplifiers are used to obtain essentially distortionless power amplification to the power level required at the antenna. In some infrequent instances, Class A RF linear amplifiers are used, but this practice is rapidly declining because of the low efficiency of this class of amplifier.

Q. 3.154. Explain briefly, how an SSSC emission is detected.

A. To detect a SSSC signal, the output of a low frequency (20 kHz) local oscillator is applied to the final receiver detector, together with the single-sideband output of the last IF amplifier (20.3 to 23 kHz). Because of the non-linear action of the detector, an amplitude-modulated wave is produced, which is then detected in the conventional manner by the same detector.

D. A single-sideband receiver is a superheterodyne and may be of the single-conversion (see Q. 3.155) or double-conversion (see Q. 3.180) type. The SSB receiver differs from the conventional type primarily in the manner of final detection, as described above. In order to faithfully reproduce the original audio signal, it is essential that the reinserted carrier have the same frequency as the transmitter carrier and have the correct amplitude. There are several ways of insuring proper frequency. As stated in the preceding question, a reduced carrier (20 kHz) may be transmitted together with the single-sideband signal. This reduced carrier may be extracted from the IF signal by a sharply tuned crystal filter and can be utilized in either of two ways. One procedure is to use the reduced carrier as the reference frequency for an AFC system to stabilize the frequency of the carrier reinsertion oscillator (20 kHz). Another possibility (after extraction) is to amplify the reduced carrier and to utilize it directly as the reinserted carrier. Both of these schemes add to the expense and complexity of the SSB receiver. A simpler arrangement, which is frequently used, utilizes a highly stable carrier reinsertion oscillator, operating at 20 kHz.

To recover the modulation information from a single-sideband signal, it is not essential to reinsert a carrier at the original low frequency (20 kHz). The carrier may be reinserted at the IF frequency (such as 455 kHz),or at the RF transmission frequency (such as 6 000 kHz, as in the preceding question). For example, in communications receivers employing a "beat-frequency oscillator" (see Q. 3.158), the BFO may be used to reinsert an IF carrier. In this case the BFO frequency is carefully adjusted to obtain an undistorted audio output. The BFO is then tuned to the precise IF frequency, 455 kHz. As an alternative, an RF oscillator may be tuned to the transmission RF carrier frequency (such as 6 000 kHz) and fed into the antenna output circuit of the receiver. In the latter case, the oscillator must be tuned to the exact RF transmission frequency of the station. This condition will be effected when undistorted audio is obtained from the receiver. As was the case for the low frequency (20 kHz) reinserted carrier, the oscillators used to reinsert the carrier must be highly stable. This is necessary because any oscillator drift will result in a distorted, "scrambled," or "inverted" audio output.

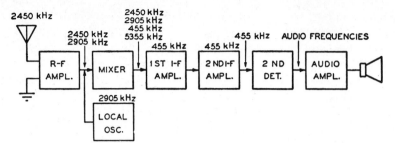

2450 kHz

2450 kHz
2905 kHz

2450 kHz
2905 kHz
455 kHz
5355 kHz
455 kHz

455 kHz
455 kHz

455 kHz   AUDIO FREQUENCIES

| R-F AMPL. | MIXER | 1ST I-F AMPL. | 2ND I-F AMPL. | 2ND DET. | AUDIO AMPL. |

2905 kHz

| LOCAL OSC. |

Fig. 3.155. Block diagram of a superheterodyne AM receiver.

Q. 3.155. Draw a block diagram of a single-conversion superheterodyne AM receiver. Assume an incident signal and explain briefly what occurs in each stage.

A. For the diagram, see Fig. 3.155.

Using the incident frequency of 2 450 kHz as shown in the diagram, a brief description of what occurs in each stage is as follows:

1. The signal, with a frequency of 2 450 kHz, is fed by the antenna system into the RF amplifier where it is amplified and separated, to some extent, from other frequencies.

2. The mixer has two signals fed to it. One of these is the incoming signal of 2 450 kHz from the RF amplifier and the other is a signal of 2 905 kHz from the local oscillator. The mixer combines these two frequencies and produces in its output the two original frequencies and their sum and differences. These are shown in the diagram.

3. The first IF amplifier is tuned, in this case, to 455 kHz and so amplifies the 455-kHz output of the mixer and rejects the remaining output frequencies. The selectivity characteristics of the IF amplifiers are such as to provide the main selectivity of the receiver.

4. The second IF amplifier provides further amplification and selectivity for the 45-kHz IF signal and presents it to the second detector.

5. The second detector demodulates the 455-kHz IF signal and extracts the original audio frequencies from it. The second detector usually derives a dc voltage from the carrier for use in the automatic-gain controlled stages of the receiver.

6. The audio amplifier raises the power level of the audio frequencies from the second detector to a value sufficient to drive the loudspeaker of the receiver.

D.

1. The purpose of the first detector is to act as a mixer by operating in a non-linear fashion and providing the action which produces the desired intermediate frequency.

If two frequencies are applied to a perfect Class A amplifier, there will be no beating action in the tube, and the only frequencies available in the output circuit will be the original two frequencies. This is because a perfect Class A amplifier is a linear circuit. In order to produce "beating," which is necessary for detection or modulation, the two frequencies must be combined in a *non-linear* device. Such a non-linear characteristic may be obtained, for example, by operating a vacuum tube on the non-linear portion of its characteristic. This is exactly what is done in the first detector of a superheterodyne (and the second detector as well). The first detector is operated with a relatively large bias, so that the operation takes place along the lower curved portion of the tube characteristic. If two different frequencies are introduced into such a non-linear device, a distortion of the input voltages will take place so that new frequencies are produced in the plate circuit, which were not originally present in the input circuit. These are mainly: (a) the *sum* of the two original frequencies, (b) The *difference* between the two original frequencies, (c) various *harmonic* frequencies. In addition, the two *original* frequencies will also be present in the plate circuit of the first detector. The desired frequency, which is usually the difference frequency in radio receivers, is selected and amplified by the intermediate frequency amplifiers.

2. Some superheterodyne receivers employ a crystal oscillator in order to insure maximum stability of receiver operation.

In a superheterodyne receiver, the correct setting and calibration of the mixer oscillator is of critical importance, since the oscillator frequency "beating" with the incoming signal produces the correct intermediate frequency. Radio-frequency circuits (RF amplifier and mixer) do not tune very sharply and can vary considerably without causing much trouble. It is, therefore, desirable whenever practical to employ a crystal-controlled oscillator to provide maximum stability. Crystal oscillators are frequently used in communications receivers operating on certain pre-determined channel frequencies. In this case a separate crystal is switched in for reception on any particular channel. This system is impractical where variable tuning is required.

3. A "superheterodyne" receiver is subject to image interference.

The intermediate frequency delivered by the first detector, and selectively amplified by the IF stages, is the difference between the input signal frequency and the oscillator frequency. There are two signal frequencies which will give the same intermediate frequency for a given oscillator frequency— one higher, and one lower than the oscillator. The input system is designed to select one and reject the other; but it sometimes happens that, due to misalignment of the receiver or to a very strong signal, the unwanted signal will get through to the first detector. When this happens, it causes an intermediate frequency signal which passes through the receiver normally. Such a signal is called "image interference." An incoming signal causing image interference is twice the intermediate frequency above or below the frequency to which the receiver is tuned, depending on whether the oscillator frequency is designed to be above or below that of the desired signal.

4. A high intermediate frequency is desirable in order to place the image frequency as far as possible from the normal received signal so that the image frequency may be effectively suppressed in the tuned RF amplifier and mixer circuits. This may be illustrated by the following example: Assume that the desired carried signal is 1 000 kilohertz, the oscillator frequency 1 050 kilohertz, and the intermediate frequency 50 kilohertz. The image frequency equals twice the intermediate frequency plus the carrier frequency or $(2 \times 50) + 1\ 000$ kilohertz = 1 100 kilohertz. Since the image is removed only 100 kilohertz from the desired carrier, the RF and mixer circuits will not offer too much rejection to the image frequency. On the other hand, if the oscillator frequency were 1 500 kilohertz, the intermediate frequency would then be 500 kilohertz and the image would equal $(2 \times 500) + 1\ 000$ kilohertz = 2 000 kilohertz. The image is now removed from the desired signal by 1 000 kilohertz and will be greatly attenuated by the RF and mixer circuits.

Q. 3.156. Explain the relation between the signal frequency, oscillator frequency and the image frequency in a superheterodyne receiver.

A.

1. Assuming the oscillator frequency to be *above* the incoming frequency, the following relations prevail:

a. Oscillator frequency = Incoming-Signal Frequency + Intermediate Frequency.

b. Image Frequency = Incoming Frequency + 2 × Intermediate Frequency.

2. Assuming the oscillator frequency to be *below* the incoming frequency (used mainly in some VHF receivers), the following relations prevail:

a. Oscillator Frequency = Incoming-Signal Frequency − Intermediate Frequency.

b. Image Frequency = Incoming Frequency − 2 × Intermediate Frequency.

D. For example, assume a receiver is tuned to an incoming frequency of 1 000 kHz; its oscillator frequency is 1 455 kHz and its intermediate frequency is 455 kHz. In this case the image frequency equals the incoming frequency plus twice the IF, or; Image = $(2 \times 455) + 1\ 000 = 1\ 910$ kHz.

For a VHF receiver operating at 120 MHz with an oscillator frequency of 109.3 MHz and an IF of 10.7 MHz, the image frequency equals twice the IF subtracted from the incoming frequency, or; Image = 120 MHz − $(2 \times 10.7$ MHz$) = 198.6$ MHz.

Q. 3.157. Draw a circuit diagram of an AM second detector and AF amplifier (in one envelope), showing AVC circuitry. Also show coupling to, and identification of, all adjacent stages.

1. Explain the principles of operation.

2. State some conditions under which readings of AVC voltage would be helpful in trouble-shooting a receiver.

3. Show how this circuit would be modified to give DAVC.

A. For the diagram, see Fig. 3.157(a).

1. a. The functioning of a diode detector depends upon the ability of an RC network (C_2, R_2, R_3) to follow the *average* diode current variations, which are directly proportional to the modulation envelope.

The secondary circuit of the last IF transformer (which acts as a generator) is connected to the diode plate and cathode in series with the parallel RC network, C_2, R_2, R_3. Assume first that an unmodulated carrier is applied to the detector. Rectification will occur with the diode plate conducting on the positive portions of the RF cycles. Capacitor C_2 will charge almost to the peak value of the unmodulated carrier. The plate side of C_2 will be negative and of a steady value, as long as the carrier amplitude remains constant.

Now assume that amplitude modulation is applied to the carrier wave. Charge on C_2 increases proportionally to the increased amplitude of the modulated carrier. Also, as the carrier amplitude decreases, charge on C_2 decreases. Thus, the charge across C_2 varies in accordance with the audio modulation changes (because of the time constant of C_2, R_2, R_3). However, the time constant is very long compared to the time of one RF cycle and the network has very little response to individual RF cycles. It does, of course, respond to the average change in amplitude of these RF cycles, which corresponds to the audio wave.

b. The detected audio wave is taken from the tap of R_2 and R_3 (to reduce distortion) and fed via the volume control, R_4, to the grid of the first audio amplifier. This functions as a conventional triode audio amplifier (see Q. 3.50(a)). The output of this stage drives the audio-power amplifier, which operates a loudspeaker.

c. As stated above, there is a rectified-

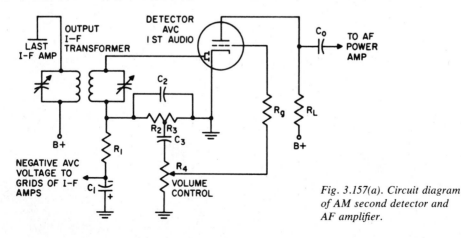

Fig. 3.157(a). Circuit diagram of AM second detector and AF amplifier.

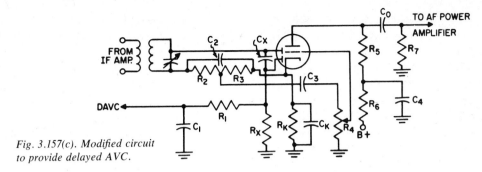

Fig. 3.157(c). Modified circuit
to provide delayed AVC.

negative voltage at the diode-plate side of C_2. This voltage varies at an audio rate, but its average value is proportional to the strength of the carrier wave. If this negative voltage is fed back to the control grids of the IF (and RF) amplifiers, it provides a method of obtaining automatic volume control.

The basis for efficient automatic volume control is the action of the variable-μ (remote cut-off) tube. This tube has a control grid which is so constructed, that changes of dc grid bias cause corresponding variations in the tube's transconductance and thus control the gain of the IF (and sometimes also RF) amplifiers. The transconductance decreases as the negative bias increases and vice versa. In the second detector, the modulated IF signal is rectified in such a way that the average value of the detector audio output is negative with respect to ground. This is accomplished by grounding the cathode of the detector, and taking the output from the plate circuit. The average negative audio output is put through a long time constant RC filter whose output is a pure, negative dc voltage. This voltage is fed through suitable decoupling filters to the grids of the various IF and RF amplifiers involved, where it becomes all or part of the bias for these tubes. The AVC filter output is a negative dc voltage whose magnitude is proportional to the average strength of the incoming modulated carrier signal. An increase of incoming signal strength creates a larger negative bias on the various controlling grids, thereby reducing the overall gain of the receiver and providing a relatively constant output. A decrease of incoming signal strength results in a *less* negative bias, an increase in overall receiver gain, and again a relatively constant output.

2. The amount of AVC voltage developed is approximately proportional to the signal strength expressed in db. The AVC voltage, therefore, can be a guide in determining the amplification of all the stages preceding the second detector. For example, with a relatively strong input signal, the AVC voltage should be relatively large. If not, there is the possibility of weak tubes, mistuned circuits, etc., in the amplifiers ahead of the second detector. In aligning a superheterodyne receiver, advantage is taken of the AVC voltage by using it as a tuning indicator. In another example of a *dead* receiver, the presence of AVC voltage but no audio output would indicate troubles in the audio frequency amplifier(s) of the receiver. This of course could be defective AF tubes or components or both.

3. The modified circuit to provide delayed-automatic volume control (DAVC) is shown in Fig. 3.157(c). Note that the two diodes are now connected independently and that cathode bias is employed for the triode amplifier. The upper diode is used only for detection and the lower diode is used only to provide DAVC.

D. In the circuit of Fig. 3.157(a), AVC voltage is developed even for very weak signals, causing a reduction in receiver gain and a loss of sensitivity. In order to obtain maximum sensitivity for weak signals, it is desirable to have zero AVC voltage. However, to maintain constant audio output, stronger signals should develop AVC. A DAVC circuit provides this action, by delaying the development of AVC voltage until the input signal level exceeds a certain predetermined level. Note that the upper-diode circuit returns to the cathode and will detect the weakest signals. However, the lower-diode circuit is returned to ground and is affected by the triode-cathode bias. Because of the normal conduction of the triode section, a positive bias is developed at the cathode. The lower diode cannot conduct until the positive peak signal applied to its plate exceeds the amount of the cathode bias (1 to 3 volts). Because of this "delay" voltage, AVC is not developed for weak signals which develop less than the cathode-bias voltage at the lower-diode plate. However, for signals strong enough to cause lower-diode conduction, DAVC voltage is developed and regulates the receiver gain in the same manner as undelayed AVC.

Q. 3.158. Draw a BFO circuit diagram and explain its use in detection.

A. For the diagram, see the accompanying figure, Figure 3.158. The main function of a beat frequency oscillator is to make it possible to hear code (A-1) reception clearly. Code which is not tone modulated would otherwise be heard at the output of a receiver as a series of hissing sounds or perhaps "thumps," which would be very difficult to interpret and easily obscured by noise. When the beat frequency oscillator is turned on, a high pitched audible note is produced which is relatively easy to "read."

A beat frequency oscillator may also be utilized in the detection of a single-sideband suppressed-carrier signal. See Q. 3.154.

Q. 3.159. Explain, step-by-step, how to align an AM receiver using the following instruments. In addition discuss what is occuring during each step.
1. Signal generator and speaker.
2. Signal generator and oscilloscope.
3. Signal generator and VTVM.

A. Regardless of whether a speaker, oscilloscope, or VTVM is used, the alignment procedure remains the same. Since a sweep generator is not mentioned, the signal generator to be used will be an amplitude-modulated CW generator. It must be assumed that the generator is properly calibrated and that the receiver is drastically out of alignment. When the speaker is used, the ear is the indicating instrument and no special connections to the speaker are required.

In using an oscilloscope, there are several points at which it may be connected to monitor the demodulated signal generator signal. One convenient place would be across the voice-coil terminals of the speaker. When a VTVM is used (dc type) it is convenient to connect it to the AVC bus or across the second detector load resistor. In the event an ac VTVM is available, this may be connected across the speaker-voice coil terminals. If the AVC voltage is not being monitored, the AVC bus should be grounded or held at a nominal fixed bias with a battery. This prevents false indications of alignment due to AVC action. Regardless of the indicating device used, a maximum indication

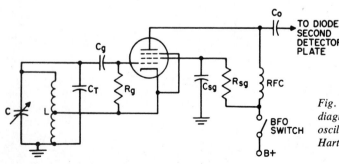

Fig. 3.158. Schematic diagram of a beat-frequency oscillator (electron-coupled Hartley).

is the sign of proper alignment. The alignment procedure follows:

1. Connect the indicating instrument as described above and proceed with the IF alignment. A common IF frequency of 455 kilohertz is assumed in this case.

a. Set the generator to 455 kilohertz and connect through a small capacitor (0.01 μF) to the grid of the last IF stage and ground. Set the generator for minimum usable output and peak the primary and secondary windings for maximum indication of the instrument being used.

b. Move the generator to the grid of the next-to-last IF stage and peak the adjustments of its transformer.

c. In a like manner, all additional IF transformers are peaked. It will be necessary to reduce the generator output as each additional stage is aligned, to prevent overloading of the amplifiers. A minimum possible generator output should always be employed.

d. The last IF transformer to be aligned is the one in the plate circuit of the mixer. In this case, the generator is connected to the grid of the mixer (which is not tuned to the IF frequency). At this point it is necessary to increase the generator output to obtain a usable alignment signal.

2. After completing the IF alignment, the RF alignment, should be undertaken. Connect the test oscillator between the antenna terminal and ground, using a small capacitor in series with the ungrounded lead. Proceed as follows:

a. Set the signal generator and the receiver dial to 1 400 kilohertz.

b. At 1 400 kilohertz first adjust the oscillator trimmer to obtain maximum indication.

Note: Do not attempt to adjust the low frequency "padder" adjustment at this time and always use the minimum possible generator output.

c. Next adjust the mixer and RF trimmers for maximum response.

d. Tune the receiver dial and the signal generator to 600 kilohertz.

e. Adjust the oscillator and low-frequency tracking trimmer for maximum response.

f. Repeat steps a through e above to achieve the optimum alignment.

D. What is being accompished in each step of the alignment when tuning for maximum response is that the circuits involved are being caused to resonate at their individual frequencies. Thus, the gain of the stages are being increased due to the increased impedance of the resonant circuits. The increased gain causes the generator signal to be amplified more, providing a greater output indication. In the case of using the AVC voltage for an indicator, the greater the gain of the stages, the higher the signal applied to the AVC detector. This results in a greater negative voltage being applied to the AVC bus. (Again, a maximum response indication.)

Q. 3.160. What would be the advantages and disadvantages of utilizing a bandpass switch on a receiver?

A.

1. Advantages. The advantage of utilizing a bandpass switch is to reduce the IF bandpass of a receiver. In so doing, the selectivity of the receiver is considerably improved. This characteristic is highly desirable in receiving signals from stations operating in a crowded spectrum. It permits separation, and therefore the intelligible reception of signals which might otherwise be lost in the confusion of overlapping channel signals.

2. Disadvantages. The disadvantage of utilizing a bandpass switch is that sideband frequencies of either voice or music broadcasts will be sharply reduced, thus reducing the intelligibility of speech and music. However, in some cases using the bandpass switch is the only way to achieve any reception at all of the desired signal.

D. By the use of regenerative IF circuits, a controllable bandpass characteristic may be achieved. This can cut the IF bandpass to as low as 1 000 hertz for use under extremely difficult signal crowding and noise conditions. Since good double-sideband voice reproduction normally requires about a 6 000 hertz bandpass, it is obvious that the intelligibility of voice (and music) will be considerably reduced. However, this technique frequently permits a signal to be received which might otherwise be covered up by interference. Since noise frequencies occupy the entire spectrum, it is seen that the sharper the bandpass, the less the noise energy that will be passed to affect the listener. In receivers used for code reception, a crystal-type IF filter is frequently employed. With this type of filter, a bandpass of only 100 to 200 hertz is passed. This bandwidth is adequate for code, but useless for voice or music reception.

Q. 3.161. Explain sensitivity and selectivity of a receiver. Why are these important quantities? In what typical units are they usually expressed?

A.

1. Sensitivity: Sensitivity is the strength of the signal, in microvolts, at the input of the receiver required to produce a specified audio power output.

2. Selectivity: Selectivity is the ability of a receiver to discriminate against frequencies other than the desired frequency.

3. Sensitivity is an important quantity because it defines the ability of a receiver to respond adequately to a weak-input signal.

4. Selectivity defines the ability of a receiver to *select* a desired signal, which may be hemmed in by adjacent frequency (undesirable) signals.

5. Sensitivity is expressed in microvolts for a certain audio output power.

6. Selectivity is expressed in hertz or kilohertz, usually in terms of the IF response curve of the receiver. The IF response curve is basically "V" shaped, being narrow at the maximum-response point and wider at the minimum-response point. Thus, it is necessary to state at what point bandwidth is to be measured. This point differs according to the purpose of the measurement.

However, for general purposes, the IF bandwidth is measured at points 3 dB (.707) down from the maximum.

Note: The following added material numbered Q. 3.161-A1 through Q. 3.161-A6 contains information that may be required to pass the General Radiotelephone Operator's License examination. This added material, as well as the new material added to other sections, has been included to help acquaint students with the current state of the electronics art. It is felt that the added material contains subject matter that may also be required of students who have obtained a General Radiotelephone Operator's License and are seeking employment. Additionally, the added material contains valuable information for private technician certification.

Q. 3.161-A1. Discuss the following: (1) full carrier, (2) suppressed carrier in AM transmissions and (3) reduced carrier.

A.

1. For full carrier, see Q. 3.149. Also see Q. 3.138 to Q. 3.142 and Q. 3.148.

2. For single-sideband suppressed carrier (SSSC), see Q. 3.152. See also Q. 3.153 and Q. 3.154.

3. For reduced carrier (RC), see Q. 3.153(3) and Q. 3.154(D).

D. With a suppressed carrier AM system, the single-sideband suppressed carrier (SSSC) scheme is the one most frequently used in communications. However, double-sideband (DS) and vestigial-sideband (VSB) suppressed carrier transmission is also used.

For example, the chrominance sub-carrier (3.58 MHz) of a television transmission is suppressed. Vestigial sideband transmission for color information is employed. The color sub-carrier is reinserted at each color TV receiver by a phase locked loop (PLL) circuit. The frequency and phase of the reinserted sub-carrier are critical if correct color reproduction is to be achieved.

A double-sideband suppressed carrier (DSSC) signal can be generated with a balanced modulator (see Q. 3.153 for balanced modulator). As for SSSC, the carrier must be reinserted at the receiver. The frequency and phase of the reinserted carrier are critical to prevent serious distortion of the detected wave.

Q. 3.161-A2. Draw a schematic diagram of a synchronous AM detector. Briefly explain its operation.

A. The schematic diagram of an AM diode synchronous detector is given in Fig. 3.161-A2.

A reference phase oscillator signal is applied at the junction of C_1 and C_2. This applies the signal with the *same phase* to opposite elements of diodes D_1 and D_2. This signal has the exact frequency and phase as the IF carrier. Simultaneously, the modulated IF signal is applied with *opposite phases* to diodes D_1 and D_2.

As a result, the output of the synchronous detector consists only of the modulation frequencies. The reference phase oscillator signal is canceled by the circuit operation and does not appear in the output. Any remaining IF carrier signal in the output is removed by the series-resonant trap, C_3 and L_1.

D. The envelope detection method has several disadvantages, including:

1. If both sidebands are not symmetrical, distortion may result.

2. If an interfering signal is present, it may also be demodulated.

3. If the received signal is small, distortion may result, with reduced sensitivity and selectivity.

Fig. 3.161-A2. Simplified schematic diagram of a synchronous AM diode detector.

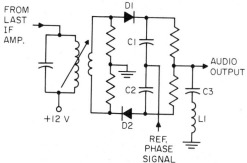

The above disadvantages can be largely overcome by increasing the strength of the carrier. This may be accomplished by adding an additional carrier of the same phase and frequency. This is obtained from the reference phase oscillator, stabilized by a phase-locked loop (PLL). With the addition of a large auxiliary carrier, the detector will operate linearly, even for weak signals.

Q. 3.161-A3. What is the signal-to-noise ratio (SNR)?

A. *Signal-to-noise ratio* may be defined generally as the ratio of the amplitude of a desired signal at any point to the amplitude of noise signals at the same point. The ratio is often expressed in decibels (dB).

D. This ratio has not been well standardized and is used interchangeably to mean the ratio of:

1. RMS signal voltage to RMS noise voltage.

2. Peak signal voltage to peak noise voltage.

3. Peak signal power to average.

4. Noise power (pulse radar systems).

5. Signal power (W) to noise power (W).

Thus, when the term "SNR" (or "S/N") is used, care must be taken to determine which ratio is being referred to.

The peak value is generally used for pulse noise. The RMS value is used for random noise.

Radio noise can be divided into two general categories: (1) noise internal to the receiving system and (2) noise external to the receiving antenna.

1. Noise *internal* to the receiving system is due to antenna losses, transmission line losses, and circuit noise developed by receiver circuits in their normal operation. These include transistor and tube noises.

2. *External* radio noise is due to (a) atmospheric disturbances, (b) galactic radiations, (c) blowing snow or dust, (d) corona, and (e) noise reradiating from any absorbing medium through which the wanted radio signal passes.

Man-made noise sources are:

1. Power lines or generating equipment.
  2. Auto ignition systems.
  3. Fluorescent lights.
  4. Switching transients.
  5. Electrical equipment in general.

At frequencies starting at about 30 MHz and above, *internal receiver noise* is a primary consideration. Most receiver noise is generated in the RF amplifiers and mixer stages. These stages require the use of low-noise transistors or tubes to obtain a suitable SNR.

The above disadvantages can be largely overcome by increasing the strength of the carrier. This may be accomplished by adding an additional carrier of the same phase and frequency. This is obtained from the reference phase oscillator, stabilized by a phase-locked loop (PLL). With the addition of a large auxiliary carrier, the detector will operate linearly, even for weak signals.

Q. 3.161-A4. With regard to receiver sensitivity, what is meant by SINAD?

A. *SINAD* is a widely accepted method of specifying receiver sensitivity. It is a ratio expressed in dB. Thus:

SINAD ratio =

$$\frac{\text{Signal + Noise + Distortion}}{\text{Noise + Distortion}} \quad \text{dB}$$

or abbreviated

$$\text{SINAD ratio} = \frac{S + N + D}{N + D} \quad \text{dB}$$

D. The noise (N) and distortion (D) are those produced by the receiver. Receiver sensitivity is limited by receiver noise. The most commonly accepted method of specifying receiver sensitivity is the 12 dB SINAD or *usable sensitivity* method. The 12 dB ratio

is a convenient reference. (Receiver sensitivity is limited by receiver noise.)

The EIA sensitivity standards for mobile receivers for three frequency bands are:

	25-54 MHz	144-174 MHz	400-470 MHz
Sensitivity μV	1.0	1.5	2.5
Audio power output	1 W	1 W	1 W

With the sensitivity figures as given in the table above, it is required that the SINAD ratio be 12 dB or better.

Man-made noise sources are:

1. Power lines or generating equipment.
  2. Auto-ignition systems.
  3. Flourescent lights.
  4. Switching transients.
  5. Electrical equipment in general.

At frequencies starting at about 30 MHz and above, *internal receiver noise* is a primary consideration. Most receiver noise is generated in the RF amplifiers and mixer stages. These stages require the use of low-noise transistors or tubes to obtain a suitable SNR.

Q. 3.161-A5. Cathode ray oscilloscopes are frequently used to register percentage modulation. Sketch the visual displays of
  1. 0% modulation.
  2. 50% modulation.
  3. 100% modulation.
  4. 120% modulation.

A. See Fig. 3.161-A5(a).
D. Additional trapezoidal waveforms illustrating modulation percentage indications on an oscilloscope are shown in Fig. 3.161-A5(b).

The percentage of modulation may be calculated as follows:

$$\% = \frac{B - A}{B + A} \times 100.$$

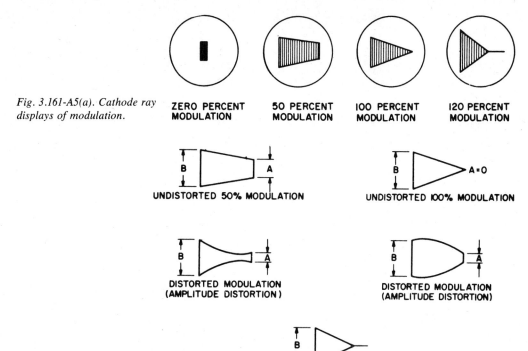

ZERO PERCENT MODULATION   50 PERCENT MODULATION   100 PERCENT MODULATION   120 PERCENT MODULATION

Fig. 3.161-A5(a). Cathode ray displays of modulation.

UNDISTORTED 50% MODULATION

UNDISTORTED 100% MODULATION

DISTORTED MODULATION (AMPLITUDE DISTORTION)

DISTORTED MODULATION (AMPLITUDE DISTORTION)

Fig. 3.161-A5(b). Trapezoidal patterns of modulation.

OVER MODULATION

Q. 3.161-A6. Why are the various RF stages usually shielded from each other in receivers?

A. Shielding of RF stages (including tube shielding) is performed to prevent or to reduce interaction between stages. This interaction can take the form of oscillation, regeneration, or degeneration. Shielding can also help to reduce interference from external, undesired signals.

RF transformers, RF stage tubes (if used), or complete RF stages may be shielded. The shield material must be a good electrical conductor, with aluminum being the most common at frequencies below about 100 MHz. Above this frequency, silver-plated copper or silver-plated brass may be used because of its better conduction.

D. Electromagnetic shielding works because the ac field inside the shield induces an ac current in the shield. This current, in turn, generates a field opposite in phase to the original field. This opposing field cancels most of the original field so that very little radiation takes place.

The same shielding is also effective against energy radiation by electrostatic fields. The shield is grounded, so capacitance exists between the shielded device (or stage) and ground. Thus, most of the electrostatic energy inside the shield is effectively grounded and little is radiated.

FREQUENCY MODULATION

Q. 3.162. Draw a schematic diagram of a frequency-modulated oscillator using a reactance-tube modulator. Explain its principle of operation.

A.
1. For the diagram, see Fig. 3.162(a).
2. The reactance tube operates as it does because an ordinary vacuum tube may act as an inductive or capacitive reactance. Furthermore the magnitude of reactance may be caused to vary in direct relationship to

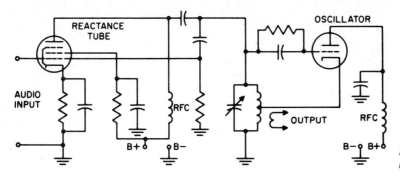

Fig. 3.162(a). A capacitive reactance tube modulator.

the speech or music which originates at the microphone. If the reactance tube is connected to the tank circuit of an oscillator, it is then possible to cause the frequency of the oscillator to vary in accordance with the modulation signal. There are several variations of the reactance tube, but only one type will be explained here. The remaining types are basically similar in operation. A basic diagram of a capacitive reactance tube modulator is shown in Figure 3.162(b). The oscillator tank circuit is made up of L and C which determines the normal frequency of the tank circuit according to the formula

$$f = \frac{1}{2\pi \sqrt{LC}}$$

This formula shows that an increase of either L or C will cause a decrease of frequency, and that a decrease of L or C will cause an increase of frequency. The reactance tube V_1 is effectively in parallel with the tank, since C_b can be considered to be a short circuit at tank frequency. If a capacitance as represented by tube V_1 is placed across the tank and caused to vary at an audio rate, then the total tuning capacitance which is made up of C plus tube V_1 will cause the oscillator frequency to vary at the same audio rate. If it can be shown that the ac plate current of tube V_1 leads the ac plate voltage by 90°, then tube V_1 represents a capacitive reactance. (See Fig. 3.162(b)). The ac tank voltage is designated as V_T. It will be seen that V_T is also the ac plate voltage of tube V_1, since it is effectively applied between plate and cathode. (C_b is effectively a short.) In the vector diagram, V_T is used as the reference. Due to the applied voltage V_T, a current I_1 is caused to flow through the series circuit $C_1 R_1$. These are so proportioned that the reactance of C_1 is made to be many times greater than the resistance R_1. Since the two are in series and the reactance predominates, we may consider $C_1 R_1$ to be a capacitive circuit. Therefore, the current I_1 will lead V_T by 90 degrees. Remember that this current I_1 flows through both C_1 and R_1 in the same phase. The grid signal of V_1 is the voltage which is developed across R_1, or in other words the IR drop across R_1. However, this IR drop is in the same phase as I_1, which is leading the ac plate voltage of V_1 by 90 degrees. Thus, as shown in the vector diagram, the ac grid voltage is leading the ac plate voltage by 90 degrees. Since the ac

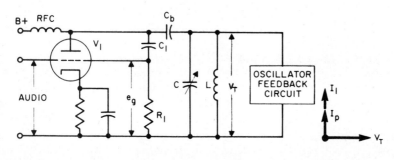

Fig. 3.162(b). Means of modulating an FM transmitter.

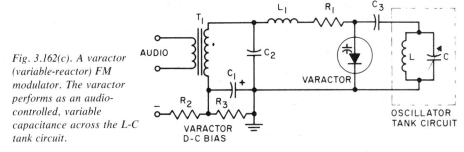

Fig. 3.162(c). A varactor (variable-reactor) FM modulator. The varactor performs as an audio-controlled, variable capacitance across the L-C tank circuit.

plate current follows the ac grid voltage in phase, it is apparent then that the ac plate current also leads the ac plate voltage by 90 degrees. Thus the tube appears to be a capacitive reactance in parallel with the oscillator tank circuit. The magnitude of this reactance is a function of the amount of ac plate current which flows. We can say that

$$X_c = \frac{V_T}{I_p}$$

Thus if the ac plate current should increase (which would happen on the positive swing of an audio wave applied to the grid, the X_c of tube V_1 would correspondingly decrease and this would be equivalent to an increase of shunt capacitance across the tank, since

$$X_c = \frac{1}{2\pi f C}$$

and therefore

$$C = \frac{1}{2\pi f X_c}$$

That is, a decrease of capacitive reactance is equivalent to an actual increase of capacitance. Since this capacitance is added in parallel with the tank capacitance, it would cause the oscillator frequency to decrease. Therefore, the amount of frequency decrease would depend upon the amplitude of the positive swing of audio grid signal. The greater the amplitude of audio grid signal, the greater would be the effective increase of capacitance and the greater the decrease in frequency. On the other hand let us take the negative swing of the audio cycle acting upon the grid of V_1. This would cause a decrease in ac plate current and

therefore X_c of V_1 would appear larger. This is equivalent to a decrease in the shunting capacitance and to an increase of oscillator frequency. It should be remembered that the *rate* at which the oscillator frequency changes is a function of the audio frequency only and not of its amplitude. The *amplitude* of the audio determines only the amount of frequency change or deviation.

A solid-state version of an FM modulator is shown in Fig. 3.162(c). This circuit employs a varactor diode, whose capacitance varies with the voltage impressed across it. The varactor is reverse-biased to the center of its linear characteristic, in order for it to function as a variable capacitance. This reverse bias is supplied by the voltage divider consisting of R2 and R3. The audio modulation signal, applied through the transformer T1, is impressed across the varactor and causes it to change its effective capacitance. The amount of capacitance change (and frequency change) is proportional to the amplitude of the audio signal, while the rate of change is proportional to the audio frequency. Thus, since the varactor capacitance is across the oscillator tank circuit, a frequency-modulated wave is produced.

Q. 3.163. Discuss the following in reference to frequency modulation.

1. The production of sidebands.

2. The relationship between the number of sidebands and the modulating frequency.

3. The relationship between the number of sidebands and the amplitude of the modulating voltage.

4. The relationship between percent modulation and the number of sidebands.

5. The relationship between modulation index or deviation ratio and the number of sidebands.

6. The relationship between the spacing of the sidebands and the modulating frequency.

7. The relationship between the number of sidebands and the bandwidth of emissions.

8. The criteria for determining the bandwidth of emission.

9. Reasons for pre-emphasis.

A.

1. When a sine wave is frequency modulated, its instantaneous frequency is varied according to the intelligence to be transmitted. The modulated wave consists of components made up of the original sine wave plus additional sine waves. These additional sine waves are of different frequencies from the original wave and are called sidebands and are symmetrically arranged above and below the original wave or carrier.

2. For a given frequency deviation, the number of sidebands is inversely proportional to the modulating frequency. For example, for a frequency deviation of plus or minus 75 kilohertz and a modulating frequency of 15 000 hertz, there will be five significant sidebands on each side of the carrier. With a modulating frequency of 150 hertz and the same deviation, there will be 500 significant sidebands on each side of the carrier.

3. For a given modulating frequency, the number of sidebands is directly proportional to the amplitude of the modulating voltage. That is, if the modulating voltage is tripled, the number of sidebands is also tripled.

4. In FM broadcast service, 100 percent modulation is defined as the modulating condition producing a frequency deviation of plus or minus 75 kilohertz. The number of sidebands produced, for any given modulating frequency, is directly proportional to the percent modulation.

5. For any given modulating frequency, the number of significant sidebands is directly proportional to the modulator index or deviation ratio. See also Discussion under (1).

6. The sidebands produced by frequency modulation are separated from one another by a frequency that is equal to the modulating frequency. The sidebands adjacent to the carrier are also separated from it by an amount equal to the modulating frequency.

7. The total number of significant sidebands multiplied by the modulating frequency equals the total significant bandwidth of emission. There are sidebands extending beyond this, but they are insignificant and contain so little power or energy that they are considered negligible.

8. The criteria for determining the bandwidth of emission are the modulation index and the modulating frequency. The product of the modulation index and the frequency of modulation equals the frequency deviation. The bandwith of emission is twice the sum of the frequency deviation and the modulating frequency.

9. In speech and music very little energy is contained in the frequencies at the upper end of the audio frequency range. However, even though such components represent very little energy, they are extremely important to the naturalness of speech as they give *definition* to the consonants and add to the identification of the different types of musical instruments. Normally, these high frequency components will be lost in transmission because of *masking* by noise unless some way is found to make them override such circuit noise. One way of accomplishing this is to amplify these components more than the low frequency sounds before introducing the complete audio signal to the modulating circuits of the FM transmitter. This process is termed *pre-emphasis*—that is, the high frequencies are emphasized before modulation and thus represent more energy during transmission. At the receiver, in order to restore these components to their original amplitude relationship with the low-frequency components, it is necessary to reverse the process after detection. This latter process is termed *de-emphasis*.

D.

1. The "modulation index" is the ratio of the amount of frequency deviation to the audio modulating frequency causing the deviation. "Deviation ratio" is simply a special case of modulation index and is defined as the ratio of the *maximum permissible* frequency deviation to the *maximum permissible* audio modulating frequency. Examples of three different deviation ratios follow.

For a standard FM broadcast station the maximum permissible deviation is 75 kilohertz above or below the average; while the maximum permissible audio modulating frequency is equal to 15 kilohertz. Therefore the "deviation ratio" for a standard FM station is equal to $^{75}/_{15}$ or 5. The FM sound carrier of a television transmitter has a maximum deviation of $\pm$ 25 kilohertz. The "deviation ratio" in this case is $^{25}/_{15} = 1.667$.

In the case of narrow-band FM used in Public Safety Radio Services, the maximum deviation is 5 000 hertz and the maximum audio frequency is 3 000 hertz. Therefore, the deviation ratio for this service is $5\ 000/3\ 000 = 1.667$.

2. In pre-emphasis, the higher audio frequencies in the modulating stages of an FM transmitter are overamplified with respect to their value and in relation to the lower audio frequencies.

Refer to Fig. 3.163(a). Studies have demonstrated that the noises which are most irritating to the listener are those which are concentrated in the upper end of the audio frequency spectrum. It is also true that these high audio frequencies represent very little

energy as compared to the low frequencies. Thus it is possible in the audio stages of an FM transmitter to over-amplify the high audio frequencies without much danger of overmodulating the transmitter. In this case overmodulation would mean a deviation in excess of ± 75 kilohertz. Since there are guard bands of ± 25 hilohertz in each FM channel, occasional overmodulation would not be too serious. A practical circuit to produce pre-emphasis is shown in Figure 3.163(a). The important part of this circuit is the parallel network R_1C_1 which is in series with resistor R_g. R_1C_1 is in effect a high pass filter. At low frequencies where C_1 is practically an open circuit, we have a voltage divider made up of R_1 and R_g. Only a small portion of the input appears across R_g at low frequencies. As the frequency increases however, the impedance of the parallel network becomes less, and more of the input signal appears across R_g. Example: At 60 cycles, the reactance of C_1 is 2 670 000 ohms and the parallel combination of R_1C_1 is then 75 000 ohms. The amount of signal now appearing on the grid is

$$v_g = V_s \frac{R_g}{R_1 + R_g} = V_s \times \frac{2\ 000}{77\ 000}$$

$$= V_s \times 2.56 \text{ percent.}$$

At 15 000 cycles the reactance of C_1 is about 10 000 ohms. The parallel impedance of R_1-C_1 is now about 8 800 ohms, and the signal voltage which appears on the grid is

$$v_g = V_s \times \frac{2\ 000}{10\ 800} = V_s \times 18.5 \text{ percent.}$$

This means that 15 000 hertz will be amplified about 7 times more than 60 hertz. The time constant for a pre-emphasis network such as $R_1 - C_1$ is standardized by the FCC at 75 microseconds, $= 0.001\ (\mu\text{F}) \times 75\ 000$ (ohms). A standard pre-emphasis chart is shown in Figure 3.163(b), and it should be noted here that the gain remains substantially constant until about 800 hertz. From then on it continues to rise until a maximum of 27 dB is reached at 15 000 hertz. (Ratio of 17dB is 7:1 approx.) The fact that the higher

Fig. 3.163(a). A standard pre-emphasis network.

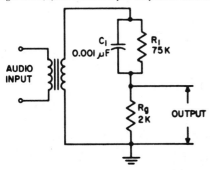

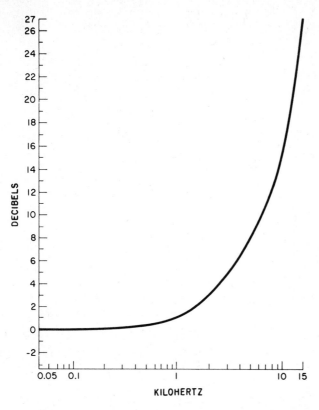

Fig. 3.163(b). A standard pre-emphasis chart.

audio frequencies are thus overemphasized makes it possible to override much of the high frequency noises which are picked up enroute to and within the receiver. However, in order to obtain the full benefits of this system and regain the correct tonal values a de-emphasis network must be incorporated into the FM receiver.

3. Refer to Figure 3.163(c). The purpose of a de-emphasis circuit is to restore the over-amplified high frequencies to their correct value, and at the same time to greatly reduce the high frequency noise output of the receiver.

Actually the de-emphasis circuit is the exact opposite in its characteristics to the pre-emphasis circuit. Where the pre-emphasis circuit amplifies high frequencies, the de-emphasis circuit attenuates them. For example the gain at 15 000 cycles is over-amplified about 7 times by pre-emphasis. In the receiver it is attenuated by the same factor of 7, thus returning the 15 000-hertz tone to its correct amplitude in comparison

with low frequencies. Were the pre-emphasis circuit was a high-pass filter, the de-emphasis circuit is a low-pass filter. A simple de-emphasis circuit is shown in the figure. This network is usually found between FM detector and the first audio amplifier. The time constant of a de-emphasis circuit is also 75 microseconds. It will be noted that the de-emphasis circuit works on the principle of a voltage divider with only that portion of the audio developed across C_1 being transmitted to the audio amplifier. At high frequencies the reactance of C_1 will be low and not much signal will be developed across C_1. For example at 16 000 hertz the reactance

Fig. 3.163(c). A de-emphasis circuit.

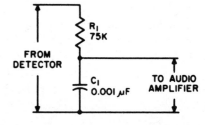

of C_1 is about 10 000 ohms. The series impedance of C_1 and R_1 equals

$$\sqrt{R^2 + X_{c1}^2} = \sqrt{75\,000^2 + 10\,000^2}$$
$$= 75\,700 \text{ ohms.}$$

The amount of voltage developed across C_1 is

$$V_{C1} = V_s \times \frac{X_{c1}}{\sqrt{R^2 \times X_{c1}^2}}$$
$$= V_s \times \frac{10\,000}{75\,700}$$
$$= V_s \times 13.2 \text{ percent}$$

At 60 hertz the reactance of C_1 is 2 654 000 ohms and the series impedance of C_1 and R_1 equals

$$\sqrt{R^2 + X_{c1}^2} = \sqrt{75\,000^2 + 2\,654\,000^2}$$
$$= 2\,655\,000.$$

The amount of voltage developed across C_1 is

$$V_{c1} = V_s \times \frac{X_{c1}}{\sqrt{R^2 \times X_{c1}^2}}$$
$$= V_s + \frac{2\,654\,000}{2\,655\,000}$$
$$= V_s \times 100 \text{ percent}$$

which is approximately 7 times more signal than for 16 000 hertz. Thus it is seen that the de-emphasis circuit works in exactly the opposite manner to the pre-emphasis circuit. It must be remembered that at the same time the high frequencies are attenuated, all high frequency noises are also attenuated by the same degree, and it is here that the greatest noise reduction takes place. It should also be borne in mind that while the high frequencies are being attenuated, they are simply being returned to their normal value and are not being suppressed in any way. After leaving the de-emphasis circuit, the audio signal is fed into a standard audio amplifier.

4. The percentage of modulation of an FM station is primarily determined by the amplitude of the audio tone. For a standard FM broadcast station, 100 percent modulation is obtained for a modulation tone which causes a deviation of $\pm$ 75 kilohertz. For any given audio tone, an increase of amplitude causes a proportional increase in the amount of frequency deviation.

5. The rate of frequency swing of an FM broadcast station depends upon the tone frequency of the modulating signal. The rate at which the carrier deviates (swings) is a direct function of the audio frequency. Thus for an audio frequency of 10 000 hertz the carrier will deviate (or swing) at the rate of 10 000 times per second.

6. One FM channel is 200 kilohertz wide. Of the allotted 200 kilohertz, 150 kilohertz is to be used for the actual transmission, while a guard band of 25 kilohertz is established on either end of each channel. The FM broadcast channels are allotted frequencies from 88 to 108 megahertz. The last FM channel has a center frequency of 107.9 megahertz.

Q. 3.164. How is good stability of a reactance tube modulator achieved?

A. In addition to the stability achieved by normal good design of the self-excited oscillator employed as a reactance tube modulated oscillator, further stability is obtained by operating the oscillator at a low radio frequency. The oscillator's operating frequency is at an integral submultiple of the desired antenna frequency. The oscillator is followed by frequency multipliers sufficient to obtain the desired final frequency.

A further advantage in stability is gained by operating the oscillator at a low frequency. This is because the frequency deviation, and hence the modulation index, is multiplied by the same factor as the carrier frequency when the signal is passed through frequency multiplying stages. Because of the low frequency deviation required, the effect of the reactance tube modulator on the stability of the oscillator is decreased.

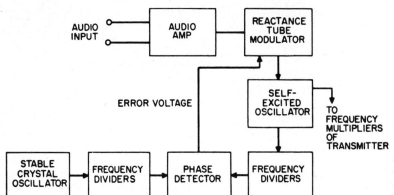

Fig. 3.164. Simplified block diagram of an AFC system used to stabilize a reactance-tube modulator.

D. Any self-excited oscillator, no matter how carefully designed is subject to some frequency drift. In addition, any variation in the parameters of the reactance tube will cause the oscillator to change frequency. To insure a completely stable reactance tube and oscillator, it is customary to employ an AFC system whose reference is an extremely stable crystal oscillator. A simplified block diagram of such an AFC system is shown in Fig. 3.164. The phase detector receives signals (divided in frequency) from both the crystal oscillator and the self-excited oscillator. The two signals are compared in the phase detector. If the frequency of the self-excited oscillator differs from that of the crystal oscillator, the phase detector develops a dc error voltage which is fed to the reactance-tube modulator. This error voltage is of the correct polarity to bring the self-excited oscillator to its correct frequency. As the oscillator approaches the correct frequency, the amplitude of the error voltage will decrease to practically zero.

Q. 3.165. Draw circuit and vector diagrams of phase modulators. Explain the operation. Label adjacent stages.

A.

1. For the diagrams, see Figs. 3.165(a), 3.165(b), 3.165(c), and 3.165(d).

2. For the explanation of the operation of one type of phase modulator, refer first to the block diagram of Fig. 3.165(a). An unmodulated RF wave is applied both to the phase-modulator amplifier and to a 90 degree phase shifter. An AF modulating signal is also applied to the phase-modulator amplifier. The latter signal causes an amplitude-modulated wave to appear at the output of the modulator. This AM wave is combined in the output load with the 90 degree shifted, unmodulated RF wave. If the amplitude of the unmodulated wave is much greater than that of the AM wave, the resultant RF will be phase shifted by an amount closely proportional to the amplitude of the AF modulating signal. Thus, the resultant RF output wave will be one whose phase is directly proportional to the amplitude of the audio modulating signal and a true phase-modulated RF wave will have been produced.

D. For a more detailed explanation of this phase modulator, refer to the schematic diagram of Fig. 3.165(b), and to the vector

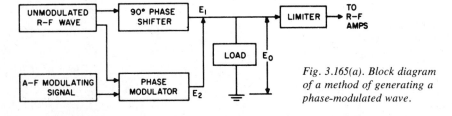

Fig. 3.165(a). Block diagram of a method of generating a phase-modulated wave.

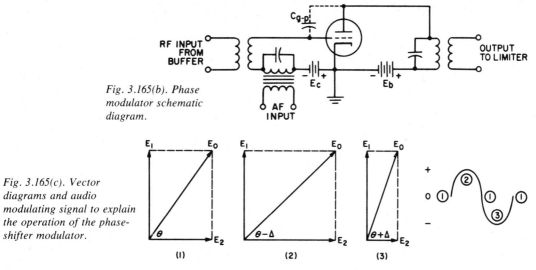

Fig. 3.165(b). Phase modulator schematic diagram.

Fig. 3.165(c). Vector diagrams and audio modulating signal to explain the operation of the phase-shifter modulator.

diagrams of Fig. 3.165(c). The numbers shown at the different points of the audio-sine wave are keyed to the three vector diagrams. In the schematic, an AM wave is developed in the triode and applied to the low-impedance tank circuit. This voltage is shown in the vector diagrams as V_2. A second voltage, V_1, is phase-shifted 90 degrees in passing through C_{gp} and is also applied to the plate tank circuit. These two voltages combine in the tank to produce their vector sum, V_0. Note in the three vector diagrams that the amplitude of V_1 remains fixed while the amplitude of V_2 varies in accordance with the amplitude and polarity of the audio-modulating wave. As a result of the variation in amplitude of V_2, the phase angle of V_0 varies in direct proportion to the amplitude and polarity of the audio-modulating wave. In vector diagram (1), the audio signal is at zero volts and a quiescent value of phase angle (θ) results for V_0. In vector diagram (2), the audio wave is at its maximum positive value. This results in a higher amplitude of V_2 and a decreased phase angle ($\theta - \Delta$) for V_0. In vector diagram (3), the audio wave is at its maximum negative value, resulting in the minimum amplitude of V_2. Note that a greater phase angle for V_0 results ($\theta + \Delta$).

V_0 varies not only in phase, but also in amplitude. These amplitude variations are removed by the following limiter, leaving only a phase-modulated wave. As discussed in the answer above, the amplitude of V_1 is normally much greater than that of V_2. However, to more graphically illustrate the phase variations shown in the vector diagrams, these voltages are shown with comparable amplitudes.

Although the modulator shown is an unneutralized triode, self-oscillation does not occur in the stage. Self-oscillation is avoided by the use of a low Q (low impedance) tank circuit and a low value of plate voltage. As explained in Q. 3.166, phase modulation produces an equivalent frequency-modulation wave. The original phase (and frequency) modulation deviation is increased to the desired value by frequency multipliers which also raise the carrier frequency to the desired final value.

A phase-modulator circuit employing a solid-state varactor (variable capacitance) diode is shown in Fig. 3.165(d). The operating principle of this circuit differs from that shown in Fig. 3.165(b). In the varactor circuit, a resonant tank circuit is made up of L, C and the varactor diode. The varactor is correctly biased (in the reverse direction) to the center of its characteristic curve. An audio input is applied to the anode of the varactor. This causes the varactor capacitance to vary

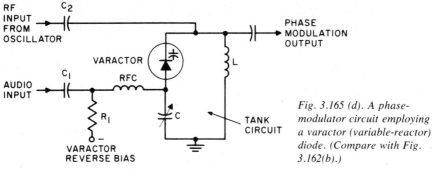

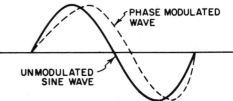

Fig. 3.165 (d). A phase-modulator circuit employing a varactor (variable-reactor) diode. (Compare with Fig. 3.162(b).)

Fig. 3.166. Effect of phase modulation on a sine wave.

above and below its quiescent value, as established by the dc bias. In addition, as shown, the RF wave from the oscillator is applied to the resonant tank circuit.

The RF input from the oscillator is always a single, fixed frequency. However, the effect of the audio wave on the varactor causes the tank circuit to be resonant both above and below its quiescent resonant frequency.

When the tank circuit is resonant above its quiescent (and oscillator) frequency, it looks like an inductance (inductive current predominates) to the RF signal. This produces a leading phase angle of the output voltage.

When the tank circuit is resonant to its normal (center) frequency (audio voltage passing through zero), it represents a pure resistance and no phase shift of the RF wave occurs.

When the tank circuit is resonant below its quiescent (and oscillator) frequency, it looks like a capacitance (capacitive current predominates) to the RF signal. This produces a lagging phase angle of the output voltage.

The amount of phase shift is proportional to the amplitude of the audio signal, while the rate of phase angle change is proportional to the audio frequency. Thus, a phase modulated wave is produced.

Q. 3.166. Explain what occurs in a waveform if it is phase modulated.

A. When a sine wave is phase modulated it becomes a distorted sine wave as

illustrated in an exaggerated manner in Fig. 3.166. As a result of this distortion, additional frequencies are created and appear in the modulated wave as sidebands.

Since frequency may be expressed as the rate of change of phase, the instantaneous frequency of the modulated wave is varied in exact accordance with the variation in the rate of change of phase. The net result of the foregoing is that phase modulation produces the same sort of modulated wave that is produced by frequency modulation. Actually, for the same modulating freqency and modulation index, the two waves will be identical.

Q. 3.167. Explain, in a general way, why an FM deviation meter (modulation meter) would show an indication if coupled to the output of a transmitter which is phase modulated by a constant amplitude, constant audio frequency. To what would this deviation be proportional?

A. Since a phase-modulated transmitter produces a wave that is frequency modulated, as explained in Q. 3.166 above, an FM deviation meter would show an indication because frequency deviation would in fact exist.

The amount of such deviation will be

proportional to the amplitude *and* the frequency of the modulating signal, whereas the deviation in an FM transmitter is proportional only to the amplitude of the modulating signal and is independent of its frequency.

D. As mentioned above, when a wave is phase modulated, the effective frequency deviation is proportional to the frequency as well as the amplitude of the audio-modulating wave. However, all FM detectors are designed to reproduce an audio wave based upon the *amplitude* only of the original audio modulating signal. As a result, when phase modulation is used in an FM transmitter, it is necessary to correct for the effect of audio *frequency* on the effective FM deviation. This is accomplished by an audio network (predistorter) which precedes the phase modulator. The "predistorter" adjusts the amplitude of the audio-modulating wave with respect to its frequency, so that the resultant effective FM deviation is proportional *only* to the *amplitude* of the audio-

modulating signal. This is accomplished by making the output voltage of the speech amplifier decrease inversely with respect to the modulating frequency.

Q. 3.168. Draw a circuit diagram of each of the following stages of a phase-modulated FM transmitter. Explain their operation. Label adjacent stages.

1. Frequency multiplier (doubler) with capacitive coupling on input and output.

2. Power amplifier with variable link coupling to antenna. Include circuit for metering grid and plate currents.

3. Speech amplifier with an associated pre-emphasis circuit.

A.

1. For the diagram of a doubler, see Fig. 3.168(a). The operation of a frequency doubler is explained in Q. 3.131. The degree of coupling to the intermediate power amplifier can be varied by changing the position of the tap on the coil or by changing the value of the output capacitor. Moving the

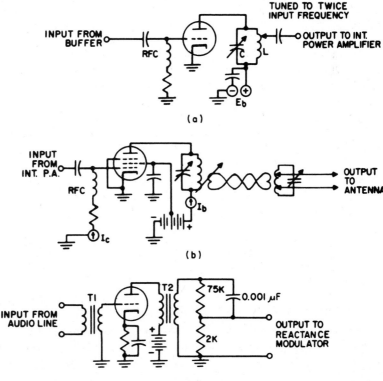

Fig. 3.168. Different stages of phase-modulated FM transmitter: (a) frequency doubler, (b) power amplifier, (c) speech amplifier.

tap toward the ground end of the tank coil will reduce the amount of coupling.

2. For the diagram of a power amplifier, see Fig. 3.168(b). For the explanation of the operation of an RF power amplifier, see Q. 3.52(a)(4). The degree of coupling to the antenna can be varied by changing the position of the small coil with respect to the tank coil. The tuned circuit at the other end of the link is resonated to the operating frequency. The taps on this coil are adjusted to match the required input impedance of the transmission line to the antenna itself.

3. For the diagram of a speech amplifier, see Fig. 3.168(c). The speech amplifier as shown is a Class A transformer-coupled stage and its operation is described in Q. 3.50(a). Following the amplifier is a network to provide pre-emphasis of the higher audio frequencies.

D. The most general use for a Class A amplifier is as a voltage amplifier, although single-ended power amplifiers which feed speakers must also be Class A. The average plate efficiency for triodes is about 20 percent, while that of pentodes is about 30 to 35 percent. Unlike either Class B or C, the average plate current and voltage remain constant regardless of the magnitude of the grid signal. The grid signal must be so confined that it does not cause grid current in its positive swing, or cut off the tube in its negative swing. The power amplification ratio is high since no grid current is drawn.

Power amplification ratio =

$$\frac{\text{power delivered to plate load}}{\text{power consumed in grid circuit}}$$

Following the speech amplifier in Fig. 3.168(c) is a network to provide "pre-emphasis" of the higher audio frequencies. Details of this network and its operation are given in Q. 3.163.

Q. 3.169. Discuss wide-band and narrow-band reception in FM voice communication systems with respect to frequency deviation and bandwidth.

A. It has been shown that the highest audio frequency used in voice communication may be limited to about 3 000 hertz without seriously impairing the intelligibility of the speech. In standard FM broadcasting (88 – 108 MHz) a deviation ratio of five is employed to provide the desired dynamic range. With a maximum transmitted audio frequency of 15 000 hertz, the maximum deviation will be 75 kHz. However, in narrow-band FM, the deviation ratio is commonly *one* so that the deviation may be limited to the audio frequency or to plus and minus 3 000 hertz. This is a considerable advantage over wide-band FM when many stations must operate within a crowded spectrum. In a narrow-band FM system, the FM receiver is also a narrow-band device. This not only improves the sensitivity and selectivity of a receiver with a given number of stages, but also makes it possible to improve the signal-to-noise ratio of the system. This is so because noise occupies the entire radio spectrum and the narrower the bandwidth of reception, the less noise energy will be delivered to the receiver output. Actually, for a voice-communications system, which requires limited frequency response and limited dynamic range, there would be no significant advantage in employing wide-band FM. On the contrary, this would require a greater deviation ratio, necessitating more complex modulating and multiplying circuits. In addition a much wider channel bandwidth would be required and fewer stations could be accommodated in a given spectrum assignment. A more complex receiver for an equal distance of communication would also be required for wide-band FM.

D. Narrow-band FM may be generally defined as FM whose sidebands do not occupy a bandwidth greater than an AM signal which has the same audio-modulating frequencies. If single-tone, narrow-band FM is employed, the modulation index may not exceed about 0.6 if the bandwidth is not to exceed that of an equivalent AM signal. However, if speech modulation is used, a complex waveform is produced. In this waveform, the energy distribution is such that the modulation index is reduced for any single frequency component. Therefore, in the case of speech modulation, a somewhat higher modulation index (1.0) may be employed with no increase in bandwidth over single-tone modulation with a lesser modulation index.

In a radio communication system, the primary object of the system is the transfer of intelligence by voice. A high signal-to-noise ratio is desirable in voice reception, but an increase of this ratio above a certain definite value will not improve the readability of the received signal. For carrier wave strengths below a certain minimum value, a low-deviation system will produce a greater signal-to-noise ratio than a high deviation system. The optimum frequency deviation for an FM system which is designed to obtain maximum distance for complete readability corresponds to a deviation ratio of *one*. Since voice frequencies are not generally of importance above 3 000 hertz, a deviation ratio of one means that the peak deviation frequency will be equal to 3 000 hertz. (See also Q. 3.163(5) through (8), Q. 3.167.

Q. 3.170. What might be the effect on the transmitted frequency if a tripler stage in an otherwise perfectly aligned FM transmitter, were slightly de-tuned?

A. The tank circuit of such a tripler would present a reactive impedance to the plate of the tube instead of a resistive impedance. The value of such a reactive impedance and the resulting phase angle will depend on the frequency at any instant. Since the instantaneous frequency varies during modulation, the detuned tripler stage will inject an additional phase modulation component into the frequency modulated wave. When such a wave is finally detected at the receiver the additional frequencies will be present at the output along with the original

frequencies. Such unwanted frequencies represent interference and noise.

D. When a tank circuit of reasonable Q (10 or more) is tuned to resonance, it presents a resistive impedance to the driving source (generator). However, if the tank is tuned to resonate either above or below the driving frequency, it will present either an inductive or capacitive reactance, respectively. The reactance presented by the detuned tank will depend upon the instantaneous frequency fed to it by the FM wave. For each frequency fed to the tank, an additional phase shift will occur. Thus, an extra phase modulation component will be added to the original FM wave, producing a distortion and interference component which will appear after detection at the receiver.

Q. 3.171. Could the harmonic of an FM transmission contain intelligible modulation?

A. The harmonics of FM transmission do contain intelligible modulation, the only difference between them and the fundamental is the increased deviation. The deviation is multiplied by the order of the harmonic.

D. In the usual FM transmitter, the carrier wave is generated at a relatively low RF frequency. In addition, this low-frequency carrier is frequency modulated at a low deviation ratio. By means of frequency multipliers in the transmitter, both the deviation and the carrier are brought to the desired waveforms. A harmonic output from the FM transmitter would merely continue this process. For example, consider an FM narrow-band transmitter operating at 31 MHz with a deviation of plus and minus 3 kHz. At the second harmonic of the radiated wave, the carrier would have a frequency of 61 MHz and a deviation of plus and minus 6 kHz. This harmonic wave contains the same intelligence as the fundamental and this intelligence may be recovered in an FM receiver tuned to 61 MHz and having a bandwidth of about 6 kHz (or more).

Q. 3.172. Under what usual conditions of maintenance and/or repair should a transmitter be retuned?

A. If tubes, RF components or RF leads are involved or disturbed during maintenance or repair, the transmitter should be retuned. Maintenance and/or repair of the power and control circuits normally do not require such retuning.

Q. 3.173. If an indirect FM transmitter without modulation was within carrier frequency tolerance, but with modulation out of tolerance, what would be some possible causes?

A. In the indirect or Armstrong system of frequency modulation, the actual modulation is obtained by employing a balanced modulator to produce sidebands, only to be combined with the carrier only after the carrier has been shifted in phase by 90°. The carrier, during modulation, is defined as the average frequency of the whole spectrum emitted. The most probable cause of the average frequency being out of tolerance during modulation is the balanced modulator not being balanced. Such an event would result in the production of unequal sidebands which would have the effect of shifting the average frequency upward or downward. Without modulation, the average frequency or carrier would be unchanged in frequency because the sidebands being added to it at this time are zero.

D. As explained in Q. 3.89 and Q. 3.98, two causes of oscillator frequency changes are supply voltage changes and oscillator loading variations. If the circumstances in the transmitter are such that either of these effects can be caused by the application of modulation, then carrier frequency changes may occur only in the presence of modulation. Supply voltage changes may occur due to a defective regulated power supply or defective decoupling circuits. Oscillator loading changes may occur due to a mistuned or defective buffer stage or to a defective phase modulator.

Q. 3.174. In an FM transmitter what would be the effect on antenna current if the grid bias on the final power amplifier were varied?

A. Normally, the final power amplifier of an FM transmitter is operated Class C. With such an amplifier, a change in its grid bias will produce a change in its output power and hence a change in the antenna current. Usually, a decrease in grid bias will increase the power output with an attendant increase in antenna current. An increase in grid bias will have just the opposite effect. Both of these effects can take place only over a rather limited range.

D. In the answer above, it was assumed that most of the bias was supplied from a fixed source. It is also possible to supply a considerable portion of the bias as "grid-leak bias" (see Q. 3.121). In this event there is a "self-regulating" effect on the antenna current if the driving signal varies between narrow limits. In this case, if the driving signal drops, the grid-leak bias decreases and causes an increase in amplifier gain which tends to maintain a constant output. If the driving signal increases, the grid-leak bias increases, decreasing amplifier gain, and again tending to maintain constant output. Outside of these limits however, the antenna current will tend to follow the amplitude of the driving signal.

Q. 3.175. Explain briefly, the principles involved in frequency-shift keying (FSK). How is this signal detected?

A.

1. Frequency-shift keying (F1 emission) is a means of keying a radiotelegraph transmitter by changing the frequency of its output when the key is depressed, rather than turning the transmitter on and off during keying. It may be accomplished by connecting a keyed reactance tube across the master-oscillator so that the resonant frequency is changed by about 850 hertz as keying takes place. Frequently, the shifted

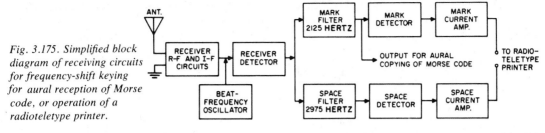

Fig. 3.175. Simplified block diagram of receiving circuits for frequency-shift keying for aural reception of Morse code, or operation of a radioteletype printer.

oscillator is at a low frequency and is only shifted a small amount to maintain good stability. The shifted oscillator frequencies are multiplied to obtain the final output frequency and the desired frequency shift.

2. One scheme of detection which may be employed either for the aural reception of Morse code or to operate a radioteletype machine is shown in block diagram form in Fig. 3.175. The frequency-shift keying (FSK) signal passes through the usual receiver RF and IF circuits and is applied to the receiver detector together with the signal from a beat-frequency oscillator (bfo) (see Q. 3.158). The bfo is adjusted to heterodyne with the IF to produce a "mark" signal of 2 125 hertz and a "space" signal of 2 925 hertz for a difference of 850 hertz. These are fed through individual filters to eliminate all other spurious frequencies. The output of the "mark" filter may be used directly or fed through an audio amplifier for aural copying of Morse code, since the dot and dash information is carried entirely by the "mark" signal. For operation of a radioteletype printer, the "mark" and "space" signals are fed to grid-leak detectors and current amplifiers, the output of which is used to operate the printer.

D. Frequency shift keying has several important advantages over "on-off" keying as follows:

1. A reduction of transmitted bandwidth, especially for high speed (machine) keying.

2. An increase of signal-to-noise ratio at the receiving end.

3. A possible reduction of fading.

When a transmitter is being keyed, frequencies other than the carrier frequency are radiated. These are called sidebands and their relative amplitude and frequency depend largely upon the rate of keying, and the shape or configuration of the keyed characters. If the keyed characters have a square shape, the side frequencies will extend out on each side of the carrier for great distances. On the other hand, if the keyed characters can be rounded off and kept that way during transmission, the sidebands will be greatly attenuated. Rounding of the keyed characters in "on-off" keying cannot be easily accomplished, since clipping and limiting in class C amplifiers effectively squares up any rounding-off which might have been originally produced.

In frequency-shift keying, rounding may be accomplished by passing the square characters through a suitable low-pass filter. The keying stage produces frequency modulation of the output, and the rounded characters are able to retain their original shape.

At the receiving end a considerable increase in signal-to-noise ratio is noted in frequency-shift keying. The main reason for this is the fact that a carrier is always present (although shifted) and noise pulses are not able to actuate the signal recorder of the receiving equipment readily.

The possible reduction of fading is due to the fact that the energy in the transmitted wave is distributed over a *band* of frequencies, each frequency of which may have somewhat different fading characteristics.

An FSK signal may be passed through a limiter (or limiters) and detected by FM discriminator. In this manner the noise reducing advantage of FM may be employed. However, in this case, the discriminator must use a dc coupled audio output to provide a dc output when the keying is stopped on either "space" or "mark".

Q. 3.176. Assume you have available the following instruments:

1. AC/DC VTVM
2. Ammeter
3. Heterodyne frequency meter (0.0002% accuracy)
4. Absorption wave meter
5. FM modulation meter

Draw and label a block diagram of a voice modulated (press-to-talk microphone), indirect (phase modulated) FM transmitter having a crystal multiplication of 12.

1. If the desired output frequency were 155.460 MHz, what would be the proper crystal frequency?

2. Consider the transmitter strip completely de-tuned; there are ammeter jacks in the control grid circuits of the multipliers and the control grid and cathode circuits of the final circuits of the final amplifier. Explain, in detail, step-by-step, a proper procedure for tuning and aligning all stages except plate circuit of final power amplifier (PA).

3. Assume a tunable antenna with adjustable coupling to the plate circuit of the final PA. With the ammeter in the cathode circuit of the PA and with the aid of a tube manual, describe a step-by-step method of obtaining maximum output power, without damage to the tube.

4. If the PA in (3). above were a pentode how would you determine the power input to the stage?

5. In (3.) above how would you determine if the PA stage were self-oscillating; if so, what adjustments could be made.

6. Assume the transmitter's assigned frequency is 155.460 MHz, with a required tolerance of plus or minus 0.0005 percent. What would be the minimum and maximum frequencies, as read on the frequency meter, which would assure the transmitter being within tolerance?

7. Assume the 1-MHz crystal oscillator

of the frequency meter has been calibrated with WWV and that the meter is tunable to any frequency between each 1-MHz interval over a range of 20-40 MHz, with usable harmonics up to 640 MHz. Explain in detail what connections and adjustments would be made to measure the signal directly from the transmitter; also by means of a receiver.

8. If in checking the frequency deviation with the modulation meter, would you expect the greatest deviation by whistling or by speaking in a low voice into the microphone?

9. If the transmitter contained a means for limiting, and were over-modulating, what measurements and adjustments could be made to determine and remedy the fault?

A. For the block diagram, see Fig. 3.176.

1. Since the transmitter employs a frequency multiplication of 12, the proper crystal frequency is the desired output frequency of 155.460 MHz divided by 12, or 12.955 MHz.

2. It is assumed that the ammeter available is actually a milliammeter and is capable of being fitted with a pair of leads terminating in a suitable plug for use in measuring electrode currents in the stages by means of the jacks available. It is further assumed that the crystal oscillator is an electron-coupled Pierce oscillator.

In aligning the transmitter it is first necessary to remove the plate and screen voltages from the power amplifier. The power is then applied to the preceding stages by operating the *Press-to-Talk* switch.

The plate circuit of the oscillator is tuned to resonance by adjusting for maximum grid current in the tripler stage. At this point check the frequency of the oscillator by loosely coupling the wavemeter to the oscillator plate coil. The frequency, by this method of measurement, should be approximately 13 MHz. This measurement is to assure us that the oscillator plate coil is tuned to the fundamental and not to a second or even third harmonic. This is possible in some

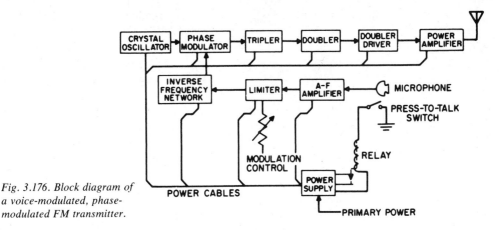

Fig. 3.176. Block diagram of a voice-modulated, phase-modulated FM transmitter.

cases due to the range of frequencies for which some oscillators are designed.

If the heterodyne frequency meter available can measure frequencies in this range, it is advisable to measure the exact frequency of the oscillator by loosely coupling the frequency meter to the oscillator plate coil. If this measurement is not feasible, the final output frequency of the transmitter can be measured later.

The milliammeter is next inserted in the jack in the control grid circuit of the first doubler and the plate circuit of the tripler adjusted for maximum grid current for this stage. Again, it is necessary to couple the wavemeter loosely to the plate coil of the tripler and check to see if the tripler output frequency approximates 39 MHz. This is to assure the stage is actually tripling the frequency and not doubling or quadrupling it.

The first doubler is adjusted in a similar fashion, again tuning for maximum grid current in the following stage. The wavemeter in this case should indicate approximately 78 MHz as the output frequency for this stage.

The procedure is again followed for the second doubler and the wavemeter used to be certain that its output is approximately 155 MHz. At this point, more than normal grid current should be indicated by the milliammeter which is inserted in the jack for the control-grid current of the power amplifier.

3. With the preceding stages of the transmitter aligned as in (2). above, and the coupling to the antenna reduced to the minimum, the plate and screen voltages to the power amplifier can be restored.

As soon as the power is applied to the transmitter, by operating the press-to-talk switch, the plate tank of the power amplifier must be adjusted for minimum cathode current. Following this, the antenna must be resonated as indicated by a maximum rise in cathode current. If little or no effect can be noted on the cathode current, it will be necessary to increase the antenna coupling slightly. When tuning the antenna results in a noticeable peak in cathode current, the cathode current and the grid current should be noted and the tube manual consulted. If the cathode current and the grid current are as specified by the tube manual, then the power amplifier will be delivering its maximum output power.

It should be borne in mind that the cathode current is the sum of the control grid, screen and plate currents. The control grid current can be measured independently by means of the jack in the grid circuit. If the applied screen and plate voltages are known, the screen current can be estimated from the information in the tube manual.

The plate current can also be estimated with a fair amount of accuracy.

If the currents thus obtained are not sufficient, according to the tube manual, the coupling to the antenna should be increased in small increments until the desired screen and plate currents are realized without excessive grid current. After each change of coupling it will be necessary to retune the plate tank of the power amplifier to resonance as indicated by minimum cathode current. If it quite often advisable to check the tuning of the doubler driver at the same time.

4. Since the input power to the power amplifier is the product of its plate current and its applied plate voltage, it is necessary to measure these quantities. The cathode current and the grid current can be measured with the aid of the milliammeter. If the applied screen and plate potentials are not given in the instruction manual they can be measured with the aid of the VTVM. From a tube manual, the screen current can be estimated and it and the grid current subtracted from the cathode current, leaving the amount of plate current. Since the screen current is usually only a small fraction of the plate current, this will make the plate current known to a fair degree of accuracy. If greater accuracy is desired and the screen voltage is obtained across a series dropping resistor of known value, the voltage drop across the resistor can be measured with the VTVM and the screen current determined by Ohm's law.

The power input to the stage can then be found by multiplying the plate current by the applied plate potential.

5. Self-oscillation of the power amplifier can be detected by removing the tube in the tripler and noting the effect on the grid and cathode currents in the power amplifier. If sufficient fixed bias is used in the power amplifier to cut off the plate and screen currents in the absence of excitation, removal of the tripler tube should result in such currents being zero. If the stage is oscillating, plate and screen currents will continue to flow in the absence of excitation.

If the power amplifier is a triode, neutralizing arrangements exist. To rid the stage of self-oscillation, the neutralizing adjustments must be performed. The exact nature of such adjustments will depend on just what type of neutralizing facilities are provided.

If the stage uses a pentode or beam power tube, conditions sometimes will cause self-oscillation. Usually, insufficient loading is the cause and increasing the loading on the stage by closer coupling to the antenna will make the circuit behave more normally.

Grid and plate currents should rise and fall smoothly as the plate circuit is tuned through resonance. Erratic behavior of these currents indicate at least a tendency toward self-oscillation.

6. Using the available frequency meter with its accuracy of plus or minus 0.0002 percent, it will be necessary to subtract this accuracy from the tolerance of plus or minus 0.0005 percent to be absolutely certain the transmitter frequency is within tolerance. Under these conditions, multiplying the carrier frequency of 155.460 MHz by plus or minus 0.0003% gives an allowable variation in frequency, as read on the meter of plus or minus 0.0004664 MHz. The maximum frequency would be 155.4604664 MHz and the minimum 155.4595336 MHz, as read on the frequency meter.

7. It is assumed, further, that the detector of the frequency meter is also tunable only over the range of 20–40 MHz. If this is so, then the meter input should be coupled to the plate coil of the transmitter's tripler and the detector (oscillating) adjusted to zero beat with the tripler's output. The detector is then adjusted to pick up the 38th harmonic of the meter's 1 MHz crystal and the detector's dial calibration adjusted to agree with this. The detector dial should then be varied to pick up the 39th harmonic and the calibration checked at this point. Returning to the frequency of the tripler output, the carrier may be read directly from the detector dial if so calibrated or interpolated if the dial is linearly divided. The frequency of the transmitter, in this case, will be four times

the frequency of the tripler output (38.865 × 4, or 155.460 MHz).

If a receiver is employed, the unmodulated transmitter is tuned in and the frequency meter's oscillating detector RF output is also coupled to the receiver. After checking the meter's calibration as described above, the detector is adjusted so its fourth harmonic is heard in the receiver at zero beat with the transmitter. The transmitter frequency, then is four times the reading as obtained in the meter's detector dial.

8. Since this is an FM transmitter, the amount of deviation produced is dependent only on the amplitude of the modulating signal and is independent of the modulating frequency. It is assumed that whistling into the microphone produces a louder signal than when speaking in a low voice and therefore the frequency deviation should be greater when whistling.

9. The *modulation control* that is shown in Figure 3.176 is used to adjust the output of the limiter stage. This control should be adjusted so that when a very loud talker is speaking into the microphone, the FM modulation meter indicates the maximum allowable frequency deviation. Assurance is then had that this deviation will not be exceeded no matter which person uses the transmitter. Care should be taken to note that when the limiter output is being *reduced* the deviation also becomes less. This makes certain that the limiter is actually limiting the maximum level of speech.

The original determination of the fault, can be made with the FM modulation meter.

Q. 3.177. Draw a schematic diagram of each of the following stages of a superheterodyne FM receiver. Explain the principles of operation. Label adjacent stages.

1. Mixer with injected oscillator frequency.
2. IF amplifier.
3. Limiter.
4. Discriminator.
5. Differential squelch circuit.

A.

1. For schematic of the mixer, see Figure 3.177(a). This circuit is frequently referred to as a "mixer-oscillator" circuit. It uses one special type tube to perform the functions of both mixer and oscillator. The oscillator section of the tube is a triode, consisting of the control grid, cathode and screen grid. The converter section is a pentode made up of the special injector grid, cathode-screen grid, suppressor grid and plate. In this type of circuit, both the control grid (oscillator voltage) and injector grid (RF voltage) signals are mixed electronically. Both of these signals modulate the electron stream going from cathode to plate. Since the tube is operated in a non-linear fashion, heterodyning of the two frequencies results and the desired IF frequency of 10.7 megahertz is selected by the tuned circuit in the converter plate.

2. For schematic of the IF amplifier, see Figure 3.177(b). This is a Class A amplifier with double-tuned plate and grid circuits resonated to the center IF of 10.7 megahertz. The bandwidth of the IF of a broadcast FM receiver will be on the order

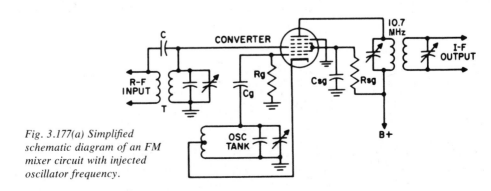

Fig. 3.177(a) Simplified schematic diagram of an FM mixer circuit with injected oscillator frequency.

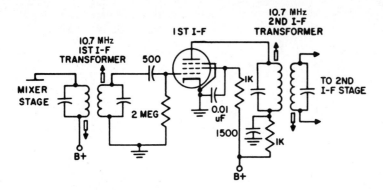

Fig. 3.177(b) Simplified schematic diagram of a first IF amplifier stage for an FM radio.

of 150 to 200 megahertz in order to pass the required modulation sidebands. Grid bias is provided by the 2 megohm resistor which produces a space-charge bias in the order of 0.5 to 1.0 volt.

3. For the schematic of a limiter, see figure, Fig. 3.177(c).

The purpose of a limiter stage is to remove the amplitude variations from the intermediate frequency signal before it is detected in the discriminator. Since most noises are amplitude modulated, they can be removed by a special IF amplifier called a limiter stage, whose output amplitude is relatively independent of input amplitude for most operating conditions. A limiter tube is easily saturated and driven below cut-off by a certain minimum value of grid swing (about .5 to 2 volts).

The limiter tube must be of the sharp cut-off type and operate with low plate and screen grid voltages in the order of 50 to 75 volts. Bias for this stage is obtained by a grid leak and capacitor network in the grid circuit. Some receivers use two limiters in

cascade to improve the sensitivity of limiting action. In this case the first limiter is grid leak biased, and the second usually operates at zero bias.

4. For the schematic of a discriminator, see Fig. 3.177(d1)

A discriminator in an FM receiver is the circuit which changes the variations in frequency of the FM wave into a conventional audio output wave which is capable of being amplified by a standard audio amplifier. The discriminator has the same relative function in an FM receiver as the second detector of a superheterodyne AM receiver. In order to detect an FM wave it is necessary to utilize a device whose dc output voltage increases when the carrier deviates in one direction and decreases when the carrier deviates in the other direction. An FM wave from a broadcast station deviates in exact accordance with the audio modulating signal, so that the variations of dc from the output of the discriminator will be a reproduction of the original modulating signal. The conventional type of discriminator does not reject

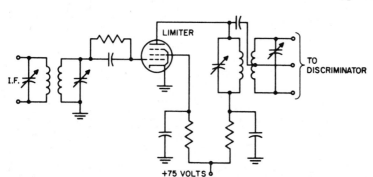

Fig. 3.177(c). A limiter stage in an FM receiver.

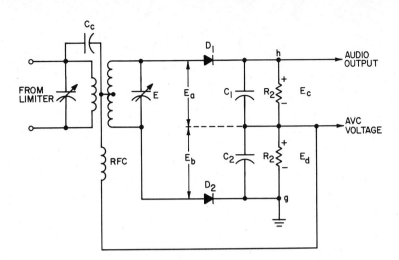

Fig. 3.177(d1). Basic circuit of the Foster-Seeley discriminator. In practice, point g is usually grounded. The audio output appears at point h and AVC or tuning eye voltage can be obtained from the center tap of the resistors. (See text for explanation of the voltage symbols.)

AM and must be preceded by one or more limiter stages for noise suppression. (See also Q. 3.223.)

To make the operation of a discriminator clear, it is necessary to review the simple relations among currents and voltages in a double-tuned IF coil, such as that shown in Fig. 3.177(d2), when both circuits are tuned to resonance. The following fundamental facts apply:

a. The resonant condition causes only resistance, and no reactance, to be reflected into the primary. The primary current I_1 will, therefore, be in phase with the primary voltage V_1.

b. The voltage across the secondary, V_2, is produced by means of a mutual reactance, M, which results from the coupling between the coils.

c. Since this mutual inductance is a reactance, *the secondary voltage V_2 is 90° out of phase with the primary voltage V_1.*

d. The secondary current, I_2, is in phase

with the secondary voltage V_2, because of the resonant condition. *The secondary current is, therefore, also 90° out of phase with V_1.*

Now suppose the secondary is center-tapped as shown in Fig. 3.177(d3). If the center point is considered as a reference, we now have a balanced circuit, that is, the voltage across the upper half is 180° out of phase with that across the lower half. Notice that with respect to the center point, V_x and V_y are equal but opposite in phase.

Now consider what happens when the frequency of V_1 changes. Suppose the frequency suddenly becomes *higher*. Since we are now off resonance in the secondary, the parallel resonant circuit becomes capacitive, causing the secondary voltage to lag behind the secondary current. This means that V_x is less than 90° away from V_1, and V_y is more than 90° from V_1. Although these phase changes have taken place, the magnitudes of V_x and V_y are substantially the same as

Fig. 3.177(d2). A diagram of a double-tuned IF coil showing currents and voltages discussed in the text.

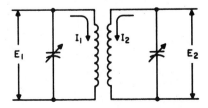

Fig. 3.177(d3). Schematic of an IF coil with a center-tapped secondary winding such as used with Foster-Seeley and ratio discriminators.

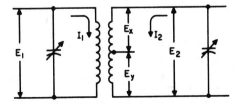

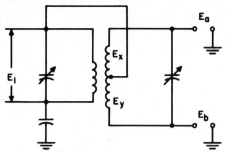

Fig. 3.177(d4). Showing how two voltages V_a and V_b are produced for application to the plates of the diodes. V_a and V_b vary in magnitude as the frequency of the input changes.

in the resonant case. If the frequency changes to lower than resonance, the situation will be reversed as far as phase is concerned. V_x will now have a phase angle of more than $90°$ while V_1 and V_y will have an angle less than $90°$.

To summarize:

a. With a signal at the resonant frequency (normally 10.7 MHz), V_x and V_y are equal and opposite, each being out of phase $90°$ with V_1 but in opposite directions.

b. When the signal gets higher than resonance, V_x and V_y are the same in magnitude, but with respect to V_1, the phase of V_x is less than $90°$, that of V_y is more than $90°$.

c. With a signal lower than resonance magnitudes are still the same, but V_x's phase is more than $90°$ while V_y's is now less than $90°$.

Now suppose we arrange the circuit as shown in Fig. 3.177(d4). The bottom of the primary coil has been grounded, and the top has been connected to the center tap of the secondary. Let us now investigate the voltage at the ends of the secondary with respect to ground. These voltages are labeled V_a and V_b. By tracing the circuit from the low side of the primary through the coil and then through one half of the secondary, it can be seen that at any given instant: $v_1 + v_x = v_a$ and $v_1 + v_y = v_b$. At resonance, when V_x and V_y are each $90°$ from V_1, V_a and V_b are equal. Under off-resonance conditions, however, the changed phase relations will cause one to be larger than the other. To clarify this, refer to Fig. 3.177(d5).

In Fig. (a) of Fig. 3.177(d5) two voltages, V_m and V_n, are plotted. They are equal in magnitude, but *less* than $90°$ apart in phase. In part (b) of Fig. 3.177(d5) the same two voltages are plotted *more* than $90°$ apart. In each case, the voltages are added, and the sum represented by the dotted line. These diagrams show that when the phase is *less* than $90°$, the sum is larger than when the phase is greater than $90°$.

The same principle applies in Fig. 3.177(d4). When the frequency is higher than resonance, the phase angle between V_1 and V_x is greater than that between V_1 and V_y. V_a, the sum of V_1 and V_x, is, therefore, greater than V_b, the sum of V_1 and V_y. When the frequency is lower than resonance, the opposite is true and V_a is less than V_b.

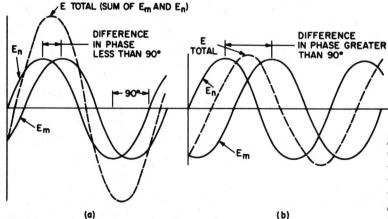

Fig. 3.177(d5). Graphs of sine waves showing how two ac voltages can produce a sum voltage whose amplitude varies with a change of phase between them.

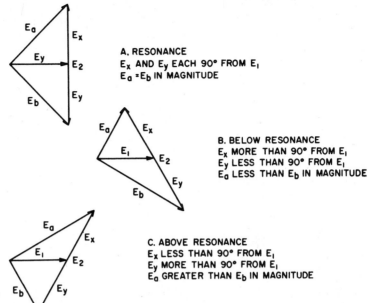

A. RESONANCE
E_x AND E_y EACH 90° FROM E_1
$E_a = E_b$ IN MAGNITUDE

B. BELOW RESONANCE
E_x MORE THAN 90° FROM E_1
E_y LESS THAN 90° FROM E_1
E_a LESS THAN E_b IN MAGNITUDE

C. ABOVE RESONANCE
E_x LESS THAN 90° FROM E_1
E_y MORE THAN 90° FROM E_1
E_a GREATER THAN E_b IN MAGNITUDE

Fig. 3.177(d6). Vector relations in the Foster-Seeley and ratio discriminators.

Another way to explain the above relations is by the use of vectors. Fig. 3.177(d6) shows a vector diagram for each of the three important conditions described above. Notice V_a and V_b are made larger and smaller according to the phase of the secondary voltage.

In Fig. 3.177(d1) we have applied the voltages V_a and V_b, which are ac, to diodes V_1 and V_2, and the circuit is a Foster-Seeley discriminator. These ac voltages are rectified and filtered and produce the vc voltage V_c and V_d. These vc voltages are proportional to V_a and V_b, respectively, and have the polarities indicated on the diagram.

Now the discriminator output is the voltage between points g and h. Since V_c and V_d oppose each other, the total voltage is equal to the difference in magnitude and will have the polarity of the larger voltage. At resonance these voltages are equal and the total voltage (g to h) is zero. At a frequency higher than resonance, V_c is larger than V_d. The total output voltage will then be V_c minus V_d with h positive and g negative. When the frequency is lower than resonance, the polarity of the output will be reversed, and the voltage will be V_d minus V_c.

Thus, when the IF changes above and below the resonant frequency, the discriminator output will vary in magnitude in the same way. This circuit is known as the Foster-Seeley type of discriminator.

Fig. 3.177(d7) shows the characteristic typical of a good discriminator. The curve of amplitude versus frequency should remain straight (linear) for all frequencies within the deviation range.

5. For schematic of a differential squelch circuit, see Fig. 3.177(e). In the absence of a receiver-input signal, considerable noise may be amplified and heard in the speaker causing an annoying condition. With

Fig. 3.177(d7). Typical discriminator characteristic.

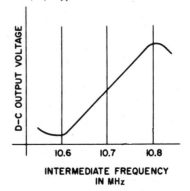

D-C OUTPUT VOLTAGE

10.6 10.7 10.8

INTERMEDIATE FREQUENCY
IN MHz

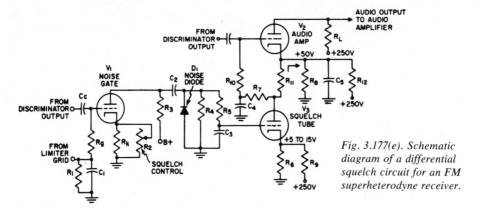

Fig. 3.177(e). Schematic diagram of a differential squelch circuit for an FM superheterodyne receiver.

a certain minimum signal level being received, the FM receiver will achieve *quieting* and only the signal will be heard. By utilizing a squelch circuit, the no-signal "noise" is prevented from being amplified. Further, a squelch control is provided to prevent weak signals from being squelched. This control is R2 in Fig. 3.177(e). In the absence of signal, the control is normally set so that the noise is barely squelched. Weak signals can then be received. However, signals in the noise level may be lost and it is sometimes desirable to operate with no squelch.

In the absence of signal, noise is amplified by the noise gate. The setting of R2 and the lack of limiter grid bias applied to R1 permits V1 to amplify normally. The amplified noise is rectified by noise diode D1 and integrated by capacitor C3. The resultant, a positive dc voltage is applied to the grid of squelch amplifier V3, causing V3 to conduct at its maximum rate. Squelch-tube current through R11, in the cathode of V2, causes V2 to be cut off and no noise output results. When a limiting signal is received, the limiter bias cuts off VI. (Capacitor C_c in the grid of V1 is very small and normally will only pass the high-frequency noise impulses.) Further, a limiting signal prevents (from the limiter or ratio detector operation) noise from appearing at V1. Under this condition, the voltage across C3 drops to zero and V3 is cut off by the fixed cathode bias across R6. With the squelch tube cut off, V2 operates normally and amplifies its audio input.

D. See Q. 3.178.

Q. 3.178. Draw a diagram of a ratio detector and explain its operation.

A. For the schematic of a ratio detector see Fig. 3.178(a). The ratio detector operation is similar to that of the discriminator (Q. 3.177(d)). However, whereas the conventional (Foster-Seeley) discriminator responds to amplitude variations and must therefore be preceded by one or more limiter stages if noise rejection is to be achieved, the ratio detector being very insensitive to amplitude variations does not require a limiter in its input circuit. The ratio detector derives its name from the fact that its output is proportional only to the ratio of the input IF voltages and not to their amplitude.

Note in Fig. 3.178(a) that the major circuit differences from a conventional discriminator are:

1. The two diodes are connected in series.

2. The addition of large capacitor C_3, which provides, in conjunction with its parallel resistors, a long time constant to maintain a relatively fixed dc voltage.

See discussion for details of the operation of this circuit.

D. A detailed operation of a ratio detector follows. Refer to the diagrams of Fig. 3.178(a) and (b).

When the FM wave is at the center or resting frequency, the potentials applied to both diodes are equal. When the FM wave deviates above resonance (10.775 MHz), V_{d1}

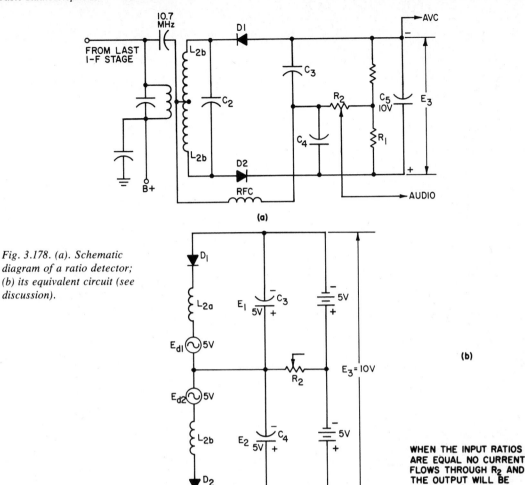

Fig. 3.178. (a). Schematic diagram of a ratio detector; (b) its equivalent circuit (see discussion).

WHEN THE INPUT RATIOS ARE EQUAL NO CURRENT FLOWS THROUGH R_2 AND THE OUTPUT WILL BE ZERO.

is greater than V_{d2} by some ratio, say 12 volts to 8 volts. When the FM wave deviates below resonance (10.625 MHz) V_{d1} will be less than V_{d2} by a ratio of 8 volts to 12 volts. Thus, except at resonance, there always exists some ratio between the voltages applied to the two diodes. A detector whose output is made proportional only to this ratio (which is changing at an audio rate), becomes independent of amplitude variations and does its own limiting. Such a device is the *ratio detector*. An equivalent circuit, Fig. 3.178(b), will simplify the discussion. The RC network R_1C_5 is connected in series with the two diodes, the direction of electron flow being such that the top of C_5 will be negative, and the bottom positive. The time constant of

R_1C_5 is quite long, about 0.2 second, so that its potential remains relatively fixed even for the lowest frequency audio variations. Actually the charge in C_5 is a function of the average carrier strength. This potential is shown as a battery of 10 volts magnitude and tapped at the center.

To this center point is connected one end of the volume control R_2. The other end of the volume control is connected to the junction of C_2 and C_4. While a fixed potential of 10 volts is used at this time, it must be remembered that this potential may vary slowly with changes in the average carrier strength. L_2 is shown in two sections with generators V_{d1} and V_{d2} representing the induced voltages for any given deviation of the FM wave. The conditions which must be present in this circuit are as follows:

First, the ratio of V_{d1} and V_{d2} must equal the ratio V_1 to V_2:

$$\frac{V_{d1}}{V_{d2}} = \frac{V_1}{V_2}$$

Secondly; the sum of V_1 and V_2 must always equal the charge in C_5, which is V_3: $V_1 + V_2 = V_3$.

Assume that

$$\frac{V_{d1}}{V_{d2}} = \frac{5}{5}$$

If no drop exists in the diodes, then

$$\frac{V_1}{V_2} = \frac{5}{5}$$

and no current can flow through R_2. Thus at the resting frequency of the f-m wave, the dc output will be zero.

Going above resonance now, assume that:

$$\frac{V_{d1}}{V_{d2}} = \frac{8}{2} = \frac{V_1}{V_2}$$

Under this condition current will flow through R_2, and the drop across R_2 will be 3 volts and positive at the junction of C_3 and C_4, thus producing the positive half of the audio cycle.

Deviating below resonance:

$$\frac{V_{d1}}{V_{d2}} = \frac{2}{8} = \frac{V_1}{V_2}$$

Current will now flow in the reverse direction through R_2 producing the negative half of the audio cycle.

In the rejection of amplitude modulation, the action is as follows. Suppose that a sharp increase in the carrier amplitude caused the ratio of

$$\frac{V_{d1}}{V_{d2}} \text{ to become } \frac{16}{4}$$

The ratio obviously remains the same but the amplitude has doubled. However, $V_1 - V_2$ remains fixed as determined by V_3, and the amplitude change cannot take place. V_3 *tends* to get higher, but the time constant of

R_1C_5 is made so large that noise pulses or amplitude modulations are too rapid to change this voltage. If the carrier level should suddenly drop, the potential V_3 would still be maintained and this drop would not appear in the output.

Since the potential across C_5 varies with the average carrier strength, it serves as an excellent source of AVC voltage.

An important advantage is the fact that there is no "threshold" effect in the ratio detector; that is, there is no minimum carrier level necessary to cause noise attenuation as with limiter circuits.

Q. 3.179. Explain how spurious signals can be received or created in a receiver. How could this be reduced in sets having sealed untunable filters?

A.
1. Spurious signals may be received from channels adjacent to the desired one due to inadequate receiver selectivity.

2. Spurious signals may be created in a receiver by regenerating or oscillating IF amplifiers. They may also be generated by the two local oscillators, mulipliers and mixers which may create numerous harmonic and heterodyne frequencies. (See Q. 3.180 below, for block diagram of a typical FM communications receiver.)

3. By the use of a sealed, untunable filter it is possible to achieve an important improvement in the selectivity of the receiver and to reject many of the undesired frequencies.

D. The sealed filter is usually placed at the input to the low-frequency IF amplifier. It has a response which is essentially flat over the necessary IF bandwidth and which drops off very steeply (skirts) on both sides. Actually, the sealed filter establishes the IF bandpass. The filters are sealed to avoid change due to atmospheric conditions and are designed to be relatively impervious to changes in their associated stages.

Two general classifications of radio-receiver interference and possible cures for each type are described below.

1. Interference due to static noises. The following methods may be employed to reduce the effect upon the receiver of such noises:

a. Insertion of a power line filter in series with the receiver supply cord close to the outlet.

b. Electrostatic shielding between primary and secondary windings in the power transformer.

c. Suitable filtering applied to the source of such noises whenever possible. (Motors, neon lights, etc.)

d. Use of horizontally polarized antennas if possible.

e. Use of shielded or well-balanced transmission lines.

f. Use of suitable noise limiters in receiver.

g. Use of crystal filter in receiver, if possible.

h. Use of highly directional antennas, if practical.

i. Complete shielding of entire receiver.

2. Interference due to undesired carrier waves. The following methods may be employed to reduce this type of interference:

a. Use of series or parallel resonant wave trap in antenna circuit.

b. Use of parallel resonant wave trap in cathode of first stage of receiver, and, if necessary, in some succeeding stages also.

c. Use of tuned RF amplifier ahead of mixer stage.

d. Use of highly directional antennas if practical.

e. Complete shielding of receiver.

Q. 3.180. Describe, step-by-step, a proper procedure for aligning an FM double conversion superheterodyne receiver.

A. A double-conversion (or double-superheterodyne) receiver is used to eliminate image interference (see Q. 3.155, Q. 3.156) from stations operating within a particular band, and to provide good adjacent channel rejection. For an FM broadcast receiver (88-108 MHz) the usual IF is 10.7 MHz. With this IF, no FM broadcast image interference is possible. Therefore, it will be assumed that the FM receiver referred to in this question is not an FM broadcast receiver, but is a VHF communications-type receiver capable of operating on one or more frequency channels. A block diagram of such a VHF receiver is given in Fig. 3.180. This is a single channel receiver, as shown, utilizing two crystal oscillators. Additional channels might be received on such a receiver by the switching of additional crystals. An input of RF signal of 160 MHz is assumed. It is also assumed that the *high* IF is 9 megahertz and the *low* IF is 460 kilohertz. The exact frequencies chosen are typical, but not critical, as the alignment procedure applies equally well to other frequencies.

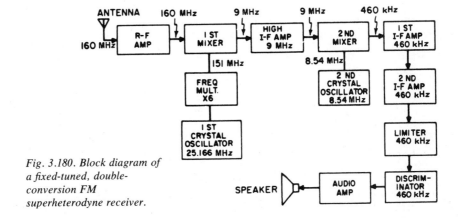

Fig. 3.180. Block diagram of a fixed-tuned, double-conversion FM superheterodyne receiver.

The equipment used for the alignment will be a properly calibrated CW signal generator and a zero-center VTVM. The alignment will be performed in steps beginning with the discriminator detector (not ratio detector).

1. Alignment of the Discriminator: Connect the zero-center VTVM between the junction of the two series-output resistors and ground. Connect the signal generator output through a small capacitor to the grid of the limiter stage and ground. Set the signal generator to 460 kilohertz. The VTVM should be set to a low scale and the generator output control adjusted to give a useful meter reading. Adjust the primary of the discriminator transformer for maximum deflection of the VTVM, reducing signal-generator output if necessary. Do not change the generator connections, but move the *hot* VTVM lead to the top of the two series-output resistors. Now, tune the discriminator secondary for a zero indication (center) between two peaks (one positive and one negative). Check the output linearity by tuning the generator equal increments on both sides of the center frequency. Equal, but opposite polarities, of voltage should occur. If this is not the case, touch up the primary adjustment to bring it about. This completes the discriminator alignment.

Note: As in most alignment procedures, use the minimum possible signal-generator output.

2. Alignment of the Limiter: Connect the VTVM between the grid of the limiter and ground. Set the meter to read a low negative voltage. Connect the signal generator (through a small capacitor) tuned to 460 kHz (unmodulated), between the grid and ground of the last IF stage preceding the mixer. The signal generator output should be the minimum possible to obtain a meter reading, in order to prevent limiter saturation which would cause broad tuning. (Maintain this low generator output throughout the entire alignment process, reducing it as nec-

essary when the circuits come into resonance.) Now tune the secondary of the last IF transformer for maximum meter deflection. Next, tune the primary in a similar manner.

3. Alignment of the IF's: (Two IF stages are present.) Maintain the meter in the limiter grid circuit. Move the signal generator (at 460 kHz) to the grid of the first IF stage (through a small capacitor). Peak first the secondary and then the primary of the IF transformer between the first and second IF stages. Next, without changing the meter position, move the signal generator (at 460 kHz) to the grid of the second mixer stage (through a small capacitor). The generator output may have to be increased at this point since the second mixer grid circuit is resonated at 9 megahertz (not 460 kHz). Peak the secondary and then the primary of the IF transformer between the second mixer and first IF stages.

4. Set the signal generator to 160 megahertz and connect it to the antenna input of the RF amplifier through a small capacitor. Maintain the VTVM at the grid of the limiter. As before, use the lowest possible signal-generator output. The frequency multiplier adjustments will result in the highest amplitude 151-MHZ signal being applied to the first mixer. This in turn will cause a 9 megahertz output from the first mixer and a 460 kilohertz output from the second mixer. Therefore, peak the multiplier adjustments for maximum VTVM readings. Next, peak the adjustments at the input and output of the *high* IF amplifier. Following this, peak the adjustments at the input and output of the RF amplifier. This completes the alignment procedure.

In the event the receiver has several channels, obtained by crystal switching, the *front-end* alignment will be slightly different. In this event, the RF amplifier and first mixer will be somewhat broadbanded and tuned to the center of the channels. Selectivity will be provided by the IF amplifiers, as usual.

D. See also Q. 3.155 through Q. 3.161.

Q. 3.181. Discuss the cause and prevention of interference to radio receivers installed in motor vehicles.

A. Interference to radio receivers in motor vehicles comes primarily from the following sources:

1. Generator brush sparking.

2. Opening and closing of breaker points.

3. Spark gap between rotor and distributor contacts.

4. Spark gap in spark plugs.

5. Static charges built up in tires and tubes while vehicle is moving.

6. Incorrect gap settings of spark plugs and breaker points.

7. Momentary interference from switches, such as dome switch, ignition switch, and heater switch and rheostat.

8. Interference from the vibrating contact points of the voltage regulator.

D. Most modern vehicles are completely bonded and so this is usually not a problem for servicemen. It is not practical to shield the ignition wires in the ordinary type of motor vehicle, but this is generally unnecessary. The following methods may be employed to minimize interference:

1. Use a by-pass capacitor across the generator output. (Usually provided by vehicle manufacturer.)

2. Have breaker points and spark plugs cleaned and correctly gapped.

3. Use anti-static springs in hub of wheels, and conducting powder inside of tire tubes, or tubeless tires.

4. By-pass all switches and long connecting wires.

5. Shield antenna transmission line.

6. Locate antenna well away from ignition system.

7. Use suppressor resistors if necessary at all spark plugs and distributor rotor connection. Some plugs (such as "Auto-Lite") have built in suppressors.

8. A capacitor is normally across the distributor breaker points and will take care of interference at this point. The value is somewhat critical and should not be varied.

9. A large part of voltage-regulator interference comes from the vibrating voltage (F terminal) and current-coil (G terminal) contacts. The reverse current relay (B terminal) rarely operates and is generally not a source of important interference. Use of a bypass capacitor at the "B" terminal of the regulator will generally eliminate this type of interference when it does occur. A small series resistor and capacitor (10 ohms and 2 500 pF) from the "F" terminal of the regulator to ground will reduce interference from this point. The "G" terminal of the regulator connects to the armature of the generator which is generally bypassed. However, additional filtering (at the regulator) may have to be installed in the "G" line since the run of wire may act as a radiating antenna.

Note: The following added material numbered Q. 3.181-A1 through Q. 3.181-A10 contains information that may be required to pass the General Radiotelephone Operator's License examination. This added material, as well as the new material added to other sections, has been included to help acquaint students with the current state of the electronics art. It is felt that the added material contains subject matter that may also be required of students who have obtained a General Radiotelephone Operator's License and are seeking employment. Additionally, the added material contains valuable information for private technician certification.

Q. 3.181-A1. Draw a block diagram of an FM broadcast receiver (88 to 108 MHz) and explain its operation.

A. Compare with AM broadcast receiver (Q. 3.155). A basic block diagram of an FM broadcast receiver, with automatic frequency control, is shown in Fig. 3.181-A1.

This receiver is a superheterodyne with many similarities to the AM broadcast receiver of Fig. 3.155. The FM broadcast band

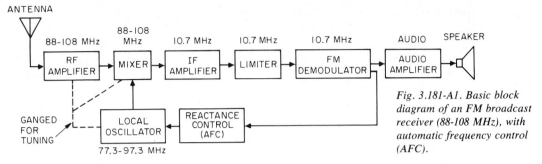

Fig. 3.181-A1. Basic block diagram of an FM broadcast receiver (88-108 MHz), with automatic frequency control (AFC).

extends from 88 to 108 MHz. Therefore, the RF amplifier and mixer must tune through this range. The IF is generally 10.7 MHz. To produce the IF, the oscillator (Q. 3.177(1)) tunes from 77.3 to 97.3 MHz. Note that these frequencies are *below* the RF frequencies. This is done to provide improved oscillator stability, which is more easily accomplished at lower frequencies.

One or more IF amplifiers tuned to 10.7 MHz, follow the mixer stage. For a broadcast FM receiver, an IF bandwidth of about 200 kHz is used. This will accommodate the transmitted bandwidth of 150 kHz in a fairly linear manner. Commercial and amateur FM receivers use a much narrower bandwidth IF strip. Typical IF bandwidths for these FM receivers range from 12 to 30 kHz. The greater selectivity is necessary to reduce adjacent channel interference on the crowded commercial and amateur channels.

The IF amplifier(s) may achieve the desired IF selectivity by using tuned over-coupled transformers (Q. 3.177(2)). These require correct alignment. An alternate method is to use crystal or ceramic IF filters. These do not require alignment and possess the necessary frequency and bandwidth.

A major advantage of the FM system is the reduction of received AM noise. This is accomplished by a limiter stage(s) tuned to 10.7 MHz or by a limiting FM demodulator. (An example of the latter is the three-transistor FM quadrature detector (Q. 3.181-A4). The limiter may consist of one or more transistor or tube stages (Q. 3.177(3)) or an IC limiter having as many as eight stages and high sensitivity. (See Q. 3.181-A3.)

Following the limiter (if not integral with the FM demodulator) is the FM demodulator stage. Two types of circuits frequently used are the Foster-Seeley discriminator (Q. 3.177(4)) and the ratio detector (Q. 3.178).

Many FM receivers incorporate an automatic frequency control (AFC) circuit. The AFC functions to maintain the local oscillator on the correct frequency regardless of minor mistuning or oscillator drift.

For a diagram and discussion of a differential squelch circuit for FM receivers, see Q. 3.177 (5). For tone-activated squelch circuit and discussion, see Q. 3.181-A7.

Q. 3.181-A2. Draw a schematic diagram of a two-stage transistor FM limiter. Briefly describe its operation.

A. The schematic diagram is shown in Fig. 3.181-A2.

Note that the first limiter stage Q_1 (PNP) has an applied forward bias of -1.3 V. This operates Q_1 close to saturation. Thus, low-level negative excursions of the IF signal (and noise) are removed by saturating the transistor. Positive signal excursions (and noise) will be limited only at moderate to high signal levels.

The signal polarities are inverted at the collector circuit of Q_1. The *limited* negative signal input is *positive* at the Q_1 collector. Also, the positive signal input to Q_1, which may have been partially limited or not at all (for very weak signals), will appear with *negative* polarity at the Q_1 collector.

Note that the signal polarities are again inverted at the secondary of IF transformer

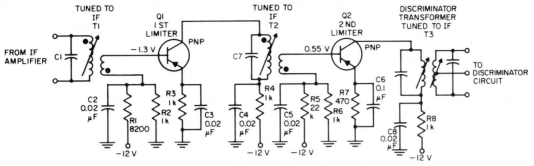

Fig. 3.181-A2. Simplified schematic diagram of a two-stage transistor FM limiter.

T_2. Now the limited original *negative* signal input excursion to Q_1 is again *negative* at the base of Q_2. The partially limited original *positive* signal input excursion to Q_1 is again positive at the base of Q_2.

The second limiter stage Q_2 has an applied forward bias of -0.55 V. This operates Q_2 close to cut-off. Thus the *limited* negative signal excursion at the base of Q_2 will drive it into greater conduction and to saturation if large enough. However, the partially limited positive signal at the base of Q_2, will drive it into cutoff, effectively limiting this portion of the signal.

As a result of the action of both limiter stages, effective limiting will occur, even for weak input signals, on both the positive and negative signal excursions.

Q. 3.181-A3. A schematic diagram of an integrated circuit (IC) FM limiter is shown in Figure 3.181-A3. Briefly describe its operations.

A. This FM limiter circuit utilizes a high-gain linear IC that contains eight active stages. The input from the IF amplifier is fed to terminal 1 of the IC. Several external parts are required. These are C_1, C_2, C_3, C_4, R_1, and discriminator transformer T_1. The limited IF signal leaves the IC at terminal 5 and is fed to the primary of T_1. The secondary of T_1 is connected to the discriminator circuit.

D. This type of FM limiter is superior in performance to either two-stage vacuum tubes or two-stage transistor limiters. The limiting threshold (knee) of this IC limiter is only about 100 uV, compared to about 1 V for a two-stage transistor limiter and about 2 to 3 V for a two-tube limiter.

Q. 3.181-A4. Explain the operation of a quadrature FM detector.

A.

1. A three-transistor quadrature FM detector is shown in Fig. 3.181-A4(1). An older version of this detector employs a single, special vacuum tube, such as a 6BN6 gated-beam tube or a somewhat more conventional pentode, the 6DT6. With either the transistors or a tube, the basic operating

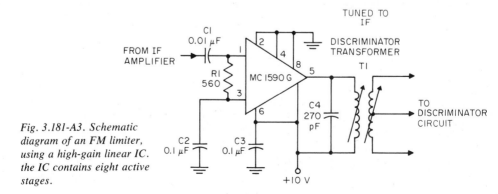

Fig. 3.181-A3. Schematic diagram of an FM limiter, using a high-gain linear IC. the IC contains eight active stages.

264 — *Element III*

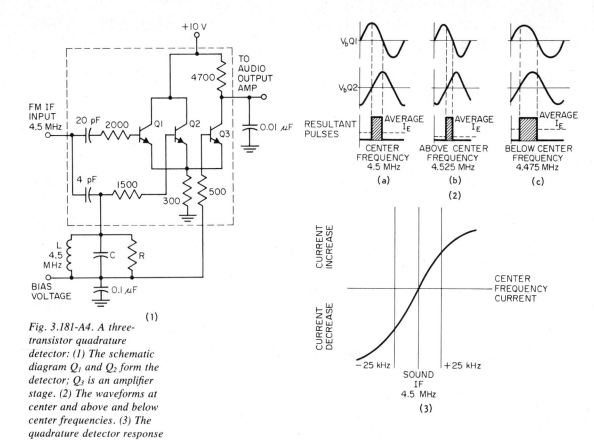

Fig. 3.181-A4. A three-transistor quadrature detector: (1) The schematic diagram Q_1 and Q_2 form the detector; Q_3 is an amplifier stage. (2) The waveforms at center and above and below center frequencies. (3) The quadrature detector response curve.

principle is the same. Since the three transistors in Fig. 3.181-A4(1) must be identical, they are usually part of an IC, which also may contain other transistors for such circuits as IF amplifiers or low-level audio amplifiers. This circuit performs the dual functions of limiter and FM discriminator.

Basically, the FM detector action is accomplished by transforming the frequency variations of the FM input wave into corresponding emitter-current variations. These emitter-current variations then represent the detected audio signal. The center FM frequency shown in Fig. 3.181-A4 is 4.5 MHz. This is the television receiver intercarrier-sound IF, here chosen because the quadrature detector is used by a number of television receiver manufacturers.

The FM detector operation is described with the aid of Fig. 3.181-A4(2). The 4.5

MHz FM IF signal is fed to the base of Q_1 in its original phase. This is V_bQ_1 in Fig. 3.181-A4(2). The 4.5 MHz signal is also fed to the base of Q_2, but it is shifted by 90° by the 4 pF capacitor. This is shown by V_bQ_2 in Fig. 3.181-A4(2). Both Q_1 and Q_2 are highly over-driven by the input signal so that their outputs are pulses that are combined at their emitters. (Q_1 and Q_2 are emitter followers.) When the FM IF wave is at its center frequency of 4.5 MHz, the condition is shown in part a of the figure. The conduction of both Q_1 and Q_2 can occur only when their input waves go above the reference line. Thus, at center frequency the output of Q_1 plus Q_2 is a series of pulses with the width as shown. (The amplitude remains constant for all pulse widths.) These pulses have a certain average current value, as shown.

Now observe the tuned circuit consisting of L, C, and R. At resonance (4.5 MHz), it does not produce any phase shift. However, for frequency changes from resonance (deviation), it does shift the phase of the signal fed to Q_2 linearly.

For frequencies above 4.5 MHz (Fig. 3.181-A4(2)), the phase of V_bQ_2 is caused to lag by *more* than 90°. Now, as shown, the pulse width is reduced and thus its average current value is *less* than in part (a).

For frequencies below 4.5 MHz (Fig. 3.181-A4(2)), the phase of V_bQ_2 is caused to lag by *less* than 90°. Now the pulse width is increased and its average current value is greater than in part (a).

From the foregoing, we see that the output of Q_1,Q_2 is an *average* current variation that follows the FM deviation. The rate of deviation is the original audio frequency. Although the individual pulses are at the 4.5 MHz frequency, these pulses after amplification in Q_3 are filtered by the 0.01 capacitor in the Q_3 output. Thus, the filtered output represents only an amplified audio wave. Q_3 is a grounded base amplifier, which acts as the first audio amplifier stage. Limiting action occurs, since both Q_1 and Q_2 are driven into saturation.

The discriminator response curve for the quadrature FM detector is shown in Fig. 3.181-A4(3)

D. See also Q. 3.177 and Q. 3.178.

Q. 3.181-A5. Explain the operation of a phase-locked loop (PLL) FM detector.

A. The basic operation of a phase-locked loop (PLL) is described in Q 3.192(U)-A28 and should first be reviewed. Fig. 3.181-A5(1) shows the block diagram of the PLL FM demodulator. (Note the similarity to the PLL in Fig. 3.192(U)-A28.) The FM IF from the last IF amplifier (or limiter) is one input to the phase comparator. This IF is generally at 10.7 MHz or 455 to 460 kHz (second IF for double conversion receivers, see Fig. 3.180).

The second input to the phase comparator is from the voltage-controlled oscillator (VCO). The free-running frequency of the VCO will be close to either 10.7 MHz or 455 to 460 kHz. The phase comparator compares the two input frequencies and generates an error voltage with a polarity and amplitude proportional to the difference between the two. The error voltage has the IF component removed by the low-pass filter and passes a relatively pure, dc error voltage to the dc error amplifier, an op amp.

The output of this op amp is fed in two directions. One output goes to the VCO to correct its frequency to be the same as the incoming FM IF signal. However, since the IF is frequency modulated, its frequency is constantly changing by an amount and rate

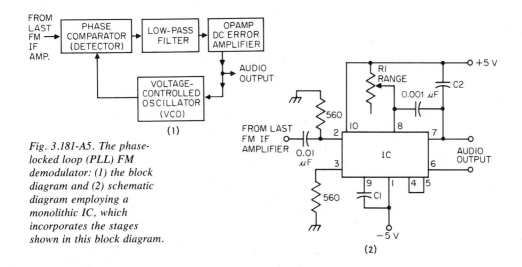

Fig. 3.181-A5. The phase-locked loop (PLL) FM demodulator: (1) the block diagram and (2) schematic diagram employing a monolithic IC, which incorporates the stages shown in this block diagram.

determined by the original audio modulation. Because of the functioning of the phase comparator, its error voltage is an exact copy of the original audio signal at the transmitter. Thus, the circuit functions as an FM detector and the audio output is taken from it as shown in Fig. 3.181-A5(1).

D. The schematic diagram of the PLL demodulator is shown in Fig. 3.181-A5(2). No transformers or tuned circuits are used. Except for the few components shown external to the monolithic IC, all the circuits of the block diagram are contained within the IC. The frequency of the VCO is adjusted approximately to 10.7 MHz or 455 to 460 kHz by R_1, which operates in conjunction with C_1. The VCO free-running frequency in hertz is

$$f_o = \frac{1.2}{4R_1C_1} \text{ Hz}$$

where

f_o = frequency in hertz
R_1 = approximately 5000 Ω
C_1 = value to obtain either 10.7 MHz, or 455 to 460 kHz

(See also Q. 3.192(U)-A28, Q. 3.177, Q. 3.178 and Q. 3.180.)

Q. 3.181-A6. With respect to FM reception, what is meant by capture effect?

A. *Capture effect* refers to the selection of the stronger of two FM signals of the same frequency. The weaker signal in this case is completely rejected.

D. The term "capture ratio" is applicable to the performance of FM tuners. Capture ratio is the ability of an FM tuner to reject the weaker of two stations on the same frequency. The lower the ratio (in dB) of the power of the desired and undesired signals, the better is the performance of the FM tuner. The best tuners have a capture ratio as low as 1 dB, but 4.5 dB is considered adequate.

Q. 3.181-A7. What is a Continuous-Tone Coded Squelch System (CTCSS)? How does CTCSS affect frequency deviation?

A.
1. The Continuous-Tone Coded Squelch System (CTCSS) is an automatic squelch system used in FM two-way radio communciations. In this system, the FM receiver sound is kept off until a specific coded transmission is received. The specific code consists of one of a series of sub-audible tone frequencies in the range of 67 to 192.8 Hz. (See Fig. 3.181-A7.)

2. The CTCSS tone produces an FM deviation of ±0.75 kHz. Since the maximum allowable deviation for FM, two-way radio is ±5.0 kHz, the maximum deviation allowed for speech in this system is ±4.25 kHz.

D. A number of sub-audible tone frequencies for CTCSS use have been designated by the EIA (Electronics Industries Association). Typical examples are 67 Hz, 103.5 Hz, 107.2 Hz, 110.9 Hz, 114.8 Hz, 118.8 Hz, 173.8 Hz, 179.9 Hz, 186.2 Hz, and 192.8 Hz.

The basic CTCSS system incorporates an encoder at the transmitter and decoder-squelch circuitry at the receiver. The specific sub-audible tone frequency is fed to the FM modulator together with the audio information. The combination of these two types of waves modulates the FM transmitter output.

At the FM receiver, the squelch circuitry cuts off the audio system, unless a signal is received that contains the specific sub-audible tone frequency. When the correct signal is received, it is accepted by the receiver's CTCSS decoder. This signal disables the squelch circuit and permits audio to be heard.

Note that the CTCSS system is known by other names, depending upon the manufacturer. Examples are, "private line" or "channel guard."

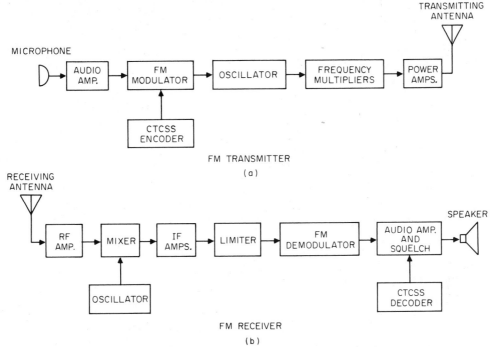

Fig. 3.181-A7. Block diagrams illllustrating the operation of the Continuous-Tone Coded Squelch System (CTCSS): (a) The CTCSS encoder output (a sub-audible tone frequency) is fed into the FM modulator together with the audio. (b) The CTCSS decoder keeps the squelch on (receiver off) until the proper tone modulation is received.

Q. 3.181-A8. What special problem is encountered when measuring the frequency of an FM carrier that contains a CTCSS tone, with a heterodyne frequency meter?

A. When measuring a carrier frequency with a heterodyne frequency meter, the variable frequency oscillator is adjusted to obtain a zero beat (see Q. 3.222) and the frequency is then read. However, if a CTCSS tone is frequency modulating the carrier, it will have a deviation of ±0.75 kHz. Under these conditions, the zero-beat will not be as sharp as indication, as if there were no carrier modulation. A method to determine the correct carrier frequency would be to adjust the variable frequency oscillator until only the CTCSS tone is heard. This will be in the center of *additional* heterodyne frequencies that will be heard on *both* sides of the carrier frequency.

D. Theoretically the CTCSS tone should be demodulated by an FM detector. However, the heterodyne frequency meter may not have an FM detector. In this case and because of the low deviation (±0.75 kHz), the meter's AM detector should serve to demodulate the FM wave. This is done by a process known as *slope detection*. Here the FM wave deviates along the non-linear response of the detector circuit and is transformed into an audio wave. (See also Q. 3.181-A7.)

Q. 3.181-A9. What is audio frequency shift keying (AFSK)?

A. AFSK is a type of radioteletype keying.

D. In AFSK the RF carrier is continuously transmitted. Keying pulses are formed by frequency shifted audio tone modulation.

Commonly used audio tones are 2.125 kHz for mark and 2.975 kHz for space. (See also Q. 3.175.)

Q. 3.181-A10. How can a varactor be used to generate direct FM in a crystal oscillator circuit?

A. A circuit used to generate direct FM (as opposed to phase modulation) is shown in Fig. 3.181-A10. The audio wave is impressed across the varactor (CR_1) and causes it to vary its capacitance. This in turn causes corresponding changes of frequency in the crystal oscillator. The output is thus an FM wave. L_1 is used to adjust the center frequency of the crystal oscillator.

D. Although the above circuit is classified as a direct FM generator, it also produces phase modulation. The reason is that only a relatively small deviation can be achieved by changing the frequency of a *cyrstal* oscillator. (See also Fig. 3.162(c), Q. 3.165, and Q. 3.176.)

DIODES, TRANSISTORS, AND DIGITAL PRINCIPLES, CIRCUITS, AND TEST EQUIPMENT

Q. 3.182 Describe the difference between positive (P-type) and negative (N-type) semiconductors with respect to:

1. The direction of current flow when an external emf is applied.

2. The internal resistance when an external emf is applied.

A.

1. As shown in Fig. 3.182(a), in P-type semiconductors, the major-current carriers are *holes* (positive charges). Hole current within the semiconductor moves from the end connected to the positive battery terminal to the end connected to the negative battery terminal. In N-type semiconductors, the majority current carriers are electrons. Electron current within the semiconductor moves from the end connected to the negative battery terminal to the end connected to the positive battery terminal. This is shown in Fig. 3.182(b)

2. In both the P- and N-types, the internal resistance may be considered to be low in the direction of the majority current carriers and high in the opposite direction.

D. The actual resistance of any semiconductor is primarily dependent upon the number of current carriers (holes or electrons) available within the material. The number of available carriers, in turn, depends upon the amount of impurities which have been added to the pure crystalline material (germanium or silicon). "Donor" materials, such as arsenic, phosphorus and antimony provide *excess electron carriers* for the crystal and classify the crystal as an "N" type. On the other hand, "acceptor" ma-

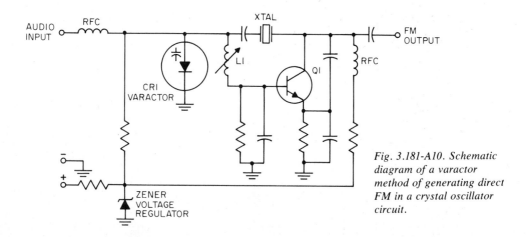

Fig. 3.181-A10. Schematic diagram of a varactor method of generating direct FM in a crystal oscillator circuit.

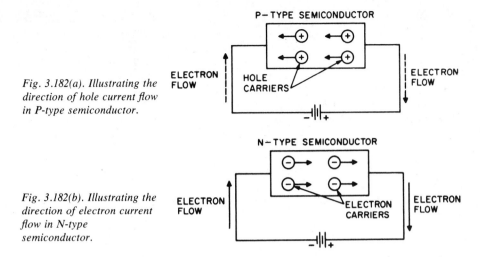

Fig. 3.182(a). Illustrating the direction of hole current flow in P-type semiconductor.

Fig. 3.182(b). Illustrating the direction of electron current flow in N-type semiconductor.

terials such as aluminum, gallium and indium cause "holes" to appear in the crystal and classify the crystal as a "P" type. Generally, a semiconductor which contains a higher degree of impurities than another semiconductor, will display a lower resistance in the direction of major carrier current flow. It is assumed that the same voltage is applied to the semiconductor in both cases.

Q. 3.183. What is the difference between forward and reverse biasing of transistors?

A.

1. When a transistor junction is *forward* biased, a continuous current flows through the junction due to the movement of the majority carriers through the P- and N-type material. (Holes in P-type and electrons in N-type constitute the majority carriers.) Fig. 3.183(a) illustrates forward biasing of the emitter-base junction and reverse biasing of the collector-base junction.

2. Reverse biasing of a transistor junction in effect prevents current from flowing in that junction. In practice a small current (in microamperes) will flow in the junction due to the movement of minority carriers. Minority carriers consist of a relatively small number of excess holes found in N-type crystals and a relatively small number of excess electrons in P-type crystals. It should

be noted that the conditions of forward and reverse biasing are normal operating conditions as shown in Fig. 3.183(a). This shows a PNP transistor. For an NPN transistor, both battery polarities would be reversed.

D. Forward and reverse biasing terminology may also be applied to the base-to-emitter bias of a transistor. In this case, forward biasing of a transistor means that the bias polarity from base-to-emitter is such as to permit relatively large current flow from the emitter to the collector.

Note: For a PNP-type the base is made negative with respect to the emitter. Opposite polarity bias is used for an NPN-type.

In this same general case, reverse bias

Fig. 3.183(a). Forward and reverse biasing of a junction transistor (PNP). Arrows indicate electron flow.

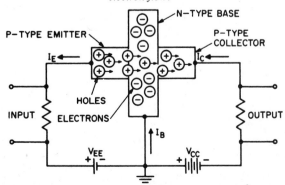

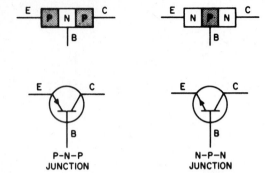

P-N-P JUNCTION   N-P-N JUNCTION

Fig. 3.183(b). The physical and symbolic representations of PNP and NPN junction transistors.

means that the base-to-emitter bias is such as to prevent emitter-to-collector current flow (except for leakage current).

Note: For a PNP-type the base is now made positive with respect to the emitter. Opposite polarity bias is used for an NPN-type.

The junction transistor is made with wafer-type construction, the complete transistor consisting of three wafers. The wafers may be arranged in positive-negative-positive sequence in the PNP type, or in negative-positive-negative sequence in the NPN type. The middle layer, or wafer of the junction transistor is called the base. On either side of the base are found the very much smaller emitter and collector wafers. The emitter corresponds to the cathode of a vacuum tube, the base to the control grid, and the collector, to the plate.

An enlarged cross-sectional view of a *PNP* junction transistor with grounded base circuit is shown in Figure 3.183(a). This view illustrates the internal operation of the unit. The *PNP* transistor utilizes "holes" (which may for simplicity be considered as positive charges) for conduction.

In the case of the *PNP* junction transistor, any voltage or current variations in the input (emitter) circuit cause corresponding variations in the number of holes in the base. Any variations in the supply of holes from the emitter can vary the number of holes traveling through the base and to the

collector element. It is found that any change in emitter current produces a substantially equal change in collector current; however, the emitter circuit has *low* impedance, while the collector circuit has *high* impedance. If the currents in the two circuits are substantially equal, it follows that the voltage (or power) variations in the collector circuit will be greater than the variations in the emitter circuit. It is by virtue of this effect that amplification is obtained in the *PNP* junction transistor.

Important characteristics of the junction transistor are: high power gain, low input power requirements and a low noise factor.

For the convenience of the reader, Fig. 3.183(b) shows the generalized physical structure and the corresponding schematic diagram for the junction *PNP* and the *NPN* transistors.

Q. 3.184. Show connections of external batteries, resistance load and signal source as would appear in a properly (fixed) biased, common-emitter transistor amplifier.

A. See Fig. 3.184(a). For an NPN transistor, the polarity of both batteries would be reversed.

D. In the simplified schematic shown (Fig. 3.184(a)), the signal input is applied between the base and emitter and the output is taken across R_L, which is connected between the collector-to-emitter circuit. As explained in Q. 3.183, the base-to-emitter junction is forward biased and the base-to-collector junction is reverse biased. The common-emitter transistor amplifier is similar in circuit arrangement to the conventional grounded cathode triode amplifier (see Q. 3.50(a)); an equivalent-tube circuit is shown in Fig. 3.184(b). Note in both the tube and transistor circuits, that a polarity reversal takes place between the input and output circuits. This polarity reversal would also occur for a common emitter NPN amplifier. (For a common base, or common collector amplifier, no polarity reversal occurs. This situation is similar to the grounded grid and cathode follower tube amplifiers.)

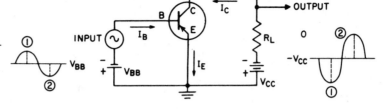

Fig. 3.184(a). Schematic diagram of a PNP common-emitter transistor amplifier using fixed bias batteries. Arrows indicate electron flow.

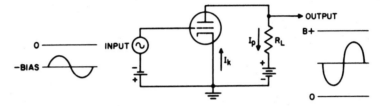

Fig. 3.184(b). Grounded cathode, triode-amplifier circuit. The common emitter amplifier (Fig. 3.184(a)) is similar.

The electron flow through a PNP common-emitter amplifier is shown by the arrows in Fig. 3.184(a). Consider the input signal going in the positive direction (point 1). This signal *opposes* the forward bias of the battery, thereby *decreasing* the total current (I_E) flowing through the emitter. The base and collector currents are now *decreased* by corresponding amounts. The decreased current in R_L will now permit the collector to become more negative (toward the negative battery potential). This effect is indicated at the output waveform by a corresponding point 1. (Note: the polarity is opposite that of the input.) Assume the input waveform to be going in the negative direction (point 2). The signal now *aids* the forward bias, *increasing* the emitter current. Corresponding increases take place in the base and collector currents. An increased current through R_L causes the collector to become less negative (more positive) which is again opposite in polarity to the input signal.

Q. 3.185. The following are excerpts from a transistor handbook describing the characteristics of a PNP alloy-type transistor as used in a common-emitter circuit configuration. Explain the significance of each item.

Maximum and Minimum Ratings:
1. **Collector-to-base voltage (emitter open)** .... **−40 max. volts**

2. **Collector-to-emitter voltage (Base-to-emitter volts = 0.5)** .... **−40 max. volts**
3. **Emitter-to-base voltage** **−0.5 max volts**
4. **Collector current** .... **−10 max. mA**
   Transistor Dissipation:
5. **At ambient temperature of 25°C for operation in free air** .... **120 max.mW**
6. **At case temperature of 25°C For operation with heat sink**.............. **140 max.mW**
7. **Ambient-temperature range: Operating and Storage** .... **−65° to + 100°C**

A.
1. Collector-to-Base Voltage: The maximum voltage which can be applied between these elements without danger of a breakdown of the collector-to-base junction.
2. Collector-to-Emitter Voltage: The maximum safe voltage which can be applied between collector and emitter (with a reverse bias of 0.5 volt between base and emitter), without breakdown occurring from collector-to-emitter.
3. Emitter-to-Base Voltage: The maximum safe forward-bias voltage, to limit emitter-to-collector current and base-to-emitter current.
4. Collector Current: The maximum

permissible collector current at which the transistor may be operated without adverse effects.

5. Transistor Dissipation in Free Air: The maximum safe thermal rating at which the transistor may be operated without a heat sink.

6. Transister Dissipation with Heat Sink: The maximum safe thermal rating at which the transistor may be operated with a heat sink.

7. Ambient-Temperature Range: The design limits for ambient temperature operation or storage of the transistor.

Q. 3.186. Draw a circuit diagram of a method of obtaining self-bias, with one battery, without current feedback, in a common-emitter amplifier. Explain the voltage drops in the resistors.

A. For the circuit diagram, see Fig. 3.186. The base-to-emitter bias (negative) is obtained by a voltage-divider scheme. Because of the dc base-to-emitter bias, emitter-to-collector current will flow through R3. Additional current flows through R3 and takes the path through R1 and the parallel combination of R2 and the base-to-emitter resistance. (Since the transistor is forward biased, current flows through the base-to-emitter junction, resulting in a low value of base-to-emitter resistance.) Because of this voltage divider action, the correct amount of base-to-emitter current is permitted to flow, thus establishing the desired forward bias. (Remember that a transistor is basically a current operated device and that we are interested in the forward bias *current,* rather than the forward bias voltage. However, these are obviously related and this current can also be established by the voltage appearing across the parallel combination of R2 and the base-to-emitter resistance.) The forward bias voltage, from base-to-emitter, has the required negative potential for a PNP transistor.

D. See Q. 3.184, Q. 3.187, and Q. 3.190(3).

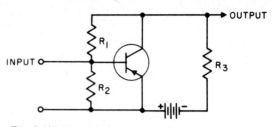

Fig. 3.186. Simplified schematic diagram of a PNP common-emitter amplifier using one battery and self bias.

Q. 3.187. Draw a circuit diagram of a common-emitter amplifier with emitter bias. Explain its operation.

A. For the circuit diagram, see Fig. 3.187(a). The input signal is applied across resistor R2 to the base-emitter circuit. Bias for the base-emitter circuit is the difference of two bias voltages. One is the voltage divider scheme described in Q. 3.186 above and the other is the drop across R3 (similar to a cathode resistor for a vacuum tube). R3 is introduced into the circuit for the purpose of bias stabilization. Reliable operation of a transistor over a wide range of temperatures, requires that the bias voltage and current remain stable. Variations of emitter-to-base junction resistance with temperature tend to cause bias changes unless external compensating circuits are used (such as R3).

Figure 3.187(b) shows the same common emitter amplifier as in Fig. 3.187(a), but modified to provide fixed emitter bias originating from an external source (V_{EE}). In Fig. 3.187(a), the drop across R3 is in opposition to the forward bias. However, in Fig. 3.187(b) an external source (V_{EE}) provides a forward bias ($+$) at the emitter. (This bias adds to the forward bias ($-$) applied to the base.) The bias at the emitter is determined by the voltage divider action of R3 and R5 in conjunction with V_{EE}. Actually, the emitter current I_E flows through R5 and tends to reduce the forward bias for the emitter. However, R3 and R5 can be easily adjusted to overcome this effect, based on the quiescent value of I_E. In addition, bias stabilization is provided by the fixed-bias

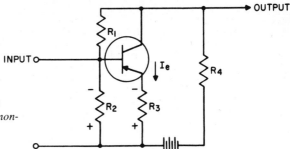

Fig. 3.187(a). Schematic diagram of a PNP common-emitter amplifier using emitter bias.

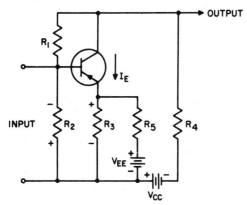

Fig. 3.187(b). The circuit of Fig. 3.187(a) modified to provide a fixed value of emitter bias from an external source. (V_{EE}).

supply and by the "swamping" resistor, as explained in the discussion. The use of an emitter resistor also tends to stabilize the quiescent collector current. Any tendency to increase collector (and emitter) current, causes a voltage drop in the emitter circuit which *reduces* the forward bias and tends to oppose such an increase. Conversely, a tendency to decrease collector current, reduces the drop in the emitter circuit and increases the forward bias. This tends to oppose the decrease of collector current. This emitter resistor function is applicable to the circuits of Fig. 3.187(a) and Fig. 3.187(b).

D. The emitter-base junction resistance has a negative temperature coefficient of resistance, which causes a bias variation with temperature changes. One method of reducing the effect of this type of bias variation is to place a large value of resistor in series with the emitter lead. This resistor is called a *swamping* resistor. It causes the variation of the emitter-base junction resistance to be a small percentage of the total resistance in the emitter circuit. This technique stabilizes the bias and provides collector current stability over a wide range of temperatures (for example, $-65°C$ to $+125°C$). For best results in this technique, the base-circuit resistance should be as near zero as possible. One method of accomplishing this is to use a low-resistance transformer input to the base.

Q. 3.188. Explain the usual relationship between collector-to-base voltage and the alpha-cutoff frequency of a common emitter transistor amplifier.

A. The alpha-cutoff frequency is only indirectly related to the collector-to-base voltage. (Refer to Q. 3.192(G) for an explanation of alpha-cutoff frequency.) This frequency is a function of the physical thickness of the base and increases as the base becomes thinner. As the base becomes thinner, the allowable base-to-collector voltage decreases. Thus it may be said that the alpha-cutoff frequency ordinarily increases as the permissible collector-to-base voltage decreases.

D. The alpha-cutoff frequency is the high frequency at which the current gain of the transistor decreases by 3 dB compared to its mid-frequency (flat) gain. The alpha-cutoff frequency is inversely proportional to the square of the base width and directly proportional to the minority carrier mobility. On this basis, NPN transistors are superior to PNP-types, because electrons have greater mobility than holes. To achieve the lowest base transit time, the base should be as thin as possible. However, this is limited by the permissible base-to-collector voltage. In transistor design, a tradeoff must be made between permissible base-to-collector voltage and the alpha-cutoff frequency.

Q. 3.189. Why is stabilization of a transistor amplifier usually necessary? How would a thermistor be used in this respect?

A.

1. Stabilization is usually necessary because transistor parameters, such as reverse-bias collector current and emitter-base junction resistance (see also Q. 3.187 above), vary with temperature. These cause changes in the transistor operating characteristics with respect to temperature. Specifically, emitter current increases with an increase of temperature.

2. A thermistor is used as part of a voltage divider in the emitter (or base) circuit. The thermistor causes the transistor bias to change with temperature, such that changes in collector current due to temperature variations, are cancelled by opposing changes in transistor bias.

D. The operation of the thermistor stabilization circuit is explained in detail with the aid of Fig. 3.189. Forward bias for the base is obtained by means of a voltage divider consisting of resistors R1 and R3. This voltage remains constant regardless of temperature variations. A reverse bias is applied

to the emitter through another voltage divider consisting of RT1 and R2. The thermistor used for this purpose has a negative-temperature characteristic. That is, its resistance decreases with an increase of temperature and increases with a decrease of temperature. Ordinarily (without stabilization), the collector current would tend to increase with an increase of temperature. This increase can be counteracted by increasing the reverse bias applied to the emitter through the voltage divider consisting of the thermistor and the emitter resistor. An increased temperature causes a decrease in resistance of the thermistor. This in turn raises the negative reverse bias applied to the emitter and decreases the net emitter forward bias. Consequently, the tendency of the collector current to increase is counteracted.

Q. 3.190. Draw simple schematic diagrams of the following transistor circuits and explain their principles of operation. Use only one voltage source: state typical component values for low power—10 MHz operation:

1. Colpitts-type oscillator
2. Class B push-pull amplifier
3. Common-emitter amplifier
4. A PNP transistor directly coupled to an NPN type.

A.

1. For the schematic of the Colpitts oscillator, see Fig. 3.190(a). For basic discussion and vacuum tube schematic, see Question 3.86(4). In the transistorized oscillator shown in the figure, positive feedback

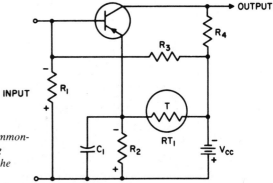

Fig. 3.189. Schematic diagram of a PNP common-emitter amplifier using thermistor control of the emitter bias.

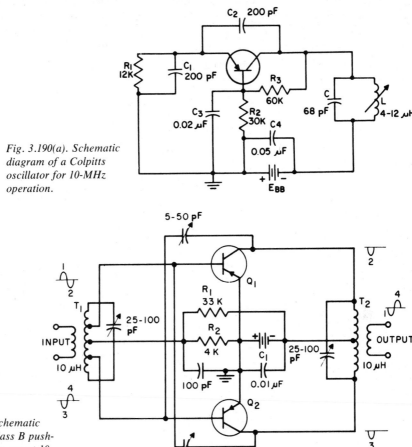

Fig. 3.190(a). Schematic diagram of a Colpitts oscillator for 10-MHz operation.

Fig. 3.190(b). Schematic diagram of a Class B push-pull amplifier for use at 10 MHz.

is provided by placing the resonant tank circuit (L-C) in parallel with the collector-to-base circuit. The circuit now becomes voltage, rather than current controlled. The feedback is taken from the junction of the two series capacitors, C1 and C2, which are effectively across the tank. R2 and C3 provide foward base bias and a degree of oscillator-amplitude stability.

2. The principle of a Class B push-pull transistor amplifier is basically the same as for this type of amplifier using vacuum tubes (see Q. 3.50(5) for a discussion of its principles). For a schematic of the transistor push-pull, Class B amplifier, see Fig. 3.190(b). Resistors R1 and R2 are proportioned so that both transistors are operated at the collector-current-cutoff point. Both transistors will amplify only the negative

portions of the applied base voltages. In this case, Q1 amplifies only the second half (2) of the sine wave and remains at cutoff during the first half (1). Q2 amplifies the first half (3) of the sine wave and is cut off during the second half (4). Note that the top and bottom of the output tank circuit receive voltage pulses of the same polarity (negative). However these occur a half cycle apart and so are correctly phased. The resulting tank circuit output is a complete sine wave, which is coupled to the succeeding circuit by means of the output portion of T2. Resonating the two transformers increases circuit efficiency and provides improved waveform (less distortion and harmonics) in the output.

The output transformer is designed to match the low-impedance input to the following transistor, from the output impedance

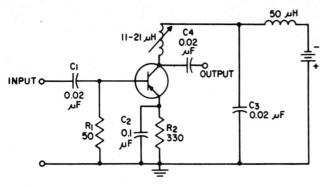

Fig. 3.190(c). Common-emitter amplifier with components for 10-MHz operation.

of the driving transistor. In general, the transistors used have a low value of input impedance. This prevents self-oscillation, due to feedback, from each collector to its associated base. (This is similar to plate-to-grid feedback in a vacuum-tube amplifier as explained in Q. 3.125 and Q. 3.128.) However, in the case of certain low-power transistors having higher values of input impedance, it may be necessary to employ "push-pull" neutralization, as is explained in Q. 3.125, part (3) of the discussion, and is illustrated for vacuum tubes in Fig. 3.125(e). In the circuit of Fig. 3.190(b) the same scheme is used, with each neutralizing capacitor connected from the collector of one transistor to the base of the other one.

3. For the schematic of a common emitter amplifier, see Fig. 3.190(c). For principles of operation, see Q. 3.186 and Q. 3.187 above.

4. For a schematic of a PNP transistor directly coupled to an NPN-type, see Fig. 3.190(d). This scheme operates by virtue of the fact that the polarity of an input signal necessary to increase the conduction of the

Fig. 3.190(d). A PNP transistor directly coupled to an NPN-type for 10-MHz operation.

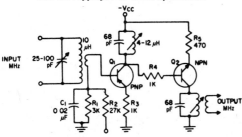

PNP-transistor is opposite to that required to increase the conduction of the NPN transistor. Since a signal polarity reversal occurs in Q1 from base to collector, this condition is satisfied. The proper bias for Q1 is established by the action of the voltage divider consisting of R1 and R2. The bias for Q2 is established by the collector current of Q1 flowing through the emitter to base circuit of Q2. The polarity of the base of Q2 is positive with respect to its emitter, thus providing forward base-to-emitter bias. Note that the collector current of Q2 is grounded for dc and the collector-to-base potential is actually applied in reverse polarity to the emitter of Q2. This is similar to a vacuum tube amplifier wherein the plate voltage is actually applied as a negative potential to the cathode.

Transistor bias stabilization is provided by resistor R3 for Q1 and by resistor R5 for Q2.

Q. 3.191. Discuss etched-wiring printed circuits with respect to the following:
 1. Determination of wiring breaks
 2. Excessive heating.
 3. Removal and installation of components.

A.
 1. Wiring breaks are determined by point-to-point continuity checking with an ohmmeter. (If voltage exists in the circuit involved, voltage tracing could be used with the aid of an ohmmeter. Signal tracing with an oscilloscope is sometimes desirable.)

Since there may be many common points permanently connected to the wire in question, a physical layout of the printed circuit board would be desirable to assist in locating the break. In many cases, the break can be repaired by soldering or by connecting an external wire across it.

2. Etched wiring printed circuit boards are constructed of various materials such as epoxy and mylar. The etched wiring is attached to the board with a cement or other bonding agent. Such boards are subject to damage caused by excessive heat. Such heat can cause distortion of the board, or stresses which may result in cracks, wire breaks, or lifting of the etched wire from the boards.

3. The components may be mounted on the boards by placing the component leads directly on a printed circuit finger and welding or soldering to the finger. Alternatively, the lead may be placed through a printed-circuit hole or eyelet. Generally, components are mounted only on one side of the board with their leads inserted into holes or eyelets. The other side of the board may then be dip soldered, or wave soldered, accomplishing all soldering in one operation. The leads of a defective component are usually removed with a small soldering iron. If the leads are welded, they are cut and the surface is cleaned in preparation for a new weld or for a solder repair. In removing transistors having three (or four leads) special attachments are available to a soldering iron so that all leads can be unsoldered simultaneously and the transistor pulled out of the board. Otherwise, one lead at a time can be unsoldered and the transistor gradually *rocked* out of the board.

Q. 3.192. What is a junction tetrode transistor? How does it differ from other transistors in base resistance and operating frequency?

A.

1. A tetrode transistor is one which is constructed in the same manner as a three-terminal PNP or NPN transistor except for the addition of an extra terminal to the base region, as shown in Fig. 3.192.

The normal emitter, base, and collector terminals are labeled (1), (2), and (3). The additional terminal to the base is labeled (4) and is supplied with a small negative voltage (0.4 V). The normal base terminal (2) is grounded as shown.

2. The base resistance is substantially lower than in a three-terminal transistor and the operating frequency is increased considerably.

D. As shown in the figure, the voltage in all portions of the emitter and collector is constant. However, because the base is supplied with 0.4 volt at the top and is grounded at the bottom, a voltage gradient appears from top to bottom of 0.4 to 0 volts. As discussed in Q. 3.183, forward biasing

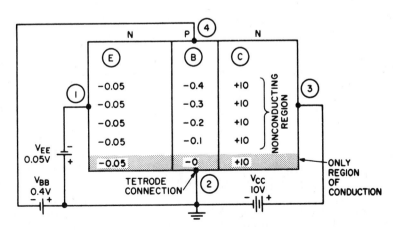

Fig. 3.192. Diagram of a tetrode (NPN) transistor, illustrating the voltage gradient of the base.

of an NPN transistor requires that the base be positive with respect to the emitter. Note in Figure 3.192 that this condition occurs only at the very bottom portion and conduction takes place only within this very restricted region of the transistor. This applies to emitter-to-base current as well as to emitter-to-collector current. Because of the small conduction areas involved, the base resistance is substantially reduced. In addition, the input and output transistor capacitances are reduced. Since both of the above factors largely determine a transistor's high frequency response, the response is substantially increased.

Note: The following questions on transistors do not appear in the current FCC Study Guide, but have been added here to improve the students' knowledge of transistor principles. It is felt that the added information will assist the student in answering certain questions on transistors which may appear in the FCC examinations.

Q. 3.192(A). What is the meaning of the term "alpha" as applied to the performance of a transistor?

A. The term "alpha" (α) is applied only to common-base amplifiers, and is a measure of the "current gain" of the circuit. The current gain is always less than one in a common-base circuit and may be commonly 0.91 to 0.99.

D. The term "alpha" (common-base only) is expressed by the simple equation

$$\alpha = \frac{\Delta I_c}{\Delta I_e}$$

This equation shows that alpha may be defined as the ratio of a change of collector current to the change of emitter current which produced the collector current change.

As an example, assume that in a common-base circuit, a change of collector current of 1 mA is caused by a change of emitter current of 1.05 mA. The alpha of this transistor is

$$\alpha = \frac{1}{1.05} = 0.95$$

Note that a common-base circuit may be compared to a grounded-grid vacuum tube circuit, which has somewhat comparable operating characteristics.

Q. 3.192(B). How is the term "alpha," as applied to transistors, expressed more specifically in terms of both dc and small-signal (ac) current ratios?

A. Alpha is a general term, referring to both dc and small signal (ac) current ratios. To distinguish between these two types of ratios, the dc ratio is commonly designated as "H_{FB}" and the small signal (ac) ratio as "h_{fb}."

D. In electronic terminology it is common to represent dc values by capital letters and ac values by small letters. In the above designations, "H" (or "h") represents current amplification; "F" (or "f") stands for forward current; and "B" (or "b") indicates a common base configuration.

Q. 3.192(C). What is the meaning of the term "beta" as applied to the performance of a transistor?

A. The term "beta" (β) is applied only to common-emitter amplifiers and is a measure of the "current gain" of this circuit. The current gain is always greater than one in a common-emitter circuit and some common values lie between 25 and 100.

D. The term beta (common emitter only) is expressed by the simple equation

$$\beta = \frac{\Delta I_c}{\Delta I_b}$$

This equation shows that beta may be defined as the ratio of the change of collector current to the change of base current which produced the change of collector current.

As an example, assume that in a common-emitter circuit, a change of collector current of 50 microamperes is caused by a change of base current of one microampere. The beta of this transistor is

$$\beta = \frac{50}{1} = 50$$

Note that a common emitter circuit may be compared to a conventional grounded-cathode vacuum tube circuit and that in this case, beta may be compared to the amplification factor of the tube, which relates the change in plate voltage caused by a lesser change in grid voltage.

Q. 3.192(D). How is the term "beta," as applied to transistors, expressed more specifically in terms of both dc and small signal (ac) current ratios?

A. Beta is a general term, referring to both dc and small signal (ac) current ratios. To distinguish between these two types of ratios, the dc ratio is commonly designated as "H_{FE}" and the small signal (ac) ratio as "h_{fe}."

D. In the above designations, "H" (or "h") represents current amplification; "F" (or "f") stands for forward current; and "E" (or "e") indicates a common emitter configuration. (See also Q. 3.192(B).)

Q. 3.192(E). A certain transistor has a small signal (ac) emitter-current gain of 0.99. What is the small signal base-current gain?

A. The small-signal, base-current gain, h_{fe}, is 99.

D. The base-current gain is beta, which for the ac case is designated h_{fe} (see Q. 3.192(D)). The emitter-current gain is alpha, which for the ac case is designated h_{fb} [see Q. 3.192(B)]. The question requires that we relate beta in terms of alpha [small signal, or ac cases). Beta is related to alpha by the simple equation

$$Beta = \frac{alpha}{1 - alpha}$$

or for the ac case

$$h_{fe} = \frac{h_{fb}}{1 - h_{fb}} = \frac{0.99}{1 - 0.99} = 99$$

Q. 3.192(F). A certain transistor has a small signal (ac) base-current gain of 49. What is the small signal emitter-current gain?

A. The small signal, emitter-current gain, h_{fb}, is 0.98.

D. (See also the preceding discussion.) The question requires that we relate alpha (emitter-current gain) in terms of beta (base-current gain) for small signal (ac) cases. Alpha is related to beta by the simple equation

$$Alpha = \frac{beta}{1 + beta}$$

or for the ac case

$$h_{fb} = \frac{h_{fe}}{1 + h_{fe}} = \frac{49}{1 + 49} = 0.98$$

Q. 3.192(G). What is meant by the alpha cut-off frequency of a transistor?

A. The alpha cut-off frequency is the high frequency at which a transistor connected in the common-base configuration drops in gain to 0.707 ($-3dB$) of its value at 1 000 hertz.

D. Note that the alpha cut-off frequency refers only to the common-base configuration (h_{fb}) emitter-current gain. Also note that the alpha cut-off frequency of any given transistor is always greater than the beta cut-off frequency (see next question) of the same transistor. This situation is somewhat comparable to the characteristics of the grounded-grid amplifier (compared to common-base), which is useful to frequencies appreciably higher than the same tube used as a grounded-cathode amplifier (compared to the common emitter). See also Q. 3.188.

Q. 3.192(H). What is meant by the beta cut-off frequency of a transistor?

A. The beta cut-off frequency is the high frequency at which a transistor connected in the common-emitter configuration drops in gain 0.707 ($-3dB$) of its value at 1 000 hertz.

D. In the cases of the beta cut-off frequency and the alpha cut-off frequency (discussed in the preceding question), the values refer only to the transistor proper and do not take into account the external circuit. As in the case of most amplifiers, the external circuit usually has the effect of further reducing the value of useful high-frequency response.

Q. 3.192(I). With reference to transistors, what is meant by the "gain-bandwidth" product?

A. The gain-bandwidth product of a transistor is a number whose magnitude is equal to the frequency (in hertz) at which the common-emitter current gain (beta) is equal to unity. Thus, if the common-emitter gain becomes equal to one at 5 megahertz, the gain bandwidth product is 5 000 000 hertz or 5 MHz.

D. The gain-bandwidth product is a commonly used measure of the approximate useful frequency range of any given transistor. It is also called a "figure of merit." for transistors.

Q. 3.192(J). Draw simple schematic diagrams comparing the common-emitter, common-base, and common-collector transistor amplifier configurations with their similar vacuum-tube configurations. Compare the advantages and disadvantages of transistors vs. tubes.

A. The diagrams are shown in Fig. 3.192(J). Note that the common-emitter am-

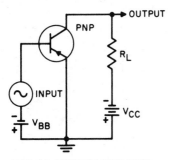

COMMON-EMITTER AMPLIFIER

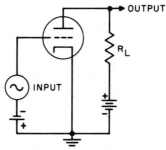

GROUNDED-CATHODE AMPLIFIER

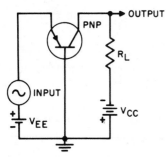

COMMON-BASE AMPLIFIER

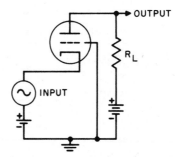

GROUNDED-GRID AMPLIFIER

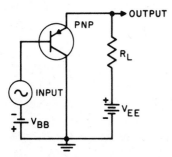

COMMON-COLLECTOR AMPLIFIER

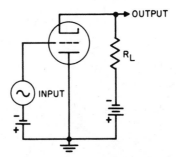

CATHODE-FOLLOWER AMPLIFIER

Fig. 3.192(J). The three transistor-amplifier configurations and their comparable vacuum-tube amplifier configurations.

plifier is similar to the grounded-cathode amplifier; the common-base amplifier is similar to the grounded-grid amplifier; and the common-collector amplifier is similar to the cathode-follower amplifier.

Some disadvantages of using transistors rather than plug-in vacuum tubes are:

1. Extreme variations of parameters due to temperature changes.

2. Need for protective diodes in many circuits.

3. Susceptible to switching-transient damage.

4. Difficult to install and replace (except where transistor sockets are used).

5. Can accept relatively low-voltage input signals.

On the side of advantages, the transistor:

1. Is smaller and lighter.

2. Is more rugged.

3. Has longer life.

4. Has greater power efficiency.

5. Requires no filament supply.

6. Is especially adaptable to use in miniaturized circuits and printed circuit boards.

7. Requires low voltage power supplies.

D. In the common-emitter amplifier configuration, the input signal is applied to the base and the output signal is taken from the collector. The emitter is at signal ground. The output signal is 180 ° out of phase with the input signal. The high-frequency response is poor, but can be improved at the expense of the voltage gain. This stage has both voltage and current gain—the only one of the three configurations that does. The common-

emitter amplifier has a lower cut-off frequency than the common-base amplifier, but it has the highest power gain of the three configurations.

The common-base amplifier output signal has the same phase as its input signal. The input signal is applied to the emitter and the output taken from the collector. The base is at signal ground. The stage has voltage gain, but a current gain of less than 1. The input circuit must present low impedance since the emitter-to-base resistance is very low. (See Q. 3.192 (K)); (See also Q. 3.50(a), Q. 3.50(c), Q. 3.50(d), and Q. 3.124.)

In the common-collector circuit, the input signal is applied to the base and the output signal is taken from the emitter. The collector is at signal ground. The emitter signal has the same phase as the base signal. This amplifier has high-input and low-output impedances. Thus, it is useful as an impedance converter or as an isolation stage. The cut-off frequency is the same as in the common-emitter amplifier. (See also 3.192K.)

Q. 3.192(K). Compare the operating characteristics of the common-emitter, common-base and common-collector transistor amplifier configurations, with respect to the following: power gain; voltage gain; current gain; input resistance; output resistance; and signal inversion.

A. The various characteristics are tabulated in Fig. 3.192(K).

D. Examining the table of Fig. 3.192(K) points up several important facts. The common-emitter configuration has intermediate values of input and output resistance, the highest level of power gain, and a fairly high

Fig. 3.192(K). Table showing typical values of transistor characteristics for the three amplifier configurations. Values are typical for selected medium-power transistors.

Characteristic	Common Emitter	Common Base	Common Collector
Power Gain	25–40 dB	20–30 dB	10–20 dB
Voltage Gain	250–1000	500–1750	Less than 1
Current Gain	25–55	Less than 1	25–55
Input Resistance	500–1500 ohms	30–150 ohms	25k–500k ohms
Output Resistance	30k–50k ohms	300k–1-M ohm	50–1000 ohms
Signal Inversion	Yes	No	No

value of voltage gain. It is also the only configuration which produces a voltage inversion of the output signal.

The common-base configuration has the lowest value of input resistance, but the highest value of output resistance. It has an intermediate value of power gain, but the highest value of voltage gain. It is the only configuration that has a current gain less than one.

The common-collector configuration has the highest value of input resistance, but the lowest value of output resistance. It has the lowest value of power gain and the only configuration with a voltage gain less than one. (See also the preceding question for a comparison of the three transistor amplifier configurations to similar vacuum-tube amplifier configurations).

Q. 3.192(L). In a common-emitter transistor amplifier, it is found that a change in the base voltage of 0.01 volt results in a change in collector voltage of 4.0 volts. What is the voltage gain of this amplifier?

A. The voltage gain (A_v) is 400.

D. The voltage gain of a commonemitter amplifier is equal to the ratio of the change of collector voltage which is caused by a change of base voltage. The simple equation for voltage gain is

$$A_v = \frac{\Delta V_c}{\Delta V_b} = \frac{4}{.01} = 400$$

Q. 3.192(M). Figure 3.192(M)(1) shows a low-to-medium power silicon transistor, with a beta of 110, connected in a common-emitter circuit and employing "fixed" bias. It is desired to operate this circuit in Class A amplification. Determine the following:

1. The required value of R_B.

2. The collector current at the "Q," or quiescent condition (dc).

3. The collector voltage at the "Q" condition.

A.

1. The required value of R_B is 200 000 ohms.

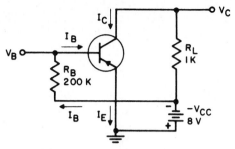

Fig. 3.192(M)(1). Common-emitter amplifier connected for "fixed" bias.

2. The collector current (I_C) is 4.4mA.

3. The collector voltage (V_C) is 3.6 volts.

D. *Note*: In this discussion, refer also to the simplified transistor characteristic curves, showing the collector-to-emitter voltage vs. the collector current for various values of base current, given in Fig. 3.192 (M) (2). These curves and the load line are used in the calculation of the required values.

In order to determine Class A operation for this transistor, it is necessary to first draw the dc load line. This load line is drawn in a manner similar to that for a vacuum tube as shown in Fig. 3.57. The transistor load line is drawn from the point of maximum collector current to the point representing the collector supply voltage. The maximum collector current occurs when the transistor is in saturation and here the collector is assumed to be shorted to the emitter. This current is

$$I_{C\ max.} = \frac{V_{CC}}{R_L} = \frac{8}{1\ 000} = 8\ mA$$

Fig. 3.192(M)(2). Load line representing dc operating conditions of the schematic in (1).

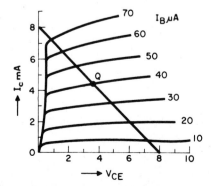

The collector supply voltage, V_{CC}, is given as 8 volts.

Once the load line is drawn, the Q point is chosen such that the base current can be varied above and below this value by an approximately equal amount. This will insure that the corresponding variations in collector current will be practically distortionless. In Fig. 3.192(M) (2), this Q point has been chosen at the intersection of the load line and the base current curve representing 40 μA. Having established the required dc base-current bias, the value of R_B is found (to a very close approximation) by

$$R_B = \frac{V_{CC}}{I_B} = \frac{8V}{40\mu A} = 200\ 000 \text{ ohms}$$

(Since dc base-to-emitter diode resistance is a small fraction of R_B, it may be ignored in this calculation).

The collector current is easily found now, and is

$$I_C = \text{beta} \times I_B = 110 \times 40\ \mu A$$
$$= 4.4 \text{ mA}$$

The collector voltage is also easily found. It is

$$V_C = V_{CC} - (I_C \times R_L$$
$$= 8V - (4.4 \text{ mA} \times 1\ 000)$$
$$= 3.6 \text{ volts}$$

Note that both the collector current and the collector voltage can be found to a very close approximation from the characteristics curves and these points on the curves should be checked to verify the calculated values. These values are found on the curves by extending a line from the Q point, horizontally to the left to obtain the collector current. The collector voltage is obtained by extending a vertical line down from the Q point, to obtain the collector voltage.

Q. 3.192(N). Figure 3.192(N) shows a low-to-medium power germanium transistor with a beta of 90, connected in a common-emitter circuit, employing voltage-divider type base bias, and an emitter bias-stabilizing resistor, R3. It is desired to operate this circuit in Class A amplification. Determine the following:

1. The magnitude of V_B required to bias the transistor Class A.

2. The values of the base-bias resistors, R1 and R2 required to provide the base-bias voltage (V_B) for Class A operation.

3. The dc (no-signal) collector current.

A.
1. The Class A, base bias (V_B) is, -3 volts.

2. R1 = 75 000 ohms. R2 = 8 500 ohms.

3. The dc collector current is 3 mA.

D. While the solution requires several steps, it is not difficult if the steps are taken in logical order, as presented below.

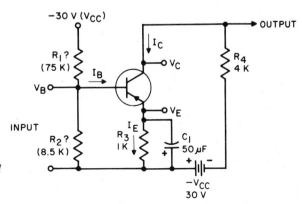

Fig. 3.192(N). Common-emitter amplifier using voltage-divider base bias and employing a bias-stabilizing emitter resistor.

STEP 1:
DETERMINE THE CLASS A BASE-BIAS VOLTAGE (V_B)

To determine this, we must first find the limits of the emitter voltage (V_E), at cut-off and saturation.

1. At cut-off, with no current in R3, V_E is at ground potential, or is zero.
2. At saturation, $V_{E\,max}$ is found by

$$V_{E\,max} = \frac{R3}{R3 + R4} \times (-V_{CC})$$

$$= \frac{1\,000}{1\,000 + 4\,000} \times (-30)$$

$$= -6\text{ V}$$

Halfway between zero volts and -6 volts is -3 volts (V_E) which is the optimum base bias for Class A operation. However, $V_E = V_B$, so $V_B = -3$ volts.

STEP 2:
DETERMINE THE VALUES FOR R1 AND R2

Resistors R1 and R2 may be selected with reasonable accuracy by assuming a value for R2 and calculating R1 on this basis.

For germanium transistors of the general type discussed in this question (beta can be greater or less), a value of R2 such as chosen here (8 500 ohms) can be assumed. (Actually any value between 5 000 and 10 000 ohms could be chosen.) Having selected R2, R1 is chosen so that the desired bias will appear at the base.

In this problem, having selected a value of 8 500 for R2, R1 is chosen at 75 000 ohms to provide the required -3 volts at the base (using practical resistors).

Note: If the transistor in question was a silicon transistor of the same general type, the value of R2 would be about 7 times greater (35 000 to 70 000 ohms). (The base-input resistance of a silicon transistor is about 7 times greater than that of a germanium transistor.)

The answer to part (2) of the question is R1 = 75 000 ohms; R2 = 8 500 ohms.

STEP 3:
WHAT IS THE DC COLLECTOR CURRENT?

In step 1, it was determined that V_B was -3 volts based on a halfway point of -3 volts for the emitter voltage. [While not stated at that time, it can be assumed for germanium transistors (only), that the dc emitter voltage is always equal to the dc base voltage because of the very small (.1 - .2 volts) base-to-emitter drop.]

Thus, there is a 3 volt drop across R3, and the emitter current is

$$I_C = \frac{V_E}{R3} = \frac{3}{1\,000} = 3\text{ mA}$$

But, practically, $I_C = I_E = 3$ mA.

Q. 3.192(O). In Fig. 3.192(N), what is the voltage gain of the circuit?

A. The voltage gain, $A_V = 460$.

D. If there is no unbypassed emitter resistance, as in this case, the voltage gain is found by

$$A_v = \frac{R4}{r_e}$$

However, r_e is found by dividing the constant 0.026 by the dc emitter current, thus

$$r_e = \frac{0.026}{3mA} = 8.7\text{ ohms}$$

and

$$A_v = \frac{4\,000}{8.7} = 460$$

Note: If the circuit contains an unbypassed emitter resistance, this must be included in the equation for voltage gain, as

$$A_v = \frac{R4}{r_e + R_E}$$

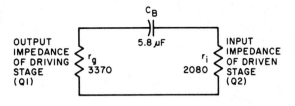

Fig. 3.192(P). Simplified diagram of a two-stage transistor audio amplifier, to facilitate calculation of the value of the interstage coupling capacitor, C_B.

Q. 3.192(P). A two-stage common-emitter transistor audio amplifier is RC coupled. The low frequency response (determined by C_B only), is to be down 3 dB at five hertz (F_1). The total output impedance r_g of the driving stage (Q1) is 3 370 ohms and the total input impedance (r_i) of the driven stage (Q2) is 2 080 ohms. Determine the value of the interstage coupling capacitor, C_B, which will provide the desired low frequency response.

A. The required value of C_B is 5.8 μF. (A commercial value of 6 μF is available.)

D. The value of C_B can be easily found from the simple equation

$$C_B = \frac{1}{2\pi \ F_1 \times R_T}$$

[Refer to the simplified diagram of Fig. 3.192(P).] We know F_1 since this is given at 5 hertz (3 dB down), but we must first solve for R_T, as follows:

$$R_T = r_g + r_i = 3\ 370 + 2\ 080$$

$$= 5\ 450 \text{ ohms}$$

$$C_B = \frac{1}{6.28 \times 5 \times 5\ 450}$$
$$= 0.0000058 \text{ farad} = 5.8 \text{ μF}$$

Note: This problem has been delib-

erately simplified for the purpose of answering similar questions as they might be asked on FCC examinations. In practice, the values of r_g and r_i would have to be calculated for the particular amplifiers involved. This process is somewhat more complicated than the simplified example given above.

Q. 3.192(Q). A transistor audio amplifier, of the common-emitter type, employs an emitter resistor and bypass capacitor. It is desired that the emitter circuit response will be −3 dB at 50 hertz (F_1). What is the required value of the emitter bypass capacitor if the *effective* value of the emitter resistance, R_{ET}, is 48 ohms?

A. The required value of the emitter bypass capacitor, C_E, is 66.3 μF. (A 60 μF capacitor would generally be adequate.)

D. The value of C_E can be easily found from the simple equation

$$C_E = \frac{1}{2\pi \ F_1 \times R_{ET}}$$

$$= \frac{1}{6.28 \times 50 \times 48}$$

$$= 0.0000663 \text{ farad}$$

$$= 66.3 \text{ μF}$$

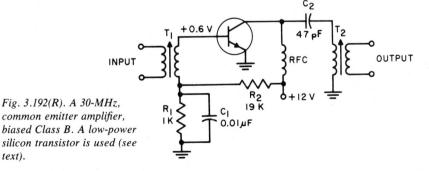

Fig. 3.192(R). A 30-MHz, common emitter amplifier, biased Class B. A low-power silicon transistor is used (see text).

Note: as in the case of Q. 3.192(P), this problem has been simplified for the purpose of answering similar questions as they might be asked on FCC examinations.

Q. 3.192(R). The schematic diagram given in Fig. 3.192(R) is a 30-MHz, low-power RF amplifier, employing a silicon transistor. Calculate the value of R1 and R2 necessary to provide Class B bias for this amplifier. Also, discuss the requirement for the value of capacitor C1.

A. The value of R1 is 1 000 ohms and R2 is 19 000 ohms. (This combination provides a forward bias of 0.6 volt.) Capacitor C1 must provide an ac ground at the bottom of the secondary of T1 and thus it must have a very low value of reactance at 30 MHz.

D. Unlike vacuum tubes, most similar transistors have an almost identical value of junction-barrier voltage. For low-power silicon transistors, the barrier voltage for the base-to-emitter junction is about 0.6 volt. This voltage, which is due to the physics of the transistor, is a "back voltage," which tends to oppose the flow of base-to-emitter current.

Base-to-emitter current cannot begin to flow until this barrier voltage is overcome (this is true also of collector current). Thus, to bias a transistor at Class B, it is necessary to supply a forward-bias voltage which will just overcome the barrier voltage of 0.6 volt. (This is equivalent to biasing a vacuum tube at cut-off bias.)

The voltage divider consisting of R1 and R2 is chosen so that it will provide a forward bias of 0.6 volt to the base. Obviously, there are an infinite number of combinations which will provide the voltage. Since the signal is grounded (for ac) by the low reactance of C1 (0.5 ohm), the value of R1 is not critical. However, the overall divider should not draw appreciable current from the power supply and for this case a bleeder current of 0.6 mA was chosen. R1 and R2 values were then based upon this bleeder current. (See also Q. 3.190(2). In the

figure, if V_{CC} was 6 volts, the forward bias would be 0.66 volt.)

In some cases of Class B operation, it is desirable to provide a small additional forward bias, since this reduces the required amount of drive.

Germanium transistors have a much lower base-to-emitter barrier voltage. For low power germanium transistors, the barrier voltage is about 0.1 volt. In this case Class B operation can be easily achieved by operating the transistor with zero forward bias.

High power silicon transistors have a barrier voltage on the order of 0.5 volt, while high-power germanium transistors have a barrier voltage in the order of 0.2 volt.

Q. 3.192(S). What is the approximate Class C bias for medium power, silicon, and germanium transistors?

A. The approximate Class C bias is 0 volts between the base and emitter.

D. The usual Class C bias is set so that approximately 120° of collector current will flow per cycle. For typical, medium power silicon and germanium transistors, this condition occurs (approximately) when the dc bias between the base and emitter is 0 volts.

A typical medium power silicon transistor [see Fig. 3.192(S)] has a base-to-emitter barrier voltage [see D. for Q. 3.192(R)] of 0.6 volt. This type of transistor reaches collector-current saturation with a base-emitter voltage of 1.5 volts. With zero bias, the signal swings around this value and varies from zero to 1.5 volts, to zero, to minus 1.5 volts. However, from zero to 0.6 volt (forward-bias direction), there will be no collector current, which will flow only when the forward bias voltage is between 0.6 and 1.5 volts (produced by higher amplitudes of the input signal). Thus Class C operation is achieved.

The same general principle applies to the medium power germanium transistor, except that the barrier is 0.2 volt and the collector current saturation occurs at 0.55 volt.

Fig. 3.192(S). Typical characteristics for low, medium, and high-power silicon and germanium transistors.

	Silicon Transistors		Germanium Transistors		Approx. B-E, Class C Bias Voltage	
	Base-Emitter, Barrier V.	Base-Emitter, Ic saturation V.	Base-Emitter, Barrier V.	Base-Emitter, Ic Saturation V.	Silicon	Germanium
Low Power	0.6	0.8	0.1	0.25	0.5 (forward)	0
Medium Power	0.6	1.5	0.2	0.55	0	0
High Power	0.5	2.0	0.2	2.0	0.25 (reverse)	0.7 (reverse)

Fig. 3.192(S) gives the values of barrier voltage, collector saturation current, and approximate Class C bias voltages for low, medium, and high-power silicon and germanium transistors. This table is based upon typical transistors used in the three power ranges.

Note that while zero bias, transistor Class C amplifiers are frequently used, this is not the only method of obtaining Class C bias. One disadvantage of this scheme is that it is not self-adjusting and thus cannot readily accommodate varying levels of input signal. The use of grid-leak bias (see Q. 3.86) in vacuum tubes operated as Class C amplifiers permits the bias to vary with the amplitude of the input signal. This method minimizes changes of output power which might occur due to variations of input power. Similar schemes are also used with transistor Class C amplifiers, as described in Q. 3.192(T). 3.192(T).

Q. 3.192(T). It is desired to operate a high power germanium transistor in a 30 MHz Class C amplifier, using a base self-bias RC

network. The peak base current (at collector saturation) is 20 mA. Determine the required values of the resistor and capacitor for the bias network.

A. The resistor, R_B = 35 ohms.
The capacitor, C_B = 0.01 μF (not critical).
D. Refer to the simplified schematic diagram of Fig. 3.192(T). Base current flows only during the positive portions of the RF input signal. It flows through the bias network in the direction shown, producing a reverse bias across the network. The value of the resistor is

$$R_B = \frac{V_B}{I_{B \ max}} = \frac{.7}{.020} = 35 \text{ ohms}$$

The value of the capacitor is not critical, but it must present a very low reactance at the operating frequency. A 0.01-μF capacitor is chosen, with a reactance of 0.5 ohm.

Q. 3.192(U). Using the same transistor and operating conditions as in Q. 3.192(T), but employing an emitter-bias network, determine the required values of the resistor

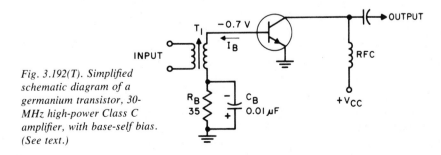

Fig. 3.192(T). Simplified schematic diagram of a germanium transistor, 30-MHz high-power Class C amplifier, with base-self bias. (See text.)

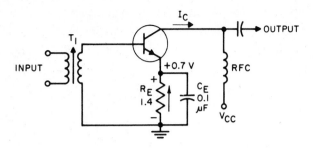

Fig. 3.192(U). Simplified schematic diagram of a germanium transistor, 30-MHz high-power Class C amplifier, with emitter self-bias. (See text.)

and capacitor for the bias network. The peak collector current is 500 mA.

A. The resistor, R_E = 1.4 ohms. The capacitor, C_E = 0.1 µF (not critical).

D. Collector current as well as base current flows only during the positive portions of the input RF signal. The collector current flows through the emitter-bias network in the direction shown in Fig. 3.192(U), producing a reverse bias across the network. The value of the resistor is

$$R_E = \frac{V_E}{I_{E\ max}} = \frac{.7}{.500} = 1.4 \text{ ohms}$$

As in the previous question the value of C_E is not critical. However, its reactance must be small compared to R_E in order to avoid degeneration in the emitter circuit. A value of 0.1 µF has been chosen, since it has a reactance at 30-MHz of only .05 ohm.

The base self-bias scheme shown in the previous question is quite widely used, but has the disadvantage that too high a value of R_B limits the usable collector-to-emitter breakdown voltage. On the other hand, the emitter self-bias arrangement described in this question does not affect the transistor breakdown characteristic and also provides thermal stability.

Some Class C amplifiers employ a combination of both the base and the emitter-bias schemes. In this design, the required bias is provided partially by each bias network.

As mentioned in the discussion of Q. 3.192(S), both the base and the emitter self-bias methods have the advantage of being self-adjusting to changes of input signal level.

With either (or both) of these schemes, an increase of input signal will result in an increase of bias and a decrease of signal level will result in a decrease of bias, with the output power remaining fairly constant.

Note: The following added material numbered Q. 3.192-A1 through Q. 3.192(U)-A40 contains information that may be required to pass the General Radiotelephone Operator's License examination. This added material, as well as the new material added to other sections, has been included to help acquaint students with the current state of the electronics art. It is felt that the added material contains subject matter that may also be required of students who have obtained a General Radiotelephone Operator's License and are seeking employment. Additionally, the added material contains valuable information for private technician certification.

Q. 3.192(U)-A1. Compare some characteristics of silicon and germanium transistors.

A. The following are some comparative characteristics:

1. For equally sized, silicon transistors can handle more power.

2. The approximate operating temperature range of a germanium transistor is −65° to +100°C, compared to that of a silicon transistor, which is approximately −65° to +200°C.

3. The germanium transistor base-to-collector (undesired) current increases at a greater rate than for a silicon transistor, as the ambient temperature increases above 25°C.

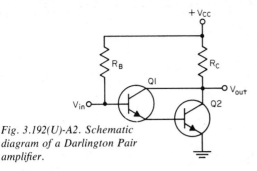

Fig. 3.192(U)-A2. Schematic diagram of a Darlington Pair amplifier.

4. Silicon transistors are capable of operating at higher frequencies than germanium transistors.

5. Germanium transistors are more susceptible to thermal runaway (increased current with temperature) than silicon transistors.

6. Of importance in dc amplifiers, variations in steady-state (no signal) collector current are considerably less in silicon than in germanium transistors. Such variations are caused by changes in leakage current due to temperature variations. An output from an amplifier due to this effect is called *zero drift*, since it occurs with no input signal.

D. See Fig. 3.192(S) for additional comparisons of the operating characteristics of silicon and germanium transistors.

Q. 3.192(U)-A2. Draw a schematic diagram of two transistors connected as a Darlington pair. What are the characteristics of this configuration?

A. For the schematic diagram, see Fig. 3.192(U)-A2. The outstanding characteristics of the Darlington pair (or super-alpha) circuit are its very high input resistance and high current gain.

D. The input signal (V_{in}) is applied to the base of Q_1, a common-collector (emitter-follower) amplifier. Base bias for Q_1 is fed through R_B. The emitter of Q_1 is direct-coupled to the base of Q_2, and both collectors are in parallel. The latter is possible, since both collector currents are in phase. The net current gain of the pair is approximately equal to the product of the individual current gains.

The input resistance of Q_1 is approximately equal to the Q_1 alpha, times the Q_1 emitter load, which here is the input resistance of Q_2. Thus, the input resistance can be very high and 1 MΩ or greater can be achieved.

The pair can be considered (for practical purposes) to be a single transistor with high input resistance and high current gain.

Q. 3.192(U)-A3. Why do power transistors require heat sinks?

A. Power transistors are usually mounted on heat sinks to prevent thermal runaway of the transistor. This could cause overheating and transistor burnout. By mounting power transistors on heat sinks, the semiconductor junction temperature is kept within safe limits. Heat sinks transfer much of the transistor heat to the surrounding atmosphere. Thus, they can greatly increase the transistor power-handling capability.

Fig. 3.192(U)-A3. Some examples of heat sinks used with power transistors: (1) TO-3 can with flat-heat sink; (2 and 3) heat sinks with fins.

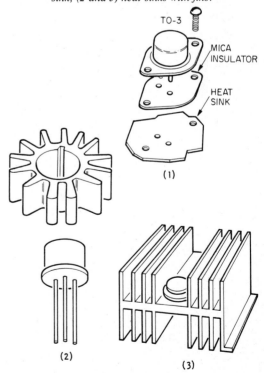

D. Some examples of typical heat sinks are shown in Fig. 3.192(U)-A3. Heat sinks may be flat, as in Fig. 3.192(U)-A3(1). In some cases, the transistors are mounted directly on a metal chassis, preferably made of aluminum, for good heat dissipation. Where chassis mounting is not feasible, the finned type of heat sink should be used. Two examples are shown in Fig. 3.192(U)-A3 (2,3).

Heat sinks are made of good heat-conductive materials. Among these are copper and aluminum, which are designed to provide the maximum heat dissipation area. In many cases, the interface between the transistor case and the heat sink must include an electrical insulator. This is because the transistor collector may be connected to the case. In such cases, the electrical insulator must be one that has low-thermal resistance. Some suitable materials are mica, anodized aluminum, and beryllia.

Q. 3.192(U)-A4. What are some of the important characteristics and uses of field effect transistors (FETs)?

A. The common term "transistor," as described in Q. 3.183, usually refers to the bipolar junction transistor (BJT). In this device, both positive (holes) and negative (electrons) charge carriers are used. The field effect transistor (FET) has current flow through it by either holes or electrons, but not by both.

The FET also differs from the BJT, in that the FET is a voltage-operated device, while the BJT is a current-operated device. The BJT is biased by base-to-emitter current. However, input current flows in the FET; thus it has practically an infinite-input resistance compared to a low-input resistance for the BJT. The FET has characteristics similar to those of a pentode vacuum tube. The term "field effect" is assigned to FETs because the current through them is controlled by a varying *electric field*. The electric field is varied by the application of a voltage to the *gate* electrode, as will be described in the Discussion section.

Types of FETs. There are two basic types of FETs. These are the *junction* FET (JFET) and the metal-oxide silicon field effect transistor (MOSFET). Some MOSFETs have one gate, while other types have two. The MOSFET is also called the *insulated gate* FET (IGFET). The JFET has no insulation between its elements and this is also true of BJTs. (See Discussion for operation.) The MOSFET has a thin insulating layer of silicon dioxide between the gate (or gates) and the channel. (See Discussion for operation.) JFETs may be N-channel or P-channel types. MOSFETs have these designations also, but, in addition, they come in *depletion* and *enhancement* types. A family tree for FETs is given in Fig. 3.192(U)-A4(1). Note that, regardless of the type of FET shown, it is either N-channel or P-channel. For N-channel FETs, the majority charge carriers are electrons. For P-channel FETs, the majority charge carriers are holes. The symbols for JFETs and MOSFETs are shown in Fig. 3.192(U)-A4(2). (All JFETs are depletion type.)

Depletion Versus Enhancement MOSFETs. Depletion and enhancement MOSFETs have different operating characteristics. A depletion MOSFET has a constructed channel and is a normally ON device. For zero gate voltage, a large drain current flows. An enhancement MOSFET has no constructed channel. It is a normally OFF device. With zero gate voltage, no drain current flows. This characteristic is useful in digital switching circuits.

Power FETs. Another class of FETs are the *power* FETs. They are known as *vertical* FETs, MOSPOWER FETs, and VMOS FETs. Among their other uses (mentioned below), a MOSPOWER FET is capable of switching a current of 1 A in less than 4 ns. These devices can be operated in Class A, AB, B, or C. Zero bias results in Class C operation.

CMOS ICs. The abbreviation CMOS ICs stands for a complementary metal oxide silicon type of integrated circuit. The IC is

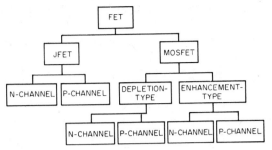

Fig. 3.192(U)-A4(1). Block diagram illustrating a family of FETs.

composed of a number of MOSFETs formed on a single chip (monolithic IC) of P- or N-type silicon. The basic chip is also known as the *substrate*. CMOS ICs consume very little power and have a very high input impedance (because of the FETs). They have very low noise characteristics. They operate on 1.5 to 16 V.

Uses of JFETs. Some uses of JFETs are as: oscillators, mixers, IF amplifiers, RF amplifiers, audio amplifiers, AGC amplifiers trigger circuits, and source followers.

Uses of MOSFETs. Some uses of MOSFETs are as: oscillators, mixers, limiters, IF amplifiers, RF amplifiers, frequency multipliers, synchronous detectors, low-level audio amplifiers, audio-power amplifiers, phase splitters, and current limiters. Dual-gate MOSFETs are used commonly as AGC controlled IF and RF amplifiers, mixers, product detectors, and variable attenuators.

Uses of CMOS ICs. Depending upon their particular configuration, CMOS ICs have a number of uses. They are found in many electronic watches, in which all functions are produced on a single chip. They are also popular in logic circuits (enhancement-MOSFET type), audio amplifiers, IF amplifiers, and RF amplifiers.

Uses of Power FETs. Power FETs can handle large amounts of power. They can be obtained for application from dc through the VHF spectrum. They can be employed as small signal amplifiers or as linear power amplifiers. This transistor is excellent for use in HF and VHF ranges. For example, one type can provide a power output of 20 W at 160 MHz. They are excellent for use in switching amplifiers.

D. The basic operation of the two basic types of FETs will now be discussed.

JFET Operation. A profile of an N-channel JFET is shown in Fig. 3.192(U)-A4(3). Figure 3.192(U)-A4(4) illustrates its operation. The characteristics of a JFET are similar to those of a pentode vacuum tube.

Fig. 3.192(U)-A4(2). Symbols for JFETs and MOSFETs.

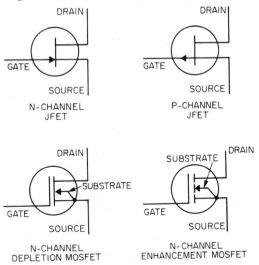

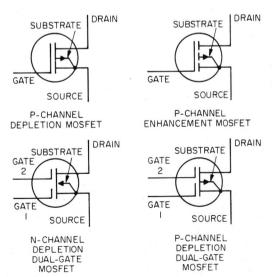

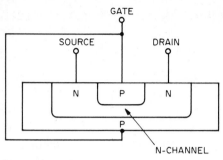

*Fig. 3.192(U)-A4(3). Profile
of an N-channel JFET.*

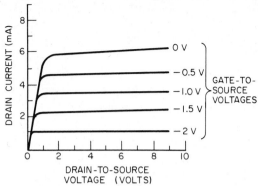

*Fig. 3.192(U)-A4(4). The gate voltage versus drain
current relationships in an N-channel JFET.*

Once the JFET drain voltage is raised to a certain level, increasing it further results in very little increase of drain current. Note this effect in the characteristic curves of Fig. 3.192(U)-A4(5).

Assuming a nominal drain-to-source voltage of + 5 V, refer to Fig. 3.192(U)-A4(5). In part a, we apply 0 V to the gate. (Remember that in an N-channel JFET, electrons are the charge carriers.)

The dotted lines around the gate in part a represent the boundaries of a depletion region that are present at the junction of the P- and N-type materials in this area. This depletion region will limit the number of electrons that can flow from the source to the drain. When no voltage is applied to the gate, the size of the depletion region is small. Under this condition, there is little opposition to the current flow through the device and the drain current will be high.

When a moderate negative voltage is applied to the gate, the PN junction is reverse-biased, and this increases the size of the depletion region as shown in part b. The result is a decrease in the drain current. The more negative the gate voltage for this type of FET, the greater the depletion region and the smaller the amount of drain current. Ultimately, a point will be reached where the depletion region is so large that it prevents any current flow through the channel. The negative voltage on the gate required to produce this situation is called the pinch-off voltage and it is shown in part c.

A P-channel JFET operates in the same manner as just described except that the voltages on the gate and the drain are reversed: the more positive the voltage on the gate, the lower the amount of the current flow in a P-channel JFET. Current flow through a P-channel JFET is due to *hole flow*, and it is toward a *negative* voltage on the source.

Depletion MOSFET Operation. A profile of an N-channel depletion MOSFET is

*Fig. 3.192(U)-A4(5). Typical drain characteristics for
an N-channel JFET.*

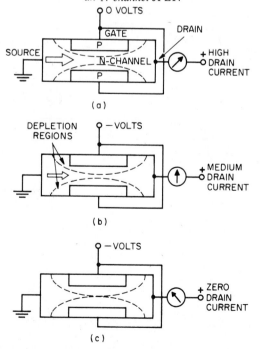

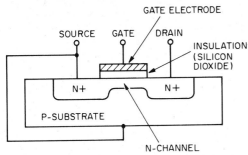

*Fig. 3.192(U)-A4(6). Profile of an N-channel
depletion MOSFET.*

shown in Fig. 3.192(U)-A4(6). Typical drain
characteristics are shown in Fig. 3.192(U)-
A4(7). You may consider that the gate electrode and the N-channel are two plates of
a capacitor, separated by the silicon dioxide
insulation. By capacitor action, if the gate
electrode is made negative, the N-channel
will be equally positive. Conversely, making
the gate electrode positive will result in the
N-channel being equally but negatively
charged.

Because of the foregoing, if we make
the gate electrode *negative* (with respect to
the source), positive charges are induced in
the N-channel. These positive charges reduce
(deplete) the majority negative charges
(electrons) in N-channel. Thus, the drain
current is reduced. Negative gate voltage
reduces drain current. This effect is clearly
seen in the characteristic curves of Fig.
3.192(U)-A4(7).

*Fig. 3.192(U)-A4(7). Typical drain characteristics for
an N-channel depletion-type MOSFET.*

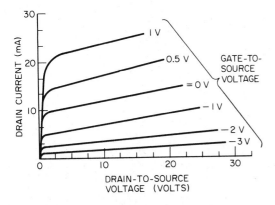

Suppose we make the gate *positive* with
respect to the source. Now negative charges
are induced in the N-channel. This causes
an *increase* of drain current. *Positive* gate
voltage increases drain current. Again, this
is clearly shown in Fig. 3.192(U)-A4(7).

The P-channel depletion-type MOS-
FET profile is basically the same as shown
in Fig. 3.192(U)-A4(6). However, in this case,
the source and drain are P+ regions, and
the channel is a P region in an N-substrate.
If we make the gate electrode *positive* with
respect to the source, negative charges are
induced in the P-channel. These negative

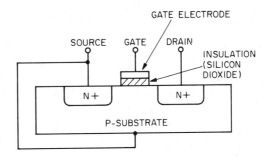

*Fig. 3.192(U)-A4(8). Profile of an N-channel
enhancement MOSFET. Note the absence of a
constructed N-channel, as in Fig. 3.192(U)-A4(6).*

charges reduce (deplete) the majority positive
charge carriers (holes) in the P-channel. Thus,
the drain current is *reduced*. Conversely,
making the gate negative will *increase* the
drain current by inducing positive charges
into the P-channel. Drain characteristics are
similar to those in Fig. 3.192(U)-A4(7).
However, the polarities of the gate to source
voltages are reversed.

Enhancement MOSFET Operation. A
profile of an N-channel enhancement MOS-
FET is shown in Fig. 3.192(U)-A4(8). Note
the similarity to the structure of the depletion-
type MOSFET in Fig. 3.192(U)-A4(6). The
difference is that in the enhancement type,
there is no *constructed* N-channel. In this
type, when a positive voltage is applied to
the gate, with respect to the source, an N-
channel is *induced* between the source, and
drain and electron current will flow between

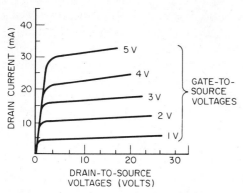

Fig. 3.192(U)-A4(9). Typical drain characteristics for an N-channel enhancement-type MOSFET.

them. (This MOSFET is a normally OFF device, as previously mentioned.) Within limits, the higher the positive gate voltage, the greater is the drain current. This may be clearly seen in the typical drain characteristics of Fig. 3.192(U)-A4(9).

The P-channel enhancement-type MOSFET profile is basically the same as in Fig. 3.192(U)-A4(8). However, in this case, the source and drain regions are P+ in an N substrate. Here a P-channel is induced by making the gate *negative* with respect to the source. Drain characteristics are similar to those in Fig. 3.192(U)-A4(9). However, the gate-to-source voltages will be negative.

Q. 3.192(U)-A5. Draw a schematic diagram of a field effect transistor (FET) radio frequency amplifier. Are its input and output impedances high or low?

A. The schematic diagram of an N-channel JFET RF amplifier is shown in Fig. 3.192(U)-A5. The input impedance is extremely high, since no gate current flows. It approaches infinity. The output impedance is fairly high and may be in the range of 20 000 to 100 000 Ωs.

D. The above JFET amplifier has a low noise figure and good dynamic range. Thus it is frequently preferred to BJT RF amplifiers. The gate and drain elements of the JFET are tapped on L_2 and L_4 to provide stability against oscillation. This circuit can provide a gain of 10 dB or greater. (See also Q. 3.192(U)-A4.)

Q. 3.192(U)-A6. What is a point-contact diode? How is it used?

A. A *point-contact diode* is one having a metal-to-semiconductor junction. They are used as mixers and detectors up to microwave frequencies.

D. The point-contact diode is the most common and basic diode. It exhibits a non-linear impedance at a metal-to-semiconductor junction. This junction is formed by forcing a pointed tungsten wire (whisker) against a silicon wafer. The silicon wafer is lightly doped at the surface (epitaxial layer).

Point-contact diodes are the preferred type of mixer at the front end of microwave receivers. This is because of their good signal-to-noise performance. They also have an inherently low capacitance. One such typical point-contact diode is the IN23E.

Q. 3.192(U)-A7. What are the properties of varactor diodes? Of zener diodes? Describe some uses of each.

A.

1. Varactor diodes (voltage-variable capacitors) are silicon diodes that use the depletion region of a reverse-biased PN junction as the dielectric of a capacitor. The two "plates" of the capacitor are formed by the P and N regions of the diode. Fig. 3.192(U)-A7(a) shows the cross-section and electrical symbol of a varactor. Note the reverse bias. As the reverse bias is increased, the capacitance is decreased and vice versa.

Varactors are used as tuning elements in TV tuners, automatic fine tuning circuits, high-power frequency multipliers, and in

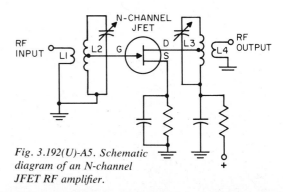

Fig. 3.192(U)-A5. Schematic diagram of an N-channel JFET RF amplifier.

general for tuning and frequency control in the VHF, UHF, and microwave ranges. In addition, varactors are used for phase or frequency modulation and as parametric (reactance) amplifiers. (See also Discussion.)

2. Zener (or avalanche) diodes operate on the basis of a reverse current breakdown. This breakdown (avalanche or zener) voltage may vary from about 2 to 200 V for different zener diodes.

Refer to Fig. 3.192(U)-A7(b). As the reverse voltage ($-V_R$) increases to a value greater than the PRV (peak reverse voltage), the diode breaks down. At this point, the reverse current ($-I_R$) increases rapidly. In the operating region from I_{ZK} (minimum zener current) to I_{ZM} (maximum zener current), the voltage *across* the zener diode is nearly constant. This voltage will be equal to the design value of the particular zener diode.

Zener diodes are used to provide fixed reference voltages, as in the circuit of Fig. 3.78-A13. They are also used as simple, shunt voltage regulating devices. (See Q. 3.78-A11). In the latter case, the output voltage will be held constant at the zener voltage (2 to 200 V). (See also Discussion.)

D.

1. The variation in capacitance with reverse voltage of a varactor, is non-linear. For example, for one type, over a range in reverse voltage from 1 to 60 V, the capacitance varies from 80 PF to 14 PF. For low-frequency applications, diode capacitances as high as 2 000 PF are available. However, microwave varactors may have a maximum capacitance of only about 0.4 PF.

Varactors can handle from 100 mW to hundreds of watts of RF power. Their breakdown voltage ranges from approximately -6 to -300 V.

2. The maximum operating zener current is limited by the permissible power dissipation of the device. Maximum zener currents range from a few milliamperes to tens of amperes. Zener diodes having a breakdown voltage less than 6 V, exhibit a negative temperature coefficient. That is, the breakdown voltage decreases with increasing temperature. For breakdown voltages above 6 V, the zeners have a positive temperature coefficient. In this case, the breakdown voltage increases with increasing temperature.

Q. 3.192(U)-A8. What is a hot carrier diode (HCD)?

A. A *hot carrier diode* (HCD) is a metal-to-semiconductor diode with a single rectifying junction. The carriers are high mobility electrons in N-type semiconductor material. A cross-sectional drawing is given in Fig. 3.192-A8(a).

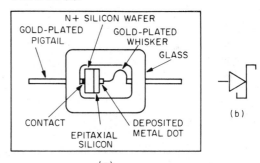

(a)

Fig. 3.192(U)-A8. (a) Cross section of a hot carrier diode. (b) Symbol of a hot carrier diode.

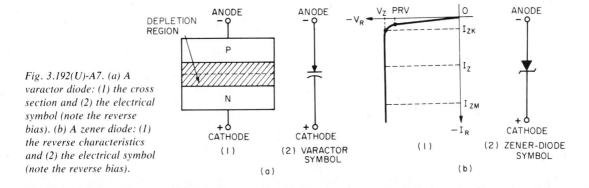

Fig. 3.192(U)-A7. (a) A varactor diode: (1) the cross section and (2) the electrical symbol (note the reverse bias). (b) A zener diode: (1) the reverse characteristics and (2) the electrical symbol (note the reverse bias).

D. The HCD has excellent high-frequency characteristics and a lower conduction voltage than a P-N junction diode (See Q. 3.192(U)-A6.) The HCD is used in mixers and detectors at VHF and above. It has lower noise, greater conversion efficiency, and lower internal capacity than a P-N junction diode. Also, it is less subject to temperature variations. (See also Q. 3.301.)

Q. 3.192(U)-A9. What is a PIN diode?

A. A *PIN diode* is constructed with highly doped P and N regions separated by an *intrinsic* region. (In an intrinsic region, the charge carriers are characteristic only of the material used.) The instrinsic region is the base material without any doping (or sometimes lightly doped). The internal structure is shown in Fig. 3.192(U)-A9. The designation PIN is derived from P for P region, I for intrinsic region, and N for N region.

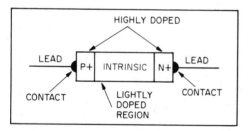

Fig. 3.192(U)-A9. Showing the internal structure of a PIN diode.

D. These diodes may be used as high-voltage rectifiers, but they will not rectify at high frequencies. This is because of the large recovery time of the intrinsic region.

The PIN diodes are used as modulators, attenuators (variable resistors), and switches at UHF and SHF. Some types are used for harmonic generation.

With maximum forward bias, the impedance is about 1 Ω. With zero bias, the impedance is about 8 000 Ω.

Failure modes are similar to those of transistors. (See Q. 3.301.)

Q. 3.192(U)-A10. What is a tunnel diode? How is it used?

A. A *tunnel diode* is a semiconductor device having a negative resistance characteristic. They are used as amplifiers, oscillators, converters, and detectors at UHF and microwave frequencies.

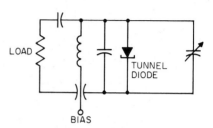

Fig. 3.192(U)-A10. A 600 MHz tunnel diode oscillator.

D. If the N and P semiconductors of a bipolar junction diode are very heavily doped, the depletion layer becomes extremely thin. Because of this, the junction breakdown occurs via a *tunneling* (penetration) process from the N side to the P side. This causes an *additional* current in the diode using a very small forward bias. It is this additional current that produces the negative resistance characteristic of the tunnel diode.

A tunnel diode oscillator circuit is shown in Fig. 3-192(U)-A10. This circuit is suitable for operation in the order of 600 MHz. It has a power output of about 0.1 W.

Q. 3.192(U)-A11. Discuss the characteristics of liquid crystal display (LCD) devices.

A. An LCD does *not* emit light. It depends upon *ambient light* for its display. The display consists of a reflective backing behind the liquid crystal material. This material is normally transparent, but it becomes opaque and black in appearance when voltage is applied across it.

D. The liquid crystal is contained within two transparent and electrically conductive layers. This forms a sandwich similar to the plates and dielectric of a capacitor. The liquid crystal material acts as a dielectric since it is an electrical insulator.

An LCD consumes only a minute amount of power. This is normally furnished by a small battery, such as that used in digital watches where this display is commonly used. The main disadvantage of an LCD display is its poor visibility in low ambient light. Sometimes a battery-operated light source is added to overcome this disadvantage.

Q. 3.192(U)-A12. What is a light-emitting diode (LED)? Why does it use a series resistor for normal operation?

A.

1. The cross-section of a light-emitting diode (LED) is shown in Fig. 3.192(U)-A12(1) and its symbol in Fig. 3.192(U)-A12(2). An LED is a special diode, which, when forward-biased, has the property of emitting light. The colors currently available are green, yellow, amber, red, and infrared. The color emitted, depends upon the type of material used in the LED.

2. The series resistor (see Fig. 3.192(U)-A12(3)) is necessary to establish the forward-bias current, which in turn determines the brilliance of the LED emission.

D. Refer to 3.192(U)-A12(1). The LED diode is forward-biased. With this bias, electrons from the N region cross the PN-junction into the P region. Similarly, some holes from the P region cross the junction into the N region. Some of the electrons that have crossed the junction recombine with holes in the P region. Also, some of the holes that have crossed the junction recombine with electrons in the N region. As a result of this recombining process, radiant energy is released and the LED emits light.

The LED is one of a group of devices in the class known as *optoelectronics*. Other devices in this class are LCDs (liquid crystal diodes), CRT displays, photo detectors, optoisolators, and photodiodes.

LEDs have low current drain, long life (up to 50 years), and small size. The operating current for maximum brilliance ranges between 10 and 20 mA.

Q. 3.192(U)-A13. Discuss the uses of LED digital readouts in displays.

A. The most common use of LEDs is in digital display units. Here, arrays of very small LEDs are arranged to provide numerical displays. There is a great variety of LED uses. Some of these are in watches

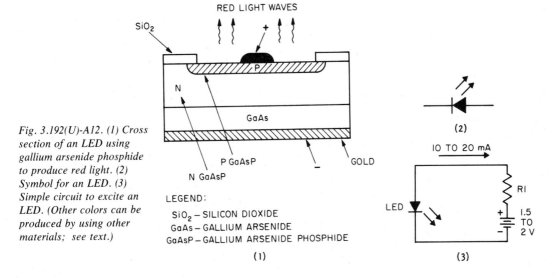

Fig. 3.192(U)-A12. (1) Cross section of an LED using gallium arsenide phosphide to produce red light. (2) Symbol for an LED. (3) Simple circuit to excite an LED. (Other colors can be produced by using other materials; see text.)

RED LIGHT WAVES

N

GaAs

P GaAsP

N GaAsP

GOLD

LEGEND:
SiO₂ – SILICON DIOXIDE
GaAs – GALLIUM ARSENIDE
GaAsP – GALLIUM ARSENIDE PHOSPHIDE

(1)

(2)

10 TO 20 mA

LED

RI

1.5 TO 2 V

(3)

and clocks, digital calculators, frequency counters, TV receiver channel number displays, digital multimeters, and the display of receiver frequencies.

Q. 3.192(U)-A14. What is the function of a Gunn diode?

A. A Gunn diode, in conjunction with a resonant cavity (as the tuned circuit), functions as a microwave oscillator.

D. The Gunn semiconductor device is called a diode, but strictly speaking it is not, because it does not have a junction. The Gunn diode is one of a family of so-called "bulk effect" semiconductor devices used in microwave oscillators. Other devices in this family are the (1) limited-space charge accumulation (LSA) diode, (2) the tunnel diode (TD), (3) the avalanche diode (AD), (4) and the transferred-electron diode (TED). These devices are capable of generating useful microwave power up to 35 GHz or more at powers from 0.1 to 1 W.

Fig. 3.192(U)-A14(1) shows the Gunn diode *mounted in a typical package.* The

diode proper is made of N-type gallium arsenide (G_aA_s). The semiconductor is actually constructed in three layers. However, the thickness of the active layer determines the frequency of operation. For example, for operation at about 16 GHz, this layer is only 8 μm thick (8×10^{-6} m) thick. The other two layers are essential for good ohmic contact and bonding into the package. The operation of a Gunn diode in an oscillator depends upon its quality of negative resistance. *Negative resistance* is another way of saying the Gunn diode can supply in-phase feedback to an oscillating circuit (cavity, in this case) to maintain sustained oscillations. This quality of negative resistance is seen when the positive applied bias voltage exceeds a "threshold" value. For the 16-GHz Gunn diode, this threshold voltage is about $+2.6$ V.

Gunn diodes may be mounted in a coaxial line cavity as shown in Fig. 3.192(U)-A14(2), or in a rectangular waveguide cavity as shown in Fig. 3.192(U)-A14(3). The coaxial line cavity is the simplest type, and the os-

Fig. 3.192(U)-A14. The Gunn diode: (1) The Gunn diode in a typical package. (Courtesy of Microwave Associates, Inc.) (2) Gunn diode in a coaxial line cavity. (3) Gunn diode in a rectangular waveguide cavity.

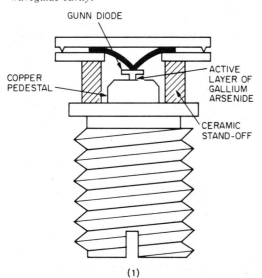

(1)

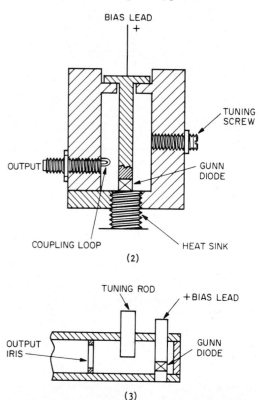

(2)

(3)

cillating frequency can be adjusted with the tuning screw. The rectangular waveguide configuration is more widely used. It provides higher Q and better performance at higher microwave frequencies. Here the frequency may be adjusted by the amount of insertion of the tuning rod: the greater the insertion, the lower the frequency.

The Gunn diode oscillator can also be tuned with a varactor diode (Q. 3.192(U)-A7), which would be mounted in the cavity near the Gunn diode. Here, tuning is accomplished by varying the reverse bias of the varactor. The varactor can vary the oscillator frequency by about ±5 percent.

An important advantage of Gunn diode oscillators is its low noise performance. It is superior in this respect to most other types of microwave sources. (See also Q. 3.246, Q. 3.247, Q. 3.248, and Q. 3.251.)

Q. 3.192(U)-A15. Draw the schematic symbol and equivalent circuit of a unijunction transistor. Discuss the characteristics of a unijunction transistor.

A. The schematic symbol and equivalent circuit are shown in Fig. 3.192(U)-A15.

D. Unlike the usual junction transistor, the unijunction transistor has no collector, but consists of a single crystal of N-type silicon mounted on a ceramic disc. The PN emitter junction is formed by alloying an aluminum wire to the top of the crystal nearest the base two contact. Base one and base two are simply defined by placing contacts at each end of the crystal.

Referring to the simplified equivalent circuit diagram of Fig. 3.192(U)-A15(b), the emitter PN junction is shown as a separate

diode connected between base one and base two. Since both bases are on a single crystal and the emitter is connected between the bases, an internal voltage divider is formed between base two and emitter, and between emitter and base one. (The total resistance between base two and base one is between 5 000 and 10 000 ohms.) With the emitter nonconducting, a typical voltage division is as shown, with $V_{B2} = 4$ V; and $V_{B1} = 6$ V (assuming a base two supply voltage of +10 V).

Note in the equivalent circuit diagram, that the resistance of base one (R_{B1}) is shown to be variable. This is true since in the absence of emitter current, R_{B1} has a fixed value, but when emitter current flows, the path is through R_{B1}, whose resistance varies inversely with the emitter current. (Typical values of R_{B1} are between 40 and 5000 ohms, depending upon the amount of emitter current which may vary between 50 and 0 mA.)

The UJT belongs to the group of semiconductors known as *thryristors*. Others in this group include the silicon-controlled rectifier (SCR) (see Q. 3.192(U)-A16), *triac* (see Q. 3.192(U)-A17), and *diac*. The diac is a three-layer, bidirectional diode. It is also called a *biswitch*. Diacs are used for triac triggering, ac phase control, and overvoltage protection.

Q. 3.192(U)-A16. What is a silicon-controlled rectifier (SCR)?

A. A silicon-controlled rectifier (SCR) is one of a group of semi conductors known as *thyristors*. Thyristors are formed with four alternate, doped semiconductor layers. These are controlled rectifiers.

Fig. 3.192(U)-A15. The unijunction transistor (UJT): (a) schematic symbol and (b) simplified equivalent circuit (see text).

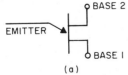

(a)

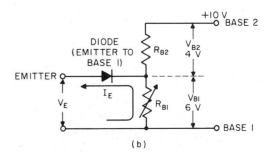

(b)

The SCR is a four-layer PNPN unidirectional device that has three terminals as illustrated in Fig. 3.192(U)-A16. Part a shows the construction and part b the electrical symbol. the *anode* connection is to the outer P region and the cathode is connected to the outer N region. The third terminal is the *gate*, which is at the inner P region.

D. The usefulness of the SCR lies in its switching characteristic. If the anode is held positive with respect to the cathode and a small pulse of current (the trigger) is applied to the gate, the SCR turns ON (conducts). In the conducting state the SCR behaves as a rectifier diode. In addition, the SCR continues to conduct even if the trigger is reduced to zero. The SCR can turn off (become non-conducting) only under one special condition—that is when the current flowing between the anode and cathode is reduced to a very low level (close to zero).

Some uses for the SCR are:

1. In electronic circuits, such as TV receiver horizontal deflection circuits.

2. Dc motor control.

3. Inverters and choppers.

4. Static switching.

5. In regulated power supplies.

Note: There is also a light-activated SCR (LASCR). In this case, the *trigger* consists of a beam of light passing through a

Fig. 3.192(U)-A16. Silicon-controlled rectifier (SCR): (a) PNPN sandwich construction, (b) electrical symbol, and (c) LASCAR (light-activated SCR) symbol.

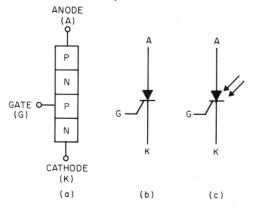

translucent window in the package. In all other respects the LASCR behaves as an SCR. The electrical symbol of a LASCR is shown in Fig. 3.192(U)-A16(c).

Failure modes are similar to those of transistors. See Q. 3.301.

Q. 3.192(U)-A17. What is a TRIAC?

A. A TRIAC is another member of the group of semiconductors known as *thyristors*. (See Q. 3.192(U)-A16). It is a bidirectional-triode thyristor. It is used with ac circuits.

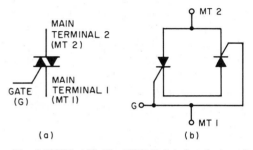

Fig. 3.192(U)-A17. The TRIAC. (a) electrical symbol and (b) equivalent circuit.

Its electrical symbol and equivalent circuit are shown in Fig. 3.192(U)-A17. Part a shows the electrical symbol and part b the equivalent circuit.

Because it is a bidirectional device, a TRIAC has no cathode-anode combination. In reference to the equivalent circuit of part b, the TRIAC is viewed as two SCRs in parallel. Here the anode of one SCR is connected to the cathode of the other.

In part a we see three terminals. The terminals for the main conductive path are designated as Main Terminal 1 (MT 1) and Main Terminal 2 (MT 2). (These are sometimes designated as Anode 1 and Anode 2, respectively.) The gate is the third terminal. Its function is associated with MT 1. The dc gate trigger voltage is 2.5 to 3.5 V.

D. Like the SCR the TRIAC must be triggered at its gate in order to conduct from MT 1 to MT 2. However, since the TRIAC is *bidirectional* it can conduct in *both* directions. That is, from MT 1 to MT 2 or from MT 2 to MT 1. Thus it is used in ac circuits. Aside from this, its characteristics are similar to those of an SCR. See also Q. 3.192(U)-A16.

Some uses for a TRIAC are:
1. Ac lamp dimmer.
2. Phase control of ac power.
3. Ac switching.
4. Ac attenuator.

Failure modes are similar to those of transistors. See Q. 3.301.

Q. 3.192(U)-A18. What is the binary number system and why is it used in digital systems?

A.
1. Semiconductor devices can be made to operate as switches. This makes them ideal for use in *digital* circuits. Such a "switch" is either ON or OFF and thus exhibits two stable states. This type of switch is also called a *bistable device*.

In order for such switches to perform arithmetic and/or logic operations, it is necessary to represent numbers by only 2 digits, or *bits*. These are 0 and 1. A group of *bits* is called a *byte*. A 0 may represent a closed switch (ON), while a 1 may represent an open switch (OFF). A number system that employs only 0s and 1s is called the *binary-number system* and is employed in digital systems. For example, all signals into and out of, as well as inside, a microprocessor must be in digital form (0s and 1s).

Digital systems process ON or OFF signals that are represented by two discrete voltage levels. These are 0 V and +5 V. Zero V is represented by digital 0, while +5 V is represented by digital 1. The 0 V and +5 V levels are practically an industry standard.

D. The decimal numbering system is "incompatible" with switching circuits. Thus, decimal numbers must be converted to equivalent binary numbers. Such a number can then be applied to computer and control circuits. The binary system may seem confusing at first, but it is actually quite simple.

We must get accustomed to working with only 2 digits (0 and 1) instead of 10 digits.

In comparing numbers having different base systems, it is customary to place the number base subscript after the number. Thus,

$$13_{10} = 1101_2$$

The binary number is *not* read as "one thousand one hundred and one, but rather as "one-one-zero-one."

Q. 3.192(U)-A19. Give a simple procedure to convert decimal numbers into binary numbers.

A. The following simple procedure illustrates how to convert a decimal number to a binary number. For example, convert decimal number 13 to binary number (See also example 1 below.)

1. Divide the decimal number by 2. The remainder is always either a 0 or a 1.

Thus, $\frac{13}{2} = 6$ with remainder 1.

2. Place the remainder to the right of the partial quotient obtained in step 1. (See example 11-1.)

3. Divide the partial quotient of step 1 (which was 6) by 2

$$\frac{6}{2} = 3 \quad \text{remainder } 0$$

Place this remainder to the right of the *new* partial quotient.

4. Repeat this process until a *quotient* of *zero* is obtained.

5. The equivalent binary number is equal to the remainders arranged so that the first significant remainder (top 1 in example 1) is the least significant bit (LSB) and the last remainder (bottom 1 in example 1) is the most significant bit (MSB) of the binary number. Thus, correctly arranging the remainders, we have

$$13_{10} = 1101_2$$

Example 1: Converting decimal 13 to a binary number.

Solution:

2)13	1
2)6	0
2)3	1
2)1	1
0	

Example 2: This is an additional exercise in which we convert decimal 103 to a binary number.

Solution:

2)103	
2)51	1
2)25	1
2)12	1
2)6	0
2)3	0
2)1	1
0	1

This is correctly written as $103_{10} = 1100111_2$.

Q. 3.192(U)-A20. Give a simple procedure to convert binary numbers into decimal numbers.

A. The following simple precedure illustrates how to convert a binary number to a decimal number.

1. Multiply the most significant bit (MSB) by 2.

2. If the next bit to the MSB is a 1, add a 1 to the *partial product* obtained in step 1. If the next bit is a 0, add a 0.

3. Multiply the *result* obtained in *step 2* by 2. Continue this process until the least significant bit (LSB) is included in the conversion. The following two examples illustrate this process.

Example 3: Convert binary number 11010 to a decimal number.

Solution: MSB   LSB
    1   1   0   1   0
$2 \times 1 + 1 = 3$ $2 \times 3 + 0 = 6$ $2 \times 6 + 1 = 13$ $2 \times 13 + 0 = 26$

Therefore, $11010_2 = 26_{10}$

Example 4: Convert binary number 110101 to a decimal number.

Solution:

    1   1   0   1   0   1
$2 \times 1 + 1 = 3$ $2 \times 3 + 0 = 6$ $2 \times 6 + 1 = 13$ $2 \times 13 + 0 = 26$
$2 \times 26 + 1 = 53$

Therefore $110101_2 = 53_{10}$

D. For your convenience, a table showing the binary number equivalents for decimal numbers from 1 through 25 is given in Table 1.

Table 1. Decimal to binary number conversion table.

Decimal	Binary	Decimal	Binary
0	0000	14	1110
1	0001	15	1111
2	0010	16	10000
3	0011	17	10001
4	0100	18	10010
5	0101	19	10011
6	0110	20	10100
7	0111	21	10101
8	1000	22	10110
9	1001	23	10111
10	1010	24	11000
11	1011	25	11001
12	1100		
13	1101		

Q. 3.192(U)-A21. What is the difference between dividers and prescalers as used in computer circuits.

A. Dividers and prescalers perform the same basic function. A prescaler, however, is a high-frequency divider that is often used to provide lower-frequency signals for succeeding dividers. Dividers may be either fixed or programmable. When fixed, they divide the input signal by a specific factor, such as 2, 5, 75, 181, 256, etc. When programmable the divide factor can be altered by changing its input logic (binary numbers); thus this type divider is generally shown as a divide by *N*. Generally speaking, integrated circuits perform these functions.

(See Fig. 3.192(U)-A22 for an example of a divide by *n* programmable divider.)

D. There are usually several inputs to dividers or prescalers, as follows:

1. The signal to be divided.
2. The binary number.
3. The "enable" (start) pulse.
4. The "reset" pulse.

Usually, the input signal to be divided is a continuous train of pulses. Thus, to accomplish the desired function, an enable pulse begins the function and a reset pulse reestablishes the starting point. If, for example, a 10-kHz signal is applied to a divide by 10 divider, the enable pulse begins the function, which is completed at the end of the 10,000th pulse. At this time, a reset pulse starts a new count, which is also divided by 10. The output is therefore 1 kHz.

Q. 3.192(U)-A22. What determines the division factor of a binary divider?

A. The division factor of the divider is determined by the binary number applied to its inputs, and it is limited by the number of bits of information it will accept. This is determined by its input ports. As an example, consider the 4-bit programs in Fig. 3.192(U)-A22.

In example 1, all input *ports* are high (binary 1); thus the division factor equals 15. (Low indicates binary 0). In example 2, only the second and fourth input ports are high, thus the division factor equals 10. Any division factor from 1 through 15 can be obtained by properly programming the input ports of this divider.

For example 3, consider an 8-bit divider, as illustrated in Fig. 3.192 (U)-A22. If all input ports are high, the divide ratio will equal 255. Thus, proper programming can provide any desired divide factor from

1 through 255. Actually, factors of several thousand are not uncommon. This becomes evident if 4 more bits are added to the above, as shown in example 4. In the latter case, we now have a 12-bit divider with all input ports high. Proper programming can provide any desired divide factor from 1 through 4 095, for the 12-bit divider.

D. The application of these circuits may be many and varied. As an example, assume that a 450-kHz signal is required for a specific purpose and that a stable 9-MHz signal is readily available. The desired signal may be obtained as shown in example 5. The 9-MHz signal is applied to a divide by 10 divider, and its output is applied to a divide by 2 divider which provides the desired 450-kHz signal.

The "latch" circuits in example 5, serve the function of turning on the dividers, when required, in response to an external switching device.

Q. 3.192(U)-A23. What are counters?

A. Counters function in a similar manner to dividers. They produce an output pulse for N-input pulses. As an example, many digital time clocks divide the power line frequency by 60 to obtain one pulse each second, then divide this pulse by 60 and its output by 60 to obtain minutes and hours.

Fig. 3.192(U)-A22. Examples 1 and 2 illustrate division by 15 and by 10. (Hi indicates binary 1 and Lo indicates binary 0.) Examples 3 and 4 illustrate division by 255 and by 4095. All inputs to examples 3 and 4 are high (binary 1). Example 4 bits are added to those of example 3. Example 5 illustrates a method of obtaining a stable 450-kHz output from a 9-MHz crystal oscillator input. (See text.)

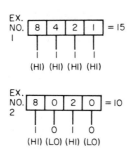

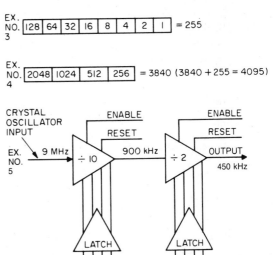

Thus, this device counts input pulses for specific time intervals.

D. Digital counters are frequently used to measure RF frequencies. These counters are available to measure frequencies up to 23 GHZ or higher. They indicate the measured frequencies numerically by a digital display.

Q. 3.192(U)-A24. What is a microprocessor (μP or MPU) and what are its basic functions?

A. A *microprocessor* is one of three major portions of a general-purpose digital computer. A basic digital computer block diagram is shown in Fig. 3.192(U)-A24. The microprocessor serves as the central processing unit (CPU) of a computer. The other two major sections are the "memory" and the "input-output" (IO) sections. The three sections working together may be called a microcomputer. The microcomputer may be on a single chip or on several separate chips.

The MPU is the "brain" of the computer. It is capable of "reading" the program stored in the memory section, interpreting each command stored there, and executing the commands.

D. The memory section of a computer stores data for future use. It also contains a sequence of instructions or commands, known as a *program*. This program is executed by the computer. As shown in the block diagram of Fig. 3.192(U)-A24, there are two types of memories, ROM and RAM. ROM stands for *read-only memory*. The ROM stores fixed and routine instructions.

Fig. 3.192(U)-A24. Simplified block diagram of a general-purpose digital computer. The system shown here is called a microcomputer. The input and output sections, shown here separately for clarity, are generally considered to be one major section, the IO section.

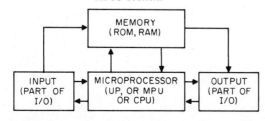

It has a program to tell the MPU what to do, but the MPU cannot change its contents. RAM stands for *random-access memory*. It is used for storing data and program information. Unlike the ROM, the RAM data can be changed by the MPU. RAM data can be erased and new data stored in its place, as required.

The input-output (IO) section interfaces with the "outside world." All information fed from an external source must pass through the input. Also, all outputs from the computer must pass through the output.

Q. 3.192(U)-A25. What is a logic probe?

A. A *logic probe* is a small, hand-held "instrument-on-a-chip," used for functional testing and troubleshooting of digital circuits.

D. Physically, a logic probe looks like an oversized pen with a needle point at one end. The needle point is placed on various digital circuit terminals to detect the presence of "logic highs" or "logic lows." From the opposite end of the logic probe, a strain-relieved power cord extends. This cord is connected to the power supply of the circuit under test.

A logic probe can detect the logic level at any point in a digital circuit. The display is by means of a band of light near the tip of the probe, as follows: (1) a logic high is indicated by a bright light, (2) a logic low is indicated by no light, (3) an incorrect signal level produces a dim light, and (4) pulsing produces a flashing light.

A logic probe is extremely useful in tracing logic levels and pulses through IC circuitry. It can instantly show whether the mode probed is "high," "low," "bad level," "open circuited," or "pulsing." (See also Q. 3.192(U)-A26.)

Q. 3.192(U)-A26. What is a logic pulser?

A. A *logic pulser* is a small, hand-held "instrument-on-a-chip." A logic pulser injects digital pulses between gates without requiring the unsoldering of components.

D. Physically, a logic pulser looks like a logic probe Q. 3.192(U)-A25. It can automatically drive "low" nodes "high" or "high" nodes "low."

A logic pulser is a pulse generator with high output current capability. It has sufficient current to override IC outputs in either the "high" or "low" state. It is a valuable instrument used for fault isolation or circuit design.

Q. 3.192(U)-A27. Describe briefly the method of testing IC digital logic circuits.

A. As with transistor and tube testers, IC digital logic circuit testers are classified as *static* or *dynamic* testers. The difference depends upon whether the circuits are tested as part of a dc or ac circuit. This type of IC tester simulates the required circuit inputs. It then tests for the proper IC-functional response at its output(s).

D. *General.* An IC may consist of combinations of many transistors on a single substrate. It may also include a number of resistors and capacitors. Consequently, the testing of ICs is a different problem from that of testing transistors or tubes. An IC is tested as a *total package.* Thus, *circuit function* is tested, rather than the characteristics of individual components.

1. *Static IC Tester.* In general, static IC testers are designed to measure the following dc parameters: (a) open circuit, (b) short circuit, and (c) leakage current I_{CBO}. These are the same dc parameters measured by static transistor testers. However, static IC testers will require a program card or knobs to identify the class of circuit, such as "digital RTL flip-flop."

Even simple circuit ICs may have 14 or 16 pins. The IC is plugged into a standard IC 16-pin socket. For 14- or 16-pin ICs, be sure to insert pin 1 of the IC into pin 1 of the IC socket.

After the IC is plugged in, a "Test" button on the static IC tester is depressed. The tester will indicate "GO" (good IC) or "NO GO" (defective IC).

2. *Dynamic Digital-IC Tester.* A front panel layout of a dynamic digital IC tester is shown in Fig. 3.192(U)-A27. Testers of this type are programmed from computer cards. A separate card is used for each IC type to be tested.

Fig. 3.192(U)-A27 shows that there are logic switches that the operator can set in accordance with the various pins of the IC. A general procedure is as follows:

a. Apply power V_{cc} and ground (or V_{ee} and ground for ECL device) to the appropriate pins. For RTL, DTL, TTL, pin 14 is used for power (also pin 4 for TTL) and pin 7 for grounds (also pin 10 for TTL). For

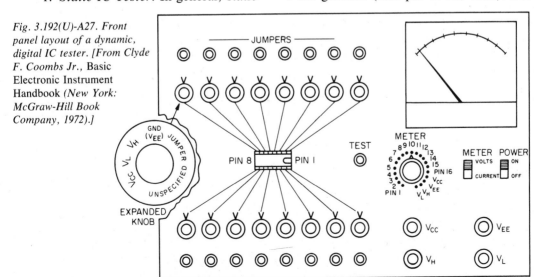

Fig. 3.192(U)-A27. Front panel layout of a dynamic, digital IC tester. [From Clyde F. Coombs Jr., Basic Electronic Instrument Handbook *(New York: McGraw-Hill Book Company, 1972).]*

ECL, pin 3 is used for power and pin 2 for ground.

b. Input logic voltage selections are made next. On Fig. 3.192(U)-A27, any voltage may be made to any pin. Then a voltmeter may be connected to any output pin to check the output voltage. Any incorrect output voltage indicates a defective IC.

Another type of dynamic digital IC tester will provide a switch to choose the logic family (RTL, DTL, TTL, or ECL). Next, logic 1s and 0s are fed to inputs and monitored at the output pins. Readouts are in the form of indicator lights for 1 and 0. Dynamic digital IC testers generally give GO, NO GO results as well as values.

Q. 3.192(U)-A28. Draw a block diagram of a phase-locked loop (PLL). Briefly describe its operation.

A. The basic block diagram is shown in Fig. 3.192(U)-A28(a). A diagram of a commercial monolithic PLL is shown in part (b) of the figure.

A PLL circuit functions to lock the frequency and phase of a voltage-controlled oscillator (VCO) to an input reference signal, V_{in}. The VCO is a free-running oscillator, which operates at a frequency close to the reference frequency, F_O.

The reference frequency and the free-running frequency are fed to the phase comparator. If they are unequal, the phase comparator generates an error voltage V_e. V_e is filtered, amplified, and applied to the VCO. This forces the VCO to operate at the reference frequency.

D. The output of the PLL can be the error voltage V_e or the stabilized VCO frequency F_o. The error voltage output can be utilized as a PLL-FM demodulator output (see Q. 3.181-A5) or a frequency shift keying (FSK) demodulator output.

The VCO output can be used in a fre-

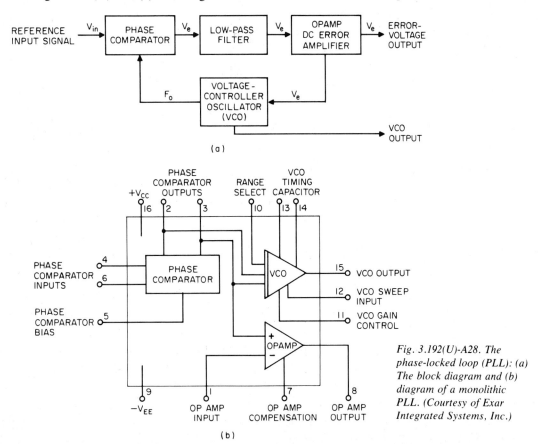

Fig. 3.192(U)-A28. The phase-locked loop (PLL): (a) The block diagram and (b) diagram of a monolithic PLL. (Courtesy of Exar Integrated Systems, Inc.)

quency synthesis system as the local oscillator for TV, CB, and commercial receivers.

Q. 3.192(U)-A29. With the aid of a simple diagram, show how crystal oscillator accuracy of 10-kHz signal is obtained using a stable 20-MHz crystal reference oscillator.

A. The diagram is given in Fig. 3.192(U)-A29. Crystal oscillator accuracy of a 10-kHz signal is required. Precision crystals at 10 kHz are not readily available and in any case would be quite expensive. However, high-frequency crystals are readily available at low cost. Thus, it would be desirable to use a 20-MHz crystal oscillator to stabilize a 10-kHz VCO.

The highly stable 20-MHz reference crystal oscillator is fed to a divide by 2000 digital frequency divider. The output of the divider is a crystal-stable 10-kHz signal. This new signal is now used as the reference to stabilize the 10-kHz VCO.

D. A crystal-controlled oscillator provides a stable reference signal to the phase comparator. The output of a voltage controlled oscillator (VCO) is also applied to the phase comparator. If the two signals are synchronized, no correction is required. However, if the VCO drifts off frequency, the phase comparator develops a correction voltage proportional to the phase difference of its input signals. The output of the phase difference of its input signals. The output of the phase comparator is filtered and applied to the VCO. This output is a dc "error" voltage. When applied to the VCO, the voltage causes it to assume to correct frequency and phase. The VCO is thus able to provide crystal oscillator accuracy. This is the basic method on which frequency synthesis is based.

Q. 3.192(U)-A30. Describe the operation of a basic digital PLL frequency synthesizer.

A. In Q. 3.192(U)-A29 we showed how a high-frequency crystal oscillator (20-MHz) could be used to help produce a crystal stable VCO frequency of 10 kHz. This is the basis

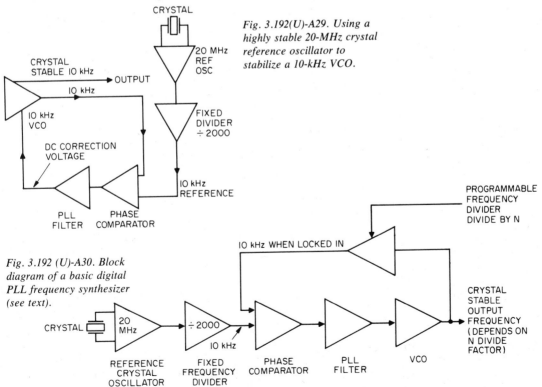

Fig. 3.192(U)-A29. Using a highly stable 20-MHz crystal reference oscillator to stabilize a 10-kHz VCO.

Fig. 3.192 (U)-A30. Block diagram of a basic digital PLL frequency synthesizer (see text).

upon which a frequency synthesizer operates. However, a frequency synthesizer is capable of providing a *number* of crystal-stable VCO frequencies with the aid of a single crystal oscillator and a single VCO. This will be explained with the aid of Fig. 3.192(U)-A30. Note the similarity to Fig. 3.192(U)-A29.

A frequency synthesizer can provide a number of crystal-stable output frequencies (one at a time) from its VCO. These frequencies can be used as the local oscillator frequencies in receivers and/or as transmitter oscillator frequencies. No adjustments are required to each frequency so obtained, since each one is the exact frequency required.

D. One popular type of PLL frequency synthesizer uses a scheme known as ''programmable, divide-by-N phase-lock synthesis.'' The circuitry consists of the following:

1. Reference crystal oscillator.
2. Fixed-frequency divider.
3. Phase comparator.
4. Programmable, divide-by-N frequency divider.
5. PLL filter.
6. VCO (voltage-controlled oscillator).

A key element in this scheme is an extremely accurate and stable, reference crystal oscillator. In our example this oscillator operates at exactly 20 MHz. This reference frequency is applied to a *fixed* digital frequency divider with a divide ratio of 2 000. The output of this divider is exactly 10 kHz, which is applied to one input of the phase comparator. The second input comes from the VCO via the divide-by-N programmable divider. This second input must also be exactly 10 kHz for the proper VCO (output) frequency to be present.

The VCO output frequency may be required to be any one of a number of specific frequencies. The desired frequency is selected by operating a channel selector switch or channel selector pushbuttons. The manner in which the desired VCO frequency output is achieved is explained by the following simplified example. Refer to Fig. 3.192(U)-

A30. Assume we wish to receive CB channel 4, which has a carrier frequency (approximately of 27 MHz. Also assume we have a single-conversion receiver with an IF of 10.7 MHz. The required local oscillator (VCO) frequency is 27 + 10.7 = 37.7 MHz. We turn the receiver channel selector switch to channel 4. The channel switch operates digital circuits, which generate the proper divide-by-N digital code for the programmable divide-by-N frequency divider. A typical digital code would be 110111.

This digital code establishes the desired divide ratio in the programmable divider. This ratio must be such that the VCO divided output that is fed to the phase comparator is exactly 10 kHz to match the fixed reference frequency of 10 kHz. This requires a divide ratio of the programmable divider of

$$\frac{37.7 \text{ MHz}}{10.0 \text{ kHz}} = \frac{37.7 \times 10^6}{10 \times 10^3} = 3\ 770$$

As we said, this required divide ratio is determined by feeding the correct digital code (here 110111) into the programmable divider. Because of the action of the PLL circuitry, the VCO frequency will be adjusted to 37.7 MHz. This happens because the programmable divider now divides by 3770. Thus the PLL will stabilize the VCO only at a frequency where the VCO frequency divided by 3770 equals 10 kHz. Any other VCO frequency would produce (through the programmable divider) a frequency other than 10 kHz. In this case the output of the phase comparator would be a dc voltage which would drive the VCO to the correct frequency (here 37.7 MHz). Once the VCO reaches the required frequency both inputs to the phase comparator will be exactly 10 kHz. Any tendency of the VC to drift from its required frequency will be quickly corrected by a dc voltage generated by the phase comparator. (The PLL filter ensures that only dc will reach the VCO.)

Q. 3.192(U)-A31. What is the logic symbol for an AND gate? An OR gate? A NAND

gate? A NOR gate? An INVERTER (NOT) gate?

A.

1. The logic symbol for an AND gate is shown in Fig. 3.192(U)-A31(a).

2. The logic symbol for an OR gate is shown in Fig. 3.192(U)-A31(b).

3. The logic symbol for a NAND gate is shown in Fig. 3.192(U)-A31(c).

4. The logic symbol for a NOR gate is shown in Fig. 3.192(U)-A31(d).

5. The logic symbol for an INVERTER (NOT) gate is shown in Fig. 3.192(U)-A31(d).

D. In digital logic systems (see Q. 3.192(U)-A22), the terms ON and OFF or HI and LO refer to discrete events. These are identified by the binary numbers 1 and 0. These discrete events are contrasted to linear (analog) signals, which have an infinite number of levels. The discrete events can be characterized by digits (1 and 0), thus the term "digital." The term "logic" applies because the circuit operation follows simple mathematical laws in which the "effect" predictably follows the "cause."

Digital circuits are packaged in ICs in which thousands of components are interconnected in a single case. Digital ICs are manufactured for specific applications. Some applications are:

1. Digital computers.
2. Switching circuits.
3. Display circuits.
4. Counting circuits.

A digital computer performs its calculations by the repeated execution of a few simple operations. The computer is actually composed of only a few different types of switching (digital) circuits. However, thousands of these basic circuits are in a computer. The basic circuits are of two general types. These are: (1) flip-flops (multivibrators) and (2) logic gates. Logic gates are used to control the flow of data in the arithmetic section of the computer. Flip-flops are used in counters and storage elements. The arithmetic (and control) functions in a digital computer (or system) are performed by three basic logic circuits. These are: (1) the OR gate, (2) the AND gate, and (3) the INVERTER (NOT) gate.

Rather than attempt to show schematic diagrams containing possibly thousands of components, logic diagrams have been developed to show *functions* of *sections* of a digital IC. This greatly simplifies the analysis and understanding of a particular IC. These logic diagrams are combinations of different types of logic "gates," some of which are shown in Fig. 3.192(U)-A31.

For the explanation of the operation of the various gates shown in Fig. 3.192(U)-A31 and the meanings of the symbols, see Q. 3.192(U)-A32.

Q. 3.192(U)-A32. Explain the operation of the logic gates shown in Q. 3.192(U)-A31 and the use of "truth" tables.

A. Logic gating operations are performed in accordance with the rules of Boolean algebra. Letters of the alphabet and other symbols are used to write Boolean equations. To avoid confusion with basic arithmetic operations, note that, for example, the Boolean expression for an AND gate is,

Fig. 3.192(U)-A31. Logic symbols for various gates: (a) the AND gate symbol, (b) the OR gate symbol, (c) the NAND gate symbol, (d) the NOR gate symbol, (e) the INVERTER (NOT) gate symbol.

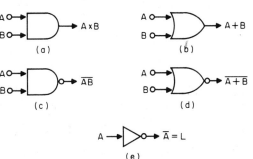

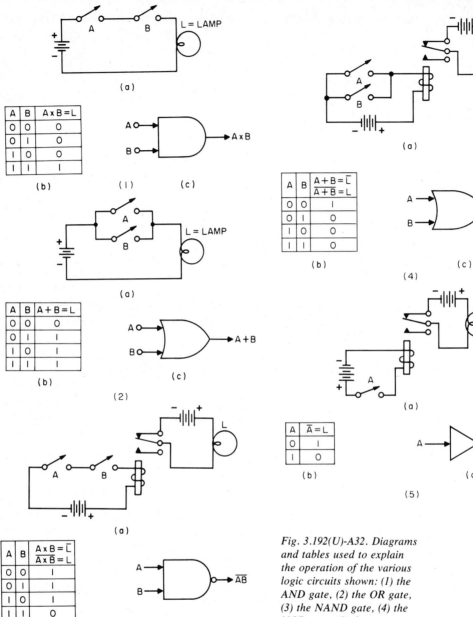

Fig. 3.192(U)-A32. Diagrams
and tables used to explain
the operation of the various
logic circuits shown: (1) the
AND gate, (2) the OR gate,
(3) the NAND gate, (4) the
NOR gate, (5) the
INVERTER (NOT) gate. (See
text.)

A × B = C (or AB = C). This is read "A *and* B is equal to C." The "×" sign (or dot) indicates the AND operation. It does *not* represent multiplication.

A *truth table* is simply a table that, at a glance, indicates all the conditions under which a particular logic circuit operates. This will be shown in the examples that follow.

1. *The AND Gate.* Figure 3.192(U)-A32(1) for the AND gate shows (a) the functional circuit, (b) the truth table, and (c) the logic symbol. The truth table entries are binary numbers with 0 corresponding to OFF and 1 corresponding to ON. In and AND gate, *both* of the inputs A *and* B must be present (in the 1 condition) to produce the

output shown in logic form as, A × B (read "A *and* B").

The circuit of Fig. 3.192(U)-A32(1)(a) shows—by means of two switches A and B, a battery, and a lamp (L)—the equivalent operation of an AND gate. Following the truth table, observe that unless switches A *and* B are in the ON (binary 1) condition, the lamp will not light (there will be no output).

2. *The OR gate*. Fig. 3.192(U)-A32(2) for the OR gate shows, (a) the functional circuit, (b) the truth table, and (c) the logic symbol.

In an OR gate, *either* the A or B input must be present (in the 1 condition) to produce the output shown in logic form as A + B (read, "A *or* B," *not* "A plus B"). The truth table shows that if either switch in part a is ON (1), the lamp will light. Also, if both switches are ON, the lamp will light. Because of this latter response, the gate is also known as an INCLUSIVE OR gate.

3. *The NAND gate*. Fig. 3.192(U)-A32(3) for the NAND gate shows (a) the functional circuit, (2) the truth table, and (3) the logic symbol.

In a NAND gate, *both* A and B inputs must be present (in the 1 condition) for the output to be in the 0 condition (no output). The output *is* expressed in logic form as $\overline{A \times B}$. An *overbar* is used to express NOT. Thus, $\overline{A \times B}$ reads "NOT A and B."

Referring to the circuit in part a and the truth table in part b, we can analyze the NAND gate operation. Note that there is an output (lamp ON) in every condition, except when *both* switches A and B are ON (1). At this time, the relay in part a is energized and the lamp goes out (output 0). In the truth table, note in the third column heading, the two logic expressions: (1) A × B = $\overline{L}$, which reads "A and B equals lamp OFF" (output 0); (2) $\overline{A \times B}$ = L, which reads, "A and B NOT equals lamp ON" (output 1).

4. *The NOR gate*. Figure 3.192(U)-A32(4) for the NOR gate shows (a) the func-

tional circuit, (b) the truth table, and (c) the logic symbol.

In the NOR gate there will be an output (1) only when *both* A and B inputs are *not* present (0 condition). The output is expressed in logic form as, $\overline{A + B}$ (read "NOT A *or* B").

To analyze the NOR gate operation, refer to the circuit in part a and the truth table in part b. Note that there is an output (lamp ON) *only* when A and B are *both* in the O condition. At this time, the relay remains unenergized and the lamp is lit (output). In any other condition, the relay is energized and the lamp goes out (output 0). In the truth table, note in the third column heading the two logic expressions: (1) A + B = $\overline{L}$, which reads "A or B equals lamp OFF" (output 0); (2) $\overline{A + B}$ = L, which reads "A or B NOT equals lamp ON" (output 1).

5. *The INVERTER (NOT) gate*. Figure 3.192(U)-A32(5) shows (a) the functional circuit, (b) the truth table, and (c) the logic symbol. An INVERTER gate is one in which the output is the inverse of the input. These gate circuits are also known as NOT gates. In an INVERTER Gate, an input "A" = 1 will result in no output (0). Conversely, if "A" = 0, there will be an output (1).

In part a, when switch A is closed (1), the relay will be energized and will open the lamp circuit (0). When switch A is opened, the relay will be deenergized and the lamp will light (1). These conditions are shown in the truth table.

The output is expressed in logic form as $\overline{A}$ = L (read "NOT A equals L"). In other words, when switch A is open (0) the lamp is ON (1).

D. Note in parts 3, 4, and 5 of Fig. 3.192(U)-A32, the small circle on the logic symbols. This means that the output (or the input, if so used) is INVERTED.

Q. 3.192(U)-A33. Why is it important that digital logic circuitry be shielded from radio frequency sources or protected from powerline noise?

A. Digital logic circuitry operates on the basis of *discrete* (pulse) signals, rather than analog signals. If either RF signals or power line noises are able to add to (or subtract from) the digital signals, they will cause malfunctioning of the digital equipment. Therefore, to insure correct operation, digital logic circuitry should be well shielded from radio frequency transmissions. In addition (where required), power line filters should be installed.

D. Not all digital logic circuitry need be protected as described above. For example, many digital calculators are battery-operated and are not normally operated in the vicinity of fairly strong radio frequency fields. Also, not all power lines are noisy enough to require filtering. However, if a particular power line is also used to operate other electrical devices, it may need to be filtered.

A term known as *noise margin* (NM) is used to determine the sensitivity of digital circuitry to interfering voltages. NM is the maximum extraneous voltage that causes a logic gate to change its state. It is measured in volts or millivolts.

Some "families" of IC digital logic devices have greater noise immunity than others. Some of these may be listed as:

1. High-threshold logic (HTL).
2. Transistor-transistor logic (TTL or T²L) (not as good noise immunity as HTL).
3. Complementary metal oxide semiconductor (CMOS).

Other families of IC digital logic devices have low noise immunity. Some of these may be listed as:

1. Resistor-transistor logic (RTL).
2. Diode-transistor logic (DCL).
3. Emitter-coupled logic (ECL).

Even though certain families may have low noise immunity, they have their own particular advantages for use in specific applications.

Q. 3.192(U)-A34. What is the CMOS digital logic integrated circuit?

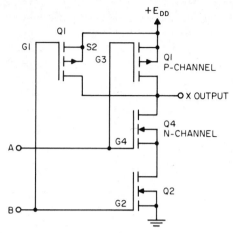

Fig. 3.192(U)-A34. A CMOS two-input NAND gate.

A. The CMOS digital logic integrated circuit is another member of the logic family. CMOS (or COS/MOS) stands for *complementary metal oxide semiconductor.* CMOS employs the enhancement-type MOSFET (see Q. 3.192(U)-A4, 3.192(U)-A27, 3.192(U)-A33, and 3.192(U)-A35. CMOS exhibits the lowest dissipation per gate and has slower speed (5 MHz) than TTL. (*Speed* refers to how fast the circuit can change states. It is measured in megahertz.)

In the CMOS logic family no resistors are used. Rather, P-channel and N-channel enhancement-type MOSFETs are used in complementary pairs. (See Discussion.) By this means, a much greater packaging density is realized than with the TTL.

D. The circuit of a CMOS, two-input NAND gate is shown in Fig. 3.192(U)-A34. Two P-channel MOSFETs (Q_1 and Q_2) and two N-channel MOSFETs (Q_3 and Q_4) are used here. In the NAND gate, the P-channel MOSFETs are in parallel and the N-channel MOSFETs are in series. There are two inputs here (a "fan-in" of two), A and B. (For each additional input desired, a P-channel MOSFET is added in parallel and an N-channel MOSFET in series. Their two gates are then connected together and become the added input point.)

The operation is as follows:

1. Assume inputs A and B are at logic 1. This turns OFF the P-channel devices and turns ON the N-channel devices. The output = logic 0. (The NOT of a one is zero.)

2. Assume either (or both) A and B inputs are at logic 0.

3. One or both P-channel MOSFETs are ON, and one or both N-channel MOSFETs are OFF. The output equals logic 1. (The NOT of a zero is one.)

Note: The CMOS can be NOR/NAND. It operates on a supply voltage from 3 to 18 V. The power dissipation per gate is only 10^{-5} mW, *Fan out* greater than 50. (*Fan out* is the maximum number of gates that may be connected to the output terminal of a single gate.) Its noise margin (NM) is classified excellent. (*Noise margin* is the maximum extraneous voltage that causes a gate to change its state. Its unit is millivolts or volts.)

Q. 3.192(U)-A35. What is the TTL digital logic integrated circuit?

A. The TTL (or T^2L) digital logic integrated circuit is one of the most widely used families of logic (gate) circuits. It has good speed and reasonably low-power dissipation per gate. (Speed refers to the rate at which the circuit can change states; it is measured in megahertz. Standard TTL equals 35 MHz.) (See also Q. 3.192(U)-A27, Q. 3.192(U)-A33, and Q. 3.192(U)-A34.) It is also known as *multiemitter transistor logic*, the reason for which can be seen in the simplified TTL schematic diagram of Fig. 3.192(U)-A35. A transistor with two or more emitters can be manufactured as part of an IC. (Four-emitter transistors for TTL gates are now uncommon.) Each emitter receives a separate input signal to determine the state of the gate (HIGH or LOW, 1 or 0). The basic TTL is a NAND gate, and operation of the gate requires that all emitters be in the LOW condition. The TTL family requires a power supply of 5V.

D. Note in the circuit of Fig. 3.192(U)-A35 that transistor Q_1 has *two* emitters serving as input points (A and B). This circuit is said to have a fan-in of two. (*Fan-in* describes the number of inputs to a gate.)

Each emitter-to-base junction acts as a diode. Therefore, these two junctions act as diodes of an AND gate to which are connected the A and B inputs. Also, the base-to-collector junction of Q_1 acts as a diode in series with the base of Q_2. Q_2 is connected as an INVERTER. The output of Q_2 is always the *opposite* (or complement) of the input logic level. Q_2 may be called a NOT gate because the input and output logic levels are *not* the same. However, the term "INVERTER" is commonly used for this circuit (Q_2).

The logic performed by TTL is positive NAND logic. Operation is as follows:

1. a. Assume input A is a logic 0. (Q_1 is an NPN transistor).

b. The "A" base-emitter junction becomes *forward biased* and the base of Q_1 assumes a low potential (near ground).

c. The collector-to-base junction of Q_1 is now *reverse-biased*, and so no base current can flow in Q_2.

d. Transistor Q_2 is now OFF. Therefore, the output at Q_2 collector rises and equals logic 1.

e. If *both* A and B inputs were at logic 0, the same condition exists as described above.

2. a. Now, assume inputs A and B are both at logic 1. Both base emitter diodes of Q_1 are reverse-biased and non-conducting.

b. The collector-base junction of Q_1 is now *forward-biased* and base emitter current flows in Q_2.

Fig. 3.192(U)-A35. The TTL (or T^2L) digital logic integrated circuit. (See text.)

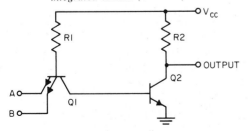

c. Now, collector current flows in Q_2 dropping its voltage to equals logic 0.

Note: There are a number of members in the TTL family. These include the standard, low-power, high-speed, and Schottky diode clamped series. The TTL is always NAND. It operates on a supply voltage of 5 V. The power dissipation per gate is 1 to 22 mW depending on the type. *Fan-out* is the maximum number of gates that may be connected to the output terminal of a single gate). Its noise margin (NM) is classified very good. (*Noise margin* is the maximum extraneous voltage that causes a gate to change its state. Its unit is millivolts or volts.)

Q. 3.192(U)-A36. What is the ASCII (American Standard Code for Information Interchange)?

A. ASCII, pronounced "ask-ee," is a standard code used extensively in computer data transmission. It is a digital code that is used for the interchange of information to or from such devices as teletypewriters or tele-(line)-printers.

D. In this scheme there is a separate ASCII digital code for each character on a typewriter or line printer, plus control codes. For example, if you want a typewriter tied to your system to type an "A," the signal that must be transmitted on the data lines to your typewriter is "1000001." Similarly, the "carriage return" the symbol is "0001101".

Each of 128 numerals, letters, symbols, and special control codes is represented by a 7-bit binary number, as shown in the above examples.

Q. 3.192(U)-A37. What is the Baudot Code?

A. The *Baudot Code* is a data transmission code in which one character (number, letter, control code) is represented by five equal-length "bits." (A *bit* is a 1 or a 0.)

D. The Baudot Code has been the standard code for telegraph communications in printing telegraph systems for many years.

The basic code has a capability of 32 discrete characters or combinations. However, by means of two special characters, (figures shift and letters shift), 56 total characters are obtained. When one of these two special characters appears, it indicates that all that follows has one of *two* possible meanings for each code combination until a new shift symbol appears.

This code is used for communication weather information and in the military.

Q. 3.192(U)-A38. What is meant by the Baud (Bd) Rate?

A. A *baud* (Bd) is a unit of signaling speed in telecommunications. It may be defined as the reciprocal of the shortest pulse duration of a data "word." (The pulses here are bits, that is, 1s or 0s. A data *word* is a set of characters that is transported by computer circuits as a *unit*. *Baud rate* is stated as a number of *baud* (Bd). For example, 110 baud, 300 baud, etc.

D. It is used frequently in serial data transmission in which the characters of a word are transmitted in sequence (one after another) over a single line. The following example will illustrate baud rate: The width of each *bit* is 9.09 m. What is the baud rate?

$$\text{Baud rate} = \frac{1}{\text{Bit time}}$$

$$= \frac{1}{9.09_{ms}} = 110 \text{ baud}$$

Note: The baud rate and the number of data bits transmitted per second are *not* the same. The above baud rate of 110 includes "start" and "stop" bits as well as data bits. For example, with a baud rate of 110, the data (information) may comprise 80 bits-per-second. (Baud rate is *not* defined in terms of bits-per-second, but data bits are. The remaining 30 bits in this case are start and stop bits.

A *start* bit is the first bit of a serial data word that signals the start of transmission of a series of *data* (word) bits.

A *stop* bit is the last bit of a serial data word that signals the end of that word. This bit is usually a 1.

Q. 3.192(U)-A39. What is meant by data rate?

A. *Data rate* is the number of *information* bits-per-second employed in a data system. (A *bit* is a 1 or a 0.) Note that *start* and *stop* bits are *not* included in the data rate. (See Q. 3.192(U)-A38).

D. The following are some common data communications system devices and their data rates.

1. *Low-speed devices* (0 to 300 bits-per-second): teleprinters, paper tape devices, card readers, and punches.

2. *Medium-speed devices* (300 to 4 800 bits-per-second): high-speed printers and paper tape devices, CRT printing display devices, magnetic ink, and optical character recognition devices.

3. *High-speed devices* (above 4 800 bits-per-second): magnetic tape, magnetic card, and magnetic drum read-in, readout devices.

Q. 3.192(U)-A40. In computer terminology, what is meant by "information"?

A. *Information* is the basic *data* and/or *program* entered into the system. It is usually measured in *bits*.

D. *Information bits:* Those bits originated by the data source that are not used for error control by the data transmission system.

Information handling: The storing and processing of information and its transmission from the source to the user.

Information rate: The minimum number of binary digits per second required to specify the source messages.

ANTENNAS

Q. 3.193. Explain the voltage and current relationships in one-wave-length antenna; half-wavelength (dipole) antenna; quarter-wave-length "grounded" antenna.

A.
1. In a one-wavelength antenna, the current is minimum at both ends and at the center of the antenna. Simultaneously, the voltage is maximum at these points. This may be seen clearly in the accompanying figure (Fig. 3.193(a)).

2. As shown in Fig. 3.193(b), the voltage is maximum and the current minimum at both ends of a half-wavelength antenna. In addition, the impedance is maximum at both ends (2500 ohms) and minimum (73 ohms) at the center. Half-wavelength antennas are invariably fed at the center with a low-impedance transmission line.

3. For a quarter-wavelength "grounded" antenna, the ground acts as a *mirror* to supply the second half of a half-wave antenna. The maximum current is therefore at the ground point, as is the minimum voltage. At the top of the antenna, the current is minumum and the voltage maximum.

The current and voltage distribution for a "grounded", quarter-wave antenna is shown in Fig. 3.193(c).

D. *General:* An antenna is a special type of resonant circuit. In the familiar type of resonant circuit where coils and capacitors are used, the dimensions of these circuit elements are generally a small percentage of a wavelength ($\frac{1}{4}$, $\frac{1}{2}$, or 1 wavelength or greater), a good deal of radiation of the electromagnetic energy will take place and for all practical purposes, the circuit represents

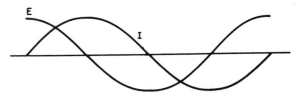

Fig. 3.193(a). Voltage and current distribution along a one-wavelength antenna (full-wave antenna).

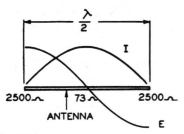

Fig. 3.193(b). *Current and voltage distribution on
Hertz antenna.*

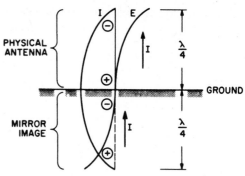

Fig. 3.193(c). *Current and voltage distribution along
a quarter wavelength, "grounded" antenna.*

an antenna. In practice, to achieve the a
wavelength (¼, ½, or one wavelength or
greater), a good deal of radiation of the electromagnetic energy will take place and for
all practical purposes, the circuit represents
an antenna. In practice, to achieve the
greatest radiation efficiency, antennas are
composed of straight resonant wires (or
rods), or combinations of such elements. As
in any resonant circuit, the greatest current
will flow when the circuit is resonated to the
applied frequency. When an antenna is resonant, it achieves the greatest amount of
radiation because maximum current then
flows in the conductor(s). The *shortest* length
of antenna wire that can be made resonant
to any given frequency is one-half wavelength. Such an antenna is commonly known
as a "dipole" (See part 2 of this discussion.
See also Q. 3.14.D. for a discussion of radiation fields from an antenna.)

If an antenna wire was infinitely long
and excited at some frequency, the RF energy
would travel down the wire and would be
dissipated in the form of radiation and heating
of the wire. However, when the wire has a
finite length and is short in terms of wavelengths, the original excitation energy (incident wave) reaches the end of the antenna
with very little attenuation. At this point, it
sees an open circuit and is reflected back
(reflected wave) toward the feed point.
However, the incident wave is continuously
present and the two waves combine to create
"standing" waves on the wire. (See Q. 3.215
and Q. 3.216.) In the three figures for this
question the "standing" waves of voltage
and current are shown for three antennas of
different wavelengths.

1. In Fig. 3.193(a), the antenna illustrated is an *electrical* wavelength long (see
Q. 3.203(4)). As such, a full wavelength of
voltage and current standing waves appear
on the antenna. The distribution of the voltage and current is sinusoidal. Also, note that
they change polarity at certain fixed points
along the antenna. The voltage changes polarity at the one-quarter and three-quarter
wavelength points. However, the current
changes its polarity at the half-wavelength
point and is always 90° out of phase with
the voltage. Note that the voltage and current
radiated fields (Q. 3.14) are also 90° out of
phase. An interesting fact is that identical
transmitting and receiving antennas have the
same standing wave pattern, impedance and
distribution and directivity pattern.

The impedance along any point of an
antenna (see Q. 3.194) is determined by the
ratio of the voltage to the current at that
point. Examination of Fig. 3.193(a) indicates
that a full-wavelength antenna has maximum
impedance at the center and both ends of
the antenna, and minimum impedance at the
one-quarter and three-quarter wavelength
points.

2. The simple dipole antenna is the basis of practically all antenna systems. As
shown in Fig. 3.193(b), it is an electrical half
wavelength long. The actual length of a dipole
in feet may be computed from the formula

$$L = 492 \times 0.95/f \text{ (MHz)}$$
$$= 468/f \text{ (MHz)}$$

The factor 0.95 is necessary because the

velocity of propagation on the antenna is less than the velocity in free space. Impedance values measured at any point on an antenna are a function of the magnitude of the current and voltage at that point. At the center of a dipole where the current is a maximum and the voltage a minimum, the impedance is equal to 73 ohms. At the ends, the impedance is about 2500 ohms. Since dipoles are usually fed at the center, the value of 73 ohms is of great importance because it must be matched to the transmission line. A common impedance for one type of coaxial line is 72 ohms and this type of line is frequently used to match correctly to the center of a dipole antenna (see D.2 of Q. 3.193).

3. The quarter-wave "grounded" antenna operates with its lower end closely coupled to ground, or to a metal ground plane (see Q. 3.204). The quarter-wave rod acts as one half of a half-wave antenna. The earth or ground plane (see Q. 3.204) acts as a mirror and supplies the other quarter-wave section, as shown in Fig. 3.193(c). This type of antenna is frequently referred to as a Marconi antenna. If a vertical grounded antenna is to show a resonant (resistive) impedance at its base, it must be an odd number (1,3,5, etc.) of quarter-wavelengths long. This antenna is fed at its base where there is a low impedance of about 38 ohms. (See Q. 3.209 for methods of feeding such antennas.) If an antenna is *less* than one-quarter wavelength high, it presents a capacitive reactance at its base. In this case an inductance must be added in series with the antenna to make it resonant. On the other hand, an antenna having a length between one-quarter and one-half wavelength will look inductive at the base. Such an antenna may be resonated with a series capacitor which will "tune out" the inductance and make the base-input impedance, resistive. (See also Q. 3.203(3) and (4).)

The concept of a "mirror" or "image" antenna is a convenient one to describe the effect of the ground plane in reflecting the original wave from the physical antenna back

into space. This ground-plane reflection causes a reflected wave to occur, which has the same characteristics as if this reflected wave originated at a second antenna. This second antenna would be identical to the real antenna, but situated under the ground directly below it. As shown in Fig. 3.193(c), the "mirror image" antenna exhibits a "mirror image" of the voltage polarity which appears across the real antenna. As a result, the current in each portion of the "antenna" flows in the same direction, producing a reinforced transmitted wave. In physical terms, what actually happens is that the vertically polarized waves will be reflected from a highly conductive ground plane without any appreciable change in phase, and tend to reinforce the wave from the physical antenna.

Q. 3.194. What effect does the magnitude of the voltage and current, at a point on a half-wavelength antenna in "free space" (a dipole), have on the impedance at that point?

A. The impedance measured at any point on a dipole in free space, is equal to the ratio of the voltage to the current at that point. The actual magnitude of the values of voltage and current is of no consequence, other than to establish the ratio

$$Z = \frac{V}{I}$$

D. See Q. 3.193(2), Answer and Discussion.

Q. 3.195. How is the operating power of an AM transmitter determined using antenna resistance and antenna current?

A. The operating (output) power is found by multiplying the square of the antenna current by the antenna resistance (radiation resistance).

D. "Radiation resistance" is a fictitious quantity of resistance which, while not present physically in the antenna, is equivalent to a resistance which if inserted in the antenna would dissipate an amount of power equal to that radiated from the antenna.

In defining the radiation resistance it is necessary to refer it to a particular point in the antenna. This point is usually taken at a current loop (maximum). The radiation resistance must be such that the square of the current times the radiation resistance will equal the power radiated. The grounded end is frequently used as the current reference point. Radiation resistance

$$R_{rad} = \frac{\text{Radiated power}}{I_{max}^2}$$

To determine antenna or radiation resistance by the resistance substitution method, a known value of non-inductive resistance is placed in series with the antenna and antenna ammeter, and a shorting switch is connected across the resistance. All circuits should be correctly tuned and the driver power and output voltage should be maintained constant during the readings. The "antenna resistance" is found from the formula

$$R_{rad} = \frac{I_2}{I_1 - I_2} \times R_1$$

where

R_1 = the known resistance.
I_2 = the antenna current with R_1 in the circuit.
I_1 = the antenna current with R_1 shorted out.

Q. 3.196. What kinds of fields emanate from a transmitting antenna and what relationships do they have to each other?

A. Two kinds of fields emanate (radiate) from a transmitting antenna. These are (1) the electric field, which lies mainly along the plane of the antenna and (2) the magnetic field, which lies mainly perpendicular to the plane of the antenna. (An "induction" field having the same relationship described above exists in proximity to the antenna wire, but is not *radiated*. Its amplitude varies inversely as the square of the distance from the antenna.) A graphical representation of the magnetic and electric fields emanating from a vertically-polarized antenna is shown in Fig. 3.196. These fields are varying in mag-

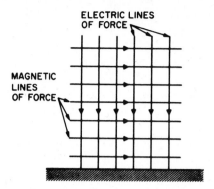

Fig. 3.196. Graphical representation of the electric and magnetic fields from a vertically polarized antenna.

nitude and direction in a sinusoidal fashion at the rate of the transmitted frequency. The arrows indicate the instantaneous directions of both fields for a wave which is traveling toward the reader. A radiated wave in *free space* decreases in strength inversely with the distance from the antenna. In practice, the attenuation is greater, due mainly to absorption of the energy by the ground and by atmospheric conditions.

D. See the discussion for Q. 3.14.

Q. 3.197. Can either of the two fields that emanate from an antenna produce an emf in a receiving antenna? If so, how?

A. This question is of a highly theoretical nature since it appears that the two fields are always present in a radiated wave (see Q. 3.196 above), and are interdependent. However, if it is assumed, for example, that only the electromagnetic wave intercepts a receiving antenna (correctly polarized) a voltage will be induced in the receiving antenna. However, this immediately sets up an electrostatic field in the receiving antenna, causing current to flow and thus produce its own electromagnetic field. This locally restores the condition of the two interdependent fields. Similarly, it might be considered that the electrostatic field only intercepts a correctly polarized receiving antenna. A potential difference will be induced across the antenna, causing current to flow in the antenna. As above, the twin and interdependent fields will again be produced.

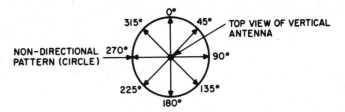

Fig. 3.198(a). Horizontal radiation pattern of a quarter-wave vertical antenna.

Q. 3.198. Draw a sketch and discuss the horizontal and vertical radiation patterns of a quarter-wave vertical antenna. Would this also apply to a similar type of receiving antenna?

A.

1. The patterns are given in Figs. 3.198(a) and 3.198(b). Note that the horizontal radiation pattern is omnidirectional and radiation is equal for all azimuth angles. In Fig. 3.198(b) (vertical pattern), observe that the strength of radiation is greatest along the horizon and is reduced practically to zero at an angle of 90 degrees above the horizon.

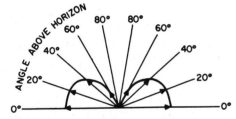

Fig. 3.198(b). Vertical radiation pattern of a quarter-wave vertical antenna.

2. The same basic patterns apply to transmitting and receiving antennas.
D. See Q. 3.193(3).

Q. 3.199. Describe the directional characteristics, if any, of horizontal and vertical loop antennas.

A.

1. A horizontal loop antenna is non-directional along the plane of the loop. It has minimum radiation or reception vertically. A loop antenna is rarely used in the horizontal plane since its primary function is to provide direction-finding. This requires a directional pattern which is discriminatory in the azimuth (horizontal) plane. (See part 2.)

2. A vertical loop antenna has a bi-directional pattern which is maximum in the directions in the plane of the loop, and minimum in the directions broadside to the loop. This directional pattern is clearly shown in Fig. 3.199.

Loop antennas are shielded in order to minimize "antenna effect" and provide a sharper indication of direction. "Antenna effect" causes a broadening of the null points because of the unsymmetrical capacity balance between the loop antenna and ground. The shield must be electrostatic only and, therefore, is electrically broken by a small section of insulating material.
D. See Q. 3.210.

Q. 3.200. In speaking of radio transmissions, what bearing does the angle of radiation, density of the ionosphere and frequency of emission have on the length of the skip zone?

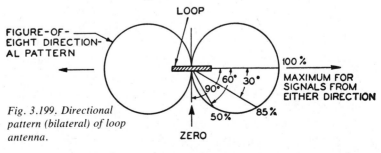

Fig. 3.199. Directional pattern (bilateral) of loop antenna.

A. See Fig. 3.200.

1. Angle of radiation: The smaller the angle of radiation at which a wave leaves the earth, the greater will be the length of the skip zone.

2. Density of the ionosphere: The greater the density of the ionosphere, the more wave refraction (bending) takes place and the shorter will be the length of the skip zone.

3. Frequency of emission: In general, the higher the frequency (below a critical value) the longer will be the skip zone.

D.

1. (Refer to the figure.) If radio waves are propagated at relatively low angles (to the earth), they require less refraction by the ionosphere to return them to earth and consequently have a relatively long "skip zone." Higher-angle radiated waves are returned to earth by greater refraction angles, producing shorter skip zones. At still higher angles (above a critical angle for the particular frequency used) the wave may pass completely through the ionized layer and may not be returned to earth at all. In this case, only the *ground wave* is effective in providing communication.

2. The amount of wave bending is proportional to the density of the ionization of a particular layer, so that shorter skip zones occur for higher densities. However, some of the wave energy is absorbed in the ionosphere and only a portion is returned to earth. The amount of absorption increases with the density of ionization, with the density of the ionized atmospheric region, and with a *decrease* of frequency.

It is interesting to note that the ionization may exist in several layers, which are designated by letters. Thus, the "D" layer exists from 30 to 55 miles high and exists only in sunlight. The "E" layer is the lowest, making possible long-distance communication and is about 65 miles high. It is minimal around midnight. The most intensely ionized layer is the F2 layer, which varies from 150 to 250 miles in height. The F2 layer maintains the most constant density over the 24-hour period and is important in long-distance communication. At high frequencies (15 to 30 MHz) the waves may pass completely through the "D" and "E" layers, but may be returned to earth by the denser F2 layer.

3. As the emission frequency increases, the amount of "wave bending" decreases, resulting in longer skip zones. However, for a given angle of radiation, as the frequency is increased, a frequency will be reached where the wave bending is not sufficient to return the wave to the earth (see the figure) and no "skip" reception is possible. However, under this condition "skip" reception may sometimes be possible by lowering the radiation angle. It should be noted in connection with "skip" reception that frequencies above about 50 megahertz are seldom of value for reliable reception.

The subject of "skip zone" is of necessity covered very inadequately by this question. Many variables and special conditions affect the phenomena of "skip." For

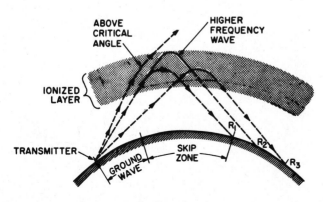

Fig. 3.200. Illustrating the refraction of radio waves and the "skip zone." Note that higher frequency wave, or lower radiation angle may increase the "skip zone."

more detailed information, it is recommended that the reader consult a book specializing in radio transmission. An excellent discussion may also be found in the ARRL Handbook, or other amateur radio handbooks.

Q. 3.201. Why is it possible for a sky wave to "meet" a ground wave 180° out of phase?

A. Since the paths traveled by the sky wave and ground wave are of different lengths, the combined waves at a receiving antenna are usually out of phase. If the sky wave arrives at the receiving antenna such that its path is exactly one-half wavelength longer (or an odd multiple thereof) than the path of the ground wave, the two waves will be 180° out of phase and severe fading will occur. Because of periodic changes in the strength and the path length of the sky wave, the signal strength at the receiving point may go through variations as the two signals change from an in-phase to an out-of-phase condition. This is a frequent cause of fading.

D. One method of minimizing fading effects is the use of a diversity antenna receiving system.

It has been determined that signals which are induced in antennas spaced 5 to 10 wavelengths apart will fade in and out independently of each other. Thus if three or more such antennas are connected to separate receivers with a combined output, the chances are very small that the received signal will ever fade out completely. The AVC voltages developed by the three receivers are added and the combined voltage is used to control the gain of three receivers simultaneously. In this manner the channel receiving the strongest signal at any instant is the one which is contributing most to the output, the other two being relatively inoperative at that instant.

Q. 3.202. What is the relationship between operating frequency and ground-wave coverage?

A. In general, ground-wave coverage decreases with increasing frequencies. For frequencies above 5 to 10 megahertz, the reliable ground-wave coverage may only be a few miles.

D. Ground-wave coverage for a given frequency may be increased by a substantial increase in transmitter power. Also, for high-frequency transmission, locating the transmission antenna at a high point will increase ground coverage. Typical examples of the latter are TV and FM broadcast antennas. Ground-wave coverage is limited by the energy absorption of the ground and other conducting mediums. The effect increases as the frequency increases and ground-wave coverage is not valuable above about 5 to 10 MHz. (See also Q. 3.200.)

Q. 3.203. Explain the following terms with respect to antennas (transmission or reception):
1. Field strength
2. Power gain
3. Physical length
4. Electrical length
5. Polarization
6. Diversity reception
7. Corona discharge

A.
1. Field strength (or field intensity): The signal voltage induced in an antenna, measured in millivolts or microvolts per meter.

2. Power gain: The power gain of a given transmitting antenna is the ratio of the power radiated (in its maximum direction of radiation), compared to the power radiated by a standard (usually dipole) antenna. Both antennas must have the same polarization.

3. Physical length: The "physical" length of an antenna is its material length as measured in inches or feet. This is generally slightly shorter than the "electrical" length of the antenna. (See discussion.)

4. Electrical length: The "electrical" length of an antenna is a descriptive and not a physical measurement. Rather, it is the wavelength (or fraction of a wavelength) to

which a given antenna is resonant. In the case of a half-wave dipole, the "electrical" half-wavelength in meters is slightly (5 percent) longer than the actual physical length of the rod. (See discussion.)

5. Polarization: The polarization of an antenna is determined by its position with respect to the earth. (The polarization is determined by the direction of the electric field which is parallel to the physical plane of the antenna.) Thus, a vertical antenna is vertically polarized and a horizontal antenna is horizontally polarized.

6. Diversity reception: See D. of Q. 3.201.

7. Corona discharge: Corona discharge is an electrical discharge which generally takes place between a conductor and its surrounding medium, which may be the atmosphere or an insulating material.

D.

1. The field strength of a standard broadcast station varies inversely as the distance from the antenna.

The field strength is a measure of the magnitude of the voltage (not power) in millivolts or microvolts per meter. The power would vary as the square of the voltage or inversely as the square of the distance. The value of field strength at moderate distances from the transmitter is found from the formula

$$V = \frac{188\,hI}{\lambda r} \text{ millivolts per meter}$$

where

h = effective antenna height in meters.
I = antenna current in amperes
λ = operating wavelength in meters.
r = distance from antenna in meters.

2. Antenna "field gain," which is a *voltage* ratio is sometimes used instead of antenna "power gain."

"Antenna field gain" is the ratio of the voltage induced into a receiving antenna under two separate transmitting conditions. The first condition is when a relatively complex transmitting antenna system is used and the

second case is when a simple dipole transmitting antenna is used.

The ratio is usually taken with respect to a dipole antenna at a reference value. The actual power output of the transmitting antenna is not increased to produce a field gain. Rather the available energy is concentrated or focused in the desired directions. According to a definition of the FCC, "antenna field gain" is defined as the "ratio of the effective free space field intensity, produced at 1 mile in the horizontal plane and expressed in millivolts per meter or 1-kilowatt antenna input power, to 137.6 microvolts per meter." The figure of 137.6 microvolts per meter is the figure used to represent an average value of field strength, at a point 1 mile from the antenna, which would be produced by 1 kilowatt radiated from a simple dipole at the mean height of the antenna being measured.

3. The physical length of an antenna is actually somewhat less than its electrical length due to "end effect," which results from the capacitance between the ends of the antenna and the earth. The end effect varies with the height of the antenna, the diameter of the antenna, and the excitation voltage. As an average figure the physical length is usually about 5 percent less than the electrical length.

4. The following discussion illustrates the reason why in the practical case, the "electrical" length is always greater than the "physical" length of an antenna.

An antenna can be considered to be a resonant circuit. Taking a half-wave (dipole) antenna in free space as a basic example, it will be found that the antenna will resonate at a frequency whose wavelength is equal to *twice* the *physical* length of the antenna. In free space the velocity of wave travel from one end of the antenna to the other and back is almost equal to the velocity of light (if wire is very thin) which is 300 000 000 meters per second. Thus in *free space* the *physical* length of a *half-wave antenna* in *meters* may be calculated from the formula

$$l = \frac{300\ 000\ 000}{2 \times (\text{Frequency in hertz})}$$

This is so because the antenna will resonate at a frequency determined by the length
of time required for a wave to travel from
one end of the antenna to the other (180°)
and to return (360°). From the above, it must
be realized that the resonant frequency of
any antenna is a direct function of the velocity
of the wave along the antenna wire. In the
practical case, the antenna is never completely isolated from the surrounding objects,
and this causes the velocity of the wave
along the antenna wire to *decrease* somewhat. Thus the *physical* length of the antenna
must be *shortened* if it is still to resonate at
the same frequency as in free space. The
exact amount of the reduction of length is
difficult to state, but a rough approximation
of 5 percent may be used as a starting point.
The approximate *physical* length of a *half-
wave* antenna in *feet* may then be found
from the formula

$$l = \frac{468}{f\,(\text{MHz})}$$

5. The physical positioning of an antenna with respect to the earth determines
the polarization of the emitted wave. An
antenna which is positioned vertically with
respect to the earth radiates a wave which
is vertically polarized, while a horizontal
antenna radiates a horizontally polarized
wave. If the antennas are located close to
the ground, vertically polarized waves will
provide a stronger signal close to the earth
than will horizontally polarized waves. If
the transmitting and receiving antennas are
more than one wavelength above the earth,
there will be little difference in signal strength
caused by the two types of polarization. If
the transmitting antenna is located at least
several wavelengths above ground, horizontally polarized waves will result in the
greatest signal strength close to the earth.

6. An important source of static produced on mobile antennas (ground or aircraft)
is the corona (electrical) discharge from such
antennas. Static charges may build up on
antennas, as well as on other conducting
surfaces and tend to discharge when their
potential is high enough for the existing conditions. Discharges tend to occur from
pointed or small dimensional surfaces because the voltage stress is greatest at such
points. To reduce corona effects, pointed
items may be balled or capped. In addition,
the use of uninsulated and small diameter
(or braided) wire should be avoided.

**Q. 3.203(A). The field intensity of a 1-
kW transmitter measured at a distance of 1
mile from the transmitter is 200 μV/meter.
The power at the transmitter was increased
so that at four miles, the field intensity became
three times as great as the original field intensity at one mile. What power increase was
made at the transmitter?**

A. The power was increased to 144
kW.

D. As stated in Q. 3.203, the field intensity (or field strength) varies inversely
with the distance from the transmitting antenna. Thus, if the distance were doubled,
the field intensity would be halved and if the
distance were quadrupled, the field strength
would be cut to ¼.

Starting with the original field strength
of 200 μV/meter at one mile, if the distance
were increased to four miles, the field intensity would then be ¼ of 200, or 50 μ/
meter.

With the increased transmitter power,
the field intensity has been increased to three
times the original value, or 3 × 200 = 600
μV/meter (at four miles).

The ratio of the increased value of field
intensity at 4 miles to the original field intensity at one mile is

$$\frac{600\ \mu\text{V/meter}}{50\ \mu\text{V/meter}} = 12:1$$

Remember that this is a voltage ratio increase
(not a power ratio increase).

This means that the antenna voltage

(or current) at the transmitting antenna has increased by 12 times. Since the transmitter power is proportional to the square of the voltage (or current), the ratio of the transmitter power increase is $12^2 = 144$ times.

The original power of the transmitter was 1 kW and the new power is therefore $144 \times 1 \text{ kW} = 144 \text{ kW}$.

Note: The above question does not appear in the current FCC Study Guide, but has been added to enhance the student's ability to solve problems of this type as they may appear on FCC License Examinations.

Q. 3.204. What would constitute the ground plane if a quarter-wave grounded (whip) antenna, 1 meter in length, were mounted on the metal roof of an automobile; mounted near the rear bumper of an automobile?

A.

1. If this antenna were mounted on the metal roof, the roof would act as the ground plane since the length of the roof is an appreciable part of a wavelength (4 meters).

2. If the antenna were mounted on or near the rear bumper, the bumper would act partially as the ground plane. Capacitive coupling to the earth would enable the earth to also act as part of the ground plane. The effectiveness of the bumper alone would depend largely upon its being an appreciable portion of a wavelength, at the frequency involved.

D. See Q. 3.193(c), Q. 3.194, and Q. 3.209.

Q. 3.205. Explain why a "loading coil" is sometimes associated with an antenna. Would absence of the coil mean a capacitive antenna impedance?

A.

1. A "loading coil" is required to operate an antenna at a lower frequency than its actual length would normally permit.

2. Absence of a "loading coil" would mean that the antenna input would *look* like a capacitive reactance and depending on the magnitude of the reactance it might not be possible to feed power into the antenna.

D. As stated in Q. 3.203, D.(4), the resonant frequency is dependent upon the velocity of the wave along the antenna. Thus any factors tending to *reduce* the velocity along a given *length* of wire will cause the antenna to resonate at a *lower* frequency. The addition of series *inductance* will produce this effect and thus reduce the resonant antenna frequency. Any factors tending to *increase* the velocity along a given length of wire will cause the antenna to resonate at a higher frequency. The addition of series *capacitance* will produce this effect and *increase* the resonant frequency of the antenna.

The following method, while possibly not strictly accurate, will provide a means of remembering the above facts. Consider the resonant frequency of an antenna as expressed by the formula

$$f = \frac{1}{2\pi\sqrt{LC}}$$

Now if *inductance* is added in *series* with the antenna (and its inductance) the effect is to *increase* the total antenna inductance. If *L increases* in the formula, the frequency *decreases*. If *capacitance* is added in *series* with the antenna (and its capacitance), the total antenna capacitance is *decreased*. If *C decreases* in the formula, the frequency *increases*. (See also Q. 3.203(3) and (4) and Q. 3.209.)

Q. 3.206. What radio frequencies are useful for long distance communications requiring continuous operation?

A. The most reliable frequencies for long distance radio communication are in the order of 15 to 30 kHz. Communication at these low frequencies is usually accomplished by means of ground waves. This requires the generation of extremely high power outputs for reliable and continuous operation.

D. These frequencies are usually produced by high speed mechanical generators.

These generators are capable of producing very large output powers. Such very low frequencies are not used much at present, because of the size of antenna required to radiate a significant amount of power. Another reliable communications system operates on VHF or UHF frequencies. This makes use of radio-relay stations operating at very high power levels. The radiation takes place by means of "scatter" propagation through the "troposphere." The "troposphere" is that layer of the atmosphere close to the earth and extending perhaps two miles above it. Wave bending in the troposphere occurs increasingly for frequencies above 50 MHz and occurs when masses of air exist in layers having differing dielectric constants. This may be caused by layers having sharply different water-vapor contents or abnormal temperature vs. altitude variations. Since the radiated waves must strike the boundaries between the layers at low (grazing) angles, the transmitting antenna is designed for maximum horizontal radiation.

Q. 3.207. What type of modulation is largely contained in "static" and "lightning" radio waves?

A. "Static" and "lightning" radio waves are mostly amplitude modulated.

D. While some frequency modulation is also present in static and lightning radio waves, the majority of the modulation components are amplitude modulated. Most of these waves are also vertically polarized. Polarization of a radio wave is determined by the direction of the electrostatic field. Antennas which are horizontally polarized reject to some extent interference caused by static and lightning radio waves.

Q. 3.208. Will the velocity of signal propagation differ in different materials? What effect, if any, would this have on wavelength or frequency?

A.

1. The velocity of propagation of radio waves differs according to the type of medium involved. It is always less than the speed of light (300 000 000 meters per second) by a factor "K" which is determined by the type of transmission material (see discussion).

2. Assuming the wave has been generated externally to the material through which it is being transmitted; the type of material has no effect on its frequency. However, considering a constant frequency and materials exhibiting a lesser propagation velocity than free space, the measured wavelength along the material will be shorter than in free space.

D.

1. The factor K mentioned above, expresses the ratio of the actual velocity of a wave through a given medium, to the velocity of light. For example the following values of K express the ratio of the actual velocity of the energy on the line to the velocity of light.

Line	K
Parallel line	0.975
Parallel tubing	0.95
Concentric line	0.85
Twisted pair	0.56 to 0.65

2. It was stated above that the measured wavelength along the material will be shorter than in free space. This is equivalent to the characteristics of "physical" and "electrical" lengths of antennas, wherein the physical length is shorter than the equivalent electrical free-space wavelength. This occurs because the transmission of energy along the antenna conductor is *slower* than the transmission of energy through free space (or through the atmosphere). See also Q. 3.203(3) and (4).

Q. 3.209. Discuss series and shunt feeding of quarter-wave antennas with respect to impedance matching.

A. Although not specifically stated, the question refers to vertical, quarter-wave antennas, ungrounded for series feed and grounded for shunt feed. For diagram of a

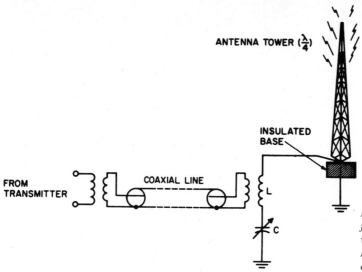

ANTENNA TOWER (λ/4)

INSULATED BASE

FROM TRANSMITTER

COAXIAL LINE

L

C

Fig. 3.209. Illustrating series-feed of a quarter-wave vertical antenna. The series LC network provides a means of impedance matching.

series-fed antenna, see Fig. 3.209. For a diagram of a shunt-fed antenna, see Fig. 3.127.

1. In the series fed case, the bottom of the quarter-wave antenna must be insulated from ground. The impedance at the base (to ground) of the antenna is about 38 ohms. If maximum efficiency is not required, the antenna can be fed directly withh a 50-ohm coaxial cable. The outer conductor is grounded (to the ground radials) and the center conductor connects to the insulated base of the antenna. For greater efficiency and lines of greater impedances, a tunable series LC network is connected between the base of the antenna and ground. The input power is inductively coupled to the series coil, which is resonated with the series capacitor to the operating frequency. This provides an excellent impedance match to the antenna, since maximum series antenna current will then be present.

2. By the use of a shunt-feed system, it is possible to ground the base of the antenna, resulting in a savings of construction costs. In this system, the transmission line is terminated at a specified distance from the base of the antenna. A wire from the center conductor of the coaxial-transmission line is then stretched upward at an angle of approximately 45 degrees to a predetermined point on the antenna. The outer conductor of the line is grounded at its end to the ground

radial system. A voltage is induced into the antenna by a magnetic field set up by a loop, consisting of the slant-wire, the lower portion of the antenna and the ground return from the base of the antenna, to the outer conductor of the coaxial line. A correct impedance match is obtained by varying the height at which the slant wire is connected to the antenna. For the common 70-ohm coaxial line, this connecting point will be approximately one-fifth of the total tower height.

D. See Q. 3.193(3) and Q. 3.198.

Q. 3.210. Discuss the directivity and physical characteristics of the following types of antennas:

1. **Single loop**
2. **V-beam**
3. **Corner-reflector**
4. **Parasitic array**
5. **Stacked array**

A.

1. Single loop (Fig. 3.210(a)): The usual type of loop antenna consists of several turns of wire enclosed in an electrostatic shield. The shape of the loop is generally circular. The loop may be considered to be an inductance coil having a large ratio of diameter to length. This inductance is frequently resonated by a variable capacitor to form the tuned-input circuit of the loop receiver. The

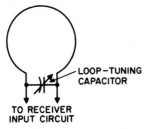

Fig. 3.210(a).Illustration of a vertical-loop antenna. Minimum pickup is perpendicular to the page.

directional characteristics are described in Q. 3.199.

2. V-beam (Fig. 3.210(b)): Consists of two heavy wires in the form of a horizontal "V." (This is one form of a so-called, "longwire" antenna.) When each leg of the "V" is made one wavelength long, the angle between the wires should be about 75°. The directivity of the "V" antenna is along a line bisecting the "V" (bi-directional). However, the ends of the wires can be terminated resistively and the antenna becomes unidirectional in the direction of the open "V." Terminated "V" antennas have a wide bandwidth and gains in the order of 10 to 15 dB. The angle of radiation is largely in the horizontal direction and the pattern may be quite sharp (highly directive) if wires several wavelengths long are employed.

3. Corner reflector (Fig. 3.210(c)): This antenna consists of the reflector and a half-wave dipole antenna. The reflector is made of two flat conducting sheets which are joined (for highest gain) at an angle of about 45°. The reflector is mounted like an open book held vertically. The dipole is mounted ver-

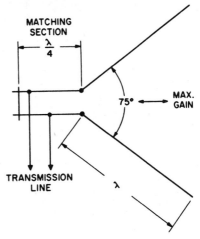

Fig. 3.210(b). A one-wavelength "V" antenna with quarter-wave impedance-matching section.

tically, a half wavelength from the joined sheets, along a line bisecting the 45° angle, inside of the "V" formed by the two sheets. This antenna has greater gain than the parabolic reflector type and is easier to construct. Maximum directivity is along the bisector of the corner angle and is mainly confined to the horizontal plane. This antenna is unidirectional.

4. Parasitic array (Fig. 3.210(d)): The simplest consists of a half-wave horizontal driven dipole and a reflector. The reflector is a rod (or tubing) about 5 percent longer than the dipole and mounted about one-quarter wavelength behind it on the same horizontal plane. However, the reflector has no direct electrical connection to the antenna and receives its energy entirely by induction.

Fig. 3.210(c). Corner reflector excited by a single dipole. (The entire assembly may also be mounted horizontally to provide horizontal polarization.)

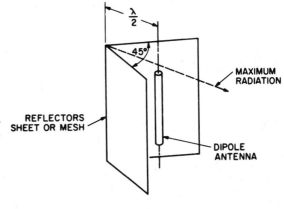

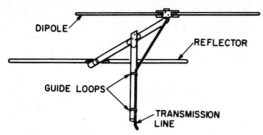

Fig. 3.210(d). Simple parasitic array consisting of a dipole and a reflector.

The practical length of the reflector may be determined by the formula

$$L = \frac{492}{f(MHz)} \text{ feet}$$

The length of a dipole may be determined by the formula

$$L = \frac{468}{f(MHz)} \text{ feet}$$

Addition of a reflector has the following effects on the normally bi-directional directivity of a simple dipole:

a. The array becomes basically unidirectional (in the direction opposite to the reflector).

b. The gain of the antenna is increased.

c. The unidirectional pattern is sharper than for the simple dipole.

d. The bandpass is reduced.

e. The dipole input impedance is reduced. The radiation of either the simple dipole or the parasitic array is mainly in the horizontal plane.

5. Stacked array (Fig. 3.210 (e)): May be formed by mounting one driven dipole

above another and is generally used with a reflector mounted behind each dipole. (Much more elaborate stackings are possible with numerous vertically stacked dipoles and reflectors. These are also frequently expanded in a broadside manner.) Stacking has the following effects compared to a single driven dipole:

a. Sharper directivity in the vertical plane.

b. Increase in gain of about 1.5 to 1.

c. Discrimination against rearward reception of about 3 to 1.

d. An increase in the dipole driving impedance.

e. Improved bandpass, compared to the single parasitic array. For a single-frequency band antenna, the vertical stacking of the elements will be about one-half wavelength. This is basically a unidirectional antenna.

Q. 3.211. Draw a sketch of a coaxial (whip) antenna; identify the positions and discuss the purposes of the following components:

1. Whip.

2. Insulator.

3. Skirt.

4. Trap.

5. Support mast.

6. Coaxial line.

7. Input connector.

A. See Fig. 3.211

1. *Whip:* The top half (quarter-wavelength) of the radiating elements. (The other half of the radiating elements is the skirt,

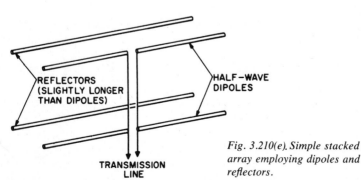

Fig. 3.210(e). Simple stacked array employing dipoles and reflectors.

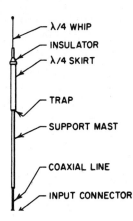

λ/4 WHIP

INSULATOR

λ/4 SKIRT

TRAP

SUPPORT MAST

COAXIAL LINE

INPUT CONNECTOR

Fig. 3.211. Coaxial (whip) antenna showing all component parts.

described below.) The whip is an electrical extension of the inner conductor of the coaxial-transmission line.

2. *Insulator:* Required to insulate the center-conductor whip from the conducting skirt.

3. *Skirt:* A metal cylinder mounted just below the insulator, and which is a quarter-wavelength long. This element, plus the whip completes the half-wave dipole radiator.

4. *Trap:* A portion of the skirt forming a shorted quarter-wave transmission line section as shown in the illustration. The open end of the quarter-wave section represents a very high impedance at the operating frequency. This effectively insulates the bottom of the skirt from the outer conductor of the coaxial line (going through its center) permitting the skirt to act as a radiating element. The skirt receives its excitation energy at the center-feed point of the coaxial-line outer conductor, which is at the extreme top of the skirt.

5. *Support Mast:* The mast supports the antenna structure. When a rigid coaxial line is employed, this item may be used as the support mast. However, for greater mechanical strength, the support mast may be a thick metal tubing or pipe, insulated from the skirt, surrounding either a rigid or flexible coax line. If a flexible coax line is used to feed the antenna, it may be supported at the skirt, using an insulated mounting support.

6. *Coaxial Line:* A transmission line which guides the RF energy from the transmitter to the coaxial-whip antenna. This is a shielded unbalanced transmission line (see discussion).

7. *Input Connector:* A coaxial-type connector for connecting the coaxial line (from the transmitter) to the coaxial-whip antenna.

D. A 72 ohm coaxial line is commonly used to feed the coaxial-whip antenna. The skirt is connected to the outer conductor of the coaxial line at its extreme upper portion, while the inner conductor continues for an additional one-quarter wavelength (electrical). Thus, effectively, the coaxial transmission line is "terminated" at the junction of the skirt and the quarter-wave, center-conductor radiator. The line feeds an actual half-wave antenna at its center point (72 ohms) and thus the impedance of the line is matched and there are practically no standing waves on the line. This helps to keep the radiation angles low, raising the efficiency of the antenna.

Q. 3.212. Why are insulators sometimes placed in antenna guy wires?

A. Insulators are placed in guy wires in order to reduce the efficiency of the guy wires in acting as unwanted radiators and reflectors of radio-frequency energy, and to reduce RF losses in these wires.

D. The guy wires should be broken up into lengths of such dimensions that they will not resonate at the fundamental or harmonics thereof of the transmitted frequency. It is considered common practice to insert an insulator near the top of each guy wire, and then cut each section of wire between the insulators so as to be non-resonant. The insulators should preferably be of the so called "egg" type which operate under compression, so that the guy wire will not separate even if an insulator breaks.

Note: The following added material numbered Q. 3.212-A1 through Q. 3.212-A22 contains information that may be required to pass the General Radiotelephone Operator's License examination. This added material, as well as the new material added to other sections, has been included to help acquaint students with the current state of the electronics art. It is felt that the added material contains subject matter that may also be required of students who have obtained a General Radiotelephone Operator's License and are seeking employment. Additionally, the added material contains valuable information for private technician certification.

Q. 3.212.A1. What is a dummy antenna? Briefly explain its use.

A. A *dummy antenna* is a non-inductive, *non-radiating* substitute antenna load. It is used as a substitute for the normal antenna when it is desired to make transmitter tests without radiation.

D. A dummy antenna usually consists either of a non-inductive resistor or of a combination of resistors (for increased wat-

tage rating). It is temporarily connected to the transmitter in place of the normal antenna for testing purposes.

The dummy antenna must have a resistance equal to the radiation resistance of the antenna (see Q. 3.195). This will ensure a correct match to the transmission line. (For a dipole fed at the center, the radiation resistance is 73 Ω.) If the transmission line is severely mismatched, this would result in a high VSWR. This could cause damage to the final amplifier or even arcing in some types of transmission lines.

In practice and for safety, the power rating of the dummy antenna is usually double the anticipated power dissipation.

Q. 3.212-A2. Draw the radiation pattern of a dipole antenna.

A. The radiation pattern of a dipole antenna is shown in Fig. 3.212-A2.

D. The radiation pattern of a dipole antenna is a figure eight, as shown in Fig.

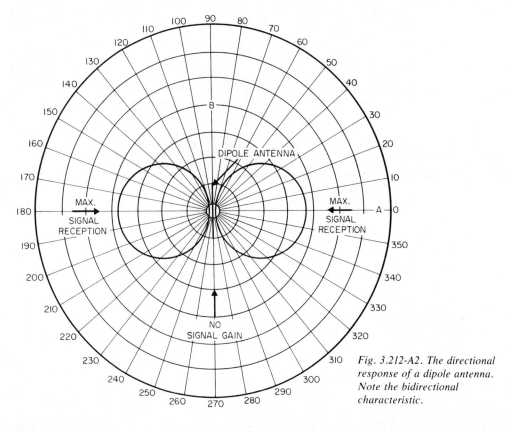

Fig. 3.212-A2. *The directional response of a dipole antenna. Note the bidirectional characteristic.*

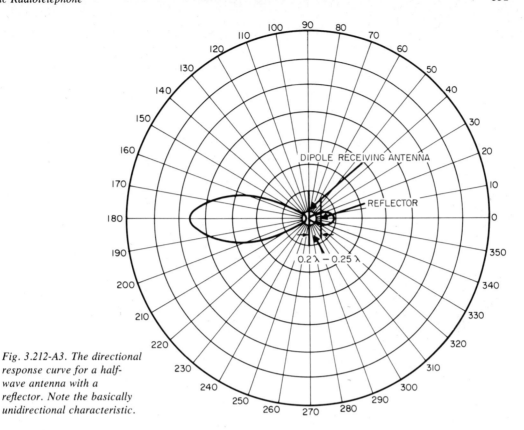

DIPOLE RECEIVING ANTENNA

REFLECTOR

$0.2\lambda - 0.25\lambda$

Fig. 3.212-A3. The directional response curve for a half-wave antenna with a reflector. Note the basically unidirectional characteristic.

Fig. 3.212-A4. A dipole antenna in conjunction with a reflector and a director, and its radiation pattern.

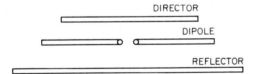

DIRECTOR

DIPOLE

REFLECTOR

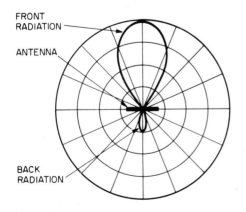

FRONT RADIATION

ANTENNA

BACK RADIATION

3.212-A2. Maximum radiation is in the directions broadside to the plane of the antenna. Note that there is little or no radiation off the ends of the antenna.

Q. 3.212-A3. Draw the radiation pattern of a dipole antenna and reflector.

A. See Fig. 3.212-A3.
D. See Q. 3.210(4).

Q. 3.212-A4. Show with simple sketches (1) A dipole with reflector and director and (2) Its radiation pattern.

A. See Fig. 3.212-A4.
D. See also Q.3.210(4) and Q.3.212-A3.

Q. 3.212-A5. Discuss the physical characteristics and directivity of the following types of antennas.
    1. ⅝ wavelength vertical.
    2. Collinear array of vertical dipoles.

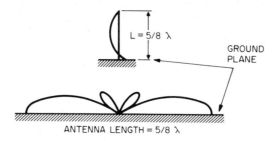

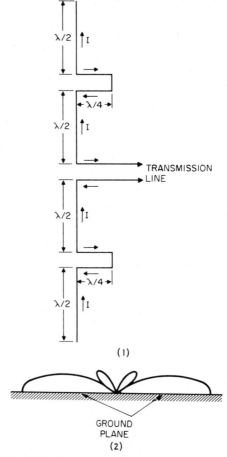

Fig. 3.212-A5(a). Directional characteristics in the vertical plane of a vertical grounded ⅝ wavelength antenna (lower drawing). View shown there is a cross section. Upper drawing shows the antenna current distribution.

A.

1. See Fig. 3.212-A5(a) for the ⅝ wavelength vertical. The ⅝ wavelength vertical antenna consists of a vertical rod, insulated at the bottom, at which point the transmission line may be attached. This antenna has omnidirectional characteristics in the horizontal plane. That is, it is horizontally non-directional. The directional characteristic in the vertical plane is shown in the lower part of the figure. The upper part shows the antenna current distribution. The directional pattern shown is true only for a vertical antenna mounted on a perfectly conducting ground.

2. Collinear array of vertical dipoles (Fig. 3.212-A5(b)(1)): The figure shows a four-element, vertical, collinear array. Collinear arrays are operated with all the elements in phase. This is accomplished by using a tuned (resonant) transmission line and two quarter-wave phasing stubs. An untuned transmission line can also be used. In this case, a quarter-wave matching stub is connected to the center of the antenna. The line is then tapped to the correct impedance point on the stub.

This antenna (as in Fig. 3.212-A5(a)) has an omnidirectional pattern. However, its antenna has an additional power gain of about 4 dB and less radiation in vertical angles. The impedance at the feed point is in the order of 400 to 600 Ω. The pattern shown in Fig. 3.212-A5(b)(2) is true only for a perfectly conducting ground plane.

Fig. 3.212-A5(b). A collinear array of four vertical dipoles. (1) The array is shown with phasing stubs and connection to a transmission line. Arrows indicate the instantaneous current direction. (2) The free space directional pattern. Antenna is omnidirectional (non-directional). View shows a cross section.

Q. 3.212-A6. Describe the physical characteristics and directivity of a phased, vertical array antenna.

A.

1. A phased vertical array antenna may consist of two quarter-wave vertical elements spaced one-half wavelength apart. If the two antennas are fed 180° out of phase, a *figure eight* radiation pattern is obtained. This pattern is *in line* with the two antenna elements. (See Fig. 3.212-A6(1).)

2. A phased vertical array antenna may also consist of two quarter-wave vertical

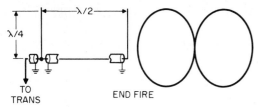

Fig. 3.212-A6(1). Antenna pattern for two quarter-wave verticals spaced one-half wavelength apart and fed 180° out of phase.

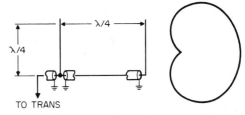

Fig. 3.212-A6(2). Antenna pattern for two quarter-wave verticals spaced one quarter-wavelength apart and fed 90° out of phase.

elements, spaced one-quarter wavelength apart and fed 90° out of phase. In this case, the radiation pattern is *unidirectional*. (See Fig. 3.212-A6(2).)

The direction of maximum radiation (or reception) is *in line* with the two antenna elements. Also, it is in the direction of the antenna element receiving the 90° phase-shifted excitation.

D. As with all vertical antennas, the ground system is critical. In moist ground areas, an 8-ft ground rod is suitable. However, in other locations a network of quarter-wave wires dispersed radially below the antennas will be more suitable.

Q. 3.212-A7. Describe the physical characteristics and directivity of a Yagi antenna.

A. A *Yagi antenna* is a highly directional, high gain, parasitic array antenna. It consists of one driven element (dipole or folded dipole), one reflector, and two or more directors. See Fig. 3.212-A7.

Fig. 3.212-A7. A Yagi antenna with three directors and one reflector. This antenna has high gain and sharp directivity.

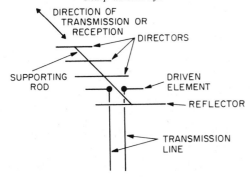

D. Because of the short wavelengths, Yagi antennas may be used in these bands when high gain and sharp directivity are required. While Fig. 3.212-A7 shows three directors, a number of additional directors may be added. A high-gain Yagi with 11 directors is not unusual.

The greater the number of directors, the higher the antenna gain and the sharper the directivity will be. Each director, extending out from the driven element, is progressively slightly shorter by about 0.70 percent.

The element spacings (typical) are as follows: (1) from driven element to first director = 0.1 wavelength, (2) between first, second, and third directors = 0.1 wavelength, (3) from third to fourth director = 0.2 wavelength, and (4) between succeeding directors = 0.4 wavelength.

Q. 3.212-A8. What is meant by the beam width of a directional antenna?

A. The *beam width* of a directional antenna is measured in degrees. It is the width in degrees of the major lobe, between the two half-power points. This is illustrated in Fig. 3.212-A8. Here the beam width is shown to be 40°.

D. At the half-power points, the field intensity is equal to 0.707 times its maximum value which is equal to 3 dB down from the maximum power point.

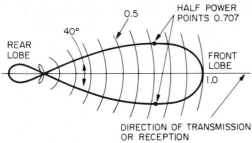

Fig. 3.212-A8. Illustrating the beam width of a directional antenna.

Q. 3.212-A9. What is meant by the directivity of an antenna?

A. The *directivity* of an antenna is its ability to transmit or receive in a specific direction while discriminating against transmission or reception from all other directions.

D. Directivity is a function of antenna beam width. See Q. 3.212-A8. The narrower the beam width, the greater is the directivity.

Q. 3.212-A10. With reference to an antenna radiation pattern, what is meant by major lobes?

A. *Major lobes* of a directional antenna pattern are those in which radiation is maximum.

D. Lobes of lesser radiation intensity are called *minor lobes*. In Fig. 3.212-A8, the major lobe is the front lobe. The minor lobe is the rear lobe.

Q. 3.212-A11. With respect to radio wave propagation what is meant by atmospheric ducts?

A. *Atmospheric ducts* are radio wave propagation paths. These paths are formed between the earth and a refracting layer of air that may exist at low altitudes (several hundred feet or less). Radio waves may be "trapped" in such a duct and may travel in it for hundreds of miles. (Far beyond the optical horizon of the transmitter).

D. In the tropics and over large bodies of water, temperature inversions* may be

* Normally, the temperature of air *decreases* with altitude. However, when a temperature inversion is present, the air temperature (in an altitude band) will actually *increase*.

almost continuously present. This forms a *refracting* layer of air, which continually bends radio waves back to earth. Thus, a transmission "duct" (similar to a waveguide) is formed between the earth and the refracting layer of air.

The frequency of a wave that can be "ducted" is dependent upon the height of the refracting air layer above the earth. The *higher* the air layer, the *lower* the frequency that can be propagated and vice versa.

If the refracting air layer is only a few feet above the earth, the lowest usable frequency may be several thousand megahertz. However, if the air layer is appreciably higher and its dielectric characteristics are proper, the lowest usable frequency can be in the order of 100 to 150 MHz.

Note that *both* the transmitting and receiving antennas must be *inside* the duct to establish successful communication by this method.

Q. 3.212-A12. What is knife-edge diffraction? How can it be used?

A. *Knife-edge diffraction* is the bending of radio waves as they pass over the upper edge of a hill or mountain. This bending effect permits some signal to be present in the "shadow" area behind a hill or mountain. The diffracted signal is always much weaker than the direct signal.

D. Diffraction, refraction, and reflection are defined as follows:

1. *Diffraction* is the bending of radio waves as they pass over a terrain feature such as a hill or mountain.

2. *Refraction* is the bending of radio waves as they pass obliquely from one medium to another in which the velocity of propagation is different.

3. *Reflection* is the return or change in direction of radio waves upon striking a surface (or traveling from one medium to another). *Mirror* reflection occurs from a smooth surface, while *diffuse* reflection occurs from a rough surface.

Q. 3.212-A13. How is the operation of a two-way radio system affected by changes

in antenna height? Antenna gain? Terrain? Urban environment? Frequency band?

A.

1. Generally speaking the higher the base and/or mobile antenna, the greater the communicating range. The antenna(s) height versus transmission distance is more critical in the VHF and UHF bands than in the HF band.

2. An antenna having a specific gain, when used at a base and/or mobile station, will increase the communicating range, when compared to an antenna(s) without a gain factor.

3. Terrain features, such as hills or mountains, that are between and higher than the base and/or mobile station (or stations) will reduce the communicating range.

4. Urban (city) environment consisting of numerous tall buildings can appreciably reduce two-way communication range. This is particularly true on the VHF and UHF bands. The situation will be improved where a base-station antenna can be appreciably elevated.

5. The frequency band used has a definite effect on two-way radio communications. On the VHF and UHF bands, the communicating range is considered to be restricted to approximately line-of-sight distances. (In practice it may be somewhat greater.) The HF band will permit appreciably greater communicating distances. In AM systems, the interference problems from atmospheric static is much less on the VHF and UHF bands than on the HF band.

D.

1. The line-of-sight distance, corrected for the actual curvature path of radio waves traveling close to the earth, is given by

$$D = 1.415 \left(\sqrt{h_t} + \sqrt{h_r} \right)$$

where

D = the line-of-sight distance in miles.
h_t = the height of the transmitting antenna in feet.
h_r = the height of the receiving antenna in feet.

Based on the above equation, if the base station antenna is 100 ft high and a mobile unit antenna is 6 ft high, the communicating range (based upon flat terrain) is about 15 miles. This range may be increased when a mobile unit is operating in an elevated position. The range may be substantially decreased if intervening hills or areas of heavy foliage exist between units.

2. Increased range due to antenna gain depends upon the particular gain figure of the base station antenna and mobile unit. For example, the base station antenna has a power gain of 6 dB (4 times). The effective radiated power (ERP) is then increased by a factor of four. In a practical case, this may increase the VHF range to a mobile unit from 25 to 35 miles. A similar improvement in range from a mobile unit to a base station will be noted if the mobile unit antenna has a gain of 6 dB. In addition, communicating range between mobile units will be increased if gain antennas are used.

3. Terrain features in the path of propagation will introduce transmission losses and thus reduce communicating range. This loss is called "shadow loss" and increases with frequency. As an example, consider a hill about 500 ft high between a base station and a mobile station. If the top of the hill is about 5 miles from the base station, the shadow loss will result in a reduction of communicating range of the base station to the mobile unit of about 12 miles.

4. Urban environment will produce a reduction of range in proportion to the number, type, and height of the intervening buildings. Buildings with metal frames will cause greater losses than wooden structures. Likewise, buildings that are close together will cause greater losses.

Gain antennas at base and mobile stations, higher-power transmitters, and elevated antennas at base stations will provide improved range. For covering large areas, many mobile systems operating in the 25- to 50-MHz band use transmitters with a power output of 30 to 100 W.

In the 150 to 173-MHz (VHF) band,

power outputs of 10 to 30 W are used to cover a medium-sized city with mobile units. In the 450- to 512-MHz (UHF) band, transmitter powers of 5 W or greater will cover a medium-sized city, when using mobile units.

5. The transmitting frequency is an important factor in the communicating range. For example, if the communicating range in the 25- to 50-MHz band is typically 25 to 50 miles, in the 150- to 173-MHz band it will be 15 to 25 miles, and in the 450- to 512-MHz band, it will be 10 to 15 miles. These figures are for base-to-mobile stations.

Q. 3.212-A14. Given, the height of a transmitting antenna (H_1) for VHF is 100 ft. What is the line-of-sight distance to the horizon?

A. See Fig. 3.212-A14. The line-of-sight distance in miles to the horizon can be found from this equation:

$$S_1 = 1.42\sqrt{H_1}$$

S_1 = distance in miles.
H_1 = height above ground of transmitting antenna in feet.

Substituting:

$$S_1 = 1.42\sqrt{100} = 1.42 \times 10$$
$$= 142 \text{ miles}$$

Q. 3.212-A15. The height of a transmitting antenna (H_1) for VHF is 100 ft and the height of a receiving antenna (H_2) is 49 ft. What is the line-of-sight communication distance between the two antennas?

A. Refer also to Fig. 3.212-A14. In this case the total line-of-sight distance is the

Fig. 3.212-A14. Method of determining total line-of-sight distance when both transmitter and receiver are elevated. (Direct ray path will be the sum of the two horizon distances, S_1 and S_2.) (See text.)

sum of *two* horizon distances as shown in Fig. 3.212-A14. This is found from the equation:

$$S_1 + S_2 = 1.42\sqrt{H_1} + 1.42\sqrt{H_2}$$

where

S_1 = distance in miles from the transmitting antenna to the horizon.
S_2 = distance in miles from the receiving antenna to the horizon.
H_1 = height in feet of the transmitting antenna.
H_2 = height in feet of the receiving antenna.

Substituting:

$$S_1 + S_2 = 1.42\sqrt{100} + 1.42\sqrt{49}$$
$$= 1.42 \times 10 + 1.42 \times 7$$
$$= 14.2 + 9.94$$
$$= 24.14 \text{ miles}$$

Q. 3.212-A16. What are the principal allocations for each of the eight major bands of the frequency spectrum?

A.
1. *VLF (10 to 30 kHz):* Radionavigation, international fixed public services, standard frequency (20 kHz), time signals.
2. *LF (30 to 300 kHz):* International fixed public services, standard frequency (60 kHz), radiolocation, radionavigation, maritime mobile, Loran C (90 to 100 kHz).
3. *MF (300 to 3 000 kHz):* Radionavigation, radio direction finding, maritime communications, standard AM broadcasting (535 to 1 605 kHz), aeronautical mobile, international, public safety, amateur, standard frequency (2500 kHz).
4. *HF (3 MHz to 30 MHz):* Aeronautical, public safety, industrial, scientific and medical, maritime, fixed services, mobile services, amateur, international, standard frequencies (5.0 MHz, 10.0 MHz, 15 MHz, and 20 MHz), CB.
5. *VHF (30 MHz to 300 MHz):* Industrial, medical, scientific and land transportation, public safety, amateur, TV broad-

casting (channels 2 through 13), aeronautical radionavigation, radionavigation satellite, space research, aeronautical mobile, maritime mobile.

6. *UHF (300 to 3 000 MHz):* Aeronautical radionavigation, communication and radionavigation satellite, meteorological aids, amateur, public safety, industrial, land transportation, domestic public, remote broadcast pickup, CB, TV broadcasting, radio astronomy, STL, space operations, telemetering.

7. *SHF (3 to 30 GHz):* Radiolocation, radionavigation, amateur, fixed satellite, domestic public, industrial, scientific and medical, amateur, fixed and mobile (except aeronautical mobile), radio astronomy.

8. *EHF (30 to 300 GHz):* Fixed and mobile, fixed satellite, radionavigation, radiolocation, aeronautical and maritime mobile satellite, amateur, radio astronomy, space research.

Q. 3.212-A17. What are the characteristics of the major bands of the frequency spectrum?

A. *Note:* Wave propagation characteristics are closely related within bands, such as 10 to 150 kHz, 150 to 1 500 kHz, etc. Consequently, such bands are used here rather than the eight major bands delineated in Q. 3.254 and Q. 3.212-A16.

1. *10 to 150 kHz:* Used for worldwide communication and navigation. Only ground waves are used. Ground wave losses are low. Very high transmission powers are used. Waves are propagated between the earth and the lower boundary of the ionosphere. Little seasonal transmission variations. Generally use vertically polarized transmission. Moist soil conditions or propagation over water improves field strengths. Not much fading.

2. *150 to 1 500 kHz:* Propagation characteristics are similar to those of the 10- to 150-kHz band. The range of ground wave is about 400 miles at 300 to 400 kHz and decreases to about 100 miles at 1 500 kHz.

Moderately attenuated ground wave. Efficient nighttime ionospheric propagation. Possibility of fading is greater than for 10- to 150-kHz band.

3. *1 500 to 3000 kHz:* There is little ionospheric propagation. Ground wave propagation is about 65 miles (3 000 kHz) to 100 miles (1 500 kHz). Vertical polarization is required. Ground waves are mainly used.

4. *3 to 30 MHz:* Minor ground wave propagation: 65 miles at 3 MHz, 10 miles at 30 MHz. Communication performed by means of skywaves (reflection or refraction). Under some conditions, the skywaves may travel many thousands of miles. Usually provides ionosphere reflections both day and night. Man-made noise from power lines is dominant. Subject to interruption by ionospheric storms. Subject to multipath propagation. Most reliable results from low-angle radiation and reception. Low atmospheric disturbances and good stability of transmission.

5. *30 to 300 MHz:* Line-of-sight transmission. No usable ground wave, high ground absorption. From 30 to 100 MHz, regular but weak propagation by ionospheric scattering. Low atmospheric disturbances and good stability of transmissions. From 100 to 300 MHz, good tropospheric propagation, up to 500 miles or more. Subject to knife-edge diffraction.* Most reliable results are from low-angle radiation. Dominant noise is from automobile ignition systems.

6. *300 to 3 000 MHz:* Generally useful only to short distance beyond horizon. But with tropospheric bending, occasional communication to 400 miles or more is possible. Uses mostly direct wave (point-to-point). Has a little static or fading. Narrow-beam antennas are employed. At higher end of band transmission is adversely affected by rain, snow, or foliage. Subject to knife-edge diffraction.

* *Knife-edge diffraction* refers to the sharp downward bend of a beam passing over an object, as the sharp top of a hill or mountain.

7. *3 to 300 GHz:* Ionospheric reflections are rare. Uses line-of-sight communications. Uses narrow antenna beams. Subject to reflections from hills or ground-based objects (multipath transmission). Subject to knife-edge diffraction. Lack of static and fading. Transmission adversely affected by rain, snow, or foliage. Little static or fading.

Q. 3.212-A18. In a 2-MHz marine installation, explain why the ground system of the boat affects the antenna impedance.

A. The ground system of a boat using a vertical, quarter-wave antenna determines its effectiveness in producing the "mirror" image (see Q. 3.193(3)). In turn, this affects the voltage and current distribution on the physical antenna. The ratio of the voltage to the current at the base of the physical antenna determines its feed point impedance. If this ratio changes due to an imperfect ground system, the feed point impedance changes proportionately.

D. We are discussing a grounded quarter-wave vertical antenna. For an explanation of this type of antenna, see Q. 3.193(3) and Fig. 3.211. The antenna impedance referred to is that at the ground end of the antenna. With an effective ground, the voltage-to-current ratio at the antenna base produces a feed point impedance of about 38 Ω. However, this impedance, as well as voltage and current distribution as shown in Fig. 3.193(c), is dependent upon an efficient ground system. If the ground system is not adequate, the "mirror image" will not be that of an "image" quarter-wave antenna. This will change the *effective* length of the antenna system. Consequently the feed point impedance will change as discussed above.

Q. 3.212-A19. What is the relationship between operating frequency and ground wave coverage? Between sunspots and skywave coverage?

A. In general, ground wave coverage decreases with increasing frequencies. For frequencies above 5 to 10 MHz, the reliable ground wave coverage may be only a few miles.

For HF and VHF frequencies, the skywave coverage may increase dramatically during periods of high sunspot activity. In addition, the maximum usable frequency (MUF) for skywave coverage will increase appreciably.

D. Ground wave coverage for a given frequency may be increased by a substantial increase in transmitter power. Also, for high-frequency transmission, locating the transmission antenna at a high point will increase ground coverage. Typical examples of the latter are TV and FM broadcast antennas. Ground wave coverage is limited by the energy absorption of the ground and other conducting mediums. The effect increases as the frequency increases, and ground wave coverage is not valuable above about 5 to 10 MHz. Giant ionic storms take place on the face of the sun. Observed through a dark lens, these storms appear as small dark spots, hence the name "sunspots." This sunspot activity has been plotted and found to peak about every 11 years. When sunspot activity is high, ultraviolet radiation from the sun is increased. This radiation increases the ionization of the earth's atmosphere and consequently skywave coverage is also increased. (See also Q. 3.200.)

Q. 3.212-A20. What percentage of antenna current increase should be expected between unmodulated conditions and 100 percent sinusoidal modulation?

A. The antenna current will increase by 22.5 percent.

D. The antenna current (rms) under sinusoidal modulation conditions is found by the formula:

$$I' = 1 + \frac{m^2}{2} \times I,$$

where

m = the modulation factor as follows:
m = 1.0 for 100 percent,
m = 0.5. for 50 percent,

m = 0.3. for 30 percent, Etc.
I = unmodulated antenna current.
I′ = modulated antenna current.

Assume the unmodulated antenna current, I, to be 10 A. Then for 100 percent modulation, I′ = 1 + ½ × 10 = 12.25 A or an increase of 22.5 percent. In practical voice or music modulation (or other types), the modulating signal is usually a complex wave rather than a sinusoidal wave. Under these practical conditions, the above formula cannot be relied upon to give any accurate indication of the modulation percentage. However, it will give a fairly reasonable approximation.

Q. 3.212-A21. What type of modulation is largely contained in static and lightning radio waves? What bands of frequencies are most affected by these waves?

A.
1. *Static* and *lightning* radio waves are mostly amplitude-modulated.
2. The bands of frequencies *most* affected are the lower-frequency bands, those below the UHF frequencies.
D. While some frequency modulation is also present in static and lightning radio waves, the majority of the modulation components are amplitude modulated. Most of these waves are also vertically polarized. Polarization of a radio wave is determined by the direction of the electrostatic field. Antennas that are horizontally polarized reject to some extent interference caused by static and lightning radio waves.

Radio disturbances caused by lightning or electrical storms are also known as static, atmospherics, or strays. These radio disturbances produce RF energy across most of the radio frequency spectrum. However, their field strength is approximately inversely proportional to frequency. Such disturbances contain considerable energy at the lower frequencies, but very little above the UHF band. Static is propagated in the same manner as other radio waves. Thus at HF, under

favorable conditions, static may be received from sources thousands of miles away.

At AM broadcast and frequencies, most static originates locally. However, on these frequencies, propagation characteristics improve at night and then static can be received from distant sources.

At LF, the static has a very high intensity. Natural sources of static generate intensities at such low frequencies. Also, at these low radio frequencies, the waves propagate over great distances under almost any conditions.

Q. 3.212-A22. Briefly discuss the types and characteristics of mobile antennas.

A. Mobile antennas are of two basic types: (1) the quarter-wave ground plane type (see Q. 3.211) and (2) the half-wave type. These are both coaxial antennas.

D. High-band (150- to 162-MHz) and 450 to 470-MHz quarter-wave ground plane antennas can be mounted on the vehicle rooftop because of their relatively short length. However, low-band (25- to 50-MHz) antennas (half-wave) are 5 to 8 ft long and must be mounted on the bumper. Loading coils are used for low-band antennas. This reduces the physical length of these antennas, permitting trunk lid mounting.

Half-wave, high-band, and 450-mHz coaxial antennas work well when mounted on a rear bumper.

Q. 3.212-A23. How does a directional antenna array at an AM station reduce radiation in some directions and increase it in other directions?

A. The following example is given for two vertical antennas spaced 180° and having equal currents in phase.

Refer to Fig. 3.212-A23. The two vertical antennas are spaced 180° apart. This is also equivalent in time to one half cycle of the exciting RF, or in distance, one half wavelength. That is to say, in the interval of time required for a radio wave to traverse

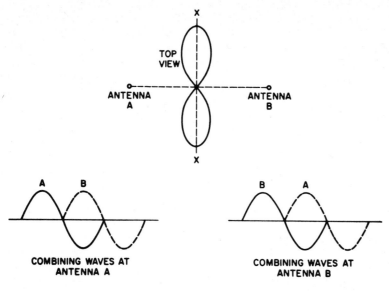

Fig. 3.212-A23. The combining action of two waves coming from vertical antennas spaced 180 degrees apart.

the distance from antenna *A* to antenna *B*, the sine wave will have completed one half or 180° of a cycle. As shown in the diagram, the currents to each antenna are of equal magnitude and are in phase. Let us assume first that the wave has left antenna *A* and is proceeding toward antenna *B*. This motion takes place along a straight line. By the time this wave arrives at antenna *B*, 180° later, the exciting current for antenna *B* has changed by 180° and the wave now radiated by antenna *B* is exactly 180° out of phase with the wave that has just arrived from antenna *A*. Thus the two waves completely cancel in the direction leading away from antenna *B*. A similar action takes place in the direction from antenna *B* to antenna *A*. That is, by the time the original wave from antenna *B* arrives at antenna *A*, the exciting current of antenna *A* has changed by 180° and again the two radiated waves will cancel out in the direction leading away from antenna *A*. Thus it is seen that the radiation along a line connecting the two antennas will always be zero. On the other hand, if we take two points such as *X* and *Y*, it may be seen that the two radiated waves must always arrive together at these points in phase and so are additive. This causes maximum radiation to take place in the direction XY.

Q. 3.212-A24. Define field intensity. Explain how it is measured.

A.

1. Field intensity is a measure of the strength of a radio wave at any given point.

2. Field intensity is measured in millivolts or microvolts per meter.

A common method of measuring field intensity utilizes a sensitive receiver, a standard signal generator and a loop antenna. The loop is connected to the receiver and oriented to give maximum reception. The receiver gain is adjusted to give a convenient reading on a microammeter which is inserted in the second detector circuit. The loop is now rotated so that no signal is received and a voltage from the signal generator is introduced in series with the loop. The signal generator is adjusted to the same frequency as the incoming signal and the generator output is varied until the receiver output indication is the same as it was when receiving the incoming signal. The signal generator output voltage is now measured with a suitable vacuum tube voltmeter and this reading, in conjunction with the effective antenna height (given in calibration data with the receiver), is the equivalent field strength indication.

D.
1. See Discussion 1 of Q. 3.203.
2. See Discussion 2 of Q. 3.203.

TRANSMISSION LINES

Q. 3.213. What is meant by the *characteristic* **(surge) impedance of a transmission line; to what physical characteristics is it proportional?**

A.
1. The characteristic (surge) impedance of a transmission line is the input impedance of a theoretically infinitely long line. In addition, if an impedance equal to this value is used to terminate a line of any given finite length, the same value of impedance appears at the input terminals of the line. The characteristic impedance also, is equal to the ratio of the voltage to the current along an infinite line, or a line terminated in its own characteristic impedance. This type of termination makes any line look like an infinitely long line.

2. The surge impedance (or characteristic impedance) of any 2-wire transmission line is dependent upon three factors. These are: (a) the diameter of the conductors, (b) the spacing between the conductors, (c) the dielectric constant of the insulating material.

D. For a two wire parallel transmission line with air dielectric the characteristic impedance is given by the formula:

$$Z = 276 \log \frac{b}{a}$$

where

Z = characteristic impedance in ohms.
b = spacing between conductors (center to center) in inches.
a = radius of one conductor in inches.

It may be seen from the above that the wider the spacing and the smaller the diameter of the conductors, the greater will be the characteristic impedance. However, an increase of dielectric constant above that of air will *reduce* the characteristic impedance. In this case the value obtained above is multiplied by a factor 1 over the square root of K, where, K is equal to the dielectric constant. For example, for polyethelene dielectric, the value of characteristic impedance in free air must be multiplied by the factor 0.675.

For a coaxial line with air dielectric, the impedance is given by the formula:

$$Z = 138 \log \frac{b}{a}$$

where

Z = characteristic impedance in ohms.
b = inner diameter of the outer conductor in inches.
a = outer diameter of the inner conductor in inches.

If polyethelyne is used as the dielectric, multiply the characteristic impedance by 0.675.

A generalized formula frequently used to describe the characteristic impedance is:

$$Z = \sqrt{\frac{L}{C}}$$

where

L = inductance per unit length.
C = capacitance per unit length.

The values of characteristic impedance may vary between 25 and 600 ohms, depending upon the type of line. Coaxial lines are generally in the range from 25 to 90 ohms. Parallel lines may vary from 100 to 600 ohms.

Q. 3.214. Why is the impedance of a transmission line an important factor with respect to matching "out of a transmitter" into an antenna?

A. For maximum power transfer from the transmitter to the transmission line, the input impedance of the transmission line must match the output impedance of the transmitter. Also, for maximum power transfer from the transmission line to the antenna, the transmission line impedance must match the input antenna impedance. This principle is no different than impedance matching for maximum power transfer in other types of circuits (i.e., audio power output circuits).

Q. 3.215. What is meant by standing waves, standing-wave ratio (SWR), and characteristic impedance as referred to transmission lines? How can standing waves be minimized?

A.

1. *Standing* waves are apparent stationary waves of voltage or current appearing on a transmission line (or antenna). They are stationary from the point of view that their maxima and minima always occur at the same physical points along the line (or antenna). Standing waves are created when a line is not terminated in its characteristic impedance. In this event, the incident waves from the generator are reflected to some degree at the end of the line. The reflected waves combine continuously with the incident waves causing *standing waves* to be formed along the line.

2. *Standing-wave ratio* (SWR) is the ratio of maximum current (or voltage) along a line to the minimum current (or voltage) along the line. The ratio is commonly expressed as a number larger than one.

3. For characteristic impedance, see Q. 3.213 above.

4. Standing waves along a line can be minimized by terminating the line in an impedance equal to the characteristic impedance of the line. If this impedance is a pure resistance, there will be no standing waves and the line will be *flat*, or will appear to be infinitely long.

D. See Q. 3.213 and Q. 3.216.

Q. 3.216. If standing waves are desirable on a transmitting antenna, why are they undesirable on a transmission line?

A. Standing waves are generally undesirable on a transmission line because of the following:

1. Their presence indicates a mismatch at the antenna and, thus, a loss of power being fed to the antenna.

2. In the case of open-type lines, radiation will occur from the line, modifying the antenna pattern.

3. A high standing-wave ratio on a transmission line may cause overheating, or arcing on the line, or in its associated circuits and traps.

4. The higher the standing-wave ratio, the greater will be the losses on the transmission line.

D. A simple straightforward answer to this question is not possible. It is true that for many antenna designs, a high standing-wave ratio is necessary and desirable. These are antennas of the "resonant" type, such as quarter-wave, half-wave, or similar antennas. On the other hand there is a class of "long-wire" antennas which may be resistively terminated to have no standing waves. Examples of these are the straight-long wire, the "V" antenna and the rhombic antenna.

On the other hand, where space is at a premium (for example, on shipboard), particularly at low frequencies, the "lead-in" to the antenna may be made a resonant portion of the antenna proper. Then again, some high frequency transmission lines are deliberately operated as "tuned" or "resonant" lines and normally require the presence of standing waves for proper operation and impedance matching. In addition, some antennas are operated on several widely varying frequencies (frequently harmonically related), causing the antenna input impedance to vary greatly. In such cases, the line is usually "tuned" (resonant) to match the antenna input impedance and standing waves necessarily exist on the line.

Q. 3.217. What is meant by stub-tuning?

A. *Stub-tuning* (or stub-matching) refers to the use of short (tuned) lengths of transmission line, which are connected to the main transmission line near the antenna. Such stubs are used to reduce or eliminate standing waves on the main transmission line. See Figure 3.217 for illustrations of stub tuning for parallel and coaxial lines.

D. If a long transmission line is used to feed an antenna, it is not always feasible to match the transmission line properly to the antenna. However, to reduce line losses, it is desirable to reduce standing waves by matching the load to the line. At some fraction of a wavelength (less than a quarter wavelength) from the antenna, the line appears as a reactance of a definite value. If a stub (shorter than one-quarter wavelength) is attached to the main line at the chosen point, it will have an equal and opposite reactance to that on the main line. Thus, the effective line reactance at the attachment point is cancelled, and the main line *sees* only a resistance equal to the characteristic-line impedance. Thus, the line is matched and minimum standing waves result.

Q. 3.218. What would be the considerations in choosing a solid-dielectric cable over a hollow pressurized cable for use as a transmission line?

A. The question appears to be worded in reverse since the performance of the pressurized cable is superior. However, considerations for choosing a solid-dielectric cable (coaxial) would include the following:
1. Less expensive.
2. Easier to install, since it is more flexible.
3. Tolerance to the higher losses.
4. Does not require special plumbing-type connections.

D. Certain types of coaxial cables are evacuated then filled with an inert gas under pressure and sealed. The reason for this is to prevent moisture from accumulating within the cable. Such moisture would reduce the normal voltage breakdown rating as well as cause increased losses within the cable. Another method sometimes used, is to continuously pump dry air under pressure through the concentric cable.

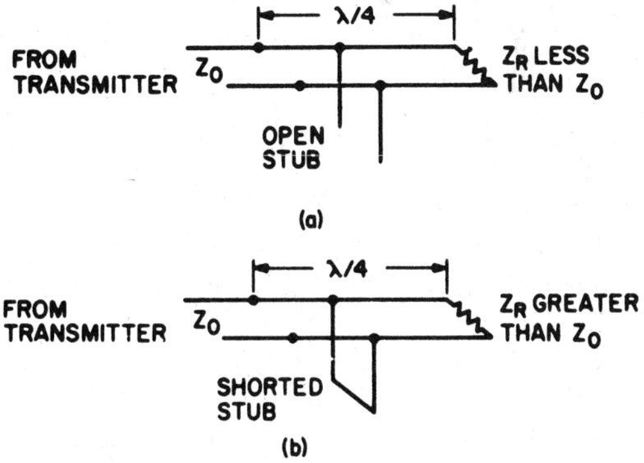

Fig. 3.217. Illustrations of "stub" tuning. Parts (a) and (b) show "stub" tuning of parallel lines. Parts (c) and (d) show "stub" tuning for coaxial lines. Z_0 is the characteristic impedance of the line. Z_R represents the antenna input impedance.

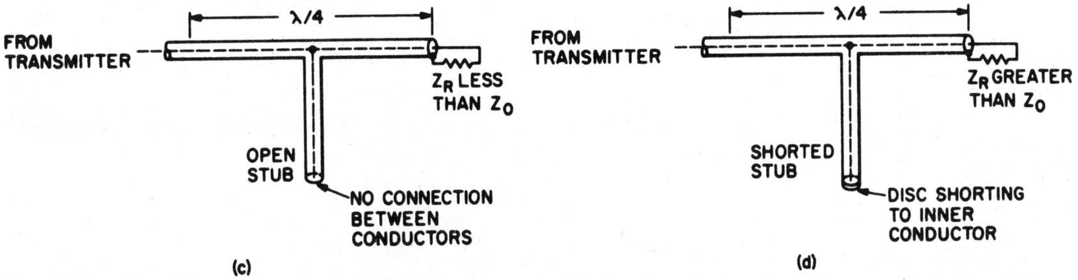

Note: The following added material numbered Q. 3.218-A1 through Q. 3.218-A9 contains information that may be required to pass the General Radiotelephone Operator's License examination. This added material, as well as the new material added to other sections, has been included to help acquaint students with the current state of the electronics art. It is felt that the added material contains subject matter that may also be required of students who have obtained a General Radiotelephone Operator's License and are seeking employment. Additionally, the added material contains valuable information for private technician certification.

Q. 3.218-A1. Why is the velocity factor of a transmission line important?

A. The *velocity factor* of a transmission line is important when determining the physical length of quarter-wave (and other length) stubs. It is also important in determining the physical length of a tuned (resonant) transmission line. In addition, sections of a transmission line may be used as resonant circuits at VHF and UHF frequencies. Here also the velocity factor must be taken into consideration in determining the physical length of the resonant sections.

D. The velocity of propagation of electromagnetic waves depends upon the medium through which it travels. With regard to transmission lines, the velocity of propagation is a function of the inductance and capacitance per unit length. Thus:

$$V = \frac{1}{\sqrt{LC}}$$

where

   V = velocity in feet per second.
   L = inductance per foot.
   C = capacitance per foot.

For example, assume a transmission line has an inductance of 0.08 μH/ft and a capacitance of 29.5 P/ft. The velocity in feet per second is:

$$V = \frac{1}{\sqrt{LC}}$$

$$= \frac{1}{\sqrt{0.08 \times 10^{-6} \times 29.5 \times 10^{-12}}}$$

$$= \frac{1}{1.536 \times 10^{-9}} = 0.651 \times 10^{-9}$$

or

   651×10^6 ft/s

Converting to meters per second (1 m = 3.281 ft) gives us

$$V = \frac{651 \times 10^6}{3.281} = 198.4 \times 10^6 \text{ m/s}$$

The velocity factor k for this transmission line is:

$$k = \frac{651 \times 10^6 \text{ ft/s}}{982 \times 10^6 \text{ ft/s}}$$

$$= 0.663$$

Note: The velocity of propagation of electromagnetic waves in free space is 982×10^6 ft/s, 186,000 mi/s, or 3×10^8 m/s. Hence the factor of 982×10^6 ft/s used above.
(See also Q. 3.193.D.(2) and Q. 3.205.)

Q. 3.218-A2. How do frequency and line length affect transmission line attenuation

A. Higher frequencies and longer line length, both increase transmission line attenuation.

D.

1. For coaxial line type RG-59U, the attenuation per 100 ft, for several frequencies is:

MHz	dB
50	2.4
100	3.4
200	4.8
300	5.8
400	6.7

For TV-type twin lead, the attenuation per 100 feet for several frequencies is:

MHz	dB
100	1.4
300	2.8
500	3.8
700	4.8
900	5.6

2. The transmission line attenuation versus length is a linear function. Thus, if the attenuation at 50 MHz for 100 ft, is 2.4 dB, it will be 4.8 dB for a 200-ft line of the same type.

Q. 3.218-A3. Do two transmission lines of the same characteristic impedance and same length necessarily have the same attenuation? Explain.

A. No. This would be true only if both lines were constructed of identical materials and in the identical physical manner.

D. The physical dimensions of a transmission line and the dielectric constant of its insulation determine the characteristic impedance. (See Q. 3.213). However, two transmission lines may have the same characteristic impedance and length, but different amounts of attenuation. The major line characteristics affecting attenuation may be summarized as follows:

1. Resistance of the conductors.
2. Dielectric material between conductors.
3. Amount of dielectric material used, solid or wafer type.
4. Radiation loss from the line.

The attenuation of a line varies logarithmically with its length. For example, if 10 percent of the input power is lost in the first 100 ft of a line, then 10 percent of the remaining power will be lost in the next 100 ft and so on. For this reason attenuation is expressed in decibels per unit length, since the decibel is a logarithmic unit. (See also Q. 3.218-A2.)

Q. 3.218-A4. Explain the use of a directional wattmeter in measuring VSWR and transmitter power.

A. A *directional wattmeter* is a calibrated RF wattmeter, which can measure separately, the incident (forward) and reflected power in a transmission line, which is connected to its antenna. The directional wattmeter is connected in series with the transmission line.

1. In measuring VSWR, the reflected and incident powers are measured and their ratio established as

$$\frac{\text{reflected power}}{\text{incident power}} = K$$

Since power is proportional to voltage squared, the equation for VSWR is

$$\text{VSWR} = \frac{1 + \sqrt{K}}{1 - \sqrt{K}}$$

For example, for a value of K of 0.1, the VSWR is 2:1. If K is 0.5, the VSWR is 5.8:1. If K equals 0, the VSWR is 1:1, a perfectly matched line condition.

2. To measure the actual transmitter power being delivered to the antenna, the incident and reflected powers are measured. The transmitter power then is the incident power minus the reflected power.

D. See also Q. 3.214, Q. 3.215, Q. 3.216, and Q. 3.217.

Q. 3.218-A5. Discuss briefly the factors causing attenuation in transmission lines.

A. The following factors can cause attenuation in transmission lines.

1. Power loss, (heating of conductors and dielectric), including skin effect.
2. Radiation losses.

D.

1. *Power loss* in a transmission line is the sum of conductor(s) loss and dielectric loss. At VHF, UHF, and EHF, the losses are greater than the dc resistance loss. This is due to the *skin effect* (see Q. 3.11), which effectively raises the ac resistance of the conductor(s).

The manufacturers of coaxial and twin-lead transmission lines furnish charts indicating the power loss of the lines. This is usually shown as the attenuation in decibels per 100 feet. For example, see the abbreviated table below:

Line Type	Freq. (MHz)	dB atten. per 100 ft.
RG-5 9/u(coaxial)	100	3.75
RG-5 9/u(coaxial)	400	8.3
Twin-Lead (TV type)	100	1.4
Twin-Lead (TV type)	400	3.0

2. *Radiation loss* from a transmission line occurs when there are standing waves on the line. See (Q. 3.214, Q. 3.215, Q. 3.216, and Q. 3.217). The higher the standing-wave ratio (SWR), the greater will be the radiation losses from a transmission line.

Additional radiation line losses due to the presence of standing waves may be calculated from charts given in various handbooks. For example, the effect of the SWR on additional radiation line loss is shown in the abbreviated table given below. Radiation line loss is for 300 ft.

SWR	Additional Line Loss (dB)
1.5:1	0.15
2.0:1	0.43
3.0:1	1.1
10:1	4.2
20:1	7.0

Q. 3.218-A6. Briefly describe the characteristics of open-end and shorted-end sections of transmission lines, one-eighth, one-quarter, three-eights, and one-half of a wavelength long.

A. The characteristics of these line sections are shown in Fig. 3.218(A).

D.

1. *Open-end lines* (refer to Fig. 3.218-A6(1)): At all *odd* quarter-wave points, an open-end transmission line acts like a series-resonant circuit. That is, it acts at these points as a low resistive impedance.

At all *even* quarter-wave points, an open-end transmission line acts like a parallel-resonant circuit. That is, it acts at these points as a very high resistive impedance.

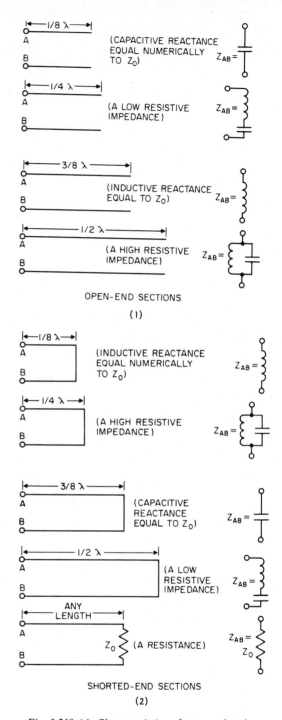

Fig. 3.218-A6. Characteristics of open-end and shorted-end sections of transmission lines: (1) open-end transmission line sections and (2) shorted-end transmission line sections. Z_o = characteristic impedance of the transmission line section.

In addition to acting as LC resonant circuits, open-end lines may also act as nearly pure capacitances or inductances. An open-end line one-eight of a wavelength long acts as a capacitance. Such a line three-eights of a wavelength long acts as an inductance. In both cases, the value of reactance is numerically equal to the characteristic impedance (Z_O) of the line section.

2. *Shorted-end lines* (refer to Fig. 3.218-A6(2)): At all *odd* quarter-wave points, a closed-end transmission line acts like a parallel resonant circuit, a high resistive impedance.

At all *even* quarter-wave points, a shorted-end transmission line acts like a series-resonant circuit; a low resistive impedance.

Like the open-end lines, shorted-end lines can also act as nearly pure capacitances or inductances. A shorted-end line, one-eighth wavelength long, acts as an inductive reactance, equal numerically to Z_O. This type of line, three-eights of a wavelength long, acts as a capacitive reactance, equal numerically to Z_O.

Q. 3.218-A7. Draw a simple sketch of a citizen's band (CB) radio phasing harness. Briefly explain its use.

A. For the sketch, see Fig. 3.218-A7. Part a of the figure shows the coaxial harness. By means of this harness, two CB antennas can be connected to a single CB transceiver. Part b of the figure shows a typical CB truck installation using two antennas.

D. When installing a CB radio on a truck or other large vehicle, it may be advantageous to use two CB antennas. This scheme will improve the radiation pattern, which is disturbed by the metal surfaces of a large vehicle. Antenna gain is not improved.

The cable lengths are designed to provide correct matching and should not be changed.

Q. 3.218-A8. What is a duplexer?

A. A *duplexer* is a circuit or device that permits the use of a single antenna for both transmission and reception.

D. See Q. 8.40 and Q. 8.41 for a radar duplexer.

Q. 3.218-A9. What is a diplexer?

A. A *diplexer* is a circuit or device that permits two different transmitters to operate with a single antenna.

D. An example of the use of a diplexer is found in television broadcasting. Here the

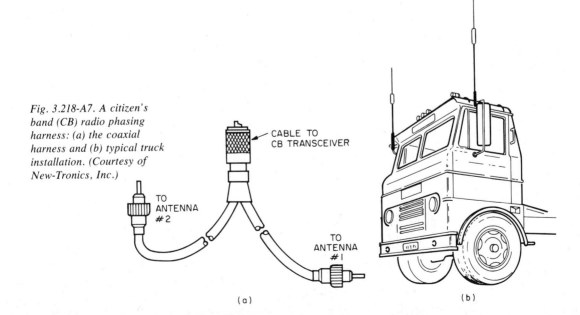

Fig. 3.218-A7. A citizen's band (CB) radio phasing harness: (a) the coaxial harness and (b) typical truck installation. (Courtesy of New-Tronics, Inc.)

CABLE TO CB TRANSCEIVER

TO ANTENNA #2

TO ANTENNA #1

(a)

(b)

picture, sound carriers, and sidebands are transmitted from a single antenna.

FREQUENCY MEASUREMENTS AND RADIO FREQUENCY INTERFERENCE

Q. 3.219. Draw a simplified circuit diagram of a grid-dip meter; explain its operation and some possible applications.

A.

1. For the circuit diagram, see Fig. 3.219.

2. The grid-dip meter is basically an oscillator (Hartley in this case) with a coil conveniently mounted so it can be easily coupled to the circuit under test. A set of plug-in coils are provided to cover a wide band of frequencies. Its operation is quite simple. When it is desired to measure the resonant frequency of a non-operating tank circuit, the probe coil is coupled loosely to the tank coil and the capacitor is varied until the meter dips to its lowest point. The frequency is then read directly from the grid-dip meter tuning dial. The meter dips because the tank circuit absorbs energy from the oscillator at the resonant frequency. This reduces the amplitude of oscillations and the oscillator grid current decreases causing a dip on the meter.

The circuit of Fig. 3.219 could easily be changed to a transistorized circuit by substituting an FET transistor (see Fig.

3.86(g3) and accompanying text) for the vacuum tube triode. The operation of the grid-dip meter remains the same.

3. Some possible applications are:

a. To measure resonant frequency of a tuned circuit.

b. To find undesired resonances in receiver or transmitter circuits.

c. Use as a signal generator to align receivers.

d. Can be used to measure RF inductances and capacitances in conjunction with a standard capacitance or standard inductance.

D. See also Q. 3.220 and Q. 3.222.

Q. 3.220. Draw a simplified circuit diagram of an absorption wavemeter (with galvanometer indicator); explain its operation and some possible applications.

A.

1. For schematic see Fig. 3.220. The wavemeter consists of a calibrated-tuned circuit (L, C1) and a simple vacuum-tube voltmeter circuit (D1, C2 and meter). In operation, the pickup coil (L) is loosely coupled to the source of RF energy and capacitor C1 tuned to provide maximum indication (resonance) on the meter. At this point, the calibrated capacitor is read in terms of the frequency of the unknown source. This may be by direct reading or taken from a calibration chart.

2. Some applications are:

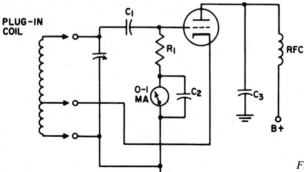

Fig. 3.219. Simplified diagram of a grid-dip meter.

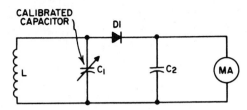

Fig. 3.220. Absorption-type wavemeter. D1 and C2 provide dc for the galvonometer.

a. To measure the frequency of a self-excited oscillator.

b. To find parasitic oscillations in transmitters.

c. To determine the frequency of operation of RF amplifiers and/or frequency multipliers.

d. To function as a general purpose RF indicator for tuning and neutralizing a transmitter.

D. In general a wavemeter is a resonant circuit which is tuned by a variable capacitor. A calibrated dial is provided on which is indicated the resonant frequency of the wave meter in terms of capacitor settings. A suitable RF indicator is connected in series or parallel with the wavemeter tuned circuit to indicate resonance. When a series connected indicator is used, the indicator may be a sensitive flashlight bulb or thermocouple meter. A better (but more complex) arrangement is the use of a diode-type vacuum tube voltmeter connected across a portion of the tuned circuit, or a solid-state crystal detector. The advantage of this type of indicator is that it consumes very little power and thus permits a higher value of Q to be developed in the wavemeter circuit. This is important because the accuracy with which readings can be made depends upon the Q.

A disadvantage of absorption type wavemeters in general is the reflected impedance they cause to appear in the measured circuit, which changes the tuning of the measured circuit and reduces the accuracy of readings.

The pickup coil of the absorption type frequency meter should be coupled as loosely as possible to the circuit under measurement in order to reduce errors in the readings. (See also Q. 3.83, Q. 3.91, Q. 3.92, and Q. 3.126 through Q. 3.128.)

Q. 3.221. Draw a block diagram, showing only those stages which would illustrate the principle of operation of a secondary frequency standard. Explain the functions of each stage.

A. For the block diagram, see Figure 3.221. The multivibrator (10 kHz) is the basic oscillator and is accurately synchronized by the 100 kHz crystal oscillator. The harmonic amplifier may have switchable tuned circuits to amplify the higher harmonic frequencies which normally decrease rapidly in amplitude. Harmonics of both 100 kHz and 10 kHz are provided, with the 100 kHz harmonics exceeding 30 megahertz in frequency.

D. To determine the operating frequency of a transmitter, the secondary-frequency standard should first be accurately calibrated as explained below.

The usual type of secondary-frequency standard will employ an accurately calibrated 100-kHz crystal oscillator with a multivibrator providing harmonics of 10 kHz. Thus, harmonics of 100 kHz and 10 kHz are provided, the 100-kHz harmonics being useful beyond 30 MHz and the 10-kHz harmonics being useful beyond 3 MHz.

1. Operate the transmitter and all test equipment for about 15 minutes to insure stability.

2. Measure the fundamental frequency of the transmitter by means of the frequency meter, obtaining an accurate zero-beat.

3. Turn off the transmitter and introduce the signals from the secondary-frequency standard into the heterodyne-frequency meter.

Fig. 3.221. Simplified block diagram of a secondary-frequency standard.

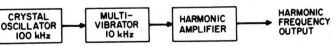

4. Turn on the secondary-frequency standard (usually a 100-kHz crystal oscillator with a 10-kHz multivibrator) and allow about a 15-minute warm-up period to insure stability.

5. Wait for the transmission period during which modulation is absent. (Receiver BFO should be off.)

6. From the heterodyne-frequency meter chart and its dial setting, determine the approximate transmitter frequency, and from this determine the harmonic of the 100-kHz oscillator from the secondary standard. (The calibration of the heterodyne-frequency meter may be checked by zero-beating it against the 100-kHz harmonics and observing the dial calibration.)

7. Using the harmonics of the 10-kHz oscillator, an audible beat will be present between the frequency of the heterodyne-frequency meter and secondary-frequency standard. This will indicate the exact frequency within a few cycles of providing a figure from zero to 5 000 hertz, to be used as the final digits of the reading provided by the heterodyne-frequency meter.

8. The exact value of the audible-beat frequency obtained in (5) above can be determined by matching this audio-frequency against that of a well-calibrated audio (or interpolation) oscillator, either by the zero-beat method or using an oscilloscope.

9. To check if the unknown frequency is greater or less than the 10-kHz frequency being used for measurement, increase the frequency of the heterodyne-frequency meter slightly. If the audio-beat frequency increases, the unknown frequency is greater than the 10-kHz harmonic involved. If the audio-beat frequency decreases, the unknown frequency is less than the 10-kHz harmonic involved.

10. In the case of frequencies above about 3 MHz, harmonics of the 10-kHz multivibrator may be too weak to be useful. In this case, set the heterodyne-frequency meter to provide a suitable harmonic to beat with the transmitter frequency. Measure the fre-

quency of the heterodyne-frequency meter, as described above and multiply the result by the appropriate harmonic.

A step-by-step explanation of how a secondary-frequency standard could be calibrated against a WWV signal is given below:

1. Using the operating frequencies of 2.5, 5, 10, 15, 20, 25, 30, and 35 MHz, select that which provides a good readable signal and tune it in accurately on the receiver. (The receiver should be warmed up for about 15 minutes to insure stability.)

2. Adjust the calibration control of the secondary-frequency standard until its harmonic is in exact zero-beat with the WWV frequency (as heard on the receiver).

3. The secondary-frequency standard is now calibrated.

Q. 3.222. Draw a block diagram of a heterodyne-frequency meter, which would include the following stages:
  Crystal Oscillator
  Crystal Oscillator Harmonic Amplifier
  Variable Frequency Oscillator
  Mixer
  Detector and AF Amplifier
  AF Modulator
  Show RF input and RF, AF, and calibration outputs. Assume a band-switching arrangement and a dial having arbitrary units, employing a vernier scale.

1. Describe the operation of the meter.

2. Describe, step-by-step, how the crystal could be checked against WWV, using a suitable receiver.

3. Under what conditions would the AF modulator be used?

4. Describe, step-by-step, how the unknown frequency of a transmitter could be determined by use of headphones; by use of a suitable receiver.

5. What is meant by calibration checkpoints; when should they be used?

6. If in measuring a frequency, the tuning dial should show an indication between the two dial-frequency relationships in the cali-

bration book, how could the frequency value be determined?

7. How could this meter be used as an RF generator?

8. Under what conditions would it be necessary to re-calibrate the crystal oscillator?

A. For the block diagram, see Fig. 3.222.

1. The unknown signal is fed to the *mixer* via the RF input where it is combined with a signal from the *variable frequency oscillator*. Due to the action in the mixer, the output not only contains the two original frequencies, but the sum and difference frequencies as well. This combination of frequencies, then, is fed to the *detector* whose output contains a signal equal to the difference of the two original frequencies—the original frequencies and their sum being bypassed. If the two original signals are close enough in frequency, the difference frequency will be in the audio range and may be heard in the output of the *AF amplifier* by means of a suitable speaker or headphones. If the variable frequency oscillator is adjusted to make the difference frequency or beat become lower and lower in pitch until it disappears, the difference in frequencies is zero and the signal from the variable frequency oscillator has the same frequency as the unknown frequency. If the variable frequency oscillator has an accurately calibrated dial, the unknown frequency will now be known by reading the dial. The process of making the difference between the two frequencies zero is known as *zero beating*.

In order to be certain of the calibration of the variable frequency oscillator dial, facilities have been incorporated into the meter to provide signals of accurately known frequency to the mixer. In the meter shown on the block diagram, a 1.0-MHz *crystal oscillator* with exceptionally good stability is used as a frequency standard. Means are provided to adjust the frequency of this oscillator to exactly 1.0 MHz when required.

The output of the crystal oscillator is delivered to a *harmonic generator* for the purpose of obtaining harmonics of the 1.0-MHz standard frequency that are of sufficient amplitude for use in the frequency range of the meter. If the meter is intended for use as high as 300 MHz, the 300th harmonic must be strong enough to be heard in the *AF output* when beat with the variable frequency oscillator. By this method, the calibration of the variable frequency oscillator dial can be checked. If the calibration is faulty, means are provided for adjusting the dial, mechanically or electrically, so that the calibration is correct at the 1.0 MHz harmonic check points.

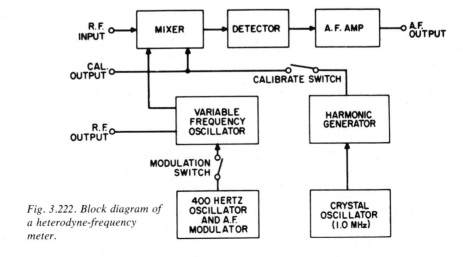

Fig. 3.222. Block diagram of a heterodyne-frequency meter.

It is often desirable to have the output of the variable frequency oscillator modulated with an audio frequency to assist in making accurate measurements. For this purpose, a *400-hertz oscillator and AF modulator* are provided. When such modulation is desired, the *modulation switch* is closed.

As shown on the diagram, an RF output terminal is shown. This output is useful for such purposes as receiver alignment, etc.

2. If a suitable HF receiver is available, the meter can be calibrated against WWV by coupling the calibration output of the meter to the antenna input of the receiver and tuning the receiver to WWV on 2.5, 5, 10, 15, or 20 MHz. The frequency choice depends on the location of the receiving site, time of day, etc. With the receiver in the AM or phone mode, the calibrate switch of the meter is closed. If the crystal oscillator is *not* on frequency, a beat note will be heard which will be the difference between WWV and the 5th, 10th, 15th, 20th, 25th or 30th harmonic of the crystal oscilator. Which harmonic is heard will depend on which WWV frequency is being received.

By adjusting the trimmer provided on the crystal oscillator its frequency can be varied until zero beat is obtained with WWV. The crystal oscillator now is within approximately plus or minus 20 hertz of being correct *at that harmonic*. For better accuracy, it is well to adjust the crystal oscillator when the WWV signal is being modulated by its 440-hertz tone. Any frequency difference will be evidenced by an apparent waxing and waning of WWV's modulation, exact zero beat being obtained when the modulation remains steady in amplitude.

3. Since the human ear cannot hear frequencies below approximately twenty hertz, the method of zero-beating the unknown signal against the output of the variable frequency oscillator produces results that are correct only to within approximately plus or minus twenty hertz. By modulating the variable frequency oscillator greater accuracy can be obtained. When the difference in the two frequencies is below audibility;

the modulation of the variable frequency oscillator will grow stronger and weaker at a rate equal to the difference frequency. By observing this and adjusting the variable frequency oscillator so that the modulation is maintained at a constant amplitude, exact equality of the known and unknown signals can be obtained. The final accuracy of the measurement is limited only by the accuracy of a frequency standard and the calibration of the dial of the variable frequency oscillator.

4. The process of using the meter and headphones to determine the frequency of a transmitter has already been described in the operation of the meter in the first paragraph of (part 1) above.

The unknown frequency of a transmitter, especially a distant one, can also be measured by using the meter in conjunction with a suitable receiver. This can be accomplished by first tuning in the transmitter on the receiver and then coupling the RF output of the meter to the antenna input of the receiver. Adjusting the variable frequency oscillator of the meter will produce a beat note in the output of the receiver between the distant transmitter and the variable frequency oscillator. Zero-beating the two signals will result in the variable frequency oscillator and the transmitter having the same frequency. The unknown frequency is read from the dial of the meter in the normal manner.

5. Calibration check points are points or dial settings at which the 1.0-MHz harmonics of the frequency standard should be heard at zero beat. They are used to assure that the frequency dial of the variable frequency oscillator is correctly adjusted to agree with the dial setting and frequency chart supplied with the meter.

For accurate and consistent results with the meter, these checkpoints should be used to check and adjust the calibration of the variable frequency oscillator *every* time a frequency is measured.

6. The calibration information usually supplied with a meter of this type is in the form of a chart where specific dial settings are listed for discrete frequencies; the fre-

quency spacing normally being uniform (100 hertz). It very often happens that the unknown frequency falls somewhere in between two listed adjacent frequencies and it is desired to know the unknown frequency more accurately than to the nearest 100 hertz. This may be determined by a process known as interpolation.

Let us suppose that the unknown frequency is zero beat at a dial setting of 173.6. Referring to the calibration chart, it is found that the dial setting for a frequency of 13248.3 kHz is 173.1 and that for 13248.4 kHz, the dial should read 174.2. It should be apparent that the unknown frequency is somewhere between 13248.3 and 13248.4 kHz. On the assumption the dial setting vs. frequency is a linear function over this small range, then the number of dial divisions per 100 hertz is 174.2 − 173.1 or 1.1. The number of dial divisions between 13248.3 kHz and the unknown frequency is 173.6 − 173.1 or 0.5. The number of *hertz* between these two points,

then, is $\frac{0.5}{1.1} \times 100$, or 45 hertz. This is

added to the lower of the two listed frequencies so that the final frequency has been determined to be 13248.345 kHz.

7. The meter may be used as an RF generator for receiver alignment, etc., by using the RF output terminal coupled to the receiver under test. The variable frequency oscillator is an accurate frequency source but may be checked for accuracy by using the normal calibration check facilities as previously described.

Either a pure continuous wave or an amplitude-modulated wave can be obtained by proper positioning of the modulation switch.

8. Normally the crystal oscillator's frequency should be checked on a routine basis; the period being determined by observation of the crystal's tendency to drift in frequency.

However, should the meter be used under unusual conditions such as high or low supply voltage or unusual climatic conditions, the crystal frequency should be checked against WWV and reset if found necessary.

Rough handling of the unit such as encountered in carrying it or shipping it dictates frequent crystal frequency checking. Any time the oscillator tube is replaced or any maintenance performed on the components of the oscillator circuit its frequency should be checked. It is good practice, also, to check the frequency when batteries are replaced in battery-powered use.

Q. 3.223. Draw a block diagram of an FM deviation (modulation) meter which includes the following stages:

Mixer
IF amplifier
Limiter
Discriminator
Peak reading voltmeter

1. Explain the operation of this instrument.

2. Draw a circuit diagram and explain how the discriminator would be sensitive to frequency changes rather than amplitude changes.

A. For the block diagram, see Fig. 3.223(a).

1. Essentially, the FM deviation meter is a very simple FM receiver. Referring to the block diagram, a sample of the output

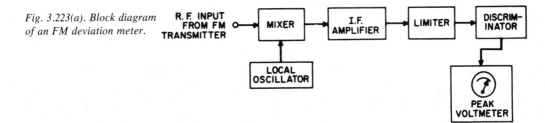

Fig. 3.223(a). Block diagram of an FM deviation meter.

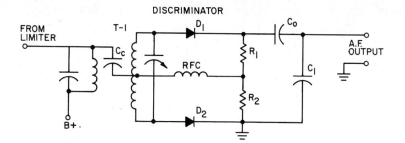

Fig. 3.223(b). Schematic diagram of an FM discriminator circuit.

of the FM transmitter and a signal from the local oscillator are combined in the mixer and the difference frequency is selected by a tuned circuit and passed to the IF amplifier. The IF amplifier provides the required amplification and selectivity for the signal and feeds the limiter. The function of the limiter is to provide an output of constant amplitude regardless of the amplitude of its input. The output of the limiter is a signal of fixed amplitude but varying in frequency according to the modulation of the original signal. The discriminator recovers the original A-F modulating signal from the modulated wave and delivers it to the peak reading voltmeter for measurement.

Since the frequency deviation is defined as the maximum instantaneous excursion of the signal frequency from the carrier frequency it corresponds to the peak amplitude of the modulating frequency. The peak amplitude of the A-F output from the discriminator is proportional to the frequency deviation. A suitable voltmeter, responding only to the *peak* amplitude of the discriminator A-F output, can be calibrated directly in terms of frequency deviation.

2. Figure 3.223(b) illustrates a typical schematic of a discriminator, while the graph in Fig. 3.223(c) shows the response of such a discriminator to varying frequency.

The response, as shown, is the actual voltage obtained across resistors R_1 and R_2 in series. As can be seen, the instantaneous voltage output is dependent on the instantaneous frequency input. The conditions shown are for sine-wave modulation.

The dashed response curve shown

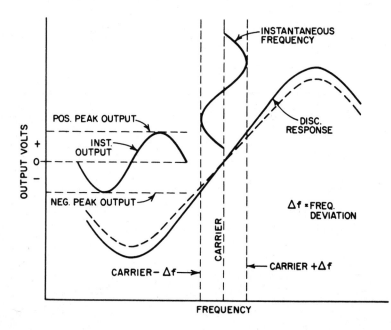

Fig. 3.223(c). The response of a discriminator to varying frequency.

would be that obtained if the amplitude of the input was somewhat reduced. This would result in a reduced output for the same frequency deviation. This possibility is eliminated by the use of a limiter ahead of the discriminator, thus assuring constant amplitude input.

D. See also Q. 3.177(1) through (4).

Q. 3.224. Describe a usual method (and equipment used) for measuring the harmonic attenuation of a transmitter.

A. One common method of measuring the harmonic attenuation of a transmitter is by use of a field strength meter. This instrument is an accurately calibrated receiver, whose output, indicated on a dB meter, is proportional to the logarithm of the input voltage. The input to the instrument is normally derived from a short wire, used as an antenna, and is thus proportional to the field strength of the signal being measured.

The actual procedure is very simple. At some distance from the transmitter site, the meter is first tuned to the fundamental frequency and the output dB noted. The meter is then tuned to the desired harmonic and the output dB again noted. The difference in the two readings, indicates the harmonic attenuation of the transmitter.

D. See Q. 3.203(1).

Q. 3.225. Why is it important that transmitters remain on frequency and that harmonics be attenuated?

A.

1. Each commercial transmitter is assigned a specific operating frequency and bandwidth channel. The purpose of such assignment is to insure that each broadcaster or broadcast service does not interfere with other stations on their assigned frequencies.

2. Harmonic frequencies must be attenuated to prevent interference with stations in the same or other services.

D. For an example of harmonic interference, an AM broadcast station operating on 660 kilohertz might cause severe interference on 1 320 kilohertz, a frequency which might be assigned to another AM broadcast station. This would occur in the case of appreciable second-harmonic radiation. In a similar manner, higher order harmonics might create interference with stations operating on the higher-harmonic frequencies. While the AM broadcast band was given as an example, harmonic radiation can occur (if not adequately suppressed) from any transmitter, causing possible interference with other services. An interesting fact, is that depending on the frequencies involved, harmonic frequencies may travel much further than the fundamental frequency, if not suppressed at the source.

Note: The following added material numbered Q. 3.225-A1 through Q. 3.225-A13 contains information that may be required to pass the General Radiotelephone Operator's License examination. This added material, as well as the new material added to other sections, has been included to help acquaint students with the current state of the electronics art. It is felt that the added material contains subject matter that may also be required of students who have obtained a General Radiotelephone Operator's License and are seeking employment. Additionally, the added material contains valuable information for private technician certification.

LAND MOBILE INTERFERENCE

Q. 3.225-A1. Discuss the use of directional antennas in reducing land mobile, co-channel interference problems.

A. 1. For "high-band" (150 to 162 MHz) and 450-MHz band operation, the base station antenna frequently consists of a vertically stacked array of folded dipoles. Such an antenna is directional and has appreciable gain. For base-to-base communication between stations employing directional antennas, co-channel (same channel) interference will be reduced. This is because each base station antenna is "beamed" at the other. Thus, each receives the maximum signal strength from the other. This tends to override other co-channel signals, which will probably be appreciably weaker.

2. Some land mobile radio systems ("backbone" systems) are used in the operation and maintenance of limited access highways, railroads, and pipelines. The system is required to cover only a narrow strip along a right of way. More than one base station is needed along the route to provide adequate coverage. Consequently, co-channel interference can occur at a mobile receiver situated in the overlap areas between adjacent base stations. The use of manually or automatically switched directional antennas in the mobile units will help to reduce interference problems. A directional antenna allows the mobile unit the option of selecting the stronger signal, while attenuating the weaker one.

D. Other techniques that help to reduce co-channel interference in "backbone" systems are as follows:

1. Maintaining accurate frequency control at the base stations to reduce the carrier frequency difference to less than 300 Hz. Thus the beat note of the carriers will be below the audio passband of the mobile receiver.

2. Installing directional antennas at the base stations having the greatest possible front-to-back ratio. This will reduce the overlap coverage area appreciably. (See also Q. 3.210, Q. 3.211, and Q. 3.137-A15.)

Q. 3.225-A2. What is intermodulation?

A. In the sense intended here, *intermodulation* is the beating together of two carrier frequencies, or one carrier and a harmonic of the other, in a non-linear device. The non-linear device in this case is either the final power amplifier (PA) stage of a transmitter, or it may be the RF or mixer stage of a receiver.

D. For a detailed discussion of trans-

mitter and receiver intermodulatio, see A. and D. of Q. 3.137-A16.

Q. 3.225-A3. Discuss some methods for reducing transmitter intermodulation? For reducing receiver intermodulation?

A.

1. For reducing transmitter intermodulation the following will be effective:

a. *Use of a push-pull final RF amplifier (PA):* This tends to cancel even-order harmonics. The second harmonic on the PA, when beating against the incoming (interfering) carrier, produces a difference frequency closest to the generated carrier frequency (Q. 3.137-A16(D).) This difference frequency is the one most likely to cause intermodulation problems when it is transmitted.

b. If the PA is operating Class C, use the smallest amount of input drive consistent with efficient operation. This will reduce the strength of the harmonics developed in the PA.

c. When possible, use a linear PA (Q. 3.144). Such amplifiers have appreciably reduced strength of their generated harmonics.

d. Use a "circulator" or an "isolator" in the antenna feedline. (See Q. 3.137-A16.)

e. A cavity filter in the feedline will be effective. (Q. 3.137-A24.)

2. For reducing receiver intermodulation, (Q. 3.137-A16(D)) the following will be effective:

a. The use of helical-tuned circuits in the RF portion of the receiver. These have high Q (narrow band) characteristics and so discriminate against unwanted signals close to the desired frequency.

b. A resonant cavity in the antenna feedline will also discriminate against unwanted frequencies (Q. 3.137-A24.)

c. A duplexer at a mobile relay (repeater) station can also help to reduce receiver intermodulation when one of the offending carriers is from the repeater transmitter. (See Q. 3.137-A24(D).) The duplexer provides a high degree of isolation between the repeater transmitter and receiver.

Note: Bipolar transistor, receiver RF amplifiers and mixers are particularly prone to intermodulation problems.

Q. 3.225-A4. What problems can electrical interference cause to CB receivers?

A. Electrical interference in either CB mobile receivers or CB base station receivers can cause the intelligibility of received signals to be appreciably reduced. In extreme cases, it may not be possible to interpret the transmission at all, especially if the signal is weak.

D.

1. CB is an AM system in the 27 MHz band using either double sideband (DSB)(A3) or single-sideband, suppressed-carrier (SSBSC)(A3J) emission. As such, the CB receivers are susceptible to various types of electrical noises. In the case of CB *mobile* receivers, some of the worst noise sources are as follows:

a. Spark plug noise is about the most severe. It peaks around 35 MHz but has a broad spectrum. This noise can be greatly reduced by the use of resistor plugs, as well as by the use of resistance ignition cable between the plugs and distributor and also between the coil and distributor. Many cars are so equipped by the factory. The use of shielded, high-voltage ignition cables and the primary coil wire and also shielding of the distributor is very effective in reducing this type of noise.

b. Alternator noise manifests itself as a high-pitched "whine" in the receiver. It varies with engine rpm. One path for this noise is through the antenna (*frontway* whine) and a second path is through the power lead (*back-way* whine). *Frontway* whine can be reduced by (1) good grounding of the antenna system, (2) a hood-grounding clip, (3) shielding any wire that may be radiating, and (4) bypassing under-dash circuits. *Backway* whine can be reduced by (1) bypass capacitor (0.5 μF) at the alternator output terminal, (2) bypass capacitor (0.5 μF) at

the accessory terminal of the fuse block, and (3) adding a commercial filter in the power line.

c. Noise from accessories—such as the wiper-motor, switches ("pops"), blower motor, and gauges—can often be reduced by the use of bypass capacitors (0.25 to 0.5 μF) and/or feedthrough capacitors.

d. Noise caused by loose or ungrounded parts of the car can be reduced by the use of copper-braided bonding straps placed as follows: (1) back corners of engine to firewall and frame, (2) hood and trunk lid to frame, and (3) muffler and tail pipes to frame.

2. CB base station receivers are subject to a range of noises, some of which may be caused by:

a. Brush motor devices, including electric shavers, hair dryers, and blenders. A 0.1-μF capacitor across the brushes usually helps.

b. Thermostats of various types can produce intermittent noises. A 0.1-μF capacitor connected across the contacts can help reduce the noise.

c. Nickel-cadmium battery chargers, such as those used in electric shavers, produce a continuous buzzing noise. A line filter is effective in suppressing this type of noise. Twenty-five-watt light bulbs can create a similar noise. Replacement is called for here.

d. Television receivers can produce interference in CB receivers. This comes from harmonics of the horizontal oscillator (15 750 Hz) and the color subcarrier oscillator (3.58 MHz). In transformer operated (non-"hot" chassis) TV sets, grounding the TV chassis will help. Additionally, the use of a line filter in the ac line cord and a high-pass filter (passes all TV channels, starting at 54 MHz) at the antenna terminals will attenuate these interfering signals.

Note: Many CB receivers contain automatic noise limiter (ANL) or automatic noise blanker circuits, which are effective in reducing impulse noise.

Q. 3.225-A5. What problems can electrical interference cause to aeronautical ground stations?

A. The basic problem is the same as stated in the answer to Q. 3.225-A4. These stations employ amplitude modulation (AM). However, CB operates in the 27-MHz band, while aeronautical-ground stations operate at the much higher (VHF) frequency range of 108 to 135 MHz.

D. Ignition interference from any stationary or transient gasoline-powered engines will cause somewhat less of a problem to aeronautical ground stations than to CB stations. As mentioned in Q. 3.225-A4, ignition noise peaks at 35 MHz and thus is much farther in frequency from the aeronautical station frequency than the CB station frequency. Nevertheless, annoying interference may be caused in this case. See Q. 3.224-A4 D1, parts (a), (b), and (c), with regard to stationary engines.

Other sources of electrical interference to aeronautical ground stations are as listed in Q. 3.224-A D2. In addition, the following may also cause interference:

1. Arcing power company transformers or high-voltage insulators.

2. Diathermy machines and industrial electric RF heaters.

3. Light dimmers using silicon-controlled rectifiers. Noise can be attenuated by the use of line chokes and capacitors.

Note: The use of automatic noise limiter (ANL) or automatic noise blanker circuits will reduce the impulse noise type of interference.

**INTERFERENCE TO
HOME ENTERTAINMENT EQUIPMENT**

Q. 3.225-A6. Why is intermediate-frequency pickup a problem when a 40-MHz transmitter is operated near a television receiver? What are some possible solutions to this problem?

A.

1. If a 40-MHz transmitter is operated near a television receiver, it may cause interference patterns such as cross-hatching or sound bars on the TV screen and distorted voice signals in the sound. The interference pattern may move or change as the radio transmitter operator talks. The TV receiver horizontal and vertical synchronization, as well as the color reproduction, may be affected.

2. Some possible solutions include:

a. A high-pass filter at the TV receiver antenna terminals (TV channels begin at 54 MHz).

b. A low-pass filter between the 40-MHz transmitter output terminal(s) and its antenna to reject harmonics.

c. Good grounding of the 40-MHz transmitter.

d. A power line filter at the 40-MHz transmitter.

e. 75-Ω (shielded) coaxial cable for the TV receiver antenna feedline, rather than unshielded-twin lead.

f. An efficient TV antenna, with good connections and an undamaged transmission line.

The two ends of a coaxial line should have the braid enclose the center conductor at the connectors. There should be no breaks in the outer shield of a coaxial line.

D.

1. The passband of the IF section of a television receiver extends roughly from 41 to 47 MHz. Many sets employ an IF trap tuned to 39.75 MHz (adjacent picture channel trap). However, a strong signal at 40 MHz would likely not be adequately attenuated by this trap. In addition, the skirts of the IF response are sloping, not sharp, and so a 40-MHz signal, especially a strong one, could pass through the IF section and be detected. Detection would occur in the TV receiver sound and picture detectors. The sound detector is an FM detector. However, there would be some sound-detector output for both FM and AM signals. This would be a distorted output.

In the TV receiver picture detector, beat frequencies would be generated that are in the video passband (about 30 Hz to 2.5–3.5 MHz). These beat frequencies are created by the mixing of the 40-MHz signal with the 45.75-MHz picture IF carrier, the 42.17-MHz color IF carrier, the 41.25-MHz sound IF carrier (monochrome sets only), and their respective sidebands. These beat frequencies could then cause the picture problems discussed above.

IF interference can be easily identified as opposed to harmonic radiation interference, intermodulation or overloading (see Q. 3.137-A16). IF interference occurs on all channels. If the TV receiver has a fine-tuning control, varying it will change the interference pattern on the screen. With the other types of interference, the fine-tuning control will not change the pattern. Also, the interference would not occur on all channels.

Q. 3.225-A7. Explain what occurs when the front end (tuner) of a television receiver is "overloaded" by a nearby CB transmitter operating at 27 MHz. What are some possible symptoms that might be observed at the television receiver?

A.

1. *Overloading* refers to a very strong carrier signal (CB or other) entering the front end (the RF amplifier and mixer portions) and creating non-harmonically related interference signals, which then cause TV sound and picture problems.

2. In the worst case (fundamental frequency overloading), the TV screen may go black during CB transmission. Or for a color set, it may be light with traces of color. The sound portion of the TV program is also affected by overloading. In this case, the TV sound may be partially or completely blotted out. Other symptoms may include beat patterns on the screen and garbled sound, in less severe cases of overloading.

D. The TV channels most affected by fundamental frequency overloading are the VHF channels, 2 through 13. However, in

severe cases, the UHF channels (14-83) can also be affected.

CB overloading interference occurs on TV channels that are *not* at harmonic frequencies of 27 MHz. A strong CB signal entering the TV receiver's front end will cause harmonics and mixing effects there. Consequently, signals are generated in the front end that are *not* harmonically related to 27 MHz. These interfering signals are generated *within* the TV receiver and cannot be suppressed by filters or other measures. To reduce this type of interference, the strength of the 27-MHz signal entering the front end must be substantially reduced, as explained in the next paragraph.

To cure fundamental frequency overloading (can also affect FM receivers), it is necessary to prevent the offending carrier from entering the front end. A high pass filter, which rejects 27 MHz but passes all TV channels, should be installed at the TV receiver antenna terminals. The filter should be shielded and well grounded.

Q. 3.225-A8. On what television channels do the 2nd and 3rd harmonics of a 27-MHz CB transmitter fall?

A. The second harmonic of 27 MHz is 54 MHz, which falls in channel 2 (54 to 60 MHz). The third harmonic of 27 MHz is 81 MHz, which falls in channel 5 (76 to 82 MHz).

D. The third harmonic of 27 MHz (81 MHz) may also affect channel 6 (82 to 88 MHz), since the front end of a TV receiver has a wide bandpass characteristic. (Selectivity is accomplished in the IF section.) The seventh harmonic of 27 MHz (189) falls in TV channel 9 (186-192 MHz) and if sufficiently strong may affect TV reception.

Harmonic interference appears on the TV screen as a cross-hatch or herringbone pattern. It may cause TV sound interference. Also, it generally affects *only* those channels that are related harmonically to 27 MHz.

Since these harmonic frequencies coincide with some TV channel frequencies, they cannot be suppressed at the TV receiver.

They must be suppressed at the CB transmitter. A low-pass filter should be placed between the CB's antenna terminal and the antenna. Such a filter will not appreciably attenuate the 27-MHz signal, but it offers high attenuation for harmonics of that frequency. In addition, it is important to connect the CB transceiver to a good ground. This can be a ground rod buried to a depth of 3 to 4 ft. In very dry earth, the area around the rod should be kept moist.

Q. 3.225-A9. What is image reception? How would it cause a 120-MHz aircraft transmission to be received on an FM broadcast band receiver having an IF of 10.7 MHz?

A.
1. For image reception, see Q. 3.156.
2. The image frequency equals twice the IF plus (for this example) the incoming frequency, or

$$\text{Image frequency} = (2 \times \text{IF}) + \text{Incoming frequency}$$
$$120 \text{ MHZ} = 21.4 \text{ MHz} + \text{Incoming frequency}$$
$$98.6 \text{ MHz} = \text{Incoming frequency}$$

Thus if the FM receiver was tuned to 98.6 MHz, the image frequency (being heard) is 120 MHz. Checking,

$$\text{Image frequency} = (2 \times \text{IF}) + \text{Incoming frequency}$$
$$= 2 \times 10.7 \text{ MHz} + 98.6 \text{ MHz}$$
$$= 120 \text{ MHz}$$

Note: The FM broadcast band is 88 to 108 MHz.
D. See Q. 3.155 D3, Q. 3.156, and Q. 3.177.

Q. 3.225-A10. Discuss the use of high-pass and low-pass filters in reducing 27-MHz CB transmission interference to television reception.

A.
1. For use of high-pass filter, see Q. 3.225-A7(D).

2. For use of low-pass filter, see Q. 3.225-A8(D).

Q. 3.225-A11. Explain how a 27 MHz CB transmission can be rectified (detected) and heard in an audio system. How can this problem be reduced or eliminated?

A.
1. A CB transmission from a CB unit fairly close to the audio system affected can sometimes be heard through the audio system. This happens because the (strong) CB modulated carrier is picked up by the audio system and is then rectified (detected) and amplified to be heard in the speaker. In most cases rectification occurs in audio pre-amplifiers. The CB signal is rectified by non-linear action of the pre-amplifier. However, rectification can also occur in following (higher-level) audio stages.
2. Some methods used to reduce or eliminate this problem are:
a. Shielding of all loudspeaker leads.
b. Shielding of all patch cords. *(Note:* Only braided shield should be used.)
c. Repair poor grounds and poor solder joints.
d. Place an RF filter in the ac power line.
e. Place an RF filter in series with the input of suspected amplifier stages.
f. Place a low-pass filter(s) between the amplifier output and the speaker(s) to prevent RF from entering the amplifier via the speaker leads. A ceramic (disc) capacitor (.01 μF) to ground at each speaker output terminal may be sufficient in this case.
D. There are a number of paths by which the 27-MHz transmission can enter an audio system and be detected. In order to solve this problem, it may be necessary to treat more than one path. Some of the more common paths are:
1. *Microphones, phono cartridges, or tape players:* A low-pass audio filter between the offending unit and the amplifier can be helpful.

2. *Ac power line pickup:* A power line filter can be quite effective.

3. *Any unshielded cables between components of a system or extension speakers:* Shield all cables and ground the shield properly at both ends.

Three types of filters that can be used to reduce or eliminate this problem are shown in Fig. 3.225-A11. The power line filter in part (a) should be installed at the input of the amplifier chassis and grounded. In part (b) is shown pre-amplifier filtering. The same scheme may be used for higher-level audio amplifiers. Both channels of a stereo amplifier may require filtering. The filter shown in part (c) prevents RF from entering the amplifier via the speaker leads. The filter should be connected directly to the amplifier output terminals and grounded.

Q. 3.225-A12. Discuss the use of open and shorted stubs to attenuate interfering signals at a receiver.

A.

1. A *quarter-wave* section (stub) of a transmission line, which is *open* at the end and connected to the receiver antenna terminals, can act as a filter. This section appears as a *short circuit* (at the terminals) to the frequency for which the section is one-quarter wavelength long. Thus, an interfering frequency can be "trapped" by a quarter-wavelength open stub, while passing the desired frequencies with little or no attenuation.

2. Similarly, a *half-wave* section (stub) of a transmission line, which is *shorted* at the end and connected to the receiver antenna terminals, can act as a filter. This section

Fig. 3.225-A11. Examples of filters to prevent CB transmissions from being heard through audio systems. (a) Power-line filter. (b) Audio preamplifier filter. (c) Speaker lead filter. Capacitors should be disc ceramic type. RFC's should be wound with heavy wire, such as #18.

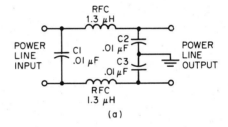

(a)

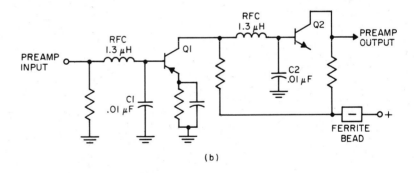

(b)

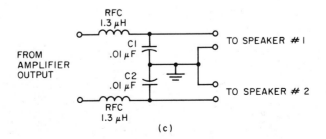

(c)

appears as a *short circuit* (at the terminals) to the frequency for which the section is one-half wavelength long. Filtering action is described in part 1 above.

D.

1. The quarter-wave open stub will also filter *odd* harmonics of the fundamental of the interfering frequency. This filter acts as a *short* circuit for stubs that are odd numbers of quarter-wavelengths long. Thus, for the third harmonic, the line that is a quarter-wavelength long at the fundamental is three-quarters of a wavelength long at the third harmonic, five-fourths of a wavelength long at the fifth harmonic, and so on.

2. The half-wave shorted stub will filter *all* harmonics of the fundamental frequency. Multiples of half-wavelength long sections act as a short circuit at the antenna terminals. For the second harmonic, the line that is a half-wavelength long at the fundamental, one-wavelength long at the second harmonic, one and one-half wavelengths long at the third harmonic, and so on.

3. Because the physical length of a stub is a function of the "trapping" frequency, it may not be practical to use for frequencies below about 60 MHz. A simple stub can be made from TV twin-lead transmission line (either open quarter-wavelength or shorted half-wavelength). The quarter-wavelength in feet can be calculated as follows:

$$\frac{\lambda}{4} L = \frac{202}{f(MHz)} \text{ ft (for open } \frac{\lambda}{4} \text{ stub)}$$

(The above is corrected for the velocity of propagation of twin-lead.) For example, assume an interfering signal of 120 MHz:

$$\frac{\lambda}{4} L = \frac{202}{120} = 1.68 \text{ ft (or 20.16 in.)}$$

The half-wavelength in feet can be calculated from:

$$\frac{\lambda}{2} L = \frac{404}{f(MHz)} \text{ ft}$$

For an interfering signal of 60 MHz,

$$\frac{\lambda}{2} L = \frac{404}{60} = 6.73 \text{ ft (or 80.76 in.)}$$

As you can see, half-wavelength (or even quarter-wavelength) stubs at the lower portion of the VHF spectrum can be quite unwieldy and inconvenient. However, at 202 MHz, a quarter-wave stub is 1 ft long and a half-wave stub is 2 ft long.

Note: If a stub is made of material other than TV twin-lead, the velocity of propagation may be different. In this case the quarter-wavelength in feet is

$$\frac{\lambda}{4} L = \frac{246}{f(MHz)} \times k \text{ ft}$$

where

k = velocity factor.

The half-wavelength in feet is:

$$\frac{\lambda}{4} L = \frac{492}{f(MHz)} \times k \text{ ft}$$

Some typical velocity factors are:

75-Ω coaxial cable with polyethelyne dielectric	0.66
300-Ω TV twin-lead	0.82
150-Ω twin-lead	0.76
75-Ω twin-lead	0.68
Two-wire line with air dielectric	0.98

(See also Q.3.203.D., Q. 3.208, and Q. 3.217.)

Q. 3.225-A13. How could improper grounding affect the harmonic radiation from a CB transmitter?

A. If the CB transmitter is improperly grounded, there would be an impedance between the chassis and ground. Under this condition, the chassis would act as an antenna and harmonic radiation would take place from it directly. Obviously, a high-pass filter at the output of the transmitter would be ineffective in reducing this harmonic radiation.

D. Substantial harmonic rather than fundamental frequency radiation would occur in this case. The reason is that, at the higher frequencies, the chassis would be a more effective antenna. By properly grounding the transmitter chassis (see below), it would be at the same potential as the earth (approximately) and not "floating" above ground. This would minimize the effectiveness of the chassis as an antenna and thus would reduce harmonic radiation. Note that grounding the chassis of a transmitter operating at, say, 100 MHz or above would not be very effective for this problem. The reason is that, at these higher frequencies, the lead(s) used to ground the chassis would then become a fairly effective antenna(s).

The following rules pertain to effective grounding:

1. All grounding should be made to a good earth ground. This may be a metal cold water pipe or a ground rod buried at least 3 to 4 ft.

2. Ground leads should be as short as possible.

3. Ground leads should be of *large* diameter wire.

4. Grounding of all items requiring it must be made to a *common* point. This avoids "ground loops" which may radiate RF energy.

BATTERIES

Q. 3.226. How does a primary cell differ from a secondary cell?

A. See Fig. 3.226. A primary cell cannot be recharged after use, while a secondary cell can.

D. A primary cell cannot be recharged because the substance of one of the electrodes is chemically eroded; this occurs because the products of the chemical reaction are soluble in the electrolyte. An attempt to recharge it would not restore it to its first condition.

A secondary, or storage, cell, when it is discharged, has undergone a chemical change, but the new products are not soluble in the electrolyte. When the charging current is supplied, the chemical action is reversed; since the electrode material has not been dissolved, the cell will be restored to its charged condition.

Q. 3.227. What is the chemical composition of the electrolyte of a lead-acid storage cell?

A. The electrolyte is a dilute solution of sulphuric acid (H_2SO_4) in distilled water, which reaches a specific gravity of about 1.300 when fully charged.

D. See also Q. 3.228 and Q. 3.229. Ammonium hydroxide (ammonia), baking soda (sodium bicarbonate), or washing soda (sodium carbonate) may be used to neutralize acid electrolyte. Great care must be taken to allow none of these substances to get inside the battery.

The level of the electrolyte in a lead-acid cell should be kept about ¼ inch above the top of the plates. During charge and discharge some of the water (not acid) evaporates and so must occasionally be replaced with pure water. If the level is allowed to be continuously low, the useful plate area will diminish and the capacity of the battery will be reduced.

Q. 3.228. Describe the care which should be given a group of storage cells to maintain them in good operating conditions?

A. The following items should be carefully checked in order to maintain a group of storage cells in good operating condition.

1. Electrolyte should be kept about ¼ in. above plates by adding pure water when needed.

2. Cells should always be kept fully charged, and on trickle charge when not in use.

3. Cells should be frequently checked to determine state of charge.

4. Any cell showing unusual conditions should be removed from the circuit.

5. If electrolyte is spilled, it should be replaced after the battery is fully charged, using electrolyte of the rated specific gravity.

6. Proper ventilation must be provided.

7. Observe correct charge and discharge rates.

8. Overcharge somewhat about once each month to remove sulphation.

9. Keep exterior of battery dry and terminals coated with vaseline or other suitable lubricant.

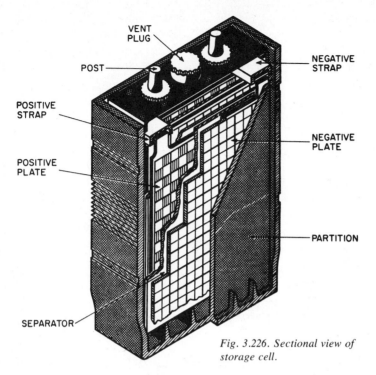

VENT PLUG

POST

POSITIVE STRAP

POSITIVE PLATE

SEPARATOR

NEGATIVE STRAP

NEGATIVE PLATE

PARTITION

Fig. 3.226. Sectional view of storage cell.

10. Keep all terminal connections clean and tight.

D. In general, the capacity of a lead-acid battery is decreased when low temperatures are present.

An important factor to be considered when lead-acid batteries are used under conditions of very low temperature is the specific gravity of the electrolyte. If the specific gravity is permitted to fall too low, there is a strong possibility that the electrolyte may freeze and split the battery. If the battery is kept fully charged, the freezing temperature is very low.

Q. 3.229. What may cause "sulphation" of a lead-acid storage cell?

A. Sulphation is a normal process in a lead-acid cell. However, excessive sulphation will be caused by overdischarging and by local action through improper charging.

The battery should be given an overcharge about once a month if in continual use, or kept on trickle charge when not in use for any extended period.

D. The effects are: (1) reduced terminal voltage, (2) increased internal resistance, (3) reduced power output, (4) possible buckling of the plates.

Sulphation is the formation of lead sulphate on the positive and negative plates of a battery during discharge. It is a normal process in the lead-acid cell and is caused by sulphuric acid molecules combining with lead dioxide and sponge lead to form lead sulphate ($PbSO_4$). If proper charging is neglected, the sulphate eventually hardens on the surface of the plates and prevents proper contact of the electrolyte with the active material of the plates. Sulphation is increased by allowing the battery to remain in a discharged condition, and by adding acid instead of properly charging the cells.

Q. 3.230. What will be the result of discharging a lead-acid storage cell at an excessively high current rate?

A. The effects are:

1. Reduction of output power. If the discharge rate is 8 times normal, the output

power is only 50 percent of the normal output power.

2. Excessive heating.

3. Excessive evaporation of water.

D. If the battery is also overdischarged; this will result in the formation of excessive sulphation which will probably be difficult to remove with normal charging.

Q. 3.231. If the charging current through a storage battery is maintained at the normal rate, but its polarity is reversed, what will result?

A. In an Edison cell, reversing the polarity of the charge will cause no damage as long as the electrolyte temperature is kept below 115°F. The cell will charge slightly the reverse way. The battery should be completely discharged and then recharged correctly.

In a lead-acid cell reversing the charging polarity will cause no damage if the discharging effect is not permitted to become excessive. If permitted to continue in reverse direction, the battery will take on a reverse charge and become very sulphated. It should be fully discharged and then charged correctly at a low rate for as much as 48 hours. If the reverse charge is excessive the negative plates will be ruined.

D. See Q. 3.228 and Q. 3.232.

Q. 3.232. What is the approximate fully charged voltage of a lead-acid cell?

A. The fully charged terminal voltage is about 2.06 volts.

D. The cell is considered to be fully discharged when the terminal voltage drops to 1.75 volts. The actual fully charged voltage depends upon temperature and individual cell characteristics, but is close to the figure given.

Q. 3.233. What steps may be taken to prevent corrosion of lead-acid storage cell terminals?

A. The cell terminals should be occasionally cleaned and coated with vaseline or other suitable lubricant.

D. Connections should be made before the terminals are coated and care must be taken to see that all terminal connections are tight. See also Q. 3.228.

Q. 3.234. How is the capacity of a battery rated?

A. In ampere-hours.

D. A typical auto battery may have a capacity of 120 ampere-hours. Such a battery can theoretically deliver 10 amperes continuously for 12 hours or 120 amperes for one hour. In practice, the performance may be somewhat less due to heating and chemical changes in the battery.

Note: The following added material numbered Q. 3.234-A1 through Q. 3.234-A4 contains information that may be required to pass the General Radiotelephone Operator's License examination. This added material, as well as the new material added to other sections, has been included to help acquaint students with the current state of the electronics art. It is felt that the added material contains subject matter that may also be required of students who have obtained a General Radiotelephone Operator's License and are seeking employment. Additionally, the added material contains valuable information for private technician certification.

Q. 3.234-A1. What is meant by the specific gravity of an electrolyte? How can the specific gravity be used to determine the state of charge of a lead acid cell?

A.

1. The specific gravity (sp gr) of an electrolyte (or any liquid) is a number which compares the weight of the electrolyte to the weight of an equal volume of water. Thus we have,

Specific gravity =

$$\frac{\text{Weight of electrolyte}}{\text{Weight of equal volume of water}}$$

The specific gravity of water is 1.000. The specific gravity of the diluted sulphuric acid electrolyte of a new, fully charged lead-acid cell is approximately 1.300.

2. The specific gravity is a good indication of the state of charge of a lead acid cell. When a cell is discharged, much of the sulphuric acid has left the electrolyte and has combined with the active material in the positive and negative plates. The cell voltage has dropped from 2.1 V. At this time the specific gravity may be 1.150. As the battery is being charged, the acid leaves the active plate material and passes back into the electrolyte. With more acid in the electrolyte, its specific gravity increases. At full charge, the specific gravity will be about 1.300 for a new battery and less for an older one.

D. To measure specific gravity, an instrument called a *hydrometer* is used. In its basic form, it consists of a sealed glass tube 3 to 5 in. long. One end is weighted so it will float in an upright position. This tube is placed in a larger glass tube, which has provision to suck up and hold some of the electrolyte. The inner glass tube is calibrated in terms of specific gravity and will float at a level indicative of the specific gravity. (See also Q. 3.227, Q. 3.228, and Q. 3.232.)

Q. 3.234-A2. How do the characteristics of lead acid and nickel-cadmium cells differ?

A.

1. Lead acid cells have the following characteristics:

a. Electrolyte of dilute sulphuric acid (H_2SO_4).

b. Positive plate of lead dioxide ($Pb O_2$).

c. Negative plate of spongy lead (Pb).

d. No-load cell voltage, 2.1 V.

e. Capacity increases initially during its early cycle life, then stabilizes.

f. End of life usually occurs when the cell's capacity falls to 60 percent of its original capacity.

g. They have the greatest capacity when discharged at about a 20-hour rate (20 hours' use to discharged condition).

h. Should not be stored at ambient temperature above 130°F.

i. Can be stored at low temperatures and yield considerable power and operation at these temperatures.

j. Available in sealed or vented units.

k. Moderate initial cost.

l. Extremely wide variety of uses, as in autos, fork-lift trucks, portable TVs, military guidance systems, and electric power tools.

2. Nickel-cadmium cells have the following characteristics. (See Fig. 3.234-A2.)

a. Electrolyte of potassium hydroxide.

b. Positive plate of nickelic hydroxide.

c. Negative plate of metallic cadmium.

d. Operating voltage of 1.25 V.

e. Can accept much more physical and electrical abuse than a lead acid cell, without permanent damage.

f. Capable of very high discharge rates.

g. Useful for "pulsed" discharges,

Fig. 3.234-A2. Schematic diagram of sintered-plate nickel-cadmium cell.

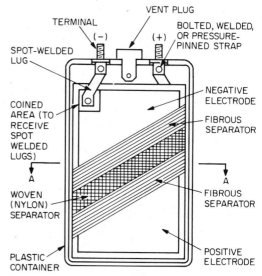

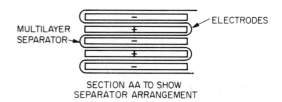

which are very high rate, very short duration discharges.

h. Can be useful down to −40°F, compared to −20°F for a lead acid cell. Thus, it is favored for low-temperature engine starting.

i. Operating voltage held nearly constant at 1.25 V until discharged.

j. Can be charged at very high rates without damage. This is not true of lead acid cells.

k. High initial cost.

l. Long life and low (or no) maintenance.

m. Available in sealed or vented units.

n. Some uses are in, jet aircraft starting, communications, medical applications, and cordless appliances such as toothbrushes and shavers.

D. See Q. 3.234-A3.

Q. 3.234-A3. Discuss the differences in charging procedures of lead acid and nickel-cadmium batteries.

A. Secondary batteries are charged by reversing the chemical action occurring during discharge. This is done by forcing a reverse dc current through the battery from a dc generator or a rectified ac source. In the charging process, the positive side of the charging source is connected to the positive battery terminal. Also, the negative side of the charging source is connected to the negative battery terminal. Of course, the charging voltage must never be less than the existing battery voltage, or the battery will discharge. A dc reverse current relay or a diode rectifier(s) will prevent this.

1. A lead acid battery that has been considerably discharged can be charged initially at a high rate (60 A or more). However, as the battery approaches full charge, its charging efficiency falls to about 5 percent. If the high rate is maintained too long, excessive gassing (with loss of water) and excessive internal heat will occur. Excessive gassing will wear active material from the plates and shorten the life of the battery.

Excessive gassing will have the appearance of boiling of the electrolyte. (Cell temperatures should be kept below about 110°F.) Consequently, as the battery approaches full charge, the charging rate must be reduced to the level that prevents excessive gassing. This process can be accomplished automatically by a charging system that senses the battery voltage and adjusts the charging rate accordingly. A good example of this system is the automobile charging system.

If possible, a so-called "trickle" charge at about a 1-A rate for several hours should follow a high-rate charge. Where conditions permit, it is always more beneficial to battery life and capacity to use low charging rates. This of course lengthens the required charging time to 8 to 14 hours. A low rate may be approximately a tenth of the ampere-hour (Ah) rating of the battery. Thus, for a 100-Ah battery, the rate would be 10 A. (A high-rate charge may be about half of the Ah rating, and a trickle charge, about one-hundredth of the Ah rating.)

2. A nickel-cadmium battery has the ability to be recharged quickly. From a fully discharged condition, this battery can be recharged in about one hour. However, with the sealed type, greater precautions must be taken to reduce the charging rate as the battery approaches gassing conditions. This can be done by automatic regulation. Generally, a sealed battery of this type will be operated with 20 to 30 percent less available capacity than the same-sized vented battery.

Although nickel-cadmium batteries are very rugged, they are subject to a condition known as "runaway" if the battery is charged in a manner to create high internal heat. This may result from excessive charge rates or from charging it in a high ambient temperature environment. When the charge is supplied from a constant voltage source, the reduction of internal resistance will result in an increase of charging current. This, in turn, will increase the heat generation and a further increase of charging current. If this situation is unchecked, the heat can destroy the battery. The runaway condition can be prevented by providing for proper charging regulation and also for adequate ventilation of the cells and their housing.

D.

1. Lead acid batteries are available in sealed units, as well as in vented types. The sealed units are made with calcium alloy. They have a cell voltage in the order of 2.8 to 3.0 V per cell when near the fully charged condition. As a result, inexpensive charge control equipment can be used to limit overcharge. In sealed batteries, very little water is used up during normal use, and none need be added for the useful life of the battery. Many automobile (and other type) batteries are made this way.

In applications such as power tools, where the battery must be operated in any position, the electrolyte must be immobilized. This is done by forming a "gel" in the electrolyte by the addition of silica gel (SiO_2). In these batteries, more care must be taken to avoid excessive gassing, which would disrupt the gel.

2. Nickel-cadmium batteries are also available in sealed and vented types. In the sealed type, the danger of physically disrupting the battery during or approaching overcharge is greater than in the vented type.

Nickel-cadmium batteries are said to have a "memory" in which the battery seems to "remember" the manner in which it has been cycled. This effect only shows up in a highly repetitive cycling routine and results in a seemingly permanent loss of reserve capacity. For example, if a 10-Ah battery is frequently cycled to use only 4 AH, the *actual* available capacity falls to 4 AH after a fairly short time. To avoid this, batteries in this type of service are periodically given conditioning cycles in which the charge and discharge are varied from the routine. This treatment avoids the memory effect and may restore the capacity of a battery already affected. Although a great number of conditioning cycles will be required. (See also Q. 3.226 through Q. 3.232.)

Q. 3.234-A4. What are the characteristics of an alkaline battery?

A. A cross-section of a typical alkaline (dry) cell is shown in Figure 3.234-A4. Some characteristics are as follows:

1. Anode: amalgamated granular zinc.
2. Cathode: manganese dioxide.
3. Electrolyte: potassium hydroxide.
4. Polarization effects are much less than in conventional (carbon-zinc) dry cells.
5. Energy can be withdrawn at higher power levels than with carbon-zinc cells.
6. Voltage variation during discharge less than for a carbon-zinc cell.
7. Good shelf life characteristics (two to three years).
8. Cells are sealed.
9. Hydrogen production is negligible.
10. Open-circuit voltage: 1.5 V.

Fig. 3.234-A4. Schematic diagram of a typical alkaline primary cell.

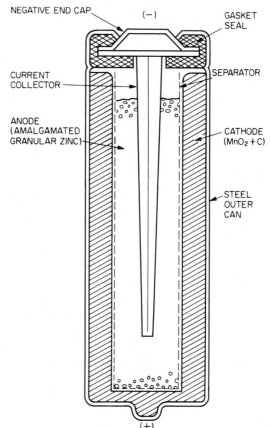

D. The voltage range under load of an alkaline cell is from 0.8 to 1.2 V. At 0°C it retains 50 percent of its capacity compared to the capacity at 25°C. A carbon-zinc cell retains only 25 percent.

Because of their ability to provide relatively high power levels and other special abilities, alkaline batteries are used to power portable radios (and TVs), photographic equipment, fractional horsepower electric motors, such as are used in shavers, toys, movie cameras, and tape recorders. They are also used to power transceivers.

Note: These are dry cells and are *not* to be recharged. Recharging may cause the cell to *explode.*

Alkaline batteries are rated by their capacity, which is cited at a particular drain rate. The capacity is expressed in milliampere hours (mAh). The capacities of three common sizes of alkaline dry cells are given below:

Size	mAH	Drain (mA)
AA	1 800	60
C	5 000	100
D	10 000	300

Example: An AA alkaline cell at a drain rate of 60 mA will operate for $\dfrac{1\,800}{60}$ = 30 hrs.

MOTORS AND GENERATORS

Q. 3.235. What is "power factor"? Give an example of how it is calculated. Discuss the construction and operation of dynamotors.

A.

1. Power factor is the factor by which the product of volts by amperes must be multiplied to obtain the true power. For an example of power factor, see the discussion.

2. A dynamotor is a combination motor and generator which utilizes a common field winding (or permanent field magnets). The two armatures (motor and generator) are mounted on a single shaft and require only two bearings. The motor is generally run by battery power, but may also be run from ac or dc lines, depending upon design requirements. The output from the generator is dc. Typical output values are 200 volts at 50 mA, 300 volts at 200 mA, and 600 volts at 300 mA.

D.

1. If a circuit is purely resistive, or the voltage is dc, its actual power consumption may be found by the formula $P = V \times I$. This is also the *apparent* power of a circuit, since V and I would be measured by a voltmeter and ammeter, respectively. However, a pure reactance consumes *no power,* so that if a circuit contains both resistance and reactance, V being alternating, the product of $V \times I$ (apparent power) is not the actual power being consumed. This is so because there is now a phase angle introduced between the voltage and current in the resistance. In order to find the "true" power, the apparent power ($V \times I$) must be corrected by a factor which takes into account the effect of the phase angle. To find the true power of a circuit multiply the apparent power ($V \times I$) by the cosine of the phase angle, which equals $\dfrac{R}{Z}$ Thus true power equals

$$V \times I \times \frac{R}{Z}$$

For example, a circuit may have one ampere flowing through an inductance and a 3 ohm resistance. If it is dc, the voltage is 3 volts, the power is 3 watts. If the inductance is such that 5 volts, ac, is required to give 1 ampere, the power is still 3 watts ($= I^2R$), but the volt-ampere product is $1 \times 5 = 5$. The power factor to give 3 watts is therefore $\frac{3}{5} = 0.6$.

The power factor is equal to $\dfrac{R}{Z}$ where Z is the ac impedance, in this case

$$5 \text{ ohms} = \frac{5 \text{ volts}}{1 \text{ ampere}}$$

$$\frac{R}{Z} = \frac{3}{5} = 0.6$$

as before.

Since the phase-angle, *A*, between the current and voltage is such that cos *A* = 0.6, *A* is about 53°.

True power is measured directly with a wattmeter, which automatically takes the phase-angle into account.

2. Normally, the output voltage of a dynamotor may be regulated only by changing the speed of the motor. A series resistance in the output line could be used to reduce the available output voltage.

The principal advantages of a dynamotor are its compactness and operating efficiency. It is possible to operate dynamotors from storage batteries. One disadvantage of a dynamotor is that its voltage output is dependent on the stability of the source voltage.

Dynamotors are used extensively in aircraft and other portable installations to supply plate and screen grid power. A dynamotor has higher efficiency than a motor-generator set, but its output voltage cannot be readily varied, and its regulation is poor.

Q. 3.236. List the comparative advantages and disadvantages of motor-generator and transformer-rectifier power supplies.

A. The advantages of motor-generator power supplies are as follows:
1. Simple output voltage control.
2. Little filtering required, due to high ripple frequency.
3. Very rugged in construction and will stand much abuse.
4. Self-rectifying, requires no tubes.
5. Can be operated from either ac or dc lines.

Disadvantages of motor-generator power supplies are:
1. High initial cost.
2. Difficult to repair.
3. Subjected to bearing troubles and other difficulties attendant with rotating machinery.

4. Equipment is noisy and causes vibration.
5. Large bulk and weight.
6. Requires comparatively frequent inspection and service, as to lubrication, brushes and commutator.
7. Limited high voltage available.
8. Causes radio frequency interference from brush sparking.

The advantages of transformer-rectifier power supplies are:
1. Low initial cost.
2. Practically unlimited high voltages available.
3. Simple to repair and replace components, compared with motor generator.
4. Completely electronic—no moving parts to service.
5. Quiet and practically vibrationless in operation.
6. Clean.
7. Can be built as an integral portion of transmitter.
8. Usually lighter and smaller than equivalent motor-generator.
9. Requires no inspection, except when trouble occurs.

Disadvantages of transformer-rectifier power supplies are:
1. Voltage output not easily controlled.
2. Requires large filter components.
3. Tubes are fragile.
4. Usually must be operated only from ac lines.
5. Tubes must occasionally be replaced.
6. High voltage windings cannot stand much overload.

D. See Q. 3.65, Q. 3.66.

Q. 3.237. What determines the speed of a synchronous motor? An induction motor? A dc series motor?

A.
1. The speed of a synchronous motor is determined by the number of pairs of poles and the line frequency.
2. The speed of an induction motor is determined by the number of pairs of poles,

the frequency, and to some extent, the load.

3. The speed of a dc series motor is determined chiefly by the load.

Q. 3.238. Describe the action and list the main characteristics of a shunt dc generator?

A. The main characteristic of a shunt-wound dc generator (Fig. 3.238) is the good voltage regulation under varying load conditions. The starting of such a generator takes advantage of the residual magnetic field of the field poles. As the armature starts rotating, an emf is induced into it due to the residual field. The first emf causes some current to flow through the high resistance field, thus increasing the field strength, and the output voltage to normal value. Most of the current is delivered to the load, due to the high field resistance. The field is composed of very many turns of fine wire. A series field rheostat is used to control the output voltage.

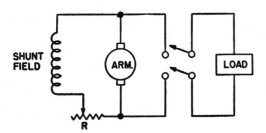

Fig. 3.238. Voltage control of shunt dc generator.

D. See also Q. 3.245.

Q. 3.239. Name four causes of excessive sparking at the brushes of a dc motor or generator.

A. Several causes are:
1. Brushes not properly set at neutral point.
2. Weak spring tension on brushes.
3. Worn brushes.
4. Motor overloaded or started too rapidly.
5. Open or short circuit in armature coil.
6. Dirt on commutator or worn brushes.

7. Commutator worn eccentric.
8. High (protruding) mica insulation between commutator bars or commutator bars of uneven height.

D.
1. "Commutating poles" or "interpoles" are added in order to reduce brush sparking without the necessity of moving the brushes.

Commutating poles are small field poles consisting of a few turns of heavy wire which are located between the main field poles of the machine. The commutating poles are connected in series with the armature, and in a motor are of the same polarity as the preceding main field pole. In a simple motor, as the load increases, the brushes have to be pushed backward to keep them in a neutral position for sparkless commutation. The commutating poles in a motor effectively twist the field forward, in proportion to the current taken, to keep the neutral position at the fixed brushes. ("Neutral position" refers to the position of the brushes on the commutator of a dc motor or generator, relative to the field poles, at which minimum brush sparking will occur.)

When the motor or generator is stationary and no current flows through the armature, the neutral position occurs when the armature coil in contact with a brush is exactly half way between two adjacent field poles. At this position no emf is induced in the armature coil. In any other position, as the brush transfers to another commutator segment, it is momentarily shorting the armature coil and causes a strong magnetic field to be set up which collapses when the brush reaches the next commutator segment. It is this collapsing field which induces a large counter-emf and causes sparking. If a heavy current is flowing through the windings, the inductance will maintain a current flow, regardless of absence of external field poles; the brushes must leave the commutator segment at the time that the induced voltage has brought the current to zero. This position is not the same for different loads. As the load increases, the brushes should be moved forward in the direction of rotation to reduce sparking, in the case of a generator, while in a motor the brushes should be moved backwards against the rotation. The commutating poles keep the neutral position fixed, by effectively shifting the field.

2. When a dc motor is first starting, a very large armature current exists due to the lack of sufficient armature cemf. This large armature current exists only until the armature reaches sufficient speed so that the cemf becomes effective in limiting the current. If too long a time is taken in starting the motor with a hand starter, the large current value will overheat and possibly burn out the starting resistors which are only rated for intermittent operation. The starter handle should be held in each position only long enough to bring the motor speed up to the value which is normally present at that particular setting.

3. A short circuit in an armature coil will cause excessive sparking at the commutator brushes, overheating of the machine, reduction of speed under load and excessive armature current.

The effects of a short circuit in an armature coil are similar to the effects of a short circuit in the windings of a transformer. A very large circulating current would be set up in the shorted portion, and the magnetic field thus produced would be in such a direction as to cancel the normal magnetic field of the armature. This would result in a decreased amount of torque and speed and an excessive armature current with attendant overheating.

Q. 3.240. How may radio frequency interference, often caused by sparking at the brushes of a high-voltage generator, be minimized?

A. By the use of brush by-pass capacitors, and high and low frequency filters.

D. Sparking interference is usually caused by the fact that certain elements within the generator form tuned circuits of various frequencies, and that connections and power leads behave as antennas to ra-

diate these frequencies. The action of the spark in this case is similar to a regular spark transmitter, supplying the energy to keep the tuned circuits oscillating. If spark interference suppression is to be successful, the radiating leads must be effectively terminated (as far as radiating frequencies are concerned) very close to the generator.

If a commutator motor is being used, a low-pass filter should be installed, close to it, in the motor supply line. With respect to the generator proper, a ripple filter (low-pass) should be connected in the high voltage line, as close to the generator as possible. Shielding of long connecting leads will reduce radiation and interference. Brush by-pass capacitors should be connected from each brush to ground. If some interference is still present, a "pi" filter made up of an RF choke and two RF by-pass capacitors can be located close to the generator in the high-voltage line and ahead of the ripple filter.

Q. 3.241. How may the output voltage of a separately excited ac generator, at constant output frequency, be varied?

A. The most practical means would be to vary the output of the dc exciting generator by means of a series field rheostat.

D. The output voltage of an ac generator depends upon (among other things) the magnetic strength of the generator field. A simple method of varying the output voltage, therefore, would be to vary the current of the exciter supply by means of a series rheostat. Any other means of varying the alternator field current would have equivalent effect.

Q. 3.242. What is the purpose of a commutator on a dc motor? On a dc generator?

A. The function of the commutator is to periodically change the armature coils which contact the brushes and thus maintain a condition of uni-directional current in the output of a generator, and an alternating current in the armature of a motor.

D. All generators and motors are essentially ac devices, and thus the commutator is really a mechanical inverter. In a dc generator, the windings have ac induced, and the output would normally be ac, were it not for the fact that the commutator action switches in a new set of armature coils just when the current in the original coil starts to reverse direction.

In a motor the switching action is such that the current in the armature is made to reverse periodically, and thus becomes ac, so that as an armature coil leaves one field pole, it will be repelled from it and attracted to the next.

Q. 3.243. What may cause a motor-generator bearing to overheat?

A. The most obvious cause would be lack of lubrication or incorrect type of lubrication. Other causes might be consistent overload, lack of ventilation, dirt in bearings, or misalignment which may result from warping or distortion of base or frame.

D. The first rule in treating an overheated bearing is never to stop the machine, as the bearings might seize (or "freeze") when contraction takes place. If possible, remove the load and slow down the machine considerably. While running slowly make every effort to cool the machine by forced air cooling or other means available. A large quantity of oil and graphite, if available, should be continuously applied while the machine is running slowly. Continue this treatment until the bearing cools to normal temperature. Flush out with flush oil or kerosene, and then lubricate with the proper grade of oil. If the heating has not been too severe the bearing will still remain in good condition. If the cause of overheating was due to any overload condition, the overload should be removed before bringing the machine back to normal speed.

Q. 3.244. What materials should be used to clean the commutator of a motor or generator?

A. The commutator may be cleaned with a piece of very fine sandpaper or commutator polishing paste; never use emery.

D. A commutator polishing agent is available, which is applied with a clean cloth. The commutator is then polished while the machine is running.

Care should be taken in the handling of any rotating machinery, and especially in the handling of high voltage generators, in order to avoid injury and shock.

Q. 3.245. If the field of a shunt wound dc motor were opened while the machine is running under no load, what would be the probable result(s)?

A. The motor would race at an ever-increasing speed; and if unchecked it may destroy itself due to centrifugal forces, provided that fuses or circuit breakers did not act sooner to protect it.

D. Ordinarily the armature current is greatly limited due to the counter-emf developed in the armature as the field is cut by the windings. Since the armature current is limited, the torque and thus the speed is limited. If the field coil opens, most of this cemf disappears, and the armature current rises to very high values, increasing the torque and speed almost without limit.

Note: The following added material numbered Q. 3.245-A1 contains information that may be required to pass the General Radiotelephone Operator's License examination. This added material, as well as the new material added to other sections, has been included to help acquaint students with the current state of the electronics art. It is felt that the added material contains subject matter that may also be required of students who have obtained a General Radiotelephone Operator's License and are seeking employment. Additionally, the added material contains valuable information for private technician certification.

Q. 245-A1. If the RF chokes in the power leads of a motor generator were shorted, what problems would result?

A. If the RF chokes were shorted, there would be an increase of radio frequency interference (RFI) at various radio frequencies.

D. It is assumed that a commutator

motor is being used. RF chokes (or low-pass filters) are usually installed in the motor power leads, close to the motor, to minimize radio frequency radiation. If such RF chokes shorted (within themselves), motor operation may not be affected, but there would be an increased radiation of radio frequencies. These radio frequencies would be generated by brush sparking. (See also Q. 3.240.)

MICROWAVE EQUIPMENT

Q. 3.246. Describe the physical structure of a klystron tube and explain how it operates as an oscillator.

A. See Q. 8.48.
D. See also Q. 3.251, Q. 3.248, Q. 8.42, Q. 8.46, and Q. 8.47.

Q. 3.247. Draw a diagram showing the construction and explain the principles of operation of a traveling-wave tube.

A. See Fig. 3.247. A traveling-wave amplifier is a micro-wave amplifier which may be used at frequencies well in excess of 7 500 megahertz. The tube in the figure was designed for a mid-frequency of 3 600 megahertz and a bandwidth of 800 megahertz. Bandwidths up to 5 000 megahertz or more are possible using tubes with higher mid-frequency design.

The tube is made up of the following major components:
1. Electron gun.
2. Helix line.
3. Focusing solenoid.
4. Collector anode.

The length of the helix may be 6 inches or more and consists of tightly wound wire. When in use, the tube is inserted into two waveguides as shown; one for input and one for output. Input and output coupling is accomplished by short stubs connected to each end of the helix and mounted so as to provide or receive energy from each waveguide (see the figure). The helix winding and collector are operated at a high positive potential (in this case, about 1 600 volts) with respect to the cathode of the electron gun. The electron gun forms a beam of electrons which is focused electrically at the gun end and magnetically along the length of the helix by the focusing solenoid. The focused and accelerated beam is shot through the inside of the helix and parallel to its axis. It is picked up by the collector anode, located at the far end of the tube.

Energy in the form of electromagnetic waves are introduced to the tube via the input waveguide, travel along the helix wire and are coupled to the output waveguide. Because the waves follow the helix wire, their actual forward velocity is only about one-tenth that of light. At the acceleration voltage chosen, the beam of electrons inside the helix moves forward at a velocity slightly greater than that of the wave. (This is the condition of maximum tube gain.) The amplification of the tube occurs by virtue of the interaction of the electrostatic component of the electromagnetic field and the electron beam. The polarity of the electrostatic component will have the effect of producing velocity modulation of the electron beam (similar to klystron operation). When the electron beam is caused to speed up (positive electric field) it removes energy from the wave. When

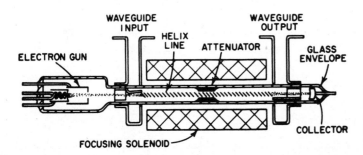

Fig. 3.247. The details of construction of a traveling-wave amplifier. (Courtesy of International Telephone and Telegraph Corp.)

it is caused to slow down, it supplies energy to the wave (negative electric field). Now remember that the electron beam velocity is slightly greater than the wave velocity. A portion of the beam originating during a positive electric field will be further accelerated and will move relatively quickly out of the positive field and into the negative field farther down the tube. It will be slowed down by the negative field, giving up energy to it. Since it remains longer (slower) in the negative field, more energy is given up to the wave than was taken from it and amplification results. Amplification is governed by the relative velocity of the beam with respect to the wave and also (within limits) by the length of the helix. A longer helix produces greater gain. An attenuator is situated at the approximate middle of the helix line. The function of this attenuator is to prevent self-oscillation from occurring in the traveling-wave tube. It does this by reducing the magnitude of feedback components to a level which is incapable of sustaining oscillations.

D. See also Q. 3.246 and Q. 3.248.

Q. 3.248. Describe the physical structure of a multianode magnetron and explain how it operates.

A.

1. A multianode magnetron consists basically of a multiple-cavity assembly, a centrally located cathode, an output-power coupling device and a very-powerful per-

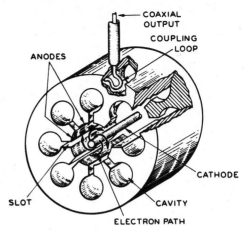

Fig. 3.248.(b). Sketch illustrating the construction of the anode cylinder of a typical magnetron.

manent magnet. A typical magnetron assembly is shown in Fig. 3.248(a).

The body of the magnetron tube is the cylindrical anode. It consists of a copper cylinder in which resonant cavities are cut with high precision and which largely determine the operating frequency of the magnetron. The frequency is influenced to a lesser extent by the strength of the magnetic and electric fields within the tube. The general arrangement of the components within the anode cylinder are shown in Fig. 3.248(b).

2. Because of the interacting electric and magnetic fields, electrons which are emitted from the cathode trace circular paths just outside of the slots leading to each cavity. Initially the cavities are shock-excited into oscillation by this electron motion. Once the cavities are oscillating, the field produced by each cavity plays an important part in the continued oscillation of the magnetron. When an electron stream is moving past one of the cavities, the field across the cavity must have a polarity capable of *slowing* down the electron stream. When this occurs, the stream *gives up energy* to the cavity to sustain oscillations. If the cavity field is such as to *speed up* the electron stream, the electrons will *remove* energy from the cavity and *reduce* the amplitude of oscillations. In practice, more electrons give up energy to the cavities than remove energy. As a consequence, magnetrons operate with efficiencies

Fig. 3.248(a). Typical assembly of a multianode magnetron. The magnetic field is perpendicular to the electric field from cathode to plate(s).

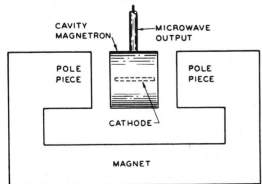

varying from 20 to 50 percent, depending upon the type of magnetron and the manner in which it is operated.

D. Magnetron oscillators (they are not used as amplifiers) are widely used in radar sets as pulsed-power oscillators of high-peak power. Moderate-power magnetrons transmit in the order of 50 to 105 kW of peak power, while peak outputs of 1 mW or more are found in high-power radar sets. (Klystrons having peak-output powers of 1 mW or more are also used in some high-power radar sets.) The frequency ranges in which magnetrons are used, range from about 1 000 MHz to well over 30 000 MHz.

In order to obtain high peak-power outputs without overloading, most magnetrons are operated at a low-*duty cycle* (see below). Typically, a moderate-power magnetron may be pulsed (at its cathode) with a negative 15 000 volt pulse, having a duration of about 1 microsecond and a pulse repetition rate of about 1 000 Hz. It may require a peak pulse current of about 20 amperes. The duty cycle may be calculated as, Duty Cycle = Pulse width × Pulse Repetition Frequency.

For the example above:

Duty Cycle = $1\mu s \times 1000 = 1 \times 10^{-6} \times 10^3 = 10^{-3} = 0.001$

Duty cycles in the order of 0.001 are very common in pulsed magnetron operation.

While Figure 3.248(b) shows a coaxial power output, it is perhaps even more common to feed a waveguide output directly from the magnetron. In this event, the coupling loop from the cavity may lead directly to a quarter-wave radiator coupled inside of a waveguide. Power is then transferred through a length of waveguide to the radar antenna. It is interesting to note that the output coupling loop is only present in one of the multiple cavities. However, the cavities are so tightly coupled together that all of the power is extracted from the magnetron.

Q. 3.249. Discuss the following with respect to waveguides:

1. Relationship between frequency and size.

2. Modes of operation.

3. Coupling of energy into the waveguide.

4. General principles of operation.

A.

1. For a rectangular waveguide, the wider dimension must be greater than one-half wavelength, while the narrow dimension should be less than one-half wavelength (see discussion). The length is not critical, however, as in any conductor, the losses increase in proportion to the length of the waveguide run.

2. The mode of operation of a waveguide defines the manner in which the electric and magnetic fields arrange themselves inside of the waveguide. Each field configuration is called a "mode." Different modes may be excited by using different schemes of excitation. (Generally, probes of some type.) The possible modes are determined by the shape of the waveguide. Modes are separated into two groups, as follows:

a. The *transverse magnetic* (TM) group has its magnetic field in the direction transverse to the direction of propagation.

b. The *transverse electric* (TE) group has its electric field transverse to the direction of propagation and has a component of magnetic field in this direction.

Each particular mode is identified by the letters from the group followed by two numerals. Examples are $TM_{1,0}$ or $TE_{1,0}$.

Figure 3.249(a) illustrates the distribution of the electric and magnetic fields in a rectangular waveguide excited in the $TE_{1,0}$ mode. Note in the end view that one-half wavelength of electric field lines appears across the wider dimension. The electric field is strongest at the center and weakest at the two ends. The electric-field lines are the vertical solid lines with arrows, while the magnetic-field lines are dashed and are perpendicular to the electric-field lines. (See also Q. 3.14, Q. 3.196 and Q. 3.197.)

3. Coupling of energy to a waveguide

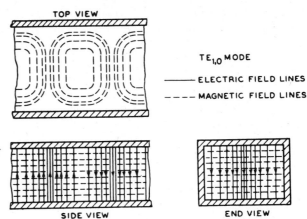

TOP VIEW

$TE_{1,0}$ MODE

——— ELECTRIC FIELD LINES

– – – – MAGNETIC FIELD LINES

SIDE VIEW   END VIEW

Fig. 3.249(a). Illustration of the electric and magnetic fields in rectangular waveguide excited in the $TE_{1,0}$ mode.

may be accomplished in one of three principal ways, as follows:

a. Insertion of a small loop of wire which couples to the electromagnetic field, as shown in Fig. 3.249(b).

b. Insertion of a small straight probe which couples to the electrostatic field, as shown in Fig. 3.249(c).

c. Linkage of the fields within the waveguide by external fields via the use of slots or holes in the wall of the waveguide.

4. The waveguide operates on its ability to conduct electromagnetic waves within its boundaries. The energy is considered to be completely contained in these waves and is not carried as a current in wires. Because of skin effect, no energy escapes through the waveguide walls. Energy is introduced

into and removed from a waveguide by one of the three methods described in (3.) above.

D.

1. In rectangular waveguides, one mode (the $TE_{1.0}$) is considered to be superior. A rectangular waveguide can easily be constructed to be excited only in this mode. As mentioned in A.(1) above, the wide dimension must be greater than one-half wavelength, but not greater than one wavelength. Also the narrow dimension must be less than one-half wavelength. (This condition is illustrated in Fig. 3.249(a).) This mode is frequently called the "fundamental" mode. Its use ensures that no unwanted, spurious modes will exist to waste power in the system. (See also Q. 8.31.)

Fig. 3.249(b). Excitation of a waveguide by means of a magnetic loop of wire.

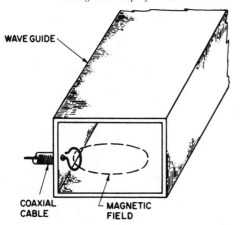

WAVE GUIDE

COAXIAL CABLE

MAGNETIC FIELD

Fig. 3.249(c) Excitation of waveguide by means of electrostatic probe.

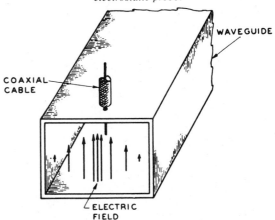

WAVEGUIDE

COAXIAL CABLE

ELECTRIC FIELD

2. For a comparison between waveguides and coaxial lines, see Q. 8.30.

3. Some advantages of waveguides are as follows:

a. Lowest losses of any conventional transmission line at the frequencies for which they are practical.

b. A hollow waveguide can transmit higher power than a coaxial line of the same size.

c. A hollow waveguide is more rugged than a coaxial line because there is no inner conductor or supports.

d. Simpler construction than a coaxial line.

e. Complete shielding.

4. Some disadvantages of waveguides are as follows:

a. The minimum size is proportional to the wavelength used. For a rectangular guide the height must be approximately ½ wavelength or more.

b. Because of the size, waveguides are not extensively used below about 3 000 megacycles (10 cm.). For 10 meter waves the pipe would have to be 25 feet wide.

c. Installation and operation of hollow waveguides is considerably more difficult than for other types of lines.

Q. 3.250. Describe briefly the construction and purpose of a waveguide. What precautions should be taken in the installation and maintenance of a waveguide to insure proper operation?

A.

1. For construction, see Q. 8.28.

2. For purpose and characteristics, see Q. 8.30 and 3.249.

3. For installation and maintenance, see Q. 8.27, 8.28, 8.29, 8.33, 8.34, 8.35.

Q. 3.251. Explain the principles of operation of a cavity resonator.

A. A cavity resonator is a resonant circuit device, having very high Q and capable of being efficiently operated in the microwave frequency region. A cavity resonator is actually a measured section of

waveguide whose resonant frequency depends upon its dimensions. Typical shapes for cavities are rectangular, cylindrical, spherical and doughnut. Cavities are energized in the same manner as waveguides, as described in Q. 3.249(3.), above. Two of the more commonly used types of cavities are illustrated in Fig. 3251(a).

D. A resonant cavity may be considered as merely another type of tuned circuit, but one which is able to function efficiently at microwave frequencies, where the conventional coil and capacitor circuit becomes virtually useless. However, as shown in Fig. 3.251(b), the resonant cavity may be considered as developed from a single turn of wire and a capacitor. Additional turns are added in parallel until a complete rhumbatron (doughnut) cavity is formed. Placing additional turns in parallel, as shown, has the effect of reducing the inductance, thereby increasing the resonant frequency and the Q of the circuit. (Note that this type of development is not strictly accurate, but is a helpful concept in the introduction to the study of resonant cavities.) Cavities are used as resonant circuits at frequencies from about 1 000 MHz to frequencies in excess of 30 000 MHz. The Q of a cavity may be in the order of several thousand.

Cavities are commonly used as the resonant circuits for:

1. Magnetrons (see Q. 3.248).

2. Klystrons (see Q. 3.246 and Q. 8.48.)

3. Echo boxes (see Q. 8.38).

4. TR and ATR tubes (see Q. 8.51)

5. Microwave wavemeters.

Q. 3.252. How are cavities installed in vertical waveguides to prevent moisture from collecting? Why are long horizontal waveguides not desired?

A.

1. To prevent moisture accumulation, the cavity may be mounted through a choke joint employing moisture-sealing gaskets. The same technique may be used at each choke-coupling flange of a waveguide run to prevent the introduction of moisture into

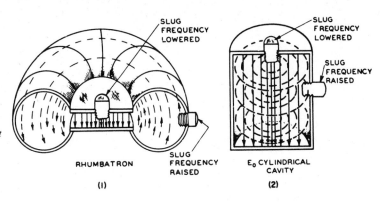

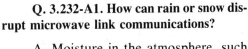

Fig. 3.251(a). Two common types of resonant cavities, showing electric-field lines (solid) and magnetic-field lines (dashed) and means of adjusting the frequency. Part (1) shows a "rhumbatron" (or doughnut) type. A cylindrical type is shown in part (2).

RHUMBATRON

(1)

SLUG FREQUENCY LOWERED

SLUG FREQUENCY RAISED

E_0 CYLINDRICAL CAVITY

(2)

the waveguide. In addition, pressurizing the waveguide with dry air or an inert gas will prevent the entrance of moisture.

2. See Q. 8.29.

D.

1. For description of choke joint, see Q. 8.35.

Choke joints are also commonly used to join such items as magnetrons, echo boxes, TR and ATR tubes and klystron outputs to waveguides (see Fig. 8.41(c)).

2. See also Q. 8.33, Q. 8.41 and Q. 3.250.

Note: The following added material numbered Q. 3.252-A1 through Q. 3.252-A4 contains information that may be required to pass the General Radiotelephone Operator's License examination. This added material, as well as the new material added to other sections, has been included to help acquaint students with the current state of the electronics art. It is felt that the added material contains subject matter that may also be required of students who have obtained a General Radiotelephone Operator's License and are seeking employment. Additionally, the added material contains valuable information for private technician certification.

Q. 3.232-A1. How can rain or snow disrupt microwave link communications?

A. Moisture in the atmosphere, such as that caused by rain, snow or fog (or simple humidity), causes attenuation of transmitted microwaves, by absorption and multipath transmission effects. These effects increase with frequency. At frequencies of 6 GHz or higher, the attenuation can be so great as to completely disrupt microwave-link communications.

D. At frequencies below about 3 GHz, the attenuation of radio wave energy by atmospheric gases and water is generally not a major consideration. However, above this frequency, such attenuation becomes greater with increasing frequency. These atmospheric qualities may also cause multipath transmission effects. Generally, rain causes greater attenuation than snow, because it is more dense. Rain can restrict reliable transmission above 30 GHz to links only a few miles in length. Oxygen and water vapor (humidity, fog) also cause attenuation. However, the attenuation due to rain usually exceeds the combined absorption of oxygen and water vapor.

Fig. 3.251(b). The development of a resonant cavity can be considered as starting with a single turn of wire and a capacitor as in (1), and putting turns in parallel until a completely enclosed volume results, as in (2); this is called a rhumbatron cavity.

(1)

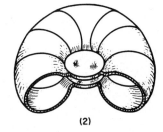

(2)

RULES AND REGULATIONS

Q. 3.253. Define the following words and phrases listed under Section 2.1 of the Commission's Rules. (R & R 2.1)

A. R & R 2.1: Definitions:

1. Authorized frequency. The frequency assigned to a station by the FCC and specified in the instrument of authorization.

2. Carrier: In a frequency stabilized system, the sinusoidal component of a modulated wave whose frequency is independent of the modulating wave; or the output of transmitter when the modulating wave is made zero; or a wave generated at a point in the transmitting system and subsequently modulated by the signal; or a wave generated locally at the receiving terminal which, when combined with the sidebands in a suitable detector, produces the modulating wave.

3. Base station: A land station in the land mobile service carrying on a service with land mobile stations.

4. Coast station: A land station in the maritime mobile service.

5. Earth station: A station located either on the earth's surface or within the major portion of the earth's atmosphere intended for communication:

a. With one or more space stations; or

b. With one or more stations of the same kind by means of one or more passive satellites or other objects in space.

6. Fixed station. A station in the fixed service.

7. Space station: A station located on an object which is beyond, is intended to go beyond, or has been beyond, the major portion of the earth's atmosphere.

8. Harmful interference: Any emission, radiation or induction which endangers the functioning of a radio-navigation service or of other safety services or seriously degrades, obstructs, or repeatedly interrupts a radiocommunication service operating in accordance with this chapter.

9. Land mobile service: A mobile service between base stations and land mobile stations, or between land mobile stations.

10. Land station. A station in the mobile service not intended to be used while in motion.

11. Mobile service. A service of radio communication between mobile and land stations, or between mobile stations.

12. Primary standard of frequency. The primary standard of frequency for radio frequency measurements shall be the National Bureau of Standards, Department of Commerce, Boulder, Colorado. The operating frequency of all radio stations will be determined by comparison with this standard or through the standard signals of stations WWV, WWVH, or WWVB, of the National Bureau of Standards.

Q. 3.254. What is the frequency range associated with the following general frequency subdivisions? (R & R 2.101)

1. VLF
2. LF
3. MF
4. HF
5. VHF
6. UHF
7. SHF
8. EHF

A.

1. VLF (very low frequency). Below 30 Hz.

2. LF (low frequency). 30 to 300 Hz.

3. MF (medium frequency). 300 to 3 000 Hz.

4. HF (high frequency). 3 to 30 MHz.

5. VHF (very high frequency). 30 to 300 MHz.

6. UHF (ultra high frequency). 300 to 3 000 MHz.

7. SHF (super high frequency). 3 to 30 GHz.

8. EHF (extremely high frequency). 30 to 300 GHz.

Q. 3.255. What is meant by the following emission designations? (R & R 2.201)

Old	New
1. A3	A3E
2. A3A	R3E
3. A5C	C3F
4. F3	F3E
5. F5	F3E
6. P3D	K3E
7. F3	G3E
8. A3H	H3E
9. A3J	J3E

A.

1. A3(A3E): Amplitude modulation, telephony, double sideband transmission.

2. A3A(R3E): Amplitude modulation, telephony, single sideband, reduced carrier.

3. A5C(C3F): Amplitude modulation, television, vestigial (partial) sideband.

4. F3(F3E): Frequency (or phase) modulation, telephony.

5. F5(F3E): Frequency (or phase) modulation, television.

6. P3D(K3E): Pulse modulation, telephony, amplitude modulated pulses.

7. F3(G3E): Phase-modulated telephony. Was formerly F3, which was also used for frequency modulation. (See 4 above.)

8. A3H(H3E): Amplitude-modulated telephony. Single sideband plus the full carrier.

9. A3J(J3E): Amplitude-modulated telephony. Single sideband plus suppressed carrier.

Note: According to the FCC, the new emission designations have been effective since October 1986. The older designations may be still somewhat in use as of the date of this edition, but are being phased out. (See R & R 2.201 in Appendix I for more details.)

Q. 3.256. What is the basic difference between type approval and type acceptance of transmitting equipment? (R & R 2.903, 2.905)

A. Type approval contemplates tests conducted by FCC personnel. Type acceptance is based on data concerning the equipment submitted by the individual prospective licensee.

Q. 3.256(A). In the private land mobile radio services, what "type acceptance" is required? (R & R 90.203)

A.

1. Except as specified in paragraph (b) of this section, each transmitter utilized for operation under this part and each transmitter marketed as set forth in section 2.803 (of part 2) must be of a type which is included in the Commission's current Radio Equipment List as type accepted for use under this part; or, be of a type which has been type accepted by the Commission for use under this part in accordance with the procedures in subparagraph (2) of this paragraph.

(1) The Commission periodically publishes a list of equipment entitled "Radio Equipment List, Equipment Acceptable for Licensing." Copies of this list are available for public reference at the Commission's offices in Washington, D.C., and at each of its field offices. This list includes type accepted equipment and, also, until such time as it may be removed by Commission action, other equipment which appeared in this list on May 16, 1955.

(2) Any manufacturer of radio transmitting equipment (including signal boosters) to be used in these services may request type acceptance for such equipment following the procedures set forth in subpart J of part 2 of this chapter. Type acceptance for an individual transmitter or signal booster also may be requested by an applicant for a station authorization by following the procedure set forth in part 2 of this chapter. Such equipment if type accepted will not normally be included in the Commission's "Radio Equipment List" but will be individually enumerated on the station authorization.

(b) Type acceptance is not required for the following:

(1) Transmitters used in developmental operations in accordance with subpart P.

(2) Transmitters used for police zone and interzone stations authorized as of January 1, 1965.

(3) Transmitting equipment used in the band 1427-1435 MHz.

Q. 3.256(B) In the private land mobile radio services, what is the transmitter carrier frequency tolerance? (R & R 90.213)

A.

(a) A licensee in the services governed by this part shall maintain the carrier frequency of each authorized transmitter within the following percentage of the assigned frequency. *(See table.)*

Frequency Tolerance

Frequency range (MHz)	Fixed and base stations		Mobile stations	
	Over 200W output power	200W or less output power	Over 2W output power	2W or less output power
Below 25..........	[1][2][3].005	.01	.01	.02
25 to 50..........	.002	.002	.002	.005
50 to 450.........	[4][5].0005	[4][5].0005	[4].0005	[6].005
450 to 470........	[7][8][9].00025	[7][8][9].00025	.0005	.0005
470 to 512........	[7].00025	[7].00025	.00035	.0005
512 to 821........	[10].00015	[10].0015	.00025	.00025
821 to 866........	.00015	.00015	.00025	.00025
1427 to 1435......	[11].03	[11].03	.03	.03
Above 2450	([12][13])	([12][13])	([12][13])	([12][13])

[1] Fixed and base stations in the Public Safety and Special Emergency Radio Services may operate with a frequency tolerance of 0.01 pct.

[2] Radio location stations operating in the 70–90 kHz or 110–130 kHz bands may operate with a frequency tolerance of 0.01 pct.

[3] For single sideband operations below 10 MHz, the carrier frequency must be maintained within 80 MHz of the authorized carrier frequency.

[4] Stations authorized for operation on or before Dec. 1, 1961. In the frequency band 73–74.6 MHz may operate with a frequency tolerance of 0.005 pct.

[5] Radio call box stations in the Local Government Radio Service in the 73–76 MHz band may operate with a frequency tolerance of 0.05 pct.

[6] Stations operating in the 154.45 to 154.49 MHz or the 173.2 to 173.4 MHz bands must operate with a frequency tolerance of 0.0005 pct.

[7] Operational fixed stations controlling mobile relays, through use of the associated mobile frequency, may operate with a frequency tolerance of 0.0005 pct.

[8] Base stations operating on the frequencies 452.925, 452.050, 457.925, and 457.950 KHz used for remote control purposes in railroad yard and terminal areas may operate with a frequency tolerance of 0.0005 pct.

[9] Central control and radio call box stations may operate with a frequency tolerance of 0.001 pct.

[10] Control stations may operate with a frequency tolerance of 0.00025 pct.

[11] Fixed stations with an output power above 120W and necessary bandwidth less than 3 kHz must operate with a frequency tolerance of 0.01 pct. Fixed stations with an output power less than 120W and using line-division multiplex, may operate with a frequency tolerance of 0.05 pct.

[12] Radio location equipment using pulse modulation shall meet the following frequency tolerance: the frequency at which maximum emission occurs shall be within the authorized frequency band and shall not be closer than 1.5 T MHz to the upper and lower limits of the authorized frequency band, where T is the pulse-duration in microseconds.

[13] To be specified in the station authorization.

(b) For the purpose of determining the frequency tolerance applicable to a particular transmittter in accordance with the foregoing provisions of this section, the power of a transmitter shall be the maximum rated output power as specified by the manufacturer.

Q. 3.256(C) In the private land mobile radio services, what is the transmitter authorized power? (R & R 90.205)

A.

(a) Applications for authorizations must specify no more power than the actual power necessary for satisfactory operation. In cases of harmful interference, the Commission may order a change in power or antenna height or both.

(b) Except where otherwise specifically provided, the maximum power that will be authorized is as follows:

Frequency range (megahertz)	Maximum output power	Maximum effective radiated power (watts)
1.3 to 3	[1] 1500	. . . .
3 to 25	[1] [3] 750	. . . .
25 to 100	300	. . . .
100 to 216	[8] 350	. . . .
216 to 220	([3] [4])	([4])
220 to 470	[3] [5] 350	. . . .
470 to 512	. . . .	1000
806 to 821	([9])	([4])
851 to 866	([7])	([8])
1427 to 1435	([8])	. . . .
2450 to 2500	5	. . . .
2500 to 10,550	([4])	([4])
10,550 to 10,680 . . .	8	. . . .
Above 10,060	([4])	([4])

[1] For single sideband operations (A3J emission) below 10 MHz, the authorized power shall be stated in terms of peak envelope power, which is the average power supplied to the antenna transmission line by a transmitter during 1 radio frequency cycle at the highest crest of the modulation envelope taken under conditions of normal operation. The maximum peak envelope power permitted is 2 k W.

[2] In the frequency band 3 to 6 MHz, stations in the industrial services and the radiolocation radio service may be authorized up to 1500 W.

[3] Except as noted in footnote 5 the maximum output in the Motor Carrier, Taxicab, Railroad, and Automobile Emergency Radio Services is 75 W.

[4] To be specified in the authorization.

[5] In the frequency band 450 to 470 MHz, stations in the land transportation radio services are limited to 75 W, however, they may be authorized up to 350 W for developmental operations in accordance with subpt. P.

[6] Specified in subpt. M.

[7] The output power of a transmitter on any authorized frequency in the band shall not exceed 2000 W.

(c) The output power shall not exceed by more than 20 percent either the output power shown in the Radio Equipment List (available in accordance with section 90.203(a)(1)) for transmitters included in this list or when not so listed, the manufacturer's rated output power for the particular transmitter specifically listed on the authorization.

Q. 3.2561(D). In the private land mobile radio services, what are the authorized types of emissions? (R & R 90.207)

A. Normally operations authorized in the services governed by this part are intended to provide voice communications between stations. Accordingly, except as otherwise provided for in the following paragraphs, stations in these services will be authorized to use only A3 or F3 emission.

(a) Authorizations to use A3 or F3 emission also include the use of emissions for tone signals or signalling devices whose whole functions are to establish and to maintain communications, to provide automatic station identification, and for operations in the Public Safety and Special Emergency Radio Services, to activate emergency warning devices used solely for the purpose of advising the general public or emergency personnel of an impending emergency situation.

(b) The use of F3 emission in these services will be authorized only on frequencies about 25 MHz.

(c) Except for Traveler's Information Stations in the Local Government Radio Service authorized in accordance with R & R 90.242, only A3J emission will be authorized for telephony systems on frequencies below 25 MHz.

(d) For tone paging operations only A1, A2, F1, or F2 emission will be authorized.

(e) For radioteleprinter operations that may be authorized in accordance with R & R 90.237, only F2 or F9 emission will be authorized.

(f) For radiofacsimile operations that may be authorized in accordance with R & R 90.237, only F4 emission will be authorized.

(g) For AVM systems that may be authorized in accordance with R & R 90.239, only F1, F2, F3, F9, or P9 emission will be authorized.

(h) For telemetry operations, when specifically authorized under this part, only A1, A2, F1, F2, or F9 emissions will be authorized.

(i) For call box operations that may be authorized in accordance with R & R 90.241, only A1, A2, F1, F2, or F3 emissions will be authorized.

(j) For radiolocation operations as may be authorized in accordance with subpart F, unless otherwise provided for any type of emission may be authorized upon a satisfactory showing of need.

(k) For stations in the Fire and Police Radio Services utilizing digital voice modulation in either the scrambled or unscrambled mode F3Y emission will be authorized. Authorization to use F3Y is construed to include the use of F9Y emission subject to the provisions of paragraphs (a), (b), and (d) of R & R 90.233.

Q. 3.256(E). In the private land mobile radio services, what are the bandwidth limitations? (R & R 90.209)

A.

(a) Each authorization issued to a station licensed under this part will specify the maximum authorized bandwidth to be occupied by the emission. The bandwidth in kilohertz will appear as a prefix to the emission classification. The specified band will contain those frequencies upon which 99 percent of the radiated power appears, extended to include any discrete frequency upon which the power is at least 0.25 percent of the total radiated power.

(b) The maximum authorized bandwidth of emission corresponding to the type of emission specified in R & R 90.207 of this part and the maximum authorized frequency deviation in the case of frequency or phase modulated emission shall be as follows:

(1) For all type A1 emission, the maximum authorized bandwidth shall be 0.25 kHz.

(2) Except as noted in subparagraph 3, the maximum authorized bandwidth for type A3 emission shall be 8 kHz.

(3) For type A3J operations below 10 MHz, the bandwidth occupied by the emission shall not exceed 8 500 Hz. The frequency coinciding with the center of the authorized frequency band of emission shall be the assigned frequency. Both the authorized carrier frequency and assigned frequency shall be specified in the authorization. The authorized carrier frequency shall be 1 400 Hz lower in frequency than the assigned frequency. Only upper sideband emission shall be used. In the case of regularly available double sideband radiotelephone channels, and assigned frequency for A3J emission is available either 1.6 kHz below or 1.4 kHz above the double sideband radiotelephone assigned frequency.

(4) For all F3 emission, on frequencies below 947 MHz, the maximum authorized bandwidth shall be 20 kHz and the maximum authorized frequency deviation shall be 5 kHz. However, stations authorized for operation on or before December 1, 1961, in the frequency band 73.0-74.6 MHz may continue to operate with a bandwidth of 40 kHz and a deviation of 15 kHz. For stations operating on frequencies above 947 MHz, except as provided in subparagraph (5), of this section the maximum authorized bandwidth and frequency deviation will be specified in the station authorization.

(5) The maximum authorized bandwidth shall be 25 MHz in the frequency band 10 550-10 680 MHz and 50 MHz in the fre-

quency bands above 16 000 MHz.

(6) For all other types of emissions the maximum authorized bandwidth shall not be more than that normally authorized for voice operations.

(c) Except as noted in paragraphs (d) and (f), the mean power of emissions shall be attenuated below the mean output power of the transmitter in accordance with the following schedule.

(1) On any frequency removed from the assigned frequency by more than 50 percent, but not more than 100 percent of the authorized bandwidth: at least 25 decibels;

(2) On any frequency removed from the assigned frequency by more than 100 percent, but not more than 250 percent of the authorized bandwidth: at least 85 decibels;

(3) On any frequency removed from the assigned frequency by more than 250 percent of the authorized bandwidth; at least 48 plus 10 Log_{10} (mean output power in watts) decibels or 80 decibels, whichever is the lesser attenuation.

(d) For single sideband operations (A8J) below 10 MHz, the carrier frequency power shall be at least 40 dB below the peak envelope power and the mean power of emissions shall be attenuated below the mean output power of the transmitter in accordance with the schedule provided by the FCC.

Q. 3.256(F). In the private land mobile radio services, what are the requirements regarding FCC applications for radio station authorizations? (R & R 90.113, 90.117, 90.119, 90.125, 90.127)

A. No radio transmitter shall be operated in the services governed by this part (part 90) except under and in accordance with a proper authorization granted by the Commission.

Persons desiring a radio station authorization must first submit an appropriate application. Prescribed application forms are listed in R & R 90.119. They may be obtained from the Washington, D.C., office of the Commission, or from any of its engineering field offices. (See R & R 90.145 for information regarding special temporary authorizations.)

D. **R & R 90.119 Application forms.**

The following application forms shall be used—

(a) Except as provided for in paragraph (c) of this section. Form 400 shall be used to apply:

(1) For new base, fixed, or mobile station authorizations governed by this part.

(2) For modification or for modification and renewal of an existing authorization. (See R & R 90.135.)

(3) For the Commission's consent to the assignment of an authorization to another person or entity. In addition, the application shall be accompanied by a letter from the

assignor setting forth his desire to assign all right, title, and interest in and to such authorization, stating the call sign and location of the station, and that the assignor will submit his current station authorization for cancellation upon completion of the assignment. Form 1046 may be used in lieu of this letter.

(b) Except as provided for in paragraph (c) of this section. Form 405-A shall be used to apply for a renewal without modification of a station license.

(c) Form 425 shall be used in lieu of Form 400 and 405(a) to submit applications specifying any frequency in the band 470-512 MHz.

(d) A separate application shall be submitted on FCC form 703 whenever it is proposed to change, as by transfer of stock ownership, the control of a corporate licensee.

R & R 90.125 Who may sign applications.

(a) Except as provided in paragraph (b) of this section, applications, amendments thereto, and related statements of fact required by the Commission shall be personally signed by the applicant, if the applicant is an individual; by one of the partners, if the applicant is a partnership; by an officer or duly authorized employee if the applicant is a corporation; or by a member who is an officer, if the applicant is an unincorporated association. Applications, amendments, and related statements of fact filed on behalf of eligible government entities, such as states and territories of the United States and political subdivisions thereof, the District of Columbia, and units of local government, including incorporated municipalities, shall be signed by such duly elected or appointed officials as may be competent to do so under the laws of the applicable jurisdiction.

R & R 90.127 Filing of applications.

(a) All applications for station authorizations and related correspondence shall be submitted to the Commission's Office at Washington, D.C. 20554, directed to the attention of the Secretary.

(b) Unless otherwise specified, an application should be filed at least 60 days prior to the desired date of Commission action. Applications for renewal should be filed no more than 90 days nor less than 30 days prior to the end of the license term. When timely and sufficient application for renewal of the license has been made, the license shall not expire until Commission action on the application has been completed.

(c) Each application shall limit its request for authorized mobile transmitters to:

(1) Transmitters which will be installed and operated immediately after authorization issuance; and to

(2) Transmitters for which purchase orders have already been signed and which will be in use within eight months of the authorization date; and

(3) In the Public Safety Radio Services and in the Special Emergency Radio Service for governmental entities only, to transmitters on which bid orders have been or will be sought and which will be in use within eight months of the authorization date, and to transmitters to be placed in operation later than eight months of the authorization date, pursuant to a specific implementation schedule which has been adopted by the

appropriate final authorities of the applicant.

(d) Failure on the part of the applicant to provide all information required by the application form or to supply the necessary exhibits or supplementary statements may constitute a defect in the application.

Q. 3.256(G). In the private land mobile radio services, what changes in authorized stations require an application for modification of license? (R & R 90.135)

A.

(a) The following changes in authorized stations require an application for modification of license:

(1) Any change in frequency.

(2) Any change in the type of emission.

(3) Any increase in output power beyond that authorized.

(4) Any increase in antenna height beyond that authorized.

(5) Any increase in the number of transmitters or control points beyond that authorized.

(6) Any change in the authorized location of the base or fixed transmitter or the area of mobile operation.

(7) Any change in ownership, control, or corporate structure.

(8) Any change in class of station.

(b) The following changes do not require an application for modification of license:

(1) Change in mailing address of licensee.

(2) Change in name only of licensee, without changes in the ownership, control, or corporate structure.

(3) Change in the number and location of station control points.

(4) Change in the number of mobile units for stations operating below 470 MHz; or in the number of mobile units operated by Radiolocation Service licensee.

(5) Any other change not listed in paragraph (a) of this section.

(6) In case of a change listed in subparagraph (1) or (2) of this paragraph, the

licensee shall promptly notify the Commission of such change. The notice, which may be in letter form, shall contain the name and address of the licensee as they appear in the Commission's records, the new name or address, the call signs and classes of all radio stations authorized to the licensee under this part and the radio service in which each station is authorized. The notice shall be sent to the Secretary, Federal Communications Commission, Washington, D.C. 20554, and to the Engineer in Charge of the Radio District in which the station is located and a copy shall be maintained with the license of each station until a new license is issued.

(7) In the case of a change listed in subparagraph (3), (4), or (5) of this paragraph the licensee shall promptly notify the Commission within 30 days of the change. The notice shall be filed on the appropriate application form (FCC Form 400 or Form 425), and shall be sent to the Secretary, Federal Communications Commission, Washington, D.C., 20554.

Q. 3.256(H). In the private land mobile radio servcies, what is the term for station licenses? (R & R 90.149)

A. Licenses for stations authorized under this part will normally be issued for a term of 5 years from the date of original issuance, modification, or renewal, except that in some instances a term of from 1 to 5 years will be applied, the term varying as may be necessary to permit the orderly scheduling of renewal applications.

Q. 3.257. Define the following words and phrases listed under Section 89.3 of the Commission's Rules.

A.

1. Authorized bandwidth: The maximum width of the band of frequencies, as specified in the authorizations, to be occupied by an emission.

2. Bandwidth occupied by an emission: The width of the frequency band (normally specified in kilohertz) containing those frequencies upon which a total of 99 percent of the radiated power appears, extended to include any discrete frequency upon which the power is at least 0.25 percent of the total radiated power.

3. Station authorization: Any construction permit, license, or special temporary authorization issued by the Commission.

Q. 3.258. May stations in the Public Safety Radio Services be operated for short periods of time without a station authorization issued by the Commission? (R & R 89.51)

A. No radio transmitter shall be operated in the Public Safety Radio Services except under and in accordance with a proper station authorization granted by the Federal Communications Commission.

Q. 3.259. What notification must be forwarded to the Engineer in Charge of the Commission's district office prior to testing a new radio transmitter in the public Safety Radio Service (which has been obtained under a construction permit issued by the Commission)? (R & R 89.59)

A. FCC Form 456 "Notification of Completion of Radio Station Construction" may be used to advise the Engineer in Charge of the local district office that construction of the station is complete and that operational tests will begin.

Q. 3.260. Where may standard forms applicable to the Public Safety Radio Services be obtained? (R & R 89.55(a))

A. To assure that necessary information is supplied in a consistent manner by all persons, standard forms are prescribed for use in connection with the majority of applications and reports submitted for Commission consideration. Standard numbered forms applicable to the Public Safety Radio Services may be obtained from the Washington, D.C. Office of the Commission, or from any of its engineering field offices.

Q. 3.261. In general, what type of changes in authorized stations must be approved by the Commission? What type does not require Commission approval? (R & R 89.75)

A. Authority for certain changes in authorized stations must be obtained from the Commission before these changes are made, while other changes do not require prior Commission approval. The following paragraphs describe the conditions under which prior Commission approval is or is not necessary.

1. Proposed changes which will result in operation inconsistent with any of the terms of the current authorization require that an application for modification of construction permit and/or license be submitted to the Commission. The request for authorization shall be submitted on FCC Form 400, and shall be accompanied by exhibits and supplementary statements as required by R & R 89.63.

2. Proposed changes which will not depart from any of the terms of the outstanding authorization for the station involved may be made without prior Commission approval. Included in such changes is the substitution of various makes of transmitting equipment at any station provided the particular equipment to be installed is included in the Commission's "List of Equipment Acceptable for Licensing." In addition it must be designated for use in the Public Safety, Industrial, and Land Transportation Radio Services. The substitute equipment must employ the same type of emission and must not exceed the power limitations as set forth in the station authorization.

Q. 3.262. The carrier frequency of a transmitter in the Public Safety Radio Service must be maintained within what percentage of the licensed value? Assume the station is operating at 160 MHz/s with a licensed power of 50 watts. (R & R 89.103)

A. The carrier frequency must be maintained within 0.0005 percent.

Q. 3.263. What is the authorized bandwidth and frequency deviation of Public Safety stations operating at about 30 MHz? At about 160 MHz? (R & R 89.107)

A.
1. For 30 megahertz, the authorized bandwidth is 20 kilohertz, and the frequency deviation is 5 kilohertz.
2. For 160 megahertz the specifications are the same as (1) above.

Q. 3.264. What is the maximum percentage modulation allowed by the Commission's rules for stations in the Public Safety Radio Services which utilize amplitude modulation? (R & R 89.109)

A. The maximum is 100 percent on negative peaks.

Q. 3.265. Define "control point" as the term refers to transmitters in the Public Safety Radio Service. (R&R 89.113)

A. A control point is an operating position which:
1. Must be under the control and supervision of the licensee.
2. Is a position at which the monitoring facilities are installed.
3. Is a position at which a person immediately responsible for the operation of the transmitter is stationed.

Q. 3.266. Outline the transmitter measurements required by the Commission's rules for stations in the Public Safety Radio Service. (R & R 89.115)

A. Transmitter measurements are as follows:
1. The licensee of each station shall employ a suitable procedure to determine that the carrier frequency of each transmitter authorized to operate with an output power in excess of 2 watts, is maintained within the tolerance prescribed in this part. This determination shall be made, and the results thereof entered in the station records, in accordance with the following:
a. When the transmitter is initially installed;

b. When any change is made in the transmitter which may affect the carrier frequency or the stability thereof:

2. The licensee of each station shall employ a suitable procedure to determine that the transmitter output power of each transmitter authorized to operate with an output power in excess of two watts does not exceed the maximum figure specified on the current station authorization. On authorizations stating only the input power to the final radio frequency stage, the maximum permissible output power is 75 percent for frequencies below 25 MHz and 60 percent of the input power for frequencies above 25 MHz. If a non-DC final radio frequency stage is utilized, then the output power shall not exceed 75 percent of the input power. This determination shall be made, and the results thereof entered into the station records, in accordance with the following:

a. When the transmitter is initially installed;

b. When any change is made in the transmitter which may affect the transmitter power output.

3. The licensee of each station shall employ a suitable procedure to determine that the modulation of each transmitter authorized to operate with an output power in excess of 2 watts, does not exceed the limits specified in this part. This determination shall be made and the results thereof entered in the station records, in accordance with the following:

a. When the transmitter is initially installed;

b. When any change is made in the transmitter which may affect the modulation characteristics;

4. The determinations required by paragraphs (1), (2), and (3) of this section may, at the option of the licensee, be made by any qualified engineering measurement service in which case the required record entries shall show the name and address of the engineering measurement service as well as the name of the person making the measurements.

5. In the case of mobile transmitters, the determinations required by paragraphs (1) and (3) of this section may be made at a test or service bench; provided, the measurements are made under load conditions equivalent to actual operating conditions, and provided further, that after installation the transmitter is given a routine check to determine that it is capable of being satisfactorily received by an appropriate receiver.

Q. 3.267. What are the general requirements for transmitting the identification announcements for stations in the Public Safety Radio Service? (R & R 89.153)

A. Station identification.

1. Except as provided in paragraphs (2) and (8) of this section, the required identification for stations in these services shall be the assigned call signal.

2. In lieu of meeting the requirements of paragraph (1) of this section, mobile units in the Police, Fire, Forestry-Conservation, Highway Maintenance, and Local Government Radio Services operating above 30 MHz may identify by means of an identifier other than the assigned call signal: *Provided*, that such identifer contain, as a minimum, the name of the government subdivision under which the unit is licensed; that the identifier is not composed of letters or letters and digits arranged in a manner which could be confused with an assigned radio station call signal; that the licensee notifies, in writing, the Engineer in Charge of the District in which the unit operates concerning the specific identifiers being used by the mobile units.

3. Nothing in this section shall be construed as prohibiting the transmission of additional station or unit identifiers which may be necessary for systems operation: *Provided,* such additional identifiers are not to be composed of letters or letters and digits arranged in a manner which could be confused with an assigned radio station call signal.

4. Except as indicated in paragraphs (5), (6), and (7) of this section, each station in these services shall transmit the required

identification at the end of each transmission or exchange of transmission, or once each 30 minutes of the operating period, as the licensee may prefer.

5. A mobile station authorized to the licensee of the associated base station and which transmits only on the transmitting frequency of the associated base station is not required to transmit any identification.

6. Except as indicated in paragraph (5) of this section, a mobile station shall transmit an identification at the end of each transmission or exchange of transmissions, or once each 30 minutes of the operating period, as the licensee may prefer. Where election is made to transmit the identification at 30 minute intervals, a single mobile unit in each general geographic area may be assigned the responsibility for such transmission, thereby eliminating any necessity for each unit of the mobile station to transmit the identification. For the purpose of this paragraph the term "each general geographic area" means an area not smaller than a single city or county and not larger than a single district of a state where the district is administratively established for the service in which the radio system operates.

7. A station which is transmitting for telemetering purposes or for the actuation of devices, or which is retransmitting by self-actuating means a radio signal received from another radio station or stations, will be considered for exemption from the requirements of paragraph (4) of this section in specific instances, upon request.

8. In lieu of the requirement of paragraph (1) of this section, base, fixed relay, repeater, and mobile relay stations shall be identified by the transmission of the call sign of the associated controlling station.

Q. 3.268. When a radio operator makes transmitter measurements required by the Commission's rules for a station in the Public Safety Radio Service what information should be transcribed into the station's records? (R & R 89.175)

A. The results and dates of the transmitter measurements and the name of the person or persons making the measurements.

Q. 3.269. What are the Commission's general requirements regarding the records which are required to be kept by stations in the Public Safety Radio Service? (R & R 89.177)

A. Form of station records.

1. The records shall be kept in an orderly manner and in such detail that the data required are readily available. Key letters or abbreviations may be used if proper meaning or explanation is set forth in the record.

2. Each entry in the records shall be signed by a person qualified to do so having actual knowledge of the facts to be recorded.

3. No record or portion thereof shall be erased, obliterated, or willfully destroyed within the required retention period. Any necessary correction may be made only by the persons originating the entry who shall strike out the erroneous portion, initial the correction made and indicate the date of the correction.

APPENDIX TO ELEMENT III

TROUBLESHOOTING RADIOTELEPHONE CIRCUITS

Some questions on analyzing circuit troubles appear on the Element III examination. These questions test the applicant's ability to analyze the effects of part failure on circuit operation. Other questions require the student to complete schematic diagrams or to identify mistakes in schematic diagrams. To assist the student in answering these questions, the following section presents in question and answer form a review of the effects of part failure on the operation of various basic circuits employing both vacuum tubes and transistors. Most of the troubleshooting questions contain references to discussions in other portions of this book. The student is strongly urged to refer to these discussions to help him attain a better understanding of the principles involved in each troubleshooting problem.

To simplify the presentation, all transistor circuits in this appendix are shown as *PNP* types. However, the same operating principles and troubleshooting procedures apply to *NPN* transistor circuits. If NPN transistors were used, it would be necessary merely to reverse all battery polarities.

OSCILLATORS

Q. 3.270 In the circuit of the tuned-plate, tuned-grid (TPTG) oscillator shown in Fig. 3.270, what will be the effect on the reading of Meter M1, if C1 becomes shorted or open?

A. Meter M1 will read 0.

D. The TPTG oscillator, like most other tube LC oscillators, employs grid-leak biasing. Grid-leak bias is developed only when the grid tank circuit is oscillating. During the positive swing of the tank circuit, the grid draws current to charge C2. During the

Fig. 3.270. TPTG oscillator.

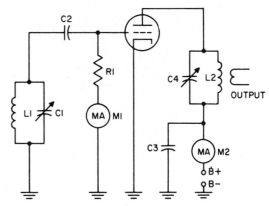

negative swing of the tank circuit, C2 discharges through R1 to provide a negative grid-bias voltage. (See Q. 3.86.) Typically this voltage is about -3 to -5 volts. If C1 shorts or opens, oscillations will cease, and grid-leak bias can no longer be developed. Therefore, M1 will read 0. (See also Q. 3.284.)

Q. 3.271 In Fig. 3.270, what will be the effect on the reading of Meter M2 with C1 shorted or open?

A. The reading of Meter M2 will increase.

D. As discussed in answer of 3.270, oscillations will cease if C1 shorts or opens and a negative bias can no longer be developed. The control grid, which was negative with respect to the cathode, will be at approximately the same potential. Therefore, plate current will increase, as indicated by an increase in the meter reading.

Q. 3.272. In the TPTG oscillator (see Fig. 3.270), what will be the effect on the reading of Meter M1 if R1 opens?

A. Meter M1 would read 0, because no current can flow through the meter with the grid circuit open.

Q. 3.273. In Fig. 3.270, what would be the effect on the reading of Meter M1 if C4 becomes shorted or open?

A. Meter M1 would read 0.

D. Oscillations in the grid tank circuit are sustained by regenerative feedback from the plate tank circuit, If C4 shorts or opens, oscillations in the plate tank circuit will cease, and no feedback will be present. This will also cause the grid tank circuit to stop oscillating. And, as explained in Q. 3.270, negative grid-leak bias is no longer produced when the grid tank circuit stops oscillating, so that no current flows through Meter M1. In addition, the reading on Meter M2 will increase because of the loss of grid-leak bias.

Q. 3.274 In Fig. 3.270, what would be the effect on oscillator operation if C2 shorted or opened?

A. In both cases, oscillation would cease. Meter M1 would read 0 and Meter M2 would show increased plate current.

D. If C2 shorted, grid-leak bias could not be developed (see Q. 3.86). The tube would operate at saturation plate current and oscillations could not build up and be sustained.

If C2 opened, the RF connection to the grid would be disconnected and L1C1 would be isolated from the oscillator circuit. Oscillations could not occur in the circuit, since C2 normally offers a low-impedance RF path between L1C1 and the grid.

Q. 3.275 In Fig. 3.270, what would be the effect on oscillator operation if L1 or L2 opened or shorted?

A. Under the conditions stated in the question, oscillations would cease.

D. If either tank coil opened or shorted, one tuned circuit would cease to function and oscillations could not be developed. (See Q. 3.86) In addition, if L2 opened, the plate voltage would be removed from the oscillator tube.

Q. 3.276 In Fig. 3.270, what would be the effect on oscillator operation if C3 opened or shorted?

A. If C3 opened, oscillations would cease; M1 would read 0, and M2 would show increased plate current. If C3 shorted, oscillations would cease; M1 would read 0, and M2 would show an excessive current.

D. Capacitor C3 normally provides a low-impedance path for the oscillator frequency signal to return to the cathode (RF plate current). If C3 opened, the only RF return path to the cathode would be through the relatively high RF impedance of the power supply to ground, which would greatly reduce the plate circuit RF current and the RF voltage across L2C4. As a result, the feedback to the grid circuit would be inadequate to sustain oscillations.

If capacitor C3 shorted, no plate voltage would be applied to V1 and the circuit would be inoperative. Meter M1 would read 0. However, a very high current would flow through M2 and capacitor C3, and the meter might be damaged.

Q. 3.277 What is a simple test to determine if an oscillator is operating?

A. Assuming no built-in meters are present (as in Fig. 3.270), the simplest test is to measure the negative grid bias of the oscillator tube with a high-resistance voltmeter.

D. The "correct" bias for any oscillator must be determined for each individual circuit. It may sometimes be obtained from manufacturer's voltage charts or may be measured and recorded when the oscillator is operating *normally*. In measuring the grid bias, a high-resistance voltmeter should be used. This should have a rating of at least 20 000 ohms per volt. A better choice is an electronic voltmeter having an input resistance of 11 megohms on all scales. Using a low-resistance voltmeter will give erroneous readings, because it will shunt the grid resistor, reducing its effective value and thus the bias (see Q. 3.86). Also, a low-resistance voltmeter will severely load the tank circuit, giving erroneous information about the condition of the oscillator. (For additional methods of checking oscillation, see Q. 3.91)

Q. 3.278 What conditions may cause weak output from an oscillator and how is this condition determined?

A. Weak output may be caused by:
1. Weak oscillator tube.
2. Low power supply voltage.
3. Increased value of plate (or screen) circuit resistor, or defective RF choke.
4. Defective tank coil or capacitor.
5. Defective grid capacitor or grid resistor.

Weak output is most easily determined by measuring the grid bias (see Q. 3.277) and comparing it with the known good value.

D. In some cases, the oscillator output may be almost normal at higher frequencies

and may decrease severely or stop entirely at lower frequencies. This occurs because in most oscillators, the amount of feedback increases as the frequency increases. Some of this effect is normal, but if it should be excessive, the troubles are usually those described above for weak oscillations.

Q. 3.279 In the crystal oscillator circuit of Fig. 3.279, what would be the effect on oscillation if C2 shorted or opened?

A. If C2 shorted, there would be no change in oscillator operation. If C2 opened, oscillation would cease; M1 would read 0, and M2 would read increased current. (See Q. 3.274 D.)

D. In Fig. 3.279, a resonant crystal has been substituted for the grid tank circuit L1C1 in Fig. 3.270. (See Q. 3.93 and Q. 3.86 (1) (c) for a discussion of the operation of this type of oscillator.)

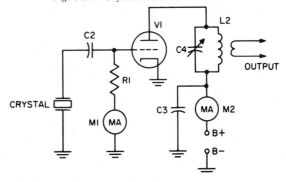

Fig. 3.279. Crystal oscillator circuit.

If C2 shorted, oscillator operation would not change because the crystal holder constitutes a capacitor and would assume the function of C2. Actually, the crystal holder capacitance and C2 are normally in series, and the effective grid-leak capacitance is the series resultant of the two capacitances. Thus, if C2 is appreciably larger than the crystal holder capacitance, very little change in the total grid-leak capacitance will take place if C2 shorts. In many crystal oscillator circuits, C2 is not used. The time constant of R1 and the total grid-leak capacitance must be at least five times as great as the period of the waveform at the oscillating frequency. If this is true, the grid-leak bias will be sustained virtually unchanged between the positive peaks of each RF cycle. (See also Q. 3.95.)

Q. 3.280. In the crystal-oscillator circuit of Fig. 3.279, what would be the effect on circuit operation of the following:
1. **R1 open?**
2. **C4 open or shorted?**
3. **L2 open or shorted?**
4. **C3 open or shorted?**

A.
1. see Q. 3.272.
2. see Q. 3.273.
3. see Q. 3.275.
4. see Q. 3.276.

Q. 3.281. In a crystal oscillator, what would be the effect(s) of a defective crystal?

A. The effect(s) might be:
1. Cessation of oscillations.
2. Variations of oscillator frequency.
3. Weak oscillations.
D. For other causes of weak oscillations, see Q. 3.278, and also Q. 3.93 and Q. 3.97.

Q. 3.282. In a crystal oscillator, what might cause the oscillator frequency to be incorrect?

A.
1. Incorrect operating temperature of the crystal.
2. Cracked or dirty crystal.
3. Improperly tuned plate tank circuit.
4. Incorrect pressure of the crystal holder.
D.
1. See Q. 3.93 and Q. 3.94.
2. See Q. 3.97.
3. Improper tuning of the plate (or screen grid in electron-coupled type) circuit may cause minor frequency changes in a crystal oscillator and may also affect its stability. The phase and amplitude of the oscillator feedback voltage are controlled by

varying the tuning of the plate tank circuit. This is the *main* function of the plate tank. Thus, both the optimum *stability* and the exact operating frequency of this crystal oscillator may be achieved only if the plate tank is tuned correctly. The plate tank is tuned correctly when it is tuned *inductively,* that is, when the natural resonance frequency of the tank is higher than the operating (crystal) frequency. This is achieved by reducing the tuning capacitance (C4) *below* the value which provides resonance at the crystal frequency.

The correct method of adjusting crystal oscillators utilizing a plate (or screen-grid) tank circuit is shown in Fig. 3.282 and Fig. 3.279. With the aid of meter M2, capacitor C4 is adjusted first for minimum plate current, shown by Point C in Fig. 3.282. At this point, the tank is practically resistive and offers maximum impedance because it is tuned to the grid (crystal) circuit frequency. This is a critical point of operation, because any small increase in C4 will make the plate tank *capacitive* instead of inductive. This will cause the feedback to be out of phase to the grid circuit, and oscillations will cease. To render the oscillator stable, capacitor C4 is decreased in value somewhat from the point of minimum plate current, and the plate current is permitted to rise as in Points A to B in Fig. 3.282. When the oscillator is adjusted in this manner, it is operating away from the unstable point at C. At the same time, the amount of feedback is reduced, further improving oscillator stability. (In practice, the plate tank should be tuned 4 to 6 per cent above the crystal frequency.)

4. Correct operation of an oscillator crystal depends upon the correct pressure being applied to the crystal. There must be adequate pressure to maintain good electrical contact during vibration. If the pressure is excessive, the crystal may stop oscillating or may oscillate at a reduced amplitude or at a different frequency. In general, the correct pressure is established by using a crystal holder specifically designed for the particular cut of crystal in use.

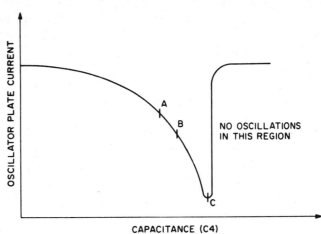

Fig. 3.282. Tuning curve for
a crystal oscillator (see text).

Q. 3.283. A schematic diagram of a transistorized (PNP), shunt-fed Hartley oscillator is given in Fig. 3.283. Describe several ways to detect oscillation in this circuit.

A. Any of the following methods may be used:

1. Tuning a radio receiver to the oscillator frequency. (If the receiver has a BFO (Q. 3.158), turn it on to hear a whistle.)

2. Tuning a heterodyne frequency meter to the oscillator frequency. A sensitive wavemeter (loosely coupled) may also be used.

3. Certain grid-dip meters have phone jacks and provisions for detecting a zero-heat condition. When the grid-dip meter is tuned to the oscillator frequency (if operating), a zero-beat condition will be observed.

Fig. 3.283. Schematic of a transistorized, shunt-fed
Hartley oscillator.

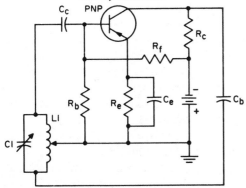

4. A neon bulb or low-current flashlight bulb connected to a loop of wire and loosely coupled to the oscillator circuit will light if the oscillator is functioning.

5. Connect a voltmeter (low scale) to measure the emitter-to-base bias voltage. Now, load down the oscillator. (A simple way to do this is to touch the base or collector end of the oscillator coil.) If the oscillator is working, there will be a noticeable change in the bias voltage. If not, the voltage will remain constant. The magnitude of the bias is not important for this test; only the change (or lack of change) of bias voltage is looked for.

D. Most vacuum-tube oscillators employ grid-leak bias. (See Q. 3.86 A. General.) With this type of circuit, it is a simple matter to determine if oscillations are present by measuring the bias. (See Q. 3.277.) Unfortunately, this simple test is not applicable to transistor oscillators, since their input resistance is very low and only a low value of "grid-leak" bias can be developed. Thus, with transistor oscillators, one of the methods described above should be used to detect the presence of oscillations.

Although the circuit shown in Fig. 3.283 is a Hartley *transistor* oscillator, the basic principles of operation are the same as described in Q. 3.86 (3) for a vacuum-tube Hartley oscillator. In addition, note that the amplifier portion of Fig. 3.283 is identical (except for RT$_1$) with the common-emitter amplifier circuit shown in Fig. 3.189.

An important feature of low-input resistance, transistor oscillators is that, to be self-starting, they must always operate with at least a small forward bias. If the transistor initially was biased beyond collector-current cut-off (Class B or C), no current would be available to initially shock the tank circuit into oscillation. A transistor oscillator must have at least a small forward bias placing the quiescent operating point in the class AB region. After the oscillations build up, the oscillation signal through base-to-emitter current may cause a Class B or Class C bias to build up in C$_C$. This is the same principle as developing a grid-leak bias in a vacuum tube (see Q. 3.86).

Q. 3.284 In the transistor, shunt-fed Hartley oscillator circuit shown in Fig. 3.283, what would be the effect on circuit operation of each of the following:
1. **Shorted or open C$_b$.**
2. **Shorted or open C$_e$.**
3. **Shorted or open C$_c$.**
4. **Shorted or open C1.**

A.
1. A shorted or open C$_b$ would render the oscillator inoperative.
2. A shorted C$_e$ may make the oscillator unstable, and the collector current would increase. An open C$_e$ would reduce the amplitude of oscillations, and in extreme cases, oscillations might cease.
3. A shorted or open C$_c$ would cause oscillations to cease.
4. A shorted or open C1 would cause oscillations to cease.
D.
1. A shorted C$_b$ would ground the collector for dc through the lower portion of L1, preventing the transistor from operating. If C$_b$ opens, the ac feedback path to L1C1 would be open and oscillations would cease. If the transistor was initially biased near cutoff, the collector current will decrease.
2. A shorted C$_e$ will short out R$_e$. The

effect of R$_e$ as a swamping resistor (see Q. 3.187) will be lost, which would tend to make the transistor characteristics unstable, with a possible resultant instability of oscillations (amplitude and frequency). Also, the shorting of R$_e$ will increase the collector current.

If C$_e$ opens, the ac voltage appearing across R$_e$ will cause degeneration, which will reduce the amplitude of oscillations. If oscillation conditions were normally marginal, oscillations might stop.

3. A shorted C$_c$ would ground (for dc) the base through the upper half of L1. This would remove the forward bias and the oscillator could not be self-starting (see Q. 3.283). The collector current would go to 0. An open C$_c$ would disconnect the tank from the base and oscillations would stop.

4. A shorted or open C1 would destroy the effectiveness of the tank circuit and cause oscillations to stop. If C1 opened, L1 would be resonated with the stray capacities across it, and the oscillator *might* operate at a much higher frequency. This frequency would be unpredictable and generally of no practical value.

Q. 3.285. In the transistor, shunt-fed Hartley oscillator circuit, shown in Fig. 3.283, what would be the effect on circuit operation of each of the following:
1. **Open R$_b$.**
2. **Open R$_f$.**
3. **Open R$_e$.**
4. **Open R$_c$.**
5. **Shorted or open L1.**

1. An open R$_b$ will not stop oscillations, but may affect oscillator stability and will increase average collector current.
2. An open R$_f$ will prevent oscillations from starting. There will be little or no collector current.
3. An open R$_e$ will stop oscillations. Collector current will be 0.
4. An open R$_c$ will stop oscillations. Collector current will be 0.
5. A shorted or open L1 will stop os-

cillations. Collector current will be reduced.

D.

1. R_f and R_b form a voltage divider to apply forward bias to the transistor base. If R_b opens, the forward bias will increase, increasing the average collector current. This may cause overheating of the transistor, some instability of transistor characteristics, and oscillator instability.

2. If R_f opens, forward-base bias will be lost, and collector current will fall to 0 (practically). Oscillations cannot start, since there will be no current impulse through the tank circuit when the oscillator is first turned on.

3. If R_e opens, the emitter-collector current path is opened and no collector current can flow. Oscillation cannot occur since the transistor is now inoperative.

4. If R_c opens, collector voltage is lost and the circuit will be inoperative.

5. If L1 shorts or opens, there will be no tank circuit and oscillations will cease. Forward bias provided by R_f and R_b will be present, resulting in a reduced value of collector current.

Q. 3.286 In the transistor, Colpitts-type crystal oscillator shown in Fig. 3.286, what would be the effect of each of the following:

1. Shorted or open C1.

2. Shorted or open C2.

3. Defective crystal.

A.

1. A failure of C1 or C2 in either the open or shorted condition would prevent the oscillator from operating.

2. See Q. 3.281.

D. The basic transistor circuit of Fig. 3.286 is very similar to that of Fig. 3.283 and the amplifier section operates in the same manner (see Q. 3.189). The major differences are: (1) in Fig. 3.286, the LC tank of Fig. 3.283 is replaced with a crystal, and (2) feedback is provided by a Colpitts arrangement. (For an explanation of the operation of a Colpitts oscillator, see Q. 3.86(4). See also Q. 386(3), and Q. 3.86(7).

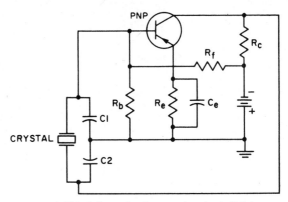

Fig. 3.286. Schematic of a transistorized, Colpitts crystal oscillator.

A shorted or open C1 or C2 would prevent the feedback circuit from operating. Thus, oscillations could not be sustained. The effects of failures of the remaining components are the same as those described in Q. 3.284 and Q. 3.285 for the corresponding parts. The methods used to detect oscillations are given in Q. 3.283.

Q. 3.287. What conditions may cause weak output from a transistor oscillator and how is the condition determined?

A. Weak output may be caused by:

1. Weak transistor (low gain).

2. Defective crystal (if used).

3. Defective tank circuit (if used).

4. Leaky base coupling capacitor (if used).

5. Open emitter-resistor, by-pass capacitor.

6. Low supply voltage.

7. Leaky collector coupling capacitor.

8. Reduced feedback from any other cause.

Output may be determined by measuring the amplitude of oscillations at a convenient point, such as the base or collector. A vacuum-tube voltmeter (ac) or oscilloscope may be used. The reading thus obtained can be compared with a reference value obtained during normal operation of this oscillator.

D. See Q. 3.91, Q. 3.278, Q. 3.281 and Q. 3.282.

AMPLIFIERS

Q. 3.288 In the triode-amplifier circuit shown in Fig. 3.228, what would be the effect of each of the following:
1. **Shorted or open C_c.**
2. **Shorted or open C_k.**
3. **Shorted or open C_f.**
4. **Shorted or open C_o.**

A.

1. A shorted C_c will probably distort the output signal and may also reduce amplifier output. An open C_c will cause either a total loss of output signal or an output of higher frequency components only.

2. A shorted C_k will distort output and may result in excessive plate dissipation. An open C_k will reduce the output amplitude, but will not cause distortion.

3. A shorted C_f will result in a total loss of amplifier output and may burn out R_f. An open C_f may distort output and possibly cause low-frequency oscillation (motorboating).

4. A shorted C_o will distort and reduce amplifier output and will also affect the following stage by shunting plate voltage to it. An open C_o will result in no output or in an output of only the higher-frequency signal components.

D.

1. If C_c shorts, the driving circuitry will be connected directly to the grid of the amplifier tube. If the driver is another amplifier stage, the plate voltage of the driver will be applied to the grid of the amplifier tube. This will cause loading of the driver by the grid-to-cathode resistance. The normally extremely high input resistance will now become very low, because the positive-driver plate voltage applied to the grid will cause it to draw a substantial amount of current. Loading of the driver will greatly reduce and distort its output. The (now) positive grid bias will drive the amplifier to saturation, and its output will be weak and highly distorted.

If C_c opens, there may be no output, or low output, from the amplifier, the exact effect depending upon the nature of the input signal. If the signal contains a wide band of frequencies, some of the higher frequency components may be coupled through the stray capacitance of C_c (and other strays), but lower frequency components will not appear in the output.

2. If C_k shorts, the bias will go to 0 and the tube will saturate (plate current), causing a highly distorted output. The rated plate dissipation may be exceeded.

If C_k opens, degeneration will occur across the now unbypassed cathode resistor R_k. For an explanation of this effect, see Q. 3.100. The degeneration does not alter the dc operating voltages, so any distortion present will be reduced, but output will be decreased.

3. If C_f shorts, the tube will not receive plate voltage. This will disable the amplifier. The full $B+$ voltage will be applied across R_f and may burn out or severely overheat R_f. A severely overheated carbon compo-

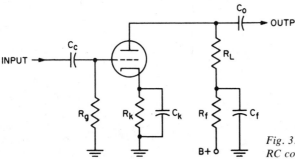

Fig. 3.288. Schematic of an RC coupled triode amplifier.

sition resistor increases in value, sometimes drastically.

If C_f opens, it no longer places an RF ground at the bottom of R_L, and the resistance of R_f is added to R_L to form the total plate-load resistance. The amplifier load line (see Q. 3.57) will be lowered. Although the amplifier gain will increase, the output may be distorted since the grid can now only accept a lower input signal if distortion is to be avoided. In addition, the high frequency response of the amplifier will be reduced. C_f and R_f are required to decouple this amplifier stage from other stages. The loss of C_f will remove this decoupling and may result in motorboating. (See Q. 3.102 for a discussion of this effect).

4. For the effects of a shorted or open C_o, see (A.4.) above.

Q. 3.289 In the triode amplifier circuit shown in Fig. 3.288, what would be the effect of each of the following:
1. **Open R_g.**
2. **Open R_k.**
3. **Open R_L.**
4. **Open R_f.**

A.
1. An open R_g will result in a distorted output, and hum or other pickup will appear in the output.

2. An Open R_k will produce no amplifier output.

3. An open R_L will produce no amplifier output.

4. An open R_f will produce no amplifier output.

D.
1. If R_g opens, the grid loses its dc ground return, leaving the grid at an extremely high impedance level. The grid-to-cathod bias will revert to the space-charge potential value. In most cases, this bias is improper for amplifier operation and will result in a distorted output. Also, the high grid-circuit impedance will make is susceptible to electrostatic pickup of hum or other extraneous voltages near the grid circuit.

2. If R_k, R_L, or R_f opens, the dc plate current circuit will be opened and the amplifier will be inoperative.

3. See Q. 3.50(1) for discussion of triode amplifier. See also Q. 3.46(2), Q. 3.47, and Q. 3.48.

Q. 3.290 In the pentode amplifier shown in Fig. 3.290, discuss the effects of shorted and open component parts.

A. Except for C_{sg} and R_{sg}, the effects of the components are as described in Q. 3.287 and Q. 3.288.

1. A shorted C_{sg} will result in little or no amplifier output. An open C_{sg} will result in a reduced amplifier output, without distortion.

2. An open R_{sg} will have the same effect as a shorted C_{sg}.

D.
1. If C_{sg} shorts, screen-grid voltage will be removed. In a pentode, plate current depends largely upon the screen grid potential. In this case, the screen grid will be *grounded* by the shorted C_{sg}. This effectively shields the plate from the control grid and cathode,

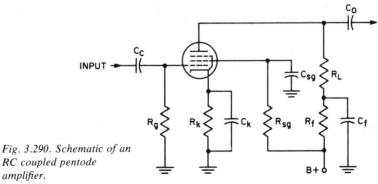

Fig. 3.290. Schematic of an RC coupled pentode amplifier.

resulting in a greatly reduced plate current. As a result, there will be little or no amplifier output.

If C_{sg} opens, screen-grid degeneration occurs across R_{sg}. The effect is basically the same as with cathode degeneration (See Q. 3.100), but is considerably reduced because the screen grid is spaced relatively far from the control grid, compared to the cathode. The effect of screen-grid degeneration is only about 10 to 15 per cent as great as cathode degeneration.

2. If R_{sg} opens, the screen-grid voltage will be removed. The screen grid will acquire a negative space-charge potential, resulting in little or no plate current, and there will be little or no amplifier output.

3. For a discussion of pentode amplifier operation, see Q. 3.50(2), Q. 3.46, Q. 3.47, and Q. 3.48.

Q. 3.291 In the pentode, Class C RF amplifier shown in Fig. 3.291, what would be the effect of each of the following:
  1. Shorted or open C1.
  2. Shorted or open C_c.
  3. Shorted or open C_{sg}.
  4. Shorted or open C_o.
  5. Shorted or open C2.

A.

1. A shorted C1 would result in no amplifier output. Meter M1 would read 0, while Meter M2 would read a high plate current.

An open C1 would result in a greatly reduced amplifier output. Meter M1 would read a low value of grid current and Meter M2 would show increased plate current.

2. A shorted C_c will result in a reduced output, increased plate current, and reduced amplifier efficiency. Meter M1 will read 0, and Meter M2 will show increased plate current.

An open C_c will result in no amplifier output. Meter M1 will read 0, and Meter M2 will show increased plate current.

3. A shorted C_{sg} will result in little or no amplifier output. Meter M1 will show a normal or slightly increased reading; Meter M2 will read very low or 0.

An open C_{sg} will result in reduced amplifier output and a slight efficiency loss. M1 will read normally, but M2 will show an increased plate current.

4. A shorted C_o will result in no amplifier output. Meter M1 will read normally, but Meter M2 will read off scale (high side) and may burn out.

An open C_o will result in no amplifier output. Meter M1 will read normally, but Meter M2 will show an appreciable increase in plate current.

5. A shorted or open C2 will result in a small output from the amplifier. Meter M1 will read normally, but Meter M2 will show an appreciable increase in plate current.

D.

1. If C1 shorts, there will be no grid drive, and therefore no grid current and no output. Without grid-leak bias (See Q. 3.86), the plate current rises substantially. A small-value resistor, R_k, is in the cathode circuit to protect the tube against excessive plate dissipation (See Q. 3.121). However, R_k does not provide operating bias, since this is a class C amplifier and the normal operating

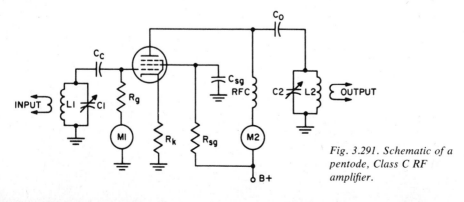

Fig. 3.291. Schematic of a pentode, Class C RF amplifier.

bias is provided through grid current rectification.

If C1 opens, the resonant circuit consisting of L1C1 is lost and the impedance of the input circuit is appreciably reduced. This reduces the grid signal and may also cause loading of the driver stage. The net result is reduced output, reduced grid current and increased plate current. The plate current increases because the negative portion of the RF plate voltage swing does not go down as much as when full output is achieved. In class C operation, plate current is drawn only at this time, and since the instantaneous plate voltage is higher, the plate current will increase. (This effect is explained in Q. 3.52(1)(d).)

2. If C_c shorts, grid-leak bias is lost and the only bias is the small amount developed across R_k. Because of the low bias, a high plate current is drawn and, although grid current is flowing, Meter M1 cannot read it, since it normally only reads the discharge current of C_c. The output will be low and the efficiency very poor.

If C_c opens, L1C1 is disconnected from the grid circuit. There can be no output, and, of course, grid-leak bias is lost (see above).

3. For a discussion of the effects of a shorted or open C_{sg}, see Q. 3.290 D.(1).

4. If C_o shorts, the plate will be grounded (for dc) through L2 and there will be no output. There will be a low resistance path to ground through M2, RFC, shorted C_o, and L2. A high current will flow through this path, which may damage M2 and possibly RFC.

If C_o opens, the plate-tank circuit L2C2 will be disconnected from the plate. There will be a low value of signal across the RFC, but this will not appear in the output. The input circuit will not be affected and M1 will read normally. However, because of the very low RF plate voltage swing, the average plate current will increase appreciably, as shown by M2 (See Q. 3.52(1)(d).)

5. If C2 shorts, the plate tank is shorted out and no amplifier output is possible. Since there is now no RF plate voltage swing, a high B+ value is continuously applied to the plate, resulting in a high reading on M2. However, the input circuit is unaffected, and M1 will read normally.

If C2 opens, the ac plate load will consist of the RFC in parallel with L2. While this combination offers some impedance, it is appreciably less than the resonant impedance of the plate tank circuit. Thus, a small output will appear and, since no tank is present, it will be very rich in harmonics, because of the Class C operation of the tube. The input circuit is unaffected and Meter M1 will read normally.

Q. 3.292 In the pentode, class C RF amplifier shown in Fig. 3.291 what would be the effect of each of the following:

    1. Shorted or open L1.
    2. Shorted or open L2.
    3. Open R_g.
    4. Open R_k.
    5. Open R_{sg}.
    6. Shorted or open RFC.

A.

1. A shorted or an open L1 would result in no amplifier output. Meter M1 would read O, and M2 would show a high plate current.

2. A shorted L2 would result in no amplifier output, and an Open L2 would result in very low amplifier output. In both cases, Meter M1 would read normally, and M2 would show a high plate current.

3. An Open R_g would result in a reduced amplifier output. If the input signal was suddenly reduced, there may be no amplifier output. Meter M1 would read 0.

4. An open R_k would result in no amplifier output. Both meters would read zero.

5. An open R_{sg} would result in little or no amplifier output.

6. A shorted RFC would result in no amplifier output. Meter M1 would read normally, but M2 would show an increased plate current.

An open RFC would result in no amplifier output. Meter M1 would read normally, but M2 would read zero. The screen-grid would draw excessive current.

D.

1. If L1 shorts, there can be no inductive coupling into the tank circuit. Also, the grid of the amplifier tube will be grounded for RF. As a result, no grid signal appears at the grid; there is no amplifier output. There is no grid current, and grid-leak bias cannot be developed. Because of the low bias across R_k, both the plate and screen-grid currents will be high.

If L1 opens, there will be no inductive coupling into the tank circuit. The amplifier operation will be described immediately above.

2. If L2 shorts, the amplifier plate will be at ac ground potential and no RF signal can be developed at the plate; therefore, no output occurs. The average plate voltage will now be maximum, resulting in a high plate current. The input circuit is unaffected and Meter M1 will read normally.

If L2 opens, the plate load will consist of the RFC in parallel with the series combination of C_o and C2. This provides a relatively low impedance plate load for RF, resulting in a very low amplifier output. Because of the low-amplitude plate RF voltage present, plate current will be high. Again, the input circuit is unaffected and grid current remains normal.

3. If R_g opens, C_c will charge to the *peak* value of the RF voltage across the grid tank. The bias will be *higher* and the grid will not be driven (practically) into the positive conduction region, thus reducing amplifier output. Assuming no leakage in C_c and a constant amplitude of input signal (all other parameters held constant), the amplifier will continue to operate with reduced output. However, if for any reason the grid drive were *appreciably* reduced, the high bias would remain across C_c and no amplifier output would be present. Since the amplifier is cut off under these reduced grid-drive conditions, M2 would read zero, and there would no screen-grid current. A lesser degree of reduced drive would result in a low amplifier output, with low plate and screen-grid

currents. In either case, because of the open R_g, M1 will read 0.

4. If R_k opens, the circuit will be opened for control grid, screen grid, and plate currents. Therefore, M1 and M2 will read 0, and the amplifier will be inoperative.

5. If R_{sg} opens, screen-grid voltage will be removed from the amplifier, resulting in little or no output. (See discussion of Q. 3.290.2.)

6. If the RFC shorts, it will effectively (through C_o) short out the plate tank. The plate circuit impedance will be practically 0. The dc path to the plate will not be interrupted, but a high average plate voltage will be present for conduction because of the absence of an RF plate swing. (See discussion of Q. 3.291.4.) Meter M2 will read high, and Meter M1 will read normally.

If the RFC opens, the dc plate current path is open and Meter M2 will read 0. Because of the absence of plate voltage, electrons normally attracted to the plate will be repelled to the screen grid, resulting in excessive screen current. This is frequently observed (glass tube) in the form of a red- or white-hot screen grid. If there is not sufficient screen-current limiting, the tube may be destroyed.

Q. 3.293 In the pentode, Class C RF amplifier shown in Fig. 3.291, discusses the effects of a loss of input-driving signal on amplifier operation.

A. Meter M1 will read zero and M2 would show a considerable increased plate current reading. There would be no amplifier output.

D. The RF driving signal normally would be provided by an oscillator or intermediate RF amplifier. If the driving source failed, grid-leak bias would be lost. The only bias remaining would be the small safety bias developed across R_k. As a result, the plate current would rise to a high value.

Q. 3.294 In the Class A, common-emitter amplifier shown in Fig. 3.294, what would be the effect of each of the following:

1. Shorted or open C_c.
2. Shorted or open C_e.
3. Shorted or open C_o.

A.

1. A shorted C_c will probably produce distortion of the output signal and may also reduce output. An open C_c will result either in a total loss of output signal or in an output of higher frequency components only.

2. A shorted C_e may cause distortion in the output. An open C_e will reduce the output amplitude, but no distortion will result.

3. A shorted or open C_o will produce results similar to those described in part 1 above.

D.

1. If C_e shorts, the circuitry of the driving source will be applied directly to the transistor base. In most cases, this will change the forward bias on the transistor, which may distort the output signal. In addition, a C_c short may cause loading of the driving stage, changing its operating characteristics as well. This may distort or reduce the output from the driver stage, which would be applied to the transistor stage in question.

If C_c opens, there may be weak or no amplifier output, depending upon the nature of the signal applied to C_c. If the signal contains a wide band of frequencies, some of the higher frequency components may be coupled through the stray capacitance of C_c

and other strays). However, lower frequency components will not appear in the output.

2. If C_e shorts, it will short out "swamping" resistor R_e. (See Q. 3.187 and Q. 3.284 (2).) The loss of the emitter resistance and the emitter-to-base junction resistance changes with temperature will result in base-to-emitter bias changes, which may distort the output. The gain will not change unless a *radical* change of bias results.

If C_e opens, degeneration will occur due to the unbypassed resistor R_e. This action is basically the same as that which occurs when a vacuum-tube cathode resistor is unbypassed. (See Q. 3.100.) Since the dc operating voltages remain, no distortion occurs (actually distortion decreases), but the degeneration results in a reduced output.

3. For the effects of a shorted or open C_o, see part 1 of answer.

Q. 3.295 In the Class A, common-emitter amplifier shown in Fig. 3.294, what would be the effect of the following:

1. Open R_b.
2. Open R_f.
3. Open R_e.
4. Open R_c.

A.

1. An open R_b will distort amplifier output and may reduce the gain.

2. An open R_f will result in severe distortion and reduced gain.

3. An open R_e will result in no amplifier output. Collector current will be 0.

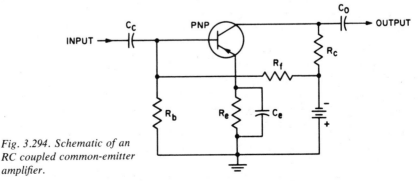

Fig. 3.294. Schematic of an RC coupled common-emitter amplifier.

4. An open R_c will result in no amplifier output. Collector current will be 0.

D.

1. If R_b opens, the forward bias will increase substantially. (See Q. 3.284 and D. (1).) The quiescent transistor operating point will be shifted to a region of high collector current, resulting in a distorted output. Since the operating point may be on the upper curved portion of the transfer characteristic curve, the transistor gain will also be reduced.

2. If R_f opens, forward-base bias will go to 0. The quiescent operating point will be in the Class B region and only (practically) the negative input half-cycles will be amplified, resulting in severe distortion. Since the quiescent operating point is now on the lower curved portion of the transfer characteristic, the transistor gain will be reduced.

3. If R_e opens, there can be no collector or base current and the amplifier will be inoperative.

4. If R_c opens, collector voltage and current are lost, and there will be no amplifier output.

Q. 3.296 In the Class C, common-emitter RF amplifier shown in Fig. 3.296, what would be the effect of each of the following:

(a) Shorted or open C_c.
(b) Shorted or open C_e.
(c) Shorted or open C1.
(d) Shorted or open C2.

A.

1. A shorted C_c would result in reduced power output and reduced amplifier efficiency. An open C_c would result in no amplifier output. Collector current would practically fall to zero.

2. A shorted C_e would have practically no effect on amplifier output. An open C_e would slightly decrease amplifier output. Operating conditions remain the same (practically).

3. A shorted C1 would result in no amplifier output. An open C1 would result in a small amplifier output. In both cases, collector current would increase appreciably.

4. A shorted C2 would result in no amplifier output; collector voltage and current go to zero. An open C2 would reduce RF output; the dc collector current would increase.

D.

1. If C_c shorts, the class C bias would be lost. C_c in conjunction with R_b provides this bias for the amplifier (R_e has a negligible effect on bias, since it is a very low value, such as 20 to 50 ohms).

For practical purposes, the emitter may be considered grounded, since R_e is very small and C_e grounds the emitter for RF. When a negative-going signal is applied to the base, current passes through the base-to-emitter diode, through C_e, and through L1 (the generator), causing C_e to charge with the polarity shown in Fig. 3.296. This results in a positive bias being applied to the base. (See Q. 3.86 for a discussion of grid-leak bias). In a PNP transistor, positive base bias cuts it off and the transistor operates as a Class C amplifier. Thus, a short circuit of C_c produces a loss of Class C bias. Since there is no fixed-forward bias provided, the transistor will now operate with substantially 0 bias, and would operate either Class B or Class AB. Since these classes are less efficient than Class C, the power output would

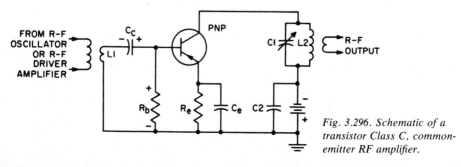

Fig. 3.296. Schematic of a transistor Class C, common-emitter RF amplifier.

be reduced. (See Q. 3.59. The same basic principles apply to transistor operation.).

If C_c opened, the RF voltage across L1 would not be able to influence the transistor base. There would be no base drive; since no forward bias is provided, the collector current would fall to 0 (practically).

1. A shorted C_c would result in reduced power output and reduced amplifier efficiency. An open C_c would result in no amplifier output. Collector current would practically fall to zero.

2. A shorted C_e would have practically no effect on amplifier output. An open C_e would slightly decrease amplifier output. Operating conditions remain the same (practically).

3. A shorted C1 would result in no amplifier output. An open C1 would result in a small amplifier output. In both cases, collector current would increase appreciably.

4. A shorted C2 would result in no amplifier output; collector voltage and current go to zero. An open C2 would reduce RF output; the dc collector current would increase.

D.

1. If C_c shorts, the class C bias would be lost. C_c in conjunction with R_b provides this bias for the amplifier (R_e has a negligible effect on bias, since it is a very low value, such as 20 to 50 ohms).

For practical purposes, the emitter may be considered grounded, since R_e is very small and C_e grounds the emitter for RF. When a negative-going signal is applied to the base, current passes through the base-to-emitter diode, through C_e, and through L1 (the generator), causing C_e to charge with the polarity shown in Fig. 3.296. This results in a positive bias being applied to the base. (See Q. 3.86 for a discussion of grid-leak bias). In a PNP transistor, positive base bias cuts it off and the transistor operates as a Class C amplifier. Thus, a short circuit of C_c produces a loss of Class C bias. Since there is no fixed-forward bias provided, the transistor will now operate with substantially

0 bias, and would operate either Class B or Class AB. Since these classes are less efficient than Class C, the power output would be reduced. (See Q. 3.59. The same basic principles apply to transistor operation.).

If C_c opened, the RF voltage across L1 would not be able to influence the transistor base. There would be no base drive; since no forward bias is provided, the collector current would fall to 0 (practically).

2. If C_e shorted, it would short out the very low value of R_e (emitter swamping resistor). The effect on base-to-emitter or emitter-to collector currents would be negligible. However, the bias would be subjected to greater changes from temperature variations, which might shift the amplifier operating point.

If C_e opened, a *minor* amount of degeneration would occur across R_e; the loss of output would be slight because of the low value of R_e.

2. If C_e shorted, it would short out the very low value of R_e (emitter swamping resistor). The effect on base-to-emitter or emitter-to collector currents would be negligible. However, the bias would be subjected to greater changes from temperature variations, which might shift the amplifier operating point.

If C_e opened, a *minor* amount of degeneration would occur across R_e; the loss of output would be slight because of the low value of R_e.

3. If C1 shorts, the collector would be grounded for RF, and no amplifier output would result. Since there is no RF swing on the collector (See Q. 3.59), the collector current will increase considerably.

If C1 opens, the RF collector load consists of only the impedance of L2. Since this is much smaller than the tank impedance, only a small output will result. Because of the small RF collector swing, collector current will increase appreciably. (See Q. 3.291.)

4. If C2 shorts, the power supply is shorted out, the collector is grounded for ac, and no output is possible. Damage to the power supply may result.

If C2 opens, the RF current-return path to the emitter would be through the power supply rather than through the very low impedance of C2. Since the power supply impedance to RF is generally much higher than the impedance of C2, the RF current through the tank would be considerably reduced, which may substantially reduce amplifier output. In addition, some of the RF energy is dissipated in the power supply and lost as useful output.

Q. 3.297 In the Class C, common-emitter RF amplifier shown in Fig. 3.296, what would be the effect of each of the following?
   1. Shorted or open L1.
   2. Open R_b.
   3. Open R_e.
   4. Shorted or open L2.

   A.
   1. A shorted or open L1 would result in no amplifier output. The collector current would drop to 0 (practically).
   2. An open R_b would result in reduced amplifier output. Collector current would increase. Amplifier bias would be unable to follow changes in the RF input from the oscillator.
   3. An open R_e will result in no amplifier output. Collector current will be 0.
   4. A shorted or open L2 would result in no amplifier output. Collector current would increase.
   D.
   1. If L1 shorted or opened, there would be no inductively coupled signal fed to the transistor base. Class C bias is lost and since no fixed-forward bias is provided, the collector current would drop to 0 (practically).
   2. If R_b opens, C_c would have no discharge path. It would charge to the peak value of the input signal and the transistor would not be driven as hard, somewhat reducing RF input. Modulation distortion may result if the output is sufficiently reduced. Without a discharge path, the bias could not follow input drive variations (See also Q. 3.291 D. (3) and Q. 3.298 D.)

3. If R_e opened, there could be no input or output transistor currents and, therefore, no amplifier output would be possible.
   4. If L2 opened, the dc collector current path would be open, resulting in a total loss of amplifier output. If L2 shorted, the collector would be at ac ground potential (through shorted L2 and C2). No output signal would be developed. Because of the lack of RF-swing at the collector, the average collector current will increase.

Q. 3.298 In the Class C, common-emitter RF amplifier shown in Fig. 3.296, discuss the effects of a loss of input-driving signal on amplifier operation.

   A. If the driving signal were lost, collector current would go to 0 (practically), and there would be no amplifier output.
   D. This operational condition is quite different from the situation where a vacuum tube is used (See Q. 3.293.) In that case the loss of grid-leak bias resulted in high plate current. In the transistor circuit, however, no fixed forward bias is provided, and when the driving signal is removed, the base-emitter bias becomes 0 and the collector current drops to 0 (practically).

TRANSMITTERS

Q. 3.299 An amplitude (plate) modulated transmitter is shown in Fig. 3.299. Describe the effects on transmitter operation of parts defect(s) in each stage.

   A.
   1. The effect of defects of each part in the individual stages of the transmitter are given in the following questions:
   a. TPTG Crystal Oscillator: Q. 3.279 through Q. 3.282.
   b. Class C RF amplifier: Q. 3.291 and Q. 3.292.
   c. Modulator preamplifier: Q. 3.288 and Q. 3.289
   d. Modulator stage: For the effect of defects of C_o, C_k, C_{sg}, R_k, R_g, and R_{sg},

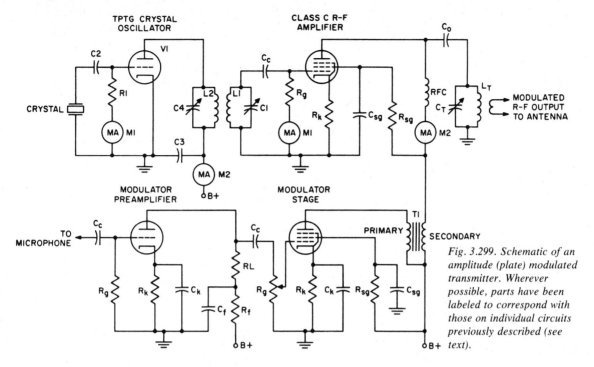

Fig. 3.299. Schematic of an amplitude (plate) modulated transmitter. Wherever possible, parts have been labeled to correspond with those on individual circuits previously described (see text).

see Q. 3.290. Except for the fact that R_g is a potentiometer and the plate load consists of a modulation transformer (T1), the modulator stage is the same as the pentode amplifier shown in Fig. 3.290. Additional faults which may occur in the modulator stage are slider-contact defects of R_g and open or short circuit conditions of T1.

(1) R_g contact defects (noisy potentiometer) may result in intermittent modulation of the RF carrier or may introduce audio-frequency noise into the transmission. The function of R_g is to adjust the amount of audio drive applied to the grid of the modulator stage, and thus to regulate the percentage of modulation.

(2) A shorted T1 primary will result in a loss of modulator stage output and thus a loss of modulation of the RF carrier. However, this will *not* affect the transmission of the RF carrier.

A shorted T1 secondary will produce the same effects as a shorted primary since the shorted secondary reflects a short into the transformer primary. There will be no

audio voltage variation across the secondary and no modulation.

An open T1 primary would result in a loss of modulator stage output and a loss of RF carrier modulation. The modulator-stage plate will be open circuited and can produce no output. The RF carrier output is unaffected. An open T1 secondary would result in a loss of modulation supplied to the RF, class C amplifier. However, this is somewhat academic since the B+ supply to the plate and screen grid of the RF amplifier will be interrupted. This stage will now be completely inoperative, resulting in a total loss of RF output from the transmitter.

D.

1. For a discussion of plate modulation of a Class C, RF amplifier, see Q. 3.143. For a discussion of modulation problems, see Q. 3.147, Q. 3.148, and Q. 3.149.

2. A totally disabled crystal oscillator (or RF amplifier) will result in no transmitter output. However a weak input into the RF amplifier or a weak output from the amplifier will result in a weak modulated RF wave

(see Q. 3.147) and will cause "downward" modulation or negative carrier shift.

3. Defects either in the modulator preamplifier or the modulator stage will in general produce:

a. No modulation, caused by a loss of output from either amplifier.

b. Overmodulation, caused by excessive output from the modulator. (For a discussion of the effects of overmodulation, see Q. 3.141. See also Q. 3.142.

c. Undermodulation, the result of a weak (but undistorted) audio being applied to the Class C RF amplifier. This does not produce any undesired sidebands in the output, but it does reduce the area consistently covered by the transmitter. (For a discussion of this effect, see Q. 3.149.)

d. A distorted audio-modulation output, causing a distorted audio at the receiving end and unwanted additional-sideband frequencies which may result in adjacent-channel interference. (See also Q. 3.139, Q. 3.140 and Q. 3.141.) Distortion of the audio output may cause negative-carrier shift (see Q. 3.147).

4. To achieve symmetrical amplitude modulation of an RF carrier wave, it is essential that the instantaneous amplitude of the RF wave follows faithfully the instantaneous amplitude of the audio-modulating voltage. Under 100 percent modulation conditions, the instantaneous positive peak of the RF envelope should reach twice the amplitude of the unmodulated RF carrier wave (see also Q. 3.142). If the RF modulated wave goes to 0, but is not able to achieve twice the unmodulated wave amplitude, the modulation wave will be compressed on the positive peak. This distorts the audio component, resulting in the radiation of undesirable harmonic-sideband frequencies. A condition of "downward" modulation or negative carrier shift will be present (see Q. 3.147). Some conditions which may prevent the instantaneous RF amplitude from achieving its required positive-peak value are as follows (Class C amplifier considered):

a. Insufficient grid excitation.

b. Insufficient bias.

c. Weak tube or excessive dc input to the RF amplifier (cannot attain desired maximum RF output).

d. Improperly tuned, plate or grid circuits.

e. Excessive loading of plate-tank circuit.

f. Inadequate regulation of power supply.

g. Insufficient screen grid and/or plate modulation.

5. If a Class C amplifier is modulated symmetrically, the plate-current reading will remain constant, with or without modulation. Any change of plate current when modulation is applied indicates a lack of modulation symmetry.

Q. 3.300 An amplitude (collector) modulated transmitter is shown in Fig. 3.300. Describe the effect(s) on transmitter operation of parts defects in each stage.

A.

1. *Crystal Oscillator:* For the effect of a defect on oscillator operation, see Q. 3.284 and Q. 3.285; C_e, R_b, R_f, R_e.

The effect of defects in the remaining parts follow.

a. Crystal defective: Oscillations cease. Collector current is reduced.

b. C_c shorted: Oscillations cease. Collector current drops to 0 (practically). C_e open; Little or no effect on oscillator operation.

c. C_T shorted or open: Oscillations cease. Collector current is reduced.

d. L_T shorted or open: Same as (c) above.

2. *Class C, RF Amplifier:* For the effect of defects in all the parts of this amplifier, see Q. 3.296, Q. 3.297. See also Q. 3.298 (loss of drive).

3. *Modulator Preamplifier:* For the effect of defects in this amplifier, see Q. 3.294 and Q. 3.295. The only difference here is that R_c is a potentiometer instead of a fixed resistor. As such, it is likely to become noisy

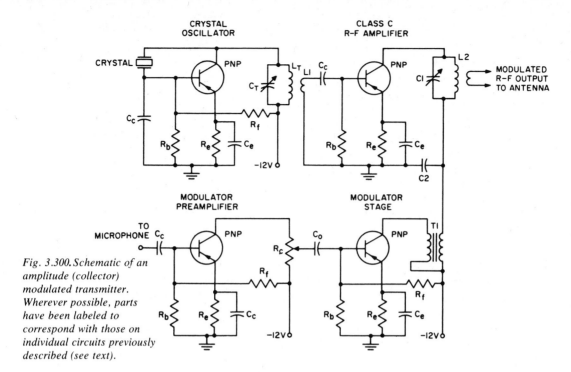

Fig. 3.300. Schematic of an amplitude (collector) modulated transmitter. Wherever possible, parts have been labeled to correspond with those on individual circuits previously described (see text).

or intermittent. The modulation will be affected in the same way. (See Q. 3.299 1. d (1).)

4. *Modulator Stage:* For the effect of defects of C_o, (C_c), C_e, R_b, R_f and R_e see Q. 3.294 and Q. 3.295. Except that the plate load of the modulator stage is a transformer (T1) instead of a resistor, this stage has the same basic configuration as Fig. 3.294. Also, the modulator stage would employ a *power* transistor to provide the modulating power for the class C, RF amplifier.

Additional problems in the modulator stage can be caused by a shorted or open modulation transformer (See Q. 3.299 1. d, (2).)

D. Note the similarity of the vacuum-tube transmitter of Fig. 3.299 and the transistor transmitter of Fig. 3.300. The stages are basically the same and the type of modulation (plate) is the same. Each stage of the transistor transmitter performs the same function as its corresponding stage in the vacuum-tube transmitter. For problems which might arise from an overall transmitter (including modulation) point-of-view, see Q.

3.298. The basic principles apply equally well for a transistorized transmitter as for a vacuum-tube transmitter.

TRANSISTOR TESTING

Q. 3.301 Describe a simple method of testing transistors using an ohmmeter.

A. The method of testing a transistor with an ohmmeter is described with the aid of Fig. 3.301. The two diodes (base-to-collector and base-to-emitter) are first tested individually and will respond to an ohmmeter test basically the same as any simple solid-state diode. If the diodes are good, there will be a high ratio between the forward and back resistance (100 to 1 or greater is common). Place the ohmmeter leads across the base-to-emitter diode (ignoring ohmmeter polarity) and record the reading. Next, reverse the ohmmeter leads and again note the reading. A ratio of less than 100 to 1 (approximately) probably indicates a leaky diode section. The same test should be made on the base-to-collector diode. Again, if a

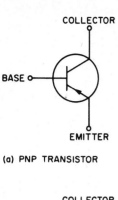

(a) PNP TRANSISTOR

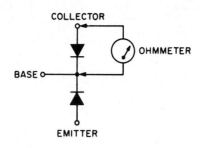

(b) REPRESENTATION OF TRANSISTOR DIODES (PNP)

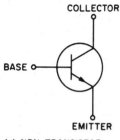

(c) NPN TRANSISTOR

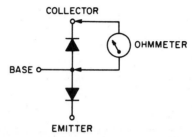

(d) REPRESENTATION OF TRANSISTOR DIODES (NPN)

Fig. 3.301. PNP and NPN schematics and their diode equivalents.

low ratio exists, the transistor should be rejected.

A short or leakage test should be made between the emitter and collector. Both readings should be quite high (may exceed several hundred thousand ohms), but one of the readings will be somewhat higher than the other. Note that with an emitter-to-collector short, the two diodes measured individually may seem perfectly normal. Therefore, the emitter-to-collector test is essential to determine the condition of the transistor.

D. In making the above tests, the ohmmeter voltages and currents should not be excessive. This is not a problem when measuring power transistors, but low-power transistors may be damaged if proper precautions are not taken. It is interesting to note that the output voltage of a typical dc, vacuum-tube voltmeter (ohmmeter function) on the R × 1 scale may be 1.5 volts and the available current 100 milliamperes or more. On the R × 10 000 scale, the voltage drops to about 0.2 volt and the available current to only 20 microamperes. A good rule to

remember is to use only the high-resistance scales for low-power transistors. The low scales may be used for testing high-power transistors.

In testing transistor diodes (or other diodes), the *ratio* of forward-to-back resistance is more important than the *actual* readings. The forward resistance should always be low, usually not more than several hundred ohms. When diode resistance is measured and the ohmmeter scales are switched, different voltages and currents are applied to the diode. Thus, scale switching may result in appreciably different resistance readings on the same diode for a given polarity of the connections.

Note: The following added material numbered Q. 3.301-A1 through Q. 3.301-A2 contains information that is *not* required to pass the General Radiotelephone Operators License examination. However, this added material, as well as the new material added to other sections, has been included to help acquaint students with the current state of the electronics art. It is felt that the added material contains subject matter that may be required of students who have obtained a General Radiotelephone Operator's License and are seeking employment. Additionally, the added material contains valuable information for future reference.

Q. 3.301-A1. Describe briefly the troubleshooting procedure known as "signal" tracing."

A. The procedure of *signal tracing* is explained with the aid of the simple block diagram shown in Fig. 3.301–A1. In this scheme, a modulated RF-signal generator is connected to the antenna terminals of a receiver. The output of the generator should be low enough not to overload the RF amplifier.

Indicating instruments as shown in the block diagram are then used to check the presence or absence of signal at the outputs of the various stages. Start checking for signal at the output of the RF amplifier and work stage by stage toward the last audio amplifier. (We are assuming a dead receiver.) When the signal indicator first shows that signal is absent, the stage immediately preceding the test point is defective. The defective stage is then checked for possible bad parts.

D. Note that, when checking stages amplifying RF or IF, an RF detector probe must be used with the indicator. If using a high-impedance headphone for audio testing, use a dc blocking capacitor (large) in series with one lead of the headphone. If AGC trouble is suspected, override the AGC with an external supply. (See also Q. 3.301–A2.)

Q. 3.301–A2. Describe briefly the troubleshooting procedure known as "signal injection."

A. The procedure of *signal injection* to locate a dead receiver stage is explained with the aid of the simple block diagram of Fig. 3.301–A2.

In this scheme, an audio signal is first fed into point H to check the speaker. If this is okay, an audio signal is injected into point G. If no output is heard, the audio power amplifier is defective. (The volume control should be set for maximum volume.) If sound is heard, the audio signal is moved to point F. If no sound is heard now, the audio pre-amplifier is defective. If sound is heard now the trouble precedes the audio pre-amplifier.

The remaining checks require the use of an IF, RF (modulated) signal generator. The procedure is basically a continuation of that described above. Using a modulated IF of the appropriate frequency, feed this signal in turn to points E, D, and C. If a point is found that produces no speaker output, the stage immediately following the point is defective. If no defective stage is found up to point C, the generator is tuned to a modulated RF frequency to which the receiver is also tuned.

Applying the RF signal to point B; if no output is heard from the speaker, the defect may be either in the mixer or the oscillator. If applying the RF signal to point B produces an output signal, the RF stage is probably defective.

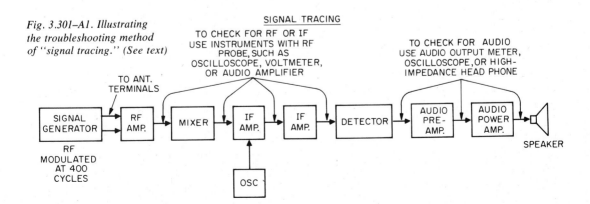

Fig. 3.301–A1. Illustrating the troubleshooting method of "signal tracing." (See text)

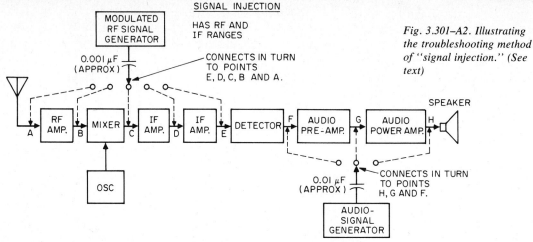

SIGNAL INJECTION

HAS RF AND
IF RANGES

Fig. 3.301–A2. Illustrating the troubleshooting method of "signal injection." (See text)

D. Although not shown in the block diagram, it should be remembered that excessive AGC voltage may disable one or more RF and IF stages. A simple test for this is to connect a low-impedance voltage source of the correct voltage, to the AGC line. This applied voltage will override the receiver's AGC voltage. (See also Q. 301-A1.)

FCC-TYPE SAMPLE TEST FOR ELEMENT III

III-1. A "difference of potential" may also be described as: (Q. 3.01)
  (a) Electrical power.
  (b) Voltage.
  (c) Electron drift.
  (d) Amperage.
  (e) Conductance.

III-2. An insulator, or non-conductor, is characterized by: (Q. 3.04)
  (a) A large number of free electrons.
  (b) Very few free electrons.
  (c) Lightly bound electrons in the outer ring of the atom.
  (d) High energy dissipation.
  (e) Large amount of skin effect.

III-3. An ac series circuit is composed of a series resistance of 20 ohms, an inductive reactance of 40 ohms, and a capacitive reactance of 15 ohms. A current of 1 ampere is flowing. What is the applied voltage? [Q. 3.09(B)]

  (a) 320 volts.
  (b) 16 volts.
  (c) 28 volts.
  (d) 32 volts.
  (e) None of the above.

III-4. A loudspeaker with a voice coil impedance of 6 ohms is fed from an emitter circuit with an impedance of 600 ohms. What is the turns ratio of a transformer which will match these two impedances? (Q. 3.13)
  (a) 10:1
  (b) 100:1
  (c) 25:1
  (d) 1 000:1
  (e) 1:1

III-5. The ratio of the amount of magnetic flux linking a secondary coil, compared to the flux generated by the primary coil, is known as the: (Q. 3.27)
  (a) Coefficient of magnetic lines of force.
  (b) Coefficient of coupling.
  (c) Coefficient of magnetism.
  (d) The magnetic coefficient.
  (e) Coefficient of self-inductance.

III-6. A filter which permits all frequencies above a predetermined cut-off frequency to be passed is called a: (Q. 3.36)
  (a) Constant-k filter.
  (b) M-derived filter.
  (c) Band-stop filter.
  (d) Power-supply filter.
  (e) High-pass filter.

III-7. A perfect op amp would have: (Q. 3.133-A23)

(a) Zero output impedance.
(b) All these characteristics.
(c) High voltage gain.
(d) Wide bandwidth.
(e) Analog and digital applications.

III-8. For a vacuum tube operating Class C, the bias should be approximately: (Q. 3.52)

(a) Cut-off bias.
(b) 10 times, cut-off bias.
(c) Twice, cut-off bias.
(d) Four times, cut-off bias.
(e) One-half cut-off bias.

III-9. A stacked antenna array will provide: (Q. 3.210)

(a) Increased vertical directivity.
(b) Decreased gain.
(c) Decreased bandpass.
(d) Decreased driving impedance.
(e) None of the above.

III-10. A wire has a cross-sectional area of 10 circular mils. It is replaced with another of the same length, but twice the diameter. The resistance will be: (Q. 3.10)

(a) Half.
(b) Twice.
(c) One fourth.
(d) Four times.
(e) The same.

III-11. Which of the following has lowest resistance to a 100 MHz signal? (Q. 3.11)

(a) 1½″ solid iron bar.
(b) Copper strip, 2″ x 4″.
(c) 1½″ solid brass bar.
(d) 2″ hollow iron bar.
(e) 1½″ solid copper bar.

III-12. If a power supply has poor voltage regulation, the effect will be: (Q. 3.72)

(a) An increased voltage under load.
(b) A constant voltage with varying loads.

(c) Appreciably varying voltage under varying loads.
(d) A decrease in output current with increasing loads.
(e) An increase in the ripple voltage with decreasing loads.

III-13. In a D'Arsonval meter movement, damping of the meter motion is accomplished by: (Q. 3.79)

(a) The two opposing springs.
(b) The jeweled meter bearings.
(c) Eddy currents in the permanent magnet.
(d) Eddy currents in the movable coil frame.
(e) Eddy current in the two springs.

III-14. Knife-edge diffraction is: (Q. 3.212-A12)

(a) The antenna pattern.
(b) Bending of radio waves.
(c) The same as refraction.
(d) The reflection of radio waves.
(e) Sky-wave reception.

III-15. A 0–1 dc milliameter is converted to a dc voltmeter with a full-scale reading of 50 volts. What value of resistance must be connected in series with the meter? (Q. 3.81)

(a) 50 000 ohms.
(b) 500 000 ohms.
(c) 5 000 ohms.
(d) 20 000 ohms.
(e) 2 000 ohms.

III-16. A 1-milliampere meter with a resistance of 50 ohms is used to measure a current by shunting the meter with a 3-ohm resistor. The meter reads 0.5 milliampere on its original scale. What is the true value of the current being measured? (Q. 3.82)

(a) 2.9 mA.
(b) 29 mA.
(c) 8.8 mA.
(d) 0.88 mA.
(e) 88.0 mA.

III-17. Rms voltage is related to peak voltage by the decimal: (Q. 3.84)

(a) 0.707
(b) 0.0707
(c) 0.636
(d) 0.9
(e) 0.7376

III-18. In the usual test oscilloscope, vertical deflection takes place by virtue of: (Q. 3.85)
(a) Electromagnetic deflection.
(b) The internally generated sawtooth wave.
(c) A 60-hertz sine wave obtained from the line voltage.
(d) The input signal being measured.
(e) The Lissajou effect.

III-19. In a Hartley-type oscillator, feedback is obtained by the use of: (Q. 3.86)
(a) A tapped capacitive circuit.
(b) A tapped resistive circuit.
(c) A tapped inductive circuit.
(d) Plate-to-grid feedback.
(e) Bridge-type feedback.

III-20. A Pierce oscillator operates in a manner similar to a: (Q. 3.86)
(a) Electron coupled oscillator.
(b) Transitron oscillator.
(c) Colpitts oscillator.
(d) Tuned-grid, tuned-plate oscillator.
(e) Armstrong oscillator.

III-21. In a multivibrator oscillator, the main frequency determining elements are: (Q. 3.86)
(a) The tubes or transistors.
(b) The RC coupling elements.
(c) The supply voltage and plate resistors.
(d) The plate and grid resistors.
(e) The plate resistors and the coupling capacitors.

III-22. The improved frequency stability gained by using a crystal in an oscillator is obtained because: (Q. 3.87)
(a) The crystal has a high positive temperature coefficient.
(b) The crystal has a high negative temperature coefficient.
(c) The crystal feedback must be strictly limited.

(d) The crystal has a very high Q.
(e) The crystal has a very low Q.

III-23. The major purpose of using a buffer amplifier in a transmitter is: (Q. 3.98)
(a) To provide a high order of RF amplification.
(b) To provide a low order of RF amplification.
(c) To isolate the final RF amplifier from the intermediate power RF amplifier.
(d) To act as a frequency multiplier.
(e) None of the above.

III-24. An overtone crystal is one which is specially ground to operate: (Q. 3.95)
(a) In a high power circuit.
(b) In an exceptionally high-stability circuit.
(c) In an audio oscillator, for precision measurements.
(d) At an odd harmonic of its fundamental.
(e) At an even harmonic of its fundamental.

III-25. In multistage audio amplifiers, decoupling networks are used: (Q. 3.102)
(a) To increase the overall gain.
(b) To provide negative feedback.
(c) To prevent audio oscillations.
(d) To prevent RF oscillations.
(e) To increase the high-frequency response.

III-26. In Fig. III-26, the voltage drop across the 3 ohm resistor is: (Q. 3.08)
(a) 1 volt.
(b) 692 mV.
(c) 962 mV.
(d) 6.92 volts.
(e) 269 mV.

Fig. III-26. Resistor network.

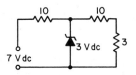

III-27. The power output of a transmitter is 30 watts and the reflected power is 5 watts.

Which figure is to be entered in the station log book? (Q. 3.85-A18, and Q 3.85-A20)

(a) 5 watts.
(b) 10 watts.
(c) 25 watts.
(d) 35 watts.
(e) 30 watts.

III-28. In true Class A operation, the output waveform is: (Q. 3.52)

(a) A perfect reproduction of the input waveform.
(b) Always a perfect reproduction of 180 degrees of the input waveform.
(c) Always inverted by 180 degrees.
(d) Always transformer coupled.
(e) Always RC coupled.

III-29. In a Class A, push-pull, audio power amplifier, the power output is:

(a) Four times the power output of one tube.
(b) The same as the power output for one tube.
(c) Twice the power output for one tube.
(d) Two and one-half times the power output for one tube.
(e) None of the above.

III-30. A carbon microphone has the disadvantage that it: (Q. 3.116)

(a) Has too high sensitivity.
(b) Has an excessive high-frequency response.
(c) Cannot be used in mobile equipment.
(d) Has a relatively poor frequency response.
(e) Does not use a power supply.

III-31. What, if anything, is wrong with Fig. III-31? (Q. 3.184)

(a) Wrong polarities.
(b) Circuit is correct.
(c) Emitter resistor is connected wrong.
(d) OK for common emitter.
(e) Wrong for common base.

Fig. III-31. Transistor stage.

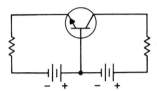

III-32. In Fig. III-32, assuming the cathode circuit to be properly connected, a complete loss of input signal would cause: (Q. 3.298)

(a) An increase of grid-leak bias.
(b) A decreased reading on meter M1.
(c) No change in plate or grid currents.
(d) A change of grid current only.
(e) None of the above.

III-33. An RF voltage amplifier, as opposed to an RF power amplifier, usually employs: (Q. 3.122)

(a) Class C bias.
(b) Class A bias.
(c) Cut-off bias.
(d) Saturation bias.
(e) Zero bias.

III-34. In Fig. III-34, what is the total capacitance? (Q. 3.29)

(a) $2.0\ \mu F.$
(b) $2.2\ \mu F.$
(c) $1.8\ \mu F.$
(d) $3.2\ \mu F.$
(e) $1.2\ \mu F.$

Fig. III-32. Incomplete schematic diagram of a low-power RF amplifier.

Fig. III-34. Capacitor network.

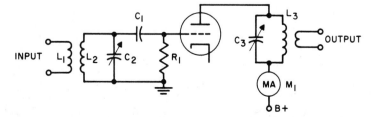

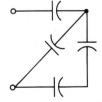

(each capacitor is 2 μF)

III-35. Triode RF amplifiers may require neutralization because of: (Q. 3.125)
(a) Cathode-to-grid feedback.
(b) Out-of-phase, plate-to-grid feedback.
(c) In-phase, plate-to-grid feedback.
(d) Their high values of g_m.
(e) The low value of plate-to-grid capacitance.

III-36. In a single-stage, frequency multiplier, the output may consist of: (Q. 3.133-A11)
(a) Either odd or even harmonics.
(b) Only odd harmonics.
(c) Only even harmonics.
(d) Only double the input frequency.
(e) Only triple the input frequency.

III-37. A Faraday screen in a transmitter is used for: (Q. 3.137)
(a) Cooling of the power tubes.
(b) Reduction of transmitted harmonics.
(c) Increasing the output power.
(d) Reducing the output power.
(e) Improving the output waveform.

III-38. Link coupling has attenuating properties for harmonic frequencies because of: (Q. 3.134)
(a) The use of physically large coupling coils.
(b) The large amount of capacity coupling.
(c) The large amount of inductive coupling.
(d) The small capacitive coupling between the link coils and the resonant circuits.
(e) The small amount of inductive coupling.

III-39. Transmitter intermodulation may occur if: (Q. 3.135)
(a) A particular transmitter has any of its stages operating above its rated power.
(b) Parasitic oscillations are occurring in any stage.
(c) The transmitter antenna is picking up energy from a second transmitter close by.
(d) The transmitting antenna is picking up energy from a second, very distant, transmitter.

(e) The transmitting antenna is not correctly matched to the final stage of the transmitter.

III-40. The following is considered a spurious emission from a transmitter: (Q. 3.136)
(a) Oscillation from an improperly neutralized RF amplifier.
(b) Radiation from the basic transmitter power supply
(c) Radiation from a directional antenna.
(d) Oscillation of the normal transmitter oscillator.
(e) Oscillation from the modulator.

III-41. High or erratic plate or grid current readings in an RF amplifier may be caused by: (Q. 3.126)
(a) A shorted power supply.
(b) The use of a dynamotor.
(c) Run-down batteries.
(d) Excessive grid bias.
(e) Parasitic oscillations.

III-42. Harmonic frequency transfer in the antenna coupling circuit of a transmitter may occur by: (Q. 3.137)
(a) Means of inductive coupling of the coils.
(b) Capacitive coupling between coils.
(c) Passing through the low-pass filter.
(d) Passing through the pi network between the final stage and the transmission line.
(e) Means of the capacitor between the output stage and the transmission line.

III-43. In amplitude modulation, the sideband frequencies consist of: (Q. 3.139)
(a) The carrier frequency and the modulation frequency.
(b) The heterodyne frequency resulting from the sum of the upper sideband frequency and the lower sideband frequency.
(c) The sum and difference frequencies between the carrier and the modulation frequencies.
(d) The sum and difference frequencies between the single sideband frequencies and the modulation frequency.
(e) The modulation frequency, plus and

minus the upper and lower sideband frequencies.

III-44. Given a carrier frequency of 1 000 kHz and a modulating frequency of 1 000 hertz, the total bandwidth of emission is: (Q. 3.140)
- (a) 2 000 hertz.
- (b) 1 000 hertz.
- (c) 20 000 hertz.
- (d) 10 000 hertz...
- (e) 900 kHz.

III-45. Given an amplitude-modulated wave with a peak-to-peak amplitude (E_{max}) of 200 volts, a minimum modulated amplitude of 100 volts (E_{min}) and an unmodulated carrier amplitude of 150 volts, the percentage of modulation is: (Q. 3.142)
- (a) 25
- (b) 100
- (c) 75
- (d) 50
- (e) None of the above.

III-46. A linear Class B RF power amplifier normally operates with a bias approximately equal to: (Q. 3.144)
- (a) Projected cut-off.
- (b) Twice cut-off.
- (c) Ten times cut-off.
- (d) 50% of cut-off value.
- (e) The Class A bias value.

III-47. The sensitivity of a receiver is an important quality because it: (Q. 3.161)
- (a) Defines the usable receiver bandwidth.
- (b) Defines the receiver's ability to discriminate against image frequencies.
- (c) Defines the receiver's ability to discriminate against adjacent-channel interference.
- (d) Defines the receiver's ability to respond efficiently to a weak signal input.
- (e) Defines the IF bandwidth of the receiver.

III-48. In Fig. III-48, when switch 1 is closed, (Q. 3.192(U)-A32)

- (a) L1 will light.
- (b) L1 will light and L2 will blink.
- (c) Both L1 and L2 will go out.
- (d) L2 will blink.
- (e) L1 will be bright and L2 will be dim.

Fig. III-48. Illustration for Question III-48.

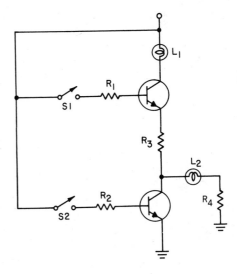

III-49. In the common emitter circuit of Fig. III-49, the following condition is present: [Q. 3.192(J)]
- (a) 180° phase reversal.
- (b) No phase change.
- (c) Very low gain.

Fig. III-49. Common emitter circuit.

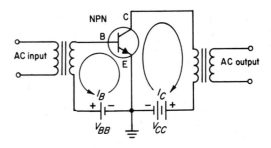

III-50. In the process of pre-emphasis: (Q. 3.163)

(a) The higher frequencies are overemphasized after detection at the receiver.

(b) The lower frequencies are overemphasized at the transmitter, before modulation.

(c) The higher frequencies are overemphasized at the transmitter, before modulation.

(d) The higher frequencies are attenuated at the transmitter, before modulation.

(e) The higher frequencies are caused to be at the same amplitude as the lower frequencies, before modulation.

III-51. If an FM deviation meter was coupled to the output of a phase-modulated transmitter: (Q. 3.167)

(a) It would show no indication at all.

(b) It would show an indication proportional to the amplitude and frequency of the modulation.

(c) It would read exactly the same, as if the transmitter were frequency modulated.

(d) It would show a reading proportional only to the amplitude of the modulation.

(e) It would show a reading proportional only to the frequency of the modulation.

III-52. In a narrow-band FM system the deviation ratio is commonly one and the highest audio frequency is generally limited to: (Q. 3.169)

(a) 15 000 hertz.

(b) 300 hertz.

(c) 10 000 hertz.

(d) 7 500 hertz.

(e) 3 000 hertz.

III-53. In an FM ratio detector, the output audio signal is proportional only to the: (Q. 3.178)

(a) Amplitude of the input IF voltages.

(b) Amplitude of the audio modulation signals.

(c) Ratio of the input IF voltages to the diodes.

(d) Ratio of the input audio voltages.

(e) None of the above.

III-54. The circuit of Fig. III-54 is an inverting op-amp. How is the gain, (A), of the circuit calculated? (Q. 3.133-A25)

(a) $A_f = R_1/R_f \times$ E in

(b) $A_f = R_f/R_1$

(c) $A_f = R_f/R_1 \times$ E out

(d) $A_f = R_f/R_1 \times$ Z in

(e) $A_f = R_1/R_f$

Fig. III-54. Inverting op-amp circuit.

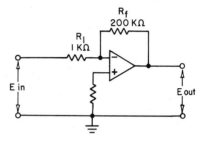

III-55. A certain transmitter has an assigned frequency of 100.00 MHz and a required tolerance of 0.0005 percent. The maximum and minimum allowed frequencies are: (Q. 3.176)

(a) 100 005 000 and 99 995 000 hertz.

(b) 100 000 500 and 99 999 500 hertz.

(c) 100 050 000 and 99 995 000 hertz.

(d) 100 000 500 and 99 999 950 hertz.

(e) None of the above.

III-56. A Gunn Diode is normally used at: (Q. 3.192(U)-A14)

(a) Microwave frequencies.

(b) Ultrahigh frequencies.

(c) Very high frequencies.

(d) Very high power.

(e) None of the above.

III-57. In a PNP, common emitter transistor amplifier, the normal operating voltages are as follows: (Q. 3.184)

(a) Negative at the emitter and negative at the collector.

(b) Positive at the base and negative at the collector.

(c) Negative at the base and negative at the collector.

(d) Positive at the base and positive at the collector.

(e) Positive at the emitter and positive at the collector.

III-58. The alpha cut-off frequency of a transistor is defined as: (Q. 3.188)
  (a) The low frequency at which the gain drops by 3 dB.
  (b) The high frequency of a compensated amplifier at which the gain rises by 3 dB.
  (c) The low frequency of a compensated amplifier at which the gain rises by 3 dB.
  (d) The high frequency at which the current gain drops by 3 dB.
  (e) The high frequency at which the current gain becomes unity.

III-59. Referring to the schematic diagram of Fig. 3.187(a) of the text, the purpose of R3 is (Q. 3.187)
  (a) To help compensate for emitter-to-base junction resistance changes with temperature.
  (b) To compensate for emitter-to collector junction resistance changes with temperature.
  (c) To provide the forward bias for the transistor.
  (d) To increase the overall gain of the amplifier.
  (e) To provide reverse bias for the collector.

III-60. The transistor, common-base amplifier is similar to the vacuum tube: [Q. 3.192(J)]
  (a) Cathode-follower amplifier.
  (b) Video amplifier.
  (c) Grounded-grid amplifier.
  (d) Grounded-cathode amplifier.
  (e) Audio amplifier.

III-61. In comparing the common-collector transistor amplifier with the common-emitter amplifier, it is found that: [Q. 3.192(K)]
  (a) The common-emitter amplifier has lower voltage gain.
  (b) The common-collector amplifier has lower power gain.
  (c) The common-collector amplifier has a current gain of unity.

(d) The common-emitter amplifier has a lower output resistance.
(e) The common-collector amplifier has a signal inversion.

III-62. In a common-emitter transistor amplifier, a change in the base voltage of 0.02 volt produces a collector voltage change of 10 volts. The voltage gain of this amplifier (A_v) is [Q. 3.192(L)]
  (a) 50
  (b) 200
  (c) 500
  (d) 50
  (e) 20

III-63. In Fig. III-63, the base current is approximately: [Q. 3.192(M)]
  (a) 12 μA.
  (b) 120 μA.
  (c) 0.0833 mA.
  (d) 83.8 μA.
  (e) 120 mA.

Fig. III-63. Common-emitter amplifier connected for "fixed" bias.

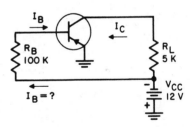

III-64. In a half-wave antenna, the center impedance is: (Q. 3.193)
  (a) 2 500 ohms.
  (b) 73 ohms.
  (c) 730 ohms.
  (d) 250 ohms.
  (e) 36½ ohms.

III-65. In the case of a Marconi antenna, the actual length of the radiating element is: (Q. 3.193)
  (a) One-quarter wavelength.
  (b) One-half wavelength.
  (c) Three-quarter wavelength.
  (d) One wavelength.
  (e) One-eight wavelength.

III-66. In a horizontal-dipole antenna, the polarization is (Q. 3.203)
(a) The same as the polarization of the magnetic field.
(b) In the vertical direction.
(c) In the horizontal direction.
(d) Circular.
(e) Measured at the center of the antenna.

III-67. If a sky wave meets a ground wave at a receiver and they are appreciably out of phase, this may cause: (Q. 3.201)
(a) Distortion of the modulation.
(b) Increased amplitude of the modulation.
(c) Increased amplitude of the received signal.
(d) Fading.
(e) Overloading of the RF stage.

III-68. The velocity of propagation of radio waves in free space is: (Q. 3.208)
(a) 300 000 000 miles per second.
(b) 300 000 meters per second.
(c) 300 000 000 meters per second.
(d) 300 000 000 yards per second.
(e) 300 000 000 000 meters per second.

III-69. In a directional antenna employing both a director and a reflector: (Q. 3.210)
(a) The reflector is placed in front and the director at the rear of the antenna.
(b) Both of these elements are placed in front of the antenna.
(c) Both of these elements are placed at the rear of the antenna.
(d) The director is placed in front and the reflector at the rear of the antenna.
(e) The driven element is placed at the rear of these other two elements.

III-70. If a transmission line is terminated in a resistance equal to its characteristic impedance: (Q. 3.213)
(a) The line loss will be maximum.
(b) The standing-wave ratio will be maximum.
(c) The standing-wave ratio will be minimum.
(d) The input impedance will be twice the terminating resistance.

(e) None of the above.

III-71. Standing waves on a transmission line: (Q. 3.216)
(a) Increase the power fed to the antenna.
(b) Result in a cooler operating line.
(c) Decrease the power fed to the antenna.
(d) Appear only with coaxial lines.
(e) Prevent arcing along the lines.

III-72. Some type of coaxial cables are filled with an inert gas, under pressure. The advantage of this is: (Q. 3.218)
(a) To increase the velocity of propagation.
(b) To prevent increased losses in the line.
(c) To reduce the internal breakdown voltage rating.
(d) To increase the characteristic impedance.
(e) To be able to use smaller diameter lines.

III-73. A grid-dip meter can be used to: (Q. 3.129)
(a) Measure the input-grid impedance of a tube.
(b) Measure the grid voltage of a vacuum-tube stage.
(c) Measure the amplitude of grid-circuit oscillations.
(d) Measure the gain of a vacuum-tube amplifier stage.
(e) Measure the resonant frequency of a tuned circuit.

III-74. The indication on an FM deviation meter is proportional to: (Q. 3.223)
(a) The peak amplitude of the AF modulation.
(b) The RMS amplitude of the AF modulation.
(c) The peak amplitude of the RF wave.
(d) The frequency of the audio modulation.
(e) The instantaneous phase of the RF wave.

III-75. Transmitter harmonics must be attenuated because: (Q. 3.225)
(a) They travel a shorter distance than the fundamental.

(b) They increase the power of the fundamental.

(c) They cause parasitic oscillations.

(d) They interfere with neutralization of RF stages.

(e) They may cause interference with other stations.

III-76. In calibrating a secondary frequency standard against WWV, you should: (Q. 3.221)

(a) Be sure that the WWV transmission is being modulated.

(b) Zero beat a harmonic of the standard against WWV.

(c) Operate all equipment for a period of one minute to ensure stability.

(d) Modulate the standard.

(e) Connect a heterodyne frequency meter to the standard.

III-77. The operation of an absorption wavemeter depends primarily upon: (Q. 3.220)

(a) A calibrated oscillator and a meter.

(b) A calibrated, variable inductor.

(c) A calibrated, tuned circuit and a vacuum-tube voltmeter.

(d) A calibrated, vacuum-tube voltmeter.

(e) The beat between two radio frequencies.

III-78. Fig. 3.222 of the text shows a block diagram of a typical heterodyne-frequency meter. The function of the 1.0-MHz crystal oscillator is: (Q. 3.222)

(a) To be zero beat against the unknown RF input signal.

(b) To verify the calibration of the variable-frequency oscillator.

(c) To check harmonics of the 400 hertz oscillator.

(d) To provide a harmonic which will beat against the unknown RF input signal.

(e) None of the above.

III-79. A primary advantage of a secondary cell as opposed to a primary cell is that a secondary cell: (Q. 3.226)

(a) Has a higher temperature of operation.

(b) Has a lower terminal voltage.

(c) Can be recharged.

(d) Has a paste-type of electrolyte.

(e) Is sealed against the entrance of air.

III-80. The approximate, fully charged voltage of a lead-acid cell is: (Q. 3.232)

(a) 2.1 volts

(b) 1.2 volts.

(c) 1.5 volts.

(d) 1.6 volts.

(e) 6.0 volts.

III-81. A certain battery has a capacity of 160 ampere-hours. If this battery is discharged continuously for 16 hours, the maximum discharge current is: (Q. 3.232)

(a) 16 amperes.

(b) 1.6 amperes.

(c) 10 amperes.

(d) 1 ampere.

(e) 10.6 amperes.

III-82. In meters, a 500 MHz radio wave is equal to: (Q. 3.203)

(a) 6 meters.

(b) 60 meters.

(c) 3 meters.

(d) 0.6 meter.

(e) 0.45 meter.

III-83. The specific gravity of a fully charged, lead-acid storage cell is: (Q. 3.227)

(a) 3.100

(b) 1.300

(c) 13.000

(d) 1.150

(e) 0.1300

III-84. The filter circuit of Fig. III-84 is the following type: (Q. 3.36)

(a) Band stop.

(b) Band pass.

(c) M-derived.

(d) High pass.

(e) Low pass.

Fig. III-84. Filter circuit.

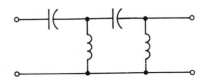

III-85. Excessive sparking at the brushes of a dc motor may be caused by (Q. 3.239)
  (a) A short circuit in an armature coil.
  (b) An open circuit in the field coil.
  (c) Excessive spring tension on brushes.
  (d) Brushes too long.
  (e) Insufficient load on motor.

III-86. A transmitter has a power output of 10 watts. 10 miles away the signal strength is 1 mV. What would be the power increase needed to increase the signal strength to 2 mV? (Q. 3.137-A13)
  (a) 20 watts.
  (b) 40 watts.
  (c) 10 watts.
  (d) 22 watts.
  (e) 30 watts.

III-87. In Fig. III-87, all inputs are low. At what point would you input a high in order to get a high out? (Q. 3.192(U)-A32)
  (a) B
  (b) A
  (c) E
  (d) C
  (e) D

Fig. III-87. Illustration for Question III-87.

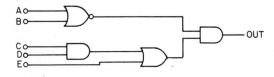

III-88. In Fig. III-88, the voltage across R_1 is: (Q. 3.08)
  (a) 21.4 V.
  (b) 23.4 V.
  (c) 1.4 V.
  (d) 30 V.
  (e) 5 V.

Fig. III-88. Resistor network.

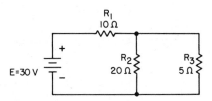

III-89. In Fig. III-89, the voltage between points A and D is 500 V. What is the voltage between points B and C? (Q. 3.66)
  (a) − 250 V.
  (b) − 500 V.
  (c) + 500 V.
  (d) + 250 V.
  (e) + 125 V.

Fig. III-89. Power supply circuit.

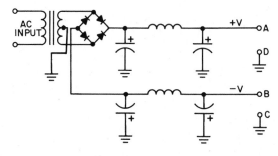

III-90. To find true power of a circuit, multiply the apparent power (V × I), by: (Q. 3.235)
  (a) The tangent of the phase angle.
  (b) The sine of the phase angle.
  (c) V/I
  (d) I × R.
  (e) The cosine of the phase angle.

III-91. The resonant frequency of a cavity resonator depends upon: (Q. 3.251)
  (a) The excitation device dimensions.
  (b) The mode of operation.
  (c) Its physical dimensions.
  (d) Its electrical dimensions.
  (e) The capacitor which tunes it.

III-92. The main frequency determining element of a klystron is: (Q. 3.251)
  (a) The repeller voltage.
  (b) The accelerating voltage.
  (c) Its mode of operation.
  (d) Its resonant cavity.
  (e) The inductance of the output probe.

III-93. Waveguides are not used extensively below about: (Q. 3.249)
  (a) 3 000 MHz.
  (b) 300 MHz.
  (c) 30 000 MHz.

(d) 1 000 MHz.

(e) 750 MHz.

III-94. A magnetron is operated at a duty cycle of .001. It has a peak power output of 100 kilowatts. Its average power is: (Q. 3.248)

(a) 1 000 watts.

(b) 1 000 000 watts.

(c) 100 watts.

(d) 10 000 watts.

(e) None of the above.

III-95. A traveling-wave tube is used at frequencies in the order of: (Q. 3.247)

(a) 8 000 MHz.

(b) 30 MHz.

(c) 300 MHz.

(d) 100 MHz.

(e) 500 MHz.

III-96. The symbol for amplitude modulation, telephony, with double-sideband transmission is: (Q. 3.255)

	Old	New
(a)	P3D.	K3E
(b)	A3A.	R3E
(c)	A3.	A3E
(d)	F3.	F3E
(e)	A5C.	C3F

III-97. The frequency range designated by the abbreviation HF is: (Q. 3.254)

(a) 3 to 30 MHz.

(b) 30 to 300 MHz.

(c) .3 to 30 GHz.

(d) 30 to 300 GHz.

(e) 3 to 30 kHz.

III-98. Figure III-98 is a schematic diagram of a transistor Colpitts crystal oscillator. If the resistor R_F were to become open, the effect would be: (Q. 3.286)

(a) The amplitude of oscillations would increase.

(b) The amplitude of oscillations would drop slightly.

(c) The collector current will become excessive.

(d) The oscillations would cease.

(e) The forward-base bias would increase.

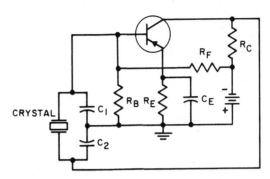

Fig. III-98. A transistor, Colpitts crystal oscillator.

III-99. To double the resonant frequency of Fig. III-99: (Q. 3.45-A29)

(a) Quadruple the value of C_1.

(b) Make C_1 $\frac{1}{4}$ of its value.

(c) Double the value of C_1.

(d) Make C_1 eight times its value.

(e) None of the above.

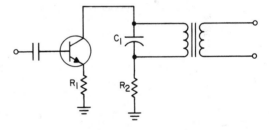

Fig. III-99. Transistor amplifier with tuned output.

III-100. Refer to Fig. 3.288 of the text. An open C_k would result in: (Q. 3.288)

(a) Increased gain of the amplifier.

(b) Increased distortion.

(c) Decreased gain and decreased distortion.

(d) Excessive plate current.

(e) Decreased low- and high-frequency response.

ELEMENT VIII

Ship Radar Techniques

Question 8.01. What are the FCC license requirements for the operator who is responsible for the installation, servicing, and maintenance of ship radar equipment? (R & R 13.61)

Answer. Such an operator must have a General Radiotelephone or first or second-class Radiotelegraph License plus a Ship Radar Endorsement (Element 8).

Discussion. Replacement of fuses and receiving-type tubes may be made by unlicensed persons.

Q. 8.02. Who may operate radar equipment in the Ship Service? (R & R 83.173)

A. The Master, or any person designated by the Master may operate a ship radar station during the course of normal rendition of service.

D. Only properly licensed personnel may supervise or be responsible for the performance of any adjustments or tests during or coincident with the installation, servicing, or maintenance of ship radar equipment while it is radiating energy.

Q. 8.03. Under what conditions may a person who does not hold a radio operator license operate a radar station in the Ship Service? (R & R 83.164)

A. The following conditions apply:

1. The radar equipment shall employ as its frequency-determining element a non-tunable, pulse-type magnetron, or other fixed-tune device.

2. The radar equipment shall be capable of being operated during the course of normal rendition of service in accordance with the radio law and the rules and regulations of the Commission by means of exclusively external controls. See also preceding question.

Q. 8.04. Who may make entries in the installation and maintenance record of a ship radar station? (R & R 83.405)

A. Entries shall be made by or under the personal supervision of the responsible installation, service, or maintenance operator concerned in each case. The station licensee is also jointly responsible for the faithful and accurate making of such entries.

Q. 8.05. What entries are required in the installation and maintenance record of a ship radar station? (R & R 83.405)

A. The following entries are required:

1. The date and place of initial installation.

2. Any necessary steps taken to remedy any interference found to exist at the time of such installation.

3. The nature of any complaint (including interference to radio communication) arising subsequent to initial installation and the date thereof.

4. The reason for the trouble leading to the complaint, including the name of any component or component part which failed or was misadjusted.

5. Remedial measures taken, and the date thereof.

6. The name, license number, and date of the ship radar operator endorsement on the first- or second-class radio operator license of the responsible operator performing or immediately supervising the installation, servicing, or maintenance.

Q. 8.06. Who has the responsibility for making entries in the installation and maintenance record of a ship radar station? (R & R 83.405)

A. See Question 8.04.

Q. 8.07. Within what frequency bands do ship radar transmitters operate? (R & R 83.404)

A. The following frequency bands are authorized: 2 900 to 3 100 MHz; 5 460 to 5 650 MHz; 9 300 to 9 500 MHz.

Q. 8.08. May fuses and receiving type tubes be replaced in ship radar equipment by a person whose operator license does not contain a ship radar endorsement? (R & R 13.61)

A. Yes. No license is required for such replacement.
D. See Q. 8.01.

Q. 8.09. Explain briefly why radar interference to a radiotelephone receiver is frequently characterized by a steady tone in the radio loudspeaker.

A. A steady tone is often heard. This is the pulse repetition rate of keying the radar transmitter (or a harmonic) which is detected in the receiver and heard as an audio tone.

D. Radar transmitters are *pulse* modulated; that is, the carrier is turned on and off (or pulsed) at regular intervals. The pulse repetition rate is determined by the timing unit and is usually within audio range. It is possible for the timing signal to reach receivers directly through power lines, etc., or by being radiated and then detected in the receiver, where it is heard as a steady tone signal. This interference cannot generally be "tuned out" of the receiver because of the harmonics present in each pulse which cause many heterodyning frequencies to be generated. Also, some of the interference is due to detection of the radar carrier signal by the communications receiver and it is not possible to tune out such interference.

Q. 8.10. Describe how various types of interference from a radar installation may be apparent to a person when listening to a communications receiver.

A. Radar interference in a communications receiver will generally take either or both of the two following forms:
1. A steady tone due to the pulsed rate. This will have a musical sound.
2. Noise or "hash." This is usually caused by such items as:
a. Radar motor generator, or
b. Improper grounding, bonding, and shielding.
D. See Q. 8.09, Q. 3.240 and also Q. 3.181.

Q. 8.11. How are the various types of radar interference recognized in (1.) auto-alarm equipment, (2.) direction-finding equipment?
A.
1. Radar interference in auto-alarm equipment may be detected by plugging the earphones into the jack provided on the auto alarm for listening purposes and listening for hash or a steady tone. The radar may be shut down temporarily to determine if it is causing the interference detected.

2. The same procedure as in (a) above may be used to detect radar interference in direction-finding equipment. It may also be advantageous to rotate the D/F loop in trying to find the source of interference, although radar interference from the same ship the D/F is on, may not have directional properties.

D. See Questions 8.09, 8.10, and 8.13.

Q. 8.12. On what frequencies should the radar serviceman look for radar interference to communication receivers on ships equipped with radar?

A. It is possible to find radar interference on practically any combination frequency because of the many harmonics produced by pulsing.

D. See Question 8.09.

Q. 8.13. In checking a direction finder for interference caused by radar equipment, would it be a good policy to check for interference while the D/F loop is being rotated?

A. It would be a good policy, although not necessarily effective as the interference may not show directional properties especially if it is coming from the power line or timer.

See Questions 8.11, 2. and 8.15.

Q. 8.14. List at least two types of indications on a loran scope that signifies that a radar installation is causing interference to the loran.

A. Two types of indications on a loran scope signifying radar interference are:

1. Narrow vertical pulses or "spikes" moving across the scope screen.

2. Hash or "grass" in the vicinity of the scanning lines.

D. The "spikes" on a loran scope are caused by the radar *pulses* originating in the timing unit. Since there is no synchronization between the loran sweep and the radar pulsing, the spikes cannot remain stationary but will move across the screen. "Grass" interference would correspond to hash or noise

if heard on a headset. It may originate in the motor generator set or be caused by poor grounding and bonding.

Q. 8.15. Is there any likelihood of a radar installation causing interference to radio receivers if long connecting lines are used between the radar transmitter and the radar modulator?

A. There is, if such lines are not shielded and terminated properly.

D. The pulses produced by the timing unit to trigger the radar transmitter (magnetron) are of extremely short duration and so contain many harmonic frequencies. Thus a pulse with a *repetition* rate of 1 000 Hz and a pulse width of 1 microsecond could easily contain harmonic frequencies of appreciable amplitude up to and beyond 30 MHz. If long connecting lines which are shielded improperly are used, the radiation of these harmonic frequencies may cause interference in any and all communications and other receivers which may tune to such harmonics.

Q. 8.16. What steps might be taken by a radar serviceman to eliminate a steady-tone of interference to radio communication receivers, or interference to loran receivers evidenced by "spikes?"

A. First check the grounding, bonding, and shielding of all units. If there are built-in filters in the radar set, check these. If not present, such filters may have to be installed.

D. The surest way to eliminate this type of interference is to prevent its *radiation*. Low-pass filters should be installed in all power lines to prevent interference from spreading through this path to other equipment. All grounding, bonding, and shielding should be thorough and well done.

It would be extremely difficult to try and filter out the radar pulses from receiving equipment. The reason for this is that the pulses are very steep and of short duration (1 microsecond or less). This means that such pulses contain *many* harmonics of the fundamental repetition rate. Radar with a pulse repetition rate of say 1 000 Hz could have harmonics of this rate every 1 000 Hz up to many megahertz. Thus, effective filtering is extremely difficult for either the radar transmitter or outside receiving equipment.

If, in this case, you tried to filter out (at the radar) all modulation frequencies above 1 000 Hz, you would completely destroy the shape of the radar pulse by removing its harmonics. Under this condition, the radar could not function usefully.

Q. 8.17. What steps might be taken by a radar serviceman to reduce "grass" on a loran scope or motor-generator noise in communication receivers?

A. Make sure that the commutators, slip rings, and brushes are all in good condition. If filters are present at the motor-generator set, check these and also bonding and grounding as well as power connections for tightness and good contact. See also Questions 8.10 and 8.14.

D. See Q. 3.240 and also Q. 3.181.

Q. 8.18. Name at least four pieces of radio and electronic equipment aboard ship that might suffer interference from the radar installation.

A. Some pieces of equipment which may suffer from radar interference are:
1. Communications receivers
2. Loran
3. Auto-alarm
4. Direction finder
5. Public-address system.
D. See Questions 8.09 through 8.17 and 8.19.

Q. 8.19. Why is it important that all units of a radar installation be thoroughly bonded to the ship's electrical ground?

A. There are two important reasons for this.
1. To place all external metal components at ship's ground and thus prevent

the possibility of shock to operators and others.
2. To reduce interference caused by the radar to other pieces of electronic equipment on shipboard.
D. See Questions 8.14 and 8.17.

Q. 8.20. What may cause bright flashing pie sections to appear on a radar PPI scope?

A. This may be caused by a defective crystal in the AFC section of the radar receiver.

D. Any other defect in an AFC system which would cause "unlocking" and "sweeping" of the AFC could also cause bright flashing to appear. A somewhat similar-appearing defect may be caused by "spoking." Generally, this refers to an irregular rotation of the deflection coil about the neck of the PPI tube. Such irregular rotation may result from a defective servo amplifier, or from mechanical binding of the deflection-coil assembly. It may also result from poor synchro slip-ring contacts or a defective deflection-coil drive motor.

Q. 8.21. What symptoms on a radar scope would indicate that the radar receiver mixer crystal is defective?

A. Any or all of the following symptoms may be present:
1. "Targets" (or echoes) will be unusually weak or will not be seen at all.
2. An excessive noise level ("grass") may be present on the scope.
3. The crystal current meter on the radar receiver will read abnormally low, or zero.
D. Great care should be taken in testing or replacing crystals as static charges may ruin them (see Question 8.49). The front-to-back resistance ratio is a measure of the condition of the crystal and may be checked as indicated in Question 8.22.

Q. 8.22 What tests may a radar serviceman make to determine whether or not the radar receiver mixer crystal is defective?

A. The serviceman may make a quick check by observing the reading on the crystal current meter of the radar receiver. Also, the front-to-back ratio of the crystal may be checked roughly by reading the forward and backward resistance on an ohmmeter.

D. One method of determining the condition of a crystal is to determine its front-to-back resistance ratio. This should be done with a high-impedance or electronic-type voltmeter. First measure the resistance across the crystal with the meter leads in either position. Then reverse the meter leads and measure it again. The larger reading, divided by the smaller reading, gives you the front-to-back ratio. In a normal crystal, this should be in the order of 20 to 1 or so. This may vary with different types, and you should find out the normal front-to-back ratios for the particular crystals in your radar. As a guide in measuring, the 1N23E crystals should read about 250 to 500 ohms for one polarity and about 10 000 ohms for the reverse polarity.

Q. 8.23. In a radar set, what are indications of (1) a defective magnetron, (2) a weak magnet in the magnetron, (3) defective crystal in the receiver converter stage?

A.

1. Defective magnetron:

a. Sweep, noise, and range marks appear, but no targets.

b. Arcing in modulator tube.

c. Low magnetron current indication.

d. Arcing in magnetron.

e. Weak signals on PPI.

f. Targets appear "fuzzy" with "spokes" present.

g. Magnetron undercurrent relay drops out.

h. Poor AFC action.

2. Weak magnet of magnetron:

a. Magnetron current meter will show an increase.

b. Oscillation may stop under extreme case of weakening.

c. Oscillation frequency will probably change.

d. AFC action may be poor.

3. Defective crystal: See Question 8.21.

D. The magnetron should never be operated without the magnet in position. To do so, may destroy the tube in a short time. To prevent this from happening, an overload relay is generally provided to protect the magnetron from damage. These relays are normally an integral part of a modulator. For example, one overload relay may appear in the modulator high-voltage dc supply to protect the supply against defects in the modulator and in the pulse-forming network. Another may be in series with the inverse-protective diode. This relay protects the modulator against defects in the magnetron or magnetron-pulse transformer, which may cause a mismatch between the pulse-forming network and the magnetron. A mismatch tends to cause reflections in the pulse-forming network. Each reflection doubles the voltage on the network and may, if unprotected by the inverse diode and its overload relay, cause a breakdown of the network or its associated components.

The inverse-diode circuit is connected to the input of the pulse-forming network in such a way as to discharge to ground any undesired reflections on the network.

Q. 8.24. What precautions should a radar serviceman take when working with or handling a magnetron to prevent weakening or damage to the magnetron?

A. The following precautions should be taken to protect the *magnet* unit of the magnetron.

1. Do not subject the magnet to extreme heat.

2. Do not subject the magnet to shocks or blows.

3. Keep all magnetic materials, such as tools, away from the immediate vicinity of the magnet.

The magnetron tube proper should be treated as any other delicate electron tube.

Q. 8.25. What precaution should a radar serviceman observe when making repairs or

adjustments to a radar set to prevent personal injury to himself or other persons?

A. First shut off all power. Then be sure to *discharge* all high-voltage capacitors *fully* by means of a suitable grounding stick or cable. Always handle cathode-ray tubes with great care. (If possible, wear gloves and goggles).

D. If adjustments or repairs must be made with power on, always have a second person at the site who can shut off the power and render immediate assistance, if required.

Q. 8.26. Is there any danger in testing or operating radar equipment aboard ship when explosive or inflammable cargo is being handled?

A. There would be some danger due to the possibility of arcing occurring in various parts of the radar equipment. It would be best to take no chances and shut off the radar when inflammable or explosive cargo is being handled.

D. In addition to the danger caused by arcing, a further possible source of ignition is the radar beam itself. This is especially true of a high-power focused beam. The energy in such a beam may be sufficient to ignite certain highly flammable material, or it may cause RF arcing between metallic surfaces, thereby creating a hazard. If any danger of flame or explosion exists, do not operate the radar set (or any other radio transmitter).

Q. 8.27. What consideration should be taken into account when selecting the location of the radar antenna assembly aboard ship?

A. There are two prime considerations:

1. The antenna proper should be located so that it will encounter a minimum number of obstructions while scanning the area around the ship. This is particularly important in the directions forward and off the bows.

2. The length of waveguide run from the antenna to the radar transmitter should be kept to the minimum practical run.

D.

1. Because of the very high frequencies and the parabolic reflector used in radar transmission, the beam is concentrated into very narrow angles. Thus, any obstruction which is in the path of the beam blocks it almost as effectively as if it were a searchlight beam. This may produce areas in which no target pickup is possible and make the radar "blind" in certain directions. This is particularly undesirable in areas directly ahead or behind the ship because of possible collision conditions.

2. The waveguide from the antenna to the radar transmitter is a form of transmission line. There are some rather difficult mechanical considerations to be met in installing waveguides and these, in general, increase as the length of run becomes greater. In addition to the installation problem, the losses of the waveguide increase with greater lengths and there is also a greater possible accumulation of moisture due to condensation, in longer lengths of waveguide.

Q. 8.28. Describe briefly the construction of a waveguide. Why should the interior of the waveguide be clean, smooth, and dry?

A. A waveguide is a form of transmission line and consists of a hollow rectangular or circular pipe. The waves are carried *inside* of the pipe. Waveguides are frequently made of copper or brass and are often plated on the interior with silver to assure a smooth and highly conducting interior surface. The interior should be kept clean, smooth, and dry in order to assure minimum losses and prevent interior arcing.

D. See Q. 3.249, Q. 3.250, Q. 8.30, Q. 8.31, and Q. 8.33 through Q. 8.35.

Q. 8.29. When installing waveguides, why should long, perfectly level sections of waveguides be avoided? Why is a small hole about ⅛ inch in diameter sometimes drilled on the underside of an elbow in a waveguide near the point where it enters the radar transmitter?

A. Long, level runs are undesirable because of the possibility of accumulating condensed moisture inside of the waveguide. A small hole at the lowest point of the waveguide may be drilled to drain out condensed moisture in the waveguide.

D. See Q. 3.250 and Q. 8.28.

Q. 8.30. Why are waveguides used in preference to coaxial lines for the transmission of microwave energy in most shipboard radar installations?

A. Waveguides are preferred over coaxial lines for transmitting microwave energy because their losses are considerably less and also because for a given size they can transmit more power than a coaxial line.

D. A simple comparison between a circular waveguide and a coaxial line of similar dimensions is made here to illustrate the two advantages mentioned above. Refer to Fig. 8.30. A coaxial line has an inner conductor which must be insulated from the outer conductor. Frequently, this is done by means of insulating beads. At microwave frequencies, the dielectric loss in the beads is considerable. A waveguide, as generally used, has only air as a dielectric. However, air has a negligible dielectric loss at practically any frequency which makes the dielectric losses in a hollow waveguide less than that of a coaxial line. The high-frequency current losses in a waveguide are also less than for a coaxial line. This is due to the elimination of the thin inner conductor in which most of the "copper losses" occur.

Fig. 8.30. Comparison between coaxial line and circular waveguide.

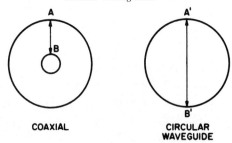

A waveguide can carry more power than a coaxial line of the same diameter. Referring again to the figure, we can see that the distance A'-B' is greater than A-B in the coaxial line. Since the maximum voltage appears between points A'-B' in a round waveguide, it is evident that a greater air space appears in the waveguide than in the coaxial line between maximum voltage points. This means a greater breakdown voltage rating for the waveguide, which, in turn, indicates a greater power handling capacity for a given outside diameter of line.

Q. 8.31. Why are rectangular cross-sectional waveguides generally used in preference to circular cross-sectional waveguides?

A. Circular waveguides are generally not used in radar because their electric field has a tendency to change direction at bends and thus change the polarization of the wave. Rectangular waveguides, on the other hand, can be made to maintain the desired polarization.

D. An exception to the above is to be found in a *rotating* joint which permits the antenna to move with respect to the fixed waveguide. This rotating joint must be circular for mechanical reasons, while the waveguide leading up to the rotating joint is usually rectangular. By means of special devices, the desired polarization is passed on to the antenna regardless of the rotating of the circular joint.

Q. 8.32. Describe how waveguides are terminated at the radar antenna reflectors.

A. There are a number of ways in which a waveguide may be terminated at the radar antenna reflector. Two methods are shown in Fig. 8.32. In part (a) are shown three variations of "horn" radiators. These horns point into the parabolic reflector, which forms the energy into a narrow beam. In part (b) of the figure, the wavelength is terminated in a polystyrene window placed at the focal point of the parabolic reflector.

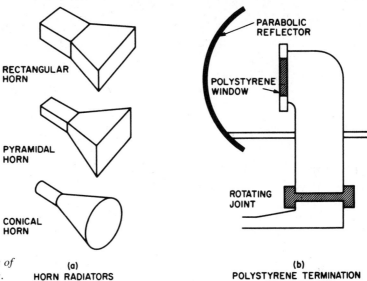

RECTANGULAR HORN

PYRAMIDAL HORN

CONICAL HORN

PARABOLIC REFLECTOR

POLYSTYRENE WINDOW

ROTATING JOINT

Fig. 8.32. Two methods of terminating waveguides.

(a) HORN RADIATORS

(b) POLYSTYRENE TERMINATION OF WAVEGUIDE

D. A brief discussion of each of the two above-mentioned systems follows:

1. Horn radiators are frequently used to obtain directive radiation in the microwave region. Their physical dimensions must be large when compared with the operating wavelength, but this becomes entirely practical at microwave frequencies. The operation of an electromagnetic horn radiator is similar to that of acoustic horns used with certain loudspeaker systems, that is, the horn serves to match the impedance of the waveguide to the impedance of external space. Horns are frequently directed toward a parabolic reflector, which then serves to concentrate the energy into a narrow beam suitable for accurate tracking purposes.

2. Another method of terminating a waveguide at the antenna reflector is by means of a polystyrene window, as shown in part (b) of the figure. The polystyrene window is placed at the focal point of the parabolic reflector. The "window" acts as an impedance-matching device between the waveguide and the parabolic reflector, and free space. The correct impedance match is obtained by selecting the correct physical dimensions of the window.

Q. 8.33. What precautions should be taken when installing vertical sections of waveguides with choke-coupling flanges to prevent moisture from entering the waveguide?

A. Moisture may be prevented from entering by inserting a suitable gasket at each choke-coupling flange and making certain that the flanges are joined tightly.

D. See Q. 3.250. Q. 3.252, and Q. 8.29.

Q. 8.34. Why are choke joints often used in preference to flange joints to join sections of waveguides together?

A. Choke joints are often used in preference to simple flange joints because they prevent loss of energy when used as expansion or rotating joints and also because they will tolerate a moderate degree of misalignment of the waveguide sections without excessive losses.

D. See next question for sketches and discussion of choke joints.

Q. 8.35. Draw a longitudinal section of a waveguide choke joint and explain briefly its principle of operation.

A. See Fig. 8.35. The choke joint includes a circular groove (or "slot") which

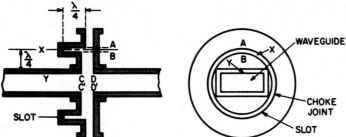

Fig. 8.35. Cross section of a choke joint.

has a depth of one-quarter wavelength. This means that the input impedance of the slot (across *A-B*) will be infinite. The distance from the center of the slot to the waveguide (*X-Y*) is also a quarter wave. The infinite impedance of *A-B* is effectively transformed through the quarter-wave section *X-Y*, into a short circuit across *C-D*. Thus, *C* and *D* are effectively connected *electrically* even though they may not be mechanically.

D. Choke joints are commonly used to connect portions of a waveguide together. Such joints are used to fulfill one or more of these functions.

1. To provide low-loss electrical connection between two parts of the system, such as the waveguide and the magnetron itself.

2. To provide mechanical isolation between two parts of the system so that vibration from one part will not damage another, for example, the antenna vibrations should be transmitted to the magnetron.

3. To permit the removal of certain sections of the waveguides to facilitate repairs and replacements.

The choke joint usually consists of two flanges. These are fixed to the waveguide at their center and face each other. The right-hand flange (in the figure) is machined flat while the left-hand flange contains the slot (described above).

In practice, the two flanges may be separated mechanically by as much as several millimeters. (One millimeter equals about 1/25 of an inch.) The separation must not, in general, exceed this distance to prevent excessive losses and reflections.

Q. 8.36. Describe how a radar beam is formed by a paraboloidal reflector.

A. A narrow beam of RF energy is formed by a parabolic reflector in a manner which is analogous to the reflection of light from a parabolic *light* reflector as used in a searchlight.

D. The RF energy is fed into the reflector at its focal point as shown in the figures of Q. 8.32. Because of the paraboloidal shape of the reflector, practically all of the RF energy which reaches the reflector will be effectively focused into a narrow beam and reflected. The parabolic reflector (or "dish") must be large in comparison with the wavelength. In general, the larger the reflector (diameter), the narrower will be the beam.

Q. 8.37. What effect, if any, does the accumulation of soot or dirt on the antenna reflector have on the operation of a ship radar?

A. A thin layer of soot or dirt has little or no effect upon the operation of a ship radar since the microwave energy is apparently able to penetrate a normal accumulation with only small losses.

D. An excessive amount of "crust" on the surface of the reflector may decrease the performance of the set, especially for weak targets and, in such cases, the reflecting surface should be wiped clean. It is more important to keep the plastic window at the end of the waveguide clean. An accumulation of soot or dirt here can introduce considerable loss.

Q. 8.38. What is the purpose of an echo box in a radar system? Explain the principle of operation of the echo box. What indications may be expected on a radar scope when using an echo box and the radar set is operating properly? When the radar set is not operating properly?

A.

1. The purpose of an echo box is to provide an artificial target which may be used to tune the receiver and also give an indication of the over-all radar system performance.

2. An echo box is a very high Q resonant cavity which is shock-excited by the transmitted pulse. In turn, its oscillations are returned to the receiver and appear as an artificial target on the radar scope.

3. Ship radars generally use a PPI scope. When the echo box is motor-tuned (see discussion), the indication consists of a series of spokes extending radially outward from the center of the PPI scope as shown in part (a) of Fig. 8.38. The spoke length is maximum when the radar is operating normally. When the echo box is simply left at

resonance, the central portion of the PPI scope will be intensified, as shown in part (b) of the figure.

4. When the radar is not operating properly, the length of the spokes (or radius of intensified area) will be less than under normal operation.

D. Normal radar target signals do not, in general, furnish a satisfactory means of checking radar system performance. Variations in atmospheric conditions, the difference in the character of various signals, and also the lack of proper reference signals make it difficult for the operator to check the performance of the radar. This is particularly true of a ship radar where the geographical location of the radar may be constantly changing. To overcome these difficulties, a so-called "echo box" has been designed to furnish a standard reference signal so that the operation of the radar can be checked periodically against the reference in any geographical location. This echo box consists of a high Q resonant cavity with means provided for coupling some transmitter energy into and out of the box. In

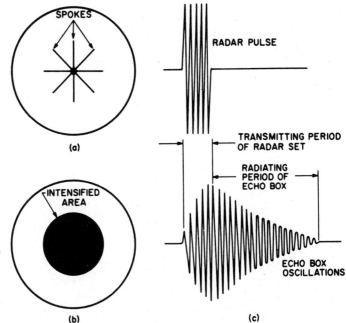

Fig. 8.38. (a) Indication on PPI due to motor-driven echo box, (b) indication on PPI due to echo box set at resonance, (c) relation between transmitted-pulse and echo-box oscillations.

(a)

(b)

(c)

addition, a plunger arrangement is provided to change the length of the cavity and thus vary its resonant frequency. In some cases, this plunger is driven by a motor through a reciprocating device so that the cavity is periodically tuned through resonance for a short period of time. As previously described, this action results in a series of spokes being produced due to the sweep rotation of the PPI scope.

The action of the echo box in providing a reference signal is briefly as follows: During the short transmitting pulse, some of the transmitted energy is fed into the echo box and shock excites it into oscillations which increase in amplitude during the pulse time. This is shown in part (c) of the figure. At the end of the transmitting pulse, the echo box continues to oscillate at a decaying amplitude and reradiates energy back to the radar receiver. A short time after the end of the transmitted pulse, the amplitude of oscillations in the echo box will decrease below the sensitivity level of the receiver. The time from the end of the transmitter pulse to the time when the oscillations no longer produce an indication on the scope through the receiver is known as the "ringing time." This ringing time is a function of the power output of the transmitter and the sensitivity of the receiver and manifests itself on the PPI in the form of spokes or as an intensified area with a certain radius. The length of these spokes (or the radius) is measured when the radar system is known to be operating at good efficiency. Using this as a standard reference, periodic measurements are made with the echo box and any radical decrease in the ringing time means that either the transmitting or receiving components of the radar may be defective and repairs are in order.

Q. 8.39. Draw a block diagram of a radar system, labeling the antenna, duplexer, transmitter, receiver, modulator, timer, and the indicator.

A. See Fig. 8.39.

Q. D. A general discussion of the radar system is presented below for the benefit of students.

Radar (radio direction and ranging) is a specialized application of the principles of radio which makes it possible to detect the presence of near or distant objects regardless of visual or atmospheric conditions; to determine their exact direction and range (distance) and to a limited extent to identify the nature of their character. Basically, a radar set consists of a transmitter and receiver located at the same point, a highly directional antenna system and an indicator (generally a cathode ray tube) to show the presence of reradiated waves and thus of objects. Detection of an object is accomplished by causing a narrow beam of RF energy to "search" a given area. Whenever the beam strikes a conducting object, it causes waves to be reradiated in many directions from the object. A very small fraction of the original radiated energy is returned to the radar set where it is picked up by the same antenna that focused the original radiation upon the object. A receiver of great sensitivity amplifies the received signal (echo) and applies it to a cathode ray tube to provide a visual indication of the presence of the object. The direction of the object will be the same as the direction of the antenna. The range can be determined with great accuracy based upon the fact that radio-frequency energy travels at the velocity of light (300 000 000 meters per second, or about 186 000 statute miles per second). Most radar transmitters employ the pulse modulation method. A radio-frequency pulse of short duration (about 1 microsecond on the average) and high peak power is transmitted at regular intervals. Between transmitted pulses, the receiver is permitted to operate and to detect the reradiated waves. The receiver output is connected to the indicator where the difference in time between the transmitted and received waves can be measured and the range determined. As an example, assume that a pulse is transmitted to an object 18.6 miles away. In one microsecond the pulse can travel .186

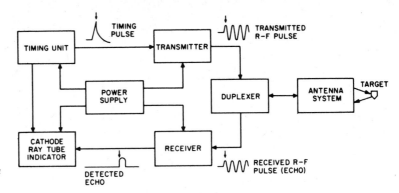

Fig. 8.39. Block diagram of a radar system.

miles (328 yards). Therefore, it will require 100 microseconds for the pulse to reach the object. When it strikes the object, it is re-radiated without loss of time and returns to the radar set in an additional 100 micro-seconds, or a total elapsed time of 200 mi-croseconds. Note that the wave actually has to travel twice the distance to the object. Because the range thus provided is twice the actual range, an allowance must be made in the indicator to measure only one-half of the elapsed time, or the true range.

The Indicator: (Discussion of the in-dicator is here restricted to that type directly applicable to marine radar sets.) The indicator must be a device which can accurately measure the elapsed time between trans-mitted and received pulses and convert it directly into range. It must also be capable of discriminating against objects with dif-ferent ranges and the same bearing, and be-tween objects with different bearings and the same range. The P.P.I. (plan-position-indicator) cathode-ray tube admirably fulfills all of the above requirements by providing a polar chart of the immediate area sur-rounding the ship from a minimum range of about 80 yards to approximately 40 miles. The P.P.I. scope provides a continuous plot of both moving and fixed objects. The sweep (time base) starts at the center of the tube at a time which is directly related to the originating time of the transmitting pulse. It travels radially out to the circumference (like the spoke of a wheel). This sweep line is divided into equal distances by means of range markers which provide indications

about a half-mile apart on low ranges, thus affording instantaneous visual checks of the range of objects. Objects are indicated (as well as range markers) by a bright spot upon the P.P.I. tube at a distance from the center corresponding to the range of the object. The radial sweep is caused to rotate (as a wheel spoke would rotate) in exact syn-chronism with the antenna, so that the object indication upon the P.P.I. tube will be of the same bearing as the antenna. The P.P.I. tube has a relatively long persistence screen, so that as the sweep rotates, a continuous picture of the surrounding area appears on the screen.

The Timer: The timer unit (or syn-chronizer or keyer is generally the most complicated part of the radar and has a num-ber of important functions to perform. A detailed discussion is beyond the scope of this book, but a general list of its functions is as follows:

1. Determines pulse repetition rate.
2. Determines range markers.
3. Provides range markers.
4. Coordinates all operations in the system.
5. Provides sweep, with blanking and unblanking.
6. Specialized functions such as "heading flash" in marine systems.

The Transmitter: The transmitter usu-ally consists of the following units:

1. A pulse shaping circuit, to determine the length of the transmitted pulse.
2. A modulator, which applies the pulse

(about 1 microsecond, 10 000 to 15 000 volts) to the magnetron, and

3. The magnetron, which is the actual RF oscillator (There are no RF amplifiers.)

The Antenna System: In order to obtain accurate bearings, it is quite necessary that the radiation pattern of the antenna be extremely narrow. Such a pattern can be most conveniently obtained by the use of a parabolic reflector of suitable dimensions, which at these frequencies is fed by means of waveguide radiators (Q. 8.27 and Q. 8.32). The parabolic reflector focuses the RF energy into a narrow beam, just as a searchlight reflector provides a narrow light beam from a light source. For the RF beam to be sufficiently narrow, the dimensions of the parabolic reflector must be in the order of many wavelengths. To accomplish this and yet restrict the overall dimensions of the antenna to a resonably small size, it is necessary that the operating wavelength be short (3 centimeters; there are 2.54 centimers per inch). A marine radar antenna has a radiation pattern which is extremely narrow with respect to azimuth (compass) directions, but is relatively broad with respect to vertical directions.

The Receiver: Radar receivers are almost always of the superheterodyne type. The receiver must have great sensitivity in order to receive and amplify the very weak reradiated RF pulse to a value suitable for use by the P.P.I. scope. Since the input signal may be in the order of one microvolt, the IF amplifier must have a gain in the order of one or two million to provide sufficient input signal to the second detector (1 or 2 volts). In order to pass the very steep and short-duration pulses, the IF amplifier must be capable of passing a band of frequencies in the order of 5 to 10 megahertz. The wide band-pass reduces the gain of the individual stages so that the number of stages in the IF amplifier is often more than six to eight.

There are no RF amplifiers in the receiver. The input signal is applied directly to a crystal mixer, and the local oscillator

is generally of the reflex klystron type (See Q. 3.246 and Q. 8.70)

The intermediate frequencies are in the order of 30 megahertz. Automatic frequency control is often employed, to compensate for frequency drift of the magnetron or local oscillator (reflex klystron), in order to maintain the proper difference frequency of 30 megahertz, and thus provide the maximum indicated response upon the P.P.I. tube at all times.

For a discussion of a duplexer, see Q. 8.41.

Q. 8.40. Explain briefly the principle of operation of a radar system.

A. Very briefly, radar operates to detect an object at a distance by directing a narrow beam of RF energy at the object and then detecting a portion of the reflected beam when it arrives back at the radar.

D. For a more complete discussion of radar, see Q. 8.39.

Q. 8.41. Draw a simple block diagram of a radar duplexer system, labeling the waveguide, the TR box, the anti-TR box, the receiver, and the transmitter.

A. See Fig. 8.41.

D. Ship radars use a common antenna system for transmitting and receiving. In such a system, it is necessary to protect the receiver from damage due to the high-power transmitter pulse and also to prevent the transmitter from absorbing too much power from the reflected echo between transmitting pulses. It is, therefore, necessary to provide some form of "switch" to disconnect the receiver effectively from the waveguide during the transmitter pulse and to disconnect the transmitter from the waveguide the rest of the time. Such a switch is often called a *duplexer*. This is not a simple switch, but is made up of certain measured lengths of waveguide and two special spark-gap tubes. How this switch operates may be seen with the aid of the simplified drawing shown in part (b) of the figure.

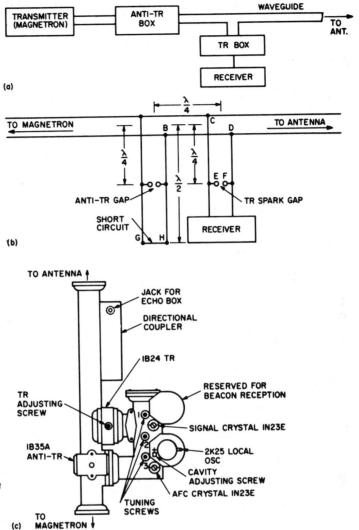

Fig. 8.41. (a) Block diagram of duplexer; (b) simplified diagram of duplexer; (c) duplexer assembly.

When the transmitter pulses, both of the spark gaps are fired and represent practically a short circuit across the gap terminals. The anti-TR connects into the waveguide a quarter-wavelength from its gap and thus reflects an open circuit across points *A* and *B*. The transmitter see a very high impedance at *A-B* and does not "pour" any appreciable power into the anti-TR. The TR gap also fires at this time producing a short across *E-F*. This prevents all but a small amount of power from entering the receiver. A high impedance appears at *C-D*, one-quarter wavelength away, and permits the transmitter power to proceed to the antenna almost without loss. Thus while the transmitter is pulsing, the receiver is protected and the full power is delivered to the antenna. After the transmitter pulse, both gaps become open circuits. The shorting bar of the anti-TR line is a half-wavelength from *A-B* and reflects a *short* across these points *(A-B)*. This short is, in turn, reflected to points *C-D*, one-quarter wavelength away, as an *open* circuit and effectively blocks received signals from passing this point toward the transmitter. Instead, the received power is effectively all shunted into the receiver. In part (c) of the figure is shown a complete drawing of a typical duplexer.

Q. 8.42. Draw a simple block diagram of a radar receiver, labeling the signal crystal, the local oscillator, the AFC crystal stage, the IF amplifier, and the discriminator.

A. See Fig. 8.42.

D. For general discussion of a radar receiver, see Question 8.39. A brief discussion of the AFC system follows. Two signals are fed into the AFC crystal detector. One is from the magnetron (greatly attenuated), the other from the local oscillator (reflex klystron). The difference frequency between these two is detected, amplified, and fed into the discriminator. The discriminator is resonated at 30 MHz, the normal IF frequency of the signal circuits. If the magnetron and local oscillator are operating at their correct frequencies 30 MHz apart (to produce 30 MHz IF). There will be no output from the discriminator. If, however, either the magnetron or klystron (or both) should drift in frequency, the output of the AFC crystal will be greater or less than 30 MHz. This will cause an output voltage from the discriminator whose sign and magnitude are proportional to the drift. This control voltage is amplified and fed back to the reflector plate of the klystron in such a way as to cause the frequency of the klystron to change to a value needed to produce again, a 30 MHz IF.

Q. 8.43. Draw a simple cross-sectional diagram of a magnetron showing the anode, cathode, and the direction of electronic movement under the influence of a strong magnetic field.

A. See Fig. 8.43.
D. See Q. 3.248 and Q. 8.70

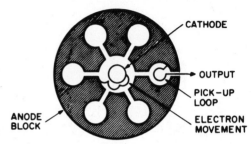

Fig 8.43. Cross section of magnetron showing electron movement.

Q. 8.44. Explain briefly the principle of operation of the magnetron.

A. See Q. 3.248.
D. See also Fig. 8.43 and Q. 8.70.

Q. 8.45. Why is the anode in a magnetron in a radar transmitter normally maintained at ground potential?

A. This is done to protect personnel from high-voltage shocks and to reduce the problem of insulating the magnetron from the chassis.

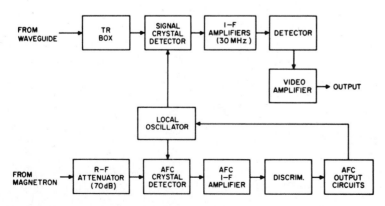

Fig. 8.42. Simplified diagram of radar receiver.

D. The anode (containing the resonant cavities) comprises the metal shell of the magnetron. This is mechanically coupled to the waveguide. If the high-voltage pulse were to be applied to the anode, it would be as a highly positive pulse. This would necessitate the insulation of the anode from the chassis as well as the insulation of the waveguide from the anode. This is difficult to do and expensive. In addition, even if the insulation were present, there would be great danger to personnel encountering the magnetron or even the waveguide. To overcome this, the metal shell of the magnetron (and waveguide) is *grounded* and a *negative* high-voltage pulse fed into the *cathode* of the magnetron. This makes construction much simpler and also is much safer for handling by personnel.

Q. 8.46. Draw a simple frequency-converter circuit (mixer) as frequently used in radar superheterodyne receivers and indicate which is the crystal stage.

A. See Fig. 8.46. (See also Fig. 8.41.)
D. See Q. 8.39.

Q. 8.47. What is the purpose of the klystron tube in a radar set?

A. The klystron tube is the local oscillator of the radar receiver. It is coupled to the mixer crystal to produce the IF as shown in Question 8.46.

Q. 8.48. Explain briefly the principle of operation of the reflex klystron.

A. A schematic of a reflex klystron is shown in Fig. 8.48. The klystron is a resonant-cavity device which is energized by the action of "bunches" of electrons. Briefly, it operates as follows. Electrons are emitted by the cathode in a steady stream and accelerated toward the cavity grids by the potential on the accelerating grid. When the stream of electrons first enters the cavity grids, the resonant cavity is shock-excited into oscillation thus producing alternating voltages across the cavity grids. The fields produced by these alternating potentials act upon the electron stream to produce "bunches" of electrons separated by spaces in which there are very few electrons. After

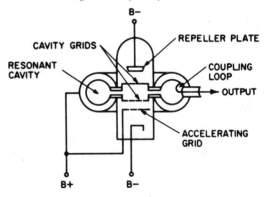

Fig. 8.48. Reflex klystron.

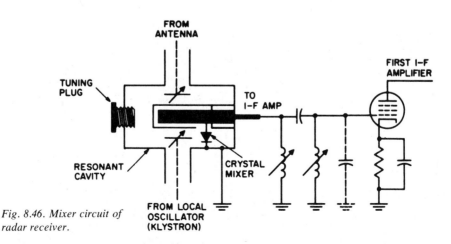

Fig. 8.46. Mixer circuit of radar receiver.

passing the cavity grids, the *bunches* are repelled by the negative potential of the repeller plate and return again to these grids. The bunches have the proper *spacing* and *timing* when returning so that oscillations are maintained in the resonant cavity. The volume of the cavity is varied to make large changes of frequency. Small changes of frequency are made by varying the repeller voltage over a narrow range.

D. See Q. 3.246 and Q. 8.70.

Q. 8.49. What care should be taken when handling silicon crystal rectifier cartridges for replacement in radar superheterodyne receivers?

A. The technician should discharge any static charge in his body by touching a convenient ground with his hands. The crystal should be handled very carefully as it may be damaged mechanically by applying excessive pressures.

D. The silicon crystals which are used as mixers (and AFC crystals) have a *low, safe* current rating. They may be damaged by static charges accumulated on the body of the person handling them. Such persons should first "discharge" themselves by touching a suitable grounding joint. The crystals are wrapped in lead foil when stored, to protect them against stray charges. This foil should not be removed, until the crystal is placed in use. The unit into which the crystal is inserted should also be grounded before installation.

Q. 8.50. What nominal intermediate frequencies are commonly found in radar receivers?

A. Radar receivers commonly use IF's of 30 or 60 MHz.

D. See Q. 8.39 and Q. 8.42.

Q. 8.51. Describe briefly the construction and operation of radar TR and anti-TR boxes. What is the purpose of a "keep alive" voltage?

A. The operation of TR and anti-TR boxes is fully described in Q. 8.41. The construction of a TR box is shown in Fig. 8.51. This consists of a TR tube mounted in a resonant cavity. The high Q of the cavity reduces the power needed to maintain the spark gap. The TR tube contains two metal electrodes which act as a spark gap. The tube itself is partially evacuated and has a small amount of water vapor inside to reduce the time of deionization.

A third electrode is placed inside of one of the main electrodes. This is known as a "keep-alive" electrode. It has a "keep-alive" voltage applied to it. This is a constant negative potential (about 1 000 volts) which keeps the gas and vapor in the tube slightly ionized at all times and accelerates the breakdown of the main gap. A TR box is similar to an anti-TR box, but may not have a "keep-alive" electrode in the TR tube.

D. See Question 8.41.

Q. 8.52. What is the purpose of the discriminator stage in a radar superheterodyne?

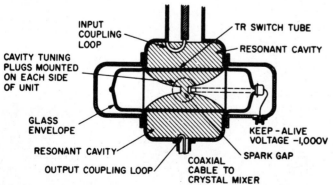

INPUT COUPLING LOOP

TR SWITCH TUBE

RESONANT CAVITY

CAVITY TUNING PLUGS MOUNTED ON EACH SIDE OF UNIT

GLASS ENVELOPE

RESONANT CAVITY

OUTPUT COUPLING LOOP

COAXIAL CABLE TO CRYSTAL MIXER

SPARK GAP

KEEP-ALIVE VOLTAGE -1,000V

Fig. 8.51. Cross section of TR switch.

A. The discriminator is part of the AFC system. Its function is to generate a corrective voltage which is sent to the local oscillator (klystron) to maintain the correct intermediate-frequency difference output from the mixer.

D. See Q. 8.42 for a discussion of the AFC system. See also Q. 3.177(4).

Q. 8.53. What type of detector is used frequently in radar receivers?

A. A silicon crystal detector (mixer) is commonly used.

D. See Q. 8.40, Q. 8.42, Q. 8.46, and Q. 8.49.

Q. 8.54. What is "sea return" on a radar scope?

A. "Sea return" is the reflection, or "echo," of radar signals bouncing off the waves of the sea and returning to the radar set.

D. Sea return response in a radar set is caused by the transmitted pulses striking the tops of waves at such an angle that they are reflected back to the radar antenna and appear on the PPI (Plan Position Indicator) scope as a solid block of interference. Due to the reflection angles involved in sea return, such interference is usually confined to areas within a few miles of the radar set.

It is, therefore, possible to discriminate to some extent against the reception of sea return in favor of targets within the interference area. This can be automatically accomplished by causing the receiver gain to be lower at times representing distances of a few miles from the radar, and automatically restoring the normal gain at times representing greater distances where sea return is not troublesome. A reduction of gain at relatively close distances is effective in this case, since a ship target reflects a signal back to the radar which is considerably stronger than the signal due to sea return. Reducing the gain in sea return areas, reduces the intensity of the PPI display due to sea return to a greater extent than it reduces the

display due to target return, and thus the target often can be observed through sea return interference.

(See also Q. 8.39 for basic discussion of radar set.)

Q. 8.55. Explain briefly the purpose of the sensitivity time control circuit in a radar set.

A. The sensitivity time control automatically reduces the gain of the radar receiver for nearby targets, to reduce interference from such effects as sea return.

D. In order to reduce sea return response in a radar set, the operator should manually adjust the "Suppressor" control (or sensitivity time control, STC) until the solid pattern of sea return is thinned out and stronger ship targets which may be present close to the radar set are more easily observed. See also Q. 8.54.

Q. 8.56. What is the distance in nautical miles to a target if it takes 123 microseconds for a radar pulse to travel from the radar antenna to the target, back to the antenna and be displayed on the PPI scope?

A. The distance to the target is 10 nautical miles.

D. A radar pulse will go out 1 nautical mile *and return* in about 12.3 microseconds. Therefore, in 123 microseconds, the distance to the target is, $123/12.3 = 10$ nautical miles.

Q. 8.57. What is the purpose of an "artificial transmission line" in a radar set?

A. An "artificial transmission line" determines the shape and duration of the transmitted pulse.

D. (See also Question 8.58.) Ship radar transmitters generally have output RF pulses varying in length from ¼ to 1 microsecond. This output RF pulse is obtained by triggering the magnetron with a high-voltage dc pulse. The pulse must have a fixed duration and a square top for good magnetron frequency stability. In order to obtain a suitable driving pulse, a "line-controlled" blocking oscillator is frequently employed. This consists of a high-voltage blocking oscillator whose pulse output duration is controlled by an artificial transmission line in its grid circuit. Briefly, the operation is as follows: A driving pulse from the synchronizer is applied to the blocking oscillator (one-shot) and forces it into conduction, thus starting the output pulse. This pulse also travels down the artificial line and is reflected when it reaches its open end. This reflected pulse comes back to the grid of the blocking oscillator with negative polarity cutting it off and terminating the output pulse. By suitable selection of the constants of the line, the time of travel up and back can be determined to a very close degree, thus controlling the length of the output pulse. The pulse from the blocking oscillator triggers a modulator tube, which actually pulses the magnetron at high voltage (10 to 15 kV). The construction of an artificial transmission line is described in Q. 8.58.

Q. 8.58. Draw a simple diagram of an artificial transmission line showing inductance and capacitance, source of power, the load, and the electronic switch.

A. See Fig. 8.58 and also Q. 8.57.

D. A convenient means of producing a very short duration rectangular pulse is to use an artificial transmission line. This is a device, which by lumped constants of capacitance and inductance, simulates an actual line with a certain characteristic impedance and wavelength. An actual line is not used because its physical length would be prohibitive. The required pulse duration is controlled by designing the line to have a certain equivalent "length." Thus, it takes an impulse a definite time to travel to the end of the line (open) and be reflected back to the load, in this case, the grid circuit of a blocking oscillator. The operation of this circuit is described in Q. 8.57. See also Q. 8.61.

Q. 8.59. What component in a radar set determines the pulse repetition rate?

A. The pulse repetition rate is determined by the timer (or synchronizer) unit.

D. See Q. 8.39 and Q. 8.40. Typical repetition rates (depending upon transmitted pulse width) are 100, 200, 500, 750, 1 000, 2 000, and 3 000 Hz. The higher the repetition rate, the narrower the transmitted pulse width must be in order not to overload the magnetron and modulator. The duty cycle (see Q. 8.62) remains fairly constant over the range of repetition rates.

Q. 8.60. What circuit element determines the operating frequency of the self-blocking oscillator?

A. See Fig. 8.60(a) for a tube-type, free-running, blocking oscillator and Fig. 8.60(b) for a transistor type.

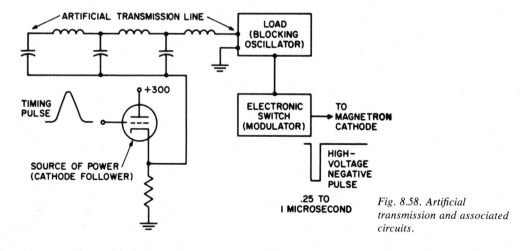

Fig. 8.58. Artificial transmission and associated circuits.

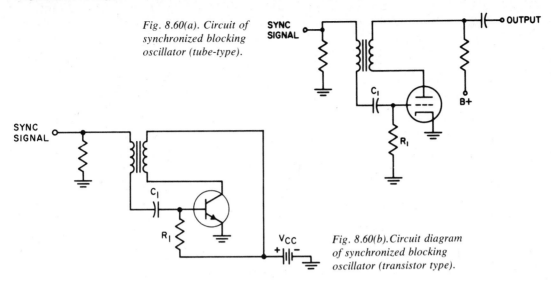

Fig. 8.60(a). Circuit of synchronized blocking oscillator (tube-type).

Fig. 8.60(b).Circuit diagram of synchronized blocking oscillator (transistor type).

D. The question is a little indefinite since there is no *single* circuit element which determines the repetition frequency. All of the circuit elements, including the tube and transformer as well as the operating potentials, affect the frequency. However, it is true that R_1 and C_1 have the greatest effect on frequency.

Note in the transistor version that R1 is returned to $+V_{CC}$, rather than to ground. This is essential for the oscillator to be self-starting, as a transistor with zero bias is biased at class C operation. Connecting R1 to $+V_{CC}$ provides the required forward bias to cause the transistor to be conducting before the start of oscillations.

In marine radar sets, a synchronized blocking oscillator is used to produce the trigger pulse for the transmitter. This will oscillate for only one cycle for each synchronizing pulse applied to the grid. In this case, the repetition frequency is determined solely by the synchronizing pulses. This would require a "one-shot" blocking oscillator, which simply means that the oscillator is biased off, in the absence of a synchronizing pulse.

Q. 8.61. What is the purpose of the rotary spark gap used in some radar sets?

A. The rotary spark gap is a mechanical system for modulating a magnetron directly at high level.

D. When an *electronic* modulator tube is used, it is frequently connected in a manner shown in the simplified drawing which is part (a) of Fig. 8.61. This operates briefly as follows:

Between triggering pulses, the modulator tube V_1 is held below cut-off by a fixed bias. During this interval, the high-voltage capacitor, C_1, charges through the charging diode, V_2, as shown by the dotted arrows, to about 12 000 volts (for example). When the triggering pulse appears, it overcomes the modulator bias, the modulator tube conducts heavily, and the high voltage of C_1 is applied to the magnetron with negative polarity. This is shown by the solid arrows. C_1 only discharges a relatively small amount, thus maintaining almost a constant voltage.

Some radar units use a spark gap and pulse-forming line instead of the blocking-oscillator modulator system. This has the advantage of generating the magnetron high-voltage dc pulse directly at high level instead of having to amplify it in several tubes. No modulator tubes are required and the efficiency is very high (80 to 90 per cent). It has, however, the disadvantages of being a *mechanical* rather than an electronic device, of generating radio-frequency interference

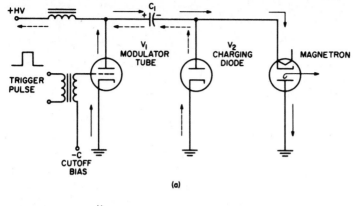

(a)

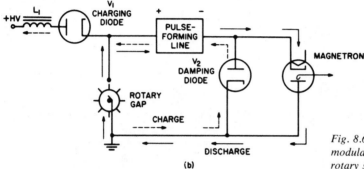

(b)

Fig. 8.61.(a) Electronic modulator for magnetron; (b) rotary spark-gap modulator.

which must be filtered, and offering no opportunities for accurate pulse shaping. A simplified drawing of such a system is shown in part (b) of the figure. The true operation of this circuit is quite complicated, but a simplified explanation follows. The rotary gap makes contacts at a very high rate, commonly at 400, 800, or 1 600 times per second. When the gap is open, the pulse-forming line charges through V_1, L_1 and V_2. This produces shock excitation of a resonant circuit consisting of L_1 and the capacitance of the pulse-forming line. Because of the diodes, the oscillation causes the line to charge to a voltage about 1.8 times the applied voltage and remain at the value. When the gap fires, the voltage at point A becomes zero and the now negative pulse-forming line voltage is applied to the magnetron for the duration of the arc. The cycle then repeats.

Q. 8.62. What is the peak power of a radar pulse if the pulse width is 1.0 microsecond, pulse repetition rate is 900 and the

average power is 18 watts? What is the duty cycle?

A. The peak power is 20 000 watts. The duty cycle is 0.0009.

D. Step 1: The duty cycle must *first* be found.

$$\text{Duty cycle} = \frac{\text{Pulse width}}{\text{Pulse repetition time}}$$

$$\text{Pulse repetition time} = \frac{1}{F} = \frac{1}{900}$$

$$\text{Duty cycle} = \frac{0.000001}{1/900} = 0.0009$$

Step 2: Find the peak power.

$$\text{Peak power} = \frac{\text{Average power}}{\text{Duty cycle}}$$

$$= \frac{18}{0.0009} = 20\ 000 \text{ watts}$$

Q. 8.63. What is meant by the bearing resolution of a radar set?

A. *Bearing resolution* may be defined

as the ability of a radar set to distinguish between targets at the same range but different azimuth directions.

D. Bearing resolution is mainly determined by the *width* of the radar beam. A narrow beam is better able to separate targets at the same radial distance than a wide beam. The resolution is also influenced by the receiving circuits and the PPI scope.

Q. 8.64. Explain how heading flash and range-marker circles are produced on a radar PPI scope.

A.

1. Heading flash is produced whenever the radar beam points dead ahead. This is accomplished by closing a switch in the antenna which causes an intensifier pulse of short duration to intensify a radial line of the PPI scope representing the heading.

2. Range-marker circles are produced on a radar PPI scope as follows: A range-marker oscillator, in conjunction with suitable squaring and peaking circuits, produces "pips" (or short positive pulses). There is a definite spacing between these pips, corresponding to range in miles (or yards), which is a function of the range-marker oscillator frequency. These pips are produced in synchronism with sweep and are applied at intensified pulses to the grid of the PPI. Each time the sweep causes the beam to go out

from the center to the edge, a series of accurately spaced intensified pips appears. Since the sweep rotates, these pips then form range-marker circles. (See Fig. 8.67.)

D.

1. The radar operator must know exactly when the radar beam is dead ahead so that he can accurately indicate the relative bearing of all targets. The PPI sweep line is normally blanked out as it rotates with only the targets intensifying the screen. To provide heading flash (or dead-ahead indication), it is necessary to intensify the sweep line momentarily each time the antenna points dead ahead. Briefly, this is accomplished by the momentary closing of a cam-actuated microswitch located in the antenna assembly. This microswitch is closed only when the antenna points dead ahead. When the switch is closed, it actuates a circuit that produces an intensifier pulse of the desired duration. This pulse (positive) is fed to the grid of the PPI scope where it causes a bright sweep line to appear on the PPI in an azimuth indication corresponding to the dead-ahead position of the antenna.

2. A block diagram of a range-marker generating system from a typical marine radar* is shown in Fig. 8.64. This operates as follows:

*Radiomarine Corp. of America.

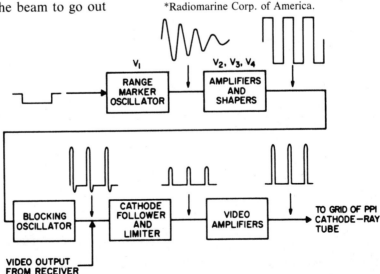

Fig. 8.64. Block diagram of a range-marker system.

a. The negative input pulse to V_1 shock excites an *L-C* tank circuit in the cathode into sine-wave oscillation. The frequency depends on the range in use and the *number* of range rings desired on that particular range. On the 1½ mile range, three rings will be seen on one model.

b. The sine waves from the *L-C* tank are then shaped by the three following stages to form *square* pulses with extremely sharp leading edges.

c. The positive output of these amplifiers is used to trigger a "one-shot" (or single-swing) blocking oscillator which generates a short duration (⅓ microsecond) pulse in synchronization with the leading edge of each squared-up pulse. These are the range-marker pulses.

d. The range-marker pulses are then fed through a cathode follower and limiter into a two-stage video amplifier. The output of the video amplifier then feeds directly into the grid of the PPI where each pip produces an intensification of the sweep.

Q. 8.65. Draw a diagram of a cathode-ray tube as used in radar showing the principal electrodes in the tube and the path of the electron beam.

A. See Fig. 8.65.
D. See Q. 8.66, Q. 8.67, and Q. 8.68.

Q. 8.66. What is the purpose of aquadag coatings on radar cathode-ray tubes?

A. (See Fig. 8.65.) The purpose of the aquadag coating is to act as an anode for the cathode-ray tube.

D. Aquadag is a graphite solution in water which is applied as a coating to the inside of a cathode-ray tube (as in Fig. 8.65). It is a good conductor and is employed in radar cathode-ray tubes as a second anode. It also acts as an electrostatic shield to protect the electron beam from stray electric fields.

Q. 8.67. Explain the principle of operation of the cathode-ray PPI tube and explain the function of each electrode.

A. 1. *Principle of Operation.* A PPI tube is one on which a "map" of the area being scanned is presented insofar as targets and fixed land echoes are concerned. (See Fig. 8.67). The center of the PPI screen represents the position of the radar antenna. The electron beam moves out radially from the center to the outer edge and is *rotated* in synchronism with the radar antenna. In practice, the scanning beam proper is blanked out and only the target indications and range rings are *intensified* on the screen. The distance from the center of the screen to the target is a measure of the *range*, while the radial *direction* indicates the target's azimuth bearing (relative).

2. *Function of Electrodes.* (See Fig. 8.65.) The PPI tube has a filament similar to that used in receiving tubes. This filament

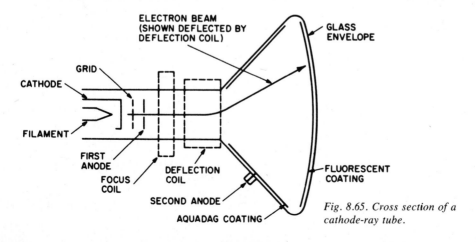

Fig. 8.65. Cross section of a cathode-ray tube.

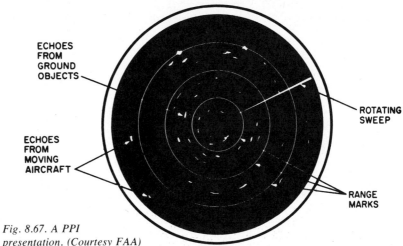

ECHOES FROM GROUND OBJECTS

ECHOES FROM MOVING AIRCRAFT

ROTATING SWEEP

RANGE MARKS

Fig. 8.67. A PPI presentation. (Courtesy FAA)

heats up and, in turn, heats a coated cathode, causing electrons to be emitted from the cathode. These electrons first encounter a grid which functions in a manner similar to the grid in a conventional triode. That is, it controls the amount of electrons passing it and, thus, the *intensity* of the spot produced on the PPI screen. After passing the grid, the electrons (now restricted to a fairly narrow stream) are acted upon by the first anode, which produces some acceleration of the electron stream toward the screen. Further and final acceleration is provided by the second anode (aquadag coating).

D. PPI tubes frequently employ *magnetic* focusing accomplished by a focus coil, which is located as indicated in Fig. 8.65. Deflection is usually accomplished by a magnetic deflection coil which moves the beam radially out from the center to the outer edge of the screen. The rotating effect of the sweep may be accomplished by *rotating* the deflection coil mechanically in synchronism with the antenna. (See Q. 8.69.)

Another method of rotating the sweep, employs fixed deflection coils. This system employs a *rotating magnetic field*, which is synchronized with the movement of the radar antenna.

Q. 8.68. What precautions should the service and maintenance operator observe

when replacing the cathode-ray tube in a radar set?

A. The radar power-supply system should be turned off and *all* high-voltage capacitors *completely discharged* by a well-insulated screw-driver or other device. Care must be taken to avoid breakage of a cathode-ray tube which may result in serious injury to the serviceman.

D. It has been demonstrated recently that cuts resulting from broken cathode-ray tubes (or other fluorescent devices) may result in serious poisoning of the bloodstream. This is due to the action of the fluorescent material. Therefore, be especially careful in disposing of such broken devices to avoid cutting the hands, arms, or face. The use of gloves is to be recommended in such cases.

Q. 8.69. Draw a simple diagram showing how a synchro generator located in the radar antenna assembly is connected to a synchro motor located in the indicator to drive the deflection coils. Show a proper designation of all leads, designating where ac voltages (if needed) are applied.

A. A. See Fig. 8.69.

D. Ship radars employ one or more PPI indicators (see Q. 8.39 and Q. 8.65). In this type of indicator, it is necessary to synchronize the rotation of the sweep line on the PPI tube with the rotation of the radar antenna. This is usually accomplished by a servo system, as illustrated in Fig. 8.69.

A synchro-control transformer has its rotor geared to the rotation of the antenna. The rotor (R_1, R_2) of this synchro is supplied with 115 volt, 400-Hz excitation. As the rotor turns, varying voltages are induced in the three-winding stator (S_1, S_2, S_3). These varying voltages are fed directly to the stator of the indicator synchro-control transformer. (Note that the rotor of the indicator synchro is mechanically coupled to the deflection coil and to the indicator-servo motor.) As a result, an "error" voltage is induced in the indicator-synchro rotor. This "error" voltage is fed to the grid of the first stage of the servo amplifier. The output of the servo amplifier is a push-pull amplifier that feeds one winding of a two-phase servo motor. The second phase (displaced by 90 degrees) is excited directly from the 115-volt, 400-Hz line. As a result of the servo-amplifier output, the servo motor is caused to rotate.

The phase of the "error" voltage is such that the servo motor rotates to drive the deflection coil in the same direction as the antenna. Further, the amplitude of the

"error" voltage is high when the antenna and deflection coil are greatly out of synchronization (in azimuth) and decreases to a very low amplitude when the two are in synchronization. In order to continuously drive the deflection coil, a small "error" voltage must always be present. This means that a very small *lag* angle always exists between the antenna and the deflection coil.

Since the indicator synchro is directly geared to the deflection coil, it "senses" when the deflection coil and antenna are approaching synchronization and automatically reduces its error voltage (to the servo amplifier) to the value just necessary to achieve and maintain synchronization.

Q. 8.70. In what range of frequencies do magnetron and klystron oscillators find application?

A. Magnetron oscillators are most generally used in the frequency range between 600 and 30 000 megahertz. Klystron oscillators are most generally used in the frequency range between 3 000 and 30 000 megahertz.

D. A magnetron oscillator derives its

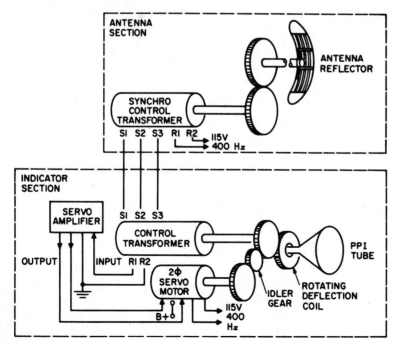

Fig. 8.69. Simplified diagram of radar servo system driving rotating indicator-deflection coil.

name by virtue of a magnetic field which is set up perpendicular to the electric field existing between cathode and plate (or plates). in a multi-anode type of magnetron, the plate segments are made up of cavity resonators. These cavity resonators receive their operating energy from the circular movement of electrons just outside of the opening of each cavity. If an electron is accelerated by the cavity fields, energy is taken from the cavity, but if an electron is slowed down by the cavity fields then energy is given up to the cavity and oscillations are thereby maintained. Magnetron oscillators are widely used in radar sets as pulsed power oscillators of high peak power. A klystron oscillator is a "velocity modulated" type of high-frequency oscillator, that is, the relative velocities of the electron beam are made to vary in such a way that "bunches" of electrons are formed. These "bunches" pass through cavity resonator grids in the proper phase relationship to maintain oscillation in the cavity resonator. Klystrons are used for local oscillators and low power transmitters. Klystron tubes are also available in the form of amplifiers. The "reflex" klystron is most widely used as a receiver local oscillator, and is also used in one type of video sweep generator. (See also Q. 3.246 and Q. 3.248.)

FCC-TYPE SAMPLE TEST FOR ELEMENT VIII

VIII-1. One of the frequency bands on which ship radars operate is: (Q. 8.07)
(a) 5 000 to 5 200 MHz.
(b) 5 460 to 5 650 MHz.
(c) 9 000 to 9 250 MHz.
(d) 3 200 to 3 450 MHz.
(e) 4 460 to 4 650 MHz.

VIII-2. Radar interference heard on a receiver frequently appears as: (Q. 8.10)
(a) Intermittent pulses.
(b) Constantly varying tone frequencies.
(c) A steady tone, always at 400 Hz.

(d) A hissing noise.
(e) A steady tone at the radar repetition rate.

VIII-3. Radar interference to communications receivers occurs: (Q. 8.12)
(a) Only at the radar transmitting RF frequency.
(b) Only at the basic radar repetition rate.
(c) On practically any communication frequency.
(d) Only below 10 MHz.
(e) Only above 300 MHz.

VIII-4. To be responsible for the installation, maintenance, and servicing of ship radar equipment, an operator must have: (Q. 8.01)
(a) A first- or second-class radiotelegraph license or a general radiotelephone license, plus a ship-radar endorsement.
(b) A third-class operator's license, plus a ship radar endorsement.
(c) A first- or second-class radiotelegraph license.
(d) A marine operator's permit plus a marine endorsement.
(e) A first-class radiotelegraph license, plus a receiver endorsement.

VIII-5. Persons who are permitted to operate a ship's radar are: (Q. 8.02)
(a) Only properly licensed individuals.
(b) Any person holding an engineer's license.
(c) Any person designated by any officer on the ship.
(d) The Master, or any person designated by him.
(e) The First Mate, or any person designated by him.

VIII-6. In joining sections of waveguide together, choke joints are often used: (Q. 8.34)
(a) To prevent moisture from entering the waveguide.
(b) To maintain the pressure of inert gas.
(c) To reduce losses caused by misalignment of waveguide sections.
(d) To permit the escape of entrapped moisture without causing excessive losses.

(e) To maintain the correct bandwidth of the waveguide.

VIII-7. When used in conjunction with a radar set, the purpose of an echo box is to: (Q. 8.38)

(a) Listen to the tone of the pulse repetition rate.

(b) Tune the magnetron to the correct frequency.

(c) Provide a second or echo pulse, which is transmitted from the radar antenna, to increase the range.

(d) Provide an artificial target, which may be used to tune the radar receiver.

(e) Provide an artificial target, which may be used to tune the radar synchronizer.

VIII-8. A radar pulse is transmitted to an object 37.2 miles away. The time required for the pulse to be returned to the radar receiver is: (Q. 8.39)

(a) 400 microseconds.

(b) 200 microseconds.

(c) 800 microseconds.

(d) 600 microseconds.

(e) 1 000 microseconds.

VIII-9. A PPI cathode-ray tube as used on a radar set: (Q. 8.39)

(a) Is used to check the percentage of modulation.

(b) Indicates only the range of a target.

(c) Indicates both the range and azimuth of a target.

(d) Indicates the range, azimuth, and altitude of a target.

(e) Is used for receiver alignment.

VIII-10. Oscillations of a klystron tube are maintained: (Q. 8.48)

(a) By plate-to-cathode feedback.

(b) By bunches of electrons passing the cavity grids.

(c) By feedback between the accelerating grid and the repeller plate.

(d) By circulating bunches of electrons within the cavities.

(e) By variations in the repeller-plate potential.

VIII-11. A radar set has a pulse width of 0.05 microsecond, a pulse repetition of 2 000 hertz, and a peak power of 100 kW. THE DUTY CYCLE IS: (Q. 8.62)

(a) 0.000 1

(b) 0.000 9

(c) 0.005

(d) 0.000 05

(e) 0.009

VIII-12. Klystron oscillators are most often used in the frequency range of: (Q. 8.70)

(a) 300 to 3 000 MHz.

(b) 30 to 30 000 MHz.

(c) 100 to 10 000 MHz.

(d) 3 000 to 30 000 MHz.

(e) 3 000 to 300 000 MHz.

VIII-13. The oscillations of a magnetron oscillator are maintained if: (Q. 8.70)

(a) Electrons are slowed down by the cavity fields.

(b) The magnet has sufficient strength.

(c) The electrostatic field matches the electromagnetic field in strength.

(d) Electrons are speeded up by the cavity fields.

(e) Electrons are formed into bunches having the proper timing.

VIII-14. A synchro generator in a radar set is used to: (Q. 8.69)

(a) Generate the synchronizing pulses.

(b) Synchronize the sweep starting time of the PPI with the synchronizer.

(c) Supply position information of an antenna, to a servo system.

(d) Supply range information to the PPI.

(e) Generate range markers for the PPI.

VIII-15. The heading flash on a radar PPI is produced: (Q. 8.64)

(a) By an oscillator in the radar synchronizer.

(b) By a flash circuit in the PPI scope.

(c) By a time-delay circuit triggered by the magnetron.

(d) By a cam-operated switch in the antenna.

(e) By a cam-operated switch in the PPI scope.

VIII-16. The function of an artificial transmission line in a radar set is to: (Q. 8.58)
(a) Conduct the RF to the radar antenna.
(b) Determine the shape and duration of the radar pulse.
(c) Determine the pulse repetition rate of the radar pulse.
(d) Connect the magnetron to the waveguide.
(e) Measure the power output of the magnetron.

VIII-17. The pulse repetition rate of a radar set is determined by (Q. 8.59)
(a) A self-pulsing magnetron.
(b) The modulator, which triggers the magnetron.
(c) The synchronizer, or timer unit.
(d) The servo unit.
(e) The range-mark generator oscillator.

VIII-18. The radar set, sensitivity-time control circuit: (Q. 8.55)
(a) Can reduce sea-return response.
(b) Make it possible to discriminate between targets that are very close together.
(c) Controls the width of the magnetron pulse.
(d) Is used to increase sea return.
(e) Is a circuit in the synchronizer that permits fine control of the radar-repetition rate.

VIII-19. Radar receivers commonly use intermediate frequencies of: (Q. 8.50)
(a) 455 kHz.
(b) 10.7 MHz.
(c) 43.0 MHz.
(d) 30 or 60 MHz.
(e) 4.5 MHz.

VIII-20. The function of the TR box in a radar system is to: (Q. 8.41)
(a) Protect the magnetron from overload.
(b) Protect the waveguide against arcing due to moisture.
(c) Protect the receiver while the magnetron is firing.
(d) Protect the antenna while the magnetron is firing.
(e) Increase the sensitivity of the receiver.

VIII-21. If the duration of the radar transmitted pulse, on a particular range of operation, is increased, the required bandwidth of the receiver's IF amplifiers: (Q. 8.39)
(a) May be decreased.
(b) Must remain as before.
(c) Must be increased.
(d) Must be doubled.
(e) None of the above.

VIII-22. In a radar set the local oscillator klystron tube is constantly kept on the correct frequency by: (Q. 8.48)
(a) A spectrum analyzer.
(b) Frequent manual adjustments.
(c) Reference to the PPI tube.
(d) An AFC system.
(e) Feedback from the range-marker oscillator.

VIII-23. In the usual radar set, the receiver RF amplifier: (Q. 8.42)
(a) Must be solid-state.
(b) Does not exist.
(c) Has a high signal-to-noise ratio.
(d) Has a low signal-to-noise ratio.
(e) Is located at the antenna, to reduce losses.

VIII-24. The maximum usable range of the usual radar set (on any particular range setting) is determined by: (Q. 8.39)
(a) The interval between transmitted pulses.
(b) The width of the transmitted pulses.
(c) The bandwidth of the receiver IF stages.
(d) The duty cycle.
(e) The horizontal resolution on the PPI tube.

VIII-25. A thin layer of dirt and grime covers the reflecting surface of the parabolic dish of a radar set. The practical effect on the performance of the radar will be: (Q. 8.37)
(a) A decrease in range.
(b) A reduction in horizontal resolution.
(c) No noticeable effect.
(d) A slightly smeary picture on the PPI.
(e) None of the above.

VIII-26. The purpose of using waveguide-choke joints is to: (Q. 8.34, 8.35)
(a) Lengthen the waveguide run.
(b) Eliminate moisture from the waveguide.
(c) Present a correct terminating impedance for the waveguide.
(d) Join two sections of waveguide with minimum losses.
(e) Pressurize the waveguide.

VIII-27. A typical value for the receiver IF of a radar set is: (Q. 8.39)
(a) 30 MHz.
(b) 130 MHz.
(c) 10.7 MHz.
(d) 455 kHz.
(e) 90 MHz.

VIII-28. In a radar set, the function of the magnetron is to: (Q. 8.43)
(a) Act as the receiver local oscillator.
(b) Produce the transmitted RF power.
(c) Modulate the transmitter.
(d) Determine the transmitted pulse width.
(e) Help determine the antenna beam shape.

VIII-29. Some waveguides are pressurized with dry air. This is done in order to: (Q. 8.28)
(a) Increase the velocity of propagation.
(b) Maintain the correct mode of operation.
(c) Keep the thin walls from bending inward.
(d) Reduce the possibility of internal arcing.
(e) Maintain pressure in the choke joints and thus ensure a better match to the magnetron.

VIII-30. When operating a magnetron in a radar set, the following precaution should be taken: (Q. 8.23, 8.24)
(a) Allow a 15-minute warm-up before applying the high voltage.
(b) Check all pulse widths before operating each time.

(c) Make certain there are no magnetic materials in the vicinity of the magnet.
(d) Bring the high voltage up very slowly to maximum.
(e) Realign the magnet each day to ensure correct operation.

VIII-31. Fuses and receiving-type tubes may be replaced: (Q. 8.08)
(a) Only by a person holding a first-class operator's license.
(b) Only by an operator who has previously obtained the permission of the master of the ship.
(c) Only by the Radio Officer in charge.
(d) Only by a person holding a ship radar endorsement.
(e) By an unlicensed person under the supervision of the licensed operator in charge of maintenance.

VIII-32. In a radar set receiver, an AFC system may be used to: (Q. 8.42)
(a) Automatically maintain the correct magnetron frequency.
(b) Maintain the desired klystron frequency.
(c) Keep the IF stages on frequency.
(d) Provide automatic control of receiver gain.
(e) Detect the radar pulse after it returns from the target.

VIII-33. In the usual PPI tube, a "map" of the scanned area is seen by virtue of: (Q. 8.67)
(a) The short persistence of the tube's phosphor.
(b) Applying the "heading flash" to the cathode.
(c) The long persistence characteristic of the phosphor of the tube.
(d) The signal applied to the second anode.
(e) None of the above.

VIII-34. The PPI tubes have an aquadag coating on the inside of the tube. The purpose of this coating is: (Q. 8.66)
(a) To prevent the escape of light.

(b) To act as the second anode.

(c) To shield the tube magnetically.

(d) To decelerate the electron beam.

(e) To deflect the electron beam.

VIII-35. A radar set has a pulse repetition rate of 2 000 hertz per second. The pulse repetition time is: (Q. 8.62)

(a) 500 μs.

(b) 5 000 μs.

(c) 2 000 μs.

(d) 200 μs.

(e) 1 000 μs.

VIII-36. The transmitted pulse length of a radar set is 0.5 microsecond. For good PPI reproduction of the received pulse, the receiver and video amplifier bandwidth should be approximately: (Q. 8.39)

(a) 10 MHz.

(b) 4 MHz.

(c) 0.5 MHz.

(d) 1.0 MHz.

(e) 455 kHz.

Hint: To reproduce sufficient harmonics so as not to distort the pulse shape, use the equation: $F = 2/T$

VIII-37. A certain radar set has a transmitted pulse width of 1.0 microsecond, a pulse repetition rate of 1 000 hertz per second and a peak power output of 100 kW. The averae power output is: (Q. 8.62)

(a) 100 W.

(b) 1 kW.

(c) 100 kW.

(d) 10 W.

(e) None of the above.

VIII-38. A radar set uses no RF amplifier and a crystal detector as the first stage of the receiver because: (Q. 8.39)

(a) An RF amplifier would produce a better signal-to-noise ratio.

(b) There are no suitable tubes or transistors available at the microwave frequencies involved.

(c) An RF amplifier would distort the incoming pulse shape.

(d) An RF amplifier would decrease the maximum range.

(e) An RF amplifier could not be matched to the waveguide output impedance.

VIII-39. In a radar system, the reciprocal of the pulse repetition time interval is the: (Q. 8.62)

(a) Pulse width.

(b) Duty cycle.

(c) Reciprocal of the duty cycle.

(d) Radar maximum range.

(e) Pulse repetition frequency.

VIII-40. The coarse frequency adjustment of a reflex klystron is accomplished by: (Q. 8.48)

(a) The AFC system.

(b) An adjustment in the synchronizer.

(c) Adjusting the flexible wall of the resonant cavity.

(d) Varying the repeller voltage.

(e) Varying the accelerator voltage.

VIII-41. In a radar AFC system, designed to keep the local oscillator frequency correct, the AFC discriminator compares the frequencies of the: (Q. 8.42)

(a) Klystron and repetition-rate generator.

(b) Klystron and magnetron.

(c) Magnetron and repetition-rate generator.

(d) Range-mark generator and the magnetron.

(e) None of the above.

VIII-42. A radar set has several switchable ranges. The following is true at the lowest switchable range: (Q. 8.39)

(a) The repetition rate is lowest and the pulse width is highest.

(b) The repetition rate is highest and the pulse width is lowest.

(c) Short-range targets cannot be resolved.

(d) Long-range targets will be seen most clearly.

(e) The repetition rate is highest and the pulse width is highest.

VIII-43. On the PPI scope of a marine radar set, it is possible to determine: (Q. 8.67)

(a) Altitude and range of the target.

(b) The instantaneous speed of the target.

(c) True North.

(d) The range and bearing of a target.

(e) The location of navigational beacons.

VIII-44. A radar PPI scope displays bright, flashing pie sections. This may be caused by: (Q. 8.20)

(a) A defect in the AFC system.

(b) Excessive gain of the receiver.

(c) Insufficient gain of the receiver.

(d) Normal rotation of the radar antenna.

(e) Interference from a Loran receiver.

VIII-45. The display on the PPI scope of a radar set will have greater intensity under the following conditions: (Q. 8.39)

(a) Higher antenna rotation speeds.

(b) Lower antenna rotation speeds.

(c) Lower pulse repetition rate.

(d) Higher pulse repetition rates.

(e) Both (b) and (d) are true.

VIII-46. The repetition rate of a pulsed-radar set refers to the: (Q. 8.62)

(a) Receiver AFC sweeping rate.

(b) Antenna rotation speed.

(c) Reciprocal of the duty cycle.

(d) Magnetron pulse rate.

(e) Klystron pulse rate.

VIII-47. In a radar-set receiver, the usual mixer stage is: (Q. 8.39)

(a) An FET.

(b) A tunnel diode.

(c) A silicon crystal.

(d) A Rochelle salts crystal.

(e) A multi-grid vacuum tube designed for microwave frequencies.

VIII-48. In order to match the output impedance of the radar receiver to the input impedance of a coaxial line, the circuit generally used is: (Q. 8.39)

(a) A step-down, video transformer.

(b) A cathode (or emitter) follower.

(c) A quarter-wave transmission line section.

(d) A common-emitter stage.

(e) A grounded grid stage.

VIII-49. When it is desired that short-range targets be clearly seen on a pulsed-radar set, it is important that the receiver and display system have: (Q. 8.39)

(a) The shortest possible recovery time.

(b) A long time constant.

(c) A restricted high-frequency response.

(d) Low-pass filters.

(e) Both (b) and (d) are correct.

VIII-50. To achieve good bearing resolution when using a pulsed-radar set, an important requirement is: (Q. 8.63)

(a) A narrow, antenna-beam width in the horizontal plane.

(b) A narrow, antenna-beam width in the vertical plane.

(c) A very narrow transmitted pulse.

(d) A low repetition rate.

(e) A high duty cycle.

Extracts from the Rules and Regulations of the Federal Communications Commission

PART 1.
PRACTICE AND PROCEDURE

R & R 1.85 Suspension of Operator Licenses. . . . Upon receipt by the Commission of such application for hearing, said order of suspension shall be designated for hearing by the Chief, Safety and Special Radio Services Bureau or the Chief, Field Engineering Bureau, as the case may be, and said order of suspension shall be held in abeyance until the conclusion of the hearing. Upon the conclusion of said hearing, the Commission may affirm, modify, or revoke said order of suspension. If the license is ordered suspended, the operator shall send his operator license to the office of the Commission in Washington, D.C., on or before the effective date of the order, or, if the effective date has passed at the time notice is received, the license shall be sent to the Commission forthwith.

* * * * * *

PART 2:
FREQUENCY ALLOCATIONS AND TREATY MATTERS: GENERAL RULES AND REGULATIONS

R & R 2.1 Definitions. The following definitions are issued*:

* Only selected definitions are given here.

Domestic fixed public service. A fixed service, the stations of which are open to public correspondence, for radiocommunications originating and terminating solely at points within: (a) the State of Alaska, or (b) the State of Hawaii, or (c) the contiguous 48 states and the District of Columbia, or (d) a single possession of the United States. Generally, in cases where service is afforded on frequencies above 72 MHz, radio-communications between the contiguous 48 States (including the District of Columbia) and Canada or Mexico, or radiocommunications between the State of Alaska and Canada, are deemed to be in the domestic fixed public service.

Experimental station. A non-amateur station utilizing radio waves in experiments with a view to the development of science or technique.

Facsimile. A system of telecommunication for the transmission of fixed images, with or without half-tones, with a view to their reproduction in a permanent form.

Industrial radio services. Any service of radiocommunication essential to, operated by, and for the sole use of, those enterprises which for purposes of safety or other necessity require radiocommunication in order to function efficiently. The radio transmitting facilities of the industrial radio services are defined as fixed, land, mobile, or radiolocation stations.

Industrial, scientific and medical equipment (ISM equipment). Devices which use radio waves for industrial, scientific, medical, or any other purposes including the transfer of energy by radio and which are neither used nor intended to be used for radiocommunication.

Land transportation radio service. Any private service of radiocommunication essential to the conduct of certain land transportation activities and operated for the use of persons engaged in those activities, the transmitting facilities of which are defined as fixed, land, mobile or radiolocation stations.

Marker beacon. A transmitter in the aeronautical radionavigation service that radiates vertically a distinctive pattern for providing position information to aircraft.

Mobile station. A station in the mobile service intended to be used while in motion or during halts at unspecified points.

Operational fixed station. A fixed station, not open to public correspondence, operated by and for the sole use of those agencies operating their own radiocommunication facilities in the public safety, industrial, land transportation, marine, or aviation service.

Personal radio services. A radiocommunication service of fixed, land and mobile stations intended for personal or business

radiocommunications, radio signaling, control of remote objects or devices by means of radio, and other purposes not specifically prohibited.

Private aircraft station. An aircraft station on board an aircraft not operated as an air carrier.

Public correspondence. Any telecommunication which the offices and stations must, by reason of their being at the disposal of the public, accept for transmission.

Public safety radio service. Any service of radiocommunication essential either to the discharge of non-Federal governmental functions or the alleviation of an emergency endangering life or property, the radio transmitting facilities of which are defined as fixed, land, mobile, or radiolocation stations.

Radio direction finding station. A radiodetermination using radio direction finding.

Radio range station. A radionavigation land station in the aeronautical radionavigation service providing radial equisignal zones.

Radiobeacon station. A station in the radionavigation service the emissions of which are intended to enable a mobile station to determine its bearing or direction in relation to the radiobeacon station.

*   *   *   *   *   *

Band No.	Frequency subdivision	Frequency range
4	VLF (very low frequency)	Below 30 kHz.
5	LF (low frequency)	30 to 300 kHz.
6	MF (medium frequency)	300 to 3000 kHz.
7	HF (high frequency)	3 to 30 MHz.
8	VHF (very high frequency)	30 to 300 MHz.
9	UHF (ultra high frequency)	300 to 3000 MHz.
10	SHF (super high frequency)	3 to 30 GHz.
11	EHF (extremely high frequency)	30 to 300 GHz.

R & R 2.201 Emission, Modulation, and Transmission Characteristics.

The following system of designating emission, modulation, and transmission characteristics shall be employed.

(a) Emissions are designated according to their classification and their necessary bandwidth.

(b) A minimum of three symbols are used to describe the basic characteristics of radio waves. Emissions are classified and symbolized according to the following characteristics:

(1) First symbol—type of modulation of the main character;

(2) Second symbol—nature of signal(s) modulating the main carrier;

(3) Third symbol—type of information to be transmitted.

Note: A fourth and fifth symbol are provided for additional information and are shown in Appendix 6, Part A of the ITU Radio Regulations. Use of the fourth and fifth symbol is optional. Therefore, the symbols may be used as described in Appendix 6, but are not required by the Commission.

(c) First Symbol—types of modulation of the main carrier:

(1) Emission of an unmodulated carrier . . . . N

(2) Emission in which the main carrier is amplitude-modulated (including cases where sub-carriers are angle-modulated):

—Double-sideband . . . . A
—Single-sideband, full carrier . . . . . . H
—Single-sideband, reduced or variable level carrier . . . . R
—Single-sideband, suppressed carrier . . . . J
Independent sidebands. . . . . B
Vestigial sideband. C

(3) Emission in which the main carrier is angle-modulated:

—Frequency modulation . . . . F
Phase modulation . . . . G
Note: Whenever frequency modulation "F" is indicated, Phase modulation "G" is also acceptable.

(4) Emission in which the main carrier is amplitude and angle-modulated either simultaneously or in a pre-established sequence. . . . . D

(5) Emission of pulses:[1]
—Sequence of unmodulated pulses. . . . . P

—A sequence of pulses:
—Modulated in amplitude. . . . . K
—Modulated in width/duration L
—Modulated in position/phase. . . . . M
—In which the carrier is angle-modulated during the period of the pulse . . . . . . Q
—Which is a combination of the foregoing or is produced by other means V

(6) Cases not covered above, in which an emission consists of the main carrier modulated, either simultaneously or in a pre-established sequence, in a combination of two or more of the following modes: amplitude, angle, pulse . . . . W

(7) Cases not otherwise covered X

(d) Second Symbol—nature of signal(s) modulating the main carrier:

(1) No modulating signal. 0

(2) A single channel containing quantized or digital information without the use of a modulating subcarrier, excluding time-division multiplex 1

(3) A single channel containing quantized or digital information with the use of a modulating subcarrier, excluding time-division multiplex 2

(4) A single channel containing analogue information 3

(5) Two or more channels containing quantized or digital information. 7

(6) Two or more channels containing analogue information 8

(7) Composite system with one or more channels containing quantized or digital information, together with one or more channels containing analogue information. 9

(8) Cases not otherwise covered X

---

[1]Emissions where the main carrier is directly modulated by a signal which has been coded into quantized form (e.g., pulse code modulation) should be designated under (2) or (3).

(e) Third symbol—type of information to be transmitted:[2]

(1) No information transmitted . . . . N
(2) Telegraphy—for aural reception . . .
. . . . A
(3) Telegraphy—for automatic reception. . . . . B
(4) Facsimile. C
(5) Data transmission, telemetry, telecommand. . . . . D
(6) Telephony (including sound broadcasting). . . . . E
(7) Television (video). . . . . F
(8) Combination of the above. . . . . .W
(9) Cases not otherwise covered X

(f) Type *B* emission: As an exception to the above principles, damped waves are symbolized in the Commission's rules and regulations as type *B* emission. The use of type B emissions is forbidden.

(g) Whenever the full designation of an emission is necessary, the symbol for that emission, as given above, shall be preceded by the necessary bandwidth of the emission as indicated in R & R 2.202(b)(1).

R & R 2.202 Bandwidths. (a) *Occupied bandwidth.* The frequency bandwidth such that, below its lower and above its upper frequency limits, the mean powers radiated are each equal to 0.5 percent of the total mean power radiated by a given emission. In some cases, for example multichannel frequency-division systems, the percentage of 0.5 percent may lead to certain difficulties in the practical application of the definitions of occupied and necessary bandwidth; in such cases a different percentage may prove useful.

(b) *Necessary bandwidth.* For a given class of emission, the minimum value of the occupied bandwidth sufficient to ensure the transmission of information at the rate and with the quality required for the system employed, under specified conditions.

[2]In this context the word "information" does not include information of a constant, unvarying nature such as is provided by standard frequency emissions, continuous wave and pulse radars, etc.

Emissions useful for the good functioning of the receiving equipment as, for example, the emission corresponding to the carrier of reduced carrier systems, shall be included in the necessary bandwidth.

(1) The necessary bandwidth shall be expressed by three numerals and one letter. The letter occupies the position of the decimal point and represents the unit of bandwidth. The first character shall be neither zero nor K, M or G.

(2) Necessary bandwidths:
between 0.001 and 999 Hz shall be expressed in Hz (letter H);
between 1.00 and 999 kHz shall be expressed in kHz (letter K);
between 1.00 and 999 MHz shall be expressed in MHz (letter M);
between 1.00 and 999 GHz shall be expressed in GHz (letter G).

(3) Examples:

0.002Hz—H002	180.5 kHz—181K
0.1 Hz—H100	180.7 kHz—181K
25.3 Hz—25H3	1.25 MHz—1M25
400 Hz—400H	2 MHz—2M00
2.4 kHz—2K40	10 MHz—10M0
6 kHz—6K00	202 MHz—202M
12.5 kHz—12K5	5.65 GHz—5G65
180.4 kHz—180K	

* * * * * *

R & R 2.402 Control of Distress Traffic. The control of distress traffic is the responsibility of the mobile station in distress or of the mobile station, which by the application of the provisions of R & R 2.403, has sent the distress call. These stations may, however, delegate the control of the distress traffic to another station.

R & R 2.403 Retransmission of Distress Message. Any station which becomes aware that a mobile station is in distress may transmit the distress message in the following cases:

(a) When the station in distress is not itself in a position to transmit the message.

(b) In the case of mobile stations, when the master or the person in charge of the ship, aircraft or other vehicles carrying the station which intervenes believes that further help is necessary.

(c) In the case of other stations, when directed to do so by the station in control of distress traffic or when it has reason to believe that a distress call which it has intercepted has not been received by any station in a position to render aid.

R & R 2.404 Resumption of Operation After Distress. No station having been notified to cease operation shall resume operation on frequency or frequencies which may cause interference until notified by the station issuing the original notice that the station involved will not interfere with distress traffic as it is then being routed or until the receipt of a general notice that the need for handling distress traffic no longer exists.

R & R 2.405. Operation During Emergency. The licensee of any station (except amateur, standard broadcast, FM broadcast, noncommercial educational FM broadcast, or television broadcast) may, during a period of emergency in which normal communication facilities are disrupted as a result of hurricane, flood, earthquake, or similar disaster, utilize such station for emergency communication service in communicating in a manner other than that specified in the instrument of authorization: *Provided,*

(a) That as soon as possible after the beginning of such emergency use, notice be sent to the Commission at Washington, D.C., and to the Engineer in Charge of the district in which the station is located, stating the nature of the emergency and the use to which the station is being put, and

(b) That the emergency use of the station shall be discontinued as soon as substantially normal communication facilities are again available, and

(c) That the Commission at Washington, D.C., and the Engineer in Charge shall be notified immediately when such special use of the station is terminated: *Provided, further,*

(d) That in no event shall any station engage in emergency transmission on frequencies other than, or with power in excess of, that specified in the instrument of authorization or as otherwise expressly provided by the Commission, or by law: *And provided further,*

(e) That any such emergency communication undertaken under this section shall terminate upon order of the Commission.

* * * * * *

R & R 2.901 Basis and Purpose. (a) In order to carry out its responsibilities under the Communications Act and the various treaties and international regulations, and in order to promote efficient use of the radio spectrum, the Commission has developed technical standards for radio frequency equipment and parts or components thereof. The technical standards applicable to individual types of equipment are found in that part of the rules governing the service wherein the equipment is to be operated. In addition to the technical standards provided, the rules governing the service may require that such equipment receive equipment authorization from the Commission by one of the following procedures: type approval, type acceptance, or equipment certification.

PART 13:
COMMERCIAL RADIO OPERATORS

R & R 13.2 Classification of operator licenses and endorsements.

(a) Commercial radio operator licenses issued by the Commission are classified in accordance with the Radio Regulations of the International Telecommunications Union.

(b) The following licenses are issued by the Commission. International classification, if different from the license name, is given in parenthesis.

(1) First Class Radiotelegraph Operator's Certificate.

(2) Second Class Radiotelegraph Operator's Certificate.

(3) Third Class Radiotelegraph Operator's Certificate (radiotelegraph operator's special certificate).

(4) General Radiotelephone Operator License (radiotelephone operator's general certificate).

(5) Marine Radio Operator Permit (radiotelephone operator's restricted certificate).

(6) Restricted Radiotelephone Operator Permit (radiotelephone operator's restricted certificate).

(c) The following license endorsements are affixed by the Commission, to provide special authorizations or restrictions. Applicable licenses are given in parenthesis.

(1) Ship radar endorsement (First and Second Class Radiotelegraph Operator's Certificates, General Radiotelephone Operator License).

(2) Six Months Service endorsement (First and Second Class Radiotelegraph Operator's Certificates).

(3) Restrictive endorsements; relating to physical handicaps, English language or literacy waivers, or other matters (all licenses).

(d) The following former licenses and endorsements are no longer issued; however, those outstanding are valid until expiration. Upon renewal, holders of these former licenses may be issued one or more of the licenses listed in paragraph (a), in accordance with R&R 13.28.

(1) Radiotelephone First Class Operator License—last issued December, 1981.

(2) Radiotelephone Second Class Operator License—last issued December, 1981.

(3) Radiotelephone Third Class Operator Permit—last issued October, 1980.

(4) Broadcast endorsement—last issued February 1979.

R & R 13.3 Holding of more than one commercial radio operator license.

*   *   *   *   *   *

(c) Each person who is legally eligible for employment in the United States may, if necessary, simultaneously hold:

(1) one General Radiotelephone Operator License and one Restricted Radiotelephone Operator Permit; or,

(2) one Marine Radio Operator Permit and one Restricted Radiotelephone Operator Permit.

*   *   *   *   *   *

R & R 13.4 Term of licenses.

(a) Commercial radio operator licenses are normally valid for a term of five years from the date of issuance, except as provided in paragraph (b) of this section.

(b) General Radiotelephone Operator Licenses and Restricted Radiotelephone Operator Permits are normally valid for the lifetime of the holder. The terms of all Restricted Radiotelephone Operator Permits issued prior to November 15, 1953, and valid on that date, were extended to encompass the lifetime of such operators.

*   *   *   *   *   *

R & R 13.6 Operator License, Posting of. The original license of each station operator shall be posted at the place where he is on duty, except as otherwise provided in this part or in the rules governing the class of station concerned.

*   *   *   *   *   *

R & R 13.11 Procedure.

(a) *General.* Applications will be governed by the rules in force on the date when application is filed. The application in the prescribed form and including all required subsidiary forms and documents, properly completed and signed, must be submitted to the appropriate office as indicated in paragraph (b) of this Section. If the application is for renewal of license, it may be filed at any time during the final year of the license term or during a 5-year period of grace after the date of expiration of the license sought to be renewed. During this 5-year period of grace, an expired license is not valid. A renewed license issued upon the basis of an application filed during the grace period will be dated currently and will not be backdated to the date of expiration and the license being renewed. A renewal application should be accompanied by the license sought to be renewed.

* * * * * *

R & R 13.21 Examination of elements.
(a) * * *
(3) General radiotelephone. Technical, legal, and other matters applicable to the operation of radiotelephone stations other than broadcast.

R & R 13.22 Required qualifications. Commercial radio operator licenses are issued only to eligible applicants found qualified by the Commission, as follows:
(a) To be qualified to hold any commercial radio operator license, an applicant must have the ability to transmit correctly and receive correctly spoken messages in the English language.
(b) To qualify for a new commercial radio operator license other than the Restricted Radiotelephone Operator Permit, an applicant must demonstrate Morse code skill, if required, and a satisfactory knowledge of the material in one or more of the elements listed in R & R 13.21, by passing all examinations required for the class of license to be issued:
(1) First Class Radiotelegraph Operator's Certificate.
(i) Transmitting and receiving Morse code tests 3 and 4.
(ii) Written examinations covering elements 1 and 2, 5 and 6.
(2) Second Class Radiotelegraph Operator's Certificate.
(i) Transmitting and receiving Morse Code tests 1 and 2.

(ii) Written examinations covering elements 1 and 2, 5 and 6.
(3) Third Class Radiotelegraph Operator's Certificate.
(i) Transmitting and receiving Morse code tests 1 and 2.
(ii) Written examinations covering elements 1 and 2, and 5.
(4) General Radiotelephone Operator License.
(i) Written examination covering element 3.
(5) Marine Radio Operator Permit.
(i) Written examination covering elements 1 and 2.
(c) No examination is required for the Restricted Radiotelephone Operator Permit. Instead, an applicant must certify that he or she:
(1) is legally eligible for employment in the United States; or, if not so eligible, holds an aircraft pilot certificate valid in the United States or an FCC radio station license in his or her name;
(2) can speak and hear;
(3) can keep, at least, a rough written log; and,
(4) is familiar with provisions of applicable treaties, laws, rules and regulations which govern the radio station he or she will operate.

* * * * * *

R & R 13.25 Examination credit for licenses held.
(a) The holder of a valid commercial radio operator license (or a license which could be renewed under the provisions of (R & R 13.28) who applies for another class of commercial radio operator license will not be required to retake the written examinations or telegraphy tests which were required to obtain the license held.

* * * * * *

R & R 13.26 Cancellation of superfluous licenses.

License Issued	License(s) Cancelled
First Class Radiotelegraph Operator's Certificate	Second Class Radiotelegraph Operator's Certificate, Third Class Radiotelegraph Operator's Certificate, Radiotelephone Third Class Operator Permit, Marine Radio Operator Permit, Restricted Radiotelephone Operator Permit
Second Class Radiotelegraph Operator's Certificate	Third Class Radiotelephone Operator's Certificate, Radiotelephone Third Class Operator Permit, Marine Radio Operator Permit, Restricted Radiotelephone Operator Permit
Third Class Radiotelegraph Operator's Certificate	Radiotelephone Third Class Operator Permit, Marine Radio Operator Permit, Restricted Radiotelephone Operator Permit.
General Radiotelephone Operator License	Radiotelephone First Class Operator License, Radiotelephone Second Class Operator License, Radiotelephone Third Class Operator Permit, Marine Radio Operator Permit.
Marine Radio Operator Permit	Radiotelephone Third Class Operator Permit.

*   *   *   *   *   *

R & R 3.28 License Renewals.

(a) Commercial radio operator licenses issued for five year terms may be renewed, by proper application, at any time during the last year of the license term or during a five year grace period following expiration. Expired licenses are not valid during the grace period.

*   *   *   *   *   *

R & R 13.61 Need for licensed commercial radio operators.
Rules which require Commission station licensees to employ licensed commercial radio operators to perform certain transmitter operating, maintenance, or repair duties are contained in Parts 73, 74, and 80 of this Chapter.

*   *   *   *   *   *

R & R 13.63 Operator's Responsibility.
The licensed operator responsible for the maintenance of a transmitter may permit other persons to adjust a transmitter in his presence for the purpose of carrying out tests or making adjustments requiring specialized knowledge or skill, provided that he shall not be relieved thereby from responsibility for the proper operation of the equipment.

*   *   *   *   *   *

R & R 13.65 Damage to Apparatus.
No licensed radio operator shall willfully damage, or cause or permit to be damaged, any radio apparatus or installation in any licensed radio station.

R & R 13.66 Unnecessary, Unidentified, or Superfluous Communications.
No licensed radio operator shall transmit unnecessary, unidentified, or superfluous radio communications or signals.

R & R 13.67 Obscenity, Indecency, Profanity.
No licensed radio operator or other person shall transmit communications containing obscene, indecent, or profane words, language or meaning.

R & R 13.68 False Signals.
No licensed radio operator shall transmit false or deceptive signals or communications by radio, or any call letter or signal which has not been assigned by proper authority to the radio station he is operating.

R & R 13.69 Interference.
No licensed radio operator shall willfully or maliciously interfere with or cause interference to any radio communication or signal.

R & R 13.70 Fraudulent licenses. No licensed radio operator or other person shall alter, duplicate for fraudulent purposes, or fradulently obtain or attempt to obtain, or assist another to alter, duplicate for fraudulent purposes, or fraudulently obtain or attempt to obtain an operator license. Nor shall any person use a license issued to another or a license that he or she knows to have been altered, duplicated for fraudulent purposes, or fraudulently obtained.

R & R 13.71. Issue of Duplicate or Replacement Licenses. (a) If the authorization is of the diploma form, a properly executed application for duplicate should be submitted to the office of issue. If the authorization is of the card form (Restricted Radiotelephone Operator Permit), a properly executed application for replacement should be submitted to the Federal Communications Commission, Gettysburg, Pa. 17325, EXCEPT for alien restricted radiotelephone operator permit applications, which must be submitted to Federal Communications Commission, Washington, D.C. 20554. In either case the application shall embody a statement of the circumstances involved in the loss, mutilation, or destruction of the license or permit. If the authorization has been lost, the applicant must state that reasonable search has been made for it, and, further, that in the event it be found, either the original or the duplicate (or replacement) will be returned for cancellation. If the authorization is of the diploma form, the applicant should also submit documentary evidence of the service that has been obtained under the original authorization, or a statement embodying that information.

(b) The holder of any license or permit whose name is legally changed may make application for a replacement document to indicate the new legal name by submitting a properly executed application accompanied by the license or permit affected. If the authorization is of the diploma form, the application should be submitted to the office where it was issued. If the authorization is of the card form (Restricted Radiotelephone Operator Permit), it should be submitted to

the Federal Communications Commission, Gettysburg, Pa. 17325, EXCEPT for alien restricted radiotelephone operator permit applications, which must be submitted to Federal Communications Commission, Washington, D.C. 20554.

R & R 13.72 Exhibiting Signed Copy of Application. When a duplicate or replacement operator license or permit has been requested, or request has been made for renewal, or a request has been made for an endorsement, higher class license or permit, or verification card, the operator shall exhibit in lieu of the original document a signed copy of the application which has been submitted to the Commission.

*   *   *   *   *

R & R 13.74 Posting Requirements for Operator Licenses. (a) Licensed commercial radio operators, on duty at a single transmitting system, shall post their radio operator license or permit in accordance with the rules governing that station when:

(1) Performing radio operating duties and in charge of the transmitting systems, or

(2) Supervising or performing service and maintenance or inspection duties at the transmitting systems.

(b) Licensed commercial radio operators, on duty at two or more transmitting systems, which are not co-located, shall post their radio operator license or permit at one of the stations, and a valid verified posting statement (FCC Form 759) at each other station in accordance with the rules governing those stations when:

(1) Performing radio operating duties and in charge of the transmitting systems, or

(2) Supervising or performing service and maintenance or inspection duties at the transmitting systems.

(c) In stations where rules for that service do not require posting, licensed commercial operators on duty and in charge of transmitting systems or performing service and maintenance or inspection duties of such transmitting systems, shall have on their person their radio operator license or permit, or a valid license verification card (FCC Form 758–F), which shall be available for inspection upon request by a Commission representative.

R & R 13.75 Record of Service and Maintenance Duties Performed. In every case where a station log or service and maintenance records are required to be kept and where service or maintenance duties are performed which may affect the proper operation of a station, the responsible operator shall sign and date an entry in the log of the station concerned, or in the station maintenance records if no log is required, giving:

(a) Pertinent details of all service and maintenance work performed by him under his supervision;

(b) His name and address; and

(c) The class, serial number and expiration date of his license: *Provided,* That the responsible operator shall not be subject to requirements in paragraphs (b) and (c) of this section in relation to a station, or stations of one licensee at a single location, at which he is regularly employed as an operator on a full time basis and at which his license is properly posted.

* * * * * *

R & R 13.77 Required endorsements.

(a) All Marine Radio Operator Permits shall bear the following endorsement:

"This permit does not authorize the operation of AM, FM or TV broadcast stations."

(b) General Radiotelephone Operator Licenses issued to persons who first qualify for that classification of license (see R & R 13.22) on or after 1985 shall bear the following endorsement:

"This license is valid for operation, maintenance, and repair of stations in the Aviation, Maritime, and International Fixed Public Radiocommunications Services only."

* * * * * *

**PART 17:
SPECIFICATIONS FOR OBSTRUCTION MARKING AND LIGHTING OF ANTENNA STRUCTURES**

R & R 17.25 Specifications for the Lighting of Antenna Structures Over 150 Feet Up To and Including 300 Feet in Height. (a) Antenna structures over 150 feet, up to and including 200 feet in height above ground, which are required to be lighted as a result of notification to the FAA under R & R 17.7 and antenna structures over 200 feet, up to and including 300 feet in height above ground, shall be lighted as follows:

(1) There shall be installed at the top of the structure one 300 m/m electric code beacon equipped with two 620- or 700-watt lamps (PS-40, Code Beacon type), both lamps to burn simultaneously, and equipped with aviation red color filters. Where a rod or other construction of not more than 20 feet in height and incapable of supporting this beacon is mounted on top of the structure and it is determined that this additional construction does not permit unobstructed visibility of the code beacon from aircraft at any normal angle of approach, there shall be installed two such beacons positioned so as to insure unobstructed visibility of at least one of the beacons from aircraft at any normal angle of approach. The beacon shall be equipped with a flashing mechanism producing not more than 40 flashes per minute nor less than 12 flashes per minute with a period of darkness equal to one-half of the luminous period.

(2) At the approximate midpoint of the overall height of the tower there shall be installed at least two 116- or 125-watt lamps (A21/TS) enclosed in aviation red obstruction light globes. Each light shall be mounted so as to insure unobstructed visibility of at least one light at each level from aircraft at any normal angle of approach.

(3) All lights shall burn continuously or shall be controlled by a light sensitive device adjusted so that the lights will be

turned on at a north sky light intensity level of about 35 foot-candles and turned off at a north sky light intensity level of about 58 foot-candles.

* * * * * *

R & R 17.27 Specifications for the Lighting of Antenna Structures Over 450 Feet Up To and Including 600 Feet in Height. (a) Antenna structures over 450 feet up to and including 600 feet in height above the ground shall be lighted as follows:

(1) There shall be installed at the top of the structure one 300 m/m electric code beacon equipped with two 620- or 700-watt lamps (PS–40, Code Beacon type), both lamps to burn simultaneously, and equipped with aviation red color filters. Where a rod or other construction of not more than 20 feet in height and incapable of supporting this beacon is mounted on top of the structure and it is determined that this additional construction does not permit unobstructed visibility of the code beacon from aircraft at any normal angle of approach, there shall be installed two such beacons positioned so as to insure unobstructed visibility of at least one of the beacons from aircraft at any normal angle of approach. The beacons shall be equipped with a flashing mechanism producing not more than 40 flashes per minute nor less than 12 flashes per minute with a period of darkness equal to one-half of the luminous period.

(2) At approximately one-half of the overall height of the tower, one similar flashing 300 m/m electric code beacon shall be installed in such position within the tower proper that the structural members will not impair the visibility of this beacon from aircraft at any normal angle of approach. In the event this beacon cannot be installed in a manner to insure unobstructed visibility of it from aircraft at any normal angle of approach, there shall be installed two such beacons at each level. Each beacon shall be mounted on the outside of diagonally opposite corners or opposite sides of the tower at the prescribed height.

(3) On levels at approximately three-fourths and one-fourth of the overall height of the tower, at least one 116- or 125-watt lamp (A21/TS) enclosed in an aviation red obstruction light globe shall be installed on each outside corner of the tower at each level.

(4) All lights shall burn continuously or shall be controlled by a light sensitive device adjusted so that the lights will be turned on at a north sky light intensity level of about 35 foot-candles and turned off at a north sky light intensity level of about 58 foot-candles.

* * * * * *

R & R Inspection of Tower Lights and Associated Control Equipment. The licensee of any radio station which has an antenna structure requiring illumination pursuant to the provisions of section 303(q) of the Communications Act of 1934, as amended, as outlined elsewhere in this part:

(a) (1) Shall make an observation of the tower lights at least once each 24 hours either visually or by observing an automatic properly maintained indicator designed to register any failure of such lights, to insure that all such lights are functioning properly as required; or alternatively.

(2) Shall provide and properly maintain an automatic alarm system designed to detect any failure of such lights and to provide indication of such failure to the licensee.

(b) Shall inspect at intervals not to exceed 3 months all automatic or mechanical control devices, indicators, and alarm systems associated with the tower lighting to insure that such apparatus is functioning properly.

R & R 17.48. Notification of Extinguishment or Improper Functioning of Lights. The licensee of any radio station which has an antenna structure requiring illumination pursuant to the provisions of section 303(q) of the Communications Act of 1934, as amended, as outlined elsewhere in this part.

(a) Shall report immediately by telephone or telegraph to the nearest Flight

Service Station or office of the Federal Aviation Administration any observed or otherwise known extinguishment or improper functioning of any top steady-burning light or any flashing obstruction light, regardless of its position on the antenna structure, not corrected within 30 minutes. Such reports shall set forth the condition of the light or lights, the circumstances which caused the failure, and the probable date for restoration of service. Further notification by telephone or telegraph shall be given immediately upon resumption of normal operation of the light or lights.

(b) An extinguishment or improper functioning of a steady burning side intermediate light or lights, shall be corrected as soon as possible, but notification to the FAA of such extinguishment or improper functioning is not required.

R & R 17.51 Time When Lights Shall Be Exhibited. All lighting shall be from sunset to sunrise unless otherwise specified.

* * * * * *

R & R 17.53. Lighting Equipment. The lighting equipment, color of filters, and shade of paint referred to in the specifications are further defined in the following government and/or Army-Navy Aeronautical Specifications, Bulletins, and Drawings: (Lamps are referred to by standard numbers). (See Table 2.)

* * * * * *

R & R 17.56 Maintenance of Lighting Equipment. Replacing or repairing of lights, automatic indicators, or automatic alarm systems shall be accomplished as soon as practicable.

PART 73:
RADIO BROADCAST SERVICES

R & R 73.14 Technical Definitions. (a) *Combined Audio Harmonics.* The term "combined audio harmonics" means the arithmetical sum of the amplitudes of all the separate harmonic components. Root sum square harmonic readings may be accepted under conditions prescribed by the Commission.

Table 2. Lighting Equipment Specifications

Outside white	TT-P-102[1] (Color No. 17875, FS-595).
Aviation surface orange	TT-P-59[1] (Color No. 12197, FS-595).
Aviation surface orange, enamel	TT-E-489[1] (Color No. 12197, FS-595).
Aviation red obstruction light—color	MIL-C-25050[2].
Flashing beacons	CAA-446[3] Code Beacons, 300 mm.
Do	MIL-6273[2]
Double and single obstruction light	L-810[3] (FAA AC No. 150/5345-2[4]).
Do	MIL-L-7830[2]
High intensity white obstruction light	FAA/DOD L-856 (FAA AC No. 150/5345-43B[4]).
116-Watt lamp	No. 116 A21/TS (6000 h).
125-Watt lamp	No. 125 A21/TS (6000 h)
620-Watt lamp	No. 620 PS-40 (3000 h).
700-Watt lamp	No. 700 PS-40 (6000 h)

[1] Copies of this specification can be obtained from the Specification Activity, Building 197, Room 301, Naval Weapons Plant, 1st and N Streets SE., Washington, D.C. 20407.

[2] Copies of Military specifications can be obtained by contacting the Commanding Officer, Naval Publications and Forms Center, 5801 Tabor Ave., Attention: NPPC-105, Philadelphia, Pa. 19120.

[3] Copies of Federal Aviation Administration specifications may be obtained from the Chief, Configuration Control Branch, AAF-110, Department of Transportation, Federal Aviation Administration, 800 Independence Avenue SW., Washington, D.C. 20591.

[4] Copies of Federal Aviation Administration advisory circulars may be obtained from the Department of Transportation, Publications Section, TAD-443.1, 400 7th St., SW., Washington, D.C. 20590.

(b) *Effective Field.* The term "effective field" or "effective field intensity" is the root-mean-square (rms) value of the inverse distance fields at a distance of 1 mile from the antenna in all directions in the horizontal plane.

(c) *Nominal power.* "Nominal power" is the power of a standard broadcast station, as specified in a system of classification which includes the following values; 50 kW, 25 kW, 10 kW, 5 kW, 2.5 kW, 1 kW, 0.5 kW, 0.25 kW.

(d) *Operating power.* Depending on the context within which it is employed, the term "operating power" may be synonymous with "nominal power" or "antenna" power."

(e) *Maximum rated carrier power.* "Maximum rated carrier power" is the maximum power at which the transmitter can be operated satisfactorily and is determined by the design of the transmitter and the type and number of vacuum tubes used in the last radio stage.

* * * * * *

(n) *Maximum percentage of modulation.* "Maximum percentage of modulation" means the greatest percentage of modulation that may be obtained by a transmitter without producing in its output harmonics of the modulating frequency in excess of those permitted by these regulations.

* * * * * *

(s) *Blanketing.* Blanketing is that form of interference which is caused by the presence of a broadcast signal of 1 volt per meter. (V/m) or greater intensity in the area adjacent to the antenna of the transmitting station. The 1-V/m contour is referred to as the blanket contour and the area within this contour is referred to as the blanket area.

* * * * * *

R & R 73.51 Antenna Input Power; How Determined. (a) Except in those circumstances described in paragraph (d) of this section, the antenna input power shall be determined by the direct method, i.e., as the product of the antenna resistance at the operating frequency (see R & R 73.54) and the square of the unmodulated antenna current at that frequency, measured at the point where the antenna resistance has been determined.

* * * * * *

(d) The antenna input power shall be determined on a temporary basis by the indirect method described in paragraphs (e) and (f) of this section in the following circumstances: (1) In an emergency, where the authorized antenna system has been damaged by causes beyond the control of the licensee or permittee (see R & R 73.45), or (2) pending completion of authorized changes in the antenna system, or (3) if changes occur in the antenna system or its environment which affect or appear likely to affect the value of antenna resistance or (4) if the antenna current meter becomes defective (see R & R 73.58). Prior authorization for the indirect determination of antenna input power is not required. However, an appropriate notation shall be made in the operating log.

(e) (1) Antenna input power is determined indirectly by applying an appropriate factor to the plate input power, in accordance with the following formula:

$$\text{Antenna input power} = Vp \times Ip \times F$$

where

Vp = plate voltage of final radio stage.
Ip = total plate current of final radio stage.
F = efficiency factor.

(2) The value of F applicable to each mode of operation shall be entered in the operating log for each day of operation, with a notation as to its derivation. This factor shall be established by one of the methods described in paragraph (f) of this section, which are listed in order of preference. The product of the plate current and plate voltage, or, alternatively, the antenna input power, as determined pursuant to subparagraph (1) of this paragraph, shall be entered in the

operating log under an appropriate heading for each log entry of plate current and plate voltage.

R & R 73.52 Antenna Input Power; Maintenance of. (a) The actual antenna input power of each station shall be maintained as near as is practicable to the authorized antenna input power and shall not be less than 90 percent nor greater than 105 percent of the authorized power; except that, if, in an emergency, it becomes technically impossible to operate with the authorized power, the station may be operated with reduced power for a period of not more than 30 days without further authority from the Commission, *Provided,* That notification is sent to the Commission in Washington, D.C. not less than the 10th day of the lower power operation. In the event normal power is restored prior to the expiration of the 30 day period, the permittee or licensee will so notify the Commission in Washington, D.C. of this date. If causes beyond the control of the permittee or licensee prevent restoration of authorized power within the allowed period, informal written request shall be made to the Commission in Washington, D.C. no later than the 30th day for such additional time as may be deemed necessary.

(b) In addition to maintaining antenna input power within the above limitations, each station employing a directional antenna shall maintain the relative amplitudes of the antenna currents in the elements of its array within 5 percent of the ratios specified in its license or other instrument of authorization, unless more stringent limits are specified therein.

*　*　*　*　*　*

R & R 73.58 Indicating Instruments. (a) Each AM broadcast station shall be equipped with indicating instruments which conform with the specifications described in R & R 73.1215 for determining power by the direct and indirect methods, and with such other instruments as are necessary for the proper adjustment, operation, and maintenance of the transmitting system.

(b) A thermocouple type ammeter, or other device capable of providing an indication of radio frequency current at the base of each antenna element, meeting requirements of R & R 7 3.1215, shall be permanently installed in the antenna circuit or a suitable jack and plug arrangement may be made to permit removal of the meter from the antenna circuit so as to protect it from damage by lightning. Where a jack and plug arrangement is used, contacts shall be made of silver and capable of operating without arcing or heating, and shall be protected against corrosion. Insertion and removal of the meter shall not interrupt the transmissions of the station. When removed from the antenna circuit, the meter shall be labeled to clearly identify the tower in which it is used, and shall be stored in a location which is readily available to that tower. Care shall be exercised in handling the meter to prevent damage which would impair its accuracy. Where the meter is permanently connected in the antenna circuit, provision may be made to short or open the meter circuit when it is not being used to measure antenna current. Such switching shall be accomplished without interrupting the transmission of the station.

(c) Since it is usually impractical to measure the actual antenna current of a shunt excited antenna system, the current measured at the input of the excitation circuit feed line is accepted as the antenna current.

(d) The function of each instrument shall be clearly and permanently shown on the instrument itself or on the panel immediately adjacent thereto.

(e) In the event that any one of these indicating instruments becomes defective when no substitute which conforms with the required specifications is available, the station may be operated without the defective instrument pending its repair or replacement for a period not in excess of 60 days without further authority of the Commission, *Provided,* That:

(1) Appropriate entries shall be made in the maintenance log of the station showing the date and time the meter was removed from and restored to service.

(2) If the defective instrument is an antenna base current ammeter of a directional antenna system, the indications required to be read and logged may be obtained from the antenna monitor pending the return to service of the regular meter, provided other parameters are maintained at their normal values.

(3) If the defective instrument is the antenna current meter of a non-directional station which does not employ a remote antenna ammeter, or if the defective instrument is the common point meter of a station which employs a directional antenna and does not employ a remote common point meter, the operating power shall be determined by the indirect method in accordance with R & R 73.51 (d), (e), and (f) during the entire time the station is operated without the antenna current meter or common point meter. However, if a remote antenna ammeter or a remote common point meter is employed and the antenna current meter or common point meter becomes defective, the remote meter shall be used in determining operating power by the direct method pending the return to service of the regular meter.

(f) If conditions beyond the control of the licensee prevent the restoration of the meter to service within the above allowed period, information requested in accordance with R & R 1.549 of this chapter may be filed with the Engineer in Charge of the radio district in which the station is located for such additional time as may be required to complete repairs of the defective instrument.

R & R 73.59 Frequency Tolerance. The operating frequency of each station shall be maintained within 20 hertz of the assigned frequency.

* * * * * *

R & R 73.67 Remote Control Operation.

* * * * * *

(3) A malfunction of any part of the remote control system resulting in improper control shall be cause for the immediate cessation of operating by remote control. A malfunction of any part of the remote control system resulting in inaccurate meter readings, shall be cause for terminating operation by remote control no longer than 1 hour after the malfunction is detected.

* * * * * *

R & R 73.93 Operator Requirements. (a) One or more operators holding a radio operator license or permit of a grade specified in this section shall be in actual charge of the transmitting system, and shall be on duty at the transmitter location, or at an authorized remote control point, or the position at which extension meters, as authorized pursuant to R & R 73.70 of this Subpart are located. The transmitter and required monitors and metering equipment, or the required extension meters and monitoring equipment and other required metering equipment, or the controls and required monitoring and metering equipment in an authorized remote control operation, shall be readily accessible to the licensed operator and located sufficiently close to the normal operating location that deviations from normal indications of required instruments can be observed from that location.

R & R 73.111 General Requirements Relating to Logs. see R & R 73.1800 (follows).

R & R 73.1800 General Requirements Relating to Logs. (a) The licensee of each station shall maintain program, operating and maintenance logs as set forth in R & R 73.1810, 73.1820 and 73.1830. Each log shall be kept by the station employee or employees (or contract operator) competent to do so, having actual knowledge of the facts required. The person keeping the log must make entries that accurately reflect the operation of the station. In the case of program and operating logs, the employee shall sign the appropriate log when starting duty and again when going off duty and setting forth the time of each. In the case of maintenance logs, the employee shall sign the log upon completion of the required maintenance and inspection entries. When the employee keeping a program or operating log signs it upon going off duty or completing maintenance log entries, that person attests to the fact that the log, with any corrections or additions made before it was signed, is an accurate representation of what transpired.

(b) The logs shall be kept in an orderly and legible manner, in suitable form and in such detail that the data required for the particular class of station concerned are readily available. Key letters or abbreviations may be used if proper meaning or explanation is contained elsewhere in the log. Each sheet shall be numbered amd dated. Time entries shall be made in local time and shall be indicated as advanced (e.g., EDT) or non-advanced time (e.g., EST).

(c) Any necessary corrections of a manually kept log after it has been signed in accordance with (a) above shall be made only by striking out the erroneous portion and making a corrective explanation on the log or attachment to it. For program logs, such corrections shall be dated and signed by the person who kept the log or the program director, or the station manager or an officer of the licensee. For operating and maintenance logs, such corrections shall be dated and signed by the person who kept the log or the station technical supervisor, the station manager, or an officer of the licensee.

(d) No automatically kept log shall be altered in any way after entries have been recorded. When automatic logging processes fail or malfunction the log must be kept manually for that period and in accordance with the requirements of this Section.

(e) No log, or portion thereof, shall be erased, obliterated or destroyed during the period in which it is required to be retained. (R & R 73.1840, Retention of logs.)

(f) Entries shall be made in the logs as required by R & R 73.1810, 73.1820 and 73.1830. Additional information such as that needed for administrative or operational purposes may be entered on the logs. Such additional information, so entered, shall not be subject to the restrictions and limitations in the FCC's rule on the making of corrections and changes in logs and may be physically removed, without otherwise altering the log in any way, before making the log a part of an application or available for public inspection.

(g) The operating log and the maintenance log may be kept individually on the same sheet in one common log, at the option of the licensee.

(h) Application forms for licenses and other authorizations require that certain operating and program data be supplied. These application forms should be kept in mind in connection with maintenance of station program and operating records.

R & R 73.112 Program Logs, see R & R 73.1810 (follows).

R & R 73.1810 Program Logs.

Commercial Stations

(a) Commercial stations shall keep a program log in accordance with the provisions of R & R 73.1800 for each broadcast day which, in this context, means from the station's sign-on to its sign-off.

(b) *Entries.* The following entries shall be made in the program log:

(1) *For each program.* (i) An entry identifying the program by name or title.

(ii) Entries which indicate the time each program begins and ends. If programs are broadcast during which separately identifiable program units of a different type or source are presented, and if the licensee wishes to count such units separately, the beginning and ending time for the longer program need be entered only once. The program units which the licensee wishes to count separately shall then be entered underneath the entry for the longer program, with the beginning and ending time of each such unit.

(iii) An entry classifying each program as to type, using the definitions given in paragraph (d) (1) of this section.

(iv) An entry classifying each program as to source, using the definitions set forth in paragraph (d) (2) of this section. (For network programs, also give name or initials of the network, e.g., ABC, CBS, NBC, Mutual.)

(v) An entry for each program representing a political candidate, showing the name and political affiliation of such candidate.

(2) *For commercial matter.* (i) An entry identifying: the sponsor(s) of the program, the person(s) who paid for the announcement or the person(s) who furnished materials or services. The entry shall constitute a representation that identification was announced on the air as required by Section 317 of the Communications Act and R & R 73.1212 of the FCC's rules. See paragraph (d) (3) of this section for the definition of commercial matter.

(ii) An entry or entries showing the total duration of commercial matter in each hourly time segment (beginning on the hour) or the duration of each commercial message (commercial continuity in sponsored programs, or commercial announcements) in each hour. See paragraph (d) (3) (iii) of this section concerning computation of commercial time.

(3) *For public service announcements.* An entry showing that a public service announcement (PSA) has been broadcast together with the name of the organization or interest on whose behalf it is made. See paragraph (d) (4) of this section for definition of a public service announcement.

(4) *For other announcements.* (i) An entry of the time that each required station identification announcement is made (pursuant to R & R 73.1201).

(ii) An entry for each announcement presenting a political candidate, showing the name and political affiliation of such candidate.

(iii) An entry for each announcement made pursuant to the local notice requirements of R & R 1.580 (pregrant), 1.594 (designation for hearing) and 73.1202 (licensee obligations), showing the time it was broadcast.

(iv) An entry for each announcement made pursuant to R & R 73.1208 concerning the broadcast of taped, filmed or recorded material.

(5) *For Emergency Broadcast System Operations.* An entry for tests of the EBS procedures pursuant to the requirements of Subpart G of this part and the appropriate station EBS checklist, unless such entries are consistently made in the station operating log.

(c) *National network programming.* A station broadcasting the programs of a national network which will supply it with all information as to such programs for the composite week need not log such data but shall record in its log the time when it joined the network, the name of each network program broadcast, the time it leaves the network, and any non-network matter broadcast which is required to be logged. The information supplied by the network for the composite week which the station will use in its renewal application, shall be retained with the program logs and associated with the logs pages to which it relates.

(d) *Definitions.* (1) *Program type.* The definitions of the first eight types of programs (i) through (viii), below, are intended not to overlap each other and will normally include all the various programs broadcast. Definitions (ix) thorugh (xi) are subcategories and the programs classified thereunder will also be classified under one of the appropriate first eight types. There may also be further duplication within types (ix) through (xi) (e.g., a program presenting a candidate for public office, prepared by an educational institution, would be classified as Public Affairs (PA), Political (POL) and Educational Institution (ED).

(i) *Agricultural programs* (A) include market reports, farming or other information specifically addressed, or primarily of interest to the agricultural population.

(ii) *Entertainment programs* (E) include all programs intended primarily as entertainment, such as music, drama, variety, comedy, quiz, etc.

(iii) *News programs* (N) include reports dealing with current local, national and international events, including weather and stock market reports; and commentary, analysis and sports news when an integral part of a news program.

(iv) *Public affairs programs* (PA) are programs dealing with local, state, regional, national or international issues or problems, including, but not limited to, talks, commentaries, discussions, speeches, editorials, political programs, documentaries, mini-documentaries, panels, roundtables, vignettes, and extended coverage (whether live or recorded) of public events or proceedings, such as local council meetings, Congressional hearings and the like.

(v) *Religious programs* (R) include sermons or devotionals; religious news; and music, drama and other types of programs designed primarily for religious purposes.

(vi) *Instructional programs* (I) are primarily intended to instruct. They further the appreciation or understanding of such subjects as literature, music, fine arts, history, geography, the natural and social sciences, hobbies and occupations and vocations.

(vii) *Sports programs* (S) include play-by-play and pre-game or post-game related activities and separate programs of sports instruction, news or information (e.g., fishing opportunities, golfing instruction, etc).

(viii) *Other programs* (O) include all programs not falling within definitions (i) through (vii).

(ix) *Editorials* (EDIT) include programs presented for the purpose of stating opinions of the licensee.

(x) *Political programs* (POL) include those which present candidates for political office or which give expressions (other than in station editorials) to views on such candidates or on issues subject to public ballot.

(xi) *Educational institution programs* (ED) include those prepared by, on behalf of, or in cooperation with educational institutions, educational organizations, libraries, museums, PTA's, or similar organizations. Sports programs shall not be included.

(2) *Program source.* (i) *A local program* (L) is any program originated or produced by the station or for the production of which the station is primarily responsible, employing live talent more than 50% of the

time. Such a program, taped, recorded or filmed for later broadcast, shall be classified as local. A local program fed to a network shall be classified by the originating station as local. Programs primarily featuring records, tapes, syndicated or feature film or other non-locally recorded programs, shall be classified as recorded (REC) even though a station announcer appears in connection with such material. However, identifiable units of such programs which are live and separately logged as such may be classified as local. For example, if during the course of a program featuring records or films, a non-network 2-minute news report is given and logged as a news program, the report may be classified as local.

(ii) *A network program* (NET) is any program furnished to the station by a network (national, regional or special). Delayed broadcasts of program originated by networks are classified as network.

(iii) *A recorded program* (REC) is any program not otherwise defined in this paragraph including, without limitation, those using recordings, tapes or films.

(3) *Commercial matter* (CM) includes commercial continuity (network and non-network) and commercial announcements (network and non-network) as follows: (Distinction between continuity and announcements is made only for definition purposes. There is no need to distinguish the two types of commercial matter when logging.)

(i) *Commercial continuity* (CC) is the advertising message of a program sponsor.

(ii) *A commercial announcement* (CA) is any other advertising message for which a charge is made, or other consideration is received. Included are bonus spots, trade-out sports, promotional announcements of a future program where consideration is received for such an announcement or where such announcement identifies the sponsor of a future program beyond mention of the sponsor's name as an integral part of the title of the program, and promotional announcements broadcast by any AM, FM or TV station for another commonly owned or controlled station serving the same community.

(iii) *Computation of commercial time:* Duration of commercial matter shall be as close an approximation to the time consumed as possible. The amount of commercial time scheduled will usually be sufficient. It is not necessary, for example, to correct an entry of a 1-minute commercial to accommodate varying reading speeds even though the actual time consumed might be a few seconds more or less than the scheduled time. However, it is incumbent upon the licensee to ensure that the entry represents as close an approximation of the time actually consumed as possible. For certain sponsored programs, it is difficult to measure the exact length of what would be considered as commercial matter, e.g., some sponsored religious and political programs. For such programs, the licensee is not required to compute the amount of commerical matter, but merely to log and announce the program as sponsored.

This exception does not apply to any program advertising commercial products or services, nor to any commercial announcements.

(4) *Public service announcement* (PSA) is one for which no charge is made and which promotes programs, activities or services of Federal, State or local governments (e.g., recruiting, sales of U.S. Savings Bonds, etc.) or the programs, activities or services of nonprofit organizations (e.g., UGF, Red Cross, Blood Donations, etc.) or any other announcements regarded as serving community interests.

Noncommercial Educational Stations

(e) A program log for stations licensed or operating as noncommercial educational stations shall be kept in accordance with the provisions of R & R 73.1810 for each broad-cast day, which in this context means from the station's sign-on to its sign-off.

(f) *Entries*. The following entries shall be made in the program log:

(1) *For each program.* (i) An entry identifying the program by name or title.

(ii) Entries which indicate the time each program begins and ends. If programs are broadcast during which separately identifiable program units of a different type or source are presented, and if the licensee wishes to count such units separately, the beginning and ending time for the longer program need to be entered only once. The program units which the licensee wishes to count separately shall then be entered underneath the entry for the longer program with the beginning and ending time for each such unit.

(iii) An entry classifying each program as to source using the definitions set forth in paragraph (h) (1) of this section. (For network programs, also give name or initials of network, e.g., PBS, NPR, etc.)

(iv) An entry classifying each program as to type, using the definitions set forth in paragraph (h) (2) of this section.

(v) An entry for each program presenting a political candidate, showing the name and political affiliation of such candidates.

(2) *For donor announcements.* An entry giving the name(s) of any donor(s) or person(s) furnishing money, service or other valuable consideration, in accordance with the provisions of R & R 73.503, 73.621, including Notes, and 73.1212; and the entry shall constitute a representation that identification was announced on the air in accordance with the provisions of those sections and Section 317 of the Communications Act. As an alternative to giving the name, an entry of the word "Donor(s)" may be made, provided that the log shall clearly indicate that the name of the donor(s) or person(s) is retained in the station's public file. Such information for a given series of programs need be entered in the public file only

once, provided the information is identical for each program in the series. The information shall be retained in the public file for a period of two years. Program logs submitted to the FCC must include a list of the names of donors indicated thereon.

(3) *For public service announcements.* An entry showing that a public service announcement (PSA) has been broadcast, together with the name of the organization or interest on whose behalf it is made. See paragraph (h) (3) of this section for definition of a public service announcement.

(4) *For other announcements.* (i) An entry of the time that each required station identification announcement is made pursuant to R & R 73.1201.

(ii) An entry for each announcement presenting a political candidate showing the name and political affiliation of such candidate.

(iii) An entry for each announcement made pursuant to the local notice requirements of R & R 1.580 (pregrant) and R & R 1.594 (designation of hearing), showing the time it was broadcast.

(iv) An entry for each announcement made pursuant to R & R 73.1208 concerning the broadcast of taped, filmed or recorded material.

(5) *For Emergency Broadcast System Operations.* An entry for each test of the EBS procedures pursuant to the requirements of Subpart G of this part and the appropriate station EBS checklist, unless such entries are consistently made in the station operating log.

(g) *Network programming.* A station broadcasting the programs of a network (see "network program," paragraph (h) (1) (iii) of this section) which will supply it with all information as to such programs necessary for the "full week of operation" (FCC Form 342) need not log such data but shall record in its log the name of each network program broadcast, the time the program was broadcast (beginning and ending) and any non-network matter broadcast which is required

to be logged. The information supplied by the network for the "full week" which the station will use in its renewal application shall be retained with the program logs and associated with the log pages to which it relates.

(h) *Definitions.* (1) *Program source.* (i) A *local program* (L) is any program originated or produced by the station or for the production of which the station is primarily responsible, employing live talent more than 50% of the time. Such a program, taped, filmed or recorded for later broadcast, shall be classified as local. A local program fed to the network shall be classified by the originating station as local.

(ii) A *record program* (REC) (Radio only) is any program not falling within the definition of "local" above, which utilizes records, transcriptions or taped music, with or without commentary by a local announcer or other station personnel.

(iii) A *network program* (NET) is any program furnished to the station by a network (national, regional or special). Delayed broadcasts of programs originated by networks are classified as network.

(iv) *Other programs* (OTHER) are any programs not defined above, including, without limitation, syndicated and feature films, and taped or transcribed programs.

(2) *Program type.* (i) *Instructional* (I) includes all programs designed to be utilized by any level of educational institution in the regular instructional program of the institution. In-school, in-service for teachers and college credit courses are examples of instructional programs.

(ii) *General Educational* (GEN) is an educational program for which no formal credit is given.

(iii) *Performing Arts* (A) is a program in which the performing aspect predominates such as drama or concert, opera or dance.

(iv) *News* (NS) programs include reports dealing with current local, national and international events, including weather and stock market reports; and commentary, analysis or sports news when an integral part of a news program.

(v) *Public Affairs* (PA) includes programs dealing with local, state, regional, national or international issues or problems, including, but not limited to, talks, commentaries, discussions, speeches, political programs, documentaries, mini-documentaries, panels, roundtables, vignettes and extended coverage (whether live or recorded) of public events or proceedings such as local council meetings, Congressional hearings, and the like.

(vi) *Light Entertainment* (LE) includes programs consisting of popular music or other light entertainment.

(vii) *Other* (O) includes all programs not falling within the definitions of Instructional, General Education, Performing Arts, News, Public Affairs or Light Entertainment. Sports programs should be reported as "Other."

(3) *Public Service Announcements* (PSA) is one which promotes programs, activities, or services of Federal, State or local governments (e.g., recruiting, sales of U.S. Savings Bonds, etc.) or the programs, activities or services of nonprofit organizations (e.g., UGF, Red Cross, Blood Donations, etc.), or any other announcement regarded as serving community interest. See, however, R & R 73.503(d) and 73.621(e) with respect to the preclusion of announcements promoting the sale of a product or service.

All Stations, Commercial and Noncommercial

(i) *Manually kept logs.* (1) Entries on a manually kept log may be made either at the time of or prior to broadcast. The employee responsible for keeping the log shall sign the log when starting duty and when going off duty and enter the time of each.

(2) If entries are preprinted prior to broadcast and any deviation therefrom occurs in what was actually broadcast, an appropriate correction must be made on the log.

(3) When the employee keeping the log signs the log upon going off duty, that person attests to the fact that the log, with any corrections or additions made before he signed off, is an accurate representation of what was actually broadcast.

(j) *Automatically kept logs.* (1) Entries on an automatically kept program log may be made by automatic logging instruments with sequential language printouts corresponding to manually kept log entries.

(2) An employee on duty shall be responsible for the automatic logging process and the keeping of the log. In the event of failure or malfunctioning of the automatic logging process, the person responsible for the log shall make the required entries in the log manually.

(3) The employee responsible shall sign the log, or a separate page to be affixed to the log, when starting duty and when going off duty and enter the time of each. The signature when going off duty constitutes a certification that, as to the automatic printout part of the log, the employee checked the automatic logging equipment periodically throughout the tour and that to the best of his knowledge and belief, at no time during his tour did it fail or malfunction, unless otherwise noted above the signature; and that, as to any part of the log which was kept manually with any correction or additions made thereon before signing off duty, it was an accurate representation of what was actually broadcast.

(k) *Automatic maintenance of logging data.* (1) An employee on duty shall be responsible for any automatic maintenance of data and the keeping of the log. In the event of failure or malfunctioning of the said automatic process, the employee responsible for the log shall make the required entries in the log manually at that time.

(2) The employee responsible shall sign, on a separate page to be affixed to the logging data, when starting duty and when going off duty and enter the time of each. The signature, when going off duty, constitutes a

certification that the employee periodically checked the automatic maintenance of data equipment throughout the tour and to the best of his knowledge and belief it did not fail or malfunction, unless otherwise noted above the signature. The signature further certifies that any part of the log which was kept manually is an accurate representation of what was actually broadcast.

(3) The licensee shall extract any required information from automatically maintained program logging data for days specified by the FCC or its duly authorized representative and submit it in written form, together with the underlying recording, tape or other means employed, within such time as the FCC may specify.

(1) *Information required.* The licensee, whether employing manual logging, automatic logging, or automatic maintenance of logging data, or any combination thereof, must be able to accurately furnish the FCC with all information required to be logged.

R & R 73.113 Operating Logs, see R & R 73.1820 (follows).

R & R 73.1820 Operating Logs. (a) Entries shall be made in the operating log either manually by a properly licensed operator in actual charge of the transmitting apparatus, or by automatic devices meeting the requirements of paragraph (b) of this section. Indications of operating parameters shall be logged prior to any adjustment of the equipment. Where adjustments are made to restore parameters to their proper operating values, the corrected indications shall be logged and accompanied, if any parameter deviation was beyond a prescribed tolerance, by a notation describing the nature of the corrective action. Indications of all parameters whose values are affected by modulation of the carrier shall be read without modulation. The actual time of observation shall be included in each log entry. The following information must be entered.

(1) *All stations:* (i) Entries of the time the station begins to supply power to the antenna and the time it ceases to do so.

(ii) Entries required by R & R 17.49(a), (b) and (c) of this Chapter concerning the time the tower lights are turned on and off each day if manually controlled, the time the daily check of proper operation of the tower lights was made if an automatic alarm system is not used, and any observed failure of the lighting system. See R & R 17.47 (a) for daily tower lighting observation or automatic alarm system requirements.

(iii) Any entries not specifically required in this section, but required by the instrument of authorization or elsewhere in this part.

(iv) An entry of each test of the Emergency Broadcast System procedures pursuant to the requirements of Subpart G of this part and the appropriate station EBS checklist, unless such entries are consistently made in the station program log.

(2) *AM stations:* (i) An entry at the beginning of operations and at intervals not exceeding 3 hours, of the following (actual readings observed prior to making any adjustments to the equipment and an indication of any corrections to restore parameters to normal operating values):

(A) Operating constants for determining the dc input power to the last radio frequency power amplifier stage of the transmitter (plate voltage and current or other parameters appropriate for the type of amplifier used).

(B) Antenna current for nondirectional operation or common point current for directional operation.

(ii) The additional entries required by R & R 73.51(c) (2) when power is being determined by the indirect method.

(iii) For stations with directional antennas, the following additional indications shall be read and entered in the operating log at the time of commencement of operation in each mode and thereafter, at successive intervals not exceeding 3 hours in duration:

(A) Antenna monitor phase or phase deviation indications.

(B) Antenna monitor sample currents, current ratios, or ratio deviation indications.

(3) *FM stations:* (i) For each station

licensed for transmitter output power greater than 10 watts, an entry, at the beginning of operation and at intervals not exceeding 3 hours, of the following (actual readings observed prior to making any adjustments to the equipment and an indication of any corrections made to restore parameters to normal operating values):

(A) Operating constants for determining the dc input power to the last radio frequency power amplifier stage of the transmitter (plate voltage and current or other parameters appropriate for the type of amplifier used).

(B) RF transmission line meter readings when the transmitter operating power is determined by the direct method.

(4) *TV stations:* (i) An entry at the beginning of operation and at intervals not exceeding 3 hours, of the following (actual readings observed prior to making any adjustments to the equipment and an indication of any corrections to restore parameters to normal operating values):

(A) Operating constants for determining the dc input power to the last radio frequency power amplifier stage of the aural transmitter (plate voltage and current or other parameters appropriate for the type of amplifier used) if power of the aural transmitter is being determined by the indirect method.

(B) RF transmission line meter readings for visual transmitter, and also for the aural transmitter when the aural transmitter operating power is determined by the direct method.

(C) For remote control operation, the results of observations of vertical interval test signal (VIT) transmissions (see R&R 73.676(f)).

(b) Automatic devices accurately calibrated and with appropriate time, date and circuit functions may be utilized to record the entries in the operating log provided:

(1) The recording devices do not affect the operation of circuits or accuracy of indicating instruments of the equipment being recorded;

(2) The recording devices have an accuracy equivalent to the accuracy of the indicating instruments;

(3) The calibration is checked against the original indicators at least once each calendar week and the results noted in the maintenance log;

(4) Provision is made to actuate automatically an aural alarm circuit located near the operator on duty if any of the automatic log readings are not within the tolerances or other requirements specified in the rules or station license;

(5) The alarm circuit operates continuously or the devices which record each parameter in sequence must read each parameter at least once during each 30-minute period;

(6) The automatic logging equipment is located at the remote control point if the transmitter is remotely controlled, or at the transmitter location if the transmitter is manually controlled;

(7) The automatic logging equipment is located in the near vicinity of the operator on duty and is inspected periodically during the broadcast day. In the event of failure or malfunctioning of the automatic equipment, the employee responsible for the log shall make the required entries in the log manually at that time.

(8) The indicating equipment conforms to the requirements of R & R 73.1215 (specifications for indicating instruments) except that the scales need not exceed 2 inches in length. Arbitrary scales may not be used.

(c) In preparing the operating log, original data may be recorded in rough form and later transcribed into the log.

(d) If required by AM or FM station operator requirements, each completed operating log shall bear a signed notation by the station's designated chief operator of the results of the review of that log, and show the date and time of such review.

R & R 73.116 Availability of Logs and Records, see R & R 73.1225 and R & R 73.1850 (follow).

R & R 73.1225. Station Inspections by

FCC. (a) The licensee of a broadcast station shall make the station available for inspection by representatives of the FCC during the station's business hours, or at any time it is in operation.

(b) In the course of an inspection or investigation, an FCC representative may require special equipment tests, program tests or operation with nighttime or presunrise facilities during daytime hours pursuant to 0.314, Part 1, of the FCC rules.

(c) The following logs and records shall be made available upon request by representatives of the FCC:

(1) *For AM stations:*

(i) Program, operating and maintenance logs.

(ii) Equipment performance measurements required by R & R 73.47.

(iii) Copy of the most recent antenna resistance or common-point impedance measurements submitted to the Commission.

(iv) Copy of the most recent field strength measurements made to establish performance of directional antennas required by R & R 73.151.

(v) Copy of the partial and skeleton directional antenna proofs of performance as directed by R & R 73.154 and made pursuant to the following requirements:

(A) Section 73.67, Remote control operation.

(B) Section 73.68, Sampling systems for antenna monitors.

(C) Section 73.69, Antenna monitors.

(D) Section 73.93, Operator requirements.

(vi) Chief operator agreements for maintenance duties.

(2) *For FM stations:* (i) Program, operating and maintenance logs.

(ii) Equipment performance measurements required by R & R 73.254 and R & R 73.554.

(iii) Chief operator agreements for maintenance duties.

(3) *For TV stations:* (i) Program, operating and maintenance logs.

R & R 73.117, see R & R 73.1201 (follows).

R & R 73.1201 Station Identification. (a) *When regularly required.* Broadcast station identification announcements shall be made: (1) At the beginning and ending of each time of operation, and (2) hourly, as close to the hour as feasible, at a natural break in program offerings. Television broadcast stations may make these announcements visually or aurally.

(b) *Content.* (1) Official station identification shall consist of the station's call letters immediately followed by the community or communities specified in its license as the station's location: *Provided,* That the name of the licensee or the station's frequency or channel number, or both, as stated on the station's license may be inserted between the call letters and station location. No other insertion is permissible.

(2) When given specific written authorization to do so, a station may include in its official station identification the name of an additional community or communities, but the community to which the station is licensed must be named first.

(3) A licensee shall not in any identification announcements, promotional announcements or any other broadcast matter either lead or attempt to lead the station's audience to believe that the station has been authorized to identify officially with cities other than those permitted to be included in official station identifications under subparagraphs (1) and (2) of this paragraph.

Note: Commission interpretations of this paragraph may be found in a separate Public Notice issued Oct. 30, 1967, entitled Examples of Application of Rule Regarding Broadcast of Statements Regarding a Station's Licensed Location. (FCC 67–1132; 10 FCC 2d 407).

(c) *Channel*—(1) *General.* Except as otherwise provided in this paragraph, in making the identification announcement the call letters shall be given only on the channel identified thereby.

(2) *Simultaneous AM–FM broadcasts.* If the same licensee operates an FM broadcast station and a standard broadcast station and simultaneously broadcasts the same programs over the facilities of both such stations, station identification announcements may be made jointly for both stations for periods of such simultaneous operation. If the call letters of the FM station do not clearly reveal that it is an FM station, the joint announcement shall so identify it.

(3) *Satellite operation.* When programming of a broadcast station is rebroadcast simultaneously over the facilities of a satellite station, the originating station may make identification announcements for the satellite station for periods of such simultaneous operation.

(i) In the case of a television broadcast station, such announcements, in addition to the information required by paragraph (b) (1) of this section, shall include the number of the channel on which each station is operating.

(ii) In the case of aural broadcast stations, such announcements, in addition to the information required by paragraph (b) (1) of this section, shall include the frequency on which each station is operating.

* * * * * *

R & R 73.252. Frequency Measurements, see R & R 73.1540 (follows).

R & R 73.1540. Carrier Frequency Measurements. (a) The carrier frequency of each AM and FM station and the visual carrier frequency and difference between the visual carrier and the aural carrier or center frequency of each TV station shall be measured or determined as often as necessary to insure that they are maintained within the prescribed tolerances. However, in any event, each station with an authorized operating power greater than 10 watts shall make at least one measurement or determination each calendar month with intervals not exceeding 40 days between successive

measurements for each main transmitter in use.

(b) The licensee of each broadcast station shall determine the method or procedures for measuring or determining the carrier frequency.

(c) The primary standard of frequency for radio frequency measurements is the standard frequency maintained by the National Bureau of Standards or the standard signals of Stations WWV, WWVB, WWVH and WWVL of the National Bureau of Standards.

* * * * * *

R & R 73.265 FM operator requirements.

(a) Transmitter duty operator requirements. (See R & R 73.1860.)

(b) Chief operator requirements. See R & R 73.1870.)

(c) Transmission system inspection requirements. (See R & R 73.1580.)

R & R 73.269. Frequency Tolerance. The center frequency of each FM broadcast station shall be maintained within 2000 hertz of the assigned center frequency.

* * * * * *

R & R 73.565. NCE-FM operator requirements.

(a) Transmitter duty operator requirements. (See R & R 73.1860.)

(b) Chief operator requirements. (See R & R 73.1870.)

(c) Transmission system inspection requirements. (See R & R 73.1580.)

● Section 73.661 is revised in its entirety to read as follows:

R & R 73.661 TV operator requirements.

(a) Transmitter duty operator requirements. (See R & R 73.1860.)

(b) Chief operator requirements. (See R & R 73.1870.)

(c) Transmission system inspection requirements. (See R & R 73.1580.)

R & R 73.764. International broadcast station operator requirements.

(a) One or more operators holding a commercial radio operator license (any class, unless otherwise endorsed) must be on duty where the transmitting apparatus of each station is located and in actual charge thereof whenever it is being operated.

(b) The licensed operator on duty and in charge of the transmitter may, at the discretion of the station licensee, be employed for other duties or for the operation of other transmitters if such duties do not interfere with the proper operation of the transmission system.

(c) Operator licenses are to be posted as specified in R & R 73.1230.

* * * * * *

R & R 73.914 Primary Station (Primary). A Primary Station broadcasts or re-broadcasts a common emergency program for the duration of the activation of the EBS at the National, State, or Operational (Local) Area level. The EBS transmission of such stations are intended for direct public reception as well as inter-station programming.

* * * * * *

R & R 73.932. Radio Monitoring and Attention Signal Transmission Requirements. (a) Monitoring Requirement. To insure effective off-the-air signal monitoring (R & R 73.931(a)(3)) all broadcast station licensees must install and operate, during their hours of broadcast operation, equipment capable of receiving the Attention Signal and emergency programming transmitted by other broadcast stations. This equipment must be maintained in operative condition, including arrangements for human listening watch or automatic alarm devices. This equipment must be installed in the broadcast station, either at the transmitter control point and/or studio location, in such a way that it enables the broadcast station staff, at normal duty locations, to be alerted instantaneously upon the receipt of the Attention Signal and

to immediately monitor the emergency programming. For situations where broadcast stations are co-owned and co-located (e.g., an AM and FM licensed to the same entity at the same location) with a combined studio facility, only one receiver is required if installed in the combined studio facility. The off-the-air signal monitoring assignment of each broadcast station is specified in the State EBS Operational Plan.

(b) Transmission Requirement. All broadcast licensees, except non-commercial educational FM Broadcast Stations of 10 watts or less, must install, operate, and maintain equipment capable of generating the Attention Signal (R & R 73.906) to modulate the transmitter so that the signal may be broadcast to other broadcast stations. This signal is used to alert other broadcast stations to the fact that the EBS is being activated at the National, State, or local level. It is also used during the Weekly Tests involving the transmission and reception of the Attention Signal and Test Script in accordance with R & R 73.961(c). This equipment must be installed in the broadcast station either at the transmitter control point and/or studio location in such a way that it enables the broadcast station staff at normal duty locations to initiate the two-tone transmission. For situations where broadcast stations are co-owned and co-located (e.g., an AM and FM licensed to the same entity at the same location) with a combined studio facility, only one generator is required if installed in the combined studio facility.

(c) The licensee has the responsibility to insure that the equipment used for off-the-air signal monitoring and generating the EBS Attention Signal is in functioning condition during all times the station is in operation, and to determine the cause of any failure to receive the Weekly Transmission Tests as described in paragraph (c) of R & R 73.961.

(d) In the event that the equipment for receiving the Attention Signal and emergency programming transmitted by other broadcast stations, or the equipment for generating the Attention Signal becomes defective, the station may operate without the defective equipment pending its repair or replacement for a period not in excess of 60 days without further authority of the Commission provided that:

(1) Appropriate entries shall be made in the station operating or program log, indicating reasons why Weekly Test Transmissions were not received or conducted, and;

(2) Appropriate entries shall be made in the maintenance log of the station showing the date and time the equipment was removed and restored to service.

(e) If conditions beyond the control of the licensee prevent the restoration of the defective equipment to service within the above allowed period, informal request in accordance with Section 1.549 of this chapter may be filed with the Engineer in Charge of the radio district in which the station is operating for such additional time as may be required to complete repairs of the defective equipment.

R & R 73.933 Emergency Broadcast System Operation During a National Level Emergency. (a) An EBS Checklist will be posted at normal duty positions where it shall be immediately available to broadcast station personnel responsible for EBS actions. This Checklist summarizes the procedures to be followed upon receipt of a National Level Emergency Action Notification or Termination Message in accordance with arrangements described in R & R 73.931(a).

(b) Immediately upon receipt of an EAN Message all licensees will proceed as follows:

(1) Monitor the radio and TV network facilities for further instructions from the network control point.

(2) Check the Radio Press Wire Service (AP and UPI). Verify the authenticity of message with current EBS Authenticator List (Red Envelope).

(3) Monitor your EBS monitoring assignment (See State EBS Operational Plan) for the receipt of any further instructions.

(4) Discontinue normal programming and follow the transmission procedures set forth in the appropriate EBS Checklist.

(i) Primary CPCS, Originating Primary Relay, Primary Relay, and Primary stations follow the transmission procedures and make the announcements under the National Level Instructions of the EBS Checklist for Participating Stations.

(ii) Non-participating stations follow the transmission procedures and make the announcements under the National Level Instructions of the EBS Checklist for Non-Participating Stations. Following the announcement, non-participating stations are required to remove their carriers from the air and monitor for the Emergency Action Termination.

(5) Upon completion of the above transmission procedures:

(i) Participating stations will begin broadcast of a common emergency program. All stations shall carry the common emergency program until receipt of the Emergency Action Termination Message. Programming priorities are set forth in R & R 73.922. Feeds will be provided by one or more of the following:

(a) Common Program Control Stations.

(b) Radio and Television Broadcast Networks.

(c) Originating Primary Relay and Primary Relay Stations in the State Relay Network.

(ii) Should it become apparent that the primary CPCS Station or Primary Relay Station of an Operational (Local) Area may not be able to provide an appropriate emergency program feed, other Primary Stations of the area may elect to assume the duties of providing a program feed. This should be done in an organized manner as designated in the State EBS Operational Plans.

(6) The Standby Script shall be used until program material is available. The text

of the Standby Script is contained in the EBS Checklist for Participating Stations.

(7) TV broadcast stations shall display an appropriate EBS slide and then transmit all announcements visually and aurally in the manner described in R & R 73.675(b) of this Part.

(8) A Station which broadcasts primarily in a language other than English shall broadcast in such foreign language following the broadcast in English.

(9) Broadcast Stations in the International Broadcast Service will cease broadcasting immediately upon receipt of an Emergency Action Notification and will maintain radio silence. However, under certain conditions they may be issued appropriate emergency authorization by the FCC with concurrence of the Director, Office of Telecommunications Policy, in which event they will transmit only Federal government broadcasts or communications. The station's carrier must be removed from the air during periods of no broadcasts or communications transmissions.

(10) Stations may broadcast their call letters during an EBS activation. State and Operational (Local) Area identifications shall also be given.

(11) All stations operating and identified with a particular Operational (Local) Area will broadcast a common emergency program until receipt of the Emergency Action Termination.

(12) Broadcast stations holding an EBS Authorization are specifically exempt from complying with R & R 73.52 (pertaining to maintenance of operating power) while operating under this subpart of the rules.

(c) Upon receipt of an Emergency Action Termination Message all stations will follow the termination procedures set forth in the EBS Checklists.

(d) Stations originating emergency communications under this Section shall be deemed to have conferred rebroadcast authority, as required by Section 325(a) of the Communications Act of 1934, as amended

and R & R 73.1207, on other participating stations.

*   *   *   *   *   *

R & R 73.961 Tests of the Emergency Broadcast System Procedures. Tests of the EBS procedures will be made at regular intervals as indicated below. Appropriate entries shall be made consistently in the station operating log or consistently in the station program log on EBS Tests received and transmitted by broadcast stations.

(a) Weekly "500" Net Test Transmissions. Test transmissions of the National level interconnection facilities will be conducted on a random basis once each week. The tests will originate on an alternate basis from one of two origination points over a dedicated government teletypewriter network to the control points of the Radio and Television Broadcast Networks, participating communications common carriers, AP and UPI. A dedicated automatic telephone network will be used for confirmation purposes between the origination points of AP and UPI. These tests will be in accordance with procedures set forth in EBS SOP-2 which is furnished to the non-government entities concerned.

(b) Periodic AP and UPI Test Transmissions. AP and UPI will separately conduct test transmissions to AM, FM, and TV broadcast stations on their Radio Wire Teletype Network, a maximum of twice a month on a random basis at times of their choice. These tests will be conducted in accordance with procedures set forth in EBS SOP-2 which is furnished to the non-government entities concerned and the EBS Checklist furnished to all broadcast stations.

(c) Weekly Transmission Tests of the Attention Signal and Test Script. Except as provided in paragraph (d) of this Section, these tests shall be conducted by all AM, FM, and TV broadcast stations a minimum of once a week at random days and times between the hours of 8:30 a.m. and local sunset. These tests will be conducted in accordance with procedures set forth in the EBS Checklist furnished to all broadcast stations.

(d) Tests of implementing procedures developed at the State and Local levels may be conducted on a day-to-day basis as indicated in State EBS Operational Plans. Coordinated tests of EBS operational procedures for an entire State or Operational (Local) Area may be conducted in lieu of the Weekly Transmission Tests of the Attention Signal and Test Script required in paragraph (c) of this section.

(e) Stations originating emergency communications under this section shall be deemed to have conferred rebroadcast authority, as required by Section 325(a) of the Communications Act of 1934, as amended, and R & R 73.1207 of this Part.

R & R 73.1515 Special Field test authorizations.

* * * * * *

(c) * * *

* * * * * *

(6) Test transmitters must be operated by or under the immediate direction of an operator holding a General Radiotelephone Operator License.

* * * * * *

R & R 73.1580 Transmission system inspections.

(a) Each AM, FM, and TV station must conduct a complete inspection of the transmitting system and all required monitors according to the following schedule:

(1) For stations not using an automatic transmission system, an inspection at least once each calendar week at intervals not exceeding 10 days.

(2) For stations using an authorized automatic transmission system (ATS) the inspections must be completed at least once each calendar month at intervals not exceeding 40 days.

(3) For Class D noncommercial edu-

cational FM stations authorized to operate with power not exceeding 10 watts, the inspections must be conducted as necessary to insure compliance with the rules and terms of the station authorization.

(b) The results of the inspections required by subsection (a) of this Section are to be entered in the station maintenance log as specified in R & R 73.1830(a)(i)(ix).

R & R 73.1830 Maintenance logs.

(a) Each AM, FM, and TV station must keep a maintenance log. Entries in the log must be made by or under the direction of the station's chief operator, and the entries are to reflect the results of all transmitter inspections, tests, adjustments, and maintenance. The following information is to be entered in the log:

(1) * * *

(ix) A signed dated statement by the chief operator upon completion of the inspections required by R & R 73.1580 showing that the inspection has been made. The statement must include details of tests, adjustments, and repairs that were accomplished to ensure operation in accordance with the technical operating rules and terms of the station authorization. If repairs could not be completed, the entry must also include details of the items of equipment concerned, the manner and degree in which they were defective, and the reasons why complete repair could not be made.

* * * * * *

(2) * * *

(iii) For stations using directional antennas, an entry of the results of field strength measurements made at the monitoring points specified in the station authorization, if such measurements are required by R & R 73.61 or the terms of the authorization.

* * * * * *

R & R 73.1860 Transmitter duty operators.

(a) Each AM, FM, and TV broadcast station must have at least one person holding a commercial radio operator license (any class, unless otherwise endorsed) on duty in charge of the transmitter during all periods of broadcast operation. The operator must be on duty at the transmitter location, a remote control point, an ATS monitor and alarm point, or a position where extension meters are installed under the provisions of R & R 73.1550.

(b) The transmitter operator must be able to observe the required transmitter and monitor metering to determine deviations from normal indications. The operator must also be able to make the necessary adjustments from the normal operator duty position, except as provided for in R & R 73.1550.

(c) It is the responsibility of the station licensee to ensure that each transmitter operator is fully instructed and capable to perform all necessary observations and adjustments of the transmitting system and other associated operating duties to ensure compliance with the rules and station authorization.

(d) The transmitter duty operator may, at the discretion of the station licensee and chief operator, be employed for other duties or operation of other transmitting stations if such other duties will not interfere with the proper operation of the broadcast transmission system.

R & R 73.1870 Chief Operators

(a) The licensee of each AM, FM, and TV broadcast station must designate a person holding a commercial radio operator license (any class, unless otherwise endorsed) to serve as the station's chief operator. At times when the chief operator is unavailable or unable to act (e.g. vacations, sickness), the licensee shall designate another licensed operator as the acting chief operator on a temporary basis.

(b) Chief operators shall be employed or serve on the following basis:

(1) The chief operator for an AM station using a directional antenna or operating with greater than 10 kW authorized power, or of a TV station is to be an employee of the station on duty for whatever number of hours each week the station licensee determines is necessary to keep the station's technical operation in compliance with FCC rules and the terms of the station authorization.

(2) Chief operators for non-directional AM stations operating with authorized powers not exceeding 10 kW and FM stations may be either an employee of the station or engaged to serve on a contract basis for whatever number of hours each week the licensee determines is necessary to keep the station's technical operation in compliance with the FCC rules and terms of the station authorization.

(3) The designation of the chief operator must be in writing with a copy of the designation posted with the operator license. Agreements with chief operators serving on a contract basis must be in writing with a copy kept in the station files.

(c) The chief operator has the following specific duties:

(1) Conduct weekly (or monthly for stations using automatic transmission systems) inspections and calibrations of the transmission system, required monitors, metering, and control systems; and make any necessary repairs or adjustments where indicated. (See R & R 73.1580.)

(2) Make or supervise periodic AM field monitoring point measurements, equipment performance measurements, or other tests as specified in the rules or terms of the station license.

(3) Review the station operating logs at least once each week as part of the transmission system inspections to determine if the entries are being made correctly or if the station has been operating as required by the rules or the station authorization. Upon completion of the review, the chief operator is to make a notation of any discrepancies observed and date and sign the log; initiate necessary corrective action, and advise the station licensee of any condition that is a repetitive problem.

(4) Make or supervise entries in the maintenance log. (See R & R 73.1830.)

PART 80:
STATIONS IN THE MARITIME SERVICES

R & R 80.5 Definitions *Associated ship unit.* A portable VHF transmitter for use in the vicinity of the ship station with which it is associated.

Automated maritime telecommunications system (AMTS). An automatic, integrated and interconnected maritime communications system serving ship stations on specified inland and coastal waters of the United States.

Automated mutual-assistance vessel rescue system (AMVER). An international system, operated by the U.S. Coast Guard, which provides aid to the development and coordination of search and rescue (SAR) efforts. Data is made available to recognized SAR agencies or vessels of any nation for reasons related to marine safety.

Bridge-to-bridge station. A radio station located on a ship''s navigational bridge or main control station operating on a specified frequency which is used only for navigational communications, in the 156–162 MHz band.

Cargo ship safety radiotelegraphy certificate. A certificate issued after an inspection of a cargo ship radiotelegraph station which complies with the applicable Safety Convention radio requirements.

Cargo ship safety radiotelephony certificate. A certificate issued after inspection of a cargo ship radiotelephone station which complies with the applicable Safety Convention radio requirements.

Categories of ships.

(1) When referenced in Part II of Title III of the Communications Act or the radio provisions of the Safety Convention, a ship is a "passenger ship" if it carries or is licensed or certified to carry more than twelve passengers. A "cargo ship" is any ship not a passenger ship.

* * * * * *

(3) The term "passenger carrying vessel," when used in reference to Part III, Title III of the communications Act or the Great Lakes Radio Agreement, means any ship transporting more than six passengers for hire.

(4) Power-driven vessel. Any ship propelled by machinery.

* * * * * *

(6) Compulsory ship. Any ship which is required to be equipped with radiotelecommunication equipment in order to comply with the radio or radionavigation provisions of a treaty or statute to which the vessel is subject.

(7) Voluntary ship. Any ship which is not required by treaty or statute to be equipped with radiotelecommunications equipment.

* * * * * *

Digital selective calling (DSC). A synchronous system developed by the International Radio Consultative Committee (CCIR), used to establish contact with a station or group of stations automatically by means of radio. The operational and technical characteristics of this system are contained in CCIR Recommendation 493.

* * * * * *

Emergency position indicating radio-beacon (EPIRB) station. A station in the maritime mobile service the emissions of which are intended to facilitate search and rescue operations.

Fleet radio station license. An authorization issued by the Commission for two or more ships having a common owner or operator.

* * * * * *

Marine utility station. A station in the maritime mobile service consisting of one or more handheld radiotelephone units licensed under a single authorization. Each unit is capable of operation while being hand-carried by an individual. The station operates under the rules applicable to ship stations when the unit is aboard a vessel, and under the rules applicable to private coast stations when the unit is on land.

*   *   *   *   *   *

Maritime mobile-satellite service. A mobile-satellite service in which mobile earth stations are located on board ships. Survival craft stations and EPIRB stations may also participate in this service.

Maritime mobile service. A mobile service between coast stations and ship stations, or between ship stations, or between associated on-board communication stations. Survival craft stations and EPIRB stations also participate in this service.

*   *   *   *   *   *

Navigational communications. Safety communications pertaining to the maneuvering of vessels or the directing of vessel movements. Such communications are primarily for the exchange of information between ship stations and secondarily between ship stations and coast stations.

*   *   *   *   *   *

On-board communication station. A low-powered mobile station in the maritime mobile service intended for use for internal communications on board a ship, or between a ship and its lifeboats and liferafts during lifeboat drills or operations, or for communication within a group of vessels being towed or pushed, as well as for line handling and mooring instructions.

*   *   *   *   *   *

Radar beacon (RACON). A receiver-transmitter which, when triggered by a radar, automatically returns a distinctive signal which can appear on the display of the triggering radar, providing range, bearing and identification information.

*   *   *   *   *   *

Safety communication. The transmission or reception of distress, alarm, urgency, or safety signals, or any communications preceded by one of these signals, or any form of radiocommunication which, if delayed in transmission or reception, may adversely affect the safety of life or property.

*   *   *   *   *   *

Selective calling. A means of calling in which signals are transmitted in accordance with a prearranged code to operate a particular automatic attention device at the station whose attention is sought.

*   *   *   *   *   *

Ship station. A mobile station in the maritime mobile service located onboard a vessel which is not permanently moored, other than a survival craft station.

*   *   *   *   *   *

Survival craft station. A mobile station in the maritime or aeronautical mobile service intended solely for survival purposes and located on any lifeboat, liferaft, or other survival equipment.

Urgency signal. (1) The urgency signal is the international radiotelegraph or radiotelephone signal which indicates that the calling station has a very urgent message to transmit concerning the safety of a ship, aircraft, or other vehicle, or of some person on board or within sight.

*   *   *   *   *   *

Vessel traffic service (VTS). A U.S.

Coast Guard traffic control service for ships in designated water areas to prevent collisions, groundings and environmental harm.

* * * * * *

R & R 80.13 Station License Required. (a) All stations in the maritime services must be licensed by the FCC.

(b) One ship station license will be granted for operation of all maritime services transmitting equipment on board a vessel.

* * * * * *

R & R 80.29 Changes During License Term. (a) The following table indicates the required action for changes made during the license term:

TYPE OF CHANGE	REQUIRED ACTION
Mailing address...................	Written notice to the Commission.
Name of licensee (without change in ownership, control or corporate structure.)	Written notice to the Commission.
Transfer of control of a corporation..	Comply with R & R 1.924 of this chapter.
Assignment of a radio station license	Comply with R & R 1.924 of this chapter.
Name of the vessel	Written notice to the Commission.
Addition of transmitting equipment which operates on a frequency or frequency band not authorized on present license....................	Application for modification of license.
Addition of replacement of transmitting equipment on a frequency or frequency band authorized on present license........	None (provided the equipment is properly type accepted and the emission characteristics remain the same.

(b) Written notices must be sent to the Federal Communications Commission, Gettysburg, Pennsylvania 17325.

* * * * * *

R & R 80.79 Inspection of Ship Station by a Foreign Government. The Governments or appropriate administrations of countries which a ship visits may require the license of the ship station or ship earth station to be produced for examination. When the license cannot be produced without delay or when irregularities are observed, Governments or administrations may inspect the radio installations to satisfy themselves that the installation conforms to the conditions imposed by the Radio Regulations.

* * * * * *

R & R 80.88 Secrecy of Communication. The station licensee, the master of the ship, the responsible radio operators and any person who may have knowledge of the radio communications transmitted or received by a fixed, land, or mobile station subject to this part, or of any radiocommunication service of such station, must observe the secrecy requirements of the Communication Act and the Radio Regulations.

R & R 80.89 Unauthorized Transmissions. Stations must not:

(a) Engage in superfluous radiocommunication.

(b) Use telephony on 243 MHz.

(c) Use selective calling on 2182 kHz or 156.800 MHz.

(d) When using telephony, transmit signals or communications not addressed to a particular station or stations. This provision does not apply to the transmission of distress, alarm, urgency, or safety signals or messages, or to test transmission.

(e) When using telegraphy, transmit signals or communications not addressed to a particular station or stations, unless the transmission is preceded by CQ or CP or by distress, alarm, urgency, safety signals, or test transmissions.

(f) Transmit while on board vessels located on land. Vessels in the following situations are not considered to be on land for the purposes of this paragraph:

(1) Vessels which are aground due to a distress situation;

(2) Vessels in drydock undergoing repairs; and

(3) State or local government vessels which are involved in search and rescue operations including related training exercises.

R & R 80.90 Suspension of Transmission. Transmission must be suspended immediately upon detection of a transmitter malfunction and must remain suspended until the malfunction is corrected, except for transmission concerning the immediate safety of life or property, in which case transmission must be suspended as soon as the emergency is terminated.

R & R 80.91 Order of Priority of Communications. (a) The order of priority of radiotelegraph communications is as follows:

(1) Distress calls including the international distress signal for radiotelegraphy, the international radiotelegraph alarm signal, the international radiotelephone alarm signal, distress messages and distress traffic.

(2) Communications preceded by the international radiotelegraph urgency signal.

(3) Communications preceded by the international radiotelegraph safety signal.

(4) Communications relative to radio direction-finding bearings.

(5) Communications relative to the navigation and safe movement of aircraft.

(6) Communications relative to the navigation, movements, and needs of ships, including weather observation messages destined for an official meteorological service.

(7) Government communications for which priority right has been claimed.

(8) Service communications relating to the working of the radiocommunication service or to communications previously transmitted.

(9) All other communications.

R & R 80.92 Prevention of Interference. (a) The station operator must determine that the frequency is not in use by monitoring the frequency before transmitting, except for transmission of signals of distress.

(b) When a radiocommunication causes interference to a communication which is already in progress, the interfering station must cease transmitting at the request of either party to the existing communication. As between non-distress traffic seeking to commence use of a frequency, the priority is established under R & R 80.91.

(c) Except in cases of distress, communications between ship stations or between ship and aircraft stations must not interfere with public coast stations. The ship or aircraft stations which cause interference must stop transmitting or change frequency upon the first request of the affected coast station.

*   *   *   *   *   *

R & R 80.95 Message Charges. (a) Charges must not be made for service of:

(1) Any public coast station unless tariffs for the service are on file with the Commission.

(2) Any station other than a public coast station or an Alaska-public fixed station, except cooperatively shared stations covered by R & R 80.503;

(3) Distress traffic;

(4) Navigation hazard warnings preceded by the SAFETY signal.

(b) The licensee of each ship station is responsible for the payment of all charges accruing to any other station(s) or facilities for the handling or forwarding of messages or communications transmitted by that station.

(c) In order to be included in the ITU List of Coast Stations public coast stations must recognize international Accounting Authority Identification Codes (AAIC) for purposes of billing and accounts settlement in accordance with Article 66 of the Radio Regulations. Stations which elect not to recognize international AAIC's will be removed from the ITU List of Coast Stations.

* * * * * *

R & R 80.99 Radiotelegraph Station Identification. This section applies to coast, ship and survival craft stations authorized to transmit in the band 405–525 kHz.

(a) The station transmitting radiotelegraph emissions must be identified by its call sign. The call sign must be transmitted with the telegraphy emission normally used by the station. The call sign must be transmitted at 20 minute intervals when transmission is sustained for more than 20 minutes. When a ship station is exchanging public correspondence communications, the identification may be deferred until completion of each communication with any other station.

(b) The requirements of this section do not apply to survival craft stations when transmitting distress signals automatically or when operating on 121.500 MHz for radiobeacon purposes.

(c) Emergency position indicating radiobeacon stations do not require identification.

* * * * * *

R & R 80.101 Radiotelephone Testing Procedures. This section is applicable to all stations using telephony except where otherwise specified.

(a) Station licensees must not cause harmful interference. When radiation is necessary or unavoidable, the testing procedure described below must be followed:

(1) The operator must not interfere with transmissions in progress.

(2) The testing station's call sign, followed by the word "test," must be announced on the radio channel being used for the test;

(3) If any station responds "wait," the test must be suspended for a minimum of 30 seconds, then repeat the call sign followed by the word "test" and listen again for a response. To continue the test, the operator must use counts or phrases which do not conflict with normal operating signals, and must end with the station's call sign. Test signals must not exceed ten seconds, and must not be repeated until at least one minute has elapsed. On the frequency 2182 kHz or 156.800 MHz, the time between tests must be a minimum of five minutes.

(b) Testing of transmitters must be confined to single frequency channels on working frequencies. However, 2182 kHz and 156.800 MHz may be used to contact ship or coast stations as appropriate when signal reports are necessary. Short tests on 2182 kHz by vessels with DSB (A3) equipment for distress and safety purposes are permitted to evaluate the compatibility of that equipment with an A3J emission system. U.S. Coast Guard stations may be contacted on 2182 kHz or 156.800 MHz for test purposes only when tests are being conducted during inspections by Commission representatives, when qualified radio technicians are installing or repairing the station radiotelephone equipment, or when qualified ship's personnel conduct an operational check requested by the U.S. Coast Guard. In these cases the test must be identified as "FCC" or "technical."

(c) Survival craft transmitter tests must not be made within actuating range of automatic alarm receivers. Survival craft transmitters must not be tested on the frequency 500 kHz during the silence periods.

R & R 80.102 Radiotelephone Station Identification. This section applies to all stations using telephony which are subject to this part.

(a) Except as provided in paragraph (d), stations must give the call sign in English. Identification must be made:

(1) At the beginning and end of each communication with any other station.

(2) At 15 minute intervals when transmission is sustained for more than 15 minutes. When public correspondence is being exchanged with a ship or aircraft station, the identification may be deferred until the completion of the communications.

(b) Private coast stations located at drawbridges and transmitting on the navigation frequency 156.650 MHz may identify by use of the name of the bridge in lieu of the call sign.

(c) Ship stations transmitting on any authorized VHF bridge-to-bridge channel may be identified by the name of the ship in lieu of the call sign.

(d) Ship stations operating in a vessel traffic service system or on a waterway under the control of a U.S. Government agency or a foreign authority, when communicating with such an agency or authority may be identified by the name of the ship in lieu of the call sign, or as directed by the agency or foreign authority.

*   *   *   *   *   *

R & R 80.114 Authority of the Master. (a) The service of each ship station must at all times be under the ultimate control of the master, who must require that each operator of such station comply with the Radio Regulations in force and that the ship station is used in accordance with those regulations.

(b) These rules are waived when the vessel is under the control of the U.S. Government.

R & R 80.115 Operational Conditions for Use of Associated Ship Units. (a) Associated ship units may be operated under a ship station authorization. Use of an associated ship unit is restricted as follows:

(1) It must only be operated on the safety and calling frequency 156.800 MHz or on commercial or noncommercial VHF intership frequencies appropriate to the class of ship station with which it is associated.

(2) Except for safety purposes, it must only be used to communicate with the ship station with which it is associated or with associated ship units of the same ship station. Such associated ship units may not be used from shore.

(3) It must be equipped to transmit on the frequency 156.800 MHz and at least one appropriate intership frequency.

(4) Calling must occur on the frequency 156.800 MHz unless calling and working on an intership frequency has been prearranged.

(5) Power is limited to one watt.

(6) The station must be identified by the call sign of the ship station with which it is associated and an appropriate unit designator.

(b) State or local government vehicles used to tow vessels involved in search and rescue operations are authorized to operate on maritime mobile frequencies as associated ship units. Such operations must be in accordance with paragraph (a) of this section except that the associated ship unit: may be operated from shore; may use Distress, Safety and Calling, Intership Safety, Liaison, U.S. Coast Guard, or Maritime Control VHF intership frequencies; and may have a transmitter power of 25 watts.

R & R 80.116 Radiotelephone Operating Procedures for Ship Stations. (a) *Calling coast stations.* (1) Use by ship stations of the frequency 2182 kHz for calling coast stations and for replying to calls from coast stations is authorized. However, such calls and replies should be on the appropriate ship-shore working frequency.

(2) Use by ship stations and marine utility stations of the frequency 156.800 MHz for calling coast stations and marine utility stations on shore, and for replying to calls from such stations, is authorized. However, such calls and replies should be made on the appropriate ship-shore working frequency.

(b) *Calling ship stations.* (1) Except when other operating procedure is used to expedite safety communication, ship stations, before transmitting on the intership working frequencies 2003, 2142, 2638, 2738, or 2830 kHz, must first establish communication with other ship stations by call and reply on 2182 kHz. Calls may be initiated on an intership working frequency when it is known that the called vessel maintains a simultaneous watch on the working frequency and on 2182 kHz.

(2) Except when other operating procedure is used to expedite safety communication, the frequency 156.800 MHz must be used for call and reply by ship stations and marine utility stations before establishing communication on one of the intership working frequencies.

(c) *Change to working frequency.* After establishing communication with another station by call and reply on 2182 kHz or 156.800 MHz stations on board ship must change to an authorized working frequency for the transmission of messages.

(d) *Limitations on calling.* Calling a particular station must not continue for more than 30 seconds in each instance. If the called station does not reply, the station must not again be called until after an interval of 2 minutes. When a called station called does not reply to a call sent three times at intervals of 2 minutes, the calling must cease and must not be renewed until after an interval of 15 minutes; however, if there is no reason to believe that harmful interference will be caused to other communications in progress, the call sent three times at intervals of 2 minutes may be repeated after a pause of not less than 3 minutes. In event of an emergency involving safety, the provisions of this paragraph do not apply.

(e) *Limitations on working.* Any one exchange of communications between any two ship stations on 2003, 2142, 2638, 2738, or 2830 kHz or between a ship station and a private coast station on 2738 or 2830 kHz must not exceed 3 minutes after the stations have established contact. Subsequent to such exchange of communications, the same two stations must not again use 2003, 2142, 2638, 2738, or 2830 kHz for communication with each other until 10 minutes have elapsed.

(f) *Transmission limitation on 2182 kHz and 156.800 MHz.* To facilitate the reception of distress calls, all transmissions on 2182 kHz and 156.800 MHz (channel 16) must be minimized and transmissions on 156.800 MHz must not exceed one minute.

(g) *Limitations on commercial communication.* On frequencies in the band 156–162 MHz, the exchange of commercial communication must be limited to the minimum practicable transmission time. In the conduct of ship-shore communication other than distress, stations on board ship must comply with instructions given by the private coast station or marine utility station on shore with which they are communicating.

(h) *2182 kHz silence periods.* To facilitate the reception of distress calls, transmission by ship or survival craft stations is prohibited on any frequency (including 2182 kHz) within the band 2173.5–2190.5 kHz during each 2182 kHz silence period.

* * * * * *

R & R 80.145 Class C EPIRB Operational Procedures. Class C EPIRB must be used for distress purposes only after use of the VHF/FM radiotelephone installation, in accordance with R & R 80.320, has proved unsuccessful or when a VHF/FM radiotelephone installation is not fitted, or when specifically requested to do so by a station engaged in search and rescue operations.

R & R 80.146 Watch on 500 kHz. During their hours of service, ship stations using frequencies in the authorized bands between 405–525 kHz must remain on watch on 500 kHz except when the operator is transmitting on 500 kHz or operating on another frequency. The provisions of this section do not relieve the ship from complying with the requirements for a safety watch as prescribed in R & R 80.304 and R & R 80.305.

R & R 80.147 Watch on 2182 kHz. Ship stations must maintain a watch on 2182 kHz as prescribed by R & R 80.304(b).

R & R 80.148 Watch on 156.8 MHz (Channel 16). Each VHF ship station, or if more than one VHF ship station is being operated from a vessel (for example, if a pilot is operating his radio equipment on board the vessel), then at least one VHF ship station per vessel must during its hours of service maintain a watch on 156.800 MHz whenever such station is not being used for exchanging communications. The watch is not required:

(a) Where a ship station is operating only with handheld bridge-to-bridge VHF radio equipment under R & R 80.143(c) of this part;

(b) For vessels subject to the Bridge-to-Bridge Act and participating in a Vessel Traffic Service (VTS) system when the watch is maintained on both the bridge-to-bridge frequency and a separately assigned VTS frequency; or

(c) For a station on board a voluntary vessel equipped with digital selective calling (DSC) equipment, maintaining a continuous DSC watch on 156.525 MHz whenever such station is not being used for exchanging communications, and while such station is within the VHF service area of a U.S.

Coast Guard radio facility which is DSC equipped.

* * * * * *

R & R 80.151 Classification of Operator Licenses and Endorsements. (a) Commercial radio operator licenses issued by the Commission are classified in accordance with the Radio Regulations of the International Telecommunication Union.

(b) The following licenses are issued by the Commission. International classification, if different from the license name, is given in parentheses. The licenses and their alphanumeric designator are listed in descending order.

(1) T-1. First Class Radiotelegraph Operator's Certificate.

(2) T-2. Second Class Radiotelegraph Operator's Certificate.

(3) G. General Radiotelephone Operator License (radiotelephone operator's general certificate).

(4) T-3. Third Class Radiotelegraph Operator's Certificate (radiotelegraph operator's special certificate).

(5) MP. Marine Radio Operator Permit (radiotelephone operator's restricted certificate).

(6) RP. Restricted Radiotelephone Operator Permit (radiotelephone operator's restricted certificate).

(c) The following license endorsements are affixed by the Commission to provide special authorizations or restrictions. Applicable licenses are given in parentheses.

(1) Ship Radar endorsement (First and Second Class Radiotelegraph Operator's Certificate, General Radiotelephone Operator License).

(2) Six Months Service endorsement (First and Second Class Radiotelegraph Operator's Certificate).

(3) Restrictive endorsements; relating to physical handicaps, English language or literacy waivers, or other matters (all licenses).

* * * * * *

R & R 80.167 Limitations on Operators. The operator of maritime radio equipment other than T-1, T-2, or G licensees, must not:

(a) Make equipment adjustments which may affect transmitter operation;

(b) Operate any transmitter which requires more than the use of simple external switches or manual frequency selection or transmitters whose frequency stability is not maintained by the transmitter itself.

* * * * * *

R & R 80.169 Operators Required to Adjust Transmitters or Radar. (a) All adjustments of radio transmitters in any radiotelephone station during or coincident with the installation, servicing, or maintenance of such equipment which may affect the proper operation of the station, must be performed by or under the immediate supervision and responsibility of a person holding a first or second class radiotelegraph or a general radiotelephone operator permit.

(b) Only persons holding a first or second class radiotelegraph operator certificate must perform such functions at radiotelegraph stations transmitting Morse code.

(c) Only persons holding an operator certificate containing a ship radar endorsement must perform such functions on radar equipment.

* * * * * *

R & R 80.175 Availability of Operator Licenses. All operator licenses required by this subpart must be readily available for inspection.

* * * * * *

R & R 80.177 When Operator License Is Not Required. (a) No radio operator authorization is required to operate:

(1) A shore radar, a shore radiolocation, maritime support or shore radionavigation station;

(2) A survival craft station or an emergency position indicating radio beacon;

(3) A ship radar station if:

(i) the radar frequency is determined by a nontunable, pulse type magnetron or other fixed tuned device, and

(ii) the radar is capable of being operated exclusively by external controls;

(4) As on board station; or

(5) A ship station operating in the VHF band on board a ship voluntarily equipped with radio and sailing on a domestic voyage.

(b) No radio operator license is required to install a VHF transmitter in a ship station if the installation is made by, or under the supervision of, the licensee of the ship station and if modifications to the transmitter other than front panel controls are not made.

(c) No operator license is required to operate coast stations of 250 watts or less carrier power or 1500 watts or less peak envelope power operating on frequencies above 30 MHz, or marine utility stations.

* * * * * *

R & R 80.213 Modulation Requirements. (a) Transmitters must meet the following modulation requirements:

(1) When double sideband emission is used the peak modulation must be maintained between 75 and 100 percent;

(2) When phase or frequency modulation is used in the 156–162 MHz and 216–220 MHz bands the peak modulation must be maintained between 75 and 100 percent. A frequency deviation of ± 5 kHz is defined as 100 percent of peak modulation; and

(3) In single sideband operation the upper sideband must be transmitted. Single sideband transmitters must automatically limit the peak envelope power to their

authorized operating power and meet the requirements in R & R 80.207(c).

(b) Radiotelephone transmitters using A3E, F3E and G3E emission must have a modulation limiter to prevent any modulation over 100 percent. This requirement does not apply to survival craft transmitters, to transmitters that do not require a license or to transmitters whose output power does not exceed 3 watts.

(c) Ship station transmitters using G3D or G3E emission in the 156–162 MHz and 216–220 MHz bands must be capable of proper technical operation with a frequency deviation of ± 5 kHz.

*   *   *   *   *   *

R & R 80.304 Watch Requirement During Silence Periods. (a) Each ship station operating on telegraphy frequencies in the band 405–535 kHz, must maintain a watch on the frequency 500 kHz for three minutes twice each hour beginning at x h.15 and x h.45 Coordinated Universal Time (UTC) by a licensed radiotelegraph officer using either a loudspeaker or headphone.

(b) Each ship station operating on telephony on frequencies in the band 1605–3500 kHz must maintain a watch on the frequency 2182 kHz. This watch must be maintained at least twice each hour for 3 minutes commencing at x h.00 and x h.30 Coordinated Universal Time (UTC) using either a loudspeaker or headphone. Except for distress, urgency or safety messages, ship stations must not transmit during the silence periods on 2182 kHz.

R & R 80.305 Watch Requirements of the Communications Act and the Safety Convention. (a) Each ship of the United States which is equipped with a radiotelegraph station for compliance with Part II of Title III of the Communications Act or Chapter IV of the Safety Convention must:

(1) Keep a continuous and efficient watch on 500 kHz by means of radio officers while being navigated in the open sea outside a harbor or port. In lieu thereof, on a cargo ship equipped with a radiotelegraph auto alarm in proper operating condition, an efficient watch on 500 kHz must be maintained by means of a radio officer for at least 8 hours per day in the aggregate, i.e., for at least one-third of each day or portion of each day that the vessel is navigated in the open sea outside of a harbor or port.

(2) Keep a continuous and efficient watch on the radiotelephone distress frequency 2182 kHz from the principal radio operating position or the room from which the vessel is normally steered while being navigated in the open sea outside a harbor or port. A radiotelephone distress frequency watch receiver having a loudspeaker and a radiotelephone auto alarm facility must be used to keep the continuous watch on 2182 kHz if such watch is kept from the room from which the vessel is normally steered. After a determination by the master that conditions are such that maintenance of the listening watch would interfere with the safe navigation of the ship, the watch may be maintained by the use of the radiotelephone auto alarm facility alone.

(3) Keep a continuous and efficient watch on the VHF distress frequency 156.800 MHz from the room from which the vessel is normally steered while in the open sea outside a harbor or port. The watch must be maintained by a designated member of the crew who may perform other duties, relating to the operation or navigation of the vessel, provided such other duties do not interfere with the effectiveness of the watch. Use of a properly adjusted squelch or brief interruptions due to other nearby VHF transmissions are not considered to adversely affect the continuity or efficiency of the required watch on the VHF distress frequency. This watch need not be maintained by vessels subject to the Bridge-to-Bridge Act and participating in a Vessel Traffic Services (VTS) system as

required or recommended by the U.S. Coast Guard, when an efficient listening watch is maintained on both the bridge-to-bridge frequency and a separate assigned VTS frequency.

* * * * * *

(c) Each vessel of the United States transporting more than six passengers for hire, which is equipped with a radiotelephone station for compliance with Part III of Title III of the Communications Act must, while being navigated in the open sea or any tidewater within the jurisdiction of the United States adjacent or contiguous to the open sea, keep a continuous watch on 2182 kHz while the vessel is beyond VHF communication range of the nearest VHF coast station, whenever the radiotelephone station is not being used for authorized traffic. A VHF watch must be kept on 156.800 MHz whenever such station is not being used for authorized traffic. The VHF watch must be maintained at the vessel's steering station actually in use by the qualified operator as defined by R & R 80.157 or by a crewmember who may perform other duties relating to the operation or navigation of the vessel, provided such other duties do not interfere with the watch. The use of a properly adjusted squelch is not considered to adversely affect the watch. The VHF watch need not be maintained by vessels subject to the Bridge-to-Bridge Act and participating in a Vessel Traffic Services (VTS) system when an efficient listening watch is maintained on both the bridge-to-bridge frequency and a VTS frequency.

* * * * * *

R & R 80.308 Watch Required by the Great Lakes Radio Agreement. Each ship of the United States which is equipped with a radiotelephone station for compliance with the Great Lakes Radio Agreement must when underway, keep a watch on

156.800 MHz whenever such station is not being used for authorized traffic. The watch must be maintained by at least one officer or crewmember who may perform other duties provided such other duties do not interfere with the watch.

* * * * * *

R & R 80.317 Radiotelegraph and Radiotelephone Alarm Signals. (a) The international radiotelegraph alarm signal consists of a series of twelve dashes sent in one minute, the duration of each dash being four seconds and the duration of the interval between consecutive dashes one second. The purpose of this special signal is the actuation of automatic devices giving the alarm to attract the attention of the operator when there is no listening watch on the distress frequency.

(b) The international radiotelephone alarm signal consists of two substantially sinusoidal audio frequency tones transmitted alternately. One tone must have a frequency of 2200 Hertz and the other a frequency of 1300 Hertz, the duration of each tone being 250 milliseconds. When generated by automatic means, the radiotelephone alarm signal must be transmitted continuously for a period of at least 30 seconds, but not exceeding one minute; when generated by other means, the signal must be transmitted as continuously as practicable over a period of approximately one minute. The purpose of this special signal is to attract the attention of the person on watch or to actuate automatic devices giving the alarm.

R & R 80.318 Use of Alarm Signals. (a) The radiotelegraph or radiotelephone alarm signal, as appropriate, must only be used to announce:

(1) That a distress call or message is about to follow;

(2) The transmission of an urgent cyclone warning. In this case the alarm signal may only be used by coast stations author-

ized by the Commission to do so; or

(3) The loss of a person or persons overboard. In this case the alarm signal may only be used when the assistance of other ships is required and cannot be satisfactorily obtained by the use of the urgency signal only, but the alarm signal must not be repeated by other stations. The message must be preceded by the urgency signal.

(b) In cases described in paragraphs (a)(2) and (3) of this section, the transmission of the warning or message by radiotelegraphy must not begin until two minutes after the end of the radiotelegraph alarm signal.

* * * * * *

R & R 80.331 Bridge-to-Bridge Communication Procedure. (a) Vessels subject to the Bridge-to-Bridge Act transmitting on the designated navigational frequency must conduct communications in a format similar to those given below:

(1) This is the (name of vessel). My position is (give readily identifiable position, course and speed) about to (describe contemplated action). Out.

(2) Vessel off (give a readily identifiable position). This is (name of vessel) off (give a readily identifiable position). I plan to (give proposed course of action). Over.

(3) (Coast station), this is (vessel's name) off (give readily identifiable position). I plan to (give proposed course of action). Over.

(b) Vessels acknowledging receipt must answer "(Name of vessel calling). This is (Name of vessel answering). Received your call," and follow with an indication of their intentions. Communications must terminate when each ship is satisfied that the other no longer poses a threat to its safety and is ended with "Out."

(c) Use of power greater than 1 watt in a bridge-to-bridge station shall be limited to the following three situations:

(1) Emergency.

(2) Failure of the vessel being called to respond to a second call at low power.

(3) A broadcast call as in paragraph (a)(1) of this section in a blind situation, e.g., rounding a bend in a river.

* * * * * *

R & R 80.409 Station Logs. (a) *General requirements.* Logs must be established and properly maintained as follows:

(1) The log must be kept in an orderly manner. The required information for the particular class or category of station must be readily available. Key letters or abbreviations may be used if their proper meaning or explanation is contained elsewhere in the same log.

(2) Erasures, obliterations or willful destruction within the retention period are prohibited. Corrections may be made only by the person originating the entry by striking out the error, initialing the correction and indicating the date of correction.

(3) The log must identify the vessel name, country of registry, and official number of the vessel.

(4) The station licenses and the radio operator in charge of the station are responsible for the maintenance of station logs.

(b) *Availability and retention.* Station logs must be made available to authorized Commission employees upon request and retained as follows:

(1) Logs must be retained by the licensee for a period of one year from the date of entry, and when applicable for such additional periods as required by the following paragraphs:

(i) Logs relating to a distress situation or disaster must be retained for three years from the date of entry.

(ii) If the Commission has notified the licensee of an investigation, the related logs must be retained until the licensee is specifically authorized in writing to destroy them.

(iii) Logs relating to any claim or complaint of which the station licensee has notice must be retained until the claim or complaint has been satisfied or barred by statute limiting the time for filing suits upon such claims.

(2) Logs containing entries required by paragraphs (e) and (f) of this section must be kept at the principal radiotelephone operating location while the vessel is being navigated. All entries in their original form must be retained on board the vessel for at least 30 days from the date of entry.

(3) Ship radiotelegraph logs must be kept in the principal radiotelegraph operating room during the voyage.

* * * * *

R & R 80.453 Scope of Communications. Public coast stations provide ship/shore radiotelephone and radiotelegraph services.

(a) Public coast stations are authorized to communicate:

(1) With any ship or aircraft station operating in the maritime mobile service, for the transmission or reception of safety communication;

(2) With any land station to exchange safety communications to or from a ship or aircraft station;

(3) With Government and non-Government ship and aircraft stations to exchange public correspondence;

(b) Public coast stations are authorized to communicate with a designated station at a remote fixed location where other communication facilities are not available.

(c) Public coast stations are authorized to transmit meteorological and navigational information of benefit to mariners.

(d) Each public coast telegraphy station is authorized to communicate with other public coast telegraphy stations to exchange message traffic destined to or originated at mobile stations:

(1) To exchange operating signals, brief service messages or safety communication;

(2) To exchange message traffic destined for a mobile station when the coast station initially concerned is unable to communicate directly with the mobile station;

(3) In the Great Lakes region, to exchange message traffic originated at a mobile station when the use of available point-to-point communication facilities would delay the delivery of such message traffic;

(4) Utilization of radiotelegraphy must not incur additional charges or replace available point-to-point communication facilities;

(5) Only authorized working frequencies within the band 415 kHz to 5000 kHz must be employed for communications between coast stations;

(6) Harmful interference must not be caused to communication between mobile stations and coast stations or between mobile stations.

* * * * *

R & R 80.507 Scope of Service. Portable units licensed as marine utility stations may be operated either on a ship or on shore. When operated on shore they must comply with all of the rules governing coast stations except that they may be operated at temporary unspecified locations. When operated on ships, they must comply with all of the rules applicable to ship stations.

* * * * *

R & R 80.855 Radiotelephone transmitter. (a) The transmitter must be capable of transmission of H3E and J3E emission on 2182 kHz, and J3E emission on 2638 kHz and at least two other frequencies within the band 1605 to 3500 kHz available for ship-to-shore or ship-to-ship communication.

(b) The duty cycle of the transmitter must permit transmission of the international radiotelephone alarm signal.

(c) The transmitter must be capable of transmitting clearly perceptible signals from ship to ship during daytime under normal conditions over a range of 150 nautical miles.

(d) The transmitter complies with the range requirement specified in paragraph (c) of this section if:

(1) The transmitter is capable of being matched to actual ship station transmitting antenna meeting the requirements of R & R 80.863; and

(2) The output power is not less than 60 watts peak envelope power for H3E and J3E emission on the frequency 2182 kHz and for J3E emission on the frequency 2638 kHz into either an artificial antenna consisting of a series network of 10 ohms resistance and 200 picofarads capacitance, or an artificial antenna of 50 ohms nominal impedance. An individual demonstration of the power output capability of the transmitter, with the radiotelephone installation normally installed on board ship, may be required.

(e) The transmitter must provide visual indication whenever the transmitter is supplying power to the antenna.

(f) The transmitter must be protected from excessive currents and voltages.

(g) A durable nameplate must be mounted on the transmitter or made an integral part of it showing clearly the name of the transmitter manufacturer and the type or model of the transmitter.

(h) An artificial antenna must be provided to permit weekly checks of the automatic device for generating the radiotelephone alarm signal on frequencies other than the radiotelephone distress frequency.

* * * * * *

R & R 80.971 Test of Radiotelephone Installation. At least once during each calendar day a vessel subject to the Great Lakes Radio Agreement must test communications on 156.800 MHz to demonstrate that the radiotelephone installation is in proper operating condition unless the normal daily use of the equipment demonstrates that this installation is in proper operating condition. If equipment is not in operating condition, the master must have it restored to effective operation as soon as possible.

* * * * * *

R & R 80.1001 Applicability. The Bridge-to-Bridge Act and the regulations of this part apply to the following vessels in the navigable waters of the United States:

(a) Every power-driven vessel of 300 gross tons and upward while navigating;

(b) Every vessel of 100 gross tons and upward carrying one or more passengers for hire while navigating;

(c) Every towing vessel of 26 feet (7.8 meters) or over in length, measured from end to end over the deck excluding sheer, while navigating; and

(d) Every dredge and floating plant engaged, in or near a channel or fairway, in operations likely to restrict or affect navigation of other vessels. An unmanned or intermittently manned floating plant under the control of a dredge shall not be required to have a separate radiotelephone capability.

* * * * * *

R & R 80.1003 Station Required. Vessels subject to the Bridge-to-Bridge Act must have a radiotelephone installation to enable the vessel to participate in navigational communications. This radiotelephone installation must be continuously associated with the ship even though a portable installation is used. Foreign vessels coming into U.S. waters where a bridge-to-bridge station is required may fulfill this requirement by use of portable equipment brought aboard by the pilot. Non-portable equipment, when used, must be arranged to facilitate repair. The equipment must be protected against vibration, moisture, temperature and excessive currents and voltages.

* * * * * *

R & R 80.1005 Inspection of Stations. The bridge-to-bridge radiotelephone station will be inspected on vessels subject to regular inspections pursuant to the requirements of Parts II and III of Title III of the Communications Act, the Safety Convention or the Great Lakes Agreement at the time of the regular inspection. If after such inspection, the Commission determines that the Bridge-to-Bridge Act, the rules of the Commission and the station license are met, an endorsement will be made on the appropriate document. The validity of the endorsement will run concurrently with the period of the regular inspection. Each vessel must carry a certificate with a valid endorsement while subject to the Bridge-to-Bridge Act. All other bridge-to-bridge stations will be inspected from time to time.

* * * * * *

R & R 80.1007 Bridge-to-Bridge Radiotelephone Installation. Use of the bridge-to-bridge transmitter must be restricted to the master or person in charge of the vessel, or the person designated by the master or person in charge to pilot or direct the movement of the vessel. Communications must be of a navigational nature exclusively.

* * * * * *

R & R 80.1009 Principal Operator and Operating Position. The principal operating position of the bridge-to-bridge station must be the vessel's navigational bridge or, in the case of dredges, its main control station. If the radiotelephone installation can be operated from any location other than the principal operating position, the principal operating position must be able to take full control of the installation.

* * * * * *

R & R 80.1011 Transmitter. The bridge-to-bridge transmitter must be capable of transmission of G3E emission on the navigational frequency 156.650 MHz (channel 13).

* * * * * *

R & R 80.1053 Special Requirements for Class A EPIRB Stations. (a) A Class A EPIRB station must meet the following:

(1) Float free of a sinking ship;

(2) Activate automatically when it floats free of a sinking ship;

(3) Have an antenna that deploys automatically when the EPIRB activates;

(4) Use A3N emission on the frequencies 121.500 MHz and 243.00 MHz;

(5) The effective radiated power must not be less than 75 milliwatts after 48 hours of continuous operation and without replacement or recharge of batteries. The effective radiated power must be determined according to FCC Bulletin OCE 45.

(6) The carrier must be amplitude modulated with an audio signal swept downward between 1600 and 300 Hz. The sweeping range of the audio signal must be 700 Hz or greater. Its sweep rate must be between 2 and 4 times per second. The modulation applied to the carrier must comply with the Radio Technical Commission for Aeronautics (RTCA) Document Number DO-183;

(7) Have a visible or audible indicator which clearly shows that the device is operating. The indicator must be activated by the RF output power. The indicator must be protected from damage due to dropping or contact with other objects;

* * * * * *

(c) If testing of an EPIRB with Coast Guard coordination is not possible, brief operational tests are authorized provided the tests are conducted within the first five minutes of any hour and are not longer than three audio sweeps or one second whichever is longer.

*   *   *   *   *   *

(e) The EPIRB must be powered by a battery contained within the transmitter case or in a battery holder that is rigidly attached to the transmitter case. The battery connector must be corrosion resistant and positive in action and must not rely for contact upon spring force alone. The useful life of the battery is the length of time that the battery may be stored under marine environmental conditions without the EPIRB transmitter output power falling below 75 milliwatts prior to 48 hours of continuous operation. The month and year of the battery's manufacture must be permanently marked on the battery and the month and year upon which 50 percent of its useful life will have expired must be permanently marked on both the battery and the outside of the transmitter. The batteries must be replaced if 50 percent of their useful life has expired or if the transmitter has been used in an emergency situation.

*   *   *   *   *   *

NOTES RE EPIRBs
(1) Class B EPIRBs must be activated manually. Also works on 121.5 MHz and 243 MHz.
(2) Class C EPIRBs operate on Channel 15 (156.75 MHz) and Channel 16 (156.8 MHz). This is intended for boats in coastal waters. The VHF-FM (156.8) Class C EPIRB transmits a brief (1.5 second) alert signal on Channel 16 to call attention to a distress. It then transmits a 15 second locating signal on Channel 15. The signals repeat periodically, the International Two-Tone Alarm Signal.

*   *   *   *   *   *

R & R 80.1175 Scope of Communications of On-Board Stations. (a) On-board stations communicate:
(1) With other units of the same station for operational communications on the ship.
(2) With on-board stations of another ship or shore facility to aid in oil pollution prevention during the transfer of 250 or more barrels of oil.
(3) With other units of the same station in the immediate vicinity of the ship for operational communications related to docking, life boat and emergency drills or in the maneuvering of cargo barges and lighters.
(b) An on-board station may communicate with a station in the Business Radio Service operating on the same frequency when the vessel on which the on-board station is installed is alongside the dock or cargo handling facility.

R & R 80.1177 Assignment and Use of Frequencies. On-board frequencies are assignable only to ship stations. When an on-board repeater is used, paired frequencies must be used. On-board repeater frequencies must be used for single frequency simplex operations.

PART 87:
AVIATION SERVICES

R & R 87.5 Definition of Terms. For the purpose of this part the following definitions are applicable:

Aeronautical mobile service. A mobile service between aeronautical stations and aircraft stations, or between aircraft stations, in which survival craft stations may also participate.

Aeronautical station. A land station in the aeronautical mobile service. In certain instances an aeronautical station may be placed on board a ship or on a platform at sea.

Aircraft station. A mobile station in the aeronautical mobile service other than a survival craft station, located on board an aircraft.

Coast station. A land station in the maritime mobile service.

Coordinated universal time (UTC). UTC is equivalent to mean solar time at the prime meridian (0 degrees longitude), formerly called GMT.

Emergency locator transmitter (ELT). A transmitter intended to be actuated manually or automatically and operated automatically as part of an aircraft or a survival craft station, with an A9 emission, as a locating aid for survival purposes.

Emergency locator transmitter test station. A land station, operated with an A9 emission on the frequencies used for testing emergency locator transmitters, for testing equipment intended to be used as emergency locator transmitters, or for training in the use of emergency locator transmitters.

Emergency position-indicating radio-beacon station (EPIRB). A station in the mobile service the emissions of which are intended to facilitate search and rescue operations.

Facsimile. A form of telegraphy for the transmission of fixed images. The images are reproduced in permanent form at the receiver.

Fixed public service. A radiocommunication service carried on between fixed stations open to public correspondence.

Fixed service. A service of radiocommunication between specified fixed points.

Fixed station. A station in the fixed service.

International fixed public radiocommunication service. A fixed service, the stations of which are open to public correspondence and which, in general, is intended to provide radiocommunication between any one of the states or U.S. possessions or any foreign point, or between U.S. possessions and any other point. This service also involves the relaying of international traffic between stations that provide this service.

Land mobile service. A mobile station in the land mobile service capable of surface movement within the geographical limits of a country or continent.

Mobile service. A service of radiocommunication between mobile and land stations, or between mobile stations.

Mobile station. A station in the mobile service intended to be used while in motion or during halts at unspecified points.

Navigational communications. Safety communications pertaining to the maneuvering of vessels or the directing of vessel movements. Such communications are primarily for the exchange of information between ship stations and secondarily between ship stations and coast station.

Operational fixed station. A fixed station, not open to public correspondence, operated by and for the sole use of those agencies operating their own radiocommunication facilities in the Public Safety, Industrial, Land Transportation, Marine, or Aviation Services.

Point of communication. A specific location designated in the license, to which a station is authorized to communicate for the transmission of public correspondence.

Radiobeacon station. A station in the radionavigation service the emissions of which are intended to enable a mobile station to determine its bearing or direction in relation to the radiobeacon station.

Radiodetermination. The determination of position, or the obtaining of information relating to position.

Radio direction-finding. Radiodetermination using the reception of radio waves for the purpose of determining the direction of a station or object.

Radio direction-finding station. A radiodetermination station using radio direction-finding.

Radionavigation. Radiodetermination used for the purposes of navigation, including obstruction warning.

Radionavigation land station. A station in the radionavigation service not intended to be used while in motion.

Surveillance radar station. A radionavigation land station in the aeronautical radionavigation service employing radar to display the presence of aircraft within its range.

Survival craft station. A mobile station in the maritime or aeronautical mobile service intended solely for survival purposes and located on any lifeboat, life raft, or other survival equipment.

*   *   *   *   *   *

R & R 87.29 Application for Aircraft Radio Station License. (a)(1) Application for new or modified aircraft radio station licenses shall be made on FCC Form 404. The purchaser or assignee of a radio-equipped aircraft shall apply for a new aircraft radio station license on FCC Form 404.

(2) An applicant, in applying for aircraft radio station licenses, may specify on a single FCC Form 404, the total number of aircraft stations in his fleet. Under these circumstances, a single instrument of authorization (fleet license) may be issued for operation of all radio stations aboard the aircraft of the fleet.

*   *   *   *   *   *

(c) The radio station on a new aircraft with factory installed radio equipment or on an aircraft which has recently undergone the initial installation of radio equipment may be operated for a period of 90 days under special temporary authority evidenced by a copy of a certificate (FCC Form 453-B) executed by the aircraft manufacturer, dealer, or distributor, in the case of new aircraft with factory installed radio equipment; or the avionics manufacturer, dealer or distributor who installs the equipment. The original of the certificate must be mailed to the Commission with an application for a new station license on FCC Form 404.

*   *   *   *   *   *

R & R 87.35 Changes in Authorized Station. (a) Except as otherwise provided in this section an application for modification of license shall be filed when any change is to be made which would result in deviation from the terms of the authorization.

(b) No application for modification of an aircraft radio station license is required to add a survival craft station using type accepted transmitters or for the addition or substitution of type accepted transmitters when the newly installed transmitters will perform the same functions and operate on the same frequencies as the transmitters specified on the license.

*   *   *   *   *   *

R & R 87.63 Power. (a) The power which may be authorized for use at any station in the Aviation Services shall not be greater than the minimum required for satisfactory technical operation.

(b) Except as indicated in paragraph (c) of this section, the power authorized for use at any station shall be specified in terms of peak envelope power at the transmitter output terminals. Peak envelope power is defined as the mean power during one radio frequency cycle at the highest crest of the modulation envelope.

(c) For stations using amplitude modulated emission and transmitting both sidebands and a full carrier, authorized power will be specified in terms of unmodulated radio frequency carrier power at the transmitter output terminals.

(d) Power may be determined either by direct measurement or by multiplying the plate input power to the final amplifier by an appropriate factor.

* * * * * *

R & R 87.65 Frequency Tolerance. In the aviation services, the transmitter frequency tolerance is 20 ppm. For survival craft, the tolerance is 50 ppm.

For shipboard transmitters, the frequency tolerance in most cases is ± 20 Hz.

* * * * * *

R & R 87.69 Bandwidth of Emission. (a) Occupied bandwidth is the frequency bandwidth such that, below its lower and above its upper frequency limits, the mean powers radiated are each equal to 0.5 percent of the total mean power radiated by a given emission.

(b) The authorized bandwidth is the maximum occupied bandwidth authorized to be used by a station.

* * * * * *

R & R 87.75 Transmitter Control Requirements. (a) Each transmitter shall be so installed and protected that it is not accessible to, or capable of operation by, persons other than those duly authorized by the licensee.

(b) Unless otherwise specifically authorized, each station shall be provided with a control point at the location of the transmitting equipment. Applications for additional control points shall specify the location of each proposed control point and any authorization which may be issued shall show the location of each such control point.

(c) A control point is a position which meets all of the following conditions:

(1) Such position must be under the control and supervision of the licensee;

(2) It is a position at which the monitoring facilities required by this section are installed and at which the transmitter can, without delay, be rendered inoperative;

(3) It is a position at which the required licensed radio operator, responsible for the actual operation of the transmitter, is stationed.

(d) At each control point the following facilities shall be installed:

(1) A device which will provide continuous visual indication when the transmitter is radiating or when the transmitter control circuits have been placed in a condition to produce radiation: *Provided, however,* That this requirement shall not apply to aircraft stations;

(2) Equipment to permit the operator to monitor, aurally, all transmissions originating at dispatch points under his supervision;

(3) Facilities which will permit the operator to disconnect any or all dispatch point circuits from the transmitter.

(e) A dispatch point is an operating position from which messages may be transmitted under the direct supervision of the licensed control point operator. Dispatch points may be installed without authorization from the Commission, and persons authorized by the station licensee to initiate messages from these points are not required to be licensed by the Commission.

R & R 87.77 Acceptability of Transmitters for Licensing. (a) From time to time the Commission publishes a revised list of type approved and type accepted equipment entitled, "Radio Equipment List—Equipment Acceptable for Licensing." Copies of this list are available for inspection at the Commission's offices in Washington, D.C., and at each of its field offices.

(b) Except as provided in paragraph (d) of this section, each transmitter used in the Aviation Services must be of a type which has been type accepted by the Commission for use in these services. *Provided, however,* That aircraft stations, when transmitting on maritime mobile frequencies, shall use transmitters which are type accepted for use in ship stations in conformity with Part 80 of this chapter.

(c) Some radio equipment which is to be installed aboard air carrier aircraft must meet requirements of the Federal Communications Commission, and those requirements of the Federal Aviation Regulations which are applicable. The applicable Federal Aviation Administration requirements may be obtained from the Federal Aviation Administration, Washington, D.C. 20553.

(d) The following exceptions to the provisions of paragraph (b) of this section are provided on the express condition that the operation of stations using transmitting equipment not type accepted by the Commission shall not result in harmful interference due to the failure of such equipment to comply with the current technical standards of Subpart A of this part.

(1) Type accepted equipment is not required at developmental stations.

(2) Type accepted equipment is not required at Civil Air Patrol stations.

(3) Equipment which has not been type accepted may be used at flight test stations for limited periods where justified on the basis of good cause shown.

(4) Equipment which is to be used exclusively under emergency and distress conditions for survival purposes and which is carried aboard aircraft in such a manner as to only be available under these conditions need not be type accepted by the Commission if it is a type which was in use prior to January 1, 1965.

Notes:

1. "Type accepted" means the manufacturer conducts tests to assure the equipment meets its specifications.

2. "Type approval" means the FCC has conducted equipment tests and that it meets its specifications.

*   *   *   *   *   *

R & R 87.93 Emergency Locator Transmitter (ELT) Tests. (See also under "Definitions" for "emergency locator transmitter.")

*   *   *   *   *

(b) An emergency locator transmitter (ELT) may be tested only under the conditions set forth below.

(1) An ELT fitted with an internal test circuit having a manually activated test switch and an output indicator may be tested provided that the switch, in the test position:

(i) Permits the operator to determine that the unit is operative;

(ii) Switches the transmitter output to a test circuit (dummy load), the impedance of which is equivalent to that of the antenna affixed to the ELT; and

(iii) reduces radiation to the minimum level that is technically feasible.

(2) An ELT not fitted with an internal test circuit may be tested in coordination with, or under the control of a Federal Aviation Administration representative to insure that testing is conducted under electronic shielding, or other conditions, sufficient to insure that no transmission of radiated energy occurs that could be received by a radio station and results in a false distress signal. If testing with FAA involvement as described above is not practicable or feasible, brief operational tests are authorized provided the tests are conducted within the first 5 minutes of any hour, are not longer than three audio sweeps, and if the antenna is removable, a dummy load is substituted during the test.

NOTE: If an ELT is accidentally activated, it must immediately be turned off. This is to preclude the possibility of this action being taken as a genuine distress signal.

R & R 87.111 Frequency Measurements. (a) Measurements of the operating frequencies of airborne transmitters may be required by the Commission in individual circumstances. The operating frequencies of all non-airborne transmitters authorized for operation in the Aviation Services shall be measured at the following times to assure compliance with the tolerances specified in these rules:

(1) When a transmitter is originally installed;

(2) When any change or adjustment is made in a transmitter which may affect an operating frequency or whenever there is reason to believe that an operating frequency has shifted beyond the applicable tolerance.

(b) A signed entry shall be made in the station's records indicating that each measured frequency is within the required tolerance. A statement that an automatic frequency monitor was in service during the period shall be deemed to meet the above requirement for any period.

(c) The determination required by paragraph (a) of this section may, at the option of the licensee, be made by any qualified engineering measurement service, in which case the required record entries shall show the name and address of the engineering measurement service and the name of the person making the measurements.

R & R 87.113 Inspection and Maintenance of Tower Marking and Associated Control Equipment.

The licensee of any radio station which has an antenna structure required to be painted or illuminated pursuant to the provisions of section 303 (q) of the Communications Act of 1934, as amended, and/or Part 17 of this chapter, shall operate and maintain the tower marking and associated control equipment in accordance with the following:

(a) The tower lights be observed at least once each 24 hours, either visually or by observing an automatic and properly maintained indicator designed to register any failure of such lights, to insure that all such lights are functioning properly as required; or, alternatively, there shall be provided and properly maintained an automatic alarm system designed to detect any failure of the tower lights and to provide indication of such failure to the licensee.

(b) Any observed or otherwise known failure of a code or rotating beacon light or top light not corrected within thirty minutes, regardless of the cause of such failure, shall be reported immediately by telephone or telegraph to the nearest Flight Service Station or office of the Federal Aviation Administration. Further notification by telephone or telegraph shall be given immediately upon resumption of the required illumination.

(c) All automatic or mechanical control devices, indicators, and alarm systems associated with the tower lights shall be inspected at intervals not to exceed three months to insure that such apparatus is functioning properly.

* * * * * *

R & R 87.115 Station Identification.

(a) Aircraft stations shall be identified by one of the following means of identification:

(1) Aircraft radio station call sign.

(2) Assigned FCC Control number (assigned to ultralight aircraft).

(3) The characters corresponding to the registration marking ("N" number) of the aircraft, omitting the prefix letter "N," preceded by the type of aircraft. When initiated by a ground station aircraft stations may use an abbreviated call sign consisting of the type aircraft followed by the last three characters of the registration marking.

(4) The radiotelephony designator of the aircraft operating agency followed by the flight identification number.

Note: The operating agency radiotelephony designators referred to in subdivision (4) of this subparagraph are designators assigned and authorized by the Federal Aviation Administration. The flight identification number is the "trip number" assigned by the company.

(5) An aircraft identification approved in advance by the FAA for use by aircraft stations participating in an organized flying activity of short duration.

(b) A land station in the aviation services shall identify by means of radio station call letters, its location, its assigned FAA identifier or the name of the city area or airdrome which it serves together with such additional identification as may be required. An aeronautical enroute station which is a part of a multistation network may also be identified by the location of its control points.

(c) Survival craft stations shall identify, so far as practicable, by transmitting an appropriate reference associating the survival craft station with its parent aircraft. No identification is required when distress signals are transmitted automatically. Transmissions other than distress or emergency signals, i.e., for equipment testing or adjustment, shall be identified by the call sign or by the official aircraft registration number of the parent aircraft followed by a single digit other than 0 or 1.

(d) Radio systems where the transmission of specific identification is considered to be impracticable are exempted from the provisions of this section; e.g., airborne weather radar, radio altimeter, air traffic control transponder, distance measuring equipment, collision avoidance equipment, racon, radiosonde, radio relay, radionavigation land test station (MTF), and automatically controlled aeronautical enroute stations.

*   *   *   *   *   *

R & R 87.133 Radio Operator Licenses. In the aviation radio services, it is not mandatory to hold a radio operator license unless operating on a frequency other than VHF, or on a flight to a foreign country. For practical purposes, most aviation station operators need only a Restricted Radiotelephone Operator Permit. However, a Marine Radio Operator Permit is required

to operate an aircraft station using frequencies below 30 MHz not exclusively allocated to the aeronautical mobile service and which are assigned for international use. This applies to stations whose power doesn't exceed 250 watts carrier power, or 1,000 watts Peak Envelope Power. If the station's power does exceed this, a General Radiotelephone Operator License is required.

*   *   *   *   *   *

R & R 87.135 Transmitter Adjustments and Tests by Operator. All transmitter adjustments or tests during or coincident with the installation, servicing, or maintenance of a radio station, which may affect the proper operation of such station, shall be made by or under the immediate supervision and responsibility of a person holding a General Radiotelephone or Radiotelegraph First- or Second-Class Operator License, who shall be responsible for the proper functioning of the station equipment: *Provided however,* that only a person holding a Radiotelegraph First- or Second-Class Operator License shall perform such functions at radiotelegraph stations transmitting by any type of the Morse Code for purposes other than automatically keyed station identification.

R & R 87.136 Operation of Transmitter Controls. (a) Operation of a station by the holder of a Marine Radio Operator Permit or Radiotelegraph Third-Class Operator Permit, or a Restricted Radiotelephone Operator Permit shall be subject to the condition that the operation of the transmitter shall require only the use of simple external switching devices, excluding all manual adjustment of frequency determining elements, and the stability of the frequencies shall be maintained by the transmitter itself within the limits of tolerance specified by R & R 87.65 or the station license. In addition, when using an aircraft radio station on maritime mobile service frequencies the carrier power of the transmitter shall not exceed 250 watts (emission A3E) or 1000 watts [emission (R3E), (H3E), (J3E)].

(b) When a station is used for telegraphy, transmitted manually by any type of the Morse Code, the transmitting telegraph key shall be manipulated only by a person who holds a radiotelegraph operator license or permit of the proper class.

* * * * * *

R & R 87.139 Operator Licenses Not Required for Certain Operations. No radio operator license is required for the operation of transmitters involving:

(1) The operation of airborne radar sets, radio altimeters, transponders, and other airborne automatic radionavigation aids,

(2) Operation of Emergency Locator Transmitters (ELTs),

(3) Operation of EPIRB transmitters;

(4) Operation of any authorized radio station which retransmits communications by automatic means,

(5) Operation of any aeronautical en-route station which transmits, by automatic means, digital communications to aircraft stations, or

(6) Operation of VHF telephony transceivers which provide domestic service or are used on domestic flights.

CAUTION: Although no operator authorization is required for the above, the transmitters must be covered by a valid *station license* or other authorization.

R & R 87.183(f) Emergency locator transmitter (ELT). (See also 87.5 "Definitions" and 87.93.)

The designation ELT is used in the aviation industry. These devices are basically the same as the Class A and Class B EPIRBs (Emergency Position Indicating Radio Beacons); so designated in the maritime industry.

Their operating frequencies are 121.5 MHz and 243 MHz. These are aeronautical emergency frequencies and are monitored by commercial, private (121.5 MHz) and military (243 MHz) aircraft.

(See also R & R 87.5, "Definitions" and R & R 80.145 and R & R 1053.)

* * * * * *

PART 89: PUBLIC SAFETY RADIO SERVICES

R & R 89.51 Station Authorization Required. No radio transmitter shall be operated in the Public Safety Radio Services except under and in accordance with proper station authorization granted by the Federal Communications Commission.

* * * * * *

R & R 89.103 Frequency Stability. (a) A permittee or licensee in these services shall maintain the carrier frequency of each authorized transmitter within the following percentage of the assigned frequency.

Frequency Range	All Fixed and Base Stations	Over 2 W	All Mobile Stations 2 W or Less
MHz	Percent	Percent	Percent
Below 25	0.01	0.01	0.02
25 to 50	.002	.002	.005
50 to 450	[1].0005	.0005	.005
450 to 470	[4].00025	.0005	.0005
470 to 512	[4].000025	.0005	.0005
806 to 820	[6].00015	.00025	.00025
851 to 866	.00015	.00025	.00025
1 427 to 1 435	[5].03	.03	.03
Above 1 435	[2,3]	[2,3]	[2,3]

[1] Stations authorized for operation on or before Dec. 1, 1961, in the frequency band 73.0–74.6 MHz may operate with a frequency tolerance of 0.005 percent.

[2] Radiolocation equipment using pulse modulation shall meet the following frequency tolerance. The frequency at which maximum emission occurs shall be within the authorized frequency band and shall not be closer than 1.5/T MHz to the upper and lower limits of the authorized frequency band were T (telsa) is the pulse duration in microseconds. For other radiolocation equipment, tolerances will be specified in the station authorization. See also R & R 89.121.

[3] The frequency tolerance for base and mobile stations will be specified in the station authorization.

[4] Operational fixed stations controlling mobile relay stations, through use of the associated mobile frequency, may operate with a frequency tolerance of 0.0005 percent.

[5] For fixed stations with power output above 120 W, the frequency tolerance is 0.01 percent if the necessary bandwidth of the emission does not exceed 3 kHz. For fixed station transmitters with a power of 120 W or less and using time division multiplex, the frequency tolerance may be increased to 0.05 percent.

[6] For control stations the frequency stability is 0.00025 percent.

(b) For the purpose of determining the frequency tolerance applicable to a particular transmitter in accordance with the foregoing provisions of this section, the power of a transmitter shall be the maximum rated output power as specified in the Commission's "Radio Equipment List."

* * * * * *

R & R 89.107 Emission Limitations.

* * * * * *

(1) For all type A3 emissions, the maximum authorized bandwidth shall be 8 kHz.

(2) For all F3 emission, the maximum authorized bandwidth and maximum authorized frequency deviation shall be as follows:

Frequency Band (MHz)	Authorized Bandwidth (kHz)	Frequency Deviation (kHz)
25 to 50	20	5
50 to 150	[1]20	[1]5
150 to 450	20	5
450 to 470	20	5
470 to 512	20	5
806 to 821	20	5
851 to 866	20	5

[1] Stations authorized for operation on or before Dec. 1, 1961, in the frequency band 73.0–74.6 MHz may continue to operate with a bandwidth of 40 kHz and a deviation of ± 15 kHz.

(3) For all type A1 emissions, the maximum authorized bandwidth shall be 0.25 kHz.

(c) The mean power of emissions shall be attenuated below the mean output power of the transmitter in accordance with the following schedule:

(1) On any frequency removed from the assigned frequency by more than 50 percent up to and including 100 percent of the authorized bandwidths: At least 25 decibels;

(2) On any frequency removed from the assigned frequency by more than 100 percent up to and including 250 percent of the authorized bandwidth: At least 35 decibels;

(3) On any frequency removed from the assigned frequency by more than 250 percent of the authorized bandwidth: At least 43 plus 10 Log_{10} (mean output power in watts) decibels or 80 decibels, whichever is the lesser attenuation.

(d) When an unauthorized emission results in harmful interference, the Commission may, in its discretion, require appropriate technical changes in equipment to alleviate the interference.

(e) The maximum authorized bandwidth of emission will be 25 MHz in the frequency band 10 550–10 680 MHz and 50 MHz in the frequency bands above 16 000 MHz.

* * * * * *

R & R 89.109. Modulation Requirements. (a) The maximum audio frequency required for satisfactory radiotelephone intelligibility in these services is considered to be 3 000 hertz.

(b) When amplitude modulation is used for telephony, the modulation percentage shall be sufficient to provide efficient communication and normally shall be maintained above 70 percent on peaks, but shall not exceed 100 percent on negative peaks.

(c) Each transmitter shall be equipped with a device which automatically prevents modulation in excess of that specified in this subpart which may be caused by greater than normal audio level: *Provided, however,* That this requirement shall not be applicable to transmitters authorized to operate as mobile stations with a maximum output power of 2 watts or less.

* * * * * *

R & R 89.175 Content of Station Records. Each licensee of a station in these services shall maintain records in accordance with the following:

(a) For all stations, the results and dates of the transmitter measurements required by these rules and the name of the person or persons making the measurements.

(b) For all stations, when service or maintenance duties are performed, the responsible operator shall sign and date an entry in the station record giving:

(1) Pertinent details of all duties performed by him or under his supervision;

(2) His name and address, and

(3) The class, serial number, and expiration date of his license, *Provided,* That the information called for by subparagraphs (2) and (3) of this paragraph, so long as it remains the same, need be entered only once in the station record at any station where the responsible operator is regularly employed on a full-time basis and at which his license is properly posted.

(c) [Reserved]

(d) [Reserved]

(e) For stations whose antenna or antenna supporting structure is required to be illuminated, a record in accordance with the following:

(1) The time the tower lights are turned on and off each day if manually controlled.

(2) The time the daily check of proper operation of the tower lights was made, if an automatic alarm system is not provided.

(3) In the event of any observed or otherwise known failure of a tower light:

(i) Nature of such failure.

(ii) Date and time the failure was observed, or otherwise noted.

(iii) Date, time, and nature of the adjustments, repairs, or replacements that were made.

(iv) Identification of the Flight Service Station (FAA) notified of the failure of any code or rotating beacon light or top light not corrected within thirty minutes, and the date and time such notice was given.

(v) Date and time notice was given to the Flight Service Station (FAA) that the required illumination was resumed.

(4) Upon the completion of the periodic inspection required at least once each three months:

(i) The date of the inspection and the condition of all tower lights and associated tower lighting control devices, indicators and alarm systems.

(ii) Any adjustments, replacements, or repairs made to insure compliance with the lighting requirements and the date such adjustments, replacements, or repairs were made.

* * * * * *

PART 90: PRIVATE LAND MOBILE RADIO SERVICES

R & R 90.145 Special temporary authority.

(a) In circumstances requiring the temporary use of radio facilities, the Commission may issue special temporary authority for new or modified operations. A request for special temporary authority may be made in letter form signed in accordance with R & R 90.125 of this part. It should be submitted, in duplicate, at least 10 days prior to the date of the proposed operation. However, in cases of emergency involving danger to life or property, or due to damage to equipment, the request may be made by telephone or telegraph under the condition that a letter request is submitted within the following 10 days. All requests for special temporary authority shall be clear and complete within themselves and shall not rely on any pending application.

(b) Every request for special temporary authority should contain the following information:

(1) Name and address of the applicant;

(2) Need for special action, including a description of any emergency or damage of equipment;

(3) Type of operation to be conducted (such as field test, dispatching, etc.);

(4) Purpose of operation;

(5) Times and dates of operation;

(6) Class of station and name of radio service;

R & R 90.155 Time in which station must be placed in operation.

(a) All stations authorized under this part, except as provided in paragraph (b) and in R & R 90.374 and 90.375(e), must be placed in operation within 8 months from the date of grant or the authorization shall be invalid and must be returned to the commission for cancellation.

(b) For local government entities only, a period longer than eight months for placing a station in operation may be authorized by the Commission on a case-by-case basis, where the applicant submits a specific schedule for the completion of each portion of the entire system, along with a showing that the system has been approved and funded for implementation in accordance with that schedule. See also R & R 90.374, 90.375(a) and 90.377(c) and (d).

R & R 90.157 Discontinuance of station operation. If a station licensed under this part discontinues operation on a permanent basis, the licensee shall forward the station license to the Commission for cancellation. A copy of the request for cancellation shall be sent to the Engineer in Charge of the district in which the station is located. For the purposes of this section, any station which has not operated for 1 year or more is considered to have been permanently discontinued.

R & R 90.215 Transmitter measurements.

(a) The licensee of each station shall employ a suitable procedure to determine that the carrier frequency of each transmitter authorized to operate with an output power in excess of two watts is maintained within the tolerance prescribed in R & R 91.213. This determination shall be made, and the results entered in the station records in accordance with the following:

(1) When the transmitter is initially installed;

(2) When any change is made in the transmitter which may affect the carrier frequency or its stability.

(b) The licensee of each station shall employ a suitable procedure to determine that each transmitter authorized to operate with an output power in excess of two watts does not exceed the maximum figure specified on the current station authorization. On authorizations stating only the input power to the final radio-frequency stage, the maximum permissible output power is 75 percent for frequencies below 25 MHz and 60 percent of the input power for frequencies above 25 MHz. If a non-DC final radio-frequency stage is utilized, then the output power shall not exceed 75 percent of the input power. This determination shall be made, and the results thereof entered into the station records, in accordance with the following:

(1) When the transmitter is initially installed;

(2) When any change is made in the transmitter which may increase the transmitter power input.

(c) The licensee of each station shall employ a suitable procedure to determine that the modulation of each transmitter, which is authorized to operate with an output power in excess of two watts, does not exceed the limits specified in this part. This determination shall be made and the following results entered in the station records, in accordance with the following:

(1) When the transmitter is initially installed;

(2) When any change is made in the transmitter which may affect the modulation characteristics.

(d) The determinations required by paragraphs (a), (b), and (c) of this section may, at the opinion of the licensee, be made by a qualified engineering measurement service, in which case the required record entries shall show the name and address of the engineering measuremen service as well as the name of the person making the measurements.

(e) In the case of mobile transmitters, the determinations required by paragraphs (a) and (c) of this section may be made at a test or service bench; Provided, That the measurements are made under load conditions equivalent to actual operating conditions; and provided further that after installation in the mobile unit the transmitter is given a routine check to determine that it is capable of being received satisfactorily by an appropriate receiver.

R & R 90.433 Operator requirements.

(a) No operator license or permit is required for the operation, maintenance, or repair of stations licensed under this part.

(b) Any person, with the consent or authorization of the licensee, may employ stations in this service for the purpose of telecommunications.

(c) The station licensee shall be responsible for the proper operation of the station at all times and is expected to provide observations, servicing and maintenance as often as may be necessary to ensure proper operation. All adjustments or tests during or coincident with the installation, servicing, or maintenance of the station should be performed by or under the immediate supervision and responsibility of a person certified as technically qualified to perform transmitter installation, operation, maintenance, and repair duties in the private land mobile services and fixed services by an organization or committee representative of users in those services.

(d) The provisions of paragraph (b) of this section shall not be construed to change or diminish in any respect the responsibility of station licensees to have and to maintain control over the stations licensed to them (including all transmitter units thereof), or for the proper functioning and operation of those stations (including all transmitter units thereof), in accordance with the terms of the licenses of those stations.

PART 94:
PRIVATE OPERATIONAL-FIXED MICROWAVE SERVICE

R & R 94.103 Operator requirements.

(a) No operator license is required for the operation, maintenance, or repair of stations licensed under this part.

* * * * * *

(c) The station licensee shall be responsible for the proper operation of the station at all times and is expected to provide for observations, servicing and maintenance as often as may be necessary to ensure proper operation. All adjustments or tests during or coincident with the installation, servicing, or maintenance of the station should be performed by or under the immediate supervision and responsibility of a person certified as technically qualified to perform transmitter installation, operation, maintenance, and repair duties in the private land mobile services and fixed services by an organization or committee representative of users in those services.

(d) The provisions of paragraph (b) of this section authorizing unlicensed persons to operate stations shall not be construed to change or diminish in any respect the responsibility of station licensees to have and to maintain control over the stations licensed to them (including all transmitter units thereof), or for the proper functioning and operation of those stations (including all transmitter units thereof) in accordance with the terms of the licenses of those stations.

PART 95:
GENERAL MOBILE RADIO SERVICE

R & R 95.129 Station Equipment.

* * * * * *

(b)(3) Has been internally adjusted or repaired by anyone except a person authorized under R & R 95.131.

* * * * * *

R & R 95.131 Service station transmitters.

(a) The station licensee shall be responsible for the proper operation of the station at all times and is expected to provide for observations, servicing and maintenance as often as may be necessary to ensure proper operation. All adjustments or tests during or coincident with the installation, servicing, or maintenance of the station should be performed by or under the immediate supervision and responsibility of a person certified as technically qualified to perform transmitter installation, operation, maintenance, and repair duties in the private land mobile services and fixed services by an organization or committee representative of users in those services.

* * * * * *

R & R 95.133 Modification to station transmitters.

* * * * * *

(b) * * *

(1) By the original manufacturer of the transmitter.

(2) In accordance with the original manufacturer's instructions by a person authorized under R & R 95.131.

R & R 95.221 (R/C Rule 21) How do I have my R/C transmitter serviced?

* * * * * *

(b) You are responsible for the proper operation of the station at all times and are expected to provide for observations, servicing and maintenance as often as may be necessary to ensure proper operation. Each internal repair and each internal adjustment to an FCC type accepted R/C transmitter (see R/C Rule 9) must be made in accord with the Technical Regulations (see Subpart E). The internal repairs or internal adjustments should be performed by or under the immediate supervision and responsibility of a person certified as technically qualified to perform transmitter maintenance and repair duties in the private land mobile services and fixed services by an organization or committee representative of users in those services.

* * * * * *

R & R 95.424 (CB Rule 24) How do I have my (CB) station transmitter serviced?

* * * * * *

(b) You are responsible for the proper operation of the station at all times and are expected to provide for observations, servicing and maintenance as often as may be necessary to ensure proper operation. You must have all internal repairs or internal adjustments to your CB transmitter made in accordance with the Technical Regulations (see Subpart E). The internal repairs or internal adjustments should be performed by or under the immediate supervision and responsibility of a person certified as technically qualified to perform transmitter maintenance and repair duties in the private land mobile services and fixed services by an organization or committee representative of users in those services.

APPENDIX II

Extracts of the Communications Act of 1934, as Amended

GENERAL POWERS OF THE COMMISSION

Sec. 303. Except as otherwise provided in this Act, the Commission from time to time, as public convenience, interest, or necessity requires, shall—

* * * * * *

(2) No order of suspension of any operator's license shall take effect until fifteen days' notice in writing thereof, stating the cause for the proposed suspension, has been given to the operator licensee who may make written application to the Commission at any time within said fifteen days for a hearing upon such order. The notice to the operator licensee shall not be effective until actually received by him, and from that time he shall have fifteen days in which to mail the said application. In the event that physical conditions prevent mailing of the application at the expiration of the fifteen-day period, the application shall then be mailed as soon as possible thereafter, accompanied by a satisfactory explanation of the delay. Upon receipt by the Commission of such application for hearing, said order of suspension shall

be held in abeyance until the conclusion of the hearing which shall be conducted under such rules as the Commission may prescribe. Upon the conclusion of said hearing the Commission may affirm, modify, or revoke said order of suspension.

(n) Have authority to inspect all radio installations associated with stations required to be licensed by any Act or which are subject to the provisions of any Act, treaty, or convention binding on the United States, to ascertain whether in construction, installation, and operation they conform to the requirements of the rules and regulations of the Commission, the provisions of any Act, the terms of any treaty or convention binding on the United States, and the conditions of the license or other instrument of authorization under which they are constructed, installed, or operated.

* * * * * *

DISTRESS SIGNALS AND COMMUNICATIONS

Sec. 321. (a) The transmitting set in a radio station on shipboard may be adjusted in such a manner as to produce a maximum of radiation, irrespective of the amount of interference which may thus be caused, when such station is sending radio communications or signals of distress and radio communications relating thereto.

(b) All radio stations, including Government stations and stations on board foreign vessels when within the territorial waters of the United States shall give absolute priority to radio communications or signals relating to ships in distress; shall cease all sending on frequencies which will interfere with hearing a radio communication or signal of distress, and, except when engaged in answering or aiding the ship in distress, shall refrain from sending any radio communications or signals until there is assurance that no interference will be caused with the radio communications or signals relating thereto, and shall assist the vessel in distress, so far as possible, by complying with its instructions.

INTERCOMMUNICATION IN MOBILE SERVICE

Sec. 322. Every land station open to general public service between the coast and vessels or aircraft at sea shall, within the scope of its normal operations, be bound to exchange radio communications or signals with any ship or aircraft station at sea; and each station on shipboard or aircraft at sea shall, within the scope of its normal operations, be bound to exchange radio communications or signals with any other station on shipboard or aircraft at sea or with any land station open to general public service between the coast and vessels or aircraft at sea: *Provided,* That such exchange of radio communication shall be without distinction as to radio systems or instruments adopted by each station.

*　*　*　*　*　*

SHIP RADIO INSTALLATIONS AND OPERATIONS

Sec. 351. (a) Except as provided in Section 352 hereof it shall be unlawful—

(1) For any ship of the United States, other than a cargo ship of less than five hundred gross tons, to be navigated in the open sea outside of a harbor or port, or for any ship of the United States or any foreign country, other than a cargo ship of less than five hundred gross tons, to leave or attempt to leave any harbor or port of the United States for a voyage in the open sea, unless such ship is equipped with an efficient radio installation in operating condition in charge of and operated by a qualified operator or operators, adequately installed and protected so as to insure proper operation, and so as not to endanger the ship and radio installation, as hereinafter provided, and in the case of a ship of the United States, unless there is on board a valid station license issued in accordance with this Act: *Provided,* That the Commission may defer the application of the provisions of this section for a period not beyond January 1, 1955, with respect to cargo ships of less than sixteen hundred gross tons not subject to the radio requirements of the Safety Convention when it is found impracticable to obtain or install equipment necessary for compliance therewith;

(2) For any ship of the United States of sixteen hundred gross tons, or over, to be navigated outside of a harbor or port, in the open sea, or for any such ship of the United States or any foreign country to leave or attempt to leave any harbor or port of the United States for a voyage in the open sea, unless such ship is equipped with an efficient radio direction finding apparatus (radio compass) properly adjusted in operating condition as hereinafter provided, which apparatus is approved by the Com-

mission: *Provided,* That the Commission may defer the application of the provisions of this section with respect to radio direction finding apparatus to a ship or ships between one thousand six hundred and five thousand gross tons for a period not beyond November 19, 1954, if it is found impracticable to obtain or install such direction finding apparatus.

(b) A ship which is not subject to the provisions of this part at the time of its departure on a voyage shall not become subject to such provisions on account of any deviation from its intended voyage due to stress of weather or any other cause over which neither the master, the owner, nor the charterer (if any) has control.

Summary of FCC Radio Operator License Rules (Effective 1984) and Field Offices

WHO NEEDS A COMMERCIAL RADIO OPERATOR LICENSE?

You need a commercial radio operator license if you operate, maintain, or repair radio transmitters in the maritime, aviation, broadcast, or international fixed public radio services. This includes:

- ship radio and radar stations on all types of vessels from small motorboats to large cargo ships;
- coast stations of all classes;
- hand-carried portable units used to communicate with ships and coast stations on marine frequencies;
- radios on all types of aircraft from small private planes to large airliners;
- aeronautical ground stations (including hand-carried portable units) used to communicate with aircraft;
- AM, FM, and TV broadcast stations including international broadcast stations;
- transmitters operated in the experimental television broadcast, experimental facsimile broadcast, developmental broadcast, low power television, television broadcast translator, FM broadcast translator, or FM broadcast booster radio services;

- international fixed public radiotelephone and radiotelegraph stations.

The FCC does *not* require you to obtain a commercial radio operator license for operation, maintenance, or repair of:

- two-way land mobile radio equipment, such as that used by taxicabs, police and fire departments, businesses, and local government agencies; or
- personal radio transceivers used in the citizens band, radio control, and general mobile radio services; or
- auxiliary broadcast stations such as remote pickup stations and others except as mentioned above.
- Stations operated in the domestic public fixed and mobile radio services. This includes mobile telephone systems, point-to-point microwave services, multipoint distribution service, etc.
- Stations operated in the cable television relay service.

TYPES OF LICENSES, PERMITS, AND ENDORSEMENTS

The FCC currently issues six types of commercial radio operator licenses and two types of endorsements, which are described briefly below:

(1) Restricted Radiotelephone Operator Permit

A Restricted Radiotelephone Operator Permit is required to operate most aircraft radiotelephone transmitters, marine radiotelephone transmitters on pleasure vessels (other than those that carry more than six passengers for hire), and AM, FM, and TV broadcast station transmitters.

There is no examination for this license, but to be eligible for it, you must:
- be at least 14 years old;
- be a legal resident (eligible for employment) in the United States or, if not so eligible, hold an aircraft pilot certificate valid in the United States or an FCC radio station license in your name (see limitation on validity below);
- be able to speak and hear;
- be able to keep at least a rough written log; and
- be familiar with provisions of applicable treaties, laws, and rules that govern the radio station you will operate.

A Restricted Radiotelephone Operator Permit is normally valid for the lifetime of the holder.

(2) Marine Radio Operator Permit

A Marine Radio Operator Permit is required to operate radiotelephone stations on board certain vessels sailing the Great Lakes, any tidewater, or the open sea. It is also required to operate certain aviation radiotelephone stations, and certain maritime coast radiotelephone stations. It does *not* authorize the operation of AM, FM, or TV broadcast stations.

To be eligible for this license, you must:
- be a legal resident of (eligible for employment in) the United States;

- be able to receive and transmit spoken messages in English; and
- pass a written examination covering basic radio law and operating procedures.

Marine Operator Permits are normally valid for a five-year term. They can be renewed at any time during the last year of the license term or up to five years following expiration. An expired permit is not valid.

(3) General Radiotelephone Operator License

A General Radiotelephone Operator License is required for persons responsible for internal repairs, maintenance, and adjustment of FCC-licensed radiotelephone transmitters in the aviation, maritime, and international public fixed radio services. It is also required for operation of maritime land radio transmitters operating with more than 1500 watts of peak envelope power and maritime mobile (ship) and aeronautical transmitters with more than 1000 watts of peak envelope power.

To be eligible for this license, you must:
- be a legal resident of (eligible for employment in) the United States;
- be able to receive and transmit spoken messages in English; and
- pass a writen examination covering basic radio law, operating procedures, and basic electronics.

The General Radiotelephone Operator License is normally valid for the lifetime of the operator.

(4) Third-Class Radiotelegraph Operator Certificate

The Third-Class Radiotelegraph Operator Certificate is required to operate certain coast radiotelegraph stations. It also conveys all of the authority of both the Restricted Radiotelephone Operator Permit and the Marine Radio Operator Permit.

To be eligible for this license, you must:

- be a legal resident of (eligible for employment in) the United States;
- be able to receive and transmit spoken messages in English;
- pass Morse code examinations at 16 code groups per minute and 20 words per minute plain language (receive and transmit by hand); and
- pass written examinations covering basic radio law, basic operating procedures (telephony) and basic operating procedures (telegraphy).

Third-Class Radiotelegraph Operator Certificates are normally valid for a renewable five-year term. They can be renewed at any time during the last year of the license term or up to five years following expiration. An expired certificate is not valid.

(5) Second-Class Radiotelegraph Operator Certificate

A Second-Class Radiotelegraph Operator Certificate is required to operate ship and coast radiotelegraph stations in the maritime services, and to take responsibility for internal repairs, maintenance, and adjustment of any FCC-licensed radiotelegraph transmitter other than an amateur radio transmitter. It also conveys all of the authority of the Third-Class Radiotelegraph Operator Certificate.

To be eligible for this license, you must:
- be a legal resident of (eligible for employment in) the United States;
- be able to receive and transmit spoken messages in English;
- pass Morse code examinations at 16 code groups per minute and 20 words per minute plain language (receive and transmit by hand); and
- pass written examinations covering basic radio law, basic operating procedures (telephony), basic operating procedures (telegraphy), and electronics technology as applicable to radiotelegraph stations.

Second-Class Radiotelegraph Operator Certificates are normally valid for a renewable five-year term. They can be renewed at any time during the last year of the license term or up to five years following expiration. An expired certificate is not valid.

(6) First-Class Radiotelegraph Operator Certificate

A First-Class Radiotelegraph Operator Certificate is required only for those who serve as the chief radio operator on U.S. passenger ships. It also conveys all of the authority of the Second-Class Radiotelegraph Operator Certificate.

To be eligible for this license, you must:
- be at least 21 years old;
- have at least one year of experience in sending and receiving public correspondence by radiotelegraph at ship stations, coast stations, or both;
- be a legal resident of (eligible for employment in) the United States;
- be able to receive and transmit spoken messages in English;
- pass Morse code examinations at 20 code groups per minute and 25 words per minute plain language (receive and transmit by hand); and
- pass written examinations covering basic radio law, basic operating procedures (telephony), basic operating procedures (telegraphy), and electronics technology as applicable to radiotelegraph stations.

First-Class Radiotelegraph Operator Certificates are normally valid for a renewable five-year term. They can be renewed at any time during the last year of the license term and up to five years following expiration. An expired certificate is not valid.

SHIP RADAR ENDORSEMENT

The Ship Radar Endorsement is required to service and maintain ship radar equipment.

To be eligible for this endorsement, you must:

- hold a valid First- or Second-Class Radiotelegraph Operator Certificate or a General Radiotelephone Operator License; and
- pass a written examination covering the technical fundamentals of radar and radar maintenance techniques.

APPLICATION FORMS AND LICENSING PROCEDURES

You must use the following FCC forms to apply for commercial radio operator licenses, permits and endorsements:

FCC Form 753—Use this form to apply for a Restricted Radiotelephone Operator Permit if you are legally eligible for employment in the United States (citizen or resident alien). It incorporates a temporary permit for immediate operating authority.

FCC Form 755—Use this form to apply for a Restricted Radiotelephone Operator Permit if you are *not* legally eligible for employment in the United States (non-resident alien, foreign aircraft pilot, etc.). It incorporates a temporary permit for immediate operating authority.

FCC Form 756—Use this form to apply for any of the commercial radio operator licenses other than the Restricted Radiotelephone Operator Permit. Also use it to apply for renewal of a license that requires renewal, replacement of a lost or mutilated license, and for a verification card, when necessary.

FCC Form 759—Use this form if you are employed at more than one radio station and each station requires the posting of your operator license. You post your license at one station and post FCC Form 759 at the other(s).

Any of the above forms may be obtained upon request from any FCC field office or from the FCC, Washington, D.C. 20554.

WHERE COMMERCIAL RADIO OPERATOR APPLICATIONS ARE PROCESSED

Applications for Restricted Radiotelephone Operator Permits are processed in Gettysburg, Pennsylvania. If you need assistance with these, contact:

Consumer Assistance Branch
Federal Communications Commission
Gettysburg, Pennsylvania 17325
Phone: (717) 337-1212

Applications for radiotelegraph licenses are processed in Washington, D.C. If you need assistance with these, contact:

Public Service Division
Radio Operator Branch
Federal Communications Commission
Washington, D.C. 20554
Phone: (202) 632-7240

Applications for the General Radiotelephone Operator License and the Marine Radio Operator Permit are processed locally by the FCC field offices. Also, all examinations are conducted by the field offices. They are listed in the next section of this bulletin. Examinations are conducted quarterly in the cities where the FCC has offices. Additionally, the offices periodically conduct examinations in certain cities where the FCC does not have offices. Advance appointments are required for all examinations. Contact your nearest FCC field office or FCC Washington, D.C. 20554 for a copy of the latest printed examination schedule.

FCC FIELD OFFICES

ALASKA, Anchorage 99510
1011 E. Tudor Rd., Room 240
P.O. Box 102955
EXAMINATION INFORMATION
  (Recording)
Phone: (907) 561-1550
OTHER INFORMATION
Phone: (907) 563-3899

CALIFORNIA, Long Beach 90807
3711 Long Beach Blvd., Room 501
EXAMINATION INFORMATION
  (Recording)
Phone: (213) 426-7886
OTHER INFORMATION
Phone: (213) 426-4451

CALIFORNIA, La Mesa (San Diego)
7840 El Cajon Blvd., Room 405
La Mesa, California 92041
EXAMINATION INFORMATION
  (Recording)
Phone: (714) 293-5460
OTHER INFORMATION
Phone: (714) 293-5478

CALIFORNIA, San Francisco 94111
423 Customhouse
555 Battery Street
EXAMINATION INFORMATION
  (Recording)
Phone: (415) 556-7700
OTHER INFORMATION
Phone: (415) 556-7701/2

COLORADO, Denver 80228
12477 West Cedar Drive
EXAMINATION INFORMATION
  (Recording)
Phone: (303) 234-6979
OTHER INFORMATION
Phone: (303) 234-6977

FLORIDA, Miami 33166
Koger Building
8675 NW 53rd Street
EXAMINATION INFORMATION
  (Recording)
Phone: (305) 593-0399
OTHER INFORMATION
Phone: (305) 350-5542

FLORIDA, Tampa 33607
Interstate Building, Room 601
1211 N. Westshore Blvd.
EXAMINATION INFORMATION
  (Recording)
Phone: (813) 228-2605

OTHER INFORMATION
Phone: (813) 228-2872

GEORGIA, Atlanta 30309
Massell Building, Room 440
1365 Peachtree Street, NE
EXAMINATION INFORMATION
  (Recording)
Phone: (404) 881-7381
OTHER INFORMATION
Phone: (404) 881-3084/5

HAWAII, Honolulu 96850
Prince Kuhio Federal Building
300 Ala Moana Blvd., Room 7304
P.O. Box 50023
Phone: (808) 546-5640

ILLINOIS, Chicago 60604
230 S. Dearborn St., Room 3940
EXAMINATION INFORMATION
  (Recording)
Phone: (312) 353-0197
OTHER INFORMATION
Phone: (312) 353-0195

LOUISIANA, New Orleans 70130
1009 F. Edward Hebert Federal Bldg.
600 South Street
EXAMINATION INFORMATION
  (Recording)
Phone: (504) 589-2094
OTHER INFORMATION
Phone: (504) 589-2095

MARYLAND, Baltimore 21201
1017 Federal Building
31 Hopkins Plaza
EXAMINATION INFORMATION
  (Recording)
Phone: (301) 962-2727
OTHER INFORMATION
Phone: (301) 962-2729

MASSACHUSETTS, Boston 02109
1600 Customhouse
165 State Street
EXAMINATION INFORMATION
  (Recording)

Phone: (617) 223-6607
OTHER INFORMATION
Phone: (617) 223-6609

MICHIGAN, Detroit 48018-1398
24897 Hathaway Street
Farmington Hills, Michigan
EXAMINATION INFORMATION
   (Recording)
Phone: (313) 226-6077
OTHER INFORMATION
Phone: (313) 226-6078

MINNESOTA, St. Paul 55101
691 Federal Bldg. & U.S. Courthouse
316 North Robert Street
EXAMINATION INFORMATION
   (Recording)
Phone: (612) 725-7819
OTHER INFORMATION
Phone: (612) 725-7810

MISSOURI, Kansas City 64133
Brywood Office Tower, Room 320
8800 East 63rd Street
EXAMINATION INFORMATION
   (Recording)
Phone: (816) 356-4050
OTHER INFORMATION
Phone: (816) 926-5111

NEW YORK, Buffalo 14202
1307 Federal Building
111 West Huron Street
EXAMINATION INFORMATION
   (Recording)
Phone: (716) 856-5950
OTHER INFORMATION
Phone: (716) 846-4511/2

NEW YORK, New York 10014
201 Varick Street
EXAMINATION INFORMATION
   (Recording)
Phone: (212) 620-3436
OTHER INFORMATION
Phone: (212) 620-3437/8

OREGON, Portland 97204
1782 Federal Building
1220 S.W. Third Avenue
EXAMINATION INFORMATION
   (Recording)
Phone: (503) 221-3097
OTHER INFORMATION
Phone: (503) 221-4114

PENNSYLVANIA, Langhorne 19047
   (PHILA)
One Oxford Valley Office Bldg., Rm 404
2300 East Lincoln Highway
EXAMINATION INFORMATION
   (Recording)
Phone: (215) 752-1323
OTHER INFORMATION
Phone: (215) 752-1324

PUERTO RICO, San Juan 00918-2251
747 Federal Building
Hato Rey, Puerto Rico
EXAMINATION INFORMATION
   (Recording)
Phone: (809) 753-4008
OTHER INFORMATION
Phone: (809) 753-4567

TEXAS, Dallas 75242
Earle Cabell Federal Building
U.S. Courthouse, Room 13E7
1100 Commerce Street
EXAMINATION INFORMATION
   (Recording)
Phone: (214) 767-0764
OTHER INFORMATION
Phone: (214) 767-0761

TEXAS, Houston 77002
New Federal Office Building
515 Rusk Avenue, Room 5636
EXAMINATION INFORMATION
   (Recording)
Phone: (713) 229-2750
OTHER INFORMATION
Phone: (713) 229-2748

VIRGINIA, Norfolk 23502
Military Circle
870 N. Military Highway
EXAMINATION INFORMATION
  (Recording)
Phone: (804) 461-4000
OTHER INFORMATION
Phone: (804) 441-6472

WASHINGTON, Seattle 98174
3256 Federal Building
915 Second Avenue
EXAMINATION INFORMATION
  (Recording)
Phone: (206) 442-7610
OTHER INFORMATION
Phone: (206) 442-7653/4

APPENDIX IV

Certification Programs for Technicians

Note: As of the time of this printing, the following organizations have been listed with the FCC as desiring to provide technician certification. A technician who possesses a certification certificate will by this means indicate that he has a certain technical competence. Thus, the certification certificate, in the future, will be used for this purpose in place of (or in addition to) an FCC Radiotelephone Operator License.

As each listed organization has its own individual requirements, interested students should contact the organization(s) directly. Also students may wish to call the FCC at (202) 632-7240 for possible new additions to the list presented herein.

1. NABER National Association of Business and Educational Radio
   Address: 1501 Duke St., Alexandria, VA 22314
   Telephone: (703) 739-0300

A test to certify technicians is given by FAA examiners or vocational instructors for the NABER Technician Certification Program. A Study Guide is also available.

2. NARTE (National Association of Radio and Telecommunications Engineers)
   Address: Box 15029, Salem, Oregon, 97309
   Telephone: (503) 581-3336

Current plans are to provide three levels of certification: First-Class, Second-Class, and Third-Class and Fourth-Class Certificates (or Licenses). The Fourth-Class Certificate is at the lowest level, and the First-Class at the highest level. NARTE also has AM, FM, and TV endorsements for all but the Fourth-Class Certificate.

3. SBE (Society of Broadcast Engineers)
   Address: Box 20450, Indianapolis, Indiana, 46260
   Telephone: (317) 842-0836

SBE has been certifying broadcast engineers since 1976. They have three levels of certification: Broadcast Technologist, Broadcast Engineer, Senior Broadcast Engineer, and Professional Broadcast Engineer (20-year). Certificates are valid for five years.

4. NRI (National Radio Institute)
   Address: 3939 Wisconsin Ave. N.W.
   Washington, D.C. 20007
   Telephone: (202) 244-1600
   Contact NRI for their current plans.

5. De Vry Inc., Industrial Training Division
   Address: 2201 W. Howard Street,
   Evanston, Illinois 60202
   Telephone: (800)323-4253
   Contact De Vry for their current plans.

6. ICET (International Society of Certified Electronic Technicians)
   Address: 2708 Westbury, Suite 8, Fort Worth, Texas 76109
   Telephone: (817) 921-9101

Two levels of tests are available:

Test I has 75 questions on such topics as basic electronics, ac, dc, transistors, and ICs. Passing this test provides an associate and temporary certificate.

Test II: Four years of experience, including education is the prerequisite for taking Test II (journeyman level). This test is available for 9 different topics. Passing a 25-question FCC legal test, plus the journeyman communications test and the associate test provides you with the ICET General Radiotelephone Certificate. Contact them for further details.

7. NICET (National Institute for Certification in Engineering Technologies)
   Address: 1420 King St., Alexandria, VA 22314
   Telephone: (703) 684-2835

NICET offers certification at several levels. Contact them for their current plans.

APPENDIX V

FCC-Type Sample Test Supplement for the General Radiotelephone Operator License and the Marine Radio Operator Permit

Note: This test includes supplementary *study information needed by applicants. This is in addition to the further requirements specified in the Preface for the above-mentioned license and permit. See also FCC Rules and Regulations, Parts 80 and 87 in Appendix I. Each question that follows is referenced to Parts 80 or 87. However, because of space limitations, not all applicable FCC Rules and Regulations appear in Appendix I. Copies of these parts can be obtained from the Superintendent of Documents, Government Printing Office, Washington, D.C. 20402. Call your regional FCC office for the latest price information.*

V-1. The following frequencies are authorized for use by shipboard EPIRB (Emergency Position Indicating Radiobeacon): (Part 80.1053)

   (a) 121.5 MHz and 243 MHz.
   (b) 500 kHz and 2182 kHz.
   (c) 121.5 MHz and 2182 kHz.
   (d) 500 kHz and 243 kHz.
   (e) 122.8 kHz and 243 kHz.

V-2. If a portable boat leaves a ship, it may only communicate with: (Part 80.1175)

   (a) Any ship or land station within range.
   (b) The ship associated with the portable boat.
   (c) The ship associated with the portable and any other portable boat.
   (d) The ship associated with the portable and any other portable boat associated with the same ship.
   (e) All of the above are true.

V-3. The power in a Bridge-to-Bridge communication radio may be increased above 1 watt, when: (Part 80.331)

   (a) There is danger in a blind situation.
   (b) Whenever the operator feels it necessary.
   (c) Never, under any situation.
   (d) To override another signal on the frequency.
   (e) None of the above.

V-4. Associated ship units (walkie-talkie portable FM radios) may be used to communicate: (Part 80.115)

   (a) Only when the ship is in port.
   (b) Only when the ship is at sea.

(c) Only with the vessel from which it is licensed.

(d) With any radio, ship, coastal station, or other portable operating on the same frequency.

(e) Only in the Great Lakes.

V-5. How often is the radiotelephone Signal Alarm Generator (SAG) tested aboard ship: (Part 80.856)

(a) Daily.

(b) Weekly.

(c) Biweekly.

(d) Monthly.

(e) Once a year.

V-6. Shipboard radiotelegraph auto-alarm (AA) systems operate on the following frequency: (Part 80.257)

(a) 500 kHz.

(b) 156.8 MHz.

(c) 2182 kHz.

(d) 2182 & 2638 kHz.

(e) 2638 kHz.

V-7. What are the maritime calling frequencies for radiotelephony? (Part 80.89)

(a) 500 kHz & 27 MHz.

(b) 1300–1500 kHz.

(c) 2182 kHz & 156.8 MHz.

(d) 2–24 mHz.

(e) 800–1364 kHz.

V-8. What is the frequency tolerance of all airborne stations (not including Civil Air Patrol) using single-sideband transmission: (Part 87.65)

(a) 10 Hz.

(b) 20 Hz.

(c) 30 Hz.

(d) 40 Hz.

(e) 50 Hz.

V-9. Survival craft radio equipment on shipboard must be tested: [Part 80.409(ii) (vi)]

(a) Once a month.

(b) Once a week.

(c) Only immediately before departure.

(d) Twice a month.

(e) Every three months.

V-10. In a survival craft radio (EPIRB), the battery must be changed: [Part 80.1053(12)]

(a) At the date marked on the battery.

(b) When 50 percent of its useful life has expired.

(c) If the transmitter has been used in an emergency situation.

(d) When the EPIRB transmitter power falls below 75 milliwatts.

(e) All of the above.

V-11. A radio operator who maintains more than one ship transmitter may satisfy the FCC requirement of posting his license by: [Part 80.407(b)]

(a) Carrying a photocopy of the license.

(b) Carrying a notarized statement attesting that he has the proper license.

(c) Posting the original license in his main shop area.

(d) Write a signed statement in the station log book to the effect that he has the proper license.

(e) Post photocopies every place he intends to be working.

V-12. A vessel of 300 to 1600 Gross Tons (G.T.) can elect to not have a radiotelegraph station. If so, what is the minimum distance the radiotelephone station must transmit? (Part 80.807)

(a) 250 miles.

(b) 150 miles.

(c) 100 miles.

(d) 350 miles.

(e) 300 miles.

V-13. When may an EPIRB (Emergency Position Indicating Radiobeacon) be tested? [Part 80.1055(4)(c)]

(a) During the first five minutes of any hour.

(b) During the second half hour of any hour.

(c) Monthly, during silence periods.

(d) During the last five minutes of any hour.

(e) On the day of departure.

V-14. The radio operator on board a ship must allow officials of foreign governments to: (Part 80.79)

(a) Examine the radio operator's license.

(b) Conduct checks of the EPIRB radio equipment.

(c) Check bridge-to-bridge radio equipment.

(d) Examine the radio station license.

(e) Restrict the radiotelephone transmitter power output.

V-15. Test transmissions should be sent every day, unless: [Part 80.409(e)(11)]

(a) The operator is prevented from doing so by official duties.

(b) The operator is ordered not to do so by the vessel master.

(c) The power output exceeds the permissible value.

(d) Normal use shows that the equipment is in need of maintenance.

(e) Normal use shows the equipment to be working properly.

V-16. If the top beacon light on an antenna 450–600 feet high burns out and it cannot be repaired in 30 minutes, whom do you notify? (Part 87.113)

(a) The owner or licensee of the station.

(b) The nearest flight service center or the FAA.

(c) The licensed operator of the station.

(d) The nearest FCC regional field office.

(e) The electric power company.

V-17. Ship stations navigating the Great Lakes and during their hours of service for telephony are required to keep watch on: (Part 80.308)

(a) 156.8 MHz.

(b) 243 MHz.

(c) 218.2 kHz.

(d) 121.5 MHz.

(e) 3000 kHz.

V-18. Maximum maritime transmitter power output is permitted when: (Part 80.311)

(a) Transmitting an urgency message.

(b) Transmitting a security message.

(c) Transmitting a distress message.

(d) The operator wants to increase his normal distance of communication.

(e) Transmitting to a commercial aircraft.

V-19. What ships require a licensed radio operator? [Part 80.159(d)]

(a) Those transporting three or more passengers for hire.

(b) Those over 300 gross tons.

(c) Only those on international voyages.

(d) Those carrying six or more passengers for hire.

(e) Those over 1250 gross tons.

V-20. The licensed operator of a ship radio station is required to: (Part 80.175)

(a) Post his license at the ship's main radio station location.

(b) Post a photocopy of his license at the ship's main radio station location.

(c) Post authorization from the ship's master at the ship's main radio station location.

(d) Always carry with him a letter of authorization from the FCC.

(e) All of the above.

V-21. When is it correct for a ship radio operator to stop listening on an international distress frequency? (Part 80.304)

(a) During silence periods.

(b) When the station is transmitting on that frequency, except during silence periods.

(c) When so directed by the chief radio operator.

(d) When in a blind situation.

(e) When the ship is within the 12 mile limit.

V-22. The authorized frequency tolerance for ship stations which use J3E(A3J) emission is: (Part 80.207)
(a) 200 Hz.
(b) 100 Hz.
(c) 50 Hz.
(d) 25 Hz.
(e) 20 Hz.

V-23. In maritime transmitters, using J3E (A3J) emission, carrier power must be suppressed below peak sideband power (PEP) by at least: [Part 80.207(3)]
(a) 40 dB.
(b) 10 dB.
(c) 30 dB.
(d) 75 dB.
(e) All of the above.

V-24. Stations using telephony may conduct operational transmitter tests: (Part 80.101)
(a) As necessary for proper maintenance, keeping emission reduced as low as possible or suppressed, and without interfering with other transmissions.
(b) As necessary and in any manner to insure the equipment is operating properly.
(c) Only under the supervision of a technician who holds a General Radiotelephone License.
(d) Only under the supervision of a technician who holds a First Class Radiotelegraph Permit.
(e) Under any of the above circumstances.

V-25. Stations using telephony in the maritime services should be operated: (Part 80.114)
(a) In any manner, provided the operator holds a valid RTCM certificate.
(b) According to the provisions set forth in the station authorization.
(c) As the operator chooses, as long as the First Mate approves it.
(d) By any member of the ship's crew, holding a General Radiotelephone License.

(e) Under none of the above conditions.

V-26. In order for the FCC to inspect a ship's radio station, they must be given how many days prior notice and by whom: (Part 80.59)
(a) 3 days by the vessel master.
(b) 1 week by the radio operator.
(c) 1 month by the vessel owner.
(d) 6 weeks by the first mate.
(e) 3 months by the operating agency.

V-27. The radiotelegraph, or radiotelephone alarm signal is used to announce: (Part 80.318)
(a) A distress call or message will follow.
(b) A cyclone warning, by a coast station.
(c) The loss of a person or persons overboard.
(d) A message preceded by the urgency signal.
(e) All of the above.

V-28. The three-minute silence periods for radiotelephone stations operating on 2182 kHz are: (Part 80.304)
(a) Xh.00 and Xh.30.
(b) Xh.15 and Xh.45.
(c) Xh.15 and Xh.30.
(d) Xh.00 and Xh.15.
(e) Xh.00 and Xh.45.

V-29. Associated ship units (walkie-talkies) are permitted to communicate with: (Part 80.115)
(a) Any other associated ship units.
(b) Its associated ship station or other associated units of the same ship station.
(c) Coast Guard associated ship units.
(d) Military associated ship units.
(e) Any ship owned and operated by the same company.

V-30. Ship radiotelephony stations are required to identify in English: (Part 80.102)
(a) Only at the end of a communication.
(b) Every five minutes during a communication.

(c) At the beginning and end of a communication.

(d) Only at the beginning of a communication.

(e) Every 10 minutes during a communication.

V-31. Associated ship units (walkie-talkies) are required to be able to transmit on: (Part 80.115)

(a) 156.8 MHz and one intership frequency.

(b) 2182 kHz and one intership frequency.

(c) 243 MHz and 156.8 MHz.

(d) Only 156.8 MHz.

(e) 156.8 MHz and 2182 kHz.

V-32. Ship's radio station logs relating to a distress situation or disaster must be retained for: (Part 80.409)

(a) 90 days.

(b) 10 years.

(c) 5 years.

(d) 3 years.

(e) 1 year.

V-33. Bridge-to-bridge communications equipment is required on: (Part 80.100)

(a) All power-driven vessels.

(b) Power-driven vessels of 300 gross tons and upward, while navigating.

(c) Towing vessels of 26 feet or over in length.

(d) Vessels of 100 gross tons and upward carrying one or more passengers for hire while navigating.

(e) (b), (c), and (d) are correct.

V-34. Use of a bridge-to-bridge transmitter is restricted to: (Part 80.1007)

(a) The chief radio operator.

(b) The master or person in charge of the vessel.

(c) A person designated by the ship's owner.

(d) Any person holding a First Class Radiotelegraph license.

(e) None of the above.

V-35. The bridge-to-bridge transmitting frequency (G3E emission) is: (Part 80.1011)

(a) 156.800 MHz.

(b) 2182 kHz.

(c) 243 MHz.

(d) 121.5 MHz.

(e) 156.650 MHz.

V-36. Bridge-to-bridge transmitter power is limited to: (Part 80.1011)

(a) 25 watts.

(b) 50 watts.

(c) 1 watt.

(d) 5 watts.

(e) 10 watts.

V-37. When phase or frequency modulation is used in a ship's transmitter, 100% modulation is defined as a deviation of: (Part 80.213)

(a) ± 75 kHz.

(b) ± 5 kHz.

(c) ± 25 kHz.

(d) ± 10 kHz.

(e) ± 2.5 kHz.

V-38. The emission designation A3E refers to: (Part 80.207)

(a) Double sideband, full carrier amplitude-modulated telephony.

(b) Vestigial sideband transmission.

(c) Frequency or phase modulated telephony.

(d) Single sideband telephony.

(e) Telegraphy.

V-39. Type-accepted transmitters may be modified as follows: (Part 80.203)

(a) To increase modulation to 100%.

(b) To increase power output by 15 percent.

(c) To change frequency as required.

(d) May not have any change to its basic design.

(e) To change the class of emission.

V-40. The radiotelephone alarm signal consists of: (Part 80.317)

(a) 12 dashes, 4 seconds each, sent in one minute.

(b) Two alternating audio tones of 2200 Hz. and 1300 Hz. for 30 and 60 seconds at a time.

(c) A continuous audio tone of 1000 Hz. for one minute at a time.

(d) The spoken word MAYDAY, repeated three times for one minute at a time.

(e) Two alternating audio tones of 400 and 1000 Hz.

V-41. For double sideband emission (A3E) or frequency or phase modulation (F3E, G3E), the modulation range is limited to: (Part 80.213)

(a) 50 to 100 percent.

(b) 50 to 75 percent.

(c) 60 to 100 percent.

(d) 75 to 100 percent.

(e) 50 to 90 percent.

V-42. In the aviation radio services, it is not mandatory to hold a radio operator license unless: (Part 87.133)

(a) Operating on a frequency other than VHF.

(b) On a flight to a foreign country.

(c) Operating on a VHF frequency.

(d) Operating across the U.S.A.

(e) (a) and (b) are correct.

V-43. A Marine Radio Operator Permit is required in the aircraft services: (Part 87.133)

(a) To operate high power airborne stations.

(b) To operate an aircraft station using frequencies below 30 MHz, which are assigned for international use.

(c) To operate an aircraft station whose power output exceeds 500 watts carrier.

(d) To operate an aircraft station using FM.

(e) To operate an aircraft station using SSBSC.

V-44. Adjustments or tests which may affect the operation of the transmitter of an aviation radio station must be made under the direct supervision of a person who holds a: (Part 87.135)

(a) Marine Radio Operator Permit.

(b) Restricted Radiotelephone Operator Permit.

(c) General Radiotelephone Operator License.

(d) Second Class Radiotelegraph Operator Certificate.

(e) (c) and (d) are correct.

V-45. In the aviation services, a radio operator holding the license or permit named below is allowed to only operate transmitters not requiring manual adjustment of frequency: (Part 87.136)

(a) Marine Radio Operator Permit.

(b) Restricted Radiotelephone Operator Permit.

(c) Third Class Radiotelegraph Operator Certificate.

(d) Third Class Radiotelephone License.

(e) (a), (b) and (c) are correct.

V-46. The universal simplex clear channel frequency for use by aircraft in distress or condition of emergency is: [Part 87.183(f)]

(a) 121.5 MHz.

(b) 2182 kHz.

(c) 243 MHz.

(d) 256.8 MHz.

(e) 221.5 MHz.

V-47. In the aviation radio services, no radio operator license is required for the operation of transmitters involving: (Part 87.139)

(a) Airborne radar sets.

(b) Radio altimeters.

(c) Transponders.

(d) Airborne automatic radionavigation aids.

(e) All of the above.

V-48. In the aviation services, measurements of the operating frequencies of non-airborne transmitters shall be measured at the following time: (Part 87.111)

(a) When the transmitter is originally installed.

(b) When any adjustment has been made that may affect an operating frequency.

(c) When it is believed an operating frequency has shifted beyond the applicable tolerance.

(d) When any change is made that may affect the operating frequency.

(e) All of the above.

V-49. Newly installed aircraft transmitters operating on frequencies different than those specified on the station license may be used for 30 days from the date of installation, provided: (Part 87.35)

(a) Application for station license to include the new equipment has been submitted to the FCC.

(b) Operation is limited to aviation frequencies authorized by the FCC.

(c) Power is kept below 5 watts.

(d) Single sideband transmission is used.

(e) (a) and (b) are correct.

V-50. The emission designation F3E stands for (Part 80.207)

(a) Frequency modulated telephony.

(b) Double-sideband AM.

(c) Single-sideband AM.

(d) Narrow-band AM.

(e) Single-sideband, suppressed carrier.

V-51. With an antenna structure which is required to be illuminated, the tower lights should be observed: (Part 87.113)

(a) Once a week.

(b) Once every two weeks.

(c) Every 48 hours.

(d) Every 24 hours.

(e) Whenever it is convenient.

V-52. With aircraft of U.S. registry, the following form(s) of identification may be used: (Part 87.115)

(a) The type of aircraft, followed by the last three characters of the registration marking "N" number.

(b) The radiotelephony designator of the aircraft operating agency (assigned by the AFA) followed by the flight identification number (assigned by the company).

(c) The name of the aircraft base city and state.

(d) The name of the aircraft captain and the flight number.

(e) (a) and (b) are correct.

Answers to the FCC-Type Sample Tests, Including Text References

Note: The question number following each answer refers to the question in the body of the text on which the sample-test question is based. In the event that the student has an incorrect answer to a sample-test question, or wishes to refresh his knowledge of the particular subject, he should study the information supplied in connection with the referenced text question.

ELEMENT I

1. (b), Q. 1.13	2. (d), Q. 1.19	3. (c), Q. 1.19
4. (a), Q. 1.15	5. (b), Q. 1.12	6. (d), Q. 1.11
7. (e), Q. 1.05	8. (d), Q. 1.01	9. (c), Q. 1.03
10. (a), Q. 1.14	11. (c), Q. 1.16	12. (d), Q. 1.06
13. (e), Q. 1.07	14. (b), Q. 1.08	15. (b), Q. 1.18
16. (b), Q. 1.17	17. (d), Q. 1.09	18. (c), Q. 1.04
19. (b), Q. 1.12	20. (c), Q. 1.02	

ELEMENT II—CATEGORY "O"— GENERAL

1. (c), Q. 2.07	2. (b), Q. 2.01	3. (c), Q. 2.14
4. (a), Q. 2.06	5. (e), Q. 2.02	6. (c), Q. 2.12
7. (d), Q. 2.05	8. (b), Q. 2.02	9. (c), Q. 2.13
10. (c), Q. 2.04	11. (e), Q. 2.02	12. (a), Q. 2.11
13. (d), Q. 2.09	14. (a), Q. 2.02	15. (c), Q. 2.02
16. (b), Q. 2.03	17. (d), Q. 2.08	18. (c), Q. 2.10
19. (d), Q. 2.02	20. (b), Q. 2.02	

ELEMENT II—CATEGORY "M"— MARITIME

1. (a), Q. 2.05	2. (c), Q. 2.09	3. (e), Q. 2.15
4. (b), Q. 2.13	5. (d), Q. 2.01	6. (d), Q. 2.01
7. (c), Q. 2.02	8. (d), Q. 2.08	9. (b), Q. 2.15
10. (d), Q. 2.12	11. (b), Q. 2.11	12. (a), Q. 2.07
13. (c), Q. 2.02	14. (a), Q. 2.04	15. (b), Q. 2.06
16. (e), Q. 2.06	17. (b), Q. 2.14	18. (a), Q. 2.03
19. (b), Q. 2.04	20. (e), Q. 2.08	

ELEMENT III

1. (b), Q. 3.01	2. (b), Q. 3.04	3. (d), Q. 3.09(B)
4. (a), Q. 3.13	5. (b), Q. 3.27	6. (e), Q. 3.36
7. (b), Q. 3.133-A23	8. (c), Q. 3.52	9. (a), Q. 3.210
10. (c), Q. 3.10	11. (b), Q. 3.11	12. (c), Q. 3.72
13. (d), Q. 3.79	14. (b), Q. 3.212-A12	15. (a), Q. 3.81
16. (c), Q. 3.82	17. (a), Q. 3.84	18. (d), Q. 3.85
19. (c), Q. 3.86	20. (c), Q. 3.86	21. (b), Q. 3.86
22. (d), Q. 3.87	23. (e), Q. 3.98	24. (d), Q. 3.95
25. (c), Q. 3.102	26. (b), Q. 3.08	27. (e), Q. 3.85-A18
28. (a), Q. 3.52	29. (c), Q. 3.110 6	30. (d), Q. 3.116
31. (b), Q. 3.184	32. (e), Q. 3.298	33. (b), Q. 3.122
34. (e), Q. 3.29	35. (c), Q. 3.125	36. (a), Q. 3.131
37. (b), Q. 3.137	38. (d), Q. 3.134	39. (c), Q. 3.135
40. (a), Q. 3.136	41. (e), Q. 3.126	42. (b), Q. 3.137
43. (c), Q. 3.139	44. (a), Q. 3.140	45. (e), Q. 3.142
46. (a), Q. 3.144	47. (d), Q. 3.161	48. (a), Q. 3.192(U)-A31
49. (a), Q. 3.192(J)	50. (c), Q. 3.163	51. (b), Q. 3.167
52. (e), Q. 3.169	53. (c), Q. 3.178	54. (b), Q. 3.133-A25
55. (e), Q. 3.177	56. (a), Q. 3.192(U)-A14	57. (c), Q. 3.184
58. (d), Q. 3.188	59. (a), Q. 3.187	60. (c), Q. 3.192J
61. (b), Q. 3.192K	62. (c), Q. 3.192(L)	63. (b), Q. 3.192(M)
64. (b), Q. 3.193	65. (a), Q. 3.193	66. (c), Q. 3.203
67. (d), Q. 3.201	68. (c), Q. 3.208	69. (d), Q. 3.210
70. (c), Q. 3.213	71. (c), Q. 3.216	72. (b), Q. 3.218
73. (e), Q. 3.129	74. (a), Q. 3.223	75. (e), Q. 3.225
76. (b), Q. 3.221	77. (c), Q. 3.220	78. (b), Q. 3.222
79. (c), Q. 3.226	80. (a), Q. 3.232	81. (c), Q. 3.232
82. (d), Q. 3.203	83. (b), Q. 3.227	84. (d), Q. 3.36
85. (a), Q. 3.239	86. (e), Q. 3.245 Q. 3.137-A13	87. (c), Q. 3.192(U)-A32
88. (a), Q. 3.08	89. (b), Q. 3.66	90. (e), Q. 3.235
91. (c), Q. 3.251	92. (d), Q. 3.251	93. (a), Q. 3.249
94. (c), Q. 3.248	95. (a), Q. 3.247	96. (c), Q. 3.255
97. (a), Q. 3.254	98. (d), Q. 3.286	99. (b), Q. 3.45-A29
100. (c), Q. 3.288		

ELEMENT VIII

1. (b), Q. 8.07	2. (e), Q. 8.10	3. (c), Q. 8.12
4. (a), Q. 8.01	5. (d), Q. 8.02	6. (c), Q. 8.34
7. (d), Q. 8.38	8. (a), Q. 8.39	9. (c), Q. 8.39
10. (b), Q. 8.48	11. (a), Q. 8.62	12. (d), Q. 8.70
13. (a), Q. 8.70	14. (c), Q. 8.69	15. (d), Q. 8.64
16. (b), Q. 8.58	17. (c), Q. 8.59	18. (a), Q. 8.55
19. (d), Q. 8.50	20. (c), Q. 8.41	21. (a), Q. 8.39
22. (d), Q. 8.48	23. (b), Q. 8.42	24. (a), Q. 8.39
25. (c), Q. 8.37	26. (d), Q. 8.34	27. (a,) Q. 8.39
	Q. 8.35	
28. (b), Q. 8.43	29. (d), Q. 8.28	30. (c), Q. 8.23
		Q. 8.24
31. (e), Q. 8.08	32. (b), Q. 8.42	33. (c), Q. 8.67
34. (b), Q. 8.66	35. (a), Q. 8.62	36. (b), Q. 8.39
37. (a), Q. 8.62	38. (b), Q. 8.39	39. (e), Q. 8.62
40. (c), Q. 8.48	41. (b), Q. 8.42	42. (b), Q. 8.39
43. (d), Q. 8.67	44. (a), Q. 8.20	45. (e), Q. 8.39
46. (d), Q. 8.62	47. (c), Q. 8.39	48. (b), Q. 8.39
49. (a), Q. 8.39	50. (a), Q. 8.63	

Answers to the FCC-Type Sample Test for Appendix V

The FCC Part 80 or 87 number following each answer refers to references in these Parts. Therein, more complete information regarding the answers can be found.

1. (a), 80.1053
2. (d), 80.1175
3. (a), 80.331
4. (c), 80.115
5. (b), 80.856
6. (a), 80.257
7. (c), 80.89
8. (b), 87.65
9. (b), 80.409(11)(vi)
10. (e), 80.1053(12)
11. (a), 80.407(b)
12. (b), 80.807
13. (a), 80.1055(4)(c)
14. (d), 80.79
15. (e), 80.409(e)(ii)
16. (b), 87.113
17. (a), 80.308
18. (c), 80.311

19. (d), 80.159(d)
20. (a), 80.175
21. (b), 80.304
22. (e), 80.207
23. (a), 80.207(3)
24. (a), 80.101
25. (b), 80.114
26. (a), 80.59
27. (e), 80.318
28. (a), 80.304
29. (b), 80.115
30. (c), 80.102
31. (a), 80.115
32. (d), 80.409
33. (e), 80.1001
34. (b), 80.1007
35. (e), 80.1011

36. (c), 80.1011
37. (b), 80.213
38. (a), 80.207
39. (d), 80.203
40. (b), 80.317
41. (d), 80.213
42. (e), 80.133
43. (b), 80.133
44. (e), 87.135
45. (e), 87.136
46. (a), 87.183(f)
47. (e), 87.139
48. (e), 87.111
49. (e), 87.35
50. (a), 80.207
51. (d), 87.113
52. (e), 87.115

Index

The index has been prepared to facilitate the use of this book for studying for a particular class of license as well as for reference and review. **Question numbers** rather than page numbers are cited for each entry. It is believed that this will make for more convenient usage.

Special headings and entries are incorporated into the index. These are, **Problems, Definitions, Diagrams, Rules and Regulations (FCC)**, and **Troubleshooting**. The reader will find these entries particularly useful for reference.